D1482689

Business, Government, and Society

NINTH EDITION

Business, Government, and Society
A Managerial Perspective
Text and Cases

George A. Steiner

*Harry and Elsa Kunin Professor of Business and Society
and Professor of Management, Emeritus, UCLA*

John F. Steiner

*Professor of Management
California State University, Los Angeles*

Boston   Burr Ridge, IL   Dubuque, IA   Madison, WI   New York   San Francisco   St. Louis
Bangkok   Bogotá   Caracas   Lisbon   London   Madrid
Mexico City   Milan   New Delhi   Seoul   Singapore   Sydney   Taipei   Toronto

McGraw-Hill Higher Education

A Division of The **McGraw-Hill** *Companies*

Previously printed under the title of *Business and Society.*

BUSINESS, GOVERNMENT, AND SOCIETY:
A MANAGERIAL PERSPECTIVE, TEXT AND CASES

This book is printed on acid-free paper.

domestic   1 2 3 4 5 6 7 8 9 0 FGR/FGR 9 0 9 8 7 6 5 4 3 2 1 0 9
international   1 2 3 4 5 6 7 8 9 0 FGR/FGR 9 0 9 8 7 6 5 4 3 2 1 0 9

ISBN   0-07-365914-2

Vice president/Editor-in-chief: *Michael W. Junior*
Publisher: *Craig S. Beytien*
Sponsoring editor: *Andy Winston*
Marketing manager: *Kenyetta Giles Haynes*
Project manager: *Carrie Sestak*
Senior production supervisor: *Lori Koetters*
Freelance design coordinator: *Laurie J. Entringer*
Cover designer: *Crispin Prebys*
Senior photo research coordinator: *Keri Johnson*
Supplement coordinator: *Mark Sienicki*
Compositor: *Shepherd Incorporated*
Typeface: *10/12 Palatino*
Printer: *Quebecor Printing Book Group/Fairfield*

Library of Congress Cataloging-in-Publication Data

Steiner, George Albert,
     Business, government, and society : a managerial perspective :
text and cases / George A. Steiner, John F. Steiner. —9th ed.
        p.   cm.
     Includes index.
     ISBN 0-07-365914-2 (alk. paper)
     1. Industries—Social aspects—United States.   2. Industrial
policy—United States.   I. Steiner, John F.   II. Title.
HD60.5.U5S8 2000
658.4—dc21   99–28375

http://www.mhhe.com

We dedicate this book
to the memory of
Jean Wood Steiner

Brief Table of Contents

Table of Contents

PART 2

THE NATURE AND MANAGEMENT OF SOCIAL RESPONSIBILITY

Part 7

BUSINESS AND THE CONSUMER

Preface

Text Overview

This book examines the interactions among business, government, and society. More specifically, it focuses on activities of firms affecting a wide range of stakeholders and the ethical and social responsibilities of these firms. In its pages are principles for judging business ethics and criteria for determining corporate social responsibility. For managers, the book has methods for analyzing forces in the sociopolitical environment, institutionalizing social responsibility, making ethical decisions, intervening in corporate cultures to elevate ethics, reducing burdens on the natural environment, and coping with diverse workforces. In every chapter we relate dramas of corporate life as cases and stories.

The passing of time has necessitated many and sometimes deep revisions in this ninth edition. All chapters have been updated and some of them have been substantially rewritten to include new events, trends, ideas, and publications. International dimensions of the subject matter have been given more prominence. Many areas of text that were formerly focused solely on the United States have been broadened to include comparative material about other nations.

We continue to emphasize current events, issues, and conditions. This edition, like previous ones, sometimes gives prominence to a historical perspective. Although we have added little new historical material, we continue to believe that discussions of the past are important for illuminating the origins of the present. We have also continued our efforts to add conceptual material not subject to rapid obsolescence by events, and we believe that this edition contains more of this basic material than do previous ones.

As in past editions, we begin each chapter with a true story or incident to illustrate key concepts. A number of these introductory stories are new. We also continue to include a case study at the end of each chapter (except for Chapter 1).

Case Writing Philosophy

Our philosophy of case writing incorporates a number of ideas. We believe that case studies should raise substantial and, if possible, multiple issues. We believe that these issues should be developed, but not in exhausting detail. So, our cases are of moderate length. We believe that cases should be written to raise questions rather than answer them. Therefore, we try to state facts and arguments without showing favor and we list central questions at the end of each case. And we believe that cases should be updated before they are republished. Therefore, except for historical cases in the first two chapters, we revised every case from the previous edition, usually substantially.

New and Updated Chapter Material

- Chapter 1 is revised to better define and introduce the field, but retains its pragmatic approach based on four models of the business-government-society relationship.
- Chapter 2 presents new material about the volatility of the business environment.
- Chapter 3 includes a new narrative about the rise of the railroads to illustrate how business power changes society.
- Chapter 5 includes new material on criteria and methods for rating corporate social responsibility.
- Chapter 6 is completely new and describes real social programs being undertaken by business.
- Chapters 7 and 8 on business ethics contain new examples, incidents, and stories to illustrate points.
- Chapters 9 and 10 on government regulation are substantially updated to include new developments.
- Chapter 13 is completely new and focuses on multiple global forces that affect corporations.
- Chapters 14 and 15 on the environment incorporate discussion of new regulatory developments such as ecological risk assessment and new methods companies use to manage environmental quality.
- Chapter 16 contains new material on the patient's bill of rights.
- Chapter 17 contains an expanded emphasis on how global forces affecting American workers also affect workers in Europe and Asia.
- Chapter 18 contains up-to-date discussion of civil rights laws, court decisions, enforcement philosophies, and the status and pay of women in management.
- Chapter 19 contains new material about issues raised by compensation of corporate directors.

New Cases

- Two cases completely new to this edition are Columbia/HCA Healthcare Corporation, which raises ethical questions about new market approaches to healthcare, and Federal Express and Congress, which raises issues about the methods that corporations use to influence politics in Washington, D.C. The case Airline Deregulation has been brought back in new form after being dropped from the last edition.

New Chapter-Opening Vignettes

- There are seven new chapter-opening stories about companies. They are on American Honda Motor Company, British Petroleum, General Electric Company, Louisiana-Pacific Corporation, McDonald's Corporation, Monsanto, and Royal Dutch/Shell.
- References to Web pages are used in the text so that students can go to the Internet for more information.

Instructor's Support Materials

An **Instructor's Resource Manual** includes the following items: sample course outlines, chapter objectives, case study teaching notes with answers to the case questions, a list of term paper topics for each text chapter, and transparency masters. The manual also contains a test bank covering chapters and case studies including multiple-choice, true/false, fill-in, short answer, and essay questions.

A **Computerized Test Bank** contains all of the questions in the printed test bank. It is a powerful system that allows tests to be prepared quickly and easily. Instructors can view questions as they are selected for a test; scramble questions; add, delete, and edit questions; select questions by type, objective, and difficulty level; and view and save tests.

A **Video Series in Business, Government, and Society** will help students connect topics covered in class with real-life events.

Acknowledgments

We are deeply indebted to many authors who have inspired and informed us. Where appropriate we have cited their works. Many people have been helpful with their contributions and suggestions in the preparation of the book. We are especially indebted to the following: Colleen Berardi, General Electric Company; Teresa Yancey Crane, Issues Management Council; Jim Croan, U.S. Department of Transportation; Robert W. Gramling, General Accounting Office; Tommy Johnson, Office of the U.S. Trade Representative; Richard Nelson, General Motors Corporation; Angela Pilkington, Correct Craft Inc.; Corey Rosen, National Center for Employee Ownership; Clay R. Sprowls, UCLA; Richard Stober, Caterpillar Inc.; Peter S. Walters, Guardian Industries Corp.; Melinda Warren, Center for the Study of American Business; Gary Watson, California State University, Los Angeles; J. Fred Weston, UCLA; Robert Williams, UCLA; Betty Wolf, U.S. Department of Transportation; and Henry Wong, General Motors Corporation.

The following reviewers provided many helpful comments and suggestions for this edition: Frank Cavaliere, Lamar University; Peggy Naumes, University of New Hampshire; Ray Vegso, Canisius College; Harvey Nussbaum, Wayne State University; Kathleen Rehbein, Marquette University.

At California State University, Los Angeles, we want to thank G. Timothy Haight, Hugh Warren, and Paul Washburn for their generous support throughout the writing of this volume. At the John F. Kennedy Memorial Library, Alan Stein gave valuable advice on the research process.

We express great appreciation for the wisdom and guidance of Karen Mellon, our editor at Irwin/McGraw-Hill and for the skill and effort put into the project by Carrie Sestak, our project manager. In addition, we are grateful to others who lent their talents to improve the manuscript greatly, especially our copyeditor, Betsy Blumenthal and our proofreader, Donna Stenitzer.

Finally, we give special thanks to Deborah Luedy for her generous assistance and support.

George A. Steiner
John F. Steiner

About the Authors

George A. Steiner is one of the leading pioneers in the development of university curriculums, research, and scholarly writings in the field of business, government, and society. In 1983 he was the recipient of the first Sumner Marcus Award for distinguished achievement in the field by the Social Issues in Management Division of the Academy of Management. In 1990 he received the Distinguished Educator Award, given for the second time by the Academy of Management. After receiving his B.S. in business administration at Temple University, he was awarded an M.A. in economics from the Wharton School of the University of Pennsylvania and a Ph.D. in economics from the University of Illinois. He is the author of many books and articles. Two of his books received "book-of-the-year" awards. In recognition of his writings, Temple University awarded him a Litt.D. honorary degree. Professor Steiner has held top-level positions in the federal government and in industry, including corporate board directorships. Past president of the Academy of Management and co-founder of *The California Management Review,* he is Harry and Elsa Kunin Professor of Business and Society and Professor of Management, Emeritus, Anderson School, UCLA.

John F. Steiner is Professor of Management at California State University, Los Angeles. He received his B.S. from Southern Oregon State College and received an M.A. and Ph.D. in political science from the University of Arizona. He has coauthored two other books with George A. Steiner, *Issues in Business and Society* and *Casebook for Business, Government, and Society.* He is also the author of *Industry, Society, and Change: A Casebook.* Professor Steiner is a former chair of the Social Issues in Management Division of the Academy of Management and former chair of the Department of Management at California State University, Los Angeles.

A Framework for Studying Business, Government, and Society

CHAPTER 1

Introduction to the Field

> **Exxon Corporation**
> www.exxon.com

Every business exists in the embrace of one or more governments and societies. Its operations affect them, and in turn, governments and societies constrain or encourage the business. The story of one large firm, Exxon Corporation, illustrates a range of business–government–society (BGS) interactions.

Exxon is one of the oldest and largest of the world's industrial enterprises. It was started in 1870 by John D. Rockefeller as Standard Oil of Ohio. Standard Oil soon dominated the American market for refined petroleum. It also became one of the first genuinely multinational corporations.

As Standard Oil grew, its power offended public values related to fairness and equity. Reformers were galvanized and in 1890 Congress passed the Sherman Antitrust Act to strike at its near monopoly. After years of legal battles, Standard Oil was finally ordered by the Supreme Court in 1911 to break up into 39 separate companies. After the breakup, Standard Oil of New Jersey continued to exist. Although it had shed 57 percent of its assets to create the new firms, it was still the world's largest oil company. Some of the companies formed in the breakup were those that came to be named Amoco, ARCO, Cheeseborough-Ponds (a company that made petroleum jelly), Chevron, Conoco, Mobil, and Sohio.[1]

---

[1] Ron Chernow, *Titan: The Life of John D. Rockefeller*, New York: Random House, 1998, pp. 557–59.

In 1972 Standard Oil of New Jersey changed its name to Exxon.

Exxon is headquartered in Irving, Texas, but it operates in 100 countries and gets most of its income from outside the United States. More than 75 percent of its gas and oil products are sold in foreign countries. It employs 80,000 people to explore for oil and gas, produce and refine oil, make chemicals, and mine coal and copper. It operates 27,000 miles of pipeline and has fleets of ships, airplanes, and helicopters. Exxon, with revenues of $122 billion in 1997, is today the world's second-largest energy company after the Royal/Dutch Shell Group. But it is poised to become the largest. In 1998 it announced a takeover of Mobil Corp., a company with $58 billion in sales. If approved by regulators, this merger would reunite two progeny of the original Standard Oil trust.

Exxon faces a competitive business environment. In oil, natural gas, and chemicals it has fierce competition from industry rivals. It also must compete with alternative forms of energy and new energy technologies.

Exxon faces a constraining government environment. Operations and earnings are affected by the laws and regulations of each country in which it does business. In the United States, for example, there are about 300 federal regulatory agencies, virtually all of which impose rules and standards. In each of the fifty states there are additional regulatory agencies. In foreign countries Exxon faces import and export restrictions, price controls, expropriation, forced divestiture of assets, and rules that restrict production. In 1996 Exxon helped to support

governments by paying $44 billion in taxes worldwide.

Exxon also faces a complex social environment. The company is subject to unpredictable international crises that interrupt energy supplies. Demographic shifts alter its markets. It is scrutinized by environmental, civil rights, animal rights, labor, and consumer protection groups—many of which are hostile. Exxon funds a wide range of programs to benefit nature and communities. One example is a $5 million campaign to save from extinction the world's five remaining tiger species. In 1997 the Exxon Foundation made charitable contributions of $55 million; this was seven thousandths of 1 percent of its $8.5 billion profits that year.

In 1989 a company tanker, the *Exxon Valdez,* spilled 11 million gallons of oil into Alaskan waters. This disaster created enormous legal, political, and social problems for Exxon. Relations became tense and bitter with the State of Alaska and several federal agencies, including the Department of Justice and the Environmental Protection Agency. In 1990 a punitive federal law, the Oil Protection Act, was passed. One provision, inserted by Senator Ted Stevens (R-Alaska), barred the *Exxon Valdez* from ever entering Prince William Sound again.

It cost Exxon $2.5 billion to clean up the spill and it paid an additional $1 billion to the State of Alaska. In 1996 a federal court ordered it to pay another $5.1 billion in damages and the company has appealed.

The spill tarnished the company's long reputation for environmental responsibility. It was accused of lax operations, a grudging response to public concerns about the spill, and a slow cleanup. The previous year Exxon had ranked sixth on *Fortune* magazine's list of most admired companies; the year of the spill, it dropped to 110.[2] Fifty thousand consumers tore up Exxon credit cards.

Exxon has angered Alaska residents by challenging the law prohibiting return of the *Exxon Valdez* to their shores. The tanker, which was renamed *SeaRiver Mediterranean*, now sails around the Mediterranean Sea, but its large capacity could benefit the company more in Alaska because profit margins on Alaskan crude are higher. Exxon believes that under maritime law there is no precedent for banning a ship from navigable waters. One of its lawyers compared the ban with a prohibition on driving a car past the point of a prior accident. Alaska residents see it differently. According to a fisheries professor at the University of Alaska, returning the ship "would be like telling the people of Hiroshima you want to bring the Enola Gay back to Japan for passenger service."[3]

Shareholders are restive as well. At the 1997 annual meeting, the Sinsi-nawa Dominicans, an order of nuns that owns Exxon stock, made a proposal to tie the compensation of Exxon's top management to social and environmental criteria. The sisters were upset that the highest-paid executives were getting millions in salary and stock options while the welfare of stockholders was clouded by a pendent $5 billion judgment for damages from the oil spill. Exxon fought with the Securities and Exchange Commission to block the sister's motion, but lost. At the meeting, CEO Lee R. Raymond (who earned $2.9 million plus 943,125 option shares that year) and the other directors recommended a vote against it. The nun's proposal was defeated; only 9.6 percent of shareholders voted for it.[4]

The story of Exxon illustrates the significance of interactions between business, government, and society. We begin the chapter with two questions: First, what is the BGS field? And second, why is the field important to managers? Then we present four basic conceptual models that are alternative ways of picturing the BGS interrelationship. Finally, we explain our approach to the subject matter of this book.

---

[2]Paul Wiseman, "Dark Days for Oil Giant," *USA Today*, April 26, 1990, p. 1B.

[3]Rick Steiner, quoted in Stanton H. Patty, "In the Wake of the Valdez," *San Francisco Examiner*, February 8, 1998, p. T-1.

[4]"1997 Proxy Season Report," *The Corporate Examiner*, July 31, 1997, p. 3.

What Is the Business–Government–Society (BGS) Field?

In the universe of human endeavor, we can distinguish subdivisions of economic activity, political activity, and social activity—that is, business, government, and society—in every nation throughout time. The interaction among these activities creates an environment in which business operates. We define the BGS field as the study of this environment and its effect on management.

First, we define the basic terms. *Business* is a broad term encompassing a range of actions and institutions. Included are enterprises that range in scale from hamburger stands to giant corporations. The term covers manufacturing, finance, trade, service, and other economic activities. The fundamental purpose of business activity is to satisfy human needs by creating wealth.

Government is a term that denotes the structures and processes through which public policies, programs, and rules are authoritatively made for society. Like business, it encompasses a wide range of organizations at the local, state, and federal levels. In this book, we focus on the economic and regulatory powers of government, especially those of the federal government, and their impact on business.

A *society* is a network of human relations with three interrelated parts: (1) ideas, (2) institutions, and (3) material things.

Ideas, or intangible objects of thought, include values and ideologies. Values are enduring beliefs that fundamental choices in personal and social life are correct. Ideologies—for example, democracy and capitalism—are bundles of values that create a particular world view. Both establish the broad goals of life expressed in terms of what is considered good, true, right, beautiful, and acceptable. Ideas shape the institutions of society, including business.

Institutions are formal patterns of relations that link people together to accomplish a goal. Examples are the corporation, government, labor unions, and universities. Complex institutions such as the legal system contain many elements. Rules and procedures determine how they work. Institutions reflect the basic ideas of a society. The U.S. Constitution, for example, contains rules for governance based on ideas prevailing among the founders in the 1780s when it was written. Since they believed that human nature was corruptible, they divided power among three branches of government to prevent tyranny by an unchecked ruler. Institutions are essential to a society because they coordinate the work of individuals who have no personal relationship with each other.[5]

The third element in society is material things, including natural resources, land, and manufactured goods. These help shape, and are partly products of, ideas and institutions. Economic institutions, together with the scale of resources, mainly determine the type and quantity of a society's material goods.

---

[5]Arnold J. Toynbee, *A Study of History*, vol. XII, *Reconsiderations*, London: Oxford University Press, 1961, p. 270.

The BGS field studies the interaction of the three broad areas defined above, and it does so primarily by focusing on the interaction of business with the other two elements. The primary focus, therefore, is on how business shapes and changes government and society, and how it, in turn, is molded by political and social pressures. Of special interest is how the manager's task is affected by the interaction of forces in the BGS nexus.

In every country, the BGS relationship is unique and changes over time. In the United States, for example, business was much more free of restraint by government 100 years ago than it is now. In Russia, due to the fall of communism, newly private companies are freer from government restraint now than just ten years ago, but they confront older socialist values hostile toward profit-making that remain widespread in the population.

Why Is the BGS Field Important to Managers?

To succeed in meeting its objectives, a business must be responsive to both its economic and its noneconomic environment. Exxon, for example, must be efficient in producing and transporting energy and chemicals to consumers. Yet swift response to market forces is not always enough. There are powerful nonmarket forces to which every business, especially a large one, is exposed. Their importance is especially clear in the two dramatic events that punctuate Exxon Corporation's history—the 1911 Court-ordered breakup and the 1989 *Exxon Valdez* oil spill. In 1911 the Supreme Court, which reflected the social and political will as well as the letter of the law, forced Standard Oil to conform with social values. In 1989, a single event instantly changed Exxon's political and social environment, resulting in sanctions by government and the public.

Recognizing that a company operates within a society is important. If the society does not accept a company's actions, that company will be punished and constrained. There exists in every era a basic agreement between business institutions and society known as the *social contract*. This contract defines broad relationships between business and society. The contract is partly expressed in legislation and law. It is also found in social values that affect business activity. To illustrate, after high unemployment throughout Europe in the 1930s, public faith in free markets was diminished and many nations nationalized companies to ensure that high employment levels would be maintained.

Unfortunately for managers, the social contract is not as clear-cut as are the economic forces a business faces, as complex and ambiguous as the latter often are. For example, it is widely recognized today that business has social responsibilities that go beyond making profits and obeying regulations. If a business does not meet them, it may suffer. But precisely what are they? To what extent must a business comply when specific obligations are not written into law? How does the social responsibility of a large company differ from that of a small one? These questions will be addressed later in the book.

It should be underscored that if a business manager ignores or violates the social contract, as vague as parts of it may be, he or she is courting disaster.

> ### The Social Contract as Corporate Policy
>
> At Procter & Gamble the existence and importance of a social contract are implicit in the following excerpts from a policy statement entitled "Our Role in Society."
>
> > A corporation like Procter & Gamble traces its existence to laws established by society. In establishing the corporation, society gave it certain rights to encourage its success and longevity. In return, we believe a corporation has certain responsibilities to society—to the governmental entities which authorize its existence, to our employees, our shareholders, our consumers, and the communities and nations where we operate . . .
> >
> > Going hand-in-hand with our responsibility to build a successful business is, of course, our responsibility to abide by the laws and regulations of the countries and communities in which we do business; and we do this everywhere we operate. In fact, we often go beyond what is required by law in how we treat our employees, the environment, and the communities where we live . . .[6]

And a manager must react not only to today's noneconomic environment but also to that of the future. During growth of the chemical industry, some leading corporations followed lawful, but comparatively lax, waste disposal procedures. Inevitably, people sought protection from dangerous chemicals and Congress passed the Superfund law in 1980. Then these companies had to pay astronomical sums to clean leaking dumps. So, the response to the question of why the BGS field is important to managers is: To be successful, business managers must understand, respond properly to, and anticipate demands of the noneconomic environment as well as the economic environment.

Four Models of the BGS Relationship

People view the BGS nexus differently. They have frames of reference, or intuitive models, through which they evaluate the interplay of economic, political, and social forces. Depending on their chosen mental model, they may reach entirely different conclusions about central issues. They may differ, for example, about the scope of business power in society, criteria for making business decisions, the extent of corporate social responsibility, the ethical duties of managers, and the need for regulation. Therefore, it is important to know the model, or conceptual framework, that a person has in mind.

---

[6]The full statement can be read at www.pg.com/docCommunity/activity/.

The following four models are basic alternatives for conceptualizing the BGS relationship. As abstractions they simplify reality, but each is a strong lens for focusing on central issues. Each model is both descriptive and prescriptive; that is, it can be seen as an explanation of how the BGS relationship does work or, in addition, as an ideal about how it should work.

The Market Capitalism Model

The market capitalism model, as shown in Figure 1-1 (below), has been popular among managers and economists for more than two centuries. It visualizes the business system as substantially sheltered from the direct impact of social forces and focuses on the primacy of economic forces. It depicts business as existing within a market environment that is influenced and shaped both by business operations and by impinging social and political forces. The market in the model is a buffer between business units and nonmarket forces.

The system depicted in this model is classical capitalism. It is a system in which most economic activity is carried on by private firms in a competitive market. The pricing system of the market allocates resources. The efficient operation of this system is based on a number of fundamental assumptions.[7]

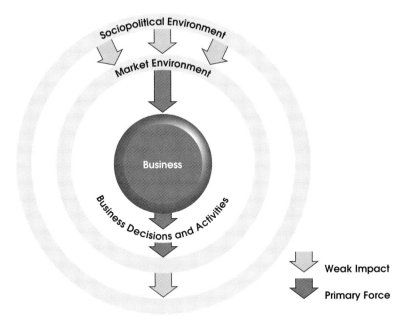

FIGURE 1-1

The market capitalism model.

---

[7]The model was built in consideration of the way in which the ideal operation of the free enterprise system was first enunciated by Adam Smith in his *Wealth of Nations* (New York: The Modern Library, 1937), first published in 1776.

One assumption is that government interference in economic life will be minimal. This is called *laissez-faire,* a term first used by the French. It meant literally that government should "let us alone." This led to the idea that government intervention in the market is both inappropriate and unnecessary. It is inappropriate because it lessens the efficiency with which free enterprise operates to benefit consumers. It is unnecessary because market forces are sufficient to channel business efforts to meet social needs. Noneconomic goals or performance measures are not legitimate yardsticks for judging business. Market performance should be the only accepted measure of social performance. It is for government, not the free enterprise system, to minister to social problems. Managers, therefore, should define company interests narrowly, as profitability and efficient use of scarce resources. Business makes its primary contribution to society by creating wealth from profitable operations.

Another fundamental assumption is that individuals have maximum freedom to pursue their own self-interest. Each individual, it is reasoned, is motivated to make money. Acting through the market, the self-interest of individuals is harnessed to create economic progress. In market competition, individuals and companies enrich themselves and society only by creating value for customers.

The model assumes also that individuals can own private property and are free to risk business investments. Under these circumstances, managers are powerfully motivated to make a profit. If there is free competition in the market, profits will be held to a minimum and the quality of products and services will rise as firms try to attract more buyers. If one enterprise tries to increase profits by charging higher prices, consumers will go to a competitor. If one producer makes higher-quality products, others will be forced to follow. The free market, therefore, is a mechanism that converts competition into broad social benefits.

Space does not permit elaboration of all the assumptions but others can be mentioned. Individuals will have full knowledge of products and prices and make rational decisions; there will be many producers in competitive markets; the interests of enterprises and consumers are closely related; pursuit of self-interest in business is accompanied by moral restraint; and there will exist basic institutions, such as a reliable banking system, to facilitate commerce.

The perspective of the market capitalism model encourages the following conclusions about the BGS relationship. There should be only limited government regulation. The market mechanism disciplines economic activity to promote social welfare. The responsibility of a corporation is to make a profit; the moral duty of a manager is to the owners of a business.

In the United States, the idea of laissez-faire economics underlying the market capitalism model dominated the public imagination from the colonial era to the 1930s depression era. Over this time the model described well the BGS relationship. Beginning in the 1930s, however, faith in the market was tarnished by visible failures of the business system. These included unemployment, monopoly, unethical behavior, income inequality, and pollution. Public disenchantment with laissez-faire led to massive intrusions of government into the market to correct these flaws.

Today the market capitalism model remains an inspiration for many, and parts of it remain valid. However, as a description of the BGS relationship it is distorted in light of current realities. Today the social responsiveness of business is not as limited as this model implies, and other assumptions upon which the model is based are contrary to reality. Government regulation is extensive. Contemporary managers must respond to sociopolitical forces outside the market. And society defines corporate responsibility much more broadly than efficient production and profit making.

Nevertheless, this model is still widely used as a lens through which many, particularly managers of small companies, view the BGS relationship. The ideology of capitalism still dominates economic values in the United States and is of growing importance in other nations.

The Dominance Model

The dominance model is a second basic way of looking at the BGS relationship. In the United States, this model represents primarily the perspective of business critics. In it, business and government dominate the great mass of people. This idea is represented in the pyramidal, hierarchical image of society shown in Figure 1-2. Those who subscribe to the model believe that a small elite sits astride a system that works to increase and perpetuate wealth and

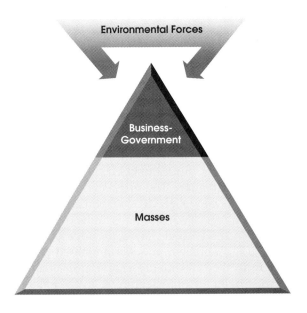

FIGURE 1-2

The dominance model.

power for a privileged few at the expense of the many. Such a system is, of course, undemocratic. In democratic theory, government and leaders represent interests expressed by the people.

Proponents of the dominance model conclude that corporations are insulated from pressures that promote responsibility to social welfare, that regulation by a government in thrall to big business is ineffectual, and that market forces are inadequate to ensure ethical management.

In the United States the dominance model gained a following during the latter half of the nineteenth century when large trusts emerged and corruptly manipulated politicians and legislatures. Beginning in the 1870s, farmers and other critics of big business rejected the ideal of the market capitalism model and based a reform movement called *populism* on the critical view of the BGS relationship in the dominance model.

This was an era when, for the first time, on a national scale the actions of powerful business magnates and financiers shaped the destinies of common people. And they openly displayed their contempt for commoners. "The public be damned," snapped William H. Vanderbilt when a reporter told him that as a railroad owner he had a responsibility to the public, "I am working for my stockholders."[8] Later, when some business leaders became

This 1900 political cartoon illustrates a central theme of the dominance model, that powerful business interests act in concert with government to further selfish money interests. Although the cartoon is old, the idea remains compelling for many.

IN THE HANDS OF HIS PHILANTHROPIC FRIENDS.

---

[8]Cited in Clifton Fadiman, ed., *The Little Brown Book of Anecdotes*, Boston: Little, Brown, 1985, p. 560

worried about federal antitrust legislation, Edward Harriman, another railroad giant, was not worried and "declared that if he wanted state legislation, he could buy it and that if necessary he could buy Congress and the judiciary as well."[9]

The populist movement in America ultimately failed to reform the BGS relationship. Marxism, an ideology opposed to industrial capitalism, emerged in Europe at about the same time as populism here and also contained ideas resonant with the dominance model. In capitalist societies, according to Karl Marx, an elite ruling class dominates the economy and other institutions. This led many business critics worldwide to advocate socialist governments that, based on Marx's theory, could achieve more equitable distributions of wealth and power.

Critical attitudes about business in a capitalist society live on. The following are the words of one recent critic.

> We are ruled by Big Business and Big Government . . . Corporate money is wrecking popular government in the United States. The big corporations and the hundred millionaires and billionaires have taken daily control of our work, our pay, our housing, our health, our pension funds, our bank and savings deposits, our public lands, our airwaves, our elections and our very government.[10]

In the United States today, the dominance model, in its most unadulterated form, is a theory opposed by considerable scholarship that holds that multiple forces in society channel and control corporate and government power. However, there is still widespread attraction to it; the American public is traditionally suspicious of centralized power in business or government. It remains one of the fundamental alternative perspectives of the BGS relationship.

At times in the past, as in the post–Civil War era, the dominance model was in close accord with reality. It is also close to the reality of the BGS relationship in some other nations, where government and business have closer formal affiliation than in the United States. In Asian countries such as Japan, China, Korea, and Singapore, governments interact closely with business to direct industrial development and trade. In the mixed economies of Europe such as France, Germany, and Great Britain, governments have nationalized companies and imposed economic planning. In many countries with tight business–government ties, social traditions are much different than in the United States, and these ties are not seen as exploitive. China, for example, has an authoritarian tradition of dominance by central political authority that most citizens accept. In Japan and Korea, the public regards close business–government cooperation as a means of accelerating economic progress. And in Europe, the mixed economy was embraced as a way of recovering from the ravages of depression and war.

---

[9]James A. Barnes, *Wealth of the American People*, New York: Prentice Hall, 1949, p. 630.
[10]Ronnie Dugger, "Welcome to Our Future," *The Progressive Populist*, January 1997, p. 1.

The Dynamic Forces Model

The dynamic forces model, shown in Figure 1-3, depicts the BGS relationship as a system of interactions. As complicated as the model seems, it does not fully reveal the extraordinary range of interactions among the major elements of society. But it does clearly show dominant flows of influence. It shows that the main influences on business come from changes in environmental forces, both economic and noneconomic; their impact on the public; and the influence of these forces on the political process, which in turn affects businesses. In addition, the model shows that business influences all other parts of society.

This is a dynamic model of multiple, or pluralistic, forces. Their strength waxes and wanes depending on factors such as the subject at issue, the power of competing interests, the intensity of public opinion, and the influence of leaders. The dynamic forces model reflects the BGS relationship in industrialized nations with democratic traditions. It differs from the market capitalism model, because it opens business directly to influence by nonmarket forces. Many forces shown as important in the dynamic forces model would be evaluated as negligible in the dominance model.

What overarching conclusions can be drawn from this model?

1. Business is deeply integrated into an open society and must respond to many forces, both economic and noneconomic. It is not isolated from its social environment, nor is it dominant.
2. Business is a major initiator of change in society through its interaction with government, its production and marketing activities, and its use of new technologies.

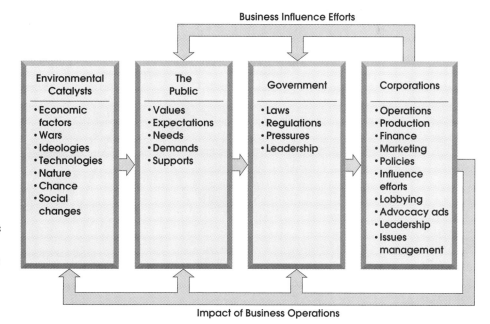

FIGURE 1-3

The dynamic forces model.

Source: Adapted from Neil H. Jacoby, *Corporate Power and Social Responsibility*, New York: The Free Press, 1973, p. 189.

3. Broad public support of business depends on its adjustment to multiple social, political, and economic forces. Incorrect adjustment leads to failure. This is the social contract at work.

4. BGS relationships continuously evolve as changes take place in the main ideas, institutions, and processes of society.

The Stakeholder Model

In the stakeholder model, as shown in Figure 1-4, the business firm is at the center of a set of mutual relationships with persons and groups known as *stakeholders.* Stakeholders are those who are benefited or burdened by the firm's operation; that is, they have a stake in it. For a large corporation, this definition of a stakeholder includes a wide range of entities, which can be divided into two categories based on their relative importance. *Primary* stakeholders have an im-

FIGURE 1-4

The stakeholder model.

mediate, continuous, and powerful impact on a firm. They are stockholders (owners), customers, employees, communities, and governments and may, depending on the firm, include others such as suppliers or creditors. *Secondary* stakeholders include a wide range of entities that have less power to influence the firm's activities, but that affect or are affected by its operations. Examples are environmentalists, the media, trade associations, universities, and religious orders.[11] Exponents of the model debate how to identify who is a stakeholder.[12] Some use a very broad definition and include, for example, future generations and natural entities such as the earth's atmosphere, oceans, terrain, and living creatures because corporations have an impact on them.[13]

The stakeholder model reorders the priorities of management away from what they are in the market capitalism model. There, the corporation is the private property of owners who invest capital. It combines capital from investors with materials from suppliers and labor from employees into products that are sold to satisfy consumer demand. The dominant purpose of the firm is to benefit one group of stakeholders—investors. In the stakeholder model, however, the welfare of each stakeholder must be considered as an end; stakeholders are not valued only as means to enrich investors. Put differently, "stakeholders are defined by *their* legitimate interest in the corporation, rather than simply by the corporation's interest in *them*."[14] Managers should be strongly responsive to multiple stakeholders, and because of this, the investor's interests receive less emphasis.

The way of looking at the corporation prescribed by the stakeholder model, then, emphasizes duties toward others in society, duties that are not recognized in traditional economic theory. The traditional theory of the corporation encourages it to dominate its environment and to maximize stockholder wealth. Stakeholder theory asserts a moral duty for management to shift its gaze beyond profits and see a range of stakeholder interests. One scholar, for example, argues that stakeholders are "moral agents" entitled to common rights and considerations. To ensure regard for these rights, corporate directors have a "duty of care" to see that the corporation is managed "in the interests of its stakeholders."[15]

---

[11]See, for example, Max Clarkson, "A Stakeholder Framework for Analyzing and Evaluating Corporate Social Performance," *Academy of Management Review,* January 1995, pp. 106–7.

[12]Ronald K. Mitchell, Bradley R. Agle, and Donna J. Wood, "Toward a Theory of Stakeholder Identification and Salience: Defining the Principle of Who and What Really Counts," *Academy of Management Review,* October 1997, pp. 853–64.

[13]See, for example, Mark Starik, "Essay by Mark Starik," *Business and Society,* April 1994, pp. 92–93.

[14]Thomas Donaldson and Lee E. Preston, "The Stakeholder Theory of the Corporation: Concepts, Evidence, and Implications," *Academy of Management Review,* January 1995, p. 76. Emphasis in original.

[15]R. Edward Freeman, "The Politics of Stakeholder Theory: Some Future Directions," *Business Ethics Quarterly,* October 1994, p. 417. See also Freeman's landmark book *Strategic Management: A Stakeholder Approach,* Boston, Mass.: Pitman, 1984.

Overall, the stakeholder model is more than a descriptive model of corporations in their environment. It is intended by its advocates to redefine the corporation. It rejects the traditional, shareholder-centered view of the corporation in the market capitalism model. "The plain truth is," write two of its advocates, "that the most prominent alternative to stakeholder theory (i.e., the 'management serving the shareowners' theory) is morally untenable."[16]

The stakeholder model seeks to create a doctrine of ethical duties toward multiple stakeholders that would shift power in the corporation, reducing that of owners and increasing that of other interests. But not everyone agrees. Critics of the model argue that it sets up too vague a guideline to substitute for market incentives. There are a number of mysteries in stakeholder theory. It is not clear who or what is a legitimate stakeholder, to what each stakeholder is entitled, or how managers should balance competing demands among a range of stakeholders. And, unlike the old criterion of return on capital in traditional capitalism, there is no single, clear, and objective measure to evaluate the combined moral/economic performance of a firm. According to one critic, this lack of a criterion "would render impossible rational management decision-making for there is simply no way to adjudicate between alternative projects when there is more than one bottom line."[17]

The stakeholder model not only rejects central elements of the market capitalism model, but is basically different from the other two models as well. It rejects the dominance model. And it is narrower than the dynamic forces model, which shows a wide range of power flows encompassing stakeholder interactions but, in addition, shows interactions with broad social forces.

What Are the Main Characteristics
of the Analysis in This Book?

The interrelationships among business, government, and society are multifaceted, and discussion could be organized in many ways. The following are the principal characteristics of our analysis in this book.

Focus on Strategic Management

Strategic management refers to actions that adapt a company to its changing environment. To compete and survive, firms must create missions, purposes, and objectives; the policies and programs to achieve them; and the methods to implement them. In this book we discuss these elements and illustrate successes and failures along the way.

---

[16]Donaldson and Preston, "The Stakeholder Theory of the Corporation," p. 88.
[17]John Argenti, "Stakeholders: The Case Against," *Long Range Planning*, June 1997, p. 444.

All broad competitive strategies consider important stakeholders and social forces. We are especially concerned with the strategic thinking in the following areas:

- Defining the social responsibilities of the company.
- Reacting to changing social values about a company's products or the changing values of workers about its policies.
- Responding to government regulations in areas such as pollution, product safety, diversity, integrity, and labor.
- Determining how the company will try to influence government.
- Establishing ethical standards within the company.

Interdisciplinary Approach with a Managerial Focus

This is a field in which the limited perspectives of single academic disciplines impede understanding. Many disciplines must be considered in dealing with theory, practice, and policy issues in the BGS interface. They include the business disciplines, particularly management; the social sciences, including economics, political science, philosophy, history, and sociology; the professional disciplines, including medicine, law, and theology; and from time to time, the natural sciences such as biology and chemistry. Our approach, therefore, is eclectic; we cross lines and boundaries to find knowledge. Our dominant orientation, however, is the discipline of management.

Comprehensive Scope

This book is comprehensive. We try to cover a large canvas, sketching the most important BGS interrelationships. This approach is in contrast to that of concentrating intensively on a few areas. Seeing a panoramic view is better for students new to the field than having an in-depth understanding of only a few areas.

Focus on Theory

Theories simplify and organize areas of knowledge by describing patterns or regularities in the subject matter. They are important in every field, but especially in this one, where innumerable details from broad areas of human experience intersect to create a new intellectual universe.

Unfortunately, there is no underlying theory integrating the entire field, nor is there likely to be one soon. The beginnings of an underlying theory of business and its relationship to society are emerging. There is growing agreement, for example, about the necessity and moral obligation of corporations to respond to social pressures and the conditions for doing so. But a comprehensive theory remains elusive. So we do not approach study in the field from any single theoretical standpoint.

Fortunately, in many areas useful theories exist in relevant disciplines. For example, there are tested legal theories concerned with manufacturer liability, economic theories about the impact of government regulation, scientific theories regarding industrial pollution, and political theories explaining corporate power. We discuss such theories where they are relevant.

Historical Perspective

History is the study of phenomena moving through time. The BGS relationship is a stream of events, of which only one part exists today. To the extent practicable, we examine the antecedents of current arrangements. Historical perspective is important for many reasons. It helps us see that today's BGS relationship is not like that of other eras; that current ideas and institutions are not the only alternative; that these ideas and institutions developed in interaction with business; that historical forces are irrepressible; that corporations both cause and adapt to change; and that the pattern of future events is being shaped today.

The historical record of the BGS relationship shows both regularity and uniqueness. One regular pattern is the rise of a new industry or technology followed immediately by outcry about the problems it creates and sometime later by government regulation to mitigate harms. Early railroads, for example, disrupted farmers when trains bisected their pastures, hit their cattle, and threw flaming cinders onto barn roofs. Soon the states set up railroad commissions and legislated to control these abuses. Similarly, the late-nineteenth-century colossus of Standard Oil developed ahead of laws to control its size and power, but the Sherman Antitrust Act eventually broke it into many pieces. Today, global corporations are said to exploit labor in poorer nations. What regulations will arise to control them? A unique event is the poison gas leak from a Union Carbide pesticide plant in Bhopal, India, in 1984 that killed and injured thousands. This leak was preventable. But because it happened, the sociopolitical environment of the chemical industry changed in ways it would not have otherwise.

Global Perspective

In this book we focus primarily on business in the United States. Yet the spread of a global economy makes it impossible to isolate the BGS relationship in one country without considering the impact of international forces. Today some large corporations that we think of as American conduct the bulk of their operations in other countries. Exxon, Mobil, IBM, Coca-Cola, McDonald's, Gillette, and Boeing are a few American-based multinationals that get more than 50 percent of their revenue overseas. The growth of global markets has had a profound impact on governments, which find their economic and social welfare policies judged by world financial markets. And on a societal plane, issues such as human rights for labor and income gaps between rich and poor countries challenge the international community. Therefore, in this book we add a global perspective to the discussion where appropriate.

The Business Environment

| **Enron Corporation** |
| www.enron.com |

In January 1995, a consortium headed by Enron Corp. (with Bechtel, Inc., and General Electric's GE Capital Corporation) completed the paperwork to begin construction of a $2.8 billion power plant at Dabhol in the state of Maharashtra, India. In February an election was held in that state and the Hindu nationalist party (BJP) teamed up with a splinter group and gained control of the government of Maharashtra. In August 1995, after Enron and its partners began construction and spent some $300 million, the new government based in Bombay "repudiated" the contracts Enron had negotiated with the previous government and with the national government in New Delhi and vowed to "throw Enron

into the sea" and not pay Enron and its partners 1 penny.

This action should be considered in light of a crippling power shortage in the state of Maharashtra, one of the major industrial areas of India, and the promise that the investment of Enron and its partners would stimulate substantial further investment in the poverty-stricken country. Furthermore, it was the previous Maharashtra state government that invited Enron to build the plant. This was in accord with a policy of the national government in New Delhi to welcome foreign investment. What happened?

The political environment for Enron changed radically. The BJP is a left-wing group that fanned the flames of anti-foreign influence that existed in Maharashtra and in other areas of India. So, it was natural that when it gained control of the government, it would reflect that sentiment.

Many charges were levied against Enron. It was accused of getting the contract without competitive bidding, of being too costly, of harming the environment, of fraud and misrepresentation, and of making bribes to get the contracts. Enron vehemently rejected these charges and none were proven.

An expert committee was formed to renegotiate the contract and agreement with the Dabhol partners which was reached and announced in early 1996. Construction was resumed and the plant was scheduled to begin commercial operations in late 1998. A second phase of the undertaking to double megawatt output is expected to begin operations in late 2000.

This story illustrates how an environment may change suddenly from bright to dark. Environment has more to do with the success or failure of a company than any other force. A slight miscalculation or unforeseen event in the environment can lead, at best, to a decline of profits and, at worst, to bankruptcy. Understanding the characteristics of the dominant environments of business, domestic and international, is of major importance to business managers and those who aspire to successful careers in business.

This chapter expands on this point. It begins with a survey of eight fundamental historical forces that underlie short- and medium-range trends in the business environment. There follows discussion of the major environments of importance to business. We conclude with comments about the impact of business on the environment.

The Volatility of the Business Environment

In 1844 Philip Hone, the mayor of New York City, was baffled by the volatility of his environment. "This world is going on too fast," he wrote. "Improvements, Politics, Reform, Religion—all fly. Railroads, steamers, packets, race against time and beat it hollow. Flying is dangerous. By and by we shall have balloons and pass over to Europe between sun and sun. Oh, for the good old days of heavy post-coaches and speed at the rate of six miles an hour!"[1]

Hone's views reflect what people have experienced throughout history, including today. From ancient to modern times, environments have been volatile and generally unpredictable. For example, the Black Death in the middle of the fourteenth century killed one-third of the population of Europe and completely changed that world. The industrial revolution in the eighteenth century in England was unforeseen and changed the world significantly for all time. Businesses in the American colonies in the seventeenth and eighteenth centuries were more and more restrained by so-called navigation acts imposed by the

---

[1]Quoted by John Steel Gordon in "When Our Ancestors Became Us," *American Heritage,* December 1989, p. 108.

British Parliament to control exports from and imports to the colonies in the interests of England. Throughout the eighteenth and early nineteenth centuries in the United States, most businesses were able to exploit a vast continent with unbounded resources and friendly governments. That freedom was considerably reduced in the late nineteenth and twentieth centuries as business became subject to ever-widening and more restrictive government regulations.

Throughout history, people in business who have been unaware of or ignored their changing environments have, at best, lost opportunities for profit and, at worst, led their companies to disaster. Look at the Baldwin Locomotive Works, for example. That firm was started by Matthias W. Baldwin, a watchmaker, to make steam locomotives. The first engine he produced—"Old Ironsides"—was built in 1832. It was one of the first steam engines made in this country. By the time of Baldwin's death in 1866, the plant had built 1,500 locomotives for American and foreign railroads. As the years went by, Baldwin's company prospered and had a virtual monopoly on the production of steam locomotives in the United States. However, its management failed to see the significance of the diesel locomotive and the company went bankrupt. On the other hand, General Electric seized the opportunity offered by diesel technology and began producing diesel locomotives. GE now dominates the worldwide market for this type of locomotive power.

Today's changing conditions in the United States and around the globe bewilder people in and out of business with their volatility and scope. Our textile, automobile, television, and many other manufacturers, for example, have felt the sting of global competition. Our pharmaceutical firms, banks, and computer firms have met foreign competition and thrived in the global marketplace. The recent financial crisis in southeastern Asian countries, and Russia, created serious economic uncertainties for managers all over the world.

Underlying Historical Forces Changing the Business Environment

We believe that in a broad sense, order can be found in the swirling patterns of current events; that there is a deep logic in the passing of history; and that change in the business environment is the result of elemental historical forces trending in roughly predictable directions. Henry Adams defined a historical force as "anything that does, or helps to do, work."[2] The work to which Adams refers is the manifest power to cause events. Change in the business environment is the work of events caused by the eight deep historical forces or streams of related events discussed below. Corporate strategy is the effect of business to adapt to the continuous changes caused by these forces.

---

[2]In the essay "A Dynamic Theory of History (1904)," in Henry Adams, *The Education of Henry Adams*, New York: The Modern Library, 1931, p. 474; originally published in 1908.

The Industrial Revolution

The first historical force is the industrial revolution. The breakup of small, local economies and the invention of new machinery and manufacturing techniques in seventeenth-century Europe led to expanded markets and mass-production technology that combined capital, labor, and natural resources in dynamic new ways. The growth of mass-consumer societies and a world economy in the twentieth century are but two recent echoes of this industrial "big bang." The ramifications of the industrial revolution ripple out through time to define the strategic business environment in many ways. For example, new and larger factories, massive capital accumulation, management techniques for organizing huge corporations, and the interdependence of financial markets all articulate its centuries-old premise. These developments, in turn, lead to changed values, institutions, land uses, and lifestyles.

Dominant Ideologies

A second historical force is the impact of dominant ideologies. An ideology is a worldview that is built upon and reinforces a set of beliefs and values. For example, the idea of progress, which has been a defining ideology in Western civilization, was built on a set of beliefs that arose with industrialism. Adam Smith taught that market economies were a great advance that harnessed human greed for the public good. Charles Darwin wrote that the biological world was characterized by constant improvement, and Herbert Spencer argued in what later came to be called social Darwinism that competition in the business world weeded out the unfit and drove humanity in upward motion toward betterment. The idea of progress reinforced values of particular importance to business such as optimism, thrift, competitiveness, individualism, and freedom from government interference.

A small number of powerful, well-developed doctrines define a worldview for millions of people. Americans and Western Europeans largely adhere to ideologies of capitalism, constitutional democracy, and the major Western religions of Catholicism and its offshoot, Protestantism. Other nations, facing different historical challenges, have been attracted to different ideologies. In Russia the populace accepted autocratic ideologies such as czarism and communism as the price of having a ruling power capable of maintaining national boundaries.

Tensions frequently arise between ideologies. For example, the accumulation of great wealth is justified by capitalism, but when this wealth is translated into social power, it conflicts with tenets of democracy that give mass populations the right to check ruling classes in the exercise of power. Tensions between these two ideologies have ignited political movements and led to redistribution of power.

Inequality of Human Circumstances

From time immemorial, societies have been marked by status distinctions, class structures, and gaps between rich and poor. Inequality is ubiquitous, as are its consequences—jealousy, demands for equality, and doctrines that justify why some people have more than others. The basic political conflict in every nation is the result of economic antagonism between rich and poor.[3] This is the conflict, manifest in the competition between Athens' democracy and Sparta's oligarchy, that debilitated and eventually tore apart ancient Hellenic civilization. In the modern world, industrialism has accelerated the accumulation of wealth without solving the persistent problem of its uneven distribution. The current emphasis on corporate social responsibility in the business environment is, in a general sense, based on the need to mitigate the appearance of remote and unresponsive concentrated wealth.

Science and Technology

The great scientific developments of civilization since Leonardo da Vinci in fifteenth-century Italy have been fuel for the powerful engine of commerce. From the water wheel to recombinant DNA, business has utilized new discoveries to more efficiently convert basic resources into equity. The development of the microchip brought changes in virtually every facet of the business environment. Like the automobile in its time, it has changed society.

Nation-States

The modern nation-state system arose in an unplanned way out of the wreckage of the Roman Empire as princes and monarchs expanded and consolidated empires in Europe after the Peace of Westphalia in 1648. The institution of the nation-state was well-suited for Western Europe, where boundaries were contiguous with the extent of languages. But the nation-state idea was subsequently transplanted to territories in Eastern Europe, Southwest Asia, and the Middle East, partly by force of colonial empires and partly by mimicry among non-Western political elites for whom the idea had attained high prestige. And where it was transplanted, nations were often irrationally defined and boundary lines divided natural groupings of culture, ethnicity, and language.

Today the world is a mosaic of independent countries, each with a separate government to impose social order and economic stability over its territory. And in each there develop feelings of nationalism or loyalty to a national identity. The dynamics of this system are a powerful force in the international business environment. Conflict among nations seeking to aggrandize their power and wealth is frequent, as occurred in the 1930s when Japan colonized South

---

[3]Mortimer J. Adler, *The Great Ideas*, New York: Macmillan, 1992, pp. 578–79.

Asian countries to gain access to oil and bauxite. Conflict between culture groupings across nation-state boundaries is today increasingly prominent.[4] The nationalistic feelings of Palestinians deposed from Israeli territory and living in other countries have affected American companies in many ways, from oil companies that have been caught in Middle East conflicts to airlines that lose passengers afraid of terrorism. For many reasons, the nation-state system is one of the major sources of turbulence in the business environment.

Great Leadership

Great leaders have brought beneficial as well as disastrous changes to societies and businesses. In the third century B.C., Alexander the Great imposed his rule on the Mediterranean world and created new routes of trade on which Greek merchants flourished. On the other hand, leaders such as Adolph Hitler in Germany and Joseph Stalin in the Soviet Union brought to their societies disaster that retarded industrial growth.

There have been many business leaders whose actions had great impact. Probably no industrial leader in American history had a more profound influence on the nation than John D. Rockefeller. His Standard Oil Company of Ohio, from its inception in 1870 to its breakup by a Supreme Court antitrust decision in 1911, grew to completely dominate the oil industry and, in the process, changed the American economic, political, and social landscape. Today William Gates of Microsoft inspires comparisons to Rockefeller as the strategies of his company increasingly define how telecommunications technologies will be used in society.

There are two views about the power of leaders as a historical force. One is that leaders simply ride the wave of history. "Great men," writes Arnold Toynbee, "are precisely the points of intersection of great social forces."[5] The other is that leaders themselves change history rather than being pushed by its tide. "The history of the world," wrote Thomas Carlyle, "is at bottom the History of the Great Men who have worked here."[6] The cases and stories of business leaders in this text provide instances for debate of this provocative clash of views.

Population

The basic population trend throughout human history is growth. World population grew very slowly until the great transition to intensive agriculture about 10,000 years ago. As more food was raised using new methods, the population

---

[4]Samuel P. Huntington, *The Clash of Civilizations and the Remaking of World Order*, New York: Simon & Schuster, 1996.

[5]*A Study of History*, vol. XII, *Reconsiderations*, London: Oxford University Press, 1961, p. 125.

[6]In "The Hero as Divinity," reprinted in Carl Niemeyer, ed., *Thomas Carlyle on Heroes, Hero-Worship and the Heroic in History*, Lincoln, Neb.: University of Nebraska Press, 1966, p. 1. This essay was originally written in 1840.

began to grow faster. Then the growth rate accelerated again in the last century. This new growth spurt had two causes: First, advances in water sanitation and medicine reduced deaths from infectious disease and, second, mechanized farming further expanded the food supply. It had taken until 1825 for the world population to reach one billion; then each one billion additional people was added faster and faster—first in 100 years, then in 35, then 15, then only 12.[7]

The world's population in 1995 was 5.7 billion, and a United Nation's study predicts that it will grow to 9.4 billion by 2050, then stabilize at around 11 billion by 2200. This stabilization will occur if the assumption in the study is accurate that fertility rates will decline with predicted economic development. Growth is fastest in developing areas. Africa will quadruple its population by 2050; Asia and Latin America will about double theirs. The industrialized nations of the West are growing more slowly. The North American population will increase by only 71 percent, and the European population will actually fall by about 22 percent. Also, as life expectancy increases, populations are expected to age, more so in the United States, Japan, and Europe than in areas of rapid growth.[8]

These figures have many implications. For one, population growth will continue to strain the ecosystem. Some economists believe that even the current scale of economic activity is unsustainable in the long run, given the finite nature of earth's resources.[9] If industrialization based on the high-pollution, resource-intense Western model occurs in currently less developed areas of high population growth, the result is problematic. For another, the West is in demographic decline relative to other peoples. In 1900 Western nations held 30 percent of the world's population and had colonial rule over another 15 percent. But today they are stripped of their former colonies and hold only 13 percent of the world's population.[10] In the future, growing non-Western peoples will be stronger economically, militarily, and politically and will push to expand their influence. This can be seen now in Islamic societies, which have young, rapidly growing populations. Although Western market values and business ideology seem ascendant now, they may be less widespread in the future as Western power wanes. Many other implications for the business environment could be discussed. For instance, immigrants will move from high- to low-growth areas; workforces will age.

---

[7]Clive Ponting, *A Green History of the World,* New York: Penguin Books, 1991, p. 240.

[8]Population Division, Department of Economic and Social Affairs, UN Secretariat, "World Population Projections to 2150," New York: United Nations, February 1, 1998; see "Executive Summary."

[9]See, for example, Herman E. Daly, "Sustainable Growth? No Thank You." in Jerry Mander and Edward Goldsmith, *The Case Against the Global Economy,* San Francisco: Sierra Club Books, 1996, p. 194.

[10]Huntington, *The Clash of Civilizations,* p. 84.

Chance

When change occurs we seek causes. If two or more lines of action intersect in an event, its cause is known, as when the technological innovation of the diesel locomotive and the steam-locomotive–based strategy of the Baldwin Locomotive Company intersected to produce failure. But where lines of action cannot be observed or seem to be random, then the concept of chance can be used to explain an event. The first Tylenol murders occurred in September 1982, when seven people died from capsules filled with cyanide. This event, perhaps the work of one person, was followed over the years by recurrent and mysteriously random product tampering to poison consumers. This tampering created a major change in the production and marketing environments of food and over-the-counter drug companies. Was the initial tampering a random act unrelated to the actions of the corporations and victims it affected? Or can its causes be explained?

Many scholars are reluctant to use the concept of chance, accident, or random occurrence as a category of analysis. Yet some changes in the business environment may be best explained as the product of unknown and unpredictable causes. No less perceptive a student of history than Niccolò Machiavelli observed that fortune determines about half the course of human events and human beings the other half.[11] We cannot prove or disprove this estimate, but we note it. The student of the world surrounding business must recognize the role of caprice.

Six Key Environments of Business

Figure 2-1 shows the six most important environments affecting business today. In each of the environments shown, there are forces of revolutionary proportion bringing epic and rapid change in their impacts on society, governments, markets, consumers, and business. Understanding and adapting to these changes is no longer the sole responsibility of a company's top managers. Managers throughout an organization must continuously pay attention to them.

We turn now to thumbnail sketches of each of the dominant environments of business and the selected forces operating in them. We will dig deeper into these environments throughout the book.

The Economic Environment

The economic environment covers a vast territory and is, of course, of primary significance to business. The economic forces of concern to a company range from overall economic activity, as measured by the gross domestic product

---

[11]Niccolò Machiavelli, *The Prince*, trans. by George Bull, New York: Penguin Books, 1961, chapter XXV, p. 78.

FIGURE 2-1

The six key environments of business.

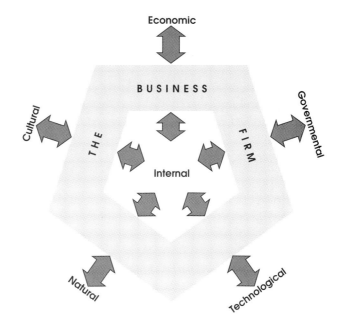

(GDP), to a competitor's actions in local and foreign areas. Following are a few dimensions to illustrate the scope, turbulence, complexity, and power of the economic environment of business.

Every important economic force has an impact on a wide range of other economic forces, which in turn affect others. The patterns of change vary with time and in intensity. To illustrate, commodity prices have fluctuated significantly in recent years and will doubtless do so again in the future, a matter of concern to business as well as consumers. But when and by how much will prices change? What will be the economic implications? No one really knows. Major changes in the general level of commodity prices will affect interest rates, consumer purchasing, stock and bond prices, basic raw material prices, and wage-rate demands, to mention but a few activities. Each of these forces affects other phenomena. For example, rising commodity prices tend to generate forces that lift interest rates. This, in turn, increases the cost of capital to business and dampens business borrowing for expansion. Rising interest rates also will bring a decline in bond prices. But rising, or lowering, interest rates result not only from commodity price increases. Higher interest rates can result from a too-rapid expansion of general economic activity and rising demand for capital, a decline in savings, or rising interest rates in a major foreign country that attract our limited capital.

These broad changes in the economic environment narrow down to specific impacts on an individual business and necessitate some difficult and often fateful decisions in dealing with them. A chief executive must answer such questions as the following: How will my costs of operations change? Wage rates? Raw materials? Health and benefit costs for my employees? Interest rates on my borrowing? What new competition will I face in the global market? How will the economic unification of Europe affect my business? Will my competitors here at home steal my market? How can I expand the demand for my products? How much research and development expenditures for new products shall I authorize?

Such underlying economic forces operate in every free enterprise and democratic country in the world, but differently in each one. For example, all countries have protective tariffs, but greater efforts are made in Japan to protect selected manufacturers and farmers from foreign competition than in the United States. In Europe, business in every country that is a member of the new European Union (see Chapter 13 for details) is being affected by the new Union rules.

The Technological Environment

New technology can and often does change the entire way of life, thinking, values, habits, and even the political processes of a nation. The automobile is a classic example of new technology that enormously affected every aspect of life here and in many other countries of the world. The United States has gone through one technological revolution after another and continues to do so: for example, computer science, biotechnology, genetic engineering, medicine, telecommunications, robotics factories, microelectronics, minerals, and astrophysics, to mention a few. In the next two decades new technologies will reshape virtually every facet of life in the United States and throughout the world. The forces generated will shake the foundations of the most secure businesses. They will powerfully affect options available to consumers, governments, the rate and growth of different business sectors, the role of business in the world, agricultural output, the health and longevity of people, and the standard of living.

A few illustrations make the point that in the immediate future there will be mind-boggling new technological inventions. New biogenetic products will cure some of the most intractable human diseases. Animal clones will be used to produce organs for human transplant. Cloning may provide an opportunity to revive important extinct species. Microbiological agents will be used to degrade dangerous wastes, such as radioactive dumps. In process today are a cornucopia of new genetically engineered plants that will revolutionize agriculture.

Advancing computer technology will be unparalleled in its impact on society. Since the 1970s, about every 2 ½ to 3 years we have had a new generation of computers. The trend has been to make them smaller and cheaper. The result, of course, will be their adoption in an expanding array of new uses. This movement, for one thing, is carrying us into what is currently called the information superhighway. It will develop into a seamless global web of communications networks, computers, databases, and consumer electronics. This infrastructure will integrate information services (voice, video, and data) into an advanced high-speed digital communications system.

These inspiring developments will not be without risks and costs with which managers must cope. For example, if a genetically engineered food were to cause an allergic reaction in consumers, a business along the chain of production of that food might be held legally liable. Such potentialities in the years ahead confront society generally and business managers in particular with dangerous risks and awesome decisions.

The Governmental Environment

Economists tell us that human wants are insatiable. Since people demand that government satisfy many of their unfulfilled wants, we can expect government to respond and issue new laws to help them. Congress today struggles with thousands of new bills covering many subjects such as health care, social security, mergers, tobacco advertising, pollution, ocean fishing, product liability, product safety, food safety, and minority employment, to mention a few. At the state and local levels, hundreds of other new laws await action in legislative halls.

There is today practically no aspect of business that governments cannot and will not regulate if the occasion arises and popular or legislative support exists. New laws, when added to past laws, have resulted in more government control of business than at any other peacetime period in our history. Furthermore, the direction of many of these laws has been to involve government in more details of managerial decision making.

U.S. companies, of course, are subject to the politics and laws of foreign governments. Illustrative of uncertainties they face was the decision by the government in the state of Maharashtra, India, concerning Enron, as explained at the beginning of this chapter.

The Cultural Environment

In 1979, when Coca-Cola returned to China, it discovered that Mao's simplification of Chinese characters translated Coca-Cola to mean "Bite the Wax Tadpole." The company solved the problem by using four Mandarin characters that translated as "Can Happy, Mouth Happy."

This simple anecdote illustrates the necessity for a company doing business in foreign countries to understand the culture of the host country. There are subtle and striking differences between the culture of the United States and the foreign cultures in which our companies do business. In addition, the cultures of individual companies differ from those of the foreign companies with whom they do business, further complicating matters. The most trivial and the most important aspects of business can be affected by those cultures.

Culture, among other things, includes the system of values, beliefs, attitudes, ideas, customs, manners, and rituals of people.[12] These aspects of a culture vary considerably in their importance to business both at home and abroad.

For example, the value of profit is basic in private enterprise throughout the world. But its concept and application differ. The old view, inherent in the market capitalism model, is no longer generally accepted in the United States, especially among managers of the largest corporations. Profit is still considered necessary by a majority, but attitudes about it are changing. Society is coming more to expect that societal interests be considered as well as business self-interest in the pursuit of profit objectives. This concept has been accepted by business leaders throughout the twentieth century.[13] This idea is inherent in the dynamic forces model and the stakeholder model discussed in Chapter 1. Business managers today take the view that concern for the interests of dominant stakeholders is the best route to expanding profits for shareholders.

The importance of profit differs among managers of the world. In a study by Hampden-Turner and Trompenaars, 15,000 managers worldwide were asked to make the following decision: Choose one of the following as an accurate statement of the proper goals of a company: "(a) The only real goal of a company is making profit. (b) A company, besides making profit, has a goal of attaining the well-being of various stakeholders, such as employees, customers, etc." Only 40 percent of the managers in the United States chose (a). But only 8 percent of the Japanese chose (a). At the lower end also were Singapore, France, and Germany. Close to the United States were Australia, Canada, and the United Kingdom.[14]

Many other managerial values vary significantly in importance among countries of the world. To illustrate, individual initiative is valued highly in American companies but it is a less dominant cultural value in Japan, France, Germany, and the United Kingdom. From the inception of this nation to the present, a laissez-faire philosophy has been imbedded deeply into the values held by business managers. Despite the fact that government today intrudes substantially in business, the fundamental value of laissez-faire is still strongly held by people in business. One result is that in the United States, business exists in an adversary relationship with government. In Japan, in sharp contrast, business

---

[12]Scholars have not agreed upon a single definition of culture, but we use this one as a working definition. Furthermore, there is a distinction between basic cultural values, attitudes, beliefs, and other words noted in our definition. For discussion of these concepts, see an old but still authoritative discussion of these concepts in Milton Rokeach, *The Nature of Human Values,* New York: Free Press, 1973.

[13]This was confirmed in interviews of chief executives of large corporations in George A. Steiner, *The New CEO,* New York: Macmillan, 1983. See also Morrell Heald, *The Social Responsibilities of Business: Company and Community, 1900–1960,* Cleveland: The Press of Case Western Reserve University, 1970.

[14]Charles Hampden-Turner and Alfons Trompenaars, *The Seven Cultures of Capitalism,* New York: Doubleday, 1993, p. 32.

and government closely collaborate on shared goals. In Germany, China, Indonesia, and many other nations of the world, the relationship is also collaborative.

There are dozens more business cultural values that vary much in importance around the world. Examples are loyalty of employees, the role of women in organizations, ethical codes, norms of giving and gratuities, organizational hierarchy, the meaning of time, the optimism of people, and clothing worn in business settings.[15]

When operating abroad, as well as at home, managers face a bewildering variety of consumer attitudes, prejudices, and preferences, many of which are constantly changing. Despite a strict no-alcohol policy, IBM and Disney permitted the use of spirits in France. Euro Disney was Disney's first large commercial venture abroad, and it returned red ink rather than profit until the company conformed more to European customs. One among many failings was the assumption that Mickey Mouse and other cartoon characters were as familiar to Europeans as to people in the United States.[16]

In the past, too many of our managers sought to do business abroad with the idea that "one size fits all"—that a good manager in this country can use the same principles and methods to duplicate his or her success anywhere in the world. That attitude has rapidly disappeared. Today there is more appreciation of the fact that a manager's ability to understand how people behave is critical for success in doing business in foreign countries.

The Natural Environment

Included in this environment are issues associated with air and water pollution, hazardous waste disposal, unsafe pesticides, automobile emissions, ozone depletion, global warming, protection of endangered species, weather, land usage, and so on. There is an intricate and significant interrelationship of industrial activity and the natural world. Industrial activity consumes, contaminates, and shapes the natural world. Interest groups pressure corporations to change impacts. This often raises difficult questions for managers who must balance their decisions about producing things people want against pressures to preserve nature. Sometimes, they face disaster from unexpected events such as floods, tornadoes, or earthquakes.

An example of how one group of environmental activists gave managers of a large corporation a headache concerns Royal Dutch/Shell Group, a giant oil company with headquarters in the Netherlands, and Greenpeace, a worldwide environmental group. Shell had an oil rig called the *Brent Spar*, built in 1970 and now obsolete, that it wanted to dump in the Atlantic Ocean 150 miles west of Scotland. There the ocean was 1½ miles deep and Shell said that any pollution resulting from the dumping would have insignificant

---

[15]See Gerald F. Cavanagh, *American Business Values With International Perspectives*, Upper Saddle River, N.J.: Prentice Hall, 1998.

[16]"The Kingdom Inside a Republic," *The Economist*, April 13, 1996.

impact on marine life. The rig had served as a floating oil tank, built to hold 300,000 barrels of oil produced in nearby fields. The oil was removed, of course, but there remained 100 tons of oil-related sludge in the tanks. Greenpeace said the dumping would release pollutants that would adversely affect sea life. Shell began towing the rig in mid-June 1995 and Greenpeace attempted to board the rig by aircraft in order to stop the towing, but was repulsed by water cannons. Pictures of the fracas were distributed worldwide and agitated environmentalists, especially in Germany. One result was a boycott of Shell products. German sales were off 20 to 30 percent. At that point Shell rescinded its decision to dump the rig in the ocean in favor of land disposal.

"You could argue in retrospect that we should have been more up front and explained what we were doing," said Christopher Fay, chairman of the Shell U.K. unit directly responsible for the *Brent Spar*.[17] Shell and observers concede that a big mistake was made in not coordinating the issue with environmental stakeholders of the company.

The Internal Environment

The internal environment, like the external environments, can change over time and, like the external environments, has a catalytic effect on business operations. It can be described in several ways. One is to view it as being coterminous with the company culture, which has been briefly mentioned. Another approach is to identify the main classes of people in an organization. This approach is shown in Figure 2-2. Each group in the chart has different goals, beliefs, needs, and so on, which managers must coordinate to achieve overall company goals. The fundamental characteristics of the groups are readily known and need no further elaboration here. Later in the book, we will intensively examine the changing internal life of organizations.

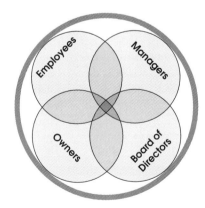

FIGURE 2-2

Major stakeholders in the internal business environment.

---

[17]Quoted in Bhushan Bahree, Kyle Pope, and Allanna Sullivan, "How Greenpeace Sank Shell's Plan to Dump Big Oil Rig in Atlantic," *The Wall Street Journal*, July 7, 1995.

Business's Impact on Its Environment

Business is not simply a passive entity that moves with historical and environmental forces like a billiard ball reacting to impacts. On the contrary, while business is strongly constrained by forces in its environment, it also has a powerful capacity to shape societies and change history.

The evolution of the automobile is a good example of how business and its products can affect our lives. The auto industry has been a prime mover of the American economy in the twentieth century, at one time accounting directly or indirectly for one of every eight jobs and a large proportion of our GDP. It encouraged an expansive highway system. It depleted world oil reserves and caused a decline in our railroads. It worsened noise, water, and air pollution. Socially, it changed patterns of crime, accelerated movement from farms to urban centers, encouraged a connection between status and ownership of material objects, and expanded tourism. It introduced assembly-line technology in manufacturing, encouraged a strong highway lobby, and expanded the field of insurance. These are but a few impacts. No business in this century up to the present time has created more intentional and unintentional changes in our society. The development of computers is now and will continue to have major impacts on societies. It is already affecting family life, production, retailing, accessibility of knowledge, entertainment, communications, transportation, and so on.

Figure 2-3 (on p. 34) illustrates the dynamic interconnection of the historical forces, business, and business environments discussed in this chapter. The deep historical forces act to shape the current major environments, both external to the corporation and internal, while the actions of corporations constantly influence not only current environments but may be powerful enough to influence the course of history. The next chapter is devoted to a discussion of the power that business has over its environment.

Concluding Observations

The environments of business have vast and profound implications for the management of business enterprises, as well as the role of the future business institution in society. Top managers today, especially of larger corporations, spend a large part of their time dealing with environmental problems. These include responding to economic environments and also addressing social concerns, complying with new social legislation, communicating with legislators and government executives about proposed laws and regulations, meeting with various interest groups concerning their demands and/or grievances, and administering their organizations in a way that is responsive to the changing attitudes of people working there. This agenda is in sharp contrast to that of a top executive of a major corporation sixty years ago, whose decision making was based almost wholly on economic and technological considerations.

FIGURE 2-3

The dynamic interaction of historical forces, business environment, and corporate actions.

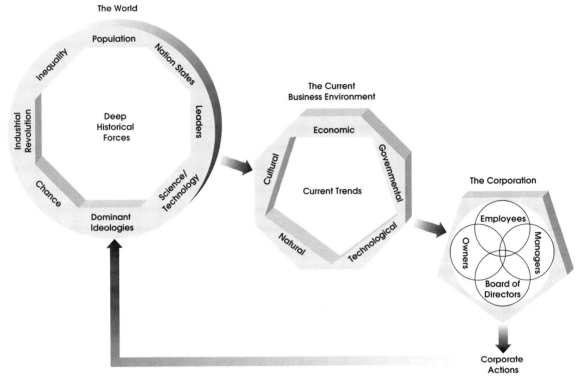

THE AMERICAN FUR COMPANY

T he American Fur Company was a relentless monopoly operating in the climactic era of the fur trade. It was created in 1808 by John Jacob Astor, a poor German immigrant, in an environment so favorable that it grew to have a larger and more powerful presence than the federal government over vast areas. But by the 1830s its situation had so deteriorated that it and a thriving 300-year-old trade in furs fell apart. Nevertheless, during the time it existed the American Fur Company shaped the young American nation and the destinies of its peoples. It made Astor America's richest citizen.

Astor Arrives in a Young Nation

Astor was born in 1763 in the small German village of Waldorf, the son of a butcher. Young John Jacob found the village dull, so at the age of 15 he left for London. There he worked for four years to save money for a trip to America and finally embarked on a ship in the winter of 1783. During the long voyage he happened to meet an expert fur trader who taught him how to appraise and handle skins. This instruction gave Astor the knowledge he needed for an occupation and he soon put it to use.

At this time the fur trade on the North American continent was almost 300 years old. It had begun early in the sixteenth century among Spanish and French explorers who made contact with native forest dwellers, and soon included the British. The Europeans wanted beaver, martin, ermine, mink, otter, bear, deer, muskrat, wolf, raccoon, and other animal skins for fashionable hats and clothing. The Native Americans, who had not yet entered the age of metal, were anxious to have even the simplest manufactured goods such as knives, mirrors, blankets, ornaments, buttons, and firearms. This simple mutual advantage proved durable over time.

For the most part the British, French, and American fur traders of Astor's time depended on the American Indians to trap animals and then negotiated with them to buy the pelts in exchange for trinkets and manufactured goods. Indian women performed the work of skinning and preparing them. In this way Indians became the production workers of the fur industry and overhead costs were reduced since no wages had to be paid. Instead of wages, trade

35

goods worth a fraction of a fur's ultimate value were used. Since furs were light and compact, they could be transported economically over long distances by mules, barges, and ships to eastern ports and thence to Europe. Profits on furs were enormous.

Typically, fur traders would pioneer trading with Indian tribes in areas on the frontiers of Euro-American settlements. Over time production in these areas fell off. Fur-bearing animals such as beaver with slow biological regeneration rates were rapidly depleted as the Indians increased their taking to meet the new demand. And Indian trappers became less productive as they were debauched with alcohol by the traders and their tribal cultures came under stress from adapting to new economic motives, tools, and technologies. When Indian productivity fell off, the Euro-American trappers moved on to work with new tribes in more productive territories, and in their wake came settlers using the maps and trails created by the fur trade. Farms and towns sprang up while the Indians were killed or stripped of their historic lands and relocated by the government. This was the unsentimental dynamic of the fur trade.

Astor Enters the Fur Business

Astor made his way to New York where he got a job selling bakery goods. He invested most of his $2-a-week pay in small trinkets and in his spare time prowled the waterfront for Indians who might have a fur to trade. Within a year he had picked up enough skins to take a ship back to London, where he established connections with fur-trading houses. This was a phenomenal achievement for an immigrant lad of 21 who had been nearly penniless on his arrival in America, but it revealed Astor's deadly serious and hard-driving personality.

Astor worked briefly with a fur dealer in New York City during which time he trekked into the forests of upstate New York to bargain for furs. He soon left his employer and by 1887 was working solely for himself. He demonstrated sharp negotiating skills in trading trinkets for furs and soon built up an impressive business. One neighbor said:

> Many times I have seen John Jacob Astor with his coat off, unpacking in a vacant yard near my residence a lot of furs he had bought dog-cheap off the Indians and beating them out, cleaning them and repacking them in more elegant and salable form to be transported to England and Germany, where they would yield him 1,000 percent on the original cost.[1]

Astor made great profits and expanded his business but, like other Americans, he was blocked from harvesting furs in the forests of the Northwest Territory. The Northwest Territory was the huge unsettled area between the Ohio

---

[1]A "Gentleman of Schenectady," quoted in John Upton Terrell, *Furs by Astor,* New York: Morrow, 1963, p. 55.

River and the Mississippi River bounded on the north by the Great Lakes. After the Revolutionary War, Great Britain had ceded this area to the United States, but continued to maintain forts and troops there because the American government was too weak to enforce its rights. British fur-trading companies exploited the area and incited Indians to attack traders and settlers who dared enter.

This imperiousness of the British pushed Congress near to declaring war. To avoid hostilities, England agreed to a treaty in 1794 that required removal of British troops and gave both British and Americans the right to trade in the Northwest Territory.[2] When Astor heard the news he said: "Now I will make my fortune in the fur trade."[3] But he was stunned when President George Washington proposed that the government promote friendly relations with Indians by setting up its own fur-trading posts to be run with benevolent trading policies. These would compete with private traders such as Astor. Congress approved the plan, which allowed trade goods to be sold at cost, prohibited the use of liquor, and required payment of fair prices for furs.

The government-run trading posts infuriated Astor, who moved quickly to undermine them with competitive tactics. He moved agents into strategic locations throughout the territory and instructed them to outprice all competitors and buy every fur they could get their hands on before others did. He bought trade goods for exchange in large quantities to lower the cost, and his agents paid for furs only with these trinkets. He also drove down the price of furs by allowing liquor to flow freely during trade negotiations.

Astor had great success using these strategies. The government moved too slowly to counter his power, and he outwitted British and American competitors. In less than ten years he was the second richest man in America (after only Stephen Girard, the shipping magnate and banker). Having accumulated huge resources, the Astor juggernaut was prepared to turn toward the far West.

The Louisiana Purchase

In 1803 the territory of the United States more than doubled with the Louisiana Purchase. President Thomas Jefferson agreed to purchase from France for $15 million approximately 800,000 square miles of land between the Mississippi River and the Rocky Mountains and running north from New Orleans to the forty-ninth parallel, which is now the Canada–U.S. boundary. At the time, little was known about the area called the Louisiana Territory. No accurate or complete maps existed; even its exact boundaries were vague. But Louisiana was beautiful in its mystery. Some geographers thought it was largely an arid desert. Others predicted a lush, fertile land over which Jefferson's ideal of an agrarian

---

[2]The treaty was negotiated for the United States in London by John Jay and is known as Jay's Treaty.

[3]Terrell, *Furs by Astor,* p. 93.

republic could spread. Rumors of geological wonders, horrific animals, and strange natives circulated, including the story of a tribe of bow-hunting, man-hating female savages in which the archers had their right breasts removed to keep them from interfering with bowstrings.[4]

Jefferson himself had a clear vision of how to use the new territory. He did not believe it could be settled right away and, until it could, he wanted to populate it with Indians and fur traders. In his 1803 message to Congress, he proposed to relocate into Louisiana eastern tribes getting in the way of American settlers, and over the next fifty years this occurred many times.[5] He also ordered an Expedition of Discovery headed by Meriwether Lewis and William Clark to explore on foot the unknown territory. A primary purpose of the Lewis and Clark expedition was to determine the suitability of Louisiana for the fur trade. The adventurers set out on a round-trip march between St. Louis and the Pacific Ocean, going where no white American had gone before, and on their return reported a wondrous land "richer in beaver and otter than any country on earth."[6] They also reported that most Indian tribes in the territory were friendly to Americans and the fur trade. These discoveries were not lost on fur traders, among them John Jacob Astor.

The American Fur Company Is Born

The Lewis and Clark expedition was a catalyst for fur-trading exploration in the new territory. Beaver production in the Northwest Territory was already beginning to fall off. Beavers reproduce slowly and their populations quickly decline when trapping begins, especially when no restraint is practiced, as was the case with all fur companies in those days. Immediately the North West Company, Astor's main competitor in the old Northwest Territory, began to move down from Canada to trade for beaver skins with Great Plains Indian tribes. Its intention was to harvest the newly discovered fur resources in the Louisiana Territory as rapidly as possible.

The beaver-rich areas discovered by Lewis and Clark covered parts of what are now North and South Dakota, Nebraska, Montana, Wyoming, and Colorado, and on the slopes of the Rocky Mountains themselves. Working in his study in New York, Astor created a plan for domination; he would build a 2,000-mile string of trading posts between St. Louis and Oregon along the route mapped by Louis and Clark.

In 1808 he cloaked this grandiose scheme in patriotic themes and approached the governor and legislature of New York seeking a charter for a

---

[4]Ben Gilbert, *The Trailblazers*, New York: Time-Life Books, 1973, p. 18.

[5]For a list of twenty-four relocations, see Cardinal Goodwin, *The Trans-Mississippi West (1803–1853)*, New York: Appleton, 1922, plate following p. 88.

[6]Quoted in David J. Wishart, *The Fur Trade of the American West (1807–1840): A Geographical Synthesis*, Lincoln: University of Nebraska Press, 1979, p. 19, citing the original journals of the trip.

company to be known as the American Fur Company. In those days state legislatures had exclusive power to create a company by issuing a charter that spelled out the conditions of its existence and operation. Astor argued that the majority of furs taken on U.S. lands went to Canadians and British, thereby depriving the Americans of revenue. His company would drive the foreigners out. He expressed plans to join with ten or twelve other wealthy entrepreneurs to capitalize the new company, which would then issue stock to others. The new company would enhance U.S. security by establishing a strong presence of American citizens over unpopulated areas. And finally, Astor promised that his company would deal honestly with the Indians and drive out smaller, irresponsible traders. The legislators of New York, responding more to Astor's open pocketbook than to the credibility of his arguments, passed a charter setting up the American Fur Company. Soon, President Jefferson wrote a letter to Astor giving his blessing to the new company also.

Astor proceeded to take on a number of partners and establish a board of directors for the American Fur Company as the charter required. However, he retained 99.9 percent of the stock, elected himself president, and subsequently declared dividends whenever he wanted to compensate himself. The partnership was a fiction; Astor never intended to share either the proceeds of the company or any portion of the fur trade that he could control.

In 1810 he made his first move. His ship, the *Tonquin,* sailed to the mouth of the Columbia River on the Pacific Coast and set up a trading post named Astoria. At this time Britain and the United States contested the area known as Oregon territory, consisting of present-day Oregon and Washington. Astor got diplomatic support for his trading post by arguing that its presence established an American claim to the territory. Secretly, however, he hoped to establish a new nation called Astoria and make himself king. In the meantime, he planned to use Astoria as one end of a vise on the new fur trade territory. All furs taken in the west would be brought to Astoria and then shipped to China, which was a huge market for fur, or to New York. By this time Astor owned a large fleet of ships with which to do this.

The other end of the vise would be operations set up in St. Louis. Furs purchased at Astor's planned string of trading posts on the eastern side of the Rocky Mountains would be sent down the Missouri River system to St. Louis, and from St. Louis overland to New York or down to New Orleans to be shipped anywhere. It was a compelling plan and Astor had the resources to carry it out. But only part of it was to work and the rest worked only until the fur trade fell apart.

The Road to Monopoly

In 1813 Astor suffered a reverse when he was forced to sell Astoria to the British during the War of 1812. He sold out at a fraction of its value because British solders were in a position to seize it as a war prize. Astor lost his foothold in Oregon territory and was unable to compete with British and Canadian fur companies in that area.

In 1816 Astor's lobbying efforts in Washington succeeded in getting Congress to pass a law forbidding foreigners from trading furs with American Indians in U.S. territory. This meant that Canadian and British companies could no longer operate in the Northwest Territory and Astor immediately bought out their interests. Astor now had a monopoly in the fur trade east of the Missouri River. Blocked from the Pacific Coast trade by the British presence, he turned his attention to the upper-Missouri fur trade.

Astor bided his time as other fur companies pioneered trading in the northern Great Plains and then, after discovery of rich valleys of beaver, in the Rocky Mountains. By 1822 Astor had established a presence selling trade goods and buying furs in St. Louis, but he waited as other companies sent expensive expeditions of traders and mountain men up the Missouri, absorbing heavy losses of men and money. Despite losses, these pioneering companies found tremendous reserves of beaver in Rocky Mountain valleys, mapped new routes, and discovered advantageous locations for trading posts.

Then he began to crush the competition. In 1826 he merged with Bernard Pratte & Company, an established firm, using it as an agent. He bought out and liquidated another competitor, Stone, Bostwick & Company. In 1827 he broke the Columbia Fur Company by building his own trading posts next to every one of theirs and engaging in cutthroat price competition for furs and plying the Indians liberally with whiskey. His trappers shadowed Columbia Fur Company trapping parties to discover where the rich sources of beaver were, then worked the areas. Using similar tactics, he bankrupted Menard & Valle. Now, according to Astor's biographer Terrell:

> Competition on the Missouri River was all but nonexistent. What remained was inconsequential, and might have been likened to a terrier yapping at a bear. The bear lumbered on, ignoring the noise until it became aggravating. Then with the sudden swipe of a paw, the yapping was forever stilled.[7]

Astor made astonishing profits. He would buy, for example, a 10-pound keg of gunpowder for $2, or 20 cents a pound, in London and transport it to his trading posts using his ships. He paid himself a 2 percent commission for buying the trade goods, or $.04 cents on the keg of gunpowder. He paid himself a freight charge for carrying the gunpowder on his ship to New Orleans. From there the keg was transported up the Missouri using the inexpensive labor of his hired trappers and traders, who were paid salaries of $150 to $300 a year. The gunpowder was valued at $4 a pound to the Indians, who were not allowed to pay money for it, but got it only by exchanging furs or on credit. In the 1820s Astor charged one 2-pound beaver skin for each pound of gunpowder, getting ten skins weighing 20 pounds for the keg of gunpowder. These skins were transported back to London, where they were worth $7 a

---

[7]Terrell, *Furs by Astor*, p. 391.

Portrait of John Jacob Astor.

pound or $140. From the $140 Astor deducted a 5 percent commission, or $7, for brokering the sale of the furs. Astor also subtracted 25 percent, or $35 from the $140, for the estimated costs of transportation and wages.

All told, this left a net profit for the American Fur Company of $97.96, or 4,900 percent on the original $2 investment.[8] And Astor owned over 99 percent of the company's shares. This profitable arithmetic was repeated on a wide range of trade goods.

The importance of trade goods lies in the nature of Indian cultures. Indians coveted them so much that they considered the whites foolish to exchange even the smallest trinkets for beaver skins in free supply. In general, the concept of material acquisition beyond basic needs was foreign to Indian cultures based on ideas of sufficiency. The Arikaras, for example, believed that a person who had more than needed to survive ought to divide it with others. It was difficult to motivate Indians to trap and process furs for Astor and other traders by using money; they were indifferent to accumulating currency. Trade goods such as rifles, knives, clothing, blankets, beads, and trinkets did have some utility for Indians, which made them attractive, but frequently native-made equivalents were just as good or better.

For the Indians, trade goods had mystic significance beyond their monetary value or utility. The appeal of trade goods in their eyes lay in certain magical, spiritual values not apparent to Europeans and Americans. They believed that

---

[8]These calculations are based on figures in Terrell, *Furs by Astor,* pp. 397–98.

the future could be divined by looking in a reflection of the self. Manufactured mirrors gave a clearer reflection than water and were, therefore, a wondrous advance in prophecy. Guns were seen as supernatural beings because they could create thunder, an event associated with the spiritual world. Kettles were regarded as having life because they rang or sang out when hit. In this way Indians found supernatural qualities in trade goods that were lost on Europeans.[9]

Astor encouraged Indians to take trade goods on credit. As a result, some tribes—the Winnebagos, Sacs, Foxes, Cherokees, Chickasaws, and Sioux—were hopelessly mired in debt, owing the American Fur Company as much as $50,000 each. Since trade goods had sky-high markups, Astor could not lose much even if tribal debts grew, but indebtedness forced tribes to trade furs with him rather than with competitors.

Astor's traders and trappers fared no better. He marked up trade goods heavily before selling them to traders. Often, traders were in debt to Astor or had mortgaged their trading posts to him and were forced to mark up trade goods heavily themselves before selling them to Indians and trappers. Trappers employed by the American Fur Company were ruthlessly exploited. They worked unlimited hours in hazardous conditions and extreme weather, but when Astor achieved dominance in an area, he cut their salaries from $100 a year to $250 every three years. They had to buy trade goods and staples at markups that were higher than those charged Indians to get furs. Whiskey costing $.30 a gallon in St. Louis was diluted with water and sold to them at $3 a pint. Coffee and sugar costing $.10 a pound was marked up to $2 at the trading posts up the Missouri. Clothes and trade goods to be used with the Indians were marked up 300 to 400 percent.

Overall, Astor had contrived a lucrative, pitiless system that amplified his fortune by diminishing those caught in its workings. Astor never ventured out west and lived in New York and Europe. He was never out of touch, however, and worked long hours, his shrewd mind obsessed with even the most minor details and squeezing out the smallest unnecessary expenses. In 1831, his son William B. wrote a letter to the Secretary of War reporting revenues for the American Fur Company of "not less than $500,000" annually.[10] Astor was now the richest man in American and had begun to buy real estate in and around New York City.

Astor Races on

In the early 1830s it seemed that nothing could slow Astor. New competing firms were organized by men who hated the American Fur Company, but few lasted. Astor destroyed them by outbidding for furs and debauching the Indians with alcohol.

---

[9]Richard White, "Expansion and Exodus," in Betty Ballantine and Ian Ballantine, eds., *The Native Americans: An Illustrated History,* Atlanta: Turner Publishing, 1993, chap. 14.

[10]Gustavus Myers, *History of the Great American Fortunes,* New York: Modern Library, 1936, p. 102. Originally published in 1909.

In 1832 Congress passed a law forbidding the import of alcohol into territories occupied by Indians, but the law was widely ignored. Astor never favored using alcohol and several times tried to negotiate with competitors to end its use. They never agreed because they could not match his resources; often alcohol was their only hope of seducing Indians with furs away from Astor's buyers. Astor was never squeamish about meeting the competition with alcohol, of course, so the American Fur Company used it freely.

Alcohol was unknown in native cultures; Indians had developed a craving for it only after European traders introduced intoxication into the process of negotiating fur prices. Some believed that spirits occupied their bodies when they drank. Among Indians who took to whiskey, a new desire was created where none had existed before, a desire that motivated them to produce furs. A few tribes, notably the Pawnee, Crow, and Arikara, never would drink. But most did and some tribes were debilitated by its effects to the point that their fur production fell and traders moved on.

Astor had no intention of obeying the new prohibition statute and smuggled as much liquor as needed past Indian Agents. One of Astor's agents built a still at the confluence of the Yellowstone and Missouri rivers that produced enough spirits to keep tribes in several states in a constant state of inebriation. The fact was that Congress could not enforce its will because the federal government had almost no presence in the vast areas of the West. Written laws were meaningless where no civil authorities existed to back them up. In Indian country the only law was the will of leaders of trading companies and brigades of trappers who wore self-designed, military-style uniforms and could rob, cheat, and murder both Indians and whites with impunity. An 1831 report to Lewis Cass, Secretary of War, stated:

> . . . The traders that occupy the largest and most important space in the Indian country are the agents and engagees of the American Fur Trade Company. They entertain, as I know to be the fact, no sort of respect for our citizens, agents, officers of the Government, or its laws or general policy.[11]

Government officials such as Cass were disinclined to thwart Astor in any case since they were frequently in his pay. Cass, who was the federal official in charge of enforcing the prohibition law, was paid $35,000 by the American Fur Company between 1817 and 1834.[12] At one time Astor even advanced a personal loan of $5,000 to President James Monroe. Over the years the Astor lobby achieved most of its objectives in Washington, D.C., and state capitals, including exclusion of foreign companies from the United States, heavy tariffs on imported furs, and abolition of the government fur-trading posts so beloved to Washington and Jefferson. Under these circumstances it is not surprising that the government failed to regulate the fur trade.

In 1831 Astor introduced a new technological innovation, the steamboat *Yellowstone*, which could travel 50 to 100 miles a day up the Missouri, transporting

---

[11]Report of Andrew S. Hughes quoted in Myers, *History of the Great American Fortunes*, p. 99.
[12]Myers, *History of the Great American Fortunes*, p. 103.

trade goods and supplies to American Fur Company posts. The keelboats used by competitors could make only 20 miles upriver on a good day and exposed the men pulling them with ropes from the bank to hostile Indian fire. Upriver Indians were awestruck by the *Yellowstone,* and traveled hundreds of miles to see the spirit that walked on water. In the north, whole tribes refused to trade with the Hudson Bay Company any longer, believing that because of the *Yellowstone* the British could no longer compete with the American Fur Company.

The Environment of the Fur Trade Changes

Although the American Fur Company was ascendant, unfavorable trends were building by the early 1830s that would bring it down. Demand for beaver was rapidly falling. The fashion trend that led every European and American gentlemen to want a beaver hat had changed. Silk hats became the new rage. Also, new methods for felting hats without using the fibrous under-hair from beaver pelts had been developed and South American nutria pelts were beginning to enter the market.

These were not the only problems. In 1832 there was a worldwide cholera epidemic. Many people believed that the disease was spread by transporting beaver pelts and trade came to a near standstill. Beaver populations were depleted by overtrapping and expanding human settlement. The fur companies had never made conservation efforts. The incentive was rather to trap all beaver in an area rather than leave any for competitors. In the 1820s the Hudson Bay Company adopted the strategy of trying to prevent Astor from moving into Oregon territory by exterminating beaver along a band of terrain to create a "fur desert" that would be unprofitable for Astor's trappers to cross. Thus, by the 1830s it was more difficult to find beaver.

In addition, losses of both horses and men to the Indians were growing. As trapping territories expanded, mountain men had to move out of areas populated by somewhat friendly Indians such as the Snake and Crow into areas frequented by more hostile tribes such as the Blackfeet. The Blackfeet, who poisoned their arrows with a deadly mixture of rattlesnake venom and antelope liver, conducted a war of attrition against trappers and by the 1830s had forced them to travel in large brigades for safety.[13] One study of 446 mountain men actively trapping between 1805 and 1845 found that 182, or 41 percent, were killed in the fur trade.[14]

By 1833 Astor realized that the fur market was doomed. In the early 1830s beaver pelts had fetched almost $6 a pound in the eastern United States, but by 1833 this had fallen to $3.50 a pound. The price would go down to around

---

[13]Trappers also attacked Blackfeet without provocation. See Osborne Russell, *Journal of a Trapper,* Lincoln: University of Nebraska Press, 1955, pp. 52, 86.

[14]William H. Goetzmann, "The Mountain Man as Jacksonian Man," *American Quarterly,* Fall 1963, p. 409.

$2 a pound in 1840.[15] Astor sold out his entire fur-trading interests and spent the rest of his years accumulating more money in New York real estate.

For a time the American Fur Company continued its ruthless dominion under new owners, but the business environment continued to deteriorate. In 1837 the American Fur Company steamboat *St. Peters* carried smallpox upriver, killing over 17,000 American Indians, and an agent observed that "our most profitable Indians have died."[16] By 1840 the American Fur Company had withdrawn from the Rocky Mountains and focused on trade in buffalo robes, which continued to be profitable for some time.

Astor's Last Years

Astor remained in New York, squeezing immense profits from rents and leases as the city grew around his real estate holdings. By 1847 he had accumulated a fortune of $20 million that towered above any other in that day. In his last years he was weak and frail and exercised by having attendants toss him up and down in a blanket. Yet despite his physical deterioration, he remained focused on getting every last penny from his tenants, poring over the rents for long hours behind barred windows in his office. When he died in 1848, his sole philanthropy was $400,000 set aside in his will for building an Astor library. This was, in the words of one critic, less than "the proceeds of one year's pillage of the Indians."[17]

The Legacy of the Fur Trade

For 300 years the fur trade shaped the economic, political, and cultural life of both native and European inhabitants of the raw North American continent. Its climactic era has often been depicted as a progressive and romantic period when trading posts represented "civilization which was slowly mastering the opposition of nature and barbarism."[18] According to historian Dan Elbert Clark:

> The fur traders, with all their faults and shortcomings, were the pathfinders of civilization. They marked the trails that were followed by settlers. They built trading posts where later appeared thriving towns and cities. They knew the Indians better than any other class of white men who came among them.[19]

The American Fur Company and its competitors did greatly advance geographical knowledge and blaze trails. But there is also a dark side to the story.

---

[15]Wishart, *The Fur Trade of the American West*, p. 141.
[16]Jacob Halsey, a clerk at Fort Pierre, quoted by Wishart, *The Fur Trade of the American West*, p. 68.
[17]Myers, *History of the Great American Fortunes*, p. 149.
[18]Arthur D. Howden Smith, *John Jacob Astor: Landlord of New York*, Philadelphia: Lippincott, 1929, p. 131.
[19]Dan Elbert Clark, *The West in American History*, New York: Thomas Y. Crowell, 1937, p. 441.

The fur companies undermined traditional Native American cultures by introducing new economic motivations. Their societies were decimated by alcohol, smallpox, and venereal disease. "The fur trade," according to Professor David J. Wishart of the University of Nebraska, "was the vanguard of a massive wave of Euro-American colonisation which brought into contact two sets of cultures with disparate and irreconcilable ways of life."[20]

The traders also depleted beaver populations and caused other ecological damage. For example, whole riverine forest areas were denuded to provide wood needed to fuel the American Fur Company's steamboats. The mentality of pillage exhibited by Astor's agents set a destructive standard. Argues Wishart: "The attitude of rapacious, short-term exploitation which was imprinted during the fur trade persisted after 1840 as the focus shifted from furs to minerals, timber, land, and water."[21]

In conclusion, the story of the American Fur Company invites reconsideration of the strategies, tactics, impacts, ethics, and precedents of the largest company in a powerful industry no longer remembered by most Americans for the formative role it played in America's early years.

Questions

1. How would you evaluate Astor in terms of his motives, his managerial ability, and his ethics? What lesson does his career teach about the relationship between virtue and success?

2. How did the environment of the American Fur Company change in the 1830s? What deep historical forces are implicated in these changes?

3. Evaluate the impact of the fur trade on society in major dimensions of the business environment, that is, economic, cultural, technological, ecological, political, and internal.

4. Who were the most important stakeholders of the nineteenth-century fur industry? Were they treated responsibly by the standards of the day? By the standards of today?

5. On balance, is the legacy of the American Fur Company and of the fur trade itself a positive legacy? Or is the impact of these companies predominantly negative?

6. How have historical forces worked since the time of the fur trade to change the business environment? What factors in the business environment today would restrict the operations of a fur company? Does the story of the American Fur Company hint at how and why capitalism has changed and has been changed over the years?

7. Do one or more models of the business–government–society relationship discussed in Chapter 1 apply to the historical era set forth in this case? Which model or models have explanatory power and why?

---

[20]Wishart, *The Fur Trade of the American West*, p. 215.
[21]Ibid., p. 212.

3

Business Power

The American Tobacco Company

James B. Duke was born in 1856 on a North Carolina farm. At the end of the Civil War, his father returned home and found a shed of tobacco miraculously intact after the Union Army occupation and began selling the contents. Soon the elder Duke built a small factory to manufacture a brand of chewing tobacco named Pro Bono Publico (a Latin phrase meaning "for the public good"). Young James Duke entered the business with his father. He was a precocious, energetic boy who became the driving force behind the company.

During the 1870s James Duke's visions of grandeur for the little factory were thwarted by the dominance of a huge rival firm, the Bull Durham Co. Its brand of chewing tobacco, Bull Durham, was so dominant and well entrenched that head-on competition seemed hopeless. So he decided on a new strategy. He would manufacture an unproven tobacco product—cigarettes. This was a venturesome move, because at the time cigarettes were a tiny segment of the tobacco market and their use was associated with degenerate dudes and dandies in big cities.

Duke brought ten professional tobacco rollers from Europe to his factory in North Carolina and set them to work. Each could roll a little over 2,000 cigarettes per day. At first he had trouble selling his Duke of Durham brand. Tobacco shops refused to buy them because customers didn't request them. So Duke innovated with his marketing strategy. In Atlanta, he put up a billboard of a famous actress holding Duke cigarettes in her outstretched hand. This was the first time a woman had been used to advertise cigarettes, and the novelty created demand. In St. Louis,

Duke's salesmen found extreme prejudice against cigarettes. Tobacco shop proprietors simply would not buy. So Duke hired a young, red-headed widow to call on the tobacconists, and she got nineteen orders on her first day.

When a young Virginia engineer, James Bonsack, invented a mechanical cigarette-rolling machine capable of rolling 200 per minute, Duke negotiated an exclusive agreement to operate the machine. With the new Bonsack machines, Duke simultaneously cut manufacturing costs from $.80 per thousand to $.30 and multiplied factory output many times.[1]

To find new markets for this swollen output, he first tried to open New York City as a foothold in the East. There he ran into competition from local firms, and he also encountered resistance to machine-rolled cigarettes among smokers. But both these barriers yielded to an array of ingenious promotional practices. He advertised widely. He put pictures of actresses and athletes in cigarette packs and numbered them so that compulsive collectors would want complete sets. He hired people to go into tobacco shops and demand his new machine-rolled Cameo and Cross Cuts brands. Immigrants entering New York were handed free samples.

Overseas, Duke's minions were at work also. One great conquest was China. At the time a few Chinese, mostly older men, smoked a bitter native tobacco in pipes. Cigarettes were unknown. Duke sent experts to Shantung Province with bright leaf from North Carolina to cultivate a milder tobacco. His sales force hired "teachers" to walk village streets showing curious Chinese how to light and hold cigarettes. He installed Bonsack machines in four huge manufacturing plants in China that soon ran twenty-four hours a day. And he unleashed on the Chinese a full range of promotional activities. At one time his cigarette packs contained pictures of nude American actresses, which proved to be a big hit with Chinese men. Duke turned China into a nation of cigarette smokers.

Back home, his tactics wore down competitors and in 1889 he engineered a combination of his firm and other large firms into the giant American Tobacco Company. As president, Duke built the company into a monopoly that controlled 93 percent of the cigarette market by 1900 and dominated the snuff, cheroot, and smoking tobacco markets as well. Duke ruthlessly swallowed or bankrupted 250 competing firms during the next twenty-two years and continued to spread the gospel of smoking around the globe.

Duke's monopoly lasted until 1911, when the Supreme Court ordered it broken up.[2] Duke himself divided the giant trust into four independent companies: Ligget & Myers Tobacco Company, P. Lorillard Company, R.J. Reynolds Company, and a new American Tobacco Company. After the breakup Duke retired from

---

[1]John K. Winkler, *Tobacco Tycoon: The Story of James Buchanan Duke*, New York: Random House, 1942, p. 56.

[2]*United States* v. *American Tobacco Company*, 221 U.S. 106 (1911).

the tobacco industry and started a new electric utility, Duke Power & Light. He also gave money to a small North Carolina college, which became Duke University.

Duke's career illustrates the power of commerce to shape society. His promotional practices accelerated the growth of smoking around the world. To find an outlet for the copious production of Bonsack machines, he turned China into a nation of cigarette smokers. His monopoly defined the structure of the tobacco industry and destroyed rivals; its financial power flattened the comparatively feeble efforts of antitobacco leagues to publicize health hazards. Duke's ads made smoking glamorous. His bribes to legislators killed antismoking laws. And, due in large measure to Duke's forcefulness, the tobacco industry resuscitated the crippled post–Civil War southern economy and created a powerful, enduring political coalition in Congress. Duke shaped society with his business strategies, but encountered the limits of business power when the Supreme Court ordered his company dismantled.

The Nature of Business Power

Business has tremendous power to change society. And the extent of its power is underappreciated. In every historical era rising companies and new industries have furrowed the social landscape, altering ideas, values, and institutions. This phenomenon is visible in the stories of dominant companies such as the American Fur Company, the Standard Oil Company, and the American Tobacco Company. These retrospective examples show the power of just one company to alter the world. The cumulative power of all business is an even more massive force for change.

What Is Power?

Power is the force or strength to act. It exists on a broad spectrum ranging from coercion at one extreme to weak influence at the other. Its use in human society creates change. Although power is sometimes exerted to prevent change, such resistance is, of course, itself a force that alters history. There are many sources of power, including wealth, position, knowledge, law, arms, social status, charisma, and public opinion. Power is unevenly distributed, and all societies have mechanisms to control and channel it for wide or narrow benefit. These mechanisms, which are not infallible, include governments, laws, police, cultural values, and public opinion. Also, the presence of multiple, competing outcrops of power limits discretion.

Business power is the force or strength behind business actions that change society. Its source is a grant of authority from society to convert resources efficiently into needed goods and services. In return for doing this, society gives corporations the authority to take proper actions and permits a return on investment. This agreement between business and society is a *social contract*.

The idea of a social contract has been used for centuries, primarily to provide a theoretical explanation of the origin of government, an event that is hidden from view in the mists of prehistory. The theory is that individuals living in a primitive, ungoverned state of nature (where, according to the philosopher Thomas Hobbes, life was "nasty, brutish, and short,") volunteered to enter a compact in which they would submit to a ruling authority. These individuals gave up the unrestrained power to act that they had in an ungoverned world and entered into a civil society in which their power was transferred to a ruling authority. In return for submitting to this power, these individuals expected the ruling authority to exercise power for the common good; they expected that their rights and property would be protected. The great advantage of this social contract was that people moved from a cutthroat, predatory, lawless situation into an ordered society.

The social contract legitimized the exercise of power by giving it a moral basis. *Legitimacy* is the rightful use of power. The power granted to the ruling authority was rightful power when it was exercised in keeping with the agreed-upon contract. The opposite of legitimacy is tyranny, which the philosopher John Locke defined as "the exercise of power beyond right."[3]

Although the social contract idea is theoretical, it defines public expectations about the exercise of power by governments and social institutions such as business. In the United States, for example, the ideal of a social contract is incorporated in historical documents such as the Declaration of Independence and the Constitution, and in various laws, customs, and beliefs. Locke, whose writings inspired the wording in the Declaration of Independence and the Constitution, believed that the social contract was established to protect the liberty and property of individuals in society.

The theory of the social contract illuminates the nature and limits of business power.[4] Business power is legitimate when it is used for the common good. The grounds for legitimacy can shift over time. For example, employing slaves is no longer permitted. As we will see in subsequent chapters, the definition of the common good that business must serve has expanded throughout American history. Social contract values can also differ between nations.

---

[3]John Locke, *The Second Treatise of Government*, New York: Bobbs-Merrill, 1952, p. 112. Originally published in 1690.

[4]For an effort to stipulate social contract norms that should guide business behavior, see Thomas Donaldson and Thomas W. Dunfee, "Toward a Unified Conception of Business Ethics: Integrative Social Contracts Theory," *Academy of Management Review*, April 1994; and the special issue of *Business Ethics Quarterly* on contract ethics, April 1995.

Levels and Spheres of Corporate Power

The actions of corporations have an impact on society at two levels, and on each level they create change. On the *surface level*, business power is the direct cause of visible, immediate changes, both great and small. Corporations expand and contract, hire and fire; they make and sell products.

On the *deep level*, corporate power shapes society over time through the cumulative changes of industrial growth. At this level, corporate power creates many indirect, unforeseen, and invisible effects. Multiple lines of action converge and interact in complex networks of cause and effect. At a deep level, the exercise of corporate power is unplanned, less controllable, and less visible, but far more significant.

On both the surface and deep levels, business power is exercised in spheres that correspond to the six business environments set forth in Chapter 2.

- *Economic power* is the ability of the corporation to influence events, activities, and people by virtue of control over resources, particularly property. At the surface level, the operation of a corporation may directly affect the well-being of its stakeholders. At a deep level, the cumulative impact of business economic power has sweeping effects. For example, over many years business has raised the standard of living in industrialized nations.

- *Cultural power* is the ability to influence cultural values, institutions such as the family, customs, lifestyles, and habits. When Calvin Klein marketed a unisex cologne, CK One, it ran ads designed to create favorable attitudes toward blurred gender distinctions. At a deep level, the cumulative impact of advertising has altered American society by reinforcing values selectively, for example, materialism over asceticism, individualism over community, or personal appearance over character development. It is estimated that the advertising expenditures of global corporations equal more than half the amount spent on public education worldwide.[5]

- *Power over individuals* is exercised over employees, managers, stockholders, consumers, and citizens. On the surface, a corporation may determine how a person works and influence buying habits. At a deep level, industrialism fixes the pattern of daily life. People are regimented, live by clocks, find their status and wealth determined by their occupation, and live in cities.

- *Technological power* is the ability to influence the direction, rate, characteristics, and consequences of technology as it develops. On a surface level, in 1914, assembly-line production techniques allowed

---

[5]Tony Clarke, "Mechanisms of Corporate Rule," in Jerry Mander and Edward Goldsmith, eds., *The Case Against the Global Economy*, San Francisco: Sierra Club Books, 1996, p. 300.

Henry Ford to introduce the transportation technology of the automobile to a consumer mass market. But at a deeper level, as the auto took hold in American society, it created extensive, uncontrolled, and unintended consequences. For example, it changed courtship patterns by allowing young couples to travel far from home and escape parental oversight.

· *Environmental power* is the impact of a company on nature. On the surface, a steel mill may pollute the air; on a deeper level, since the seventeenth century, the burning of wood, coal, and oil to power industrial processes has altered the chemical composition of the earth's atmosphere.

· *Political power* is the ability to influence government decisions. On the surface, corporations give money to candidates and lobby legislatures. At a deep level, market economies require that great freedom with the use of property be given to managers. Free markets chaff at repressive government, and their spread has contributed to the decline of authoritarian regimes.

The Story of the Railroads

Activity in the economic sphere is the primary force for change. From this, change radiates into other areas. The story of the railroad industry in the United States illustrates how this works.

Small railroads began to run in the 1820s. At this time most passengers and freight moved by horse and over canals. The railroad was a vastly superior conveyance and was bound to revolutionize transportation. Tracks cost less to build than canals and did not freeze in winter. Routes could be more direct. Trains were faster; for the first time people and cargo traveled overland at faster than the speed of a horse. The trip from New York to Chicago was reduced from three weeks to just three days. And the cost of moving goods and passengers was less; in a day a train could go back and forth many times over the distance that a canal boat or wagon traversed once.[6]

The initial boom in railroading came in the 1850s. In 1850 trains ran on only about 9,000 miles of track, but by 1860 more than 30,000 miles of track had been laid down. During this decade, more than thirty railroad companies completed route systems. Tracks were expensive, and each of these enterprises was a giant for its day. Many needed $10 to $35 million in capital, and the smallest at least $2 million. Companies in other industries did not approach this size; only a handful of textile mills and iron and steel plants had required capitalization of more than $1 million.[7]

---

[6]Alfred D. Chandler, Jr., *The Visible Hand: The Managerial Revolution in American Business*, Cambridge, Mass.: The Belknap Press, 1977, pp. 83, 86.

[7]Ibid., pp. 83, 90.

American Landscape, *a 1930 oil painting, depicts Ford Motor Company's giant River Rouge plant. In this painting, American artist Charles Sheeler makes a comment on the power of business to change and shape society. Outwardly this scene seems to beautify, venerate, and ennoble the architecture of industry, making it appear almost pastoral. But on another level the scene provokes anxiety. Nature has been run off the scene by factory buildings dominating a landscape that is now entirely artificial. The tiny human figure in the middle ground is overwhelmed and marginalized by the massive factory; its movement is limited and regimented by the surrounding industrial structure. Here, then, art invokes the anxiety at the root of fear of industrial growth in a way that words cannot.*

Source: Sheeler, Charles, "American Landscape." 1930. Oil on Canvas, 24" × 31" (61 × 78.8 cm). The Museum of Modern Art, New York. Gift of Abby Aldrich Rockefeller. Photograph © 1996.

The need for this much money transformed capital markets. The only place such huge sums could be raised was in large northeastern cities. Since interest rates were a little higher in Boston at the time, New York became the center of financial activity and has remained so to this day. Railroads sold bonds and stocks to raise capital, and a new investment banking industry was created. The New York Stock Exchange went from a sleepy place where only a few hundred shares of stock might change hands each week to a roaring market. Speculative techniques such as margin trading, short-selling, and options trading appeared for the first time. Later, the financial and speculative mechanisms inspired by railroad construction were in place when other industries began to need more capital. This changed American history by accelerating the industrial transformation of the late 1900s. It also put New York bankers such as J. P. Morgan in a position to control access to capital. This would have many consequences.

At first, the railroads ran between existing trade centers, but as time went on and track mileage increased, they linked more and more points. In 1860 there were 30,626 miles of track. By 1880 that had increased to 93,267 miles and by 1890 to 163,597 miles.[8] The consequence was a transformed society.

Before the growth of railroads, the United States was a nation of farmers and small towns held together by the traditional institutions of family, church, and local government. Since long-distance travel was time-consuming and arduous, these towns were comparatively isolated. Populations were stable. People identified more with local areas than with the nation as a whole. Into this world came the train.

Trains destabilized rural society. They took away young people who would have stayed but for the lure of wealth in distant cities. In their place, they brought strangers who were less under the control of community values and who never permanently settled in. The intimacy of small-town life gave way to the growth of impersonal crowds, a unique and new phenomenon in American life. Trains violated established customs. In small towns Sunday was a day of worship. Many churchgoers were offended when huffing and puffing trains intruded on services. But new capital accounting methods used by railroad companies showed increased return on investment from using equipment an extra day each week. This imperative trumped devoutness. In early America, localities set their own time standards, with the result that train travelers passed through a patchwork of time zones. However, in 1882 a General Time Convention standardized the time of day for the convenience of the railroads.

As the railroads grew, they spread impersonality and an ethic of commerce. Towns reoriented themselves around the train station. Shops and restaurants were placed nearby so that strangers would spend money before moving on. The railroads gave more frequent service to cities with commercial possibilities and bypassed small towns or left them withered by less frequent service. This speeded urbanization and the centralization of corporate power in cities. Rural areas were redefined. Whereas once they had been the cultural heartland, they soon were seen as backwards and rustic—places best used for vacations from urban stress.

The railroads also changed American politics. On the surface their lobbyists could dominate legislatures. On a deep level the changes were more

---

[8]Bureau of the Census, *Statistical Abstract of the United States,* 77th ed., Washington, D.C.: Government Printing Office, 1956, table 683.

profound. Congress had always selected nominees before presidential elections, but now trains brought delegates to national nominating conventions, changing the nature of party politics. Trains enabled all sorts of associations to have national meetings, and this galvanized interest groups, which, after the 1850s, began asserting themselves more at a national level. The rails also spread issues that might have remained local. The movement to give women the vote, for example, succeeded after Susan B. Anthony took trains to all parts of the country, spreading her rhetoric and unifying the cause.[9]

At first government encouraged and subsidized railroads. All told, federal and state governments gave them land grants totaling 164,000,000 acres, an area equal to the size of Nevada and California combined.[10] But later, the challenge was to control them. When Congress passed the Interstate Commerce Act in 1887 to regulate the railroads, the independent regulatory commission set up by the act, with its strengths and weaknesses, soon became the model for regulating other industries.

Many other changes in American society are traceable to railroads. They were the first businesses to require modern management structures. Due to the need for precise coordination of speeding trains over extended areas, railroads pioneered professional management teams, division structures, and present-day cost accounting.[11] These innovations were later adopted by other industries. Railroads lay behind Indian wars. For the plains Indians, the tracks that divided old hunting grounds were the main barrier to peace.[12] Thousands of laborers came from China to lay rail, and their descendants live on in communities along the lines. Railroads changed the language. The word "diner," meaning a place to eat, appeared after the introduction of George M. Pullman's first dining car in 1868.[13] And social values changed. Railroads were pathways into America that inserted and gave prominence to the commercial values of Eastern business.

The story of the railroads illustrates the power of an industry to change society, not just through its operations, but through the impact of those operations as they ripple in unpredictable and unaccountable ways through social and political institutions. The cumulative effects on a deep level of all industrial activity are, of course, far greater in sum than the effects of just one industry. New industries have changed our lives, institutions, and values in more ways than we know. Today, although our vision lacks the clarity of hindsight, industries such as the microchip industry promise to have an impact as great as that of the railroads.

---

[9]These and other social and political changes are treated at length in Sarah H. Gordon, *Passage to Union,* Chicago: Ivan R. Dees, 1996.

[10]Page Smith, *The Rise of Industrial America,* vol. 6, New York: Viking Penguin, 1984, p. 99.

[11]Chandler, *The Visible Hand,* Chapter 3.

[12]Ibid., p. 89.

[13]Daniel J. Boorstin, *The Americans: The Democratic Experience,* New York: Random House, 1973, p. 335.

erspectives on Business Power

There is agreement that business has great power, but considerable disagreement about whether this power is adequately checked and well-harnessed for the public good. Views about business power cover a wide spectrum, but most fall into one of two opposing positions.

The first is the *dominance theory,* which holds that business is preeminent in American society, primarily because of its control of wealth, and that its power is inadequately checked. Hence, corporations can alter their environments in self-interested ways that are detrimental to the general welfare. This was the thesis of Karl Marx, who wrote that unrestrained economic power exercised by a tiny capitalist class results in the exploitation of workers and lower social classes. This dominance theory is the basis of the dominance model of the BGS relationship set forth in Chapter 1.

The second is the *pluralist theory,* which holds that business power is exercised in a society where other institutions such as markets, government, labor, education, and public opinion also have great power. So, business power is counterbalanced, restricted, controlled, and sometimes defeated. Adam Smith was convinced that by market forces alone, business power could be adequately channeled to benefit society.

The Dominance Theory

The idea that concentration of economic power results in abuse arose, in part, as an intellectual reaction to unprecedented economic growth late in the nineteenth century. Until then, the United States had been primarily an agricultural economy. But between 1860 and 1890, industrial progress transformed the country. The statistics illustrating this are striking. During these thirty years, the number of manufacturing plants more than doubled, growing from 140,433 to 355,415; the value of what they made rose more than 400 percent, from $1.8 billion to $9.3 billion; and the capital invested in them grew more than 600 percent, from $1 billion to $6.5 billion.[14]

The population doubled from 31 million to 62.6 million; the number of wage earners nearly quadrupled, from 1.3 million to 4.2 million. Life was never the same again.[15] Large cities formed around industry, bringing slums, crime, disease, impersonality, and other affronts to the folksy, rustic values of a largely agrarian country. Social tensions resulted, and the dislocations of industrial development were often blamed on business, the most visible force for change.

---

[14]Figures in this paragraph are from Arthur M. Schlesinger, *Political and Social Growth of the United States: 1852–1933,* New York: Macmillan, 1935, pp. 132, 144.

[15]Ibid., p. 132.

Large companies, in particular, suffered public criticism because at the end of the century, between 1895 and 1904, an unprecedented merger wave created dominant firms in industry after industry. Since then there have been other merger waves, but this was the first. It made a definitive impression on the American mind, and its legacy is an enduring fear of big companies.

Merger waves are caused by changes in the economic environment that create incentives to combine. The stimulus for the 1895–1904 wave was the growth of the transcontinental railroads, which reduced transportation costs, thereby creating new national markets. Companies rushed to transform themselves from regional operations to national ones. Combinations such as James Duke's American Tobacco Company gorged themselves swallowing competitors. They crowded into formerly regional markets, frequently wiping out small family businesses. The story was repeated in roughly 300 commodities including oil, copper, cattle, smelting, and such items as playing cards and tombstones. A 1904 study of the ninety-two largest firms found that seventy-eight controlled 50 percent of their industry, fifty-seven controlled 60 percent or more, and twenty-six controlled 80 percent or more.[16]

The economic imperative of that era can, in retrospect, be understood. At the time, the public did not see the growth of huge firms as a natural, inevitable, or desirable response to new economic incentives. Instead, it saw them as colossal monuments to greed. Companies of this size, or "trusts" as they were called then, were something new. They inspired a mixture of awe and fear. In 1904, when the United States Steel Corporation became the first company with more than $1 billion in assets, people were astounded. Previously, astronomers, not managers, had dealt with such numbers!

Antibusiness intellectuals of the era popularized the idea that growing industry power breeds abuse. The notion stuck and remained an article of public faith during subsequent periods of rapid growth between 1900 and 1929 and after World War II. It is now axiomatic that industrial growth encourages popular belief in the dominance theory, or the theory that economic power is too concentrated in the hands of a few wealthy individuals and the leaders of giant corporations.

In recent years mergers have again reached record heights, and again advocates of the dominance theory fear growing concentration of corporate power. In 1996, there were more than 5,600 mergers between U.S. firms, and their value exceeded $1 trillion, almost double that of two years earlier. There were 364 acquisitions of foreign companies, worth a total of $59 billion, almost triple the value of such mergers two years earlier.[17] The current merger wave is impelled by globalization of markets, rapid technology change, and fierce competition.[18]

---

[16]John Moody, *The Truth about Trusts: A Description and Analysis of the American Trust Movement*, New York: Greenwood Press, 1968, p. 487. Originally published in 1904.

[17]Bureau of the Census, *Statistical Abstract of the United States: 1997*, Washington, D.C.: Government Printing Office, 1997, table 859.

[18]Roger C. Altman, "Mergers Unlimited, Inc.," *Los Angeles Times*, April 12, 1998, p. M1.

Consolidation allows corporations to expand market reach, absorb technological innovation, and lower costs by axing redundant plants and workers. Adherents of the dominance theory, however, believe that the financial power of global corporations is converted into harmful influence on consumers and societies worldwide.

Corporate Asset Concentration

A frequent measure of the extent of corporate economic power is asset concentration. The first creditable compilation was made by economists Adolph Berle and Gardner Means in 1932.[19] They showed that the 200 largest nonfinancial corporations in the United States in 1929 (less than 0.7 percent of all nonfinancials) controlled nearly 50 percent of all corporate wealth. They predicted that asset concentration would increase, with dangerous consequences.

Yet they were wrong; asset concentration has fallen and is less today than it was in 1929. By 1947 concentration of wealth in the nation's top 200 corporations had fallen to 46 percent, and it continued to fall, going as low as 34 percent in 1984. Since then it has risen only slightly to 36 percent in 1996.[20] Note also that the large, top-200 company of yesteryear was usually in a single business such as steel or railroading; sometimes it did have power to fix prices or adjust quality to the consumer's detriment. Today, however, the largest firms are often diversified and put their assets in multiple, separate, and even unrelated markets rather than in only one market.

A different statistical measure of concentration is the share of sales of the top four firms in an industry. For many years it was argued that if the top four firms had more than 40 percent of sales, competition was too anemic to protect the public. Although the extent of concentration varies widely in the roughly 450 U.S. manufacturing industries, they have for years averaged a four-firm ratio of about 40 percent.

There are two reasons not to be alarmed by a high concentration in some industries. First, research has failed to show that the performance of firms in such industries injures the public. In fact, such firms tend to be more productive, pay higher wages to workers, and raise prices more slowly than firms in less concentrated industries.[21] Second, the growth of a world economy has lowered concentration. Even though the top four firms in a wide range of

---

[19]*The Modern Corporation and Private Property,* New York: Macmillan, 1932.

[20]J. Fred Weston, Kwang S. Chung, and Juan A. Siu, *Takeovers, Restructuring, and Corporate Governance,* 2nd ed., Upper Saddle River, N.J.: Prentice Hall, 1998, p. 116. See also J. Fred Weston, "Mergers and Economic Efficiency," in *Industrial Concentration, Mergers, and Growth,* vol. 2, Washington, D.C.: Government Printing Office, June 1981. These figures allow rotation of new firms into the top-200 firms. If the same 200 firms had been followed over the years, asset concentration would have fallen even faster.

[21]See Richard Schmalensee, "Interindustry Studies of Structure and Performance," in Richard Schmalensee and Robert D. Willig, eds., *Handbook of Industrial Organization,* vol. 2, Amsterdam: Elsevier, 1989, pp. 951–1009.

industries average a 50 percent market share in the American market, this share declines to an average of only 25 percent when calculations are based on international markets.

Also, no corporation or personal fortune, no matter how large, is assured of survival. Over time, underlying forces such as poor management, competition, and technological change have continuously revised the roster of America's biggest companies. Of the 100 largest corporations in 1909, only 36 remained on the list until 1948. Between 1948 and 1958, only 65 of the new top-100 held their place. The winnowing continues. Only 116 company names remained on the Fortune 500 list of industrials from its inception in 1955 to 1994, when industrial and service corporations were combined. Now attrition is beginning on the new list. Between 1995 and 1998, 108 companies, or more than 20 percent, have been dropped.[22]

Corporate bigness may be dangerous, but it is difficult to show how power derived from asset concentration is regularly abused. The overall implications of the undeniable concentration of assets in a few firms are elusive, complex, and not clearly negative.

Concentration in Other Countries

Concentration of economic resources is characteristic of other industrialized nations. Sometimes it far exceeds that in the United States. Japan is an example.

The Japanese economy is dominated by a handful of *keiretsu* (CARE et soo), or groups of companies centered around large banks. The six largest keiretsu—Mitsubishi, Mitsui, Sumitomo, Fuyo, Dai-Ichi Kangyo, and Sanwa— are descended from old, family-controlled holding companies called *zaibatsu* (ZIE bot sue) that dominated Japan's economy before World War II. The zaibatsu were created by government policy beginning in the 1880s, because the Japanese wanted an industrial base that would support a strong military. After World War II, the zaibatsu carried the stigma of Japanese militarism and during the post-1945 Allied occupation they were dismantled. Still, the antitrust ethic that bigness is bad is foreign to the Japanese. So during the 1950s the traditional pattern of industrial concentration reasserted itself as keiretsu formed with the encouragement of the new Japanese government.

Keiretsu are not formally consolidated, as were the old zaibatsu, but they are linked and coordinated. Each is centered around a large bank and includes major trading, transportation, and manufacturing companies. Mitsubishi, the largest, includes 190 companies centered around Mitsubishi Corp., a trading

---

[22]Figures in this paragraph are derived from Neil H. Jacoby, *Corporate Power and Social Responsibility,* New York: Macmillan, 1973, p. 32; John Paul Newport Jr., "A New Era of Rapid Rise and Ruin," *Fortune,* April 24, 1989, p. 77; Carol J. Loomis, "Forty Years of the 500," *Fortune,* May 15, 1995, p. 182; and successive listings of the Fortune 500. Of the 108 companies dropped in the past three years, 59 shrank in size, 46 were acquired or merged, two failed to file a Form 10-K, and one became foreign-owned.

company, which is the fourth largest company in the world in revenues. Four other companies in the Mitsubishi keiretsu rank in the top 100 and five more in the top 500.[23] To each major company in a keiretsu is tied a network of thousands of dependent suppliers. It has been estimated that, together, the big six keiretsu control about 100,000 companies and account for approximately one quarter of the sales and assets of all Japanese companies.[24] The main body of firms, excluding smaller suppliers, is tied together by reciprocal stock ownership and shared directors. Its activities are coordinated at monthly presidential councils, where top executives meet to adopt reinforcing strategies.

The South Korean government followed a similar path of encouraging industrial growth. After the 1953 truce agreement ending the Korean war, South Korea decided to industrialize in order to raise living standards. Like the Japanese, it used controls and incentives to promote asset concentration in strong, export-oriented companies.

The country's economy was soon dominated by a group of mammoth conglomerates, or *chaebol* (CHA bool). Explosive economic growth raised per capita GNP from $82 in 1961 to $6,498 in 1991.[25] Korea became the world's eleventh-largest economy.[26] In 1996 the top 30 chaebol controlled 669 major companies. Concentration of assets in these companies is so great, however, that sales of just the top four—Hyundai, Samsung, Lucky-Goldstar, and Daewoo—accounted for approximately 80 percent of Korean GDP.[27]

Japan and Korea are examples of how historical and cultural factors guide the expression of corporate power. The intercorporate ties permitted in either country would be illegal in the United States. Americans would be paranoid and outraged to learn that the CEOs of Fortune 500 companies were discussing strategic cooperation in monthly meetings at which no note-taking was permitted. Yet the presidential council meetings of Japan's keiretsu are accepted in that country. This shows that the benefits and dangers of economic concentration are evaluated quite differently in other cultures.

Recently, both the Japanese and South Korean economies have suffered from severe problems related in part to the government policies that encouraged asset concentration. In both countries governments used protectionist measures to free the big corporate groups from domestic competition with foreign firms. The governments also gave the keiretsu and chaebol access to low-cost capital based on decisions by government agencies about which industries should grow and, particularly in Korea, these decisions were based on corrupt political contributions to high officials.

---

[23] "Global 5 Hundred: The World's Largest Corporations," *Fortune,* August 3, 1998, p. F1.

[24] Kenichi Miyashita and David W. Russell, *Keiretsu,* New York: McGraw-Hill, 1994, pp. 78, 80.

[25] Chan Sup Chang and Nahn Joo Chang, *The Korean Management System,* Westport, Conn.: Quorum Books, 1994, p. 31.

[26] "South Korea: The End of the Miracle," *The Economist,* November 29, 1997, p. 21.

[27] Steven V. Brull and Catherine Keumhyun Lee, "South Korea: Why Seoul Is Seething," *Business Week,* January 27, 1997, p. 45.

Inefficiencies grew in the big corporate groups that were unexposed to the full force of competition in global markets. In Korea, corporate leaders bought companies just so their children could run a business. A former president, Roh Tae-Woo, received $650 million in bribes from the chaebol. In Japan the ponderous keiretsu became riddled with cross-guaranteed loans given out of loyalty, not business sense, to prop up anemic companies in their groups. When economic downturn recently hit both countries, the problems with the pampered industry groups suddenly became visible as stock markets fell and workers were laid off.

For many years the decisions of Japan and South Korea to promote asset concentration in export industries worked well and harmonized with values supporting hard work and sacrifice to create a richer nation. This is how corporate power was harnessed to transform societies for the better. In Korea, for instance, life expectancy increased from 47 in 1955 to 71 in 1997.[28] The policies that promoted this, however, allowed corporate power to grow while simultaneously shielding it from important checks and balances in government and the market. Eventually, this led to abuse of that power.

Elite Dominance

Another argument that supports the dominance theory is that there exists a small number of individuals who, by virtue of wealth and position, control the nation. The members of this elite are alleged to act in concert and in undemocratic ways. There is a long history of belief in an economic elite dominating American society. In the debates preceding adoption of the Constitution in 1789, some opponents charged that the delegates who wrote it were wealthy aristocrats designing a government favorable to their businesses. Later, farmers suspected the hand of an economic elite in the pro-business policies of Alexander Hamilton, George Washington's secretary of the treasury, who had many ties to wealth and commercial power. Since the colonial era, charges of elitism have surfaced repeatedly in popular movements opposed to big business.

The modern impetus for the theory of elite dominance comes from the sociologist C. Wright Mills, who wrote a scholarly book in 1956 describing a "power elite" in American society. "Insofar as national events are decided," wrote Mills, "The power elite are those who decide them."[29] Mills described American society as a pyramid of power and status. At the top was a tiny economic-military elite, the power elite, composed primarily of the leaders of the largest corporations. Mills never gave a specific estimate of its numbers, but said it was very small. Just below was a group of lieutenants who implemented the elite's policies. They included the professional managers of corporations, powerful politicians beholden to the economic elite for their

---

[28]"South Korea: The End of the Miracle," *The Economist,* November 29, 1997, p. 21.
[29]C. Wright Mills, *The Power Elite,* New York: Oxford University Press, 1956, p. 18.

J. P. Morgan and the Panic of 1907

In the first decade of the twentieth century, J. P. Morgan (1837–1913), head of J. P. Morgan & Co. in New York, was often called the most powerful man in the country. He specialized in buying competing companies in the same industry and merging them into a single, monopolistic firm. He joined separate railroads into large systems. He combined smaller electrical concerns into General Electric in 1892 and consolidated diverse manufacturers into the International Harvester Company, which started with 85 percent of the farm machinery market. In 1901 he created the first billion-dollar company when he merged competing firms to form the United States Steel Company with capitalization of $1.4 billion (it would not be until 1911 that the annual appropriations of the federal government reached $1 billion).

Morgan and two of his close associates together held 341 corporate directorships. He dominated American banking and finance in an era of finance capitalism. His power was very independent of government controls. At the turn of the century the Sherman Antitrust Act was unenforced, there was no national bank to regulate the money supply, and existing securities and banking laws were rudimentary. One awestruck writer said he was "a kind of unelected economic president of this country."[30]

In October 1907, panic swept Wall Street and stocks plummeted as anxious investors sold shares. Soon a number of banks suffered runs of withdrawals and were on the verge of failure. Liquidity, or the free flow of money, was fast vanishing from financial markets, and the nation's banking system was on the verge of collapse. So influential was Morgan that he commanded the New York Stock Exchange to stay open all day on October 24 to maintain investor confidence. To support it, he raised $25 million of credit.

There was little the federal government could do to ease the crisis. President Theodore Roosevelt was off hunting bears in Louisiana, an ironic pursuit in

election, and government bureaucrats appointed by the politicians. The large base of the pyramid was composed of a mass of powerless citizens, including ineffectual groups and associations with little policy impact. This image of a pyramid corresponds to the dominance model in Chapter 1.

Mills' book inspired considerable scholarly research. Several years later another sociologist, Floyd Hunter, estimated the size of the top elite to be "between one and two hundred."[31] In the mid-1990s, political scientist Thomas R. Dye tried to find out precisely which individuals occupied positions of great power. In America today, power comes with leadership roles in government, corporations, and other large organizations. So Dye defined a "national institutional elite" that consists of

---

[30]Alex Groner, *American Business and Industry,* New York: American Heritage Publishing, 1972, p. 213.

[31]In his book *Top Leadership U.S.A.,* Chapel Hill: University of North Carolina Press, 1959, p. 176.

light of the crashing stock market. Without a national bank, the government had no capacity to increase the money supply and restore liquidity. Powerless, Secretary of the Treasury George B. Cortelyou traveled to New York to get Morgan's advice.

On the evening of October 24, Morgan gathered members of the New York banking elite at his private library. He played solitaire while in another room the assembled bankers discussed methods for resolving the crisis. Periodically, someone came to him with a proposal, several of which he rejected. Finally, a plan was hatched in which $33 million would be raised to support the stock exchange and failing banks. Where would this money come from? The secretary of the treasury was to supply $10 million in government funds, John D. Rockefeller contributed $10 million, and Morgan the remaining $13 million.

This action stabilized the economy. Perhaps it demonstrates that elite power may be exercised in the common good. It should be noted, however, that the panic of 1907—and other panics of that era—came after Morgan and other titans of finance repeatedly choked the stock exchange with the colossal stock offerings needed to finance their new combinations.

Morgan was widely criticized for his role in ending the panic of 1907. Conspiracy theorists, suspicious of so much power resident in one man, attacked him. Upton Sinclair, for example, accused him of inciting the panic for self-gain, a wildly erroneous accusation. In 1912, Morgan was the focus of congressional hearings by the Pujo Commission, which concluded that he led a "money trust" that controlled the nation's finances and that this was unfortunate. Death claimed him in 1913 just before Congress passed the Federal Reserve Act to set up a central bank and ensure that no private banker would ever again be sole caretaker of the money supply.

. . . individuals who occupy *the top positions in the institutional structure of American society.* These are the individuals who possess the formal authority to formulate, direct, and manage programs, policies, and activities of the major corporate, governmental, legal, educational, civic, and cultural institutions in the nation. . . . For purposes of analysis, we have divided American society into twelve sectors: (1) industrial corporations, (2) utilities and communications, (3) banking, (4) insurance, (5) investments, (6) mass media, (7) law, (8) education, (9) foundations, (10) civic and cultural organizations, (11) government, and (12) the military.[32]

Based on this approach, Dye identified 7,314 elite positions and found that they were held by 5,778 individuals, because some persons, for example business leaders who served on several boards of directors, held more than one position. This is a much larger elite than that suggested by Mills and Hunter, but it is still only two ten-thousandths of 1 percent of the American population.

---

[32]Thomas R. Dye, *Who's Running America? The Clinton Years,* 6th ed., Englewood Cliffs, N.J.: Prentice Hall, 1995, pp. 8–9. Emphasis is in the original.

Dye and other researchers have also noted that elite members originate predominantly in an upper class with identifiable traditions and mechanisms for concerted action. G. William Domhoff has researched for over thirty years a "governing class" in American society that perpetuates its power through a range of social mechanisms. Domhoff argues:

> There is a social upper class in the United States that is a ruling class by virtue of its dominant role in the economy and government. . . . This ruling class is socially cohesive, has its basis in the large corporations and banks, plays a major role in shaping the social and political climate, and dominates the federal government through a variety of organizations and methods.[33]

Members of Domhoff's governing class attend one of thirty-three exclusive private preparatory schools in the Northeast that are either secular or Episcopalian, the religious affiliation identified by sociologists as most common in the American upper class. These schools inculcate upper-class mores and begin life-long contacts. Prep school graduates later attend elite universities. During those years, the schools and also upper-class social functions such as debutante parties bring adolescents of both sexes together and the marriage institution subsequently perpetuates upper-class cohesion. Later in life, when members of the upper class ascend to positions of institutional power, they join exclusive private social clubs.

The working of these mechanisms is shown in Dye's study of institutional leaders. Dye found that 10 to 20 percent of the top leaders in business and government had attended one of thirty-three prep schools, a figure he calls "astonishing . . . since these schools educate an infinitesimal proportion of the nation's population."[34] Fifty-six percent of the 5,778 institutional leaders had attended one of just twelve prestigious universities; another 18 percent had attended private colleges.[35] Thirty-five percent held membership in one of thirty-seven exclusive clubs in cities around the country.[36]

Pluralist Theory

The counterpoint to the dominance theory is the *pluralist theory,* or the argument that although American economic interests are powerful, they must compete in an open society and open markets with other strong interests and institutions. Even if corporations and industries are asset-laden and controlled by elites, they cannot engage in tyranny because they are hemmed in by many countervailing forces.

A *pluralistic society* is one that has many groups and institutions through which power is diffused. No one group has overwhelming power, and each

---

[33]G. William Domhoff, *Who Rules America Now? A View for the 80s,* Englewood Cliffs, N.J.: Prentice Hall, 1983, p. 1.

[34]Dye, *Who's Running America?* p. 173.

[35]Ibid., pp. 171–173. The schools were Harvard, Yale, Chicago, Stanford, Columbia, M.I.T., Cornell, Northwestern, Princeton, Johns Hopkins, Pennsylvania, and Dartmouth.

[36]Ibid., p. 192.

may have direct or indirect impact on others. The dynamic forces model in Chapter 1 illustrates how, in such a society, business must interact with many constraining forces in its environments. It may have considerable influence over some of these forces, but over most it has limited influence and over some none at all. Several features of American society contribute to its pluralistic nature.

First, it is infused with democratic values. Unlike many European and Asian societies, America never had a long period of feudal rule by a powerful monarchy during which traditions of deference toward wealthy aristocrats could develop. From colonial days onward, Americans adopted the then-revolutionary doctrine of natural rights, which held that all persons were created equal and entitled to the same opportunities and protections. The French aristocrat Alexis de Tocqueville, who wrote an insightful book about American customs following a tour in America in 1831–32, called equality "the fundamental fact" in American culture. He wrote that "it creates opinions, gives birth to new sentiments, founds novel customs, and modifies whatever it does not produce." It was, he wrote, "the fundamental fact from which all others seemed to be derived."[37] Thus, in America laws apply equally to all. No person or interest is above the law. Power should be exercised for the public good through open, participative processes.

Second, American society encompasses a large population spread over a wide geography and engaged in diverse occupations. It is, therefore, characterized by a great mixture of interests, more than some other countries. Ethnic groups press for their aspirations. Economic interests, including labor, banking, manufacturing, agriculture, and consumer groups, are a permanent fixture. A rainbow of voluntary associations (whose size, permanence, and influence vary) compete in governments at all levels.

Third, the Constitution creates a government that encourages pluralism. Its guarantees of rights protect the freedom of individuals to form associations and to freely express and pursue their interests. Thus, business has been challenged by consumer, labor, environmental, and other groups. In addition, the Constitution diffuses political power through several branches of the federal government and between the federal and state governments and to the people of the United States. This is a remarkably open system.

Besides these factors, in a capitalist economy business is exposed to market forces that constrain managers. These forces can be implacable. Henry J. Kaiser, the son of German immigrants, worked his way up from store clerk to owner of 32 companies, including seven shipyards that turned out one finished ship each day during most of World War II. When he started an auto company in 1945, nobody thought he would fail. Eager customers put down 670,000 deposits before a single car was built.[38] But his cars, the Kaiser and the Frazier, were underpowered and overpriced and the market registered this. The venture failed.

---

[37]*Democracy in America*, New York: New American Library, 1956, p. 26. Originally published as two volumes in 1835 and 1840.

[38]Robert Sobel, "The $150 Million Lemon," *Audacity*, Winter 1997, p. 11.

Market forces are the most significant restraints on managerial decisions. They force a stream of resource allocation decisions to center on cost reduction and consumer satisfaction. Kaiser never got costs under control; he had to negotiate many parts prices with competing auto companies that made them. Toward the end, he built a model that was sold at Sears as the Allstate. This proved to be a terrible mistake because it gave the car a low-quality image with consumers.

In sum, a pluralistic, free-market society imposes immediate, concrete, and strong boundaries on the discretionary exercise of business power. Wise managers anticipate that, despite having considerable influence on governments and markets, their power will often be restricted, blunted, challenged, or shared by others. Overall, there are four boundaries on managerial power.

1. *Governments* at all levels and in all countries establish competitive rules and regulate business activity. They provide incentives for business, but they are the ultimate arbiters of legitimate behavior in the marketplace and can act rapidly to blunt the exercise of corporate power.

2. *Social interest groups* exist to represent every segment of society and can restrain business using an array of methods including product boycotts, lawsuits, picket lines, press conferences, and lobbying for more regulation. Prominent in recent years have been labor, environmental, civil rights, religious, consumer, and public interest groups.

3. *Social values* are embedded in civil and criminal law, reflected in public opinion, and found in literature and the media. They are internalized by managers in schools and churches. Social values include norms of duty, justice, truth, and piety that may direct a manager's behavior as powerfully as laws. In the 1960s shifting generational values gave film studios license to experiment with brazen nudity and violence, but Walt Disney's films never did. No financial incentive was enough to make him forsake his personal values about the importance of family life, morality, and the small-town decency he saw in his Kansas boyhood.[39]

4. *Markets and economic stakeholders* impose strong limits. Stockholders, employees, suppliers, creditors, and competitors can take a range of actions when corporate decisions jeopardize their interests.

Figure 3-1 illustrates the boundaries of managerial power. Just as in the solar system the planets move freely within but cannot escape their gavitational fields, so major corporations in American society move within orbits constrained by plural interests.

---

[39]Richard Schickel, *The Disney Version,* 3rd ed., Chicago: Ivan R. Dee, 1997, p. 39.

FIGURE 3-1

Boundaries of managerial power.

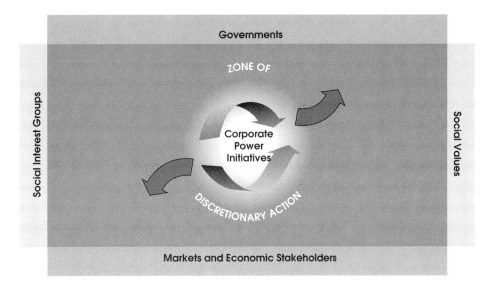

Concluding Observations

In this chapter we emphasize how important corporate power is as a force for change and how, at a deep level, economic growth shapes society in sweeping, unplanned ways. We also set forth two opposing perspectives about this power. One, dominance theory, holds that inadequately restrained economic power is concentrated in large corporations dominated by a wealthy elite. The other, pluralist theory, holds that corporate power is encircled by multiple restraining forces in an open society. These theories have clashed for many years. Both are molds into which varieties of evidence must be fitted. Both contain insights, and neither has a lock on accuracy. As useful a conclusion as any is this: As long as corporate power remains generally accountable to democratic controls, society will continue to accord it legitimacy. If rule by law and a just economy exist, corporate power will broadly and ultimately be directed toward the public welfare.

JOHN D. ROCKEFELLER AND THE STANDARD OIL TRUST

This is the story of John D. Rockefeller, founder of the Standard Oil Company. It is the story of a small-town boy who dominated the oil industry by dint of brilliant strategic insight and ruthless, methodical execution. He became the richest man in America and, for a time, one of the most hated.

Rockefeller's life spanned ninety-eight years. When he was born, Martin Van Buren was president, Andrew Jackson was the nation's preeminent hero, and settlers followed the Oregon Trail in covered wagons. He lived to see Franklin Roosevelt's New Deal, watch the rise of the Nazi party in Germany, and hear Frank Sinatra and *The Lone Ranger* on network radio.

The historical backdrop of this lifetime is an economy gripped by the fever of industrial progress. Rockefeller built his fortune in an era that lacked many of today's ethical norms and commercial laws, an era when the power of a corporation and of its founder could be exercised with fewer restraints.

The Formative Years

John Davison Rockefeller was born on July 8, 1839, in a small village in southern New York. He was the second of six children and the oldest boy. His father, William Rockefeller, was an itinerant quack doctor who sold worthless elixirs and engaged in a wide variety of businesses. He was jovial, slick, and cunning and made enough money to keep the family in handsome style until he had to flee and live away from home to avoid arrest on a charge of raping a local woman. After that, he visited only in the dark of night. But he taught young John D. and his brothers lessons of business conduct, especially, that sentimentality should not influence business transactions. "I cheat my boys every chance I get," he once said. "I want to make'em sharp."[1] John D.'s mother was a somber, religious woman who gave the children a strict

---

[1]David Freeman Hawke, *John D.: The Founding Father of the Rockefellers*, New York: Harper & Row, 1980, p. 13.

upbringing emphasizing manners, church attendance, and the work ethic. She preached homilies such as "Willful waste makes woeful want." And she taught charity to the children; from an early age John D. made regular contributions to worthy causes.

Young John D. was not precocious in school. In high school he was an uninspired student, little interested in books and ideas, but willing to work hard. He grew into a somber, intense lad nicknamed "the Deacon" by his classmates because he faithfully attended a Baptist church and memorized hymns. In the summer of 1855 he attended a three-month course at a business college in Cleveland, Ohio, and then set out looking for a job. In addition to his formal schooling, he carried the contradictory temperaments of his parents—the wily, self-assured boldness of his father and the exacting, pietistic character of his mother. He internalized both, and the combination was to prove formidable. Here was a man with the precision of an accountant and the cunning of Cesare Borgia.

Early Business Career

Rockefeller's first job was as a bookkeeper at a Cleveland firm where he meticulously examined each bill submitted and pounced on errors. He also recorded every cent he earned and spent in a personal ledger. Its pages show that he was parsimonious and saved most of his $25-a-month salary, but that he still gave generously to the Baptist church and the poor. In 1859 he formed a successful partnership with two others in the produce business in Cleveland and proved himself an intense negotiator, described by an acquaintance as a person "who can walk right up on a man's shirt bosom and sit down."[2] The business boomed from supplying food to the Union army during the Civil War. Although in his early twenties at the time, the steady, unemotional lad was never touched by patriotic fervor. In those days, the law permitted any man of means to pay someone else to serve in his place, and this he did.

Beginnings of the Oil Business

Profits from the produce business were high, and John D. looked around for a promising new investment. He soon found one—a Cleveland petroleum refinery in which he invested $4,000 in 1863. At the time, petroleum production and refining was an infant industry. A new drilling technology had led to an 1859 oil strike in nearby Pennsylvania, followed by a frenzied boom in drilling

---

[2]Jules Ables, *The Rockefeller Billions,* New York: Macmillan, 1965, p. 35.

and refining. Soon Rockefeller devoted himself full time to the oil business, and he began conforming his refinery to his principles of parsimony. One of his basic principles was to avoid paying a profit to anyone. For example, instead of buying barrels and paying the cooper $2.50 each, Rockefeller set up his own barrel-making factory and made them for $.96. He even purchased a tract of forest and made the staves from his own trees. Another basic principle was methodical cost cutting. Lumber for barrel staves was kiln-dried before shipment to the cooperage plant, and because water evaporated from the wood, it became lighter and transportation costs were lower.

Though obsessed with details and small economies, Rockefeller also proved aggressive in larger plans. He borrowed heavily from banks to expand the refinery, taking risks that scared his partners, whom he bought out. In 1865 he borrowed more to build a second refinery. Soon he incorporated an export sales company in New York.

Dynamics of the Oil Industry

By the late 1860s the new industry was in a chaotic state. A basic cause was overproduction in the oil regions of Pennsylvania, which were the only source of crude oil. The price of a barrel of crude oil fluctuated wildly but gradually declined over time. Drillers rushed to pump their wells as fast as possible, fearing that neighboring wells tapped into the same pool would pump the oil first. As supply increased, prices fell. Falling prices spurred drillers to increase output even more to maintain their income. As this chain of events continued, it led to long-term price declines. Drillers had a hard time making money.

Every drop in crude oil prices encouraged construction of new refineries. Hence, by the late 1860s refining capacity was three times greater than oil production; this encouraged vicious price wars. Many refiners tried to stay in business by selling products at a loss to raise cash for continued payment on debt. In doing so, they dragged down profit margins for all refiners. Rockefeller had the insight to invest in large-scale refineries and, because he cut costs tenaciously, his refineries made money. But even with the efficiencies of his business, the workings of the marketplace were inexorably eating away at his net earnings. In addition to economies of cost-reduction and scale in his facilities, Rockefeller believed that it was necessary to "rationalize" the entire industry in order to end its tendency to destructive competition.[3] His method for fixing the problem would be monopoly. His tactics would be controversial.

---

[3]Ron Chernow, *Titan: The Life of John D. Rockefeller, Sr.*, New York: Random House, 1998, pp. 130 and 149–52.

Rockefeller's Competitive Strategies

Rockefeller used a number of common competitive strategies. He became a low-cost, high-volume producer. He used debt financing to expand. He also attempted to make his refined petroleum products of high and consistent quality, since fly-by-night refiners turned out inferior distillates, and cheap kerosene with a low ignition point had burned many a home after exploding in a wick lamp. In 1870 he incorporated the Standard Oil Company of Ohio; the name was intended to imply a "standard oil" of uniformly good quality. He engaged in vertical integration by making wooden barrels. As time went on, he also bought storage facilities and a fleet of tank cars. In furtherance of these strategies, he used tactics common to the commercial environment of that time, including secret rebates.

One of Rockefeller's tactics for lowering costs was to strong-arm the railroads. An important cost to refiners was transportation. They had to pay the railroads to ship in crude oil and ship out refined products such as kerosene and lubricating oil. In the 1860s the railroads were highly competitive and altered freight rates to attract business. There were no regulatory restrictions and published rates were often only the starting point for negotiations.

Railroads often granted *rebates* to shippers; that is, they returned part of their freight charge after shipment. These rebates were usually secret and given in return for the guarantee of future business. The rebate system provided an incentive to increase volume, since large-volume shippers could get the biggest rebates. In the 1860s oil refineries often received rebates, and Standard Oil was no exception.

At this time Rockefeller is described by biographers as being a prepossessing man with penetrating eyes who drove a hard bargain. He would take the measure of a person with a withering stare, and few were his match. He was formidable in negotiations because he was invariably informed in detail about the other's business. And he was still a pious churchgoer who read the Bible every night before retiring.

Late in 1871 Rockefeller hatched a brazen plan for stabilizing the oil industry at the refining level. In clandestine meetings he worked out a rebate scheme between a few major refiners and the three railroads that connected to the Pennsylvania oil regions. This scheme was called the South Improvement Plan. In it the railroads agreed to a big increase in published rates for hauling oil. But Rockefeller's Cleveland refineries and a small number of major refineries in other states would be given large rebates on every barrel shipped. For example, the regular rate between the oil regions and Cleveland would be $.80 a barrel and between Cleveland and New York $2.00 a barrel. It would cost a total of $2.80 per barrel for any other refinery in Cleveland to bring in a barrel of crude oil and ship a barrel of refined oil to New York for sale or export. Rockefeller, on the other hand, would be charged $2.80 but would receive a rebate of $.90. The other conspiring refineries got similar rebates.

In addition, the refineries participating in the South Improvement Plan received *drawbacks,* or payments made on the shipment of oil by competitors! Thus Rockefeller would receive a drawback of $.40 on every barrel of crude oil his competitors shipped into Cleveland and one of $.50 on every barrel of refined oil shipped to New York. Under this venal scheme, the more a competitor shipped, the more Rockefeller's transportation costs were lowered. While competitors paid $2.80 for this critical transportation route (Pennsylvania oil regions–Cleveland–New York), Rockefeller paid only $1.00. Also nefarious was the requirement that railroads give the conspirators waybills detailing competitors' shipments—a more perfect espionage system could not be imagined.

Why did the railroads agree to this scheme? There were several reasons. First, it removed the uncertainty of cutthroat competition. Oil traffic was guaranteed in large volume and apportioned so that the Pennsylvania got 45 percent of eastbound shipments from the oil regions, the Erie 27.5 percent, and the New York Central 27.5 percent. Second, the refiners agreed to provide services to the railroads, such as tank cars, loading facilities, and insurance. And third, railroad executives were offered stock in the participating refineries. This gave them a large stake in their success.

The consequences of the South Improvement Plan were predictable. Nonparticipating refineries would face unreasonably high transportation costs and be noncompetitive with the conspirators. They would have two choices. Either they could sell to Rockefeller and his cohorts, or they could stand on principle and go bankrupt. The appeal of the former would encourage horizontal integration, the acquisition of other firms at the refining level. Refinery capacity would be limited and price stabilization would occur because a combination of refiners could keep down the price of crude. Rockefeller believed that the industry could thus be "rationalized."

The Conspiracy Plays Out

In February 1872 the new freight rates went into operation. Their advent was greeted by widespread and explosive rage in the industry, and the full outlines of the agreement were quickly revealed. Producers and refiners in the oil regions rebelled and boycotted the conspirators and the railroads. Rockefeller was correctly regarded as the prime mover behind the South Improvement Plan, and his reputation was scorched by public attacks. His wife feared that Rockefeller's life was in danger, but he was steadfast in his belief that the plan was right. He said of the plan: "It was right. I knew it as a matter of conscience. It was right between me and my God."[4] Indeed, as historian Ida Tarbell noted, Rockefeller was not squeamish about such business affairs.

---

[4]Peter Collier and David Horowitz, *The Rockefellers: An American Dynasty,* New York: New American Library, 1976, p. 11.

Mr. Rockefeller was "good." There was no more faithful Baptist in Cleveland than he. Every enterprise of that church he had supported liberally from his youth. He gave to its poor. He visited its sick. He wept with its suffering. Moreover, he gave unostentatiously to many outside charities of whose worthiness he was satisfied. . . . Yet he was willing to strain every nerve to obtain himself special and unjust privileges from the railroads which were bound to ruin every man in the oil business not sharing them with him.[5]

Within a month the weight of negative public opinion and loss of revenue caused the railroads to cave in. They rescinded the discriminatory rate structure. All appearances were of a Rockefeller defeat. But in this case appearances deceived. After the South Improvement Plan had been drawn up, but before it was exposed, Rockefeller quickly met one by one with rival refiners in Cleveland. Because of overcapacity and vicious price-cutting most were doing poorly. He explained the rebate scheme and its salutary effect on the industry and then asked to buy out his competitor. He offered the exact value of the business in cash or, preferably, in stock of the Standard Oil Company.

By the time the railroads reset their rates, Rockefeller had purchased twenty-one of his twenty-six Cleveland competitors. Some acquisitions were simply dismantled to reduce surplus capacity. He now dominated Cleveland, the country's largest refining center, and controlled over a quarter of U.S. capacity. Furthermore, he soon negotiated a secret new rebate agreement with Commodore Vanderbilt's Erie Railroad, giving him renewed advantage in transportation costs. Of these actions Ida Tarbell noted sardonically: "He had a mind which, stopped by a wall, burrows under or creeps around."[6] If any circumstance cast a shadow over this striking victory, it was that public opinion had turned against him. Henceforth, he was reviled as an unfair competitor, hatred of him growing apace with his burgeoning wealth. He never understood why.

Onward the Course of Empire

By this time Rockefeller, now 33, was a wealthy man. But he drove on, compelled to finish a grand design, to spread his pattern over the entire industry landscape, to conform it to his vision.

He continued the strategy of horizontal integration at the refinery level by absorbing more and more of his competitors. He branched out from Cleveland and began a relentless campaign of refinery acquisitions in other cities.

As the size of Standard Oil increased, Rockefeller gained added leverage over the railroads. Like an orchestra conductor he played them against each other, granting shares of the oil traffic in return for rebates and drawbacks that gave him a decisive advantage over competitors.

---

[5]Ida M. Tarbell, *The History of the Standard Oil Company*, Gloucester, Mass.: Peter Smith, 1963, vol. 1, p. 43.
[6]Ibid., p. 99.

Some competitors stubbornly clung to their businesses, but Rockefeller made them "sweat" and "feel sick" until they sold.[7] He owned large numbers of tank cars and these were often "unavailable" to ship crude oil to competing refiners. Rockefeller kept many of his acquisitions a secret to conceal the full sweep of his drive to monopoly. These companies were the Trojan horses of Rockefeller's war against independent refiners. They appeared to be independent, but secretly conspired to undermine Standard's competitors by participating in elaborate conspiracies involving code words used in letters and telegrams such as "morose" for Standard, "doubters" for refiners, and "mixer" for railroad drawbacks. The phantom competitors bought some refiners who refused in principle to sell out to Standard Oil. Their existence confronted independents with a dark, mysterious force that could not be brought into the light in order to be fought.

The Standard Oil Trust

By 1882 Rockefeller's company was capitalized at $70 million and produced 90 percent of the nation's refining output. Its main product, illuminating oil, was changing the way people lived. Prior to the availability of affordable illuminating oil of good quality, most Americans had gone to bed at dark because they could not afford expensive candles or whale oil and feared using the explosive kerosene made by Standard's early, small competitors. They now had inexpensive light and stayed up, and their lives were changed.

Rockefeller reorganized Standard Oil as a trust.[8] His purpose in doing so was to make state regulation more difficult. The trust form that he adopted became the model for many other dominant firms of that era. Rockefeller directed his far-flung empire from headquarters at 26 Broadway in New York City. He worked with a loyal inner circle of managers. As he had absorbed his competitors, so had he co-opted the best business minds in industry, and business historians attribute much of Standard's success to this stellar supporting cast. Though dominant, Rockefeller delegated great responsibility to his managers by running the giant company with a system of committees.

His management style was one of formal politeness. He never spoke harshly to any employee. The perfectionist instinct remained strong. He insisted on having a statement of the exact net worth of Standard Oil on his desk every morning. Oil prices were always calculated to three decimal places. On the way to work he penciled notes on the cuff of his sleeve. At night he

---

[7]Abels, *The Rockefeller Billions,* p. 35.

[8]A trust is a method of controlling a number of companies in which the voting stock of each company is transferred to a board of trustees. The trustees then have the power to coordinate the operations of all companies in the group. This organizing form is no longer legal in the United States.

prowled the headquarters turning down oil lamps. Compared to other moguls of that era he lived simply. He had two large estates, in Cleveland and New York, but neither was overly ostentatious. He read the Bible daily, continued regular attendance at a Baptist church, and gave generously to charities.

Extending Domination

By the 1880s Standard Oil had overwhelming market power. Its embrace of refining activity was virtually complete, and it had moved into drilling, pipelines, storage facilities, transportation, and marketing of finished products. By now the entire world was becoming addicted to kerosene and other petroleum products and Standard branched out into international sales.

In all these efforts, Rockefeller's dominating competitive philosophy prevailed. Regional marketing agents, for example, were ordered to destroy most independent suppliers. To suppress competition, Rockefeller's employees pioneered fanatical customer service. More questionable tactics were used as well. A competitor intelligence-gathering network was established. A bookkeeper at one independent refinery was offered $25 to pass information to Standard Oil. Railroad employees were turned into company detectives and bribed to misroute shipments. Standard employees climbed on competitor's tank cars and looked into the contents. Price warfare was used. A competitor often found Standard selling kerosene to its customers at a price substantially below production cost.

Rockefeller himself was never proved to be personally involved in any flagrant misconduct. He blamed criminal and unethical actions on overzealous employee behavior. His critics said the strategy of suffocating small rivals and policies such as that requiring regular written intelligence reports encouraged degenerative ethics among his minions.

Rockefeller, however, saw Standard Oil as a stabilizing force in the industry and as a righteous crusade to illuminate the world. How, as a good Christian devoted to the moral injunctions of the Bible, was Rockefeller able to suborn such vicious behavior in business? His biographer Allan Nevins gives one explanation:

> From a chaotic industry he was building an efficient industrial empire for what seemed to him the good not only of its heads but of the general public. If he relaxed his general methods of warfare . . . a multitude of small competitors would smash his empire and plunge the oil business back to chaos. He always believed in what William McKinley called "benevolent assimilation"; he preferred to buy out rivals on decent terms, and to employ the ablest competitors as helpers. It was when his terms were refused that he ruthlessly crushed the "outsiders." . . . It seemed to him better that a limited number of small businesses should die than that the whole industry should go through a constant process of half-dying, reviving, and again half-dying.[9]

---

[9]Allan Nevins, *Study in Power: John D. Rockefeller*, New York: Scribner, 1953, vol. 2, p. 433.

The Standard Oil Trust under Attack

Standard Oil continued to grow, doubling in size before the turn of the century and doubling again by 1905.[10] But eventually its very size brought a flood of criticism that complicated operations. Predatory monopoly was at odds with prevailing social attitudes about individual rights and free competition. The states wanted to regulate Standard Oil and filed antitrust cases against it. Muckraking journalists scorched Standard Oil as a company by whose acts, in the words of one, "hundreds and thousands of men have been ruined."[11] Rockefeller was the personification of greed in political cartoons. Some politicians not suborned by his bribery lambasted him.

Rockefeller, by now the richest man in the nation, was shaken by public hatred. Feeling that his life was endangered, he hired bodyguards and slept with a revolver. At church on Sundays gawkers and shouters appeared, forcing the hiring of Pinkerton detectives to guard services. He developed a digestive disorder so severe that he could eat only a few bland foods, and upon his doctor's advice he stopped daily office work. By 1896 he appeared only rarely at 26 Broadway. Soon he was afflicted with a nervous disorder and lost all his hair.

As attacks on Rockefeller grew, the vise of government regulation slowly tightened on Standard Oil. A swarm of lawsuits and legislative hearings hung about the company. Finally, in 1911, the Supreme Court in an 8–1 opinion ordered its breakup under the Sherman Antitrust Act, holding that its monopoly position was an "undue" restraint on trade that violated the "standard of reason."[12] The company was given six months to separate into thirty-nine independent firms. The breakup consisted mainly of moving the desks of managers at 26 Broadway and was a financial windfall for Rockefeller, who received stock shares in all the companies, the prices of which were driven up by frenzied public buying. All the companies prospered primarily because of skyrocketing demand for gasoline to run a growing number of automobiles. Prior to 1910 kerosene sales had buoyed the company. But just as electric light bulbs were replacing oil lamps, the automobile jolted demand for another petroleum distillate—gasoline. In 1900 only 8,000 autos were registered, but by 1910 the number had grown to 458,000, by 1915 to 2,491,000, and by 1925 to 19,941,000.[13] Rockefeller, who was seventy-one at the time of the breakup and would live another twenty-six years, would earn new fortunes simply by maintaining his equity in the separate companies.

---

[10]Ibid., vol. 2, app. 3, p. 478.

[11]Henry Demarest Lloyd, "Story of a Great Monopoly," *The Atlantic*, March 1881, p. 320.

[12]*Standard Oil Company of New Jersey* v. *United States*, 31 U.S. 221.

[13]Hastings Wyman Jr., "The Standard Oil Breakup of 1911 and Its Relevance Today," in Michael E. Canes, ed., *Witnesses for Oil: The Case against Dismemberment*, Washington, D.C.: American Petroleum Institute, 1976, pp. 72–73.

John D. Rockefeller at age 65. This photograph was taken shortly after a disease, generalized alopecia, caused him to lose his hair.

The Great Almoner

Since childhood Rockefeller had made charitable donations and, as his fortune accumulated, he increased them. After 1884 the total was never less than $100,000 a year and after 1892 it was usually over $1 million and sometimes far more. In his mind these benefactions were linked to his duty as a good Christian to uplift humanity. To a reporter he once said:

> I believe the power to make money is a gift from God—just as are the instincts for art, music, literature, the doctor's talent, yours—to be developed and used to the best of our ability for the good of mankind. Having been endowed with the gift I possess, I believe it is my duty to make money and still more money and to use the money I make for the good of my fellow-man according to the dictates of my conscience.[14]

Over his lifetime, Rockefeller gave gifts of approximately $550 million. He gave, for example, $8.2 million for the construction of Peking Union Medical

---

[14]Quoted in Abels, *The Rockefeller Billions*, p. 280.

College in response to the need to educate doctors in China. He gave $50 million to the University of Chicago. He created charitable trusts and endowed them with millions. One such trust was the General Education Board, set up in 1902, which started 1,600 new high schools. Another, the Rockefeller Sanitary Commission, succeeded in eradicating hookworm in the South. The largest was the Rockefeller Foundation, established in 1913 and endowed with $200 million. Its purpose was "to promote the well-being of mankind throughout the world." Rockefeller always said, however, that the greatest philanthropy of all was developing the earth's natural resources and employing people. Critics greeted his gifts with skepticism, thinking them atonement for years of plundering American society.

In his later years Rockefeller lived a secluded, placid existence on his great Pocantico estate in New York, which had seventy-five buildings and 70 miles of roads. As years passed the public grew increasingly fond of him. Memories of his early business career dimmed, and a new generation viewed him in the glow of his huge charitable contributions. For many years he carried shiny nickels and dimes in his pockets to give to children and well-wishers. On his eighty-sixth birthday he wrote the following verse.

> I was early taught to work as well as play,
> My life has been one long, happy holiday;
> Full of work and full of play—
> I dropped the worry on the way—
> And God was good to me every day.

He died in 1937 at the age of ninety-seven. His estate was valued at $26,410,837. He had given the rest away.

Questions

1. With reference to the levels and spheres of corporate power discussed in the chapter, how did the power of Standard Oil change society? Was this power exercised in keeping with the social contract of Rockefeller's era?

2. How does the story of Standard Oil illustrate the limits of business power? Does it better illustrate the dominance theory or the pluralist theory discussed in the chapter?

3. Did Rockefeller himself ever act unethically? By the standards of his day? By those of today? How could he simultaneously be a devout Christian and a ruthless monopolist? Is there any contradiction between his personal and business ethics?

4. In the utilitarian sense of accomplishing the greatest good for the greatest number in society, was the Standard Oil Company a net plus or a minus? On balance, did the company meet its responsibilities to society?

5. Did strategies of Standard Oil encourage unethical behavior? Could Rockefeller's vision have been fulfilled using "nicer" tactics?

Critics of Business

McDonald's Corporation
www.mcdonalds.com

The gulf between corporations and their critics can be remarkably wide. Perceptions of McDonald's Corporation illustrate this.

In the business world and to millions of customers, McDonald's success is legendary. It all started in 1948 when two brothers, Richard and Maurice "Mac" McDonald, built several hamburger stands with golden arches in southern California. One day a traveling salesman named Ray Kroc came by selling milkshake mixers. Kroc was impressed by the popularity of their $0.15 hamburgers, so he bought world franchise rights from them and soon spread the golden arches around the globe.

Today, McDonald's is one of the world's best-known brand names. In 1997 its 237,000 employees served 14 billion meals in 23,132 restaurants in 106 countries, taking in $11.4 bil-

lion in total revenues.[1] The key to the company's success has been its ability to standardize a formula of "Quality, Service, Cleanliness, and Value," and apply it everywhere.[2] About 60 percent of operating income now comes from outside the United States.

Despite its extent, McDonald's is not among the largest of American companies. In 1997 it ranked only 397 in the *Fortune* Global 500; its revenues were only one-fifteenth those of General Motors and one-tenth those of Wal-Mart.[3] But for many its penetration of global markets symbolizes the

---

[1]McDonald's Corporation, *The Annual: McDonald's Corporation 1997 Annual Report,* Oak Brook, Ill.: McDonald's Corp., 1998, inside front cover.

[2]Ibid., p. 8.

[3]"The Global 500 List," *Fortune,* August 3, 1998, p. F8.

spread of American values. The power of McDonald's to influence foreign cultures is well documented. For example, a group of anthropologists studying the impact of McDonald's in east Asia found that in Hong Kong and Taiwan, the company's clean rest rooms and kitchens set a new standard that elevated expectations throughout the country. In Hong Kong, children's birthdays had traditionally gone unrecognized, but McDonald's introduced the practice of birthday parties in its restaurants, and now birthday celebrations are widespread in the population. In Japan dining at McDonald's has reduced an old stigma against eating while standing.[4]

Critics claim that McDonald's presence is a form of American cultural imperialism that manipulates foreigners, particularly gullible children, into buying junk food that they don't need. Social and environmental activists around the world have targeted it for protest. An example of such a protest was one undertaken in England by a group called London Greenpeace. In 1986 the group wrote a six-page leaflet entitled "What's Wrong with McDonald's?" to be handed out at the company's restaurants. It was illustrated with a grotesque caricature of a businessman hiding his leering face behind a Ronald McDonald clown mask. A parody of the golden arches logo replaced the company's name with the words "McDollars" "McGreedy," "McCancer," and "McMurder." The

contents accused McDonald's of destroying rainforests to raise beef; littering cities; exploiting children with its ads; encouraging the "torture and murder" of food animals; serving fatty, cancer-causing food; and abusing employees with low wages. In short, the company hid its "ruthless exploitation of resources, animals and people behind a facade of colorful gimmicks and 'family fun.' "[5]

McDonald's executives suffered indigestion over this brochure and brought a suit for libel against two young social anarchists who had been handing it out, David Morris and Helen Steel. McDonald's said that the leaflet contained lies and sought damages of £120,000. Before trial, McDonald's offered to drop the suit if the two signed an apology. But they wouldn't; on principle, Steel and Morris elected to fight. Under British libel law, they would have to prove every statement in the leaflet. The trial began in 1994. McDonald's was represented by a prominent British libel lawyer; Morris and Steel could not afford counsel and defended themselves.

The court proceedings revealed that the corporation and its critics lived in different worlds. Morris and Steel called witnesses who said that a diet of the high-fat, low-fiber foods such as those on McDonald's menu could cause cancer and heart disease. A McDonald's vice president testified that all foods are nutritious, even Coca-Cola because it contains water. Morris and Steel got testimony from a

---

[4]James L. Watson, ed., *Golden Arches East: McDonald's in East Asia,* Stanford, Calif.: Stanford University Press, 1997, pp. 103, 134.

[5]The leaflet is at http://www.mcspotlight.org/case/pretrial/factsheet.html.

vegetarian group that children were enticed to eat junk food at McDonald's by ads that encouraged them to pester their parents into going there. A McDonald's senior vice president proudly testified that ads all over the world were designed to create brand loyalty in children between the ages of two and eight. The company believed it was promoting pro-family values. The activists said that each year McDonald's used up to 30,855 square miles of forest to meet its paper needs; the company estimated that it was just 9.46 square miles.[6] And so it went as the opposing parties dueled over one sentence after another in the leaflet.

In 1997, after three years of trial, Justice Rodger Bell issued an 800-page Judgement holding that many statements in the leaflet were libelous. But he fined Morris and Steel just £60,000, half the damages sought by McDonald's, because he felt that some statements were accurate. In particular, he found compelling evidence of cruelty to cows and chickens, of ads that manipulated susceptible children to pressure their parents, and of low pay for workers. McDonald's CEO Paul Preston was "broadly satisfied with the Judgement"; Morris and Steel said that "[b]y standing up to the company's bullying we turned the tables on them and all their dirty laundry was aired in public, exposing the reality behind the glossy image."[7] The company never tried to collect the monetary damages.

The McLibel trial, as it became known, was the longest trial of any kind in British history, and the spectacle of a giant corporation suing two people galvanized anticorporate activists. They created a McSpotlight Web site containing the "What's Wrong with McDonald's" leaflet and 19,000 pages of trial transcripts. This web site now contains new brochures and is used to coordinate worldwide anti-McDonald's demonstrations.[8]

Corporations today are attacked by a wide spectrum of critics. The story of the activists versus McDonald's is just one of many that could be told. It illustrates the difficulty of conflict resolution where the philosophies, values, and ideologies of the critics are irreconcilable with those of corporations. There are, however, many types of critics and innumerable criticisms. In this chapter we will elaborate on both.

Historical Attitudes toward Business

Throughout recorded history, merchants and businesses have been regarded with suspicion. We preface our discussion of types and sources of current business criticism with a look at the past. Although criticism of business has always existed, it deepened and changed its character after the industrial revolution.

---

[6]John Vidal, *McLibel*, New York: New Press, 1997, p. 207.

[7]Ibid., pp. 318, 319.
[8]http://www.mcspotlight.org.

The Ancient and Medieval Worlds

The earliest societies such as ancient Egypt and Mesopotamia, the Inca and Aztec societies, old China, and the ancient Hindu kingdoms of Southeast Asia were agrarian in nature. An *agrarian society* is a preindustrial society in which economic activity, government, and culture are based on traditions arising from agriculture. In these societies the great mass of people tilled land for subsistence. Upper social classes were comprised of wealthy landowners. No industry or mass-consumer markets existed, so business activity was only a tiny part of these ancient economies. In this setting the activities of merchants were often viewed as indecent because their sharp trading practices and temporizing ethics clashed with the traditional, more altruistic values of family and clan relations among farmers. Merchants were typically given lower class status than government officials, farmers, soldiers, artisans, and teachers.

Both Greece and Rome were also based on subsistence agriculture, and economic activity by merchants, bankers, and manufacturers was limited. The largest factory in Athens, for example, employed 120 workers making shields.[9] Commercial activity was greater in Rome, but it was still fundamentally an agrarian society. Merchants in both societies achieved middle-class status below an upper class of landed aristocrats.

Because industrial activity was so limited in Hellenic civilization, no accurate, coherent economic doctrines were developed to explain or justify commercial activity.[10] Into this vacuum of economic understanding stepped some of the great philosophers who encoded the idea that wealth, particularly wealth from commercial activity, was associated with greed and corruption—an idea that has left a lasting legacy of cynicism about business in Western society.

Greed was suspect in the limited economy of ancient Greece because of the popular belief that the amount of wealth was fixed. If so, an individual seeking to increase wealth did it only at the expense of the share of others. This belief was responsible for the idea that material acquisitiveness is not a noble motive in the same way as, say, desire for knowledge. The latter does not create social injustice; the former may, and is dangerous to society. The Greeks also believed that the acquisition of wealth freed individuals from certain restraints and let them pursue selfish desires that might be immoral.

These views were reflected in Greek—and later Roman—culture. In the utopian society described in *The Republic*, for example, Plato prohibited the possession of private property by its rulers for fear of corruption and the rise of tyrants; they were forbidden even to touch gold or silver.[11] In his *Politics*, Aristotle argued that retail activity for the purpose of accumulating wealth—

---

[9]Will Durant, *The Life of Greece*, New York: Simon & Schuster, 1939, p. 272.
[10]John Kenneth Galbraith, *Economics in Perspective*, Boston: Houghton Mifflin, 1987, pp. 9–10.
[11]Trans. F. M. Cornford, New York: Oxford University Press, 1945, pp. 155–68.

as opposed to simply acquiring necessities—is a "perverted or unsound" activity.[12] He also viewed the lending of money for interest as "hateful."[13]

Later, Roman law would forbid the senatorial class from making business investments (and the law would be widely circumvented). Likewise, the Stoic philosophers of Rome, such as Epictetus and Marcus Aurelius, taught that the truly rich person possessed inner peace rather than capital or property.[14] These thinkers looked down on merchants of their day as materialists who, in pursuit of wealth, sacrificed the opportunity to develop character. Needless to say, this did not deter the merchants from accumulating fortunes and neglecting the study of ideals.

During the Middle Ages, the prevailing theological doctrines of the Roman Catholic Church were intolerant of profit making. Christianity created a doctrine opposed to the values of the wealthy ruling class, which had debilitated Rome in its waning years. It rejected a focus on wealth accumulation and sought special status for the poor. The Church was deeply suspicious of commerce because it diverted merchants from devoutness. Merchants were exhorted to charge a *just price* for their wares, a price that was just adequate to maintain them in the social station to which they were born. The just price stands in contrast to the modern idea of a *market price* determined by supply and demand. But today we hear echoes of medieval theology when consumers complain that high prices for a product are unjust, unfair, or unethical. The Roman Church also condemned *usury,* or the lending of money for interest. By the twelfth and thirteenth centuries, however, the money supply and economic activity had expanded greatly and interest-bearing loans were commonplace. "Commercial activity," notes historian Will Durant, "proved stronger than fear of prison or hell."[15] Church scholars such as St. Thomas Aquinas began to back away from the dogma of the just price and the sin of usury, though they never fully embraced market pricing or lending for interest. In fact, Church doctrine making lending money for interest a sin was not officially repealed until 1917.

As business activity accelerated during the Renaissance, new economic theories arose to justify practices that had previously been condemned. In particular, Adam Smith's theory that free markets harnessed greed for the public good contradicted Aristotle's belief that the pursuit of money was corrupting. Smith's theory that competitive markets protected consumers from price gouging contradicted the Church's insistence on the idea of a just

[12]Trans. Ernest Barker, New York: Oxford University Press, 1962, p. 27. Originally written c. 335 BC.

[13]Ibid., p. 29.

[14]"Asked, 'Who is the rich man?' Epictetus replied, 'He who is content.'" *The Golden Sayings of Epictetus,* trans. Hastings Crossley, in Charles W. Eliot, ed., *Plato, Epictetus, Marcus Aurelius,* Danbury, Conn.: Grolier, 1980, p. 179.

[15]In *The Age of Faith,* New York: Simon & Schuster, 1950, p. 631.

price. And the notion that only a fixed amount of wealth existed in a society was countered by evidence of wealth creation in thriving economies.

However, just when old beliefs lost their hold, the industrial revolution created new tensions that led to critical attitudes about business. These new tensions arose as industrialism transformed agrarian societies and challenged traditional values with modern alternatives.

Agrarian societies are fundamentally different from industrial societies; in the fire of industrialization they undergo rapid change. Agrarian societies are rural and slow-paced; they are stable and cling to traditional ethics and values passed down over generations. They revere nature, value independence and equality, put the community before the individual, and emphasize humanitarian ethics of interpersonal relations such as the Golden Rule. During industrialization such societies are swiftly and dramatically altered. They become urban and fast-paced; the complexity of institutions grows. Awe of nature is replaced by conquest of nature. New values and habits arise; consumption, for instance, replaces thrift and saving. More emphasis is placed on growth, development, and commerce. Historian Henry Adams described this change colorfully in 1905 when he took a backward look at the rise of big business in America:

> The Trusts and Corporations . . . were obnoxious because of their vigorous and unscrupulous energy. They were revolutionary, troubling all the old conventions and values, as the screws of ocean steamers must trouble a school of herring. They tore society to pieces and trampled it underfoot.[16]

Although the antiquarian values of Greece and Rome may still shine through in the charges of critics, fundamental societal change from industrialization soon became the great source of raw material for their attacks. We will examine the impact of this change in the United States.

Attitudes toward Business in American History

High levels of public confidence in business existed during the early years of this nation. Historians record generally positive feelings toward entrepreneurs, companies, and the business system until the growth of giant trusts in the latter half of the nineteenth century.

The earliest colonies were established by privately owned English companies. Sometimes the motive for colonization was to avoid religious persecution, but the backers of the Pilgrims, for instance, hoped to make a profit. The commercial spirit manifested itself in different ways in colonial America, but it was dominant in most walks of life. The farmer was not a peasant bound to the soil with a pattern of life dictated by custom. Although his way of life was different from that of the retail merchant in the town, they both engaged in buying and

---

[16]Henry Adams, *The Education of Henry Adams,* New York: Modern Library, 1931, p. 500. This passage was written in 1905.

selling. As the farmers accumulated wealth, they built and ran grain .
in other ways employed their capital exactly like the merchants. Merc₁
great wealth rose to top status in colonial society in part because there w ₁₁o
tradition of a landed or hereditary aristocracy, as in Europe.

By 1850, America was a predominantly rural, agrarian society of small,
local businesses. But explosive industrial growth rapidly reshaped it, creating
some severe social problems in the process. Cities grew as farmers left the land
and immigrants swelled slum populations. Most cities were run by corrupt political machines that failed to ameliorate parlous conditions. Simultaneously, in
many industries companies merged into huge national monopolies. These
changes were the raw material of two movements critical to big business.

The first was the *populist movement,* a farmers' protest movement that
began in the 1870s and led to formation of a new political party, the People's
party, which met its ultimate defeat in 1896. Here is how the movement started.
Soon after the Civil War, farmers began to suffer from a persistent drop in crop
prices. Falling prices were caused mainly by overproduction because of the efficiencies of new farming machinery, and by competition from foreign farmers
because of new transportation methods. At the time, farmers did not understand these factors and blamed their distress on railroad companies, the largest
and most visibly corrupt businesses of the day, which frequently overcharged
farmers when hauling crops, and on "plutocrats" such as J. P. Morgan and others in the eastern banking community, who controlled finance and industry
and sometimes foreclosed on their farms. In a typical tirade, Mary Lease,
speaking on behalf of the Farmers' Alliance ticket in 1890, complained:

> Wall Street owns the country. It is no longer a government of the people, by the
> people and for the people, but a government of Wall Street and for Wall Street.
> The great common people of this country are slaves, and monopoly is the mas-
> ter. The West and South are bound and prostrate before the manufacturing
> East.[17]

To solve agrarian ills, the populists advocated government ownership of
railroads, abandonment of the gold standard, and measures to control the influence of big business in politics, including direct election of U.S. senators.

Historian Louis Galambos believes that despite the populist critique, there
existed a great reservoir of respect for and confidence in business until the late
1880s.[18] Thereafter, analysis of newspaper and magazine editorials shows
mounting hostility toward large trusts. Soon the populists succeeded in electing many state and local officials, who enacted laws to regulate the railroads

---

[17]In John D. Hicks, *The Populist Revolt,* Minneapolis: University of Minnesota Press, 1931, p. 160.

[18]Louis Galambos, *The Public Image of Big Business in America, 1880–1940,* Baltimore: Johns
Hopkins University Press, 1975, chap. 3. Galambos examined 8,976 items related to big business
that were printed in eleven newspapers and journals between 1879 and 1940 using content
analysis to reconstruct a rough measure of public opinion among influential groups in the
population.

The Wonderful Wizard of Oz

The Wizard of Oz is known as a book for children.[19] But it has another dimension. Written by an author of children's books, Lyman Frank Baum (1856–1919), in 1900 as an allegory of the populist dream, it satirizes the evils of an industrial society run by a moneyed elite of bankers and industrialists. "Oz" is the abbreviation for ounce, a measure of gold. It and the Yellow Brick Road allude to the hated gold standard. The characters all represent major groups in society. Dorothy represents the common person. The Scarecrow is the farmer. The Tin Woodsman is industrial labor. His rusted condition recalls the closing of factories in the depression years of the 1890s and his lack of a heart reminds readers that factories dehumanized workers. The Cowardly Lion is William Jennings Bryan, the defeated People's party candidate, whom Baum regarded as lacking sufficient courage. The Wicked Witch of the East was intended by Baum to parody the capitalist elite. She kept the munchkins, or "little people," in servitude. At the end of the Yellow Brick Road lay the Emerald City, which was Washington, D.C. When the group arrived, it was met by the Wizard, who stood for the president of the United States. At the end Dorothy melted the Wicked Witch of the East, the Wizard flew off in a balloon, the Scarecrow became ruler of Oz, and the Tin Woodsman took charge of the East. This ending was the unrealized populist dream.

and provided the political groundswell behind the creation of the Interstate Commerce Commission in 1887 to regulate railroads. Despite efforts, populists were never able to forge a national coalition with labor organizations. The movement died in 1896 with the decisive defeat of William Jennings Bryan, the People's party candidate for president. But it had refined a logic and lexicon for spotlighting the business system as the source of social ills. Populists blamed adverse consequences of industrialization on monopoly, trusts, Wall Street, "silk-hatted Easterners," the soulless "loan sharks" and shameless "bloodhounds of money" who foreclosed on farms, and corrupt politicians who worked as errand boys for the "moneybags" in a system of "plutocracy" (or rule by the wealthy). Their criticisms were harsh and colorful. In an essay on the superior virtues of farming as an occupation, Bryan wrote that for farmers "even the dumb animals are more wholesome companions than the bulls and bears of Wall Street."[20]

---

[19]First published in 1900 under the title *The Wonderful Wizard of Oz*, Chicago: Reilly & Britten, 1915. Eventually there were fourteen Oz books. The classic interpretation of symbolism in *The Wizard of Oz* is Henry W. Littlefield, "The Wizard of Oz: Parable on Populism," *American Quarterly*, Spring 1964.

[20]"Farming as an Occupation," *Cosmopolitan*, January 1904, p. 371.

It was, of course, too late in the day for America to return to farming. This did not diminish the appeal of the populist message. On the contrary, continued industrial growth has caused it to resurface time and again up to the present day, each time its critical message refurbished to fit current circumstances.

The second movement was the *progressive movement,* a broader reform movement lasting from about 1900 until the end of World War I in 1918. Fueled by great moral indignation about problems of industrialization, it incorporated the urban middle class as well as farmers. Although a short-lived Progressive party was formed and unsuccessfully nominated Theodore Roosevelt for president in 1912, both the Democratic and Republican parties had powerful, dominant progressive wings. Unlike populism, progressivism was a mainstream political doctrine. Like populism, it was at root an effort to cure social ills by controlling perceived abuses of big business.

Because of broad popular support, progressives were far more effective than populists in their reform efforts, and during their era a reform tide washed over business. Progressives broke up trusts and monopolies, made federal campaign contributions by corporations illegal, imposed federal regulation on consumer products, restricted child labor, started a corporate income tax and inheritance taxes, and regulated safety conditions in factories. "Turn the waters of pure public spirit into the corrupt pools of private interests," wrote Ernest Crosby, editor of *Cosmopolitan* magazine, "and wash the offensive accumulations away."[21] Progressivism further refined the antibusiness lexicon of the populists and carried their legacy into the twentieth century.

After the triumph of progressive reforms, there was a period of high public confidence in big business during the prosperous, expansive 1920s. This rosy era ended abruptly with the stock market crash of 1929, and business once again came under sustained attack. During the 1920s, the idea that business knew how to achieve continuing prosperity had been advanced and widely accepted. The depression of the 1930s disproved this view and, in addition, brought to light much ineptness, criminal negligence, and outright fraud on the part of prominent business executives. There was a popular feeling that the economic collapse would not have occurred if business managers had been more capable. Criticism of business was intensified by the callous-appearing reaction of the conservative business community, which believed that government should not intervene to relieve human misery caused by the depression.

As anger at business grew, the old rhetoric of populism reemerged. In the Senate, for example, Huey Long, a colorful populist Democrat from Louisiana who claimed to be the advocate of the poor against the rich, rose to condemn a "ruling plutocratic class" controlled by the "fortune-holding elements of Morgan, Mellon, and Rockefeller."[22] In 1934, Long introduced a

---

[21]"The Man with the Hose," August 1906, p. 341.
[22]*Congressional Record,* 73d Cong., 2d sess., 1934, p. 6081, speech of April 5.

Art Young, a radical cartoonist of the Progressive era, had an impish ability to highlight the excesses of the industrial age. This cartoon, typical of many at that time drawn by Young and others, first appeared in 1912.

CAPITALISM

plan to redistribute wealth that would annually tax large fortunes and corporate assets and redistribute the money by guaranteeing every family a gift of $5,000 and an annual income of $2,500. To promote his plan, Long established a Share Our Wealth Society that attracted over 5 million members in 1935, but he was assassinated before its enactment, and the milder reforms of President Franklin D. Roosevelt's New Deal proved sufficient to placate his supporters.

During World War II support for business rebounded. Industry wrapped itself in patriotism, and its high output of war material proved essential to Allied victory. As a result, business was seen as the "arsenal of democracy," not as a bloated plutocracy. In a postwar poll, only 10 percent of the population believed that where "big business activity" was concerned "the bad effects outweighed the good."[23] This renascence of respect lasted into the 1960s before the populist seed sprouted once again.

Recent Antibusiness Sentiment

Strong public support for business collapsed in the mid-1960s. It was a time of unrest. Social movements attacked basic institutions for their failure to solve major problems. Government, labor, the military, churches, higher education, medicine, the press, and, of course, business all suffered diminished public confidence. Here are examples of polls that reflect the extraordinary negative trend in public attitudes toward business.

- In 1968, 70 percent agreed that business tried to strike a fair balance between profits and the public interest. By 1970 the figure had declined to 33 percent, and in 1976 it had plummeted to 15 percent. This was a drop of 55 points in eight years.[24]
- Two polls, the first in 1966 and the second in 1979, showed that the percentage of Americans expressing a "great deal of confidence" in the leaders of major companies declined from 55 percent to 19 percent.[25]
- Between 1965 and 1977, the average favorability ratings for eight industries fell from 68 percent to 36 percent. Approval of twenty-two large companies declined from an average rating of 74 percent in 1965 to 48 percent in 1975.[26]

Scholars who studied the polls theorized that the period of turmoil in American society in the 1960s created a "confidence gap," or a gap between public expectations about how institutions *should* perform and public perceptions of how they actually *did* perform. This gap has now existed for more than thirty years, and it continues to define the climate of public opinion. In 1997 only 28 percent of Americans expressed "a great deal" or "quite a lot" of confidence in big business, just 2 percent more than in 1973; and only 17 percent had "very high" or "high" confidence in the ethics of business executives, three points less than in 1979.[27]

---

[23]Burton R. Fisher and Stephen B. Withey, *Big Business as the People See It,* Ann Arbor, Mich.: University of Michigan Microfilms, December 1951, p. xiii.

[24]Seymour M. Lipset and William Schneider, "How's Business? What the Public Thinks," *Public Opinion,* July–August 1978.

[25]Philip Shaver, "The Public Distrust," *Psychology Today,* October 1980.

[26]Seymour M. Lipset and William Schneider, *The Confidence Gap,* New York: Free Press, 1983, p. 31.

[27]Frank Newport, "Small Business and Military Generate Most Confidence in Americans," and Leslie McAneny, "Pharmacists Again Most Trusted; Police, Federal Law Images Improve," Gallup Poll Archives, August 1997 and December 1997, http://www.gallup.com/archive.htm.

Factors Underlying Negative Attitudes toward Business

What causes this confidence gap to persist? Sometimes negative opinions about business are based on recent events or personal experiences. However, complex historical, cultural, and psychological factors are also at work. One of the most fundamental factors, which we have already discussed, is the stress of industrialization on the social fabric. Beyond this, the following are also important.

Traditional American Antipathy to Centralized Power

Fear of concentrated power is deeply fixed in the bedrock of American political culture. Sources of this fear are the experiences of colonial America with an imperious England and the popularity in the revolutionary era of the English philosopher John Locke, who wrote that human beings are naturally free and equal. Political power should be accountable to the consent of the governed and be used to protect individual rights to life, liberty, and property. Locke believed that popular majorities have the right to influence and check powerful executives and legislators.[28]

After the Civil War, when trusts grew to dominate markets and suborn politicians, Locke's ideology of popular checks on centers of power was applied to them by critics. To this day many critics fear the motives of managers and regard giant multinationals as remote, impersonal entities that cannot be trusted any more than the colonists could trust King George. In 1941 a poll found that 59 percent of Americans agreed that "there is too much power in the hands of a few rich men and large corporations."[29] Over fifty years later, the perception of oppressive corporate power was even more widespread: 76 percent of those surveyed in 1992 agreed that "there is too much power concentrated in the hands of a few big companies."[30]

Tension between Capitalism and Democracy

There is a natural, built-in tension between capitalist economies and democratic governments because they embody equally legitimate but competing value systems. Capitalist values include economic efficiency, self-interest as a major motive, and resource allocation through an impersonal market mechanism. Unfettered, these values can lead to enormous inequalities of wealth and circumstance. Democracy is a combination of popular sovereignty, political equality, and majority rule. These characteristics are leveling forces. American society continuously seeks to reconcile these competing value sets.

---

[28]See *The Second Treatise of Government*, Thomas P. Reardon, ed., Indianapolis: Bobbs-Merrill, 1952. Originally published in 1690.

[29]George H. Gallup, ed., *The Gallup Poll: Public Opinion 1935–1971*, vol. 1, New York: Random House, 1972, p. 27.

[30]A Gallup/Times Mirror poll cited in "Opinion Outlook," *National Journal*, July 25, 1992, p. 1750.

In capitalist–democratic societies, business can expect persistent attack. This attack occurs because democracies tend to drift leftward over time as more have-nots are included in the electoral process. Political parties win support with promises to increase the well-being of the lower strata. In this process, leftist politicians and political parties appeal to the masses by attacking wealth and privilege. Since the early 1990s, this trend has been eclipsed in Western democracies by the success of market economies and conservative parties, but it has not been eliminated.

Operation of the Business Cycle

Recurrent recession and depression in American history have ensured periodic concern about economic institutions and their performance. Panics in the nineteenth century led to public rage directed at the financial community. The stock market scandals of the 1930s associated with the 1929 market crash tainted business for years. Opinion polls show that people rate economic problems among the most important problems and sometimes blame business for their economic ills.

Historically, periods of economic decline have fed fear of business power and belief in business conspiracy.[31] Lipset and Schneider showed that confidence in leaders of major companies and other institutions declined with the rise of unemployment and inflation between 1966 and 1980.[32] Although the American economy has been strong and both unemployment and inflation are low, current high levels of criticism are related to insecurity over job loss and a long-term decline in real wages for blue-collar workers.

The Image of Business in Media and the Arts

Values are both shaped and reflected by images of business in journalism, literature, and the visual arts.

A longstanding adversarial relationship exists between business and journalists representing the print and broadcast media. Corporations want to see positive images conveyed through newspapers, magazines, radio, and television. The job of editors, reporters, and producers, on the other hand, is to seek out and publish accurate information in a way that attracts audiences. The result of this difference of mission is that companies sometimes accuse the news media of distortion, bias, simplification, and omission in business reporting. Journalists, in turn, complain of executives "unavailable" for comment, unreturned phone calls, terse news releases, and overprotective public relations offices that shield top managers from the press. Three other basic factors underlie the friction between journalism and business.

---

[31]W. W. Rostow, "Business Cycles, Harvests, and Politics," *Journal of Economic History*, November 1941.

[32]Lipset and Schneider, *The Confidence Gap*, p. 62.

First, many business stories are complex, yet strong forces in the media work against in-depth, sophisticated reporting. Television journalists are usually generalists, not specialists in business affairs. They face short deadlines, and unless the story is a blockbuster, news program editors rarely give it more than ninety seconds. Television news, due to its visual nature, tends to emphasize colorful, emotional, visually exciting, and dramatic stories involving conflict, but not all or even the most important business news is of this nature. The dynamics of print journalism are less restricting. The most sophisticated daily newspapers, such as the *New York Times* and the *Washington Post*, have specialist business reporters and can devote many pages to a story to achieve in-depth reporting, although their deadlines are also short. Weekly news magazines have longer deadlines and can do more research on stories.

Second, surveys show that journalists have different values than business executives. They tend to be liberals and Democrats, whereas executives are the reverse. They have lower income and different educational backgrounds than the managers they cover, and they tend to have different policy preferences.[33] Thus, journalists may filter issues and events through a value system that abets bias. On the other hand, large media corporations frequently own the news organizations that employ journalists. Such ownership ties raise delicate issues. In corporate-owned media, owners and editors do not hamhandedly forbid certain topics or kill big stories. But they have the more subtle power to choose subjects that will be treated in greater depth and with more frequency.

A third factor underlying friction between business and journalism is the tradition of muckraking in the profession. This tradition began during the progressive era after 1902 when a group of moralistic writers published exposés of business corruption in emergent mass-circulation magazines. Ida M. Tarbell, for instance, began her famous two-volume *History of the Standard Oil Company* as a series of articles in *McClure's* beginning in 1903[34] Other writers skewered trusts in meat packing, railroading, tobacco, banking, and life insurance. Basic to the writings of the muckrakers was faith in the righteousness of an informed, aroused public. Today's journalists carry on this tradition.

The image of business in literature reflects a mixture of attitudes among novelists. It is often negative, and business values have been derided by some of the most famous American novelists. At the turn of the century Frank Norris, in his aptly titled novel *The Octopus*, portrayed railroads as corrupt and evil.[35] Upton Sinclair attacked greed and disregard for workers in the meat-packing industry in *The Jungle*, his tragic narrative of an immigrant's life in Chicago's slaughterhouses.[36] A few years later, Sinclair Lewis used the vacant

---

[33]Karlyn Bowman, ed., "Opinion Pulse: The Political Views of Journalists," *The American Enterprise,* March/April 1996, p. 88.

[34]Ida M. Tarbell, *The History of the Standard Oil Company,* Gloucester, Mass.: Peter Smith, 1963, 2 vols. Originally published in 1904.

[35]New York: Doubleday, Page, 1901.

[36]New York: Doubleday, Page, 1906.

character George Babbitt to show a business world that lacked excitement and meaning.[37] This tradition continues. A study of business novels written since 1975 concludes that managers are shown as "opportunistic 'valueless' individuals devoid of ethical and social awareness."[38] Tom Wolfe's *Bonfire of the Vanities* rose to the top of the *New York Times* bestseller list in 1987 with just such a protagonist. It is the story of a rich, pretentious Wall Street bond trader whose life in business is frivolous and amoral.[39] As the plot unfolds, his pretensions of superiority are destroyed by the "little people," the street punks, police, and courts of New York. This is a novel the populists would have loved.

Although some of America's greatest novelists have treated business with scorn and contempt, others have affirmed business values. Horatio Alger's popular formula novels about business success are an example. Alger wrote more than 100 novels between 1867 and 1899, all with the same inspirational story line. In books with titles such as *Mark the Matchboy* and *Ragged Dick,* impoverished street urchins display strong character values of integrity and hard work. Fortuitously, these values attract the attention of titans of industry who then open the doors to opportunity and boundless wealth. One literary historian, who studied 450 novels with business themes, concludes that novelists have admired virtues such as hard work, achievement, and integrity. Some writers, however, portrayed these traits as being at odds with business life.[40]

By contrast, on entertainment television the image of business is often strikingly negative. A landmark study of 620 prime-time shows in the thirty seasons between 1955 and 1986 found that business characters were depicted more negatively than any others. Though making up only 12 percent of the characters, they committed 32 percent of the crimes, including 40 percent of the murders. Only 37 percent of businesspeople on TV played positive roles.[41] The researchers found a trend over the seasons toward increasingly negative depictions, whereas other types of characters remained unchanged. This was attributed to a shift in program content that paralleled growing public cynicism about business; story lines increasingly reflected the antibusiness, liberal, left-wing attitudes of Hollywood writers and producers. More recent studies show that TV still uses stereotypes of villainous executives.[42]

---

[37]Sinclair Lewis, *Babbitt,* New York: Harcourt, Brace, Jovanovich, 1922.

[38]Bernard Sarachek, "Images of Corporate Executives in Recent Fiction," *Journal of Business Ethics,* March 1995, p. 203.

[39]New York: Farrar, Straus, & Giroux, 1987.

[40]Howard P. Smith, "Novelists and Businessmen: Schizophrenia in the Complex Society," *Journal of Contemporary Business,* Autumn 1976.

[41]S. Robert Lichter, Linda S. Lichter, and Stanley Rothman, *Watching America: What Television Tells Us about Our Lives,* New York: Prentice-Hall Press, 1991, pp. 131–33.

[42]Marc Gunther, "Business Is TV's Newest Bad Guy," *Fortune,* July 7, 1997, p. 32.

"Modern Man Followed by the Ghosts of His Meat," by Sue Coe. Coe is an artist who attempts to provoke anger and unease. Her paintings are often bleak because she believes that the presence of injustice in her subjects leaves no beauty to be depicted. This painting is one of a series Coe did after visiting slaughterhouses and meatpacking plants. The image challenges values that support meat eating and includes a McDonald's logo that implicates corporations in the slaughter of animals.

Source: Sue Coe. "Modern Man Followed by the Ghosts of His Meat." 1988. Copyright © 1988 Sue Coe. Courtesy Galerie St. Etienne, New York.

Conspiracy Theories

Throughout American history, it has been alleged that some group (and the list includes Jesuits, city women, European monarchs, immigrants, Jews, blacks, Communists, Masons, Darwinians, munitions manufacturers, international bankers, oil companies, and Wall Streeters), acting in secret for its own self-interest, is out to do the public in. This mindset, which has been called the "paranoid style" by historian Richard Hofstadter, is distinguished by the belief that a vast conspiracy is the motive force of history.[43]

The number of people who believe that conspiracies exist can be large. In 1974, for instance, 43 percent of Americans believed that the energy shortage was "contrived" by the oil companies to exploit the public.[44] In 1985, according to 67 percent, "the oil companies are just waiting for a chance to create another oil shortage so they can increase their prices again like they did in the 1970s."[45] In 1990 the public affirmed its suspicious prophecy. When oil

[43]*The Paranoid Style in American Politics and Other Essays*, New York: Knopf, 1966.

[44]In Clarence H. Danhoff and James C. Worthy, eds., *Crisis in Confidence II: Corporate America*, Proceedings of the Second Annual Intersession Public Affairs Colloquium, Springfield, Ill.: Sangamon State University, 1975, p. 39.

[45]Edward Byers and Thomas B. Fitzpatrick, "Americans and the Oil Companies: Tentative Tolerance in a Time of Plenty," *Public Opinion*, December/January 1986, p. 44.

companies raised gasoline prices after Iraq invaded Kuwait, 84 percent believed that "they deliberately tried to rip off the American motorist."[46]

Conspiracy theories such as these are difficult to combat because their circular logic is airtight. Because undiscovered conspiracies are by definition secret, they cannot be directly observed or verified. The most straightforward appeal of conspiracy theories is that they provide simple explanations for complex events and relieve the mind of the necessity for stenuous thought. Hence, intricate reality is reduced to the existence of a hidden conspiracy that explains everything. The persistence of conspiracy theories is a factor underlying cynicism toward business.

Current Criticism of Business

The list of specific criticisms of corporations is virtually endless, but all are based on the same idea, which is that people in business place profit before enduring values such as honesty, truth, justice, love, devoutness, aesthetic merit, tranquility, and respect for nature. For example, commercialism has eroded the meaning of Christmas, according to two critics who say it has turned "the day commemorating the birth of Jesus Christ into an unparalleled orgy of consumption."[47] In this instance, devoutness is sacrificed for profit. To critics the profit motive is less noble than humanitarian motives because it is seen as selfish. This idea, an echo from ancient Greece, is at the root of the following generic categories of criticism. Each broad category, in turn, includes many specific criticisms.

- The largest corporations have too much power. This power is concentrated in too few hands and is inadequately checked in global corporations that have the leverage to pit nations and workers against each other.
- Corporations have too much influence in government. They use their wealth to corrupt politicians and undermine democratic processes. We have what Ralph Nader has called "a government of the Exxons, by the General Motors and for the DuPonts."[48]
- Market values create corporate cultures in which people feel pressured to carry out amoral actions. Good human beings put into corporate roles turn into minions who prioritize return on capital even when it conflicts with social welfare.

---

[46]"Opinion Outlook," *National Journal,* February 2, 1990, p. 295.

[47]Michael F. Jacobson and Laurie Ann Mazur, *Marketing Madness: A Survival Guide for a Consumer Society,* San Francisco: Westview Press, 1995, p. 203.

[48]Hector Tobar and Bill Stall, "Green Party Nominates Nader for President," *Los Angeles Times,* August 20, 1996, p. A3.

- Corporations exploit stakeholders. "To ask corporations to behave better by making growth and profit a lower priority or to act foremost in the interests of local communities, the environment, or the workers is like asking armies to give up guns," notes one critic.[49]
- Corporations spread a gospel of Western-style development around the world, erasing distinct local cultures. Capitalism creates undesirable structural trends such as industrialization, growth of mass consumer markets, and reliance on intrusive, large-scale technologies ranging from autos to nuclear power plants. This cannot define progress because it reduces the life-satisfactions of those it affects.

Classifying business critics is difficult. They exhibit a wide range of values, opinions, methods, and goals. It is important to distinguish between average people who have some cynicism about business but largely accept it and a small number of others who have deep-seated, emotional, and principled objections to the system and who want to change it. To oversimplify, there are four basic groups of these more vociferous critics.

Activist Reformers

The first group, activist reformers, is composed of individuals and groups who accept the legitimacy of the business system, but see flaws and work with companies and through political processes for reform. They are often motivated by principle, focused on emotional issues, and willing to crusade selflessly. The philosophy of the activist reformer is exemplified by consumer advocate Ralph Nader, who accepts American capitalism in its democratic setting but sees an "imbalance of power between the people and the plutocracy."[50] For more than thirty years, Nader has worked to redress this imbalance by building an organization of public interest groups called Public Citizen through which he and his disciples push for reforms.

Some activism is the product of lone individuals, but the most effective pressure on companies comes from groups. Civil rights activist Rev. Jesse Jackson, for example, has worked for years through a group called Operation PUSH (People United to Serve Humanity) to pressure corporations into including more minorities and women as executives, suppliers, and franchisees.

Activists use a wide range of tactics. Common pressure tactics include negotiation, letter writing, speeches, lobbying, research, and editorial writing. Labor unions frequently picket companies. A few groups use lawsuits to challenge business. Sometimes, activists resort to harassment, as when they sue corporations based on trumped-up charges such as racketeering or disrupt the

---

[49]Jerry Mander, "The Rules of Corporate Behavior," in Jerry Mander and Edward Goldsmith, *The Case Against the Global Economy,* San Francisco: Sierra Club Books, 1996, p. 309.

[50]Ralph Nader, "Breaking Out of the Two-Party Rut," *The Nation,* July 20/27, 1992, p. 8.

lives of executives and their families by picketing their homes, protesting at their children's schools, and interrupting services at their churches. Activist groups are adept at redefining issues, creating symbolism, and attracting media attention. INFACT, a group "whose purpose is to stop life-threatening abuses by transnational corporations," inducts companies into its "Hall of Shame." When it picked Dow Chemical Co., a member of the group attended the company's annual shareholders meeting and attempted to present the "award" to Chairman Frank Popoff. Popoff declined to accept, and the INFACT representative was "escorted" from the meeting.[51]

There are additional tactics used by activists that take advantage of the corporation's market orientation.

- *Shareholder Resolutions.* Rules permit individuals and groups owning the stock of public companies to sponsor resolutions on which all shareholders may vote at annual meetings. If the resolutions pass, they are binding on management. Religious groups have led in sponsoring such resolutions. The Interfaith Center on Corporate Responsibility in New York coordinates a coalition of 275 Protestant, Roman Catholic, and Jewish denominations that, in 1998, generated 210 shareholder resolutions on social issues aimed at 143 companies.[52]

- *Boycotts.* A boycott is a call to pressure a company by not buying its products and services. In 1998 there were more than 100 ongoing boycotts organized by a wide range of groups. Here are some examples. An animal rights group, People for the Ethical Treatment of Animals, organized boycotts of American Express, for selling fur coats through catalogues, and *Vogue* magazine, for depicting fur as fashionable and glamorous. An environmental group, Rainforest Action Network, called for a boycott of Mitsubishi Corporation because a subsidiary logged tropical forests. A human rights group, Honor Our Neighbors Origins and Rights (HONOR), boycotted G. Heileman Brewing Co. for selling Crazy Horse malt liquor because the name disgraced the memory of the legendary warrior. And the American Family Association, a group on the Christian right, organized a boycott of Circle K for selling *Playboy*, *Penthouse*, and *Hustler* magazines.[53]

- *Selective Purchasing and Investment Laws.* Governments and pension funds are pressured by groups to stop them from buying from or investing in allegedly irresponsible corporations. For instance, in the 1980s the Africa Fund, Transafrica, labor unions, and civil rights groups were successful in getting more than 100 laws passed in

---

[51]"Campaign Report," *INFACT Update,* Summer 1996, p. 3.
[52]"Corporate Responsibility Challenges 1998," *The Corporate Examiner,* March 10, 1994, p. 1.
[53]See "On-Going Boycotts," *The Boycott Quarterly,* Spring 1998, pp. 33–39.

states, counties, and cities prohibiting purchase of anything from companies doing business in South Africa. Although these laws have been rescinded, new ones based on other causes have proliferated.

In recent years antibusiness critics have created a growing number of *transnational advocacy networks*, which are fluid, global coalitions of entities that are focused on correction of problems or abuses. Activist groups are always at the core of these networks that may also include churches, labor unions, intellectuals, researchers, and government officials. In the 1800s, an advocacy network led the global antislavery campaign, so the idea is not new. But in recent years, they have grown in number and sophistication.[54] An example is the International Campaign to Ban Landmines, composed of 800 groups in 50 countries. As part of its work, activist groups such as Human Rights Watch have attacked corporations that make antipersonnel mines. One of them, Raytheon Co., got out of the business of making mine components and others, including Motorola Inc., Hughes Aircraft Co., and General Electric, have adopted rules prohibiting the sale of components to make antipersonnel mines.[55]

Liberal Intellectuals

This group is composed of thinkers who share a broad approach to social problems that they express with the pen rather than the sword of activism. Often they are in the vanguard; they see emerging social problems caused by corporate activity, frame issues for public discussion, and suggest reforms. Usually they believe in protection of human rights, restraint of corporate power, and solution of social problems through government action.

The liberal reform tradition surfaced as America industrialized. In that era and subsequently, intellectuals have attacked social ills. When economic activity accelerated in the nineteenth century, intellectuals began to be bothered. "Commerce," complained Ralph Waldo Emerson in 1839, ". . . threatens to upset the balance of man and establish a new, universal Monarchy more tyrannical than Babylon or Rome."[56]

By the end of the last century, factories had proliferated and a mass consumer society formed to buy their output. In 1899 Thorstein Veblen gave an unflattering description of "conspicuous consumption" in *The Theory of the Leisure Class.* He argued that in an industrial society, material possessions replaced knowledge and character as sources of status. Therefore, people bought expensive things to compete with their neighbors. The more extravagant and

---

[54]Margaret E. Keck and Kathryn Sikkink, *Activists Beyond Borders,* Ithaca, N.Y.: Cornell University Press, 1998, pp. 8–12.

[55]Christina Del Valle and Monica Larner, "A New Front in the War on Land Mines," *Business Week,* April 28, 1997, p. 43.

[56]Quoted from Emerson's *Journals,* vol. V, pp. 285–86, in Vernon Louis Parrington, *Main Currents in American Thought,* New York: Harcourt, Brace, 1927, p. 386.

wasteful a possession, the more it gave "pecuniary strength" to its owner. A circuitous driveway over flat land, for example, was much preferred to a straight one. The indirect route was less efficient, but the wasteful extra expense of constructing it showed that the owner was opulent and inspired "invidious comparison."[57] As a critic of consumer society, Veblen was decrying the deterioration of thrift as a central value.

By the 1950s a new class of white-collar workers had emerged. In his 1956 book, *The Organization Man*, sociologist William H. Whyte Jr. argued that big corporations forced conformity on their employees.[58] Industry was whittling away at the American tradition of rugged individualism. At this time, economist John Kenneth Galbraith wrote the first of many books over forty years advocating government control of business to reverse the loss of consumer sovereignty that he attributes to the growth of corporations.[59]

Some writers never challenge business directly, but their work changes social values. In the 1962 book *Silent Spring*, naturalist Rachael Carson warned of the danger of pesticides, and wrote at just the right time to galvanize a dawning environmental movement and quicken the attack on industrial pollution.[60] Peter Singer's 1975 philosophical tract *Animal Liberation* created a moral justification for animal rights that changed the environment for the animal agriculture, cosmetics, fur, and restaurant industries.[61]

Socialists

Socialist critics reject current institutions and demand replacement with a collectivist state. Unlike reform-oriented critics, this group believes that the faults of capitalism cannot be ameliorated through gradual reform. Basic institutions such as the free market and private capital must be swept away.

Socialists base their critique on the philosophical and economic theories of Karl Marx (1818–1883). They attack classical economists for blindness to the abusive aspects of markets. Orthodox views of the market, they say, fail to acknowledge worker exploitation, imperialist expansion overseas, resource waste, race and sex discrimination, income inequality, militarism, and other evils.

Historically, socialist critics have been persistent antagonists of business. An early landmark of American socialism was Edward Bellamy's popular 1888 novel, *Looking Backward*. Bellamy began the book with a metaphor comparing industrial society "to a prodigious coach which the masses of humanity were harnessed to and dragged toilsomely" while the privileged few sat in

---

[57]New York: Penguin Books, 1979, pp. 27 and 137. Originally published in 1899.
[58]New York: Simon & Schuster, 1956.
[59]See, for example, *The Affluent Society*, Boston: Houghton Mifflin, 1958, and *The New Industrial State*, Boston: Houghton Mifflin, 1967.
[60]Boston: Houghton Mifflin, 1962.
[61]New York: New York Review of Books, 1975. Revised edition by Avon Books, 1990.

"breezy and comfortable seats on the top."[62] But the plot made its way to a new cooperative society in the year 2000, in which businesses nationalized by the government worked for the benefit of everyone, not to satisfy the greed of a few. The book ignited the public's imagination and sold more copies—over 500,0000—than any book ever had before. It spawned "Nationalist" clubs across the country and inspired several hundred people to form a colony in Tennessee to bring Bellamy's alternative future to life. This living critique of modern capitalism required its members to pass a socialist entrance exam, used a loud steam whistle to wake them and bring them to meals and work, and tried to instill values with communal readings of the Declaration of Independence.[63] It lasted only seven years.

Although the tide of history has gone against socialism, its advocates reached high-water marks in three historical eras. The first was during the progressive era, when in 1912 the Socialist party presidential candidate, Eugene V. Debs, attracted 6 percent of the popular vote. The second was in the depression era of the 1930s, when attacks on free enterprise abounded. And the third was during the 1960s and 1970s, when social movements challenged the establishment, including business. In each case, however, moderate reform defeated the socialist agenda.

Today the influence of Marxist thinkers has waned as formerly socialist countries convert to market economies. This historical development blunts the appeal of its critique. Though the movement is moribund, to dismiss it now might be premature.

Radical Nonsocialists

Radical nonsocialist critics see industrial society as beyond redemption and want to replace its basic principles and restructure its institutions. Unlike socialists, however, they do not coalesce around a specific theory of what is wrong, what should be done, and how to do it.

Radical criticism of industry has a long history in American society; in the last century, the first radical critics tried to cling to the values and life of an agrarian society being swept away before their eyes. In the 1840s, Brook Farm in Massachusetts and similar agrarian communes were founded to demonstrate an alternative way of life. In them, values prized in industrial society—materialism, competition, individualism, and tireless labor—were rejected. Instead, an effort was made to substitute moderation, group harmony, and leisure. These utopias soon failed, their example fated by industrialization.

---

[62]*Looking Backward: 2000–1887,* Boston: Ticknor and Company, 1888, p. 6. Bellamy advocated "nationalism" and avoided the word socialism because he believed it had frightening connotations for Americans.

[63]W. Fitzhugh Brundage, *A Socialist Utopia in the New South,* Urbana: University of Illinois Press, 1996, pp. 50, 109, 125.

In 1863, Henry David Thoreau wrote to reject a world where the poetry and grace of everyday life was being smothered by business values.

> This world is a place of business. What an infinite bustle! I am awakened almost every night by the panting of the locomotive. It interrupts my dreams. There is no sabbath. It would be glorious to see mankind at leisure for once. It is nothing but work, work, work. I cannot easily buy a blank-book to write thoughts in; they are commonly ruled for dollars and cents . . . I think that there is nothing, not even crime, more opposed to poetry, to philosophy, ay, to life itself, than this incessant business.[64]

The ideas of Brook Farm and Thoreau failed to spread. But the tradition of radical rejection of industrial society has been continuously renewed. In 1896, Henry Demarest Lloyd wrote *Wealth Against Commonwealth,* a popular book that moved public sentiment against big business. The argument in Lloyd's book makes the same points as today's critics. He attacked the drive of "corporate caesars" to "control production, not by the needs of humanity, but by the desires of a few for dividends"; he wrote that across the globe "corporations are grown greater than the State," and that common people are "slaves to market tyrants."[65] Lloyd rejected government as a solution, advocating instead a curative based on brotherly love. Like many radical critics of industrialism, the arc of reasoning never returns to earth; the faults of capitalism are laid bare, but the cure is nebulous. He was unable to offer a concrete substitute for the way of life he rejected.

More recently, E. F. Schumacher wrote *Small Is Beautiful,* in which he urged a new society of small-scale organizations in which people harmonize with nature instead of dominating it.[66] Dave Foreman, a founder of the radical activist group Earth First! believes in dismantling much of industrial civilization, tearing up roads, and returning to an earlier kind of life.[67] Another recent radical critic, Kirkpatrick Sales, writes that corporations must be reoriented to have "spiritual identification" with all species, large organizations with global perspectives must be replaced by small communities, and industrial capitalism must be converted to a system of cooperation rather than competition.[68] These ideas could have been found at the Brook Farm commune 150 years ago.

Concluding Observations: What to Think of Critics

In this chapter we have set forth a long history of negative attitudes toward business and discussed specific criticisms. In doing so, we have not analyzed the merits of particular criticisms, but have simply noted them. The fundamental response to critics of industrial society is as follows.

---

[64]Henry David Thoreau, "Life Without Principle," *The Atlantic Monthly,* October 1863, pp. 484–85.
[65]New York: Harper & Brothers Publishers, 1989, pp. 2, 1, 494, and 521.
[66]New York: Harper & Row, 1973.
[67]Dave Foreman, *Confessions of an Eco-Warrior,* New York: Harmony Books, 1991.
[68]Kirkpatrick Sales, *Rebels Against the Future,* Reading, Mass.: Addison-Wesley, 1995, pp. 276–77.

There is no question that industrial capitalism as it exists in the United States and elsewhere is a historical force that creates fundamental, continuous social change; it is, as the economist Joseph Shumpeter wrote in 1942, "a perennial gale of creative destruction," which destroys institutions and challenges existing authority.[69] The great issue is how to regard this change.

The defense of industrial capitalism is that the changes in companies, governments, values, technologies, and living patterns that it creates represent progress, a condition of improvement for humanity. As against promoting greed and avarice, it has rather promoted positive cultural values such as imagination, innovation, organized cooperation, hard work, and the interpersonal trust necessary to conduct millions of daily business transactions on faith. It operates in a democratic political system which has ably reformed abuses over the years. And it has improved living standards for millions. As one defender of the "spirit of capitalism" notes, during the last century even as critics attacked its deplorable impact, it was actually

> . . . prompting inventions and improvements that systematically came to the assistance of the neediest: eyeglasses for those of weak eyesight, lamps for those in darkness, new medicines for the ill, mechanical aids to replace brute human strength, and ever-greater ease of transport. Life became softer, even as intellectuals described it in terms of the jungle. The spirit of capitalism may in fact be portrayed more accurately as leading to excessive comfort than as reincarnating the law of survival.[70]

Whether or not we agree with their ideas, business critics play an important role. There are legitimate criticisms of business that demand attention by both corporations and governments. If criticism is properly channeled, it can preserve the best of the business institution and bring wide benefit.

---

[69]*Capitalism, Socialism and Democracy,* New York: Harper & Row, 1976, p. 143. Originally published in 1942.

[70]Michael Novak, *The Catholic Ethic and the Spirit of Capitalism,* New York: Free Press, 1993, p. 26.

TIME WARNER AND RAP CRITICS

Rap music is a tiny sliver of total revenue for the giant entertainment conglomerate Time Warner Inc. Yet the lyrics of some rap artists on its labels have made it a big target for critics, who believe that the company profits by selling violent, degrading, and sexist lyrics that undermine community values. "Like a junkie quivering toward a fix," wrote one critic, "Time Warner simply can't resist cashing in on the amoral singers who work tirelessly to tear the culture apart, glorifying brutality, violence and the most hateful attitudes toward women the public culture has ever seen, ranging from rape to torture and murder."[1]

Time Warner counters that rap lyrics contain ideas that deserve to be heard. In a company brochure, Gerald Levin, chairman of the board and CEO of Time Warner, writes: "Creative expression results from an environment that nurtures imagination, encourages debate, welcomes dissent, and is always striving to reconcile the responsibilities of a publicly owned business with the aspirations of the artistic spirit."[2] This response has never satisfied the critics.

What follows is the story of Time Warner's confrontations with critics, first with law enforcement groups and then with conservatives who think that rap degrades society.

Time Warner

Time Warner, with 1997 revenues of $13.3 billion from 70 countries, is one of a handful of global corporations that dominate the entertainment industry. It describes itself as "the world's leading media and entertainment company."[3] It is not the largest; Sony and Walt Disney are much larger and Bertelsmann, its German rival in publishing and music, is slightly larger. But it has a formidable portfolio of entertainment assets and distribution channels.

---

[1]John Leo, "The Leading Cultural Polluter," *U.S. News & World Report,* March 27, 1995, p. 16.

[2]Time Warner, *Factbook,* "Introduction," undated, www.pathfinder.com/corp/fbook/fbintro.html.

[3]Time Warner Inc., Form 10-K, December 31, 1997, p. I-1.

Time Warner was put together by a merger of Time Inc. and Warner Communication in 1989; in 1996 it absorbed Turner Broadcasting System. It is a complex company. Time Warner itself is a holding company that controls more than 200 wholly or majority-owned subsidiaries. The subsidiaries are organized into four business segments. The *publishing segment* encompasses book publishers Little, Brown and Warner Books, Book-of-the-Month-Club, and thirty magazines including *Time, People, Sports Illustrated,* and *Fortune.* Its *cable network segment* broadcasts HBO, Cinemax, CNN, and other channels. The *entertainment segment* includes Warner Bros. Pictures and Music Group, which hold the rights to 6,000 films, 28,500 television programs, and music productions ranging from Cole Porter to LeAnne Rimes. The Music Group has a 22 percent domestic market share, more than any competitor. Finally, the *cable systems segment* gets fees from 12.6 million cable subscribers around the country.

Time Warner, as an intricate collection of businesses, may be a difficult company to manage. It took on enormous debt to complete the 1989 merger, and since then CEO Levin has incurred more debt by buying new businesses such as cable companies. Today the entertainment industry is dominated by large conglomerates that bring together under one corporate banner all forms of making and delivering entertainment. As rivals grow, Time Warner must develop similar size and diversification to remain competitive. The company has not performed well in the stock market and has turned in losses in recent years. But, while growing, it has also been cutting costs, generating cash, paying debt, and moving closer to profitability. In this overall strategic situation, a few rap albums are insignificant elements in a larger mechanism until they endanger overall performance. An example is the "Cop Killer" controversy.

The "Cop Killer" Controversy

In March 1992, Warner Bros. Records released *Body Count*, a new album by rap artist Ice-T and his heavy metal band. *Body Count* was a crossover album from rap to rock. Later, it would be misrepresented as rap because its lyrics fit the rap mold. A theme in *Body Count* was black anger toward racist police. One song, "Smoked Pork," was about shooting police responding to a false call for help. Another, "Cop Killer," had lyrics about getting a sawed-off shotgun and a knife—and driving a car with the lights off, being ready to kill a police officer. The refrain included the phrase "Die Pig, Die!" followed by eight repetitions of "F- - - the police!"

At the time, the release of *Body Count* was unremarkable. It did not stretch boundaries for popular music. Its content had been pioneered years earlier by, among others, the rap group N.W.A. in its song, "F- - - tha Police." The album was an immediate hit and ultimate sales were 310,000.[4] There was no hint of a tempest brewing.

---

[4]Ice-T's royalty rate was estimated to be less than $1.25 per album. If so, he collected royalties of somewhat less than $387,500 on *Body Count* albums with "Cop Killer." *Body Count* sales were about $4.6 million, or approximately four one-thousandths of 1 percent of Time Warner's 1992 revenues.

Then, on April 11, a Texas state trooper stopped a stolen truck and was shot to death by the driver, a 19-year-old black man who was playing on the truck's tape deck the rap album *2pacalypse Now* by Tupac Amaru Shakur. A song on the album, "Soulja's Story," told of "blasting" a police officer and "droppin' the cop" during a traffic stop. The driver later told police that these lyrics incited him to kill the trooper. *2pacalypse Now* was distributed by Time Warner for Interscope Records. The trooper's family sued Interscope and rap artist Shakur for lyrics that incited "imminent lawless action," and the incident received national media coverage.[5] Vice President Dan Quayle called on Interscope to take *2pacalypse Now* out of distribution. Suddenly, black anger toward police in rap music was seen as more than artistic license; it became a concrete danger. Public fear grew later that month when blacks in south central Los Angeles attacked white motorists during riots following the Rodney King trial.

Critics Target "Cop Killer"

Since its release, "Cop Killer" had met with some reproach here and there from police, but now a firestorm of criticism rolled out of Texas. There, Ronald G. DeLord, president of the Combined Law Enforcement Officers of Texas (CLEAT), saw that an attack on "Cop Killer" was an opportunity to fight police bashing in the wake of the Rodney King acquittal.

DeLord's wrath focused on Time Warner, not on Ice-T. He intensely disliked Ice-T's message in "Cop Killer," but he believed that it represented only a fringe mentality. Ice-T, or someone like him, would always be contemptuous of social standards. The critical problem was that when a leading corporation marketed an antisocial recording, it found greater legitimacy and larger audiences than it would otherwise. So DeLord decided to strike at Time Warner, depicting it as a greedy corporation promoting pathological ideas disguised as entertainment.[6]

Early in June, DeLord held a press conference and, on behalf of his 12,000-member group, he demanded that Time Warner stop distributing "Cop Killer" and that it apologize to police and to the families of slain officers everywhere. If the company failed to comply by July 16, the day of its annual shareholder's meeting, CLEAT would call a nationwide consumer boycott of its products. Mark Clark, CLEAT's director of government relations, added: "Our goal is to educate the average Time Warner shareholder as to how low this corporation has sunk to earn a dollar."[7]

---

[5]John Broder, "Quayle Calls for Pulling Rap Album Tied to Murder Case," *Los Angeles Times,* September 23, 1992. Subsequently, a jury convicted the shooter, rejecting his defense that rap music caused him to kill.

[6]Ronald G. DeLord, "In My View," *Texas Police Star,* Autumn 1992, p. 3.

[7]Quoted in Chuck Philips, "Texas Police Call for Boycott of Time Warner," *Los Angeles Times,* June 12, 1992, p. F7.

Over 300,000 copies of the Body Count *album were sold.*

In response to the CLEAT press conference, Time Warner released this statement:

> Time Warner is committed to the free expression of ideas for all our authors, journalists, recording artists, screenwriters, actors and directors. We believe this commitment is crucial to a democratic society, where the full range of opinion and thought—whether we agree with it or not—must be able to find an outlet.[8]

The press conference created a story line of confrontation and the national media jumped on it. In DeLord's words, "it just went like a bullet."[9] Michael Jackson and Rush Limbaugh did shows about it. Police groups across the country supported CLEAT's demands; some boycotted Time Warner. The National Rifle Association took out newspaper ads pledging legal assistance "to the interests of any police officer shot or killed if it is shown that the violence was incited by Ice-T's 'Cop Killer.'"

---

[8]Ibid.

[9]Author's telephone interview with Ronald G. DeLord, February 15, 1993.

Defending "Cop Killer"

A few voices were raised in support of "Cop Killer." The National Black Police Association refused to support CLEAT. Jesse Jackson argued that "rap music and the rhythms mirror the reality we would rather not see."[10] A rap magazine, *The Source*, editorialized that Ice-T was "not polite," but said that he was "describing the way many people in the community feel."[11]

Soon politicians began to exploit the issue. Sixty members of the House and Senate issued a statement denouncing Time Warner, and the Los Angeles City Council passed a motion asking it to withdraw the song. President Bush said, "It's wrong for any company . . . to issue records that approve of killing a law enforcement officer."[12] Over 1,000 record stores refused to sell *Body Count*.

Nevertheless, Time Warner was defiant. Within a week, Gerald Levin (who was co-CEO then) responded to critics by writing a piece for *The Wall Street Journal*.[13] In it, he made two arguments for "Cop Killer." First, it contained a message that Americans needed to hear. The anger, rage, and obscenity in rap music were a warning from the inner-city black community. He wrote:

> [N]early 30 years ago, Malcolm X expressed his amazement at the surprise with which white Americans confronted the insurrections that racked American cities. He wondered how whites could have failed to grasp the nature and extent of the long-fermenting anger in our ghettos. Malcolm X's question still haunts us. Why can't we hear what rap is trying to tell us.

Levin's second justification for the distribution of "Cop Killer" was that Time Warner was committed to freedom of expression.

> [T]he test of any democratic society lies not in how well it can control expression but in whether it gives freedom of thought and expression the widest possible latitude, however controversial or exasperating the results may sometimes be . . . Time Warner is determined to be a global force for encouraging the confrontation of ideas. . . . In the short run, cutting and running would be the surest and safest way to put this controversy behind us and get on with our business. But in the long run it would be a destructive precedent.

Levin's reasoning failed to change minds. At Time Warner's shareholder meeting ten days later, twenty speakers rose to challenge *Body Count*. Charleton Heston gave a theatrical recitation of profane lyrics from the album trying to embarrass Time Warner executives and directors. Police officers who had been shot in the line of duty rose to speak. Ron DeLord of CLEAT argued that rap lyrics could dehumanize police just as anti-Semitic propaganda had dehumanized the Jews in Nazi Germany. In response, Levin read a prepared statement defending "Cop Killer" as protected speech.

---

[10]Jesse Jackson, "From Pain to Power," *Liberal Opinion Week,* July 13, 1992, p. 19.

[11]James Bernard, quoted in Philips, "Texas Police Call for Boycott of Time Warner," p. F7.

[12]Quoted in Chuck Philips, "The Uncivil War," *Los Angeles Times/Calendar,* July 19, 1992, p. 6.

[13]Gerald M. Levin, "Why We Won't Withdraw 'Cop Killer,'" *The Wall Street Journal,* June 6, 1992, p. A20.

"Cop Killer" Bites the Dust

The pressure, however, was overwhelming. On July 28, just four months after the release of *Body Count*, Time Warner announced that at the request of Ice-T, it would produce a new version of the album without the song "Cop Killer." Though Time Warner issued no apologies for the song, CLEAT decided it had won a victory and never called a boycott. Within six months, Ice-T and Warner Music Group parted company.

Freedom of Speech

Freedom of speech is a central value in American culture. It derives from a long philosophical tradition, exemplified in John Stuart Mill's classic essay *On Liberty*. Mill believed that freedom of opinion and expression were necessary to maintain a free society, the kind of society that could protect liberty and promote happiness. He wrote that a natural tendency existed to silence discomfiting or unorthodox views. But this is wrong, because no person is in possession of ultimate truth. Restricting debate deprives society of the opportunity to find new ideas that are more valid than prevailing ones. Even bizarre or hurtful comments can contain partial truth and should be valued. Censorship of any kind is wrong because no person, society, or generation is infallible. It is better to leave open many avenues for challenging mainstream views so that falsehood and pretention can be exposed. Truth, said Mill, needs to be "fully, frequently, and fearlessly discussed."[14]

In American society, the philosophy of free speech is given legal force in the First Amendment, which prohibits government from abridging the spoken or printed expression of ideas. Over the years, the Supreme Court has given expansive protection to all forms of expression. Indeed, Justice William O. Douglas once wrote that free speech may "best serve its high purpose when it induces a condition of unrest, creates dissatisfaction with conditions as they are, or even stirs people to anger."[15] And the Court has been faithful to his argument. It has, for example, permitted racist language,[16] burning of the American flag,[17] sexually explicit material,[18] malicious parodies of public figures,[19] and the right of the Ku Klux Klan to advocate race war on television.[20]

---

[14]John Stuart Mill, *On Liberty*, ed. Currin V. Shields, Indianapolis: Bobbs-Merrill, 1956, p. 43. Originally published posthumously in 1907.

[15]In *Terminiello* v. *Chicago*, 337 U.S. 4 (1949).

[16]*Terminiello* v. *Chicago*, 337 U.S. 1.

[17]*Texas* v. *Johnson*, 57 LW 4770 (1989).

[18]*Sable Communications* v. *FCC*, 57 LW 4920 (1989).

[19]*Hustler Magazine* v. *Falwell*, 485 U.S. 46 (1988).

[20]*Brandenburg* v. *Ohio*, 395 U.S. 447 (1969).

The First Amendment, however, protects speech only from government censorship. Time Warner is a corporation, not a government. Therefore, the First Amendment is a barrier to any government body that tries to stop it from publishing rap music. Critics cannot prevail on Congress or state legislatures to ban the sale of songs with offensive lyrics. They must force Time Warner to self-censor lyrics.

Ice-T was unimpressed by First Amendment arguments. He wanted the debate to focus on the idea or "reality" that he was trying to express, that is, that inner-city blacks were angry with police. In his words, "That's what needed to be said. Not, 'Ice-T has free speech.' That's bull- - - -"[21]

There are others who fault the doctrine of free speech itself for permitting insults to minorities and women. Some rap lyrics are criticized for demeaning women. Feminist scholars such as Catharine A. MacKinnon attack free-speech doctrine for permitting this. MacKinnon argues that degrading references to women are not simply an expression of opinion, but are a form of discrimination that robs women of equality and dignity. She believes that modern free-speech doctrine related to obscenity was developed by men to keep pornography available. As a result, it protects abusive words about women that diminish their stature and threaten their rights. She recommends that in such cases, speech rights of men should not be absolute, but should be balanced against rights of women to equality. Similarly, the rights of Klan members to hate speech should be balanced against the rights of minorities to be protected from discrimination. Her view is that words are not only ideas, but they are actions with consequences to the welfare of real persons.[22]

The Rap Music Phenomenon

Rap emerged in the 1970s in the South Bronx as black youths created a form of musical expression to voice feelings about inner-city life. It depicts harsh realities of that life, including drugs, crime, violence, and poverty. But at its core it is more than descriptive. It is also an aggressive narrative of rebellion against an American culture perceived as racist.[23] Rap challenges cultural oppression by voicing forbidden narratives such as those in which young black men kill police. The brash, loud sound of rap, played through huge speakers with heavy bass, projects the assertive confrontation intended by some rap artists.

Rap music is part of a broader urban youth culture known as hip hop. Hip hop is a lifestyle that confronts mainstream values. Baggy clothing and heavy gold jewelry subvert Fifth Avenue style. Graffiti give voice to those who lack access to traditional media. Rapidly evolving slang is used as a code for criticizing oppressive social structures. Today, elements of hip hop are moving

---

[21]Ice-T, "The Controversy," in Adam Sexton, ed., *Rap on Rap*, New York: Dell, 1995, p. 181.

[22]Catharine A. MacKinnon, *Only Words*, Cambridge: Harvard University Press, 1993, Part III.

[23]Chuck D, *Fight the Power: Rap, Race, and Reality*. New York: Delacorte Press, 1997.

into the mainstream, including fashion trends and rap. In 1998 rap accounted for more than 10 percent of U.S. record sales, and its popularity was growing. Almost 75 percent of it was purchased by white consumers, 50 percent of them under 18 years old.[24] According to one critic, rap is "the first musical style since the '50s to truly rival rock 'n' roll as the primary music of choice for American youth culture."[25] This gives entertainment corporations a strong financial incentive to get involved.

Conservative Critics Focus on Time Warner

Not long after the *Body Count* controversy died down, a new attack on Time Warner was mounted by conservative defenders of civic virtue. These new critics did not focus on one artist or song; instead, they fought against violent, profane, sexist, and explicit lyrics found in many rap albums.

The initiative for this new attack on Time Warner came from C. Delores Tucker, a civil rights activist and head of the National Political Congress of Black Women. In 1993 Tucker began a crusade against violent and obscene music that she believed was degrading to black women and black culture. She soon made Time Warner the target of her wrath because of its 50 percent ownership of Interscope Records, a record label with a stable of rap artists whose work she found particularly egregious. One of Interscope's subsidiaries, called Death Row Records, had a cohort of gangsta rappers unparalleled in the industry both for its market success and for its explicit lyrics. As one anti-rap columnist wrote, Time Warner's half-ownership of this group was "the cultural equivalent of owning half the world's mustard-gas factories."[26]

By 1995 Tucker had assembled an anti-rap coalition that included William J. Bennett, the former secretary of education, who headed a conservative group called Empower America and was editor of a best-selling work on moral education, *The Book of Virtues;*[27] and Barbara Wyatt, who headed the Parents' Music Resource Center, an organization founded to protect children from exposure to sex and violence in music. Bennett proposed to escalate the campaign against Time Warner by attacking it in the media and creating a new confrontation at the company's annual shareholder's meeting.

Confrontation

At the shareholders' meeting, Tucker rose for a seventeen-minute denunciation of Time Warner. She recited explicit rap lyrics and asked shareholders to stop investing in "sexually explicit, pornographic music."[28] She accused the

---

[24]Christopher John Farley, "Songs in the Key of Lauryn Hill," *Time,* September 7, 1998, p. 70.
[25]Marc Weingarten, "Large and In Charge," *Los Angeles Times/Calendar,* July 26, 1998, p. 9.
[26]Leo, "The Leading Cultural Polluter," p. 16.
[27]New York: Simon & Schuster, 1993.
[28]Quoted in Sallie Hofmeister, "Time Warner Defends Rappers," *Los Angeles Times,* May 19, 1995, p. D3.

company of being "devoid of social conscience and citizen responsibility,"[29] and of "putting profit before principle."[30] After Tucker's speech, CEO Gerald Levin rose to defend the right of rap artists to be heard, asserting that "music is not the cause of society's ills" and announcing that the company would campaign for industrywide labeling standards to identify music that could be considered objectionable.

Afterward, Levin agreed to a private meeting with Tucker, Bennett, and Wyatt. The meeting was a disaster. Tucker handed printed lyrics from "Big Man with a Gun" by Nine Inch Nails to Michael Fuchs, chairman of Warner Music Group, and offered to give him $100 if he would read them out loud. The lyrics read in part, "Maybe I'll put a hole in your head / You know, just for the f- - - of it."[31] Fuchs refused and Tucker briefly left the room in anger.

Bennett was also confrontational. When Levin said that the meeting would have occurred even without the pressure of public criticism, Bennett replied, "Baloney!" After the meeting Fuchs said of Bennett: "He came in with no information and no credentials to discuss any of this intelligently. . . . I guess he thought he was the self-appointed marshall riding in on a white horse to be the arbiter of morals." Bennett retorted: "I was impressed with the lack of candor. . . . It was extremely pompous. Here were these guys in $4,000 suits making us feel like we were lucky to be getting the time of day."[32]

Pressure on Time Warner Grows

In late May, Tucker and Bennett launched a series of television ads in big cities attacking Time Warner and urging parents to boycott it. Then, on May 31, presidential candidate Senator Robert Dole (R-Kansas), seeking to appeal to his conservative constituency, gave an address at a fund-raising event in Los Angeles in which he attacked depravity and violence in the entertainment industry. Dole cited as examples rap groups distributed by Time Warner and singled out the company for "marketing evil through commerce."[33] Dole posed rhetorical questions for Time Warner executives. "Is this what you intended to accomplish with your careers? . . . You have sold your souls, but must you debase our nation and threaten our children as well?"[34]

Time Warner made little response to its critics, and the moves it made only played into their hands. In early June, Danny Goldberg, chairman of Warner Bros. Records, said that rap's critics were "a bunch of middle-aged people who don't like the music."[35] Tucker demanded that Goldberg be fired.

---

[29]Quoted in Richard S. Dunham and Michael Oneal, "Gunning for the Gangstas," *Business Week,* June 19, 1995, p. 41.

[30]Quoted in Patrick Rogers and Rochelle Jones, "Gunning for Gangstas," *People,* June 26, 1995, p. 105.

[31]Richard Zoglin, "A Company under Fire," *Time,* June 12, 1995, p. 39.

[32]Both are quoted in Zoglin, "A Company under Fire," p. 39.

[33]Quoted in John M. Broder, "Dole Indicts Hollywood for Debasing Culture," *Los Angeles Times,* June 1, 1995, p. A15.

[34]Quoted in Zoglin, "A Company under Fire," p. 37.

[35]Quoted in Dunham and Oneal, "Gunning for the Gangstas," p. 41.

Goldberg had been scheduled to appear on *Face the Nation* to debate Bennett, but Time Warner ordered him not to. On the broadcast, Bennett homed in on Time Warner for distributing music "not fit for human consumption." He read rap lyrics by the Geto Boys. "Her body is beautiful, so I'm thinking rape. Shouldn't have had her curtains open, so that's her fate." Bennett zeroed in on the reason for Goldberg's absence. "I think," he said, "the reason is that the world's largest communication company is virtually speechless on this issue. They cannot defend themselves in public."[36]

Later in the month, Tucker threatened to demonstrate at the homes of Time Warner executives and play gangsta rap. "We will," she threatened, "march in their neighborhoods and let their neighbors hear the music."[37]

Exit Interscope

Although Time Warner continued to support the speech rights and creative freedoms of its rappers, the criticism had created inner tension. Some directors and executives expressed concern about rap lyrics. Soon, the company's top music executive was fired. His replacement asked Interscope for a preview of lyrics on a forthcoming album by a gangsta rap group called Tha Dogg Pound. Interscope refused, saying that this would constrain the artistic freedom of its acts. So Time Warner sold its interest in the label for $100 million to the two entrepreneurs who had started it. All ties between the two companies were severed.

Tucker sent letters to Time Warner's rivals in the music business warning them not to buy Interscope. But in less than a year, a subsidiary of Seagram Co., MCA, Inc., bought a half-interest for $200 million, giving the two entrepreneurs a quick $100 million profit. However, Interscope soon moved out of gangsta rap. In 1996 it cut its ties to Death Row after the label's biggest star, Tupac Shakur, was murdered and its top executive, Marion "Suge" Knight, was jailed. Since then, Interscope has increased its revenues by recording other kinds of music; ironically, it now handles God's Property, one of the hottest gospel acts.

Tucker Keeps the Pressure On

After Time Warner severed ties with Interscope, it still recorded some rap on other labels. In May 1997 Delores Tucker, this time with her husband William, returned to Time Warner's annual meeting. When they got the microphone, she set upon Lil' Kim, a rap artist who used graphic lyrics to express sex fantasies. Lil' Kim's album, *Hardcore,* had been characterized by a review in *Billboard* as "aural porn grooves" that were "raw deluxe."[38]

---

[36]Quotes in this paragraph are from David G. Savage, "GOP Presses Attack on Film, Music Businesses," *Los Angeles Times,* June 5, 1995, pp. A1, A10.

[37]Quoted in Dunham and Oneal, "Gunning for the Gangstas," p. 41.

[38]"Hardcore," *Billboard,* December 14, 1996.

Tucker recited lyrics before the assembled stockholders and accused Levin of condoning "the destruction of our children, especially African-American children." Many shareholders responded to Tucker's remarks with sustained applause. Levin responded: "We have to balance artistic integrity and freedom with corporate consciousness," and lectured Tucker: "You do not have the right to demean me or my family. You cannot look into my heart." In response, Tucker's husband told Levin: "If you had a thread of decency, you would be outraged by it."[39]

In December, Tucker was in action again, this time demonstrating in front of Time Warner's headquarters in New York to denounce the song "Smack My Bitch Up" by a British rock group named Prodigy. The song had been released by the Maverick label, a joint venture between Madonna and Warner Bros. Records, and was manufactured, distributed, and publicized by Time Warner. It was on the group's *Fat of the Land* CD that had sold over two million copies and was one of the year's hottest sellers. The phrase "smack my bitch up" is the only lyric in the song and is repeated over and over. The group had taken it from the phrase "smack my bitch up like a pimp" in a rap album by another group.[40] The band's producer said that the phrase did not refer to hitting women; it was slang for having high energy. Feminists doubted this, especially since Prodigy had made a video with "images of women being manhandled."[41] Wal-Mart and Kmart had already refused to sell the CD.

Tucker was joined on the sidewalk by women's advocates, including Gloria Steinem and Eleanor Smeal. The group sang a song to the tune of "Santa Claus Is Coming to Town." A sample verse: "You have a right to publish, as Klan and Nazis do. But you would never publish what endangers men like you." She demanded a meeting with Gerald Levin. This was refused. So she issued a statement.

> The song "Smack My Bitch Up," promoted by Time Warner, reflects a long-standing policy of distributing misogynistic lyrics which denigrate and endanger women of all races. The refusal to meet with us is symbolic of the anti-woman corporate policy promoted by Time Warner.[42]

Warner Bros. and Maverick issued a statement saying that "the lyric in question was never intended to be harmful or disrespectful," adding that they were "saddened that those who exercise their right to express themselves freely would deny it to others."[43] On albums sold in Target stores, the two companies agreed to add parental advisory labels about the lyrics. And to get the albums back in Wal-Mart stores, they modified the artwork on CDs to cover the word "bitch."

---

[39]Quotes are in Keith J. Kelly, *Daily News (New York)*, May 16, 1997, p. 72.

[40]Chuck Philips, "Time Warner Again Faces the Music over Song Lyrics," *Los Angeles Times,* December 4, 1997, p. A34.

[41]Ibid.

[42]Press release, "Coalition of Women Leaders Protest Against Time-Warner Policies," National Political Congress of Black Women, Washington, D.C., December 18, 1997, p. 1.

[43]Quoted in Thomas S. Mulligan, "Women's Rights Activists Go A-Protesting," *Los Angeles Times,* December 19, 1997, p. D4.

Postscript

Since the "Smack My Bitch Up" outcry, Time Warner has not had a major confrontation with its critics. But its detractors keep up a steady drumbeat. Foremost is C. Delores Tucker, who continues her "Gansta Rap Crusade."

A National Commission on Civic Renewal, co-chaired by William Bennett, published a report on the health of American society that included this passage:

> . . . [T]here is no guarantee that the operation of market forces will prove wholly compatible with the requirements of civic health. For example, many Americans believe that the market-driven decisions of giant media corporations have diminished the quality of our public culture and have greatly complicated the task of raising children.[44]

After two young boys were arrested in Chicago and charged with murdering a young girl, an irate newspaper column accused Time Warner of producing song lyrics that were part of a toxic cultural atmosphere corrupting children's values. "America requires industries that pollute the air and water to regulate themselves," he wrote, "but any talk of regulation . . . of industries that pollute America's soul is greeted with squeaks of censorship."[45]

In 1998, eleven states had pending legislation either to stop investment of public pension funds in Time Warner or similar companies or to make it a crime to sell to a minor any record with a parental advisory logo.[46]

The corporate response to criticism has been limited, but significant. First, for many years the Recording Industry Association of America (RIAA) has promoted the use of parental advisory labels on records. These are black and white labels reading "PARENTAL ADVISORY: EXPLICIT CONTENT" to be placed on the front of an album. There is no industry ratings board, so each company voluntarily decides when a label is necessary. Some companies have set up lyrics review committees to make these decisions. In 1995 the labeling program was given greater emphasis by the RIAA. Second, Time Warner and other large corporations produce less rap now. Most "hardcore" rap now comes from smaller labels that operate independently and make difficult targets for Tucker and like critics. The largest is Priority Records in Los Angeles, which quietly puts out the kind of rap that Time Warner might not touch.[47]

---

[44]National Commission on Civic Renewal, *Final Report: A Nation of Spectators,* College Park, Md.: National Commission on Civic Renewal, 1998, p. 40.

[45]Dick Feagler, "Kids Infected by Our Toxic Pop Culture," *St. Louis Post-Dispatch,* August 16, 1998, p. B3.

[46]Press release, "RIAA Battles First Amendment Threats in State Legislatures," Washington, D.C.: Recording Industry of America, March 5, 1998.

[47]Neil Strauss, "The White Face Behind Big-Time Rap," *New York Times,* September 3, 1998, p. B2.

Questions

1. What ideas are being expressed by rap artists mentioned in the case who use violent, profane, or explicit lyrics? Do you believe that these ideas have artistic or social merit? Or do you believe that they erode decency?

2. The central criticism of business is that enduring social values are sacrificed for profits. Is Time Warner undermining cultural values when it sells rap music?

3. Do you agree with Ice-T's and Time Warner's decision to stop selling "Cop Killer" and with Time Warner's decision to sever its ties with Interscope? Why or why not?

4. Did Time Warner handle its critics well? Should it have stood more firmly behind the principle of artistic freedom? Should it have met the demands of critics sooner?

The Nature and Management of Social Responsibility

Corporate Social Responsibility

There are many stories of social responsibility in business. The one that follows is singular and remarkable.

For centuries river blindness, or onchocerciasis (on-ko-sir-KIE-a-sis), has tortured humanity in equatorial regions. The disease is caused by a parasitic worm that lives only in humans. When bitten by female blackflies, which swarm near fast-moving rivers and streams, people are infected by the worm's tiny, immature larvae. The larvae settle in human tissue and form colonies, where adults grow up to 2 feet long. These colonies are often visible outside the body as lumps the size of tennis balls. Mature adults live for 7 to 18 years intertwined in these internal nodes, where they mate and continuously release tens of thousands of microscopic new worms, called microfilariae. These offspring migrate from the internal nodes back to the skin, where they cause disfiguring welts, lumps, and discoloration. The itching they cause is so terrible that suicide is not uncommon. Eventually they migrate to the eyes, causing blindness. The cycle of infection is renewed when blackflies bite victims, ingesting tiny microfilariae from their blood, and later bite uninfected individuals passing parasitic larvae to them.

More than 18 million people have the disease, most of them in river regions of African nations. The disease saps economic activity by blinding and enervating many in the labor force and by driving people away from some of the most fertile areas.

Extensive regions in these countries are abandoned, regions that if farmed could feed millions.

Until recently, there was no effective treatment for river blindness. Two drugs existed, one to kill adult worms and one to kill their larvae, but both had frequent, dangerous side effects—including death. The World Health Organization had undertaken ambitious pesticide spraying programs to kill blackflies, but it was tough going. Winds carried flies up to 100 miles from their breeding grounds.

Then in 1975 researchers at Merck & Co., a pharmaceutical firm headquartered in New Jersey, discovered a compound that killed animal parasites. By 1981 this compound had been synthesized and introduced as a successful animal drug. But Merck scientists had a strong hunch that it also would be effective in humans against *Onchocerca volvulus*, the river blindness parasite.

Merck faced a hard decision. It cost an average of $230 million to bring a new drug to market and more to manufacture it later.[1] Yet the people who had the disease were among the world's poorest. Their villages had no doctors. Should Merck develop a drug that might never be profitable? The company chose to go ahead, in large measure because its research scientists were motivated by humanitarian and scientific goals and it was difficult to restrain them in a corporate culture that strongly rewarded innovation. Donations from governments and international foundations

could pay for much of the cost later, management reasoned.

Clinical trials of the drug, called ivermectin, were held in Senegal and other countries beginning in 1981 and confirmed its effectiveness. A single low dose dramatically reduced the population of the tiny worms migrating through the body and impaired reproduction by adult worms.[2] Ivermectin did not cure river blindness, for it did not kill the adult worms, but it miraculously stopped itching, prevented blindness, and did so with no major side effects.[3]

Merck concluded that neither those in need nor their governments could afford to buy ivermectin. So in 1987 Merck announced that it would manufacture and ship it at no cost to areas where it was needed for as long as it was needed to control river blindness. Governments and private organizations were asked to set up distribution programs.

Over the next decade, Merck gave away millions of doses in a treatment program put together by humanitarian groups and foundations with the help of the United Nations and the World Bank. As a result, about 40 million persons have been protected from debilitating disease and 600,000 have been spared blindness. The disease has been almost eradicated in eleven African countries, and 25 million

---

[1]David Bollier, *Merck & Company*, Stanford, Calif.: Business Enterprise Trust, 1991, p. 5.

[2]Mohammed A. Aziz et al., "Efficacy and Tolerance of Ivermectin in Human Onchocerciasis," *The Lancet*, July 24, 1982.

[3]See, for example, Michel Pacque et al., "Community-Based Treatment of Onchocerciasis with Ivermectin: Safety, Efficacy, and Acceptability of Yearly Treatment," *Journal of Infectious Diseases*, February 1991.

In countries ravaged by river blindness, young children sometimes lead the blind by having them hold on to a stick. Merck commissioned this bronze sculpture, which stands at its headquarters in New Jersey, to symbolize the concern for humanity in its program to develop and give away a river blindness drug.

Source: Reprinted with permission from Merck & Co., Inc.

hectares of farmland, enough to grow food for 17 million people a year, has returned to production.[4]

For a drug company to go through the new drug development process and then give the drug away was unprecedented. However, Merck's management believes that although developing and donating ivermectin has cost hundreds of millions of dollars, humanitarianism and enlightened self-interest vindicate the decision.

Few corporations have such a singular opportunity to drive evil from human life, but most today initiate activities that go beyond normal business to improve society in some way. The idea underlying these activities is *corporate social responsibility*, which may be defined as the duty a corporation has to create wealth by using means that avoid harm to, protect, or enhance societal assets.[5]

The Evolving Idea of Social Responsibility

Every business must use its power in keeping with a social contract. This is an abstract rule, but valid in practice. When rioting spread over Los Angeles after the verdict in the 1992 Rodney King trial, many businesses were looted and burned. Before the disorder, a condition of McDonald's franchise agreements was that owners employ people in nearby neighborhoods and get involved in community activities. They did and during the riots, not a single McDonald's restaurant was damaged. Sometimes local gang members protected them.

---

[4]World Health Organization, "The Control of River Blindness: The Leopard Must Change Its Spots," press release, April 17, 1998.

[5]The phrase *corporate social responsibility* is a modern one. It did not enter common usage until it appeared in academic literature in the 1960s. The phrase "social responsibility" was not generally used until well into the twentieth century.

Inner-city Shell Oil stations were a different story. Fifty-eigh'
aged, eight destroyed by fire. Many stations were owned by Ko..
cans who did not employ blacks and Latinos or get involved in nearby communities. This story illustrates that every business must use its power in
keeping with a social contract. Shell Oil Products Inc. learned this lesson and
developed a conscience in inner-city Los Angeles. The centerpiece of its new
social program is a multimillion-dollar Shell Youth Training Academy that
prepares south-central Los Angeles high school students for jobs and college.

It has taken American business a long time to accept an expansive definition of corporate social responsibility. The idea has grown over time with a
changing social contract. Here, we briefly review this evolution.

Social Responsibility in Classical Economic Theory

Throughout American history, classical economic theory, which is the basis
for the market capitalism model in Chapter 1, has been the basic inspiration of
people in business. In the classical view, a business is socially responsible if it
maximizes profits while operating within the law, because an "invisible hand"
will direct economic activity to serve the good of the whole.

The ideology of market capitalism, derived from Adam Smith's *Wealth of Nations,* is compelling in its simplicity and its resonance with self-interest.[6] In nineteenth century America, it was elevated to the status of an immutable law. But
the idea that selfishness in markets creates social prosperity has always existed in
tension with morality-based ideas about business's responsibility. Smith himself
voiced a surprising number of reservations about the ability of markets to protect
social welfare.[7] And throughout American history, business and businesspeople
have modified the strict profit-maximization rule to address social concerns—not
much at first, but more and more over time. Today the classical ideology remains
entrenched as a guiding principle, though, as we shall see, ethical theories of
broader responsibility have worn away some of its prominences.

The Charitable Impulse of the Eighteenth and Nineteenth Centuries

The idea that corporations had social responsibilities awaited the rise of corporations themselves. Meanwhile, the most prominent expression of responsibility was charity by owners.

In the colonial era businesses were very small. Merchants practiced thrift
and frugality, which were dominant virtues then, to an extreme. The penny-
pinching nature of the time is reflected in Benjamin Franklin's advice to a business acquaintance: "He that kills a breeding sow, destroys all her offspring to
the thousandth generation. He that murders a crown, destroys all that it might

---

[6]Adam Smith, *An Inquiry into the Nature and Causes of the Wealth of Nations,* New York: Modern
Library, 1967. Originally published in 1776.

[7]Jacob Viner, "Adam Smith and Laissez-Faire," *Journal of Political Economy,* April 1927.

have produced, even scores of pounds."[8] But charity was a coexisting virtue, and respectability came to owners of these tiny enterprises who contributed to churches, orphanages, and poorhouses. In doing this they exemplified the historical lesson that although American business is often depicted as a jungle of profit maximization, people in business have always been concerned citizens.[9]

In the early nineteenth century, companies were not effusive in their social concerns. Charitable contributions by owners continued and grew over time as fortunes were made. Mostly, entrepreneurs endowed social causes without reference to the companies that were the fountainheads of their wealth. One of the earliest was Steven Girard, a shipping and banking tycoon. When he died in 1831, the richest person in the nation, he made generous charitable bequests in his will, the largest of which was $6 million for a school to educate orphaned boys from the earliest grades through high school.[10] This changed the climate of education because it came at a time when no state yet provided free elementary schooling and when a high-school education was still the province of children of the wealthy. Following Girard, others donated money to social endeavors, and they began to do so before rigor mortis set in. The first great living philanthropist was George Peabody, a merchant and financier, who gave $9 million in the 1850s to promote education and provide housing for the poor.[11]

Other, better-remembered business donors followed Peabody's example. For instance, John D. Rockefeller, who accumulated a fortune in the second half of the nineteenth century, gave in his lifetime more than $550 million. Andrew Carnegie gave $350 million during his lifetime to social causes, built 2,811 public libraries, and donated 7,689 organs to American churches. Carnegie wrote a famous article entitled "The Disgrace of Dying Rich" and said that it was the duty of a man of wealth ". . . to consider all surplus revenues . . . as trust funds which he is called upon to administer."[12]

However, Carnegie's philosophy of giving was highly paternalistic. He believed that big fortunes should be used for grand purposes such as endowing universities and building concert halls like Carnegie Hall. They should not be wasted by paying higher wages to workers or giving gifts to poor people; the riches would be dissipated on small indulgences and would not, in the end, elevate the intellectual and moral heritage of society. Thus, one day when a friend of Carnegie's came upon a beggar and gave him a quarter, Carnegie thought it was one of "the very worst actions of his life."[13]

---

[8]Benjamin Franklin, "Advice to a Young Tradesman [1748]," in *The Autobiography of Benjamin Franklin and Selections from His Other Writings*, ed. Nathan G. Goodman, New York: Carlton House, 1932, p. 219. A crown was a British coin on which appeared the figure of a royal crown.

[9]For an excellent overview of the charitable impulse in business, see Mark Sharfman, "The Evolution of Corporate Philanthropy, 1883–1952," *Business & Society*, December 1994.

[10]The school became known as Girard College, which the senior author of this book attended; it still exists in Philadelphia.

[11]Franklin Parker, *George Peabody: A Biography*, Nashville, Tenn.: Vanderbilt University Press, 1994.

[12]Andrew Carnegie, *The Gospel of Wealth*, Cambridge, Mass.: Harvard University Press, 1962, p. 25. Originally published in 1901.

[13]Quoted in Page Smith, *The Rise of Industrial America*, vol. 6, New York: Penguin Books, 1984, p. 136.

In this view, Carnegie was championing the doctrine of social Darwinism, which held that charity interfered with the natural evolutionary process in which society shed its less fit to make way for progress by the better adapted. Well-meaning people who gave to charity interfered with this natural law by propping up failed examples of the human race. The leading advocate of this astringent doctrine, Herbert Spencer, wrote in a tremendously popular book in 1850:

> It seems hard that a laborer incapacitated by sickness from competing with his stronger fellows should have to bear the resulting privations. It seems hard that widows and orphans should be left to struggle for life or death. Nevertheless, when regarded not separately, but in connection with the interests of universal humanity, these harsh fatalities are seen to be full of the highest beneficence—the same beneficence which brings to early graves the children of diseased parents and singles out the low-spirited, the intemperate, and the debilitated as the victims of an epidemic.[14]

Spencer did approve of some charity, though only because it raised the character and superiority of the giver. Nevertheless, the overall effect of Spencer's arguments was to moderate charity by business leaders and retard growth of social responsibility.

More than just belief in classical economics and social Darwinism constrained business from undertaking voluntary social action. State laws and charters required that managers give priority to shareholders. Courts consistently held company charity to be *ultra vires,* that is, "beyond the law." To use shareholder funds for charity or social works invited a shareholder lawsuit. Thus, when Rockefeller had the humanitarian impulse to build the first medical school in China, he paid for it out of his own pocket; to avoid lawsuits, not a penny came directly from Standard Oil. A few exceptions to this doctrine were granted by courts to permit the building of schools and churches in company towns. But social programs that corporations undertake today, for example, Merck's program to halt river blindness, would have clashed with the ultra vires doctrine had they been tried in the 1800s.

As the twentieth century approached, classical ideology was still a mountain of resistance to expanding the idea of business social responsibility. Overall, the spirit of the time is captured by a poet of that era, James Russell Lowell.

> Not a deed would he do
>   Not a word would he utter
> Till he weighed its relation
>   To plain bread and butter.

Social Responsibility in the Late Nineteenth and Early Twentieth Centuries

During the late nineteenth century and early twentieth, forces converged that pushed business leaders, especially of the largest corporations, to create

---

[14]Herbert Spencer, *Social Statics,* New York: Robert Schalkenbach Foundation, 1970, p. 289. First published in 1850.

new responsibility doctrines. Industrialization brought with it massive social problems—child labor, political corruption, labor unrest, city slums, inequality, and stock frauds. Critics questioned the ultimate benevolence of a doctrine as cruel and aloof as social Darwinism. Business feared calls for more government regulation and sought to blunt their urgency. Business leaders, many of whom by this time were not the original entrepreneurs, but owned only a small part of the stock of the companies they managed, felt freer to use corporate assets for social action. Business sought and found arguments to circumvent the ultra vires doctrine.

By the 1920s, three interrelated themes had emerged to justify broader business social responsibility. First, managers were *trustees,* that is, agents whose corporate roles put them in positions of power over the fate of not just stockholders, but of others such as customers, employees, and communities. This power implied a duty to promote the welfare of each entity. Second, managers believed they had an obligation to *balance* the interests of these groups. They were, in effect, coordinators who reconciled the competing claims of multiple interests. And third, many managers subscribed to the *service principle,* a principle with two distinct definitions. One definition was a near-spiritual belief that business, simply by pursuing profit, had the power to redeem society by creating general welfare. Individual managers served society by making each business successful; if they did this, the aggregate effect would be eradication of social injustice, poverty, and other ills. A second understanding of the service principle, however, was that although capitalism elevated humanity, companies and managers were still obligated to undertake social programs to benefit, or serve, the public.[15]

These three interrelated ideas—trusteeship, balance, and service—were accepted by more and more business and opinion leaders. Although uplifting, they did not foster lavish spending on social programs, nor did they divert most managers from their laissez-faire attitudes and dominant emphasis on profits. Railroad car manufacturer George M. Pullman hired an architect to use the latest principles of science and public health in building a model community for his employees, Pullman, Illinois. Pullman was hailed for creating blissful living conditions for workers, but his actions soon revealed that he saw the town mainly as an investment.

In the depression of 1893, he laid off half his workers and cut the wages of the rest by 25 percent. Despite this, he refused to reduce rent on company-owned houses. Payments had been pegged to give the company a 6 percent return on investment. When union leaders demanded rent reduction, he fired them. This led to the Pullman strike of 1894, a long, bloody deadlock that paralyzed the nation's economy. Although the workers no longer lived in unsanitary, crime-plagued tenements, they were now being shot at by thugs hired to discourage strikers and, as the strike dragged on, they became malnourished from hunger. Pullman, previously known as a great humanitarian, became, in

---

[15]Rolf Lunden, *Business and Religion in the American 1920s,* New York: Greenwood Press, 1988, pp. 147–50.

the eyes of the *Chicago Tribune*, "a cold-hearted, cold-blooded autocrat" whose "small piggish eyes" contained "the glitter of avarice."[16]

Like Pullman, there were many others for whom profits came first, service to society a distant second. One was Henry Ford, who had the ability to cover cruelty toward workers with a shining veneer of citizenship. In the winter of 1914, Ford thrilled the public by announcing the "Five-Dollar Day" for Ford Motor Co. workers. Five dollars was about double the daily pay for manufacturing workers at that time and seemed very generous. In fact, although Ford took credit for being bighearted, the $5 wage was intended to cool union organizing and was not what it appeared to be on the surface. Nevertheless, it attracted hordes of job-seekers to Highland Park, Michigan, from all around the country. One sub-zero morning in January, there were 2,000 lined up outside the Ford plant by 5:00 AM; by dawn there were 10,000. Disorder broke out, and the fire department turned hoses on the freezing men.

The few who were hired had to serve a six-month apprenticeship and comply with the puritanical Ford Motor Co. code of conduct (no drinking, marital discord, or otherwise immoral living) to qualify for the $5 day. Many were fired on pretexts before the six months passed. Thousands of replacements waited outside each day hoping to fill a new vacancy. Inside, Ford speeded up the assembly line. Insecure employees worked faster under the threat of being purged for a younger, stronger, lower-paid new-hire. The workers who did hang on to qualify for the $5 wage had to face merchants, landlords, and realtors in the surrounding area who raised rents and prices.

In 1926 Ford announced the first five-day, 40-hour week for his workers, but with public accolades still echoing for this "humanitarian" gesture, he speeded up the line still more, cut wages, and announced a program to weed out less-efficient employees. These actions were necessary, he said, to compensate for Saturdays off. Later that year, Ford told the adulatory public that he had started a social program to fight juvenile delinquency. He proposed to employ 5,000 boys 16 to 20 years old and pay them "independence wages."[17] This was trumpeted as citizenship, but as the "boys" were hired, older workers were pitted against younger, lower-paid replacements.

A few business leaders, however, implemented practices consistent with the new themes of business responsibility. One was General Robert E. Wood, who led Sears, Roebuck and Company from 1924 to 1954. He believed that a large corporation was more than an economic institution; it was a social and political one as well. In the Sears *Annual Report* for 1936, he wrote:

> In these days of changing social, economic, and political values, it seems worthwhile . . . to render an account of your management's stewardship, not merely from the viewpoint of financial reports but also along the lines of those general broad social responsibilities which cannot be presented mathematically and yet are of prime importance.

---

[16]Smith, *The Rise of Industrial America*, vol. 6, p. 524.

[17]Keith Sward, *The Legend of Henry Ford*, New York: Rinehart & Company, 1948, p. 176.

He outlined the ways in which Sears was discharging its responsibilities to what he said were the chief constituencies of the company—customers, the public, employees, sources of merchandise supply, and stockholders.[18] In speaking about constituents, General Wood repeatedly put the stockholder last "not because he is least important," he said, "but because, in the larger sense, he cannot obtain his full measure of reward unless he has satisfied customers and satisfied employees."[19]

General Wood was an exemplar of the theory of business responsibility in his day, but in his actions he was far ahead of most managers. Nevertheless, in the 1920s and thereafter, corporations found various ways to support communities. Organized charities were formed, such as the Community Chest, the Red Cross, and the Boy Scouts, to which they contributed. In many cities, companies gave money and expertise to improve schools and public health. In the 1940s, corporations began to give cash and stock to tax-exempt foundations they set up to carry out philanthropic work. Then, in 1953, the moribund ultra vires doctrine breathed its last gasp when the Supreme Court of New Jersey found it unreasonably restrictive and refused to uphold it.[20]

The Late Twentieth Century

Over the last fifty years, the idea of business social responsibility has continued to evolve and broaden. The view that total responsibilities are broader than simple economic responsibilities has become more compelling, more accepted by managers, and more widely practiced.

The underlying cause of expanded social responsibility is the historical force of economic growth. Social responsibilities arise from the impacts of corporations on society, and as corporations grow larger, their impacts are greater. Impacts have also become more visible in this century. Two examples are pollution and discrimination. Before the 1960s, both scientists and the public had limited understanding of carcinogens in industrial waste. Statistics that would have shown racism in hiring were not yet kept.

An early and influential statement of the modern idea of social responsibility was made in 1954 by Howard R. Bowen in his book, *Social Responsibilities of the Businessman.* Bowen defined social responsibility as "obligations . . . to pursue those policies, to make those decisions, or to follow those lines of action which are desirable in terms of the objectives and values of our society."[21] In the book, he made a strong case that managers were increasingly aware of public expectations to act in ways that went beyond profit-seeking and were, in fact, acting to meet these expectations.

---

[18]James C. Worthy, *Shaping an American Institution: Robert E. Wood and Sears, Roebuck,* Urbana: University of Illinois Press, 1984, p. 173.

[19]Ibid., p. 63.

[20]*A. P. Smith Manufacturing Co. v. Barlow,* 98 A.2d 581 (N.J. 1953).

[21]New York: Harper, 1953, p. 6.

Bowen made the basic arguments that underlie the current doctrine of corporate social responsibility: (1) managers have an ethical duty to consider the broad social impacts of business decisions, (2) businesses are reservoirs of skill and energy for improving civic life, (3) corporations must use power in keeping with a broad social contract, or lose their legitimacy, (4) it is in the enlightened self-interest of business to improve society, and (5) voluntary action may head off negative public attitudes and undesirable regulations. This book, despite being nearly fifty years old, remains an excellent encapsulation of the modern justification for corporate social responsibility. If it were unburdened of its sexist title, given fresh examples, and rereleased, it would shine forth as better argued than some more recent tracts.

The Case against Expansive Social Responsibility

Not everyone accepted the arguments made by Bowen, and in the 1960s there was considerable debate about their validity. Arguments against expanding social responsibility were made by some economists and executives who held that business is *most* responsible when it operates efficiently to make profits, not when it misapplies its energy on social projects.

The argument against assuming greater responsibilities is that business is an economic institution. Its core functions are to produce goods and services efficiently and to enrich stockholders. Economic values should be the sole determinant of performance. This argument hews closely to classical economic theory. A pertinacious exponent of this view, then and now, is Nobel laureate Milton Friedman, a respected economist who makes the following argument:

> There is one and only one social responsibility of business—to use its resources and engage in activities designed to increase its profits so long as it stays within the rules of the game, which is to say, engages in open and free competition, without deception or fraud . . . Few trends could so thoroughly undermine the very foundations of our free society as the acceptance by corporate officials of social responsibility other than to make as much money for their stockholders as possible. This is a fundamentally subversive doctrine.[22]

Friedman argues that in a free-enterprise, private-property system, a manager is an employee of the owners of the business and is directly responsible to them. Because stockholders want to make as much profit as possible, the manager's sole objective should be to try to do this. If a manager spends stockholder money in the public interest, he or she is spending it without stockholders' approval and perhaps in ways they would oppose. Similarly, if the cost of social action is passed on to consumers in higher prices, the manager is spending their money. This "taxation without representation," says Friedman,

---

[22]*Capitalism and Freedom,* Chicago: University of Chicago Press, 1962, p. 133.

should be rejected.[23] Furthermore, if the price on the market for a product does not truly reflect the relative costs of producing it, but includes costs for social action, the allocative mechanism of the marketplace is distorted. The rigors of the market will endanger the competitive position of any firm that adds to its costs by assuming social responsibilities.

Friedman and others also warned that social responsibility poses a great danger to political freedom. A company running social programs is performing a political function and also an economic one. The fusion of both political and economic power in the hands of corporate executives is dangerous. The two kinds of power ought to be kept separate. The market mechanism, which fragments economic power, is a counterbalance to political power. If both realms are fused under the control of unelected managers who have never kissed the cheek of a voter's baby, a powerful barrier to tyranny is removed. Others who take Friedman's position have included Peter Drucker:

> Milton Friedman's position that business should stick to its business . . . is indeed the only consistent position in a free society. Any other position can only mean that business will take over power, authority, and decision making in areas outside of the economic sphere, in areas which are or should be reserved to government or to the individual or to other institutions.[24]

The opposition of Friedman and adherents of classical economic doctrine to corporate social responsibility has been a principled, rearguard action. The futility of it was evident when business leaders began to articulate a vision of expanded duty. In 1971 the Committee for Economic Development (CED), an old organization of prominent business leaders throughout the nation, issued a milestone statement that boldly stated that "business functions by public consent, and its basic purpose is to serve constructively the needs of society— to the satisfaction of society." Society today, said the report, has broadened its expectations of business into what may be described as "three concentric circles of responsibilities:"[25]

- The *inner circle* includes the clear-cut basic responsibilities for the efficient execution of the economic function—products, jobs, and economic growth.
- The *intermediate circle* encompasses responsibility to exercise this economic function with a sensitive awareness of changing social values and priorities: for example, with respect to environmental conservation; hiring and relations with employees; and more rigorous expectations of customers for information, fair treatment, and protection from injury.

---

[23]"The Social Responsibility of Business Is to Increase Its Profits," *New York Times Magazine,* September 13, 1970.

[24]Peter Drucker, *Management: Tasks, Responsibilities, Practices,* New York: Harper & Row, 1973, p. 348.

[25]Committee for Economic Development, *Social Responsibilities of Business Corporations,* New York: CED, 1971, p. 11.

- The *outer circle* outlines newly emerging and still amorphous responsibilities that business should assume to become more broadly involved in actively improving the social environment.[26]

Classical ideology focused solely on the first circle. The new view is that managerial responsibilities go much beyond this point. But this does not mean diminished profits. On the contrary, say top executives in larger corporations, it is in the self-interest of corporations to assume social responsibilities.

In its 1981 *Statement on Corporate Responsibility,* the Business Roundtable, a group of 200 leaders of the largest corporations, said that the pursuit of profit and assumption of social responsibilities were compatible:

> Economic responsibility is by no means incompatible with other corporate responsibilities in society. In contemporary society all corporate responsibilities are so interrelated that they should not and cannot be separated. . . .
>
> A corporation's responsibilities include how the whole business is conducted every day. It must be a thoughtful institution which arises above the bottom line to consider the impact of its actions on all, from shareholders to the society at large. Its business activities must make social sense just as its social activities must make business sense.[27]

These statements by business groups encouraged corporate responsibility. Since their publication, the range of social programs assumed by business has continuously expanded until today corporations carry out a wide spectrum of activities including programs for education, the arts, public health, employees, housing, urban renewal, crime prevention, literacy, and the environment. In each of these areas, corporations have implemented literally thousands of programs, and efforts continue to multiply.

The Basic Elements of Social Responsibility

Figure 5-1 illustrates the relative magnitudes of three basic elements of social responsibility. The proportions are our estimates for three historical eras and change as the elements of social responsibility have evolved over time.

The first element is actions taken in response to market forces. The magnitude of these actions in all three eras shows that market forces have always dominated corporate activity and continue to do so. When a corporation responds to the marketplace, it is being socially responsible. Some critics believe that certain businesses, for instance, gambling, defense, tobacco, animal agriculture, and alcohol, are irresponsible no matter how well conducted. Such value judgments do not invalidate the general rule that the largest impact on society, hence, the greatest test of responsibility, comes from normal market operations.

---

[26]Ibid., p. 15.
[27]New York: The Business Roundtable, October 1981, pp. 12, 14.

FIGURE 5-1

Principal elements of social responsibility and their evolving magnitudes.

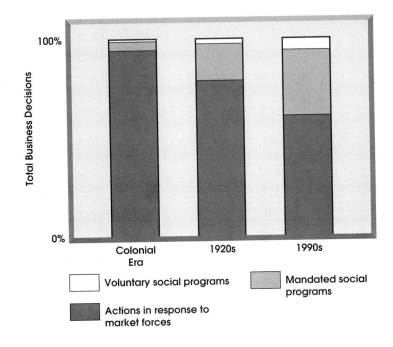

This is illustrated by General Motors. In 1997, GM employed 608,000 people in 56 countries and had a worldwide payroll of $30.4 billion. It made 8.6 million vehicles that were sold through 14,900 dealers. The dealers, in turn, employed another 542,000 people. GM paid $1.1 billion in taxes of all kinds to governments. General Motors customers paid another $6.8 billion in taxes worldwide when purchasing GM products. In the United States, GM withheld an additional $4.9 billion from employee's paychecks, which it remitted to the federal government for income and social security taxes. It also paid $3.7 billion in benefits to its U.S. workers.[28] These statistics illuminate the huge aggregate impact of GM's routine, everyday business operations, operations that broadly support the general welfare and are, in a sense, GM's biggest social program.

The second element includes mandated social programs. These are programs that either are required by government regulation, such as equal opportunity hiring, or are required by agreements negotiated with stakeholders, such as benefits programs in union contracts. The size of this category has grown over the years, primarily due to accumulating regulation.

---

[28]Figures in this paragraph are taken from General Motors Corporation, Form 10-K 1997, filed March 20, 1998. Figures for dealer employees, U.S. withholding, and customer taxes paid are prorated from figures in General Motors Corporation, *1994 Public Interest Report,* Detroit: General Motors Corporation, 1994, p. 3.

GM is exposed to multiple regulations in many nations, dictating a range of decisions. For example, in the United States, GM vehicles must comply with tailpipe emission standards; its fleet must achieve a federally mandated average fuel economy of 27.5 miles per gallon (it was over by 0.7 mpg in 1997). It must meet state and local noise standards for light vehicles of 80 decibels at 50 feet and another standard for large trucks. Its plants must comply with rules limiting air and water discharges. Its workforce must meet equal opportunity standards. So regulatory guidelines codify for GM many societal expectations for responsible operations. General Motors has also responded to stakeholder pressures. In 1994 it became a signatory of the CERES principles,[29] a set of 10 environmental guidelines supported by a coalition of environmental and religious groups. Compliance with these principles requires actions and reporting standards that exceed government mandates.

The third element is voluntary social programs. Within the voluntary area are three zones of action. In the first zone are voluntary programs or efforts that accompany and exceed regulations or mandates, which might be called "legal plus." They go in the same direction as, but beyond, existing requirements in areas such as minority advancement, worker safety, and pollution control. In the second zone are voluntary programs that respond to a national consensus, such as contributing to charities and improving adult literacy. In the third zone are actions taken in areas where there is no public consensus. There are few programs in this area, but an example is advertising designed by Benetton Group to promote discussion about controversial issues. Benetton's 1995 ads of people with "H.I.V. Positive" tatoos were so incendiary in Germany that sales slumped badly for a time.[30]

General Motors, of course, undertakes many voluntary social programs. Some of these fall into the legal plus category, such as its WE CARE (or Waste Elimination and Cost Awareness Reward Everyone) program to reduce pollution and waste beyond legal requirements. Others commit GM to help society in nonregulated areas related to its primary business. The GM Mobility Program gives $1,000 to disabled persons installing adaptive driving equipment on GM vehicles. In 1996, GM gave $67 million to educational, cultural, and arts programs, many of which were unrelated to making cars and trucks. GM has not undertaken some activities for which there is no consensus in society. For example, it has opposed demands by religious groups that it adopt controversial guidelines for hiring Protestants in a Northern Ireland plant.

---

[29]CERES stands for the Coalition for Environmentally Responsible Economics.

[30]Nathaniel C. Nash, "Benetton Touches a Nerve and Germans Protest," *New York Times*, February 3, 1995, p. C1.

General Principles of Corporate Social Responsibility

No universal standard for social responsibility exists; managers must think carefully about what their companies need to do. The following are six general principles to guide them.

First, all firms must comply with two bodies of law: one is the body of corporation law that creates a fiduciary duty toward shareholders; the other is the body of regulation that protects all other stakeholders.[31] Beyond this, there is no one formula for all business or a single business; often, situations are unique. In Colombia, the government gave Occidental Petroleum the legal right to explore in a remote area, but U'wa Indians claimed that drilling would defile sacred ground. Five thousand U'was threatened to commit collective suicide if Occidental went ahead. Occidental executives were unsettled by tribal history, which records a mass suicide to protest Spanish colonization in the seventeenth century.[32] Each firm must decide for itself what it will and will not do. So far, Occidental has not moved into U'wa territory.

Second, corporations are economic institutions with strong profit motives; they should be judged primarily by economic criteria. They should not be expected to meet noneconomic objectives in a major way without financial incentives. As the Business Roundtable says in its *Statement on Corporate Responsibility:* "If the bottom line is a minus, there is no plus for society."[33] Companies may responsibly incur substantial short-run costs to correct social problems that threaten long-term profitability. And they may be encouraged to make profits by solving social problems.

Third, corporations have a duty to correct the adverse social impacts they cause. Without this duty the exercise of corporate power is illegitimate. For example, a corporation should try to internalize *external costs,* or costs of production borne by society. A factory dumping toxic effluent into a stream creates costs—perhaps human and animal disease, perhaps the destruction of natural beauty—borne by innocents, not by the company or its customers. Corporations should not "maximize" profits by imposing external costs, but should seek to reduce these costs.

Fourth, social responsibility varies with company characteristics such as size, industry, strategies, marketing techniques, locations, internal cultures, stakeholder demands, and managerial values. Thus, a global chemical manufacturer has a much different impact on society than a small, local insurance company, and its social responsibilities are both different and greater. Responsibilities also vary with national problems. A survey of

---

[31]On this point, see Robert B. Reich, "The New Meaning of Corporate Social Responsibility," *California Management Review,* Winter 1998, pp. 15–16.

[32]Russell Mokhiber and Robert Weissman, "Beat the Devil: The Ten Worst Corporations of 1997," *Multinational Monitor,* December 1997, p. 9.

[33]Business Roundtable, *Statement on Corporate Responsibility,* p. 5.

12,000 managers in twenty-five countries revealed great national variations concerning the priority managers give to different social issues.[34]

Fifth, managers should try to meet the legitimate needs of stakeholders. Managers generally agree that their primary responsibilities are to five groups, which may be called dominant stakeholders: customers, stockholders, employees, governments, and communities.[35] Managers often express their responsibilities to these groups in statements of corporate philosophy or, as they are also called, mission statements or credos. A well-known example is the credo of Johnson & Johnson shown on the following page. This credo is chiseled in stone at corporate headquarters.

However, as noted in Chapter 1, there are many other stakeholders, some of whom may from time to time become dominant. For example, when a firm is heavily in debt, the financial community and creditors may take the forefront. For a large corporation there are many stakeholders whose multiple demands conflict and cannot be completely met. So each company must set priorities to determine where, within its limited resources, it will meet legitimate demands. Research suggests that the effort made by companies to respond to these primary stakeholders varies significantly among firms and between industries.[36]

Sixth, managers can be guided by the general direction of a nation's public policy. Lee Preston and James Post believe that managers should follow a "principle of public responsibility"; that is, they should figure out responsibility by studying the overall "framework" of public policy, which includes "not only the literal text of the law and regulation, but also the broad pattern of social direction reflected in public opinion, emerging issues, formal legal requirements, and enforcement or implementation practices."[42]

Specific Criteria for Rating Social Responsibility

At the level of specific actions, social responsibility is highly situational, so developing objective criteria for grading and ranking firms is hard. However, there have been many attempts to judge corporate performance. The most

---

[34]Rosabeth Moss Kanter, "Transcending Business Boundaries: 12,000 World Managers View Change," *Harvard Business Review*, May–June 1991, p. 156.

[35]This is the order of priority revealed in surveys of 220 CEOs of large U.S. companies. See Linda D. Lerner and Gerald E. Fryxell, "CEO Stakeholder Attitudes and Corporate Social Activity in the Fortune 500," *Business & Society*, April 1994, table 2. See also Tammie S. Pinkston and Archie B. Carroll, "Corporate Citizenship Perspectives and Foreign Direct Investment in the U.S.," *Journal of Business Ethics*, March 1994, showing that managers of chemical firms headquartered in seven countries rank stakeholders similarly.

[36]Catherine Lerme Bendheim, Sandra A. Waddock, and Samuel Graves, "Determining Best Practice in Corporate Stakeholder Relations Using Data Envelopment Analysis: An Industry-Level Study," *Business & Society*, September 1998. (This research includes the environment as a stakeholder and not government.)

[42]Lee E. Preston and James E. Post, *Private Management and Public Policy: The Principle of Public Responsibility*, Englewood Cliffs, N.J.: Prentice Hall, 1975, p. 57.

Our Credo

We believe our first responsibility is to the doctors, nurses and patients,
to mothers and fathers and all others who use our products and services.
In meeting their needs everything we do must be of high quality.
We must constantly strive to reduce our costs
in order to maintain reasonable prices.
Customers' orders must be serviced promptly and accurately.
Our suppliers and distributors must have an opportunity
to make a fair profit.

We are responsible to our employees,
the men and women who work with us throughout the world.
Everyone must be considered as an individual.
We must respect their dignity and recognize their merit.
They must have a sense of security in their jobs.
Compensation must be fair and adequate,
and working conditions clean, orderly and safe.
We must be mindful of ways to help our employees fulfill
their family responsibilities.
Employees must feel free to make suggestions and complaints.
There must be equal opportunity for employment, development
and advancement for those qualified.
We must provide competent management,
and their actions must be just and ethical.

We are responsible to the communities in which we live and work
and to the world community as well.
We must be good citizens — support good works and charities
and bear our fair share of taxes.
We must encourage civic improvements and better health and education.
We must maintain in good order
the property we are privileged to use,
protecting the environment and natural resources.

Our final responsibility is to our stockholders.
Business must make a sound profit.
We must experiment with new ideas.
Research must be carried on, innovative programs developed
and mistakes paid for.
New equipment must be purchased, new facilities provided
and new products launched.
Reserves must be created to provide for adverse times.
When we operate according to these principles,
the stockholders should realize a fair return.

Johnson & Johnson

Aaron M. Feuerstein and Albert Dunlap

Employees and stockholders are both vital to a firm. When their interests conflict, which group should have priority? Two executives profiled here exemplify very different answers to this question.

Aaron M. Feuerstein.   Late in 1995, a fire in Lawrence, Massachusetts, burned three buildings at Malden Mills Industries. Feuerstein, the owner and CEO of Malden Mills, immediately announced that he would rebuild and that all 3,200 employees would have a job waiting. Meanwhile, he promised full pay and benefits for 90 days to 1,400 idled workers; moreover, he paid everyone a $275 Christmas bonus.

Feuerstein was hailed in the media as an exemplar who put loyalty to employees over short-term gain. "I feel that I am a symbol of the movement against downsizing and layoffs," he told a *New York Times* reporter.[37] Profiles of him appeared in the *Reader's Digest, Parade*, and *People*; he received two honorary degrees; and he sat with Hillary Clinton during the State of the Union Address in January 1996.

Is Feuerstein a saint who put people before profits? At 70, he could have taken the insurance and retired to a favorite pastime—memorizing Shakespeare. The factory was insured at its replacement cost, but without rebuilding, insurance would cover only its depreciated value, a lesser sum. In addition, Malden Mills had a growing business making Polartec, a warm, lightweight fabric used in brands such as L. L. Bean, Eddie Bauer, and Polo by Ralph Lauren. In the year before the fire, it had made a pre-tax profit of $20 million on sales of $400 million. The long-term income stream to owner Feuerstein and his family from a rebuilt business was attractive.

Still, Feuerstein needed a big loan from BankBoston to begin rebuilding, and the salaries he paid to idle workers increased his risk of default. He continued to pay a basic wage of $12 per hour, $2 above the prevailing rate in the area. And he resisted the idea of outsourcing production to a low-wage country. Feuerstein ascribes his actions to enlightened self-interest. He believes that loyal workers are more productive and make better goods. Though he could have done less, he chose to do more.

Reconstruction was complete in 1997 but, unhappily, Malden Mills has been suffering huge losses. Its Polartec unit thrives, but other products are uncompetitive. The velvet upholstery unit was closed and 300 jobs were lost and, overall, the company now employs only 2,000. BankBoston has pressured Feuerstein to pledge his own assets and Malden Mills stock he owns to secure the loan. He has refused to do so.[38]

Albert Dunlap.   Al Dunlap is a managerial hired gun. He turned around eight struggling companies by ruthlessly prioritizing shareholder gain. At these

(continued)

---

[37]Louis Uchitelle, "The Risks of Keeping a Promise," *New York Times,* July 4, 1996, p. C3.

[38]Steve Baily and Steven Syre, "For Malden Mills, A Painful Fight Back," *Boston Globe,* August 11, 1998, p. C1.

Aaron M. Feuerstein and Albert Dunlap (concluded)

companies, he laid off so many people that nicknames such as "Chainsaw Al," "Rambo in Pinstripes," and "The Shredder" have stuck to him.

On his first day at Scott Paper, he called a meeting of eleven top managers, asking each for a self-introduction. Then, based on one prior briefing and what he calls "instincts," he fired nine of them. "Looking around the room," he writes, "I kept my remarks simple and pointed my index finger at the people I wanted to remain. 'You two stay—the rest of you are fired. Good-bye.'"[39] He cut 70 percent of upper-management jobs and 11,200 other jobs, or 35 percent of Scott's workforce.

Dunlap did turn Scott Paper around, increasing its stock market value from $2.9 billion to $9 billion. He liked to point out that although he cut jobs, he also secured the remaining 20,000 jobs by restoring the company's health. His pay and stock options netted him about $100 million, less than 2 percent of the value he created. The rest enriched Scott's shareholders. In his book, *Mean Business*, he asks: "Was I worth [it]?" He answers: "Go ask the shareholders."

Focused narrowly on profits, Dunlap rejected the stakeholder theory of social responsibility. "The most ridiculous term heard in boardrooms these days is 'stakeholders,'" he wrote. "If you see an annual report with the term 'stakeholders,' put it down and *run,* don't walk, away from the company. It means that the company has its priorities upside down. CEOs who bow to multiple constituencies are shirking their duties."[40] Besides firing employees, Dunlap pressured suppliers to trim bids and banned corporate charity donations (even after profitability returned).

In 1996 appliance-maker Sunbeam Corp. was losing money and its board hired Dunlap to turn it around. Sure enough, the chainsaw materialized and 6,000 of Sunbeam's 12,000 workers disappeared. But this time the formula failed. Sunbeam missed quarterly earnings targets. Morale sagged. Dunlap began to use dubious accounting measures to inflate earnings reports. From a high of $53, Sunbeam's shares fell below $10 (Dunlap owned 1.5 million shares and this cost him $65 million). Sunbeam's directors fired him in 1998 with a one-minute phone call.

It is not clear that a focus on profit maximization backfired on Dunlap or that he could not eventually have fixed the company. A *Business Week* investigation of his firing suggested that a critical factor was the board's perception of emotional instability.[41]

These two managers—Feuerstein and Dunlap—represent opposing philosophies about responsibility to employees. The media tend to brand one a saint and the other a devil. But the labels are too stark; both are effective managers, though in very different ways. Both prioritize stakeholders, but different ones.

---

[39] Albert J. Dunlap, *Mean Business,* New York: Random House, 1996, p. 127.
[40] Ibid., pp. 196–97. Emphasis in the original.
[41] John A. Byrne, "How Al Dunlap Self-Destructed," *Business Week,* July 6, 1998.

prominent and systematic evaluations are made by analysts with groups and companies that assemble portfolios of "good" companies for principled investors.

Companies are included in socially responsible portfolios if they pass through "screens," or tests. A prominent socially responsible mutual fund, the Domini Social Equity Fund, includes 400 companies. To pick these 400 companies, analysts examined about 650 firms, sifting through them to weed out the less responsible ones. An exclusionary "sin" screen blocks companies in alcohol, tobacco, and gambling. Two other exclusionary screens cut companies that produce military weapons or nuclear power. Remaining companies are subjected to positive screens that assess philanthropy, employee relations, diversity, environmental performance, product quality, and support for human rights in non-U.S. operations.

The Council on Economic Priorities (CEP) runs a research service for investors that evaluates the social performance of 700 companies in eight areas—environmental responsibility, women's advancement, minority advancement, charitable giving, community outreach, family benefits, workplace issues, and disclosure of information. In each category, detailed information is gathered from public records and questions sent to the companies. For example, environmental performance is rated in ten categories, each with specific measures ranging from pounds of toxins released to whether employees can win awards for reducing pollution. Companies are ranked or graded in five categories corresponding to letter grades A through F. (See the box on page 138 for a sample evaluation.)

Other funds for principled investors use screens that reflect different social values. The Timothy Plan Mutual Fund for conservative Christian investors screens out companies that pursue "an unholy agenda."[43] It cuts out companies in the alcohol, tobacco, and gambling businesses and, in addition, eliminates firms such as Sony Corporation, which produces sexually explicit and violent entertainment; Prudential Insurance, which supports Planned Parenthood; and Johnson & Johnson, which makes medical products used in abortions. The Noah Fund, whose investments are based on Judeo-Christian principles, also uses alcohol, tobacco, pornography, gambling, and abortion-related screens. Conservative Christian funds also eliminate companies such as Walt Disney Company that recognize gay employee groups and give benefits to domestic partners.

The use of screens is an art. Exclusionary screens invite in-or-out choices, but their boundaries are not always sharp. For example, if on principle a screen excludes tobacco companies, should it also block forest products firms that make cigarette paper or the cellulose in filters? Chemical companies that make cellophane for cigarette packs? Supermarket chains that sell cigarettes?

---

[43]Jacob Heilbrunn, "Moral Capital: The Prophets of Biblical Investing," *New Republic,* October 6, 1997, p. 20.

Grading the Social Performance of Compaq

The SCREEN Research Service for Investors at the Council on Economic Priorities recently published detailed social performance evaluations of 250 companies. Here, as an example, are the grades for Compaq Computer.

Environment	A
Women's Advancement	D
Minority Advancement	C
Charitable Giving	F
Community Outreach	C
Family Benefits	B
Workplace Issues	A
Social Disclosure	A

Compaq received an A in environmental performance because it is in the top 20 percent of companies evaluated. Among other things, environmental goals are included in employee performance reviews, and it has won several awards. The D in women's advancement was given because none of the twelve top officers, only one of the twelve directors, and only three of the 25 highest-paid employees were women. Similarly, the C in minority advancement came because only one top officer, no directors, and two of the top 25 highest-paid employees were minorities—but the company started a promising diversity program. Compaq gave only $7 million to charity, just 0.4 percent of its pretax earnings. This put it in the bottom 20 percent of companies and earned it an F. Compaq was above average in family benefits because it supported child care and flexible work schedules. The A in workplace issues came in part because Compaq had 50 percent fewer worker injuries than the average for the computer industry. Finally, the A in social disclosure was earned by forthcoming responses to questions submitted during the evaluation process.

The overall grade point average for Compaq is 2.6, or a C+.

Source: CEP, *The Corporate Report Card: Rating 250 of America's Corporations for the Socially Responsible Investor*, New York: Dutton, 1998, p. 63.

Companies in unrelated industries owned by tobacco companies? To what extent should principled objection travel a chain of complicity in the disfavored product? The Amana Growth Fund invests according to Islamic law and screens out not only companies that produce alcohol, but also restaurant chains, hotels, and supermarkets that get sales revenue from it. The fund also screens out banks, because in Islam it is considered wrong to profit from interest. However, tobacco and nuclear power companies are acceptable.[44] Positive screens may also present difficult choices. How should various actions be weighed? What criteria should be evaluated in each area? How much can information from a company be trusted?

When the definition of corporate social responsibility moves from abstract principle to specific criteria, it is evident that there is disagreement about it. The disagreement is caused by diverging values and illustrates that there can be sharp conflicts among stakeholders about what a company should do. At this level of specific criteria, the definition of and criteria for measuring responsibility are subjective.

Are Social Responsibility and Financial Performance Related?

Is there a reward for virtue? Are socially responsible companies more profitable than those less responsible? Is their stock a better investment? Or is there a cost penalty for social responsibility? We address these questions by looking at the performance of social investments, scholarly studies, and the profit implications of specific corporate programs.

Performance of Socially Responsible Investment Funds

Investing on principle is noble but has been less profitable. There are about 150 mutual funds in the United States that use screens for social responsibility.[45] They are only a tiny sliver of the 6,500-fund universe. And they are very small. In 1997, all social responsibility funds combined took in $530 million from investors, only 6 percent of the $9 billion inflow into just one of the most popular ordinary funds, the Vanguard Index Trust 500 Portfolio.[46]

A mutual fund rating service, Morningstar, Inc., tracked 17 social responsibility funds having a five-year performance record. Only five had returns in the top half of all funds in similar investment categories (such as growth, value, or growth and income) and only two ranked in the top quarter.[47] There was no evidence that liberal-leaning funds outperformed conservative ones, or vice versa.

---

[44]"Finding an Oasis of Profit for Islamic Investors," *Los Angeles Times*, December 29, 1996, p. D13.

[45]Social Investment Forum, *1997 Report on Responsible Investing Trends in the U.S.*, Washington, D.C.: Social Investment Forum, November 5, 1997, Executive Summary.

[46]Charles Gasparino and Pui-Wing Tam, "Feel-Good Mutual Funds Haven't Yet Found Favor," *The Wall Street Journal*, February 12, 1998, p. C1.

[47]Lloyd Kurtz, "No Effect, or No Net Effect? Studies on Socially Responsible Investing," *Journal of Investing*, Winter 1997, p. 37.

These findings reinforce analyses over many years showing that social responsibility funds lag behind other funds. Some believe that they do not attract the most experienced and talented managers. Also, their expenses and fees tend to be above average. But there is no inherent reason why such funds cannot yield market average or higher returns.[48] Even with multiple screens, the number of companies that qualify for investment is always large and varied enough to include many with strong financial and share-price performance. So far, however, the overall showing of socially screened funds does not prove that investment returns rise when stocks are screened with specific criteria perceived to show social responsibility.

Scholarly Studies

To explore the relationship between virtue and profit, scholars compare the financial performance of corporations with a high reputation for social responsibility to the financial performance of corporations with a lower reputation. As many as 100 such studies have been undertaken over the past twenty-five years. A recent review of fifty-one of them notes that although most revealed a positive relationship between social performance and profitability, a significant number of them—twenty—contained some negative correlations, and some others were inconclusive.[49] A second review of twenty-one studies found that in twelve studies, highly responsible firms were more profitable; in only one study were responsible firms less profitable; and in eight studies, no relationship between responsibility and profits was shown. From this, the reviewers concluded that "socially responsible firms certainly perform no worse and, perhaps, perform better than non-socially responsible firms."[50] This is as accurate a conclusion as any.

The inconsistency of results from study to study is not surprising because researchers face extraordinary problems. To begin, defining social responsibility in an objective way so that corporations can be ranked as more or less responsible is difficult. Many academic studies use rankings of social responsibility of the Council on Economic Priorities or the Domini Social Equity Fund, which have liberal perspectives. Others rely on social responsibility rankings made by executives of Fortune 500 firms who have a more conservative perspective.[51] In addition, it may seem objective to quantify financial performance,

---

[48]R. Bruce Hutton, Louis D'Antonio, and Tommi Johnsen, "Socially Responsible Investing: Growing Issues and New Opportunities," *Business & Society,* September 1998, p. 294.

[49]Jennifer J. Griffin and John F. Mahon, "The Corporate Social Performance and Corporate Financial Performance Debate," *Business & Society,* March 1997, p. 6.

[50]Moses L. Pava and Joshua Krausz, *Corporate Responsibility & Financial Performance: The Paradox of Social Cost,* Westport, Conn.: Quorum Books, 1995, pp. 8, 56.

[51]See, for example, Lee E. Preston and Douglas P. O'Bannon, "The Corporate Social–Financial Performance Relationship," *Business & Society,* December 1997. For an analysis of ranking systems, see Eugene Szwajkowski and Raymond E. Figlewicz, "The Social Performance Component of Corporate Reputation Ratings," paper delivered at the Annual Meeting of the Academy of Management, San Diego, CA, August 12, 1998.

but among measures of profitability such as return on assets, earnings per share, or net income, which should be used?

While most academic studies suggest that more responsible companies are more profitable, some do not, and there are still enough methodological questions and mixed results to reserve final judgment.

Individual Corporate Programs

Specific social programs may or may not be profitable for companies. McDonald's, for example, has a McPride program to promote academic achievement in which employees earn an hour's wages for coming in and doing schoolwork for an hour before their shifts. This program is a cost. On the other hand, at Ben & Jerry's a recycling program has reduced the company's use of paper and plastic, saving considerable sums.

British Airways has a program to provide books, toys, and clothes for street children in the Philippines. Donors of clothing are given discount vouchers on flights on the Manila–London route for every kilo (2.2 pounds) they turn in. This helps the poor, but it also offsets some of the project's cost by encouraging loyalty to the airline.

The impact of still other social programs on profits is unmeasurable. To teach teamwork, many companies have outdoor retreats at which teams of managers compete in races and aggressive games. But the Plastics Division at General Electric has its managers work together refurbishing decaying urban neighborhoods. Once, when GE Plastics had just bought Borg-Warner Chemicals, it brought 500 managers from both companies to San Diego and mixed them together in 30 teams. The teams renovated an aging downtown YMCA, making it useful to the community again. The exercise seemed to promote acceptance of GE among skeptical Borg-Warner managers who had feared entering GE's fanatically aggressive company culture.[52] Did this citizenship exercise lead to better morale, wiser decisions, and a stronger competitive team at GE? The answer is probably yes, but the bottom-line impact is unclear.

Overall, the connection between responsibility and profits for individual corporate programs is complex and varied.

Corporate Social Responsibility in Other Nations

Businesses in every nation must meet social obligations. But the idea of corporate social responsibility has developed differently around the world because of unique histories, cultures, and institutions. These factors combine to create singular social contracts.

---

[52]David Bollier, "Building Corporate Loyalty While Rebuilding the Community," *Management Review,* October 1996, p. 17.

European Nations

To understand the social contract in the developed nations of the West, it is necessary to revisit the depression years of the 1930s. Millions were unemployed worldwide and economies ran down to a near standstill. Left alone, markets failed to correct the downward spiral as their advocates had promised. Because of economic hardship, Adolph Hitler rose to power in Germany and Joseph Stalin was able to consolidate power in Russia. The Japanese became convinced that they needed more self-sufficiency in natural resources, the military gained more power, and the country pursued expansionist policies in southeast Asia. The world plunged into war. There is no greater historical lesson about the importance of the economic function of business to the health of society than the story of this era.

In post-war Europe, economies and cities lay in ruins. Much of the blame was placed on the market failures that preceded the war. European governments sought even closer control over companies to ensure that they met not only economic goals, but also social goals such as full employment and income equality. In England, some, but not all, industries were nationalized. In France, industrial sectors were also nationalized, as were businesses that had belonged to Nazi collaborators. In Germany, corporations were required to have supervisory boards with members from labor and government as well as industry. Thus, so-called mixed economies were created.

In European nations with mixed economies, governments have taken broad responsibility for alleviating societal problems. Traditionally, these governments have used high taxes to fund broad social programs and have tried to achieve social objectives through state-owned firms. As a result, there has not been great pressure on private European companies to address as broad a range of social problems as have American firms. The development of an ideology of social responsibility similar to that in the United States has, therefore, been slower. European companies are more likely to believe that they have met their obligations by paying taxes and following regulations.

In France, and to a lesser extent in Britain, Germany, and Italy, social responsibility came to refer primarily to labor issues such as wages, working conditions, and employment security. In these countries, conflict between labor unions and employers is old and deep, and reflects a socialist tradition in which corporate capitalism is seen as exploiting workers who therefore need government protection.

Unique industrial regulations reflect this responsibility toward workers. In France, for example, companies must spend 1 percent of total wages on worker education programs. In Germany, workers receive benefits that would be considered astounding in the United States. The provisions of a Social Chapter in the Maastricht Treaty that set up the European Union in 1992 extend such generous workers' rights throughout the European Union, but this is being resisted by much of industry.

In the 1990s, European industries struggled to compete in global markets. Nationalized firms that were being run for both economic and social objectives had grown inefficient. This led to reduced faith in the ability of governments to steer industries and more faith in markets. Companies are now being privatized and some regulations rolled back. Under these circumstances, business may be called on to assume a wider range of voluntary programs as governments take less responsibility for promoting social welfare.

Japan

In Japan, because of historical circumstance and the influence of Confucianism, the idea of corporate social responsibility has developed slowly. Before 1800, Japan was a divided society ruled by feudal lords, deeply influenced by Chinese culture, but virtually isolated from contact with Western nations. After 1800, America and European nations aggressively pursued trade with the Japanese. When the xenophobic Japanese tried to stop the influx, they were militarily crushed. Feudal samurai were no match for Western industrial-era weapons. The defeats of the 1850s and 1860s are to this day seen in Japan as a source of shame.

In 1868 Emperor Meiji issued an "imperial oath" that called upon the people to overcome feudal divisions and to rise above their humiliation by making Japan a world power. He called for modernization, to be achieved by borrowing business acumen and technology from the West. The emperor's plan became a national obsession and has been a guiding principle for Japan for over 130 years. Its significance for business, and for defining corporate social responsibility in Japan, is profound.

Following the emperor's declaration, government began to play a major role in promoting economic development. The central role of business became to make the country dominant and ensure preservation of the Japanese race in a hostile world. After the collapse of the military in 1945, the role of business became even more central. The people, previously loyal to feudal lords, in time transferred their loyalty to companies. In Japan, individuals believe that they make a national contribution by their work in a corporation. Large corporations in turn adopt a paternalistic attitude toward employees.

Since the time of Emperor Meiji, big companies have built housing, roads, and public facilities for workers. The Japanese company accepts all-encompassing responsibility for its community of employees. But while it cossets employees, it does not have a broad conception of societal involvement. This limited conception of social responsibility is based partly on Confucian doctrine. Confucianism spells out strict ethical duties and responsibilities, but traditionally they apply only to persons in direct relationships. Thus, companies embrace responsibility for workers, but do not feel as obligated to external stakeholders. Government must legislate solutions for other groups, and corporate responsibility is then to follow the law.

The Japanese cultural environment has supported an emphasis on corporate economic performance. The tax code does not make charitable contributions tax-deductible. Compared with the United States, stakeholder groups apply less pressure for social performance. Consumer and environmental interests have far less support. Labor unions are weak; to challenge the economic juggernaut would be unpatriotic. There are few minorities in Japan, where racial purity is openly discussed as a virtue. No strident civil rights movement confronts business. Wide acceptance of the Confucian teaching that women are lesser beings has slowed a nascent feminist movement.

Professor Richard E. Wokutch believes that because in Japan stakeholders are less demanding, Japanese firms are unprepared for the more turbulent U.S. environment and make major blunders. Sumitomo Bank and Honda, for example, engaged in sex and race discrimination that led to negative publicity. Hitachi was caught by the FBI trying to get trade secrets from IBM employees.[53] More recently, a Mitsubishi auto plant, operating with supervisory attitudes toward women that might not have raised eyebrows in a Japanese plant, was forced into a consent decree to settle major sexual harassment charges.

With the maturation of Japan's industrial society, its corporations are adopting more expansive social programs.[54] Some of them are ingeniously related to the firm's business activity. The Yakult Honsha Corporation, which employs 56,000 "Yakult ladies" to deliver its milk-based drinks door-to-door throughout Japan, has them check up on elderly persons who live alone as they do their routes. The Asahi Beer Co. has established a lavish clinic in Tokyo for backache sufferers. Liquor store delivery people must climb countless flights of stairs in the city's many high-rise buildings and frequently develop backaches. The Asahi Tower Clinic can treat them. Overall, and despite recent expansion, the Japanese idea of social responsibility is narrower than the American.

Less-Industrialized and Industrializing Nations

In less developed countries (LDCs), there is often no indigenous sense of corporate responsibility. For example, many small African and Latin American nations have massive social problems, and their economies limp along because of low incomes, high inflation, weak currencies, and capital flight. Economic success is the primary duty of business in such situations. Professor James E. Austin, an expert on LDCs, argues that "the extremity and pervasiveness of poverty in LDCs places a special social responsibility on business as a vehicle for creating economic progress that will help alleviate this deprivation."[55]

---

[53]Richard E. Wokutch, *Worker Protection, Japanese Style,* Ithaca, N.Y.: ILR Press, 1992, pp. 47–54.

[54]Kazuo Inamori, *For People and For Profit,* trans. T. R. Reid, Tokyo: Kodansha International, 1997, pp. 54–55.

[55]*Managing in Developing Countries,* New York: Free Press, 1990, p. 47.

Because local industry may be weak in such countries, the burden of responsibility can be felt by foreign multinationals. For example, about 90 percent of those who are HIV positive or have AIDS live in the developing world. In African countries such as Zambia, some companies lose most of their executives to AIDS and find that large percentages of their workers test HIV positive. Shell Oil, Unilever, and Levi Strauss, among other transnational firms, sponsor programs to fight the disease. At Shell facilities throughout Africa, Asia, and Latin America, employees receive information, counseling, anonymous testing, and condoms.[56]

Less-industrialized nations may emphasize strong corporate social responsibility if this is supported by their history, culture, and stage of development. One example is the Philippines, where in 1970 a group of corporations joined to fight poverty and social problems in the country. Today there are 180 firms in Philippine Business for Social Progress. Each company agrees to give one percent of its net income before taxes to social programs.

India is another example. In that country, thinking is deeply influenced by the doctrine of trusteeship set forth by Mahatma Gandhi in the 1940s. Gandhi believed that all money and property belong to society and are held in trust by rich people and business organizations. Persons or businesses that accumulate great wealth are obligated to use it for social welfare activities. Ownership of private property has a narrow meaning, and Gandhi intended the doctrine of trusteeship to moderate the tendency toward disparities of wealth and poverty in capitalism. Said Gandhi:

> Suppose I have earned a fair amount of wealth either by way of legacy or by means of trade and industry. I must know that all that belongs to me is the right to an honourable livelihood no better than that enjoyed by millions of others. The rest of my wealth belongs to the community and must be used for the welfare of the community.[57]

Since the mid-1960s, Indian business groups have held conferences and produced a series of statements that connect Gandhi's doctrine to the ideology of business responsibility. Indian companies undertake widespread and significant social actions to an extent unusual for a developing nation.

India is a largely rural and agricultural nation that suffers from poverty and bad infrastructure, so many corporate programs are in these areas. For example, Ahmadabad Industries built twelve textile mills to employ rural workers. Associated Cement Companies Ltd. builds and donates cattle sheds, wells, and manure pits for rural farms. Brooke Bond, Ltd., a tea company, sends a mobile artificial insemination unit to rural areas to help impoverished farmers breed more

---

[56]Arnold S. Tenorio, "Companies Do Their Share in AIDS Prevention through Inclusion in HRD Programs," *Business World,* October 31, 1997, p. 29; Gustavo Capdevila, "AIDS a Major Threat to Emerging Markets," *Inter Press Service,* February 11, 1997.

[57]In *Young India,* November 6, 1932, quoted in K. M. Mital, *Social Responsibilities of Business,* Delhi: Chanakya Publications, 1988, p. 134.

cattle. Cadbury India, Ltd., buys otherwise useless apples that peasants pick up from the ground and makes a carbonated apple drink from them. Other companies build roads and schools and operate buses between towns.

Summation

In sum, the idea of corporate social responsibility has different meanings throughout the world based on the context of history, culture, and institutions in which it exists. Professors Steven L. Wartick and Donna J. Wood write that principles of corporate responsibility are universal. Transnational corporations must mitigate problems they cause, follow laws, behave ethically, perform economically, and in general meet social contract expectations.[58] This is correct, but when these broad guidelines are implemented with concrete actions, managers around the world will interpret them differently.

The most expansive development of corporate responsibility is in the United States. In countries with more government intervention in markets, its development has been narrower, as in Europe and Japan where the focus is on duties to workers. In less-developed nations, its meaning is largely defined as economic performance.

Concluding Observations

Throughout American history, corporations have been driven primarily by the classical economic ideology. As they have grown in size and power, the concept of social responsibility has expanded to justify responding to public expectations. This has also been the experience in foreign countries. This dynamic interaction between corporate power and values of corporate social responsibility will continue. Corporations will be expected to assume more voluntary social programs, become more sensitive to a larger array of impacts on stakeholders, and conform to more regulatory mandates. At the same time, they will be expected to manage efficiently the resources at their disposal and be highly competitive in both local and global markets. Exceptional managers will be required to do all these things.

---

[58]Steven L. Wartick and Donna J. Wood, *International Business & Society*, Malden, Mass.: Blackwell, 1998, p. 76.

UNION CARBIDE CORPORATION AND BHOPAL

On December 3, 1984, operations went awry at a Union Carbide pesticide plant in Bhopal, India. Rapidly, a sequence of safety procedures and devices failed. Fugitive lethal vapors crossed the plant boundaries, killing 4,037 people and seriously injuring 60,000 more.

Bhopal is the worst sudden industrial accident ever in terms of human life lost. Industry critics were galvanized by the incredible event. "Like Auschwitz and Hiroshima," wrote one, "the catastrophe at Bhopal is a manifestation of something fundamentally wrong in our stewardship of the earth."[1] The gas leak raised major questions of responsibility, not just for Carbide, but for its Indian subsidiary, the Indian government, Bhopal officials, and others.

Union Carbide before Bhopal

In 1984, the year of the tragic events in Bhopal, Union Carbide was the nation's thirty-fifth-largest industrial corporation. The giant firm, founded in 1886, had grown from a small dry-cell-battery company into the nation's third-largest chemical producer, with a net profit of $199 million on $9.5 billion in sales. It employed 98,366 "Carbiders" at 500 facilities in thirty-seven countries, and foreign sales were 31 percent of total sales. The company had a variety of product lines, including petrochemicals, industrial gases, welding equipment, and popular consumer products such as Prestone antifreeze, Eveready batteries, Glad bags, and Simoniz wax. These multiple businesses gave Carbide strength. When one business, such as commodity chemicals, took a cyclical downturn, other businesses, particularly the popular name-brand consumer products, steadied earnings.

---

[1]David Weir, *The Bhopal Syndrome,* San Francisco: Sierra Club Books, 1987, p. xii.

Union Carbide's Bhopal Plant

Union Carbide first entered India in 1934 and operated through an Indian subsidiary. It owned a 50.9 percent majority interest in this subsidiary, which was named Union Carbide India, Ltd. (UCIL). The greatest part of the other 49.1 percent was owned by the Indian government; those shares not owned by the government traded on the Bombay Stock Exchange. In 1984, UCIL had fourteen plants and 9,000 employees, including 120 at the Bhopal plant in central India. Although UCIL contributed less than 2 percent to Carbide's revenues, it was the fifteenth-largest in sales among all Indian companies in 1984. Most of its revenues came from sales of Eveready batteries.

Union Carbide elected to build a pesticide plant in Bhopal in 1969. At that time there was a growing demand in India and throughout Asia for pesticides because of the "green revolution," a type of planned agriculture that requires intensive use of pesticides and fertilizers in the cultivation of special strains of food crops such as wheat, rice, and corn. Although pesticides may be misused and pose some risk, they also have great social value. Without pesticides, damage to crops, losses in food storage, and toxic mold growth in food supplies would cause the loss of many lives from starvation and food poisoning in developing countries such as India.

In the early 1970s, the small Bhopal plant formulated pesticides from chemical ingredients imported to the site. The plant was encouraged by the government of the city of Bhopal and the state of Madhya Pradesh with tax incentives. In 1975, however, UCIL was pressured by the Indian government to stop importing chemical ingredients. The company therefore proposed to manufacture methyl isocyanate (MIC) at the plant rather than ship it in from Carbide facilities outside the country. This was a fateful decision.

Methyl isocyanate, CH_3NCO, is a colorless liquid with a sharp odor. At the Bhopal plant it was used as an intermediate chemical in pesticide manufacture. It was not the final product; rather, MIC molecules were created and then pumped into a vessel to react with other synthetic organic chemicals. The reaction process creates uniquely shaped molecules that interfere with the natural chemistry of insect nervous systems and thus act as chemical weapons within pests. The two pesticides made by an MIC reaction process at Bhopal, with the trade names Sevin and Temik, are carbamate pesticides that disable a critical enzyme in the nervous systems of pests, leading to convulsions and death.

In 1975, Carbide received a permit from the Ministry of Industry in New Delhi to build a methyl isocyanate unit at the Bhopal plant. Two months prior to approval of this permit, the city of Bhopal enacted a development plan that required relocation of dangerous industries to an industrial zone 15 miles outside the city. Pursuant to the plan, M. N. Buch, the Bhopal city administrator, tried to relocate the UCIL pesticide plant and convert the site to housing and light commercial activity use. For reasons that are unclear, this effort failed and Buch was shortly thereafter transferred to forestry duties elsewhere.

Between 1975 and 1980, the MIC unit was constructed from a design package provided by Union Carbide's engineering group in the United States.

Detailed design work was done by an Indian subsidiary of a British firm. The unit was built by local labor using Indian equipment and materials. The reason for such heavy Indian involvement with the plant was an Indian law, the Foreign Exchange Regulation Act of 1973, that requires foreign multinationals to share technology and use Indian resources.

In 1980 the project was finished and the MIC unit began operation. During construction, large, unplanned slums and shantytowns called *jhuggis* had grown up near the plant, inhabited mainly by manual laborers and unemployed people seeking work. But the plant had become far more dangerous; it now made the basic chemicals used in pesticides rather than using shipped-in ingredients. One step in the manufacture of MIC, for example, creates phosgene, the lethal "mustard gas" used in World War I. The slum dwellers crowding up against the plant were ignorant of these dangers.

In 1981, a phosgene gas leak at the Bhopal plant killed one worker, and a crusading Indian journalist wrote a series of articles about the plant and its potential dangers to the population. No one took any action. In 1982, a second phosgene leak forced temporary evacuation of some surrounding slum areas. Also in 1982, a safety survey of the plant by three Carbide engineers from the United States cited approximately fifty safety defects, most of them minor, and noted "no situation involving imminent danger or requiring immediate correction."[2] Subsequently, all suggested changes in safety systems and procedures were made (except one troublesome valve outside the accident area). Worker safety and environmental inspections of the plant were carried out by the Department of Labor in Madhya Pradesh. The agency had only fifteen factory inspectors to cover 8,000 plants and had a record of lax enforcement.[3] This was typical of the generally low commitment to pollution control in India by regulators at all levels.

A downturn in the Indian economy and stiff competition from other pesticide firms marketing new, less expensive products soon caused the Bhopal plant to lose money for three years in a row. As revenues fell, its budgets were cut, and it was necessary to defer some maintenance, lessen the rigor of training programs, and lay off workers. At the time of the accident, the MIC unit was operating with a reduced crew of six workers per shift rather than the normal twelve—a condition some process-design engineers thought unsafe.

Union Carbide's Relationship with the Bhopal Plant

The Bhopal pesticide plant fit into the Union Carbide management hierarchy as depicted in the organization chart in Exhibit 1. Although some Americans had staffed the plant and had conducted safety inspections in its early years,

---

[2]L. A. Kail, J. M. Poulson, and C. S. Tyson, *Operational Safety Survey,* CO/MIC/Sevin Units, Union Carbide India Ltd., Bhopal Plant, South Charleston, W. Va.: Union Carbide Corporation, July 28, 1982, p. 1.

[3]Sheila Jasanoff, "Managing India's Environment," *Environment,* October 1986, p. 33.

Exhibit 1

Union Carbide's organization structure as related to the Bhopal plant.

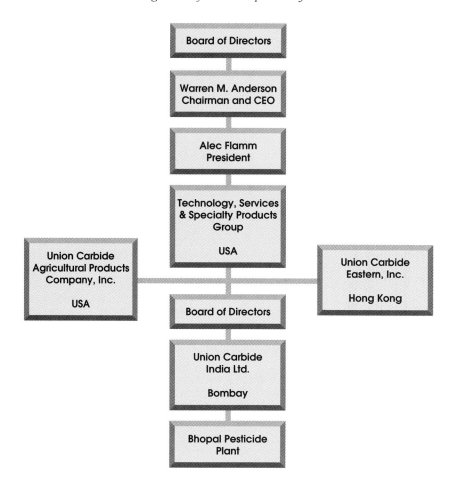

Carbide turned the plant completely over to Indian personnel after 1982. It did so under Indian government pressure to increase national self-sufficiency. Plant safety inspections after 1982 were the responsibility of the Indian subsidiary, UCIL. At the time of the accident, therefore, line responsibility for the day-to-day operations and safety of the plant rested with the plant manager, an Indian employee of UCIL. The plant operated with a great deal of autonomy. But Union Carbide had majority ownership of UCIL and, in addition, was represented by five members on the UCIL board of directors—four from Union Carbide Eastern, Inc., and the fifth from the international headquarters group. The Bhopal plant was also in close contact with the management of Union Carbide Agricultural Products Company, Inc., Carbide's arm for the production and marketing of pesticides.

Top management at Union Carbide's Danbury, Connecticut, headquarters received monthly reports from the Bhopal plant and approved major financial, maintenance, and personnel decisions. Carbide engineers also provided UCIL and the Bhopal plant with the processing manual on MIC that was supposed to guide plant operations.

In the reporting relationship, Union Carbide's top management in Connecticut had ultimate, formal responsibility for the operation of the Bhopal plant. Shortly after the accident, chairman Warren M. Anderson stated in interviews that Carbide accepted "moral responsibility" for the tragedy. Nevertheless, the Bhopal plant was but one of hundreds of sites worldwide in which the company had an equity interest. For this reason, and because of the vast physical distances separating the two sites, Carbide's U.S. management team delegated considerable authority over operations to UCIL's management team on the spot.

The Gas Leak

On the evening of December 2, 1984, storage tank 610, one of three storage tanks at the MIC unit, was filled with 11,290 gallons of MIC. The tank, which had a capacity of 15,000 gallons, was a partly buried, stainless steel, pressurized vessel. The purpose of tank 610 was to store large batches of MIC. MIC was produced elsewhere at the plant and routed through pipes into tank 610. At an appropriate time, operators in a control room would open and close valves to move 1-ton batches of MIC through a transfer pipe to the area where pesticides were made. The MIC would then be converted to Sevin (or Temik).

At about 9:30 PM, a supervisor ordered R. Khan, an operator in the MIC complex, to unclog four filter valves near the MIC production area by washing them out with water. Khan connected a water hose to the piping above the clogged valves, but neglected to insert a slip blind above the point of water entry. A slip blind is a simple device that seals lines to prevent water leakage into adjacent pipes. Khan's omission violated instructions in the MIC processing manual, the technical manual that sets forth procedure established by the chemical engineers who set up the plant.

Because of either this careless washing procedure or the introduction of water elsewhere, 120 to 240 gallons of water entered tank 610, initiating a powerful exothermic (heat-building) reaction. Initially, operators were unaware that the reaction was proceeding that night. At 10:20 PM, tank pressure was logged at 2 pounds per square inch. Then, at 10:45, a new shift came on duty. At 11:30 PM, a new operator in the MIC control room noticed that the pressure in tank 610 was 10 pounds per square inch, but was unconcerned because this was within tolerable limits, the gauges were often wrong, and he did not read the log to discover that pressure was five times greater than it had been one hour earlier.

As the reaction continued, the temperature in tank 610 rose. Unfortunately, the refrigeration units that cooled the tanks had been shut down for five months as an economy measure. Had the tanks been refrigerated, as the MIC processing manual required, the heat buildup from the reaction with the water might have taken place over several days instead of several hours.

As pressure built in the tank, a leak developed. At about 11:30, workers smelled MIC, and their eyes watered. At 11:45, one operator spotted a small, yellowish drip of MIC from some high piping and informed his supervisor. The supervisor suggested fixing the leak after a tea break scheduled for 12:15 AM on December 3.

At 12:40 the tea break ended. But by this time a gauge in the control room showed that the pressure in tank 610 was 40 pounds per square inch. It rose in a short time to 55 pounds per square inch, the top of the scale. A glance at the tank temperature gauge brought more bad news: the MIC was vaporizing at 77° F, 36° higher than the safety limit specified in the MIC processing manual. After reading the gauges, an operator ran out to look at tank 610. He felt heat radiating from the tank and heard the concrete over it cracking. Within seconds, a pressure-release valve opened and a white cloud of deadly MIC vapor shot into the atmosphere with a high-decibel screech.

Operators back in the control room turned a switch to activate the vent gas scrubber, a safety device designed to neutralize any escaped toxic gases from the MIC unit by circulating them through a caustic soda solution. The scrubber, however, failed to operate because it was down for maintenance. Subsequent investigation established that even if the scrubber had been on-line, it was not designed to handle the temperature and pressure reached by the MIC in the tank and would have been quickly overwhelmed. A flare tower designed to burn off toxic gases before they escaped into the atmosphere was also off-line; it had been disassembled for maintenance, and an elbow joint was missing. Another emergency measure, the transferring of MIC from tank 610 to one of two other storage tanks, was impossible, because both of those tanks were full or nearly so. This situation also violated procedure in the MIC processing manual, which called for leaving one tank empty as a safety measure.

At about 1:00 AM, an operator turned on an alarm to warn workers of danger from escaping gas. The plant superintendent, who had arrived in the control room, directed that a water spray be turned on the escaping MIC vapor to knock it down, but this had little effect. At this time most workers in the plant ran in panic, ignoring four parked buses that they were supposed to drive through the surrounding area to begin evacuation of residents. Only two workers stayed in the MIC control room. They shared the only available oxygen mask when the room filled with MIC vapor. Finally, at about 2:30 AM, the pressure in the tank dropped, the leaking safety valve resealed, and the MIC leak stopped.

Over a two-hour period, roughly 10,000 gallons, or about 90 percent of the MIC in tank 610, vaporized and blew out in a white cloud. The cloud spread for miles across the sleeping city. That night the wind was calm, the temperature was about 60°, and the heavy chemical mist lingered just above the ground. The gas attacked people in the streets and seeped into their homes. Those who panicked and ran into the night air suffered higher doses of toxic vapor. Because MIC is so reactive with water, simply breathing through a wet cloth would have saved many lives. But people lacked this simple knowledge.

Animals died. Trees were stripped of leaves. Crowds of Bhopal residents fled the city. As the poisonous cloud enveloped victims, MIC reacted with water in their eyes. This reaction created heat that burned corneal cells, rendering them opaque. Residents with cloudy, burning eyes staggered into aid stations.

Many victims suffered shortness of breath, coughing fits, inflammation of the respiratory tract, and chemical pneumonia. In the lungs, MIC molecules reacted with moist tissues, causing chemical burns. Fluid oozed from seared lung tissue and pooled, a condition called pulmonary edema, and many victims literally drowned in their own secretions. When they did not suffocate from edema, chemical burns destroyed cells that facilitate the exchange of gases. In survivors, the burned tissue eventually healed over with a tough protein substance called fibrin, which created areas of pulmonary fibrosis that diminished breathing capacity.

Treatment consisted of administration of oxygen, mechanical ventilation of the lungs, diuretics to maintain fluid balance, and short-term use of steroids to decrease lung inflammation. Unfortunately many residents of the slums around the plant were already suffering from malnutrition, tuberculosis, and a variety of infections. Their chronic ill health compounded the effects of MIC injury.

How many died at Bhopal? In the hysteria immediately following the accident, estimates by Indian officials ranged as high as 10,000. Eight years later, in 1992, the Indian government fixed the immediate death toll at 4,037. Eventually, over 600,000 residents would make a gas-related death or injury claim.[4] Many of these were fraudulent.

Union Carbide Reacts

Unprecedented management problems faced Warren M. Anderson, then age 63, chairman and CEO of Union Carbide. Awakened early on Monday, December 3, he rushed to Carbide's Danbury, Connecticut, headquarters and learned of the rising death toll. In the early morning hours, when the extent of the disaster was evident, an emergency meeting of a senior management committee was held. The committee sent emergency medical supplies, respirators, oxygen (Carbide products), and an American doctor with extensive knowledge of MIC to Bhopal.

The next day, Tuesday, December 4, Carbide dispatched a team of technical experts to examine the plant. On Thursday, Anderson departed for India.

---

[4]Many Bhopal residents reported injuries other than to the respiratory tract and eyes, including miscarriages, birth defects, immune diseases, blood disorders, and neuromuscular effects. High rates of psychiatric disorders have been observed. Over 100 scientific and medical studies have yielded a body of evidence that MIC can attack other body organs in addition to the eyes and lungs. For a summary, see Pushpa S. Mehta et al., "Bhopal Tragedy's Health Effects: A Review of Methyl Isocyanate Toxicity," *Journal of the American Medical Association,* December 5, 1990, pp. 2781–87. See also, "The Bhopal Legacy: An Interview with Dr. Rosalie Bertell," *Multinational Monitor,* March 1997, pp. 26–28.

But upon arriving in Bhopal, he was charged with criminal negligence, placed under house arrest, and then asked to leave the country.

With worldwide attention focused on Bhopal, Carbide held daily press conferences. Christmas parties were canceled. Flags at Carbide facilities were flown at half-mast. All of Carbide's nearly 100,000 employees observed a moment of silence for the victims. Employees contributed to a relief fund. Carbide gave $1 million to an emergency relief fund and offered to turn its guest house in Bhopal into an orphanage. Months later, Carbide offered another $5 million to the state of Madhya Pradesh, but the money was refused because Indian politicians thought they would appear to be in collusion with the company. The political climate was so hostile that anything associated with Carbide was reviled. Later, when the government learned that Union Carbide had set up a training school for the unemployed in Bhopal, the facility was flattened with bulldozers.

Carbide Fights Lawsuits and a Takeover Bid

No sooner had the vapor cleared than American attorneys arrived in Bhopal seeking litigants for damage claims. They walked the streets signing up plaintiffs. Just four days after the gas leak, the first suit was filed in a U.S. court; soon cases seeking $50 billion in damages for 200,000 Indians were filed against Carbide.

But soon after these filings, the Indian Parliament passed a law giving the Indian government the exclusive right to represent victims.[5] A week later India filed a suit in the United States. Union Carbide offered $350 million to settle existing claims (an offer rejected by the Indian government) and brought a motion to have the cases heard in India. Both Indian and American lawyers claiming to represent victims opposed the motion, knowing that wrongful death awards in India were small compared to those in the United States. In May 1985, a federal court ruled that the cases should be heard in India rather than in the United States, noting that "to retain the litigation in [the U.S.] . . . would be yet another example of imperialism, another situation in which an established sovereign inflicted its rules, its standards and values on a developing nation."[6] This was a victory for Carbide and a defeat for American lawyers, who could not carry their cases to India in defiance of the government.

---

[5]Indian courts rarely awarded more than $10,000 for a wrongful death, and families of Indians killed by buses usually received $100 to $200. By contrast, in U.S. courts there have been hundreds of awards exceeding $1 million. See R. Clayton Trotter, Susan G. Day, and Amy E. Love, "Bhopal, India and Union Carbide: The Second Tragedy," *Journal of Business Ethics,* June 1989, p. 447.

[6]*In re Union Carbide Corporation Gas Plant Disaster,* 634 F.Supp. 867. This opinion was upheld on appeal to the U.S. Court of Appeals, Second Circuit, on January 14, 1987. The appeals court did, however, strike several procedural conditions imposed on Union Carbide related to discovery, parallel jurisdiction, and satisfaction of eventual judgment. Left intact was an order that Union Carbide waive defenses based on the statute of limitations. In October 1987, the U.S. Supreme Court, without comment, let the judgment stand.

In September 1986, the Indian government filed a $3.3 billion civil suit against Carbide in the Indian courts. The suit alleged that Union Carbide Corporation, in addition to being majority shareholder in Union Carbide India Ltd., had exercised policy control over the establishment and design of the Bhopal plant. The Bhopal plant was defective in design because its safety standards were lower than similar Carbide plants in the United States. Carbide had consciously permitted inadequate safety standards to exist. The suit also alleged that Carbide was conducting an "ultrahazardous activity" at the Bhopal plant and had strict and absolute liability for compensating victims regardless of whether the plant was operating carefully or not. Carbide countered with the defense that it had a holding company relationship with UCIL and never had exercised direct control over the Bhopal plant; it was prohibited from doing so by Indian laws that required management by Indian nationals.[7] In addition to the civil suit, Carbide's chairman, Warren Anderson, and several UCIL executives were charged with homicide in a Bhopal court. This apparently was a pressure tactic, since no attempt to arrest them was made. The Indian court had no power to extradite and try Anderson, a United States citizen.

On top of its legal battle, Carbide had to fight for its independence. The depressing effect of Bhopal on its stock price made the company a takeover candidate. In December 1985, GAF Corporation, which had been accumulating Carbide's shares, made a takeover bid. After a suspenseful month-long battle, Carbide fought off GAF, but only at the cost of taking on enormous new debt to buy back 55 percent of its outstanding shares. This huge debt had to be reduced because interest payments were crippling. So in 1986 Carbide sold $3.5 billion of assets, including its most popular consumer brands— Eveready batteries, Glad bags, and Prestone antifreeze. It had sacrificed stable sources of revenue and was now a smaller, weaker company more exposed to cyclical economic trends.

Investigating the Cause of the MIC Leak

In the days following the disaster, there was worldwide interest in pinning down the precise cause of the gas leak. A team of reporters from the *New York Times* visited Bhopal and interviewed plant workers. Their six-week investigation concluded that the accident was caused by a large volume of water entering tank 610 and reacting with the MIC.[8] The water entered because the operator

---

[7]*Union of India* v. *Union Carbide Corp. and Union Carbide India Ltd.*, Bhopal District Court, No. 1113 (1986).

[8]Stuart Diamond, "The Bhopal Disaster: How It Happened," *New York Times*, January 28, 1985; Thomas J. Lueck, "Carbide Says Inquiry Showed Errors but Is Incomplete," *New York Times*, January 28, 1985; Stuart Diamond, "The Disaster in Bhopal: Workers Recall Horror," *New York Times*, January 30, 1985; and Robert Reinhold, "Disaster in Bhopal: Where Does Blame Lie?" *New York Times*, January 31, 1985.

who had washed out piping earlier in the evening violated procedure and failed to use a slip blind. So water from the hose simply backed up and eventually flowed about 400 feet into the MIC storage tank. The *Times* account was widely accepted as authoritative, and this theory, called the "water washing theory," gained wide currency.

Immediately after the accident, Union Carbide also rushed a team of investigators to Bhopal, including scientists, chemical engineers, attorneys, and accident investigation experts. But the team got little cooperation from Indian authorities operating in a climate of anti-Carbide, anti-American popular protest. They were denied access to plant records and workers.

The Carbide investigators were, however, given access to tank 610 and took core samples from the bottom residue. These samples were sent to the United States, where over 500 experimental chemical reactions were undertaken to explain their chemical composition. In March 1985, Carbide finally released its first report on the accident. The report concluded that the accident had been caused by the entry of water into the tank, but did not accept the water washing theory. It stated that "the source of the water is unknown" but mentioned the possibility of entry through misconnection of a water line at a utility station, or "service drop" near the tank.[9]

Service drops are located throughout chemical plants and provide needed services. Typically they contain headers for compressed air, water, nitrogen, and steam—all essential for chemical plant operation. At the utility station near tank 610, the nitrogen and water lines are located together (see the lower left-hand corner of Exhibit 2). The Carbide investigation team hypothesized that if a worker had deliberately or accidentally connected piping leading to tank 610 with the water line at the service drop, the resulting flow could have released an amount of water sufficient to cause the reaction. Carbide investigators rejected the water washing hypothesis for several reasons. The piping system was designed to prevent water contamination. Valves between the piping being washed and tank 610 were found closed after the accident. And the amount of water contamination required to create the reaction—1,000 to 2,000 pounds—was too great to be explained by valve leakage.

The Carbide report contradicted the water washing theory, but within nine months an investigation sponsored by the Indian government embraced it once again. This study, made by Indian scientists and engineers, stated that the entry of water into tank 610 was the cause of the accident and that water had gotten into the tank as a result of improper water washing procedure.[10] (See Exhibit 3.)

There matters stood until December 1985, when a U.S. court ordered the Indian government to give Carbide access to plant records and the names of

---

[9]*Bhopal Methyl Isocyanate Incident Investigation Team Report,* Danbury, Conn.: Union Carbide Corporation, March 1985, p. i.

[10]*Report on Scientific Studies on the Release Factors Related to Bhopal Toxic Gas Leakage,* Bombay: Indian Council of Scientific and Industrial Research, December 1985.

EXHIBIT 2

The tank storage area and safety equipment in Bhopal. Unfortunately, the refrigeration unit was off, and the vent gas scrubber, flare tower, and water spray failed to prevent disaster. The service drop in the lower left corner is a possible source of water that caused the reaction.

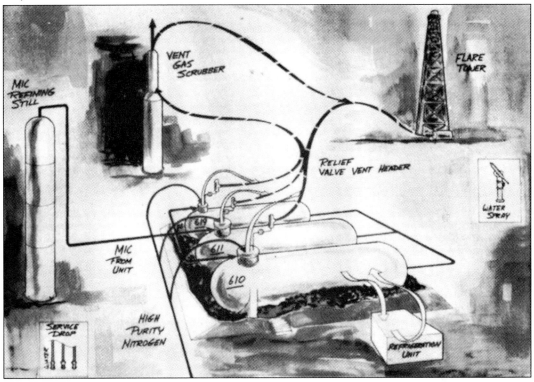

workers. This order corrected an unfairness in the litigation process—that the government of India was suing Carbide yet also barred Carbide from access to critical evidence that might prove its innocence. Carbide renewed its investigation, sending a team of interviewers to India to seek out and interview plant workers. Over seventy interviews, plus careful examination of plant records and physical evidence, led the investigators to conclude that the cause of the gas leak was sabotage by a disgruntled employee who intentionally hooked up a water hose to tank 610.

Here is the sequence of events on the night of December 2–3 that Carbide set forth. At 10:20 PM, the pressure gauge on tank 610 read 2 pounds per square inch. This meant that no water had yet entered the tank and no reaction had begun. At 10:45 the regularly scheduled shift change occurred. Shift changes take half an hour and the MIC storage area would have been deserted. At this time, an operator who had been angry for several days about

EXHIBIT 3

Two theories clash on water entry into MIC tank.

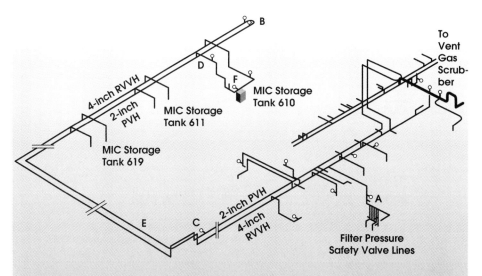

According to the water washing theory of Indian government, water was introduced through a hose into bleeder A at filter pressure safety valve lines. As hose kept running, water proceeded through leaking valve in that area and rose up into the relief valve vent header line (RVVH). It took a turn at the jumper line, B, and moved into the process vent header line (PVH), filling it in the reverse direction all the way to the slip blind, C. When PVH was completely filled, water rose at line D and proceeded into MIC storage tank 610.

On Feb. 8, 1985, two months after the leak, India's Central Bureau of Investigation drilled a hole in the PVH line at point E to drain any water left in the line. No water emerged. Carbide says this fact alone disproves the water washing theory. The fact various valves in the pathway to the tank were closed also disproves the theory, according to Carbide.

Carbide espouses an alternate theory: The company says it has proof that water was introduced by a "disgruntled employee" who removed pressure gauge F, attached a hose to the open piping, and ran water into the MIC tank. Gas then escaped through a rupture disk and proceeded through the RVVH and out the vent gas scrubber.

Source: Courtesy of Union Carbide.

his failure to get a promotion stole into the area. He unscrewed the local pressure indicator gauge on tank 610, hooked up a rubber water hose, and turned the water on. Five minutes would have sufficed to do this. Carbide claims to know the name of this person, but has never revealed it.

Why did he do it? Carbide speculated that his intention was simply to ruin the MIC batch in the tank; it is doubtful that this worker realized how toxic MIC vapor was or intended any loss of life. The interviews had revealed that the workers thought of MIC chiefly as a lachrymator, a chemical that produces tearing; they did not regard it as a lethal hazard. Indeed, there had been no prior experience with fatalities from MIC, and after the venting of tank 610 into the air, operators felt some relief. They believed the threat had passed and informed town authorities there was no danger to life.

A few minutes after midnight, MIC operators noted a strong pressure rise in tank 610. Walking to the tank, they found the hose connected and removed it, then informed their supervisors. The supervisors tried to prevent a catastrophic pressure rise by draining water from tank 610. Between 12:15 AM and 12:30 AM, just minutes before the major gas release, they transferred about 1 metric ton of MIC from tank 610 to a holding tank in the Sevin manufacturing area. Water is heavier than MIC and the transfer was accomplished through a drain in the bottom of tank 610; thus, the supervisors hoped to remove the water. They failed. At 12:45 AM the gas leak occurred.

Union Carbide investigators had physical evidence to support this scenario. After the accident, the local pressure gauge hole on tank 610 was still open and no plug had been inserted, as would have been normal for routine maintenance. When written records for the MIC unit were examined, a crude drawing of the hose connection was found on the back of one page from that night's log book. Also, operators outside the MIC unit told the investigation team that MIC operators had told them about the hose connection that night.

Log entries in the MIC unit had been falsified, causing the Carbide team to conclude that the operators engaged in a crude cover-up. The major falsification was an attempt to hide the transfer of MIC from tank 610 to the Sevin production area. The operators on duty that night made clumsy efforts to show that the transfer had come from tank 611 instead and had been done more than an hour earlier, before the shift change. But the entries were out of chronological sequence and in the handwriting of operators who did not come on until the night shift. Further, analysis of the contents of the MIC transferred into the Sevin area showed it to be contaminated with reaction byproducts. The MIC in tank 611, from which the operators claimed to have made the transfer, was found to be on-specification and untainted. The transfer had to have come from tank 610.

Why did the supervisors and operators attempt a cover-up? One Carbide investigator has written this explanation.

> Not knowing if the attempted transfer had exacerbated the incident, or whether they could have otherwise prevented it, or whether they would be blamed for not having notified plant management earlier, those involved decided on a cover-up. They altered logs that morning and thereafter to disguise their involvement. As is not uncommon in many such incidents, the reflexive tendency to cover up simply took over.[11]

This theory of deliberate sabotage became the centerpiece of Carbide's legal defense. The Indian government made no public comment, but Srinivason Varadarajan, lead investigator in the 1985 study by the Indian Council of Scientific and Industrial Research, commented: "We have other evidence showing the likelihood that water came in by the water washing. I don't think

---

[11]Ashok S. Kalelkar, *Investigation of Large-Magnitude Incidents: Bhopal as a Case Study*, paper presented at the Institution of Chemical Engineers Conference on Preventing Major Chemical Accidents, London, England, May 1988, p. 27.

we'll have any difficulty showing it."[12] And some observers noted that the sabotage theory failed to mitigate management responsibility for equipment failures and procedures inadequate to contain the MIC reaction.

A Settlement Is Reached

The case never came to trial. In 1989, a settlement was reached in which Carbide agreed to pay $470 million to the Indian government, which would distribute the money to victims. In return, India agreed to stop all legal action against Carbide, UCIL, and their executives. India agreed to this settlement, which was far less than the $3.3 billion it was asking for, because a trial and subsequent appeals in the Indian court system might have taken twenty years. Carbide was pleased with the settlement. It had $200 million in insurance and took a charge of $.50 per share against 1988 net earnings of $5.31 per share.

Victims' groups were upset at the settlement, which they thought was too little, and mounted legal appeals. In late 1991, the Indian Supreme Court rejected these appeals, but permitted reinstatement of criminal proceedings against Warren Anderson. An arrest warrant for Anderson on manslaughter charges was issued in India in 1992, but no action against him has been taken.

Postscript

The Indian government has been slow in distributing settlement money to gas victims. It assigned the job to a government agency that did not begin to award much of the money until 1994. In the intervening five years, the settlement's value increased due to strengthening of the dollar and interest payments. By 1997, an average of $1,600 had been paid in 11,267 death claims and an average $650 had been paid on 318,657 injury claims.[13] Over 350,000 claims remained to be considered.[14]

The compensation process is riddled with corruption. It is common for healthy people to bribe physicians for false medical records and then use these to receive compensation. One estimate is that only 6 percent of the roughly 600,000 claimants filing so far suffered permanent injury; of the rest, 52 percent suffered temporary injury and 42 percent suffered no injury.[15]

In 1994, Union Carbide sold for $90 million its 50.9 percent equity in UCIL to the Indian subsidiary of a British company. As a condition of sale agreed to

---

[12]Will Lepkowski, "Union Carbide Presses Bhopal Sabotage Theory," *Chemical & Engineering News*, July 4, 1988, p. 11.

[13]Figures are from Corporate Watch website (www.corpwatch.org) citing data from the Welfare Commission, Bhopal Gas Victims, as of October 14, 1997.

[14]Bharat Desai, "Bhopal Gas Tragedy: A Mockery of Compensation," *India Today*, April 15, 1997, p. 78.

[15]"Bhopal Gas Tragedy Victim's Woes Continue," *The Statesman* (*India*), February 25, 1998, p. 1.

by Indian courts, Carbide put $20 million into a charitable trust fund to build a Bhopal hospital. With the sale of its assets, Carbide believes it no longer has any involvement with India. Victims' groups in India keep demanding further justice from the company and its officers, but Indian courts have refused to re-open the settlement. Though charges remain open, the Indian government has never tried to serve a warrant on Warren Anderson. In recent years, India has tried to create a more friendly climate for foreign multinationals. Pursuing a vendetta against Carbide would work against its goal of encouraging more foreign trade and investment.

Union Carbide today is a smaller, less resilient company. The post-Bhopal need for debt reduction combined with later strategic thinking has led to the sale or spin-off of a number of its parts. In 1984, the year of the gas leak, Carbide had 98,366 employees and sales of $9.5 billion; in 1997, it had only 11,745 employees and sales were $6.5 billion. It is now among the smallest of international chemical companies, and its loss of diversification leaves it more vulnerable to cyclical downturn.

The Bhopal plant never reopened. It has been dismantled and some of its equipment sold. UCIL was renamed Eveready Industries India Limited by its new owners.

Questions

1. Who is responsible for the Bhopal accident? How should blame be apportioned among the parties involved, including Union Carbide senior management, UCIL managers, workers at the MIC unit in Bhopal, governments in India that issued permits and provided incentives for the plant, Bhopal community officials who permitted slum dwellers to move near the plant in illegal settlements, Indian environmental and safety inspectors, and others?
2. What principles of corporate social responsibility and business ethics are applicable to the actions of the parties in question?
3. How well did the legal system work? Do you agree with the decision to try the lawsuits in India? Were victims fairly compensated? Was Carbide sufficiently punished?
4. Did Union Carbide handle the crisis well? How would you grade Carbide's performance in facing uniquely difficult circumstances?
5. What lessons can other corporations learn from the story of Union Carbide and Bhopal?

6

Implementing Corporate Social Programs

Royal/Dutch Shell was the fifth largest company in the world as measured by revenues of $128.1 billion in 1997, and it ranked third in profits of $7.8 billion. There are over 1,700 companies in the Shell Group. They range from companies that control gasoline stations to owners of tankers for road and sea and those drilling for and distributing oil, gas, and coal. They are in over 100 countries and employ 105,000 people.

Bruising criticisms of Shell's activities have been voiced by human rights and environmental groups, stockholders, and investors. Shell has been severely criticized for its actions in Nigeria—its support of the author-

itarian government, its pollution of the environment, and its indifference to human rights. The company faced worldwide criticism over the Brent Spar incident, as noted in Chapter 2. There were many other sources of concern about the company's pollution and human rights actions, in Turkey, Peru, and other countries.[1]

These complaints, supported by stockholder resolutions, led the com-

---

[1]For instance, Council on Economic Priorities, *The Corporate Report Card*, New York: Dutton, 1998; "Remember Shell, Boycott Shell," *Multinational Monitor*, December 1997; and "Shellman Says Sorry," *The Economist*, May 10, 1997, p. 65.

pany to make major changes in its policies. Cor Herkstroter, chairman of Royal Dutch, organized a review of the company's basic business principles. The result was a new *Statement of General Business Principles* (SGBP) formulated in 1997. Like most other mission statements, which is what this document really is, the main objective stated for the company is to engage efficiently in production and be responsible to its main stakeholders—shareholders, customers, employees, and society.

Of interest here is the section of the SGBP devoted to expressed responsibilities for social programs and what the companies need to do about them. To its employees, the company commits itself to respect their human rights, to provide them with good and safe conditions of work, and to promote and develop their best talents. To society the policy is:

> To conduct business as responsible corporate members of society, to observe the laws of the countries in which they [Shell companies] operate, to express support for fundamental human rights in line with the legitimate role of business and to give proper regard to health, safety and the environment consistent with their commitment to contribute to sustainable development.[2]

The SGBP expresses "[o]ur intention . . . to develop ways for consistently monitoring, measuring and reporting performance in a manner aligned to the expectations of society and our Statement of General Business Principles." The company realizes that this is a pioneering effort but pledges to seek acceptable measures of performance. Shell has formed a social accountability unit to publish a "Shell Report." This will be similar to a financial report, said the company, but will assess social accountability and environmental performance. In developing suitable measures of performance, the committee will communicate widely with employees and others.[3]

Currently, Shell companies are undertaking hundreds of different social programs throughout the world, tailored to the particular local circumstances. Here are but a few examples. In 1991, the government of Singapore gave the first Distinguished Partner in Progress award to Shell for its economic and social contributions to the country. The social contributions covered activities in education, the arts, the environment, and the community. Shell made substantial cash contributions in 1998 to a number of programs in Malaysia, including cash to subsidize surgery for young heart patients and various charities for young

---

[2]The words "sustainable development" have a special meaning. The first definition was made by The World Commission on Environment and Development (called The Brundtland Commission) in 1987. The definition was ". . . to meet the needs of the present without compromising the ability of future generations to meet their own needs." This definition has been accepted by The President's Council on Sustainable Development. For companies it means such things as reducing energy use, reducing negative environmental impacts of products, recycling scarce resources, reclaiming waste products, or reducing use of scarce resources when sensible.

[3]Royal/Dutch Shell, http://www.shell.com, July 8, 1998.

people. In Gabon, Shell for years has been developing infrastructure for the country, educating entrepreneurs, and providing them with financial support.[4]

The policies set forth in the SGBP, although at a high level of abstraction, are laudable. Noteworthy are the policies concerning human rights, social responsibilities, and the intent to measure performance. How well the Shell companies comply with these policies and how successful the top management is in developing creditable measures of performance remain to be seen. *The Economist*

pointed out that while the policies seem vague, there is in the SGBP "a glint of steel underneath."[5] Previous statements of policy were considered only guides to company action. This statement is mandatory.

In this chapter we begin with observations about the changing attitudes of companies in assuming social programs. We then discuss major pressures on companies to meet social demands, what they are doing to determine which ones to address, and how they are implementing programs.

Changing Attitudes toward Undertaking Social Programs

As pointed out in the last chapter, there is general acceptance in society today, including most business managers, that business enterprises do have social responsibilities. Precisely what they are and whether and to what extent a corporation should accept them are complex and controversial questions. Attitudes of corporate managers to such questions have changed significantly in recent years.

Two evolving attitudes are of most significance here. The first is that more corporations are adopting a proactive strategy to undertaking and implementing social programs. The second is that more corporate managers believe this will benefit their company.

Patterns of Social Response

These views are not accepted by all managers nor for all demands made on an individual company, even in the most enlightened firm. For example, corporate response to pressures to undertake social programs can be classified into six broad basic categories, as follows.

First is *rejection,* a strategy in which a company denies any responsibility for taking action on a social issue. Although Philip Morris conducts extensive

---

[4]Ibid.
[5]Ibid.

voluntary social programs to help communities and funds a wide range of charities, it rejects demands to stop advertising cigarettes. Sometimes a strategy of rejection is justified, as when fringe groups make unreasonable demands on corporations. In other cases, rejection and other defensive strategies invite more pressure and a fight in which the corporate image can be damaged.

Second is the *adversary* strategy, in which a firm fights to avoid having to take social actions but will, under severe pressure, grudgingly give in. The National Highway Traffic Safety Administration (NHTSA) told Chrysler Corp. in 1996 to recall more than 91,000 Chryslers and Dodges because of unsafe seat belts. Chrysler told the agency it would not comply because it believed the belts were safe. The result was continuing controversy between Chrysler and the government. In August 1998, Chrysler was fined $800,000 for disobeying NHTSA's order. Chrysler said it would appeal this decision made by a U.S. District Court judge after two years' litigation.

Third is a *resistance* strategy in which a corporation may make token moves or act slowly to satisfy demands that it considers are beyond its social responsibilities. Animal rights activists have complained that discarded Yoplait containers endangered skunks and have asked General Mills to redesign the containers. The Animal Protection Institute says that every year about 100 skunks die because the container's rim curves inward and traps the skunks when they poke their nose and head inside. Some modification of the container was made by General Mills, but a spokesperson for the Institute said skunks were still at risk because the new design continued to be dangerous to the animals. General Mills said it was impractical to make the containers larger, which the Institute urged, because that might entrap larger animals.[6]

Fourth is *compliance.* In this posture the company simply decides to abide by a government request or a reasonable demand of some stakeholder group. For most government regulations, of course, companies have little choice but to comply to avoid penalties.

Fifth is the *accommodation* strategy in which a firm voluntarily undertakes social programs to meet public expectations. Firms in this category do not oppose, strongly resist, or act reluctantly. They develop social programs to meet the observed or expressed needs of communities. Hewlett-Packard, for example, is responsive to needs of universities for advanced computer equipment. Coca-Cola is responsive to civil rights causes.

Sixth is the *proaction* strategy in which a company takes actions designed to address potential future stakeholder demands or other pressures. Polaroid, for example, has developed a program that groups chemicals it uses into toxicity categories and develops plans to reduce or eliminate them. In this way, the company may avoid future demands for such action. Management also

---

[6]Susan Abram, "Yogurt Container Redesigned, but Animal Advocates Turn Up Their Noses," *Los Angeles Times,* July 22, 1998.

found it saved the company money.[7] Procter & Gamble expresses the attitude of many managers about proactive programs in these words:

> . . . we often go beyond what is required by law in how we treat our employees, the environment and the communities where we live. When we see things that need changing, we work within the system of established laws and regulations of the duly constituted government.[8]

Pressures for Undertaking Social Programs

There is literally no end to the actions that individuals and organized groups want corporations to take. The point is underscored in Figure 6-1, which shows major areas of pressures on companies to undertake social programs. In each area there are many specific needs and demands. The areas identified are not mutually exclusive. Thus, demands for environmental action may be made by government agencies, interest groups, sometimes stockholders, and, on occasion, competitive situations. With this chart, it is easy to visualize the huge number of potential demands placed on a large multinational corporation. Here are a few.

Government Programs

Governments (domestic and foreign) are the most significant forces pressuring business for social programs. Most government pressures concern compliance with existing regulations. But governments are also major sources of potential rules, a fact with which business must be concerned. Governments ask businesses to volunteer to help them with their problems. In January 1997, for example, President Clinton was joined by former president George Bush at a White House "summit" to launch a program to boost corporate and private volunteer efforts. Retired Army General Colin Powell agreed to lead the effort. Companies immediately responded. Columbia/HCA Healthcare said it would immunize 1 million children by 2000. AT&T pledged $150 million to connect 110,000 schools to the Internet. KPMG pledged 160,000 hours and $20 million to paint classrooms, renovate playgrounds, and tutor children in 1,000 communities.[9]

President Clinton in April 1997 announced a coalition of industry, human rights, and labor groups to end sweatshops. Foreign governments exert pressures on companies to abide by codes of conduct that they and international

---

[7]James Maxwell, Sandra Rothenberg, Forrest Brisco, and Alfred Marcus, "Green Schemes: Corporate Environmental Strategies and Their Implementation," *California Management Review,* Spring 1997.

[8]Procter & Gamble, "Our Role in Society," http://www.pg.com/docCommunity/activity/index.html.

[9]Margaret Carlson, "Colin Powell Finds a Cause Worthy of His Star Power—Calling on America to Volunteer," *Time,* March 17, 1997.

FIGURE 6-1

Clusters of pressures for business to undertake social programs.

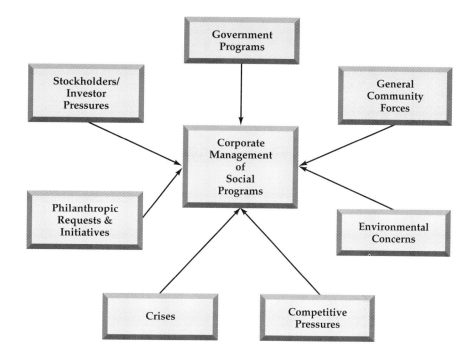

organizations have drafted.[10] These codes are heavily weighted with broad charges on corporations to respect human rights and social justice, pay "fair" wages, protect the environment, ensure the health and safety of workers, improve worker living conditions, behave ethically, and so on. Beyond the pressure upon corporations to respect these codes, countries are making more specific demands in areas such as these.

Community Interests and Demands

Corporate managers realize that their companies will not prosper in unhealthy communities. They therefore undertake many programs of direct benefit to the communities in which they operate. Programs can range widely, from helping to rebuild disadvantaged communities to providing executive talents to local governments. Procter & Gamble's contributions in the United States amounted to $45.6 million in 1997. In addition it contributed $7 million of products, equipment, and personnel. This supported a wide range of activities from scholarships for talented children of P&G employees to civic organizations.[11]

---

[10]For details of many codes, see *Principles for Global Corporate Responsibility: Bench Marks for Measuring Business Performance,* New York: Interfaith Center on Corporate Responsibility, 1998.

[11]Procter & Gamble, "Summary of Procter & Gamble 1996–97 Contributions," http://www.pg.com/docCommunity/activity/index.html.

As U.S. corporations do more business abroad, their contributions to the communities in which they operate have risen substantially. A study of The Conference Board revealed a wide range of programs in foreign communities: for example, "creating scholarship programs that allow poor but deserving students in Korea, Malaysia, and Mexico to study engineering at local educational institutions" and, in another case, "providing computers to the New Zealand Symphony orchestra to enable it to manage its business more effectively."[12]

Environmental Concerns

Most of the environmental programs of corporations result from standards established by government agencies, especially the Environmental Protection Agency. Many corporations understand the need to improve the quality of the environment. In 1992, Bristol-Myers Squibb launched a new strategic direction for worldwide operations, called "Environment 2000." The goals were set to prevent pollution, minimize waste, and reduce use of scarce resources while maintaining product quality and market competitiveness. Central in its planning is the examination of every aspect of the company's business for each stage of a product's life cycle. This means from product development through marketing, manufacturing, packaging, sales and distribution, consumer use, and final disposition of the product.[13]

Competitive Pressures

Some companies have found that by eliminating toxic wastes, they can reduce their costs and thereby strengthen their competitive position. Procter & Gamble found that when it sought to improve the recyclability of its packaging, it was able to reduce costs with alternative designs and packing materials. The company estimated it saved $300 million between 1994 and 1995 through waste and material loss reductions. Its 1997/98 goal was to introduce packaging reduction programs to eliminate 22 million pounds of materials.[14] Some companies believe that by taking social actions, they can improve their image and thereby advance their competitive position.

Stockholder/Investor Pressures

Large stockholders such as pension funds have long-range interests in the financial success of their investments. In this light, some of them exert pressure on corporations to respond appropriately to community social interests. For example, shareholders of PepsiCo launched a campaign to force the company to pull

---

[12]The Conference Board, *Benchmarking Corporate International Contributions,* New York: The Conference Board, 1996, p. 17.

[13]Thomas M. Hellman, "Integrating the Environment into Business Planning," Report No. 1066, New York: The Conference Board, 1994.

[14]Procter & Gamble, http://www.pg.com/docInfo/enviro/goals.htm.

out of Myanmar because of the human rights violations of the military regime in that country. Franklin Research & Development Corp. examined the opinions of PepsiCo shareholders and found almost unanimous belief that doing business in Myanmar was immoral. They said, among other things, that consumers were boycotting PepsiCo beverages and the losses that created were greater than any gains from sales in Myanmar. PepsiCo stopped doing business in Myanmar.[15]

Philanthropic Requests and Initiatives

Today, as public funding for charitable causes has been restrained, there is increasing pressure for greater giving by the private sector. Corporations have responded, as will be discussed later in the chapter.

Crises

The lesson of experience is clear. Companies that do not plan to deal with crises may suffer seriously. So crisis management is an area where proactive preparation may prevent a crisis or deal with it effectively if it comes.

How Do Companies Evaluate These Pressures?

There is no one simple way to evaluate the many demands on a typical large company. In some cases, a CEO may make a decision without consulting anyone in the company.[16] In a large corporation, there are many staffs that are concerned not only with evaluation of proposals made to the company but also with generating proposals of their own. For example, a Community Affairs Department staff might be concerned about demands from all the communities in which the company operates. This staff might receive recommendations from local managers to evaluate. The Public Affairs Department also often gets involved in this process. The Manufacturing Department deals with issues concerned with establishing production facilities in disadvantaged areas. The Purchasing Department evaluates ways to help minority businesses by purchasing their products. Employees also often get involved in the process. Outside consultants can be engaged in evaluation. In some companies, the evaluation and methods of implementation are coordinated in a central corporate or division planning system.

A Conceptual Model of the Corporate Planning Process

Figure 6-2 shows the sequence of events in a central corporate planning process. While this is a conceptual model, it is also operational. The model is

---

[15]Louisa Wah, "Treading the Sacred Ground," *American Management Association International, Management Review,* July/August 1998.

[16]Mark P. Sharfman, "The Effects of Managerial Values on Social Issues Evaluation: An Empirical Examination," *Academy of Management Proceedings '97,* Boston, August 8–13, 1997.

FIGURE 6-2

*Model of a
corporate planning
process.*

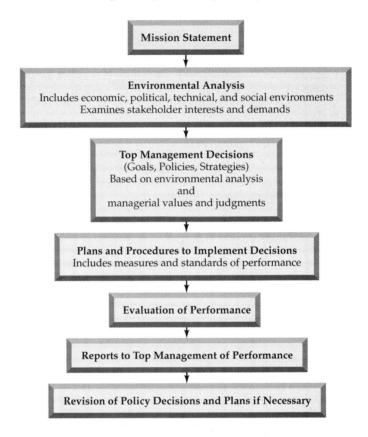

an oversimplified sketch of what usually is a complex and time-consuming process. But it is more or less followed in most companies in one form or another. Actual practices vary widely.

In this process, decisions with respect to social programs are but one part of a much larger effort that covers all major activities of an enterprise. Decisions with respect to social activities, which are our concern here, can be and are made in this system. In larger corporations, however, there are usually many different types of social activities, and they may be evaluated and implemented in different ways. Many of them, even when following different decision paths, are coordinated with other departments and planning systems.

Implementation Procedures Vary with Types of Social Programs

Alternative implementation procedures are followed for various types of social programs. These include, for example, aiding educational institutions,

K through 12 as well as universities; giving equipment and/or products; funding medical research; working in partnerships with other companies; giving charitable contributions; lending executives to local governments; developing employee volunteer programs; installing pollution controls; recycling materials used in production and product packaging; and preventing teen pregnancies. Simple programs of cash gifts to the local YWCA or a community church involve less complicated implementation procedures than engaging in partnership with other companies to improve the community educational system. Space does not permit an extended description of all these alternative programs. We choose only the following for further details: issues management, crisis management, corporate/strategic philanthropy, and education.

Issues Management

In the 1970s there arose an atmosphere of hostility to corporations and their products. Critics of the corporation were organizing product boycotts, filing law-suits, igniting adverse publicity, and pressuring legislators for new business regulations. Managers reacted to this environment by developing strategies to respond to the issues before they resulted in harm to the company. This was called *issues management.* The main purpose of issues management at that time was narrowly defined. It was to identify issues that could result in legislative action that would restrict a corporation and to forge strategies to counter them. Since then a second definition has evolved. This is the view that issues management means the identification of all important environmental issues of concern to the company and the methods to deal with them. The implementation of action could follow many different procedures, as described throughout this chapter.

Today perhaps one-third of the larger companies have issues management programs conforming to the narrow definition. There are enough issues management practitioners to have their own organization, The Issues Management Council, which numbers several thousand participants in its activities.

The importance of issues management is clear. There is literally no end to the list of actions that individuals and organized groups want business to take. Some of them, if not addressed, may result in severe damage to business. It therefore becomes very important for a company to identify critical issues and decide what action, if any, should be taken.

The Issues Management Process

If the company adopts the narrow definition of issues management, the process follows the life cycle of an issue. There is general agreement about

FIGURE 6-3

Issue life cycle.

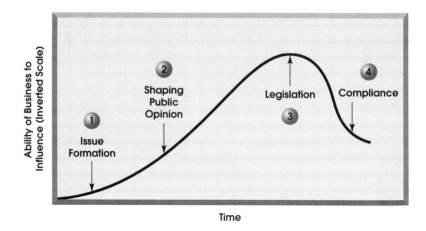

the stages of an issues life cycle but no consensus of the precise details.[17] The conceptual steps, which are also generally followed in practice, are shown in simplified form in Figure 6-3.[18]

Issue Formation.   The first step in issues management is to identify issues that may require company action. This may not be easy. Some issues, such as activities of an activist group focused on the company, may be obvious. Others, however, currently may be vague, have little focus, and have no clear dimension of urgency. These may turn out to be serious. Many important issues do not suddenly appear. There are underling forces and changes in society that may lead to problems that demand concerted attention either by business acting alone or by new government regulations. These conditions may continue for years before there is sufficient public agreement that something should be done. There are many illustrations in our history. For example, in the latter part of the nineteenth century, the merger of companies into giant monopolies at first generated no public concern. Eventually, however, public outrage at their perceived excesses led to government antitrust controls.

Today a large company is faced with hundreds of issues that could impact its operations immediately or sometime in the future. There are many ways to make early identification. An issues management staff, of course, can do this. This staff might be helped by committees. In Weyerhaeuser and Procter & Gamble, issues management program committees are employed. Outside consultants may help.

---

[17]For an early listing, see James E. Post, *Corporate Behavior and Social Change,* Reston, Va.: Reston Publishing Company, 1978. For a later exposition of steps, see Barbara Bigelow, Liam Fahey, and John Mahon, *A Typology of Issue Evolution,* Monograph No. 5, in a Series on Issues Management, Leesburg, Va.: The Issue Exchange, circa 1995.

[18]See, for example, Gary O'Malley, "Issue Management Adds Value at Weyerhaeuser," *Corporate Public Issues and Their Management,* 21, no. 18, 1997; and Deborah D. Anderson, "Key Concepts in Anticipatory Issues Management," *Corporate Environmental Strategy, The Journal of Environmental Leadership,* Autumn 1997. The latter article explains the system at Procter & Gamble Company.

Methodology in Making Evaluations of Social Issues

The palette of analytical techniques that can be employed in making evaluations is large, ranging from the intuitive search to comprehensive, systematic, and interdisciplinary computer models. In a comprehensive analysis, a great many separate techniques can be employed. Space and time allow us to mention but a few of the methodologies.

Intuitive Search.   For analyses in which the dominant focus is sociopolitical, both short- and long-range, the most widely employed method by far is the intuitive search. This technique is used by all managers who concern themselves with the changing environment. It involves a random, unsystematic, qualitative search for information, by means of which the manager comes to conclusions about forces in the environment of concern to him or her and the company. The selection of information and its evaluation are based upon experience, judgment, insight, and "feel." When done by experienced managers who continuously survey the evolving environment, it is more powerful than any other technique.

Scenarios.   These are credible descriptions of the future based on careful analysis of complex, interacting forces. They are not predictions of the future but disciplined and structured judgments of future possibilities. They set forth fundamental projections about anticipated trends and their outcomes. Generally, they describe different possible pictures, or alternatives. They are stories of what might happen in the future.[19] Scenarios can be used to look at possible social, political, and ecological events, but more frequently they embrace all relevant environmental forces. They can be made for rather narrow subjects, such as the future of the automobile, or for more comprehensive events such as the outlook for family life in the United States in the year 2025.

Scenarios have been an important part of strategic management at Royal Dutch/Shell for more than twenty-five years. Indeed, this company was one of the originators and perfecters of this methodology. This company has a staff with responsibility for scenario planning and is continuously engaged in this activity.[20] Many of our large corporations either prepare scenarios with their own staffs or employ outside consultants to work with staff to create scenarios for their management. Government agencies also use scenarios to look ahead. For example, Battelle consultants worked with the Los Angeles Department of

---

[19]It should be noted that the nomenclature of assessments or projections of sociopolitical phenomena varies widely among academicians and practitioners. For example, scenarios have been referred to as futures research, futures explorations, alternative futures, survey research, scanning, exploratory planning, vision, and environmental forces.

[20]See Peter Schwartz, *The Art of the Long View*, New York: Doubleday Currency, 1991. Schwartz helped Shell establish its scenarios, and this book contains a detailed series of steps in producing scenarios. For a current account of Shell's development of scenarios, see John Elkington and Alex Trisoglio, "Developing Realistic Scenarios for the Environment: Lessons from Brent Spart," *Long Range Planning*, December 1996.

Figure 6-4

Probability/impact matrix.

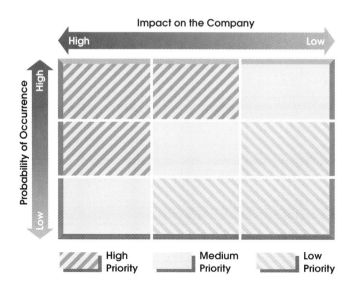

Water and Power to prepare scenarios concerning energy requirements for Los Angeles by the year 2007.[21]

Probability/Impact Matrix.   In this technique, events foreseen for the future are analyzed in terms of their probability and potential impact on the company. The matrix used is shown in Figure 6-4. This is a straightforward but really powerful tool. If an evaluation places an issue, likely occurrence, or trend in the upper left corner of the matrix, it should be a matter of concern to a company. If, on the other hand, an event is judged to fall in the lower right-hand corner, it will be given a low priority for action. Forces falling in the medium-priority areas raise questions about what action, if any, should be taken. The General Electric Company used a matrix like this for a number of years with significant results.

Setting Priorities.   Once issues are identified, priorities must be set to focus on those of most immediate or long-range impact on the company. Weyerhaeuser uses criteria to identify and analyze the most important ones. Issues are chosen for further analysis if (1) they have an important impact (positive or negative) on the company, (2) there is a high likelihood of public or government action, (3) the company's participation can influence the outcome, and (4) there is potential for divergent views within the company.[22]

Once priorities are decided, then strategies for company action can be determined. The first decision, of course, is to determine whether the company should do anything currently. If so, then there are a great many options. One is to act before an issue gets to the point of hearings and legislation. In 1993 Home

---

[21]Wally Wood, "So Where Do We Go from Here?" *Across the Board,* March 1997.
[22]O'Malley, "Issue Management Adds Value," p. 106.

Depot, a worldwide home-supply chain, mailed a questionnaire to its 300 foreign suppliers asking whether they employed children and/or prison convicts. A reply was demanded within seventy-two hours. Home Depot took this action because the media were accusing some U.S. companies of purchasing products from foreign enterprises that employed children as young as nine years old. Home Depot wanted to make sure that its own suppliers were free of child labor or other rights abuses. The company obviously wished to avoid charges that it was selling products made under such circumstances. This is by no means an isolated case of preemptive action by a company to avoid damaging publicity.

Shaping Public Opinion. During this phase of the life cycle, the company has a free hand in devising policies to deal with controversial social issues. It can conduct a wide range of publicity campaigns, including advocacy advertising, press releases, public policy speeches by managers and staffs, public reports and studies, and participation in TV and radio talk shows. The actions chosen should, of course, be coordinated throughout the company.

Legislation. When the issue moves into legislative hearings and the drafting of bills, a company has fewer options, but still some powerful ones. To influence the legislative process, activities may include coalition building with other like-minded companies and groups, lobbying, making political contributions, and issuing public statements. The firm also can challenge the legality of a law when it is being drafted.

Compliance. Finally, when laws are passed, options are limited to methods of compliance and engaging in litigation. After a bill has become law, corporations can and do seek to influence the drafting of detailed rules to implement the law and the way regulators go about implementing the rules. Also, a company may marshal its resources to attempt a revision of the law.

Crisis Management

Crisis management arises when some event becomes dramatically critical to the stability or survival of a company. An example that did much to initiate crisis management occurred in 1982 to Johnson & Johnson. The company was shocked to learn that someone in the Chicago area had injected deadly poison into capsules of its painkiller Extra Strength Tylenol. Tragically eight people died after taking only one capsule apiece. J&J immediately went into action. A top executive was named to head a committee to deal with the crisis, all Tylenol capsules were removed from the market, and the company executives made themselves available to the media to respond to massive consumer concerns and interest. Heretofore, the company had remained aloof from the media. But not with this crisis. The team brought in others from around the company to design a new "tamper-resistant" package. This was marketed, but unfortunately in 1986 another capsule was filled with poison and one person died. Lessons learned in the earlier crisis helped in this crisis. The capsule form of pill was abandoned and J&J decided to make a solid, smooth, capsule-shaped pill that would be difficult to contaminate. The monetary costs of these crises to J&J were about $500 million. No estimate exists, of course, for the costs of the deaths, the emotional strains of the families, and consumer anxieties. This contrasts with a number of other crises where the managements of the companies involved were unprepared and did not deal well with the crisis. Many families of the victims of the TWA 800 crash in 1996 did not think that TWA management responded promptly to their concerns.[23]

There are many different types of crises, and they range widely in their potential impact on a company. For instance, one can include product or service defects, sabotage, natural disasters, industrial accidents, and unexpected substantial pollution of air or water.[24] Crisis management is as necessary to nonprofit organizations as to profit enterprises.[25]

At no time in our past history have the probabilities of such crises been greater for corporations. There is no way to forecast the type and timing of crises that could have serious or even terminal implications for a company. But they do occur, and wise managements lay plans to meet them on a when-as-and-if basis.

Here are three basic conceptual steps companies take in preparing for crises:

First, assess realistic possibilities of crises. It is especially important to identify, if possible, warning signs of trouble ahead. J&J, of course, had no warning signs. But in other crises there were. For example, there were warnings that dangerous leaks might occur in the Union Carbide plant in Bhopal, India. When a major leak did occur, thousands of people were killed or injured. Evaluations in this step can be similar to those made in the first step in issues management noted above.

Second, prepare plans for meeting the crisis when it occurs. Usually, in the event of a severe crisis such as that described for J&J, a top-management team is identified to go into action. For a major fire in the computer room, a different, more detailed type of plan might be made, such as making arrangements with another company to use its computers, or duplicating critical records and locating them outside the company.

We do not mean that a set of plans must be prepared to be followed without deviation. The idea here is to prepare an organization to think about crises and to be ready to act appropriately in an emergency. As Christine M. Pearson and Ian I. Mitroff note, on the basis of interviews in 200 companies, "A fixed preparation for all crises is not a sensible target. However, a systematic,

---

[23]Kathleen Flynn, "Keeping Families in the Dark," *New York Times,* July 23, 1996.

[24]For examples of many actual crises, see Michael Regester and Judy Larkin, *Risk Issues and Crisis Management: A Casebook of Best Practice,* London: Kogan Page Limited, 1997; Ian I. Mitroff and Ralph H. Kilmann, *Corporate Tragedies: Product Tampering, Sabotage, and Other Catastrophes,* New York: Praeger, 1984; Steven Fink, *Crisis Management: Planning for the Inevitable,* New York: Amacom, 1986; and Gerald C. Meyers, *When It Hits the Fan,* Boston: Houghton Mifflin, 1986.

[25]See, for example, Judith Blumenthal, "Crisis Management in University Environments," *Journal of Management Inquiry,* September 1995.

integrative process of crisis management is a proper and attainable goal. Anything less invites disaster."[26] This suggests the following step.

Third, game the crisis. This follows the military practice of simulating situations. A scenario of a crisis is prepared and the team goes into action just as if a crisis actually occurred. This means, for example, not only the event itself, but make-believe frightened and irate consumers (if the crisis deals with a product), TV cameras, newspaper reporters, and coordinating action required by the crisis among major functions (production, marketing, finance, etc.).[27]

Hopefully, when a crisis does actually take place, the plans and experience with gaming will provide the specifications for getting the coordinating team in place, satisfactorily dealing with the crisis, and creating the means to repair or alleviate the damage to the company.

Corporate Philanthropy

Through most of our corporate history, businesses have made charitable contributions for social purposes, but the amounts were not large.[28] One reason was that courts held that such actions by a business were ultra vires acts (beyond the powers of the corporation) and illegal.

The first major break from the narrow interpretation of the legality of corporate giving came in 1935 with the passage of the Revenue Act of that year. Congress made it possible for corporations to deduct from taxable earnings their charitable contributions, up to 5 percent of net profits before taxes. (This was raised to 10 percent by the Economic Recovery Tax Act of 1981.) The legal requirement that directors of corporations must exercise sound business judgment and act in a fiduciary capacity to corporate interests was not relaxed.

The legality of using corporate funds for purposes other than clearly charitable giving under the Revenue Act, however, continued to be very doubtful, and corporations were not particularly generous for fear of stockholder suits. The legal restraint on corporate giving was removed in 1953 by the case of *A. P. Smith v. Barlow* in which the Supreme Court refused to review a decision of the highest court in New Jersey allowing the A. P. Smith Company to give Princeton University money for general maintenance. The New Jersey Supreme Court, affirming a lower-court decision, said in part, "Such giving may well be regarded as a major,

---

[26]Christine M. Pearson and Ian I. Mitroff, "From Crisis Prone to Crisis Prepared: A Framework for Crisis Management," *Academy of Management Executive,* February 1993, p. 29. For another excellent article, see Christine M. Pearson and Judith A. Clair, "Framing Crisis Management," *Academy of Management Review,* January 1998.

[27]For other steps, see Pearson and Mitroff, "From Crisis Prone to Crisis Prepared," p. 58; Ian I. Mitroff, Paul Shrivastava, and Firdaus E. Udwadia, "Effective Crisis Management," *The Academy of Management Executive,* November 1987; Ian I. Mitroff, L. Katharine Harrington, and Eric Gai, "Thinking About the Unthinkable," *Across the Board,* September 1996; and Jennifer R. Hickman and William "Rick" Crandall, "Before Disaster Hits: A Multifaceted Approach to Crisis Management," *Business Horizons,* March–April 1997.

[28]See Morrell Heald, *The Social Responsibilities of Business: Company and Community, 1900–1960,* Cleveland, Ohio: Press of Case Western Reserve University, 1970.

though unwritten, corporate power. It is even more than that. In the Court's view of the case, it amounts to a solemn duty."[29]

Corporate Philanthropic Allocations

Corporate giving, which includes cash (from the company as well as its foundations) as well as in-kind gifts such as company products, was $8.2 billion in 1997, a 7.5 percent rise from 1996. This compares with total individual giving of $109.2 billion in 1997. The top five corporate givers were: Merck & Co., $140.5 million; IBM Corporation, $100.8 million; Johnson & Johnson, $88.5 million; Pfizer Inc., $85.5 million; and Hewlett-Packard Co., $71.6 million.

In 1997 corporate contributions were distributed as follows: education, 30 percent; health and human services, 25 percent; unallocated 17 percent; civic and community, 10 percent; culture and arts, 9 percent; and all other, 9 percent. This pattern of distribution has been rather steady for a number of years.

Few individual corporations have ever come close to giving the 10 percent of their pretax revenues to philanthropic purposes as permitted by law. Actually, business contributions have averaged between 1 and 2 percent of pretax revenue over the past twenty years. In only one year was it over 2 percent; that was in 1986 when it was 2.38 percent.[30]

It is worth mentioning here that throughout our history, wealthy business-people have contributed large fortunes for philanthropic purposes. Among the earliest and largest were Rockefeller and Carnegie. More recently, a number of large foundations have been created. An example is J. Paul Getty's endowment for the arts (now estimated at $7 billion). He made his fortune in oil. David Packard, cofounder of Hewlett-Packard, recently established the Packard Foundation with a grant of $6.6 billion.

The accompanying box shows a list of the largest individual donors to philanthropic purposes in 1997. The individual gifts are impressive, especially those of Ted Turner and George Soros, both of which represented a substantial share of their net assets. When the contributions of Turner and Soros are eliminated from the list, the result is a much different relationship between gift and assets. Wayne M. O'Leary calculated that the other eight gave in 1997 0.6 percent of their total net assets. Bill Gates, the richest man in the world, gave 0.53 percent of his net holdings. Many billionaires gave even less. Warren Buffett, the second richest person in the United States gave less than 0.06 percent of his assets to charity.[31]

---

[29]*A. P. Smith Manufacturing Company* v. *Barlow et al.*, 26 N.J. Super. 106 (1953), 98 Atl. (1962). For an excellent short article on the history of corporate philanthropy during the 1883–1953 period, see Mark Sharfman, "Changing Institutional Rules: The Evolution of Corporate Philanthropy, 1883–1953," *Business & Society*, December 1994.

[30]*Giving USA 1998, The Annual Report on Philanthropy for the Year 1997*, New York: AAFRC Trust for Philanthropy, Inc., 1998.

[31]Wayne M. O'Leary, "Those Generous Billionaires," *The Progressive Populist*, March 1998, p. 23.

The Ten Top Philanthropists of 1997

Fortune magazine identified the top 25 philanthropists of 1997. Altogether they gave $3.3 billion, more than double the amount of the top 25 of 1996. Maybe wealthy people were stimulated by Ted Turner, who, when he announced a gift of $1 billion, said that rich people ought to give more. Maybe there were other reasons for the increase, such as recognition or favorable tax laws that encouraged giving. At any rate, here are the top 10 as listed by *Fortune.*

Ted Turner. $1 billion. Owner of sizeable amount of Time Warner stock. Gave 11 percent of his stock holdings to the United Nations. He also gives grants through a foundation for environmental causes and family planning.

Kathryn Albertson. $660 million. Heir to Albertson's grocery. The gift was to support public education in Idaho.

George Soros. $500 million. To Russia for, among other things, health and educational programs necessary to create a functioning democracy. He has long been interested in supporting democratic institutional developments. He also gave $25 million in support of education and drug policy initiatives.

Bill Gates. $200 million to Gates Library Foundation to provide Internet access to public libraries. He also gave $10 million to Lakeside School for the same purpose.

Leonard Abramson. $100 million to the University of Pennsylvania for cancer research. He is the founder of U.S. Healthcare.

Michael & Jane Eisner. $89 million. To the Eisner Foundation to support underprivileged children. He is CEO of Disney.

Mitchell Wolfson Jr. $75 million to Florida International University. His fortune came from the sale of Wometco Enterprises, an entertainment conglomerate.

Phyllis Wattis. $70 million. She is the great-granddaughter of Brigham Young. Her husband sold his Utah Mining & Construction Co. to General Electric in 1976, and she is a large holder of General Electric stock. This gift was to various cultural institutions in the Bay Area and to the Salt Lake City museum.

Raymond Nasher. $50 million to the Nasher Foundation. A real estate developer, he made this gift to the foundation to build a facility to house his sculpture collection.

Dwight Opperman. $50 million to Drake University. His fortune was from the sale of West Publishing (for $3.4 billion), in which he was a large shareholder.

Source: Anne Faircloth and Caroline Bollinger, "*Fortune's* 40 Most Generous Americans," *Fortune,* February 2, 1998.

The Story of George Feeney

Since 1984 George Feeney, 65, has given away over $610 million. In a technique reminiscent of the old television program "The Millionaire," he donates the money anonymously using cashier's checks that do not reveal the name of the source.

Feeney, who grew up in a working-class neighborhood in New Jersey, came to own 38.75 percent of the Duty Free Shoppes Ltd. stores found in airports. In 1984 he decided that he "had enough money."[32] Without even informing his partner in the business, he set up two foundations in Bermuda, where they would not be subject to U.S. laws that require disclosure of contributions. Into them, he irrevocably transferred his ownership interest in the Duty Free Shoppes. At the time this was worth about $500 million; today the foundations have assets of $3.5 billion.

Feeney now could be worth over $4 billion, but his personal assets total only about $5 million. According to a friend, he does not own a house or car and wears a watch worth about $15. He prefers casual clothes and calls himself a "shabby dresser."[33]

Most of Feeney's gifts have gone to hospitals, universities, and mainstream charities, although he has given $280,000 to the Irish Republican Army on condition it not subsidize violent activity.

His passion for secrecy stems from a desire to live life without constant importuning from seekers of funds and his belief in the teachings of Maimonides, a twelfth-century philosopher who taught that the highest form of giving was anonymous and selfless. The staff at Feeney's foundations carefully scrutinizes programs that get donations. He sometimes attends meetings with potential recipients who do not recognize the nondescript member of the team as the benefactor himself.

Feeney's charitable giving only came to light in 1997 when Duty Free Shoppe's Ltd. was sold and a lawsuit regarding the sale was about to make public his financial affairs. He talked to the *New York Times*, but even then refused to have his picture taken.

Although Feeney is unique, there is a tradition of anonymous contribution in American history. Another example is Chester F. Carlson, the inventor of xerography, who gave away $300 million in the 1960s (in today's dollars, about $1 billion).

Community Economic Development Programs (CED)

A large part of philanthropic giving goes for community activities. Companies also contribute cash from operating budgets, products, and employee time. CED programs often go far beyond the run-of-the-mill charity drives, pet projects, and ephemeral undertakings. The forms of these programs vary widely among companies, but almost all of them involve partnerships with other corporations, governments, community-based groups, and national nonprofit

---

[32]Judith Miller, "He Gave Away $600 Million, and No One Knew," *New York Times*, January 23, 1997, p. A13.

[33]David Cay Johnston, "An Entrepreneur Driven to Repay a Debt to Society," *New York Times*, January 23, 1997, p. A13.

organizations. Within companies, the organizational structures to undertake CED programs vary widely, but most of them involve other functions, such as public affairs, human resources, purchasing, finance, manufacturing, legal, real estate, and marketing.

The methods of implementing CED programs range from a passive contribution, such as Alcoa's donation of its thirty-one-story headquarters building in Pittsburgh to a group of community development organizations, to complex partnership arrangements. A good example is the activities of Deere & Company to rejuvenate downtown Moline, Illinois. In the late 1980s, the area was devastated—many buildings were abandoned, infrastructure was crumbling, obsolete factories were operating only part time, and retail merchants were losing customers. Today the area is thriving with new construction, green and inviting spaces, tourists, and jobs. This was made possible by leadership of Deere & Company in partnership with many people and organizations.

Many other companies have initiated similar programs. Lincoln National Life Insurance Company, for example, initiated a substantial program to address problems of youth violence, drugs, guns, and vocational education in Fort Wayne, Indiana. Pfizer Inc. started a major CED program in Williamsburg, Brooklyn; and Binney & Smith (makers of Crayola products) assumed a lead role in rejuvenating downtown Easton, Pennsylvania. Many companies through their foundations or divisions have organized programs by means of which employees engage in voluntary community services. The Polaroid Foundation and the Mitsubishi Electric America Foundations are two illustrations. Why do companies make major commitments to CED programs? Figure 6-5 answers this question for 88 *Fortune* 500 companies in a study made by The Conference Board. This study is also the source of the above material concerning CEDs.[34]

Relating Philanthropy to Self-Interest

Corporate philanthropic giving did expand following the *A. P. Smith* decision. Much of it went to organized charities without reference to corporate interests. But in recent years, more and more contributions have been made to benefit directly corporate interests. This has been labeled *strategic philanthropy,* a phrase we think was first expressed by Craig Smith, president of Corporate Citizen.[35] Strategic philanthropy tries to tie giving to the major strategies and goals of a company.[36]

Here are a few examples of aligning philanthropy with corporate goals. Coca-Cola launched a multi-million-dollar sponsorship of Boys & Girls Clubs

---

[34]The Conference Board, *Building the Corporate Community Economic Development Team,* Research Report 1205-98-RR, New York: The Conference Board, 1998.

[35]Craig Smith, "The New Corporate Philanthropy," *Harvard Business Review,* May–June 1994, p. 105.

[36]See The Conference Board, *The Corporate Contributions Plan: From Strategy to Budget: A Research Report,* Report Number 1192-97-RR, New York: The Conference Board, 1997.

FIGURE 6-5

Goals of CED investments.

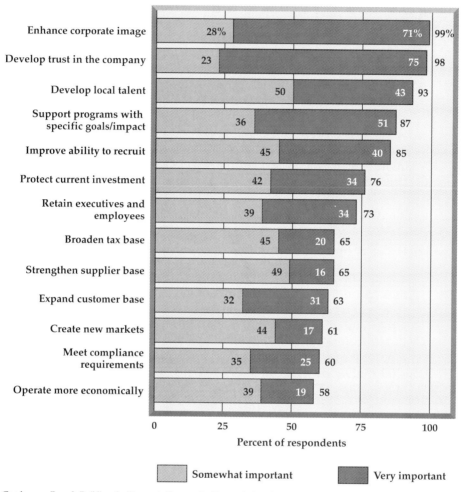

Source: The Conference Board, *Building the Corporate Community Economic Development Team,* Research Report 1205-98-RR, New York: The Conference Board, 1998, p. 14.

of America in 1997. The company believes the program will enhance its image and lift sales of Coke throughout the nation. Avon Products used to give money principally to alleviate human suffering. Now it ties its programs specifically to women, its primary customers. American Express has a program to preserve historical sites through which it hopes to increase tourism and its business. Bristol-Myers Squibb used to support almost exclusively medical research. Now the company also focuses on women's health programs, a tie to its Clairol line of women's products. Hewlett-Packard each year gives millions of dollars' worth of computers and other equipment to schools and universities, which correlates with its core business.

Cause-Related Marketing

Cause-related marketing is another type of philanthropy practiced by a number of companies. It seeks to have customers reach for products because of the maker's support of some worthwhile cause. For example, General Foods has donated 25 cents to scholarships for African American college students with the use of a specially marked coupon for Stove Top stuffing and other products. These programs have been criticized as being insincere since such a small fraction of the sales price goes to the worthy cause. However, consumers have responded favorably to many of these cause-related marketing campaigns. For some products, the programs have not affected sales.[37]

Business in Education

As noted above, the largest category of corporate philanthropy is for education. In surveying what companies are doing in this area, several conclusions seem warranted. First, managers are increasingly interested in improving education. Second, companies are contributing not only cash but also managerial and employee volunteers in support of their programs. Third, whereas in the past companies focused the major part of their educational philanthropy on higher education, they are now increasing their support to grades K through 12. Fourth, many companies have established a staff position at their headquarters to implement educational policies. Fifth, the educational programs do benefit companies in the long run, but some programs can also help companies achieve short-term goals. An example of the latter is training skilled workers for employment in the company.

Aside from cash grants, the programs being undertaken by business cover virtually every important facet of the educational system. Programs range from preventing school dropouts to broad educational reform. Employees of companies volunteer as tutors and mentors, classroom teachers, teachers of teachers, and advisers in preparing new curricula. Companies arrange partnerships with schools and form coalitions to aid education.

A good example is the CIGNA Corporation, which, through its CIGNA Foundation, has dedicated significant efforts and resources to improving educational opportunities for children. It has a multiyear cooperative partnership with five schools in Philadelphia that supply employees to the company. The partnership provides planning, financial support, and encouragement to students

---

[37]Geoffrey Smith and Ron Stodgill II, "Are Good Causes Good Marketing?" *Business Week,* March 21, 1994, p. 64.

throughout their academic careers. It contributes computers and trains students in their use. Company volunteers tutor students, help them with homework, and serve as role models. More than 6,000 students have benefited from the partnership programs.[38]

Here are a few other examples. IBM makes grants to schools to improve technical education, to stimulate improved student achievement, and to build a bridge between home and school. Procter & Gamble has many projects involving hundreds of mentors, tutors, and other volunteers. Seventeen companies (among them AT&T, General Motors Corporation, Chubb Corporation, and General Electric) have sponsored a program called INROADS in the Chicago area to aid minority students who are interested in careers in business and engineering.

Some companies have established schools to aid education. For example, Merck set up the Merck Institute for Science Education where employees train to became mentors in local schools where teachers can advance their knowledge of science. Ford Motor Company established the Ford Academy of Manufacturing Sciences at Michigan's Novi High School to prepare students for careers in manufacturing, engineering, and skilled trades.

Critics of Business Educational Activities

Not everyone approves all that business is doing for education. On the one hand are those educators who resent businesspeople "getting into our sandbox." They believe they know more about how to educate young people than people in business. There are those who seriously question the propriety of mixing business gifts that further education while advertising the company's products. When school budgets are strained, as they are today, businesses have become more aggressive in lending support for promoting their brands and products. On the other hand, there are those who not only welcome corporate support but hope it will expand.

Measuring and Evaluating Corporate Community Involvement

In the 1960s and 1970s, the idea of a *corporate social audit* was widely discussed in business and government, as well as academic circles. This was based on the concept that corporations should be held accountable for their social performance; the audit was intended to measure it.[39] The idea lost supporters but

---

[38]*CIGNA Foundation Annual Report, 1994,* Philadelphia: CIGNA Foundation, 1995, plus printed descriptions of programs.

[39]See, for example, John J. Corson and George A. Steiner, *Measuring Business's Social Performance: The Corporate Social Audit,* New York: Committee for Economic Development, 1974; and George A. Steiner, *Business and Society,* 2nd ed., Chapter 12, New York: Random House, 1975.

has been revived in different forms by some companies. Royal/Dutch Shell, as noted previously, is one of them.

Behind this trend is the fact that executives are becoming more interested in evaluating what they are getting for their strategic giving. The Alcoa Foundation has developed a practice of including goals and milestones in its grants. This places more responsibility for performance on the grantee and makes evaluation by Alcoa much easier.[40] Pfizer Inc. follows the same practice. In a survey of 177 companies by The Conference Board in 1996, 44 percent said they had some form of program evaluation and 56 percent said they conducted benchmarking exercises to determine how well they were doing. (Benchmarking is a phrase used widely in business to mean measuring one's performance against that of what they consider the best in the industry.) There were mixed levels of satisfaction expressed. Generally, the obstacles to better measurement, they said, were insufficient time, staff, and budgets. Five university professors have advanced a methodology for measuring consumer sensitivity to corporate social performance.[41] It is likely that efforts such as these will grow.

Concluding Observations

In the last chapter, the nature of and case for corporations to assume social responsibilities were made. In this chapter, in examining what corporations are actually saying and doing, it is apparent that companies in the United States not only have accepted the idea of social responsibilities but are anticipating new social demands and taking appropriate action to address them. Not only are United States–based corporations taking the lead in these trends, but they are also applying them in their foreign operations.[42] Social demands will increase in the future, which makes all the more important the type of programs examined in this chapter.

---

[40]The Conference Board, *Measuring Corporate Community Involvement,* Report No. 1169-96-RR, New York: The Conference Board, 1996.

[41]Karen Paul, Lori M. Zalka, Meredith Downes, Susan Perry, and Shawnta Friday, "U.S. Consumer Sensitivity to Corporate Social Performance," *Business and Society,* December 1997.

[42]Jeffrey E. Garten, "Globalism Doesn't Have to Be Cruel," *Business Week,* February 9, 1998, p. 26.

LEVI STRAUSS & CO. IN CHINA

I n May 1993 Levi Strauss announced that it would phase out operations in China over several years. The reason was that company values were in conflict with "pervasive human rights abuses." In 1997, however, the company decided to reenter China.

Levi Strauss has long been admired for its high social and ethical standards and the way it incorporates these values in its decisions. This case describes these values and how they were applied to doing business in China.

The Company

Levi Strauss is the largest apparel producer in the world. In 1997 it had revenues of $6.9 billion, operated in more than 50 countries, and employed over 30,000 people. There were approximately 20,500 in the Americas Division, 7,000 in the European Division, and 2,400 in the Asia Pacific Division. Its foreign operations include wholly owned-and-operated businesses, joint ventures, licensees, and distributors. It had fifty-three production facilities and thirty customer service centers in forty-six countries. The company generally manufactures goods in countries in which they are sold.

This global giant had humble beginnings. In the 1850s a Bavarian-born immigrant and dry goods merchant named Levi Strauss moved from New York to San Francisco. In San Francisco he began to make sturdy work pants from the canvas-like material he used making tents for miners. This was the origin of the pants now known throughout the world as blue jeans. Rivets were first used on the jeans in 1873 because miners complained that their pockets ripped under the weight of ore samples.

The company prospered as a privately held firm and by 1970 sales reached approximately $350 million. At that time opportunities for significant growth seemed apparent, but the company needed cash to exploit them. To finance expansion the company in 1971 offered 13 percent of its stock to the public. In 1985, however, following a year in which sales and profits dropped precipitously, the company bought back the publicly held stock for $1.45 billion. The company said this was the best way to continue its long tradition of following its basic values.

A Socially Concerned Company

Social concern began with founder Levi Strauss. For example, when the great earthquake of 1906 devastated San Francisco, Levi Strauss bought space in newspapers to notify his 350 employees that their paychecks would continue. He was one of the first to integrate his plants and he paid his employees salaries above the average for the industry. Levi Strauss was known in San Francisco as a generous supporter of charities and education.[1]

Levi Strauss's current Chairman and Chief Executive Robert D. Haas, the great-great-grandnephew of Levi Strauss, follows the founder in the tradition of corporate social responsibility. In one of his speeches, he quoted with favor from Henry David Thoreau's essay on civil disobedience a passage that argues that a corporation "has no conscience, but a corporation of conscientious men is a corporation with a conscience." This value was clearly demonstrated when, in 1997, the company decided on a substantial layoff of personnel but tempered it with a generous cash severance settlement.

In 1997 the company reported fiscal year sales of $6.9 billion, down from $7.1 in 1996. Competitors were selling comparable products at substantially lower prices than Levi Strauss and it's market share was dropping. So the company decided in November 1997 to close 11 U.S. facilities in 1998 to bring to balance a long-felt need to match manufacturing capacity with U.S. production demands and to cut costs. The discharged employees totaled 6,395, a third of the U.S. workforce. At the same time, the company said it would allocate $200 million for employee benefits and have the Levi Strauss Foundation make $8 million in grants to communities affected by plant closings. Employees were given eight months' notice; up to three weeks' severance pay per year of service; continuation of health benefits for 18 months; a $6,000 allowance for education, retraining, and other severance costs; and early retirement. Bruce Raynor, executive vice president of the Union of Needletrades, Industrial and Textile Employees, said this was "by far the best severance settlement apparel workers have ever gotten, which will enable the affected workers to move forward with their lives."[2]

Ethical and Social Responsibility Foundations of Levi Strauss & Co.

A "Mission Statement" and "Aspiration Statement" formulated in 1987 are the written foundation of Levi's ethical and social values. They read as follows:

Mission Statement
The mission of Levi Strauss & Co. is to sustain responsible commercial success as a global marketing company of branded apparel. We must balance goals of superior

---

[1]"Levi Strauss: A Biography," San Francisco, Levi Strauss & Co., undated.

[2]Quoted in David Cay Johnson, "At Levi Strauss, a Big Cutback, with Largess," *New York Times*, November 4, 1997.

profitability and return on investment, leadership market positions, and superior products and service. We will conduct our business ethically and demonstrate leadership in satisfying our responsibilities to our communities and to society. Our work environment will be safe and productive and characterized by fair treatment, teamwork, open communications, personal accountability and opportunities for growth and development.

Aspiration Statement

We all want a Company that our people are proud of and committed to, where all employees have an opportunity to contribute, learn, grow and advance based on merit, not politics or background. We want our people to feel respected, treated fairly, listened to and involved. Above all, we want satisfaction from accomplishments and friendships, balanced personal and professional lives, and to have fun in our endeavors. When we describe the kind of LS&CO. we want in the future, what we are talking about is building on the foundation we have inherited: affirming the best of our Company's traditions, closing gaps that may exist between principles and practices and updating some of our values to reflect contemporary circumstances. What type of leadership is necessary to make our Aspirations a reality?[3]

This statement is followed with details about what leadership is required to meet Levi's mission and aspiration. This includes policy with respect to employees, product, service, and foreign operations.

In the 1980s Levi Strauss moved to foreign countries to take advantage of low wages. It was obliged to do this because of severe competition in the industry and the pressure on all companies to reduce costs. In 1991 one of Levi Strauss's contractors in Saipan was accused of employing Chinese women and paying them below the island's legal minimum wage, among other violations of human rights. The contractor was fired and the company formed a committee of top managers to establish standards for its contractors in foreign countries. After nine months the committee produced a policy statement that has been slightly revised, as shown in Exhibit 1.

These statements are not rhetorical gloss at the company but are the core of decision making. Haas explained the process as follows:

Today, at Levi Strauss & Co., we base our approach to ethics upon six ethical principles—honesty, promise-keeping, fairness, respect for others, compassion and integrity. . . . We're integrating ethics with our other corporate values, which include diversity, open communications, empowerment, recognition, teamwork and honesty, into every aspect of our business—from our human resource practices to our relationships with our business partners.[4]

When the original guidelines for country engagement were completed in 1991, the company sent audit teams to inspect 700 contractors worldwide. They found that 70 percent of the contractors were in compliance with the guidelines,

---

[3]"All about Levi Strauss & Co.," *Vision: Responsible Commercial Success,* www.levistrauss.com/about/vision.html, September 20, 1998.

[4]Robert D. Haas, "Ethics—A Global Business Challenge," speech delivered before The Conference Board, New York City, May 4, 1994.

EXHIBIT 1

Terms of Engagement and Guidelines for Country Selection.

BUSINESS PARTNER TERMS OF ENGAGEMENT

Terms of Engagement address issues that are substantially controllable by our individual business partners.

We have defined business partners as contractors and subcontractors who manufacture or finish our products and suppliers who provide material (including fabric, sundries, chemicals and/or stones) utilized in the manufacture and finishing of our products.

1. ENVIRONMENTAL REQUIREMENTS

We will only do business with partners who share our commitment to the environment and who conduct their business in a way that is consistent with Levi Strauss & Co.'s Environmental Philosophy and Guiding Principles.

2. ETHICAL STANDARDS

We will seek to identify and utilize business partners who aspire as individuals and in the conduct of all their businesses to a set of ethical standards not incompatible with our own.

3. HEALTH & SAFETY

We will only utilize business partners who provide workers with a safe and healthy work environment. Business partners who provide residential facilities for their workers must provide safe and healthy facilities.

4. LEGAL REQUIREMENTS

We expect our business partners to be law abiding as individuals and to comply with legal requirements relevant to the conduct of all their businesses.

5. EMPLOYMENT PRACTICES:

We will only do business with partners whose workers are in all cases present voluntarily, not put at risk of physical harm, fairly compensated, allowed the right of free association and not exploited in any way. In addition, the following specific guidelines will be followed.

• WAGES AND BENEFITS

We will only do business with partners who provide wages and benefits that comply with any applicable law and match the prevailing local manufacturing or finishing industry practices.

• WORKING HOURS

While permitting flexibility in scheduling, we will identify prevailing local work hours and seek business partners who do not exceed them except for appropriately compensated overtime. While we favor partners who utilize less than sixty-hour work weeks, we will not use contractors who, on a regularly scheduled basis, require in excess of a sixty-hour week. Employees should be allowed at least one day off in seven.

• CHILD LABOR

Use of child labor is not permissible. Workers can be no less than 14 years of age and not younger than the compulsory age to be in school. We will not utilize partners who use child labor in any of their facilities. We support the development of legitimate workplace apprenticeship programs for the educational benefit of younger people.

• PRISON LABOR/FORCED LABOR

We will not utilize prison or forced labor in contracting relationships in the manufacture and finishing of our products. We will not utilize or purchase materials from a business partner utilizing prison or forced labor.

• DISCRIMINATION

While we recognize and respect cultural differences, we believe that workers should be employed on the basis of their ability to do the job, rather than on the basis of personal characteristics or beliefs. We will favor business partners who share this value.

• DISCIPLINARY PRACTICES

We will not utilize business partners who use corporal punishment or other forms of mental or physical coercion.

6. COMMUNITY BETTERMENT

We will favor business partners who share our commitment to contribute to the betterment of community conditions.

GUIDELINES FOR COUNTRY SELECTION

The following country selection criteria address issues which we believe are beyond the ability of the individual business partner to control.

1. BRAND IMAGE

We will not initiate or renew contractual relationships in countries where sourcing would have an adverse effect on our global brand image.

2. HEALTH & SAFETY

We will not initiate or renew contractual relationships in locations where there is evidence that Company employees or representatives would be exposed to unreasonable risk.

3. HUMAN RIGHTS

We should not initiate or renew contractual relationships in countries where there are pervasive violations of basic human rights.

4. LEGAL REQUIREMENTS

We will not initiate or renew contractual relationships in countries where the legal environment creates unreasonable risk to our trademarks or to other important commercial interests or seriously impedes our ability to implement these guidelines.

5. POLITICAL OR SOCIAL STABILITY

We will not initiate or renew contractual relationships in countries where political or social turmoil unreasonably threatens our commercial interests.

Revised 1994

25 percent were in need of improvements, and 5 percent were not in compliance. Contracts with the latter were stopped. The evaluations led to severed relations with 30 business partners and demands for changes in 120 others in various countries. For example, human rights violations were clear and pervasive in both Burma and China. Work in Burma, which was minor in total company revenues, was phased out in several months. The situation in China was more complex, and a twelve-member China Policy Group (CPG) was created in 1992 to make recommendations about what should be done.

The Situation in China

Levi Strauss had three types of arrangements in China: (1) contracts with local companies to produce a certain number of garments, (2) contracts for a company in China to import fabric for further production of garments in China, and (3) contracts for the purchase of fabrics. Although the company had been buying from China since 1986, the 1992 volume of garment purchases was only about 2 percent of Levi Strauss's total output. Fabric purchases were about the same percentage.[5] Levi Strauss purchased about 5 million items of clothing from Chinese sewing and laundry contractors with a value of around $50 million.[6]

Human rights violations were found to be widespread in China. Here are a few illustrations. Freedom of association and expression were severely restricted. Dissidents were jailed without due process and fair trial procedures. Arrests were often arbitrary and capricious. Prisoners were subject to maltreatment, sometimes torture, and impressed into forced labor. Employers were expected to help enforce the one-child-per-family law of 1979, which was designed to curb soaring population growth. Enforcement sometimes took the form of abortions and involuntary sterilization. Communist party representation on boards of directors was pressed upon companies. Communist party organization took place in the workplace, although union organizations were illegal. There was little protection of intellectual property.[7]

Conditions within individual companies varied. In general, however, they were unsatisfactory in terms of Levi's values. The specifics of conditions among Levi's contractors are not known, but studies for other companies revealed such conditions as child labor, long hours, absence of trade unions, authoritarian management, inadequate communications between managers and workers, excessive unpaid overtime often without compensation, fines for

[5]Abraham Wu, "Levi Strauss & Co. in China," S-P-13, Palo Alto, Calif.: Stanford University, Graduate School of Business, July 1994, p. 2.

[6]Jane Palley Katz, "Levi Strauss & Co.: Global Sourcing (A)," Boston, Mass.: Harvard Business School, 1995.

[7]Lawrence W. Beer, "Current Human Rights Issues in Asia," speech delivered at Lehigh University, Bethlehem, Pa., April 11, 1995.

minor infractions (such as being late to work by a few minutes), and unsafe and unhealthful conditions.

The question before Levi Strauss's top management in 1991 was: Can we operate in China without violating our policies?

U.S.-China Human Rights Issues

The decision in answer to this question must be viewed against the larger canvas of human rights issues between the United States and China. Issues concerning human rights in China first received significant attention in the federal government during the Carter administration (1976–1980). President Carter campaigned with the pledge to pressure foreign countries dependent on the United States to improve their human rights behavior. At the time, the human rights situation in China was appalling to many people, a view supported by such China observers as Amnesty International in a 1978 evaluation.[8]

Within the Carter administration, there were two distinct views concerning what the U.S. position should be with respect to human rights in China. On the one hand were those who wanted to exert as much pressure on China as possible with whatever leverage the United States had. On the other hand were those who wanted to leave human rights issues out of any negotiations with China. Their assumption was that negotiations would be more amicable and trade development would open the way for U.S. institutions to stimulate human rights advances. In mind, for example, were student exchanges that resulted in thousands of Chinese students entering our educational institutions.[9] In later years this argument evolved into the idea that peaceful trade and cultural exchanges would stimulate economic growth and, eventually, political freedom and protection of human rights. This argument continues to be advanced in human rights discussions.

Tiananmen Square

Hopes that the United States could advance human rights in China were shattered when the Chinese People's Liberation Army on the evening of June 3 and early morning of June 4, 1989, crushed a student demonstration for democracy in Tiananmen Square in Beijing. Hundreds of people were killed and thousands imprisoned. Democratic governments around the world condemned the massacre and human rights issues were brought into sharp focus in the United States. It turned out, of course, that little progress had been made following the Carter administration.

---

[8]Amnesty International, *Political Imprisonment in the People's Republic of China*, London: Amnesty International, 1978.

[9]See Richard Madsen, *China and the American Dream*, Berkeley: University of California Press, 1995, for an excellent discussion of this point.

Conflicting Views on Human Rights in the United States and China

People and governments in the United States and China see these rights in fundamentally different ways. Our way of thinking is anchored in the idea espoused by John Locke, a seventeenth-century philosopher, that all men have certain "inalienable rights to life, liberty, and the pursuit of happiness." This idea was carved in our Declaration of Independence, and in the Constitution, especially the Bill of Rights.

Views of human rights in China are derived from the philosophy of Confucius, who lived in the fourth century B.C. but whose ideas are still alive; and from the pragmatism of communist ideology. Confucius taught that the government was like a patriarch in a family. The ruler ruled and the people submitted to his authority. Society rests on the obedience of children to their parents, and wife to husband. These bedrock ideas provided justification for authoritarian government. Government under communism decides what is best for the people, the welfare of individuals is administered by the state, individuals function for the good of the whole community, and individuals themselves have few rights. The primary objective of government is to secure order in society and not individual freedom. These are oversimplified summaries of complex philosophical and political thinking but useful to understand why differences in respect for human rights developed.

Continuing Tensions between the United States and China

Tensions between the two nations following World War II continued with periodic ups and downs. Issues not only involved human rights, but trade, sales of munitions to rogue nations, nuclear testing, and geopolitics (especially with respect to Taiwan and North Korea). Up to 1994, the United States refused to grant China most-favored-nation (MFN) status until it improved its human rights behavior. (MFN status provides for substantially lower tariffs to the nation having it.) In 1994 President Clinton, under pressure from American business interests, and in recognition of the growing economic and political strength of China, delinked MFN status from China's human rights record.

This delinking was based on the idea widespread in the Carter and subsequent administrations that if economic progress takes place in China, economic freedoms inherent in the process will inevitably lead to enhancement of individual freedoms. Tiananmen Square punctured but did not destroy that assumption.[10] We will return to this issue later in the case.

China's Response to Accusations of Human Rights Abuse

Any evaluation of human rights problems must consider that within China criticism is seen as anti-Chinese. Richard Hornik, formerly *Time*'s bureau chief

---

[10]Ibid.

in Beijing and Hong Kong, says, "Simply to question the accomplishments of a 4,000-year-old civilization is taken as evidence of bias and, generally speaking, broad-gauge attacks on China's ancient political culture, particularly by foreigners, are dismissed out of hand."[11]

There is a strong belief among Chinese leaders that human rights concerns in U.S. policy toward China are used as a pretext to contain its growing geopolitical influence. There is a conviction that we wish to contain China economically, politically, and militarily. Economically, they see excessive and unjustified pressures to open their markets, to resist their entrance into the World Trade Organization, and to stop human rights abuses. Politically, they strongly resent what they see as closer relationships with Taiwan, which might lead to our recognizing that country as an independent nation. This is an idea they condemn in the strongest terms because they insist Taiwan is a renegade province and a part of China. Militarily they resent our efforts to stop their sales of munitions to aggressive countries and condemnation of their nuclear testing and their military exercises off Taiwan and in the South China Sea. The confinement strategy, they say, is confirmed by the strong anti-China rhetoric among some members of our Congress.[12]

Furthermore, some Chinese say that the United States is guilty of the very things it condemns in China. They remember how missionaries in the nineteenth century lectured them on values while we tolerated slavery in the United States. They point to incidents today where virtual slave labor exists in some companies in our textile industry. Use the energy in lecturing us to improve conditions in your own country, they assert.

In sum, what the United States sees as "constructive engagement" they see as a policy of containment. Mutual distrust exists.

Levi Strauss Decides to Leave China

In March 1993, the China Policy Committee gave its recommendations to the Executive Management Committee of Levi Strauss. A majority of the committee recommended staying in China. A minority recommended leaving. The final decision was left to Robert Haas, who presented his recommendation to leave China to his board of directors in April 1993. It approved the recommendation.

Reasons for Staying

The most important arguments made for staying were as follows:

- China is a rapidly growing economy that some observers believe will be the largest economy in the world in the early twenty-first century. Levi Strauss should be in a position to take advantage of the great opportunities presented there.

---

[11]Richard Hornik, "Bursting China's Bubble," *Foreign Affairs,* May/June 1994, p. 28.
[12]Dick Kirschten, "Prodding China," *National Journal,* August 12, 1995.

- If Levi Strauss leaves now, it may be difficult to get back when and if human rights conditions improve.
- Finding alternative sources in Asia will be costly. We will be obliged to rely on smaller firms, economies of scale will be lost, and labor costs will be higher.
- If the firm stays, it may have potential leverage in improving human rights in conformance with the company's basic values. If the firm stays, it should insist that provisions of the terms of engagement be met and monitored.

Reasons for Leaving

- Staying in China means tolerating a climate of repression inconsistent with company fundamental values.
- More and more customers of Levi Strauss's products are concerned about human rights and if the company stays in China, the brand loyalty to Levi Strauss could be seriously damaged.
- Economic growth in China has not been without costs. It has been accompanied by price inflation and the impaired infrastructure raises costs of operations.
- China has little protection from piracy of intellectual property, patents, or products.
- Political instability is always possible in China and is expected by some observers when Deng Xiaoping, China's leader who is now in his nineties, dies and a power struggle ensues.

The Final Decision

The final decision of the board was to phase out contracting in China and make no direct investments, but continue to buy fabric until the company's sourcing guidelines were reviewed for these products. In announcing the decision, Haas explained in a memorandum to all employees that Levi Strauss had "always been willing to hold ourselves to a higher standard than the general business community, and that is a source of pride for employees and shareholders."[13]

Levi Strauss Decides to Return to China

The company announced on April 8, 1998, that it would end its self-imposed restrictions on manufacturing in mainland China.

---

[13]Jane Palley Katz, "Levi Strauss & Co.: Global Sourcing (B)," Boston, Mass.: Harvard Business School, March 10, 1995.

Reasons for Returning

- Levi Strauss has operations in Hong Kong and since the return of that city to China, the decision to expand operations in the mainland becomes compelling. (Actually, Levi Strauss never fully withdrew from China. Through contractors in Hong Kong, it produced in China only 800,000 units a year, a relatively small number, compared with 2,648,000 a year at the time of pullout.)

- The company believes it can identify business allies who will honor the Levi Strauss code. However, the company will pursue business opportunities in China only if it can function in a way that conforms with its rules for engagement.

- To not return to China would threaten the commercial interests of the company because competitors would solidify a foothold in this fast-growing economy.

- The 1993 decision was not intended to change human rights policies in China or to impose Levi Strauss's values on others. It was essentially a business decision. So is the decision to return.[14]

Peter A. Jacobi, president and chief operating officer of Levi Strauss, in announcing the pullout said that the environment in China was improving and "We basically felt that we should untie our hands." He also said that Levi Strauss is not in the human rights business but is concerned when abuses affect the company's business. The company does not own factories in China but does manufacturing through subcontractors. With this arrangement, China can become a key point for the company's expansion of sales in Japan and South Korea. These two countries generate two-thirds of Levi Strauss's $468 million Asian revenues.[15] Levi Strauss has made clear that it will monitor facilities in China to ensure that operations are in conformance with its engagement code.

Reaction of Activists

Fifty-one human rights organizations and activists sent Haas a letter expressing deep disappointment in the decision. They said the human rights situation in China has not improved. Indeed it is worse, they said, than when Levi Strauss pulled out in 1993. The letter noted that a National Labor Committee study of U.S. companies in China published in March 1998 "documents widespread physical abuse, forced overtime, grueling 10- to 15-hour shifts, and

---

[14]"Talking Points on Conducting Business in China," Press Release, April 8, 1998: http://www.levistrauss.com/press/pr_pressrelease.asp?releaseid=15.

[15]Mark Landler, "Reversing Course, Levi Strauss Will Expand Its Output in China," *New York Times*, April 9, 1998.

wages as low as 13 cents an hour." If the company is to do business in China the activist groups said it should take such steps as:

1. Disclosing subcontractor factories used, and the wages and work hours.
2. Allow independent human rights groups to verify compliance with the company's Code of Conduct . . .
3. Pay a living wage.
4. Ask about jailed political and labor leaders. Chinese authorities are more likely to respond positively to questions by foreign companies than human rights groups.[16]

David Samson, Vice President of Communication, Levi Strauss, replied to the letter and reiterated some of the reasons for the return, as given above. In addition he said: "If we return, we will move back in a measured and cautious way. If we can't operate in ways consistent with our values, we won't be there any long period of time."[17]

Not all activists, however, were critical of the return. Han Dongfang, a prominent Chinese labor activist who formed the first independent labor union during the Tiananmen Square uprising, said that "he believed that the company could do more good by providing jobs in China, rather than by shunning the country."[18]

There were others who were disappointed. Labor rights groups accused Levi Strauss of letting the bottom line supersede its concern for worker welfare. The Canadian Catholic Organization for Development and Peace said there were doubts that the company is capable of policing its factories. Charles Kernaghan, executive director of the National Labor Committee said, "It sounds like Looney Tunes to me that they think they can go in there and guarantee the rights of those workers."[19]

United States Department of State Assessment of Conditions in China in 1997

The U.S. Department of State each year prepares a detailed report on human rights practices in China, as well as in many other countries. Its report for 1997 establishes a background for the decision of Levi Strauss to return.[20] The report says that positive steps were recorded in human rights but serious prob-

---

[16]Published in "Letters," *Business Ethics,* July/August 1998, p. 5.

[17]Ibid.

[18] Landler,"Reversing Course."

[19]Carol Emert, "Levi's Expanding in China; 5-Years Ago, Company Restricted Operations," *The San Francisco Chronicle,* April 9, 1998.

[20]U.S. Department of State, "China Country Report on Human Rights Practices for 1997," Released by the Bureau of Democracy, Human Rights, and Labor, January 30, 1998: http://www.state.gov/www/global/human_rights/1997_hrp_report/, September 26, 1998.

lems remain. Widespread abuses are documented about human rights abuses. Prison conditions remain harsh. Documented were torture and mistreatment of prisoners, forced confessions, and arbitrary arrest. Tight restrictions exist on freedom of speech, the press, assembly, religion, privacy, and worker rights. Citizens have no means to change government legally nor means to change laws that govern them. The government does not welcome any investigation or criticism of its human rights situation. There are laws to protect women, but in practice there is widespread discrimination against them.

In Chinese workplaces, there is very poor enforcement of occupational safety and health conditions. Workers' lives are at risk. Child labor is prohibited, and that is enforced effectively by the government. There is no national minimum wage. Local governments can determine their own standards. In general, the level is higher than the local poverty relief ceiling but under the wage level of the average worker. Monthly rates vary from $12 in poor rural areas to $100 in parts of special economic zones for skilled workers. The law sets a standard workweek from 44 to 40 hours, excluding overtime, and mandates a 24-hour rest period weekly, but the enforcement of these provisions varies among regions.

What Is the Responsibility of a Company for Improving Human Rights in China?

A corporation does have social responsibilities, but precisely what they are is not always clear. This is particularly so with respect to China. A multinational company's social responsibilities for human rights in that country are complex questions, the answers to which depend upon many variables.

For example, there are numerous non-Chinese entities with influence in China aside from MNCs, including other nations, the United Nations, and nongovernment organizations such as human rights groups. Each has some responsibility, but how much?

An important factor in determining the responsibility of an MNC is the type of human rights in question. For example, a company has responsibility for worker rights associated with employment, such as safety conditions, but not for the Chinese government using prison labor.

The government is far more sensitive to criticisms of the latter type of human rights than the former. As Michael A. Santoro of Rutgers Graduate School of Management writes: "The rights of workers to minimum wages, safe working conditions, and limited working hours are not as problematical for the Chinese government as the rights to association and expression. Hence, when foreign companies uphold minimal labor standards through business partner terms of engagement, the risk of alienating the Chinese government is not nearly as great as when companies attempt to uphold the political rights of Chinese workers."[21] However, the

---

[21]Michael A. Santoro, "Engagement with Integrity: What We Should Expect Multinational Firms to Do About Human Rights in China," *Business & The Contemporary World*, 10, no. 1, 1998, p. 40.

human rights issue may be extremely difficult for a company when the government seeks its help in enforcing a penalty for a worker's exercise of freedom of speech or association contrary to government rules. Santoro says executives of MNCs "need not concern themselves with human rights violations that have nothing to do with the firm's operations."[22] But what if the government insists?

Multinational firms employ only a small percentage of all workers in China and encounter only a small fraction of human rights abuses. Furthermore, few if any MNCs are invulnerable to retaliation from the Chinese government. The typical MNC is weak, therefore, in its ability to influence the government to change its actions respecting human rights outside the workplace. China is interested in attracting foreign capital and seems little concerned with the working conditions set up by MNCs so long as the companies do not get involved in political promotion of human rights.

Santoro suggests what he called a "fair share" theory of corporate responsibility for human rights issues in China. This theory requires an allocation of responsibilities among major entities operating there. As noted above, MNCs do have responsibilities, particularly those concerning working conditions in their organizations. The greatest influence on human rights conditions in China, however, rests with international institutions.

Can Economic Freedom Bring Political Freedom?

U.S. policy toward China today is based partly on the assumption that improving economic conditions in that country will inevitably bring political, economic, and social freedom. That will clearly be in the United States national interest. This is a fundamental assumption that has been held by mainstream economic thinkers for centuries. Is it true?

Scholars of capitalism generally believe that the freedoms that must exist in a competitive economic system do not coexist easily with political repression. Michael Novak, for example, points out that capitalism requires what he calls "civic space," or freedom in society to organize resources, create organizations, take voluntary action, innovate, and exercise initiative.[23] The existence of this civic space is incompatible with a government that represses liberties and fears challenge to established traditions.

Milton Friedman argues that throughout history, every society with political freedom has also had something like a free market economy. But he points out that free markets do not necessarily, by themselves, create political freedom. Countries such as Fascist Italy, Fascist Spain, and Czarist Russia prior to World War I had free enterprise economies coexisting with governments that

---

[22]Ibid, p. 45.
[23]Michael Novak, *The Catholic Ethic and the Spirit of Capitalism,* New York: Free Press, 1993, pp. 50, 54.

repressed individual liberties. Modern China might be added to this list. For Friedman, the relationship between political liberty and free markets is "complex" and he believes that while "capitalism is a necessary condition for political freedom . . . it is not a sufficient condition."[24]

The best conclusion may be that even if capitalism in China is not certain to lead to political democracy, it will create economic power that exists independently of the central regime and can challenge its authoritarian controls.

When Deng Xiaoping decided to permit the creation of a few free economic zones in western China in the 1970s, he made a strategic decision that a certain amount of economic freedom could exist without the central government losing its strong controls. He encouraged economic freedom because he believed that economic development was essential for China to improve living conditions. However, he also took a significant gamble that this could be done while at the same time maintaining the control of the central government over the country.

Questions

1. Do you believe the guidelines shown in Exhibit 1 are appropriate for most or all U.S. companies doing business abroad? Explain your position. Are companies that lack such guidelines irresponsible?
2. Evaluate the pros and cons of Levi Strauss's decision to stay in or leave China in 1993. Did the company make the right decision?
3. Evaluate the decision to reenter China in 1998. Did Levi Strauss make the right decision?
4. What is the responsibility of a company like Levi Strauss for improving human rights in China?
5. What do you think of Santoro's "fair share" theory?
6. Argue the question: Does economic freedom result in political freedom?

---

[24]Milton Friedman, *Capitalism and Freedom,* Chicago: University of Chicago Press, 1962, p. 10.

Business Ethics

7

Ethics in the Business System

Correct Craft

www.skinautique.com

Walter C. Meloon dropped out of high school to work in a print shop. The boss's daughter was a devout Christian, so he became a convert to win her hand in marriage. When, in 1925, Meloon started a small boat-making business in Florida, he resolved to glorify God and follow the Golden Rule in his business dealings.

Meloon's company, Correct Craft, barely survived the depression years of the 1930s, but during World War II it prospered making boats for the armed services. In January 1945, General Dwight D. Eisenhower was driving toward Berlin ahead of schedule and set March 10, 1945, as the date for crossing the Rhine. However, there was a critical shortage of the 17-foot, spoon-shaped assault boats that carried soldiers on such river crossings.

Correct Craft was given an urgent order for 300 of these boats by the Army. The company had only eighteen days to build them; its normal output was forty-eight boats per *month!* Immediately, a government expediter demanded that Meloon go to a seven-day workweek, but he refused, saying that it was not God's plan to work on the Sabbath. The expediter gave in. Correct Craft went on to produce 306 boats four days ahead of schedule, without working on Sundays, and another 100 boats when other companies were unable to meet their schedules.

At a second Correct Craft plant, where Meloon built boats for the U.S. Navy, a government inspector tried to speed production by stopping weekly chapel services for the employees. Meloon told him: "If we can't serve

This picture from the December 1945 National Geographic magazine shows the road in front of Correct Craft littered with finished plywood assault boats. It was taken on Wednesday, February 21, 1945.

the Lord and the U.S. Navy at the same time, we just won't serve the Navy."[1] The inspector relented.

After World War II, Correct Craft prospered as the second largest builder of sport boats and yachts in the nation. Then, in 1957, the company got a big U.S. Army contract for 3,000 fiberglass boats. One day a government inspector demanded that the Meloons set up a special account for "inspector's expenses." This was a request for a bribe.

By this time W. C.'s equally principled sons, Walter O. and Ralph, managed daily operations. The family

prayed for guidance. The payments were small compared to the income at stake. But bribery was wrong. The payments were not made. "If you have made a decision based only on money," said W. C., "you have made a bad decision."[2] Soon the inspectors began to use trivial blemishes as pretexts for rejecting finished boats. In the end they rejected 640 boats. Correct Craft lost $1 million on the contract and in 1958 went into Chapter 11 bankruptcy proceedings. It owed $500,000 to 228 creditors.

Knowing the situation, every Correct Craft employee resigned. Walter O.

---

[1]Quoted in Robert G. Flood, *On the Waters of the World: The Story of the Meloon Family,* Chicago: Moody Press, 1989, p. 18.

[2]Quoted in John S. Tompkins, "These Good Guys Finish First," *Reader's Digest,* June 1992, p. 140.

and Ralph rehired only those with essential jobs. The two brothers' wives worked at the switchboard. Walter O. returned his new Lincoln to the dealer. Other family members mortgaged their homes and sold their cars. All adopted a frugal lifestyle.

The company barely avoided liquidation. First came a loan from a friend. Then the government of Pakistan bought 239 of the fiberglass boats that the inspectors had rejected. In early 1965, after years of hardship, the bankruptcy judge released the company from Chapter 11 when 127 remaining creditors agreed to repayment at 10 cents on the dollar.

But despite the agreement, the Meloons struggled for the next nineteen years to repay 100 percent of their debt. As the years passed, it became hard to locate some creditors. The family worked to find them. In some cases they were deceased and payments were made to surprised widows or relatives. In one case Ralph flew to Michigan to search for a creditor when telephone calls proved fruitless. In May 1984 the last payment was made. The family had paid 100 percent of its debt!

Today Correct Craft is a profitable company known for its line of inboard-engined recreational boats, including the Ski Nautique, a towboat preferred by water skiers because of its flat wake. Correct Craft boats are sold worldwide. The third generation of Meloons is in charge; Walter N., son of Walter O., is president. Walter O. and Ralph remain on the board of directors and a third brother, Harold, has been company chaplain since 1974.

Correct Craft is a company driven by ethical values. These values, derived from the philosophy and example of its founder, permeate the company culture to direct employees and influence strategic decisions. Its story illustrates how ethical values can have a continuous impact on the fortunes of a business.

In this chapter we locate the sources of ethical standards that constrain business, discuss ethical behavior in companies, and explain methods of managing used to promote higher ethics. The next chapter focuses on methods that people in business can use for making decisions about ethical matters.

What Are Business Ethics?

Ethics is the study of what is good and evil, right and wrong, and just and unjust. *Business ethics,* therefore, is the study of good and evil, right and wrong, and just and unjust actions in business. Ethical managers try to do good and avoid doing evil. A mass of principles, values, norms, and thoughts concerned with what conduct *ought* to be exists to guide them. But in this vaporous mass, the outlines of good and evil are indistinct. Usually they are clear enough, but often not. Hence, the application of ethics in business is an art, an art that requires judgement about both the motivations behind an act and the act's consequences.

Discussions of business ethics frequently emphasize refractory and unclear situations, perhaps to show drama and novelty. Although all managers face difficult ethical conflicts, the vast majority of ethical problems yield to resolution through the application of clear guidelines. The Eighth Commandment, for example, prohibits stealing and clearly makes unethical practices ranging from theft of a competitor's trade secrets to taking a screwdriver home from work. A misleading or lying advertisement violates a general rule of the Western business world that the seller of a product should not purposely deceive the buyer about its price or quality. This general understanding stems from the Mosaic law, the Code of Hammurabi, Roman law, and other sources and is part of a general ethic favoring truth that has remained unchanged for at least 3,000 years.[3]

In general, ethical traditions that apply to business favor truth telling, honesty, protection of human and animal life and rights, respect for law, and operation in accord with policies adopted by society to achieve justice for citizens. Some of these touchstones go back thousands of years. Other ethical standards, such as the principle that a corporation is responsible for worker safety and health, have emerged only recently. In keeping with this long and growing ethical heritage, most business actions can be clearly judged ethical or unethical; it may be difficult to eliminate some unethical behavior, such as bribery or embezzlement, but knowing the rightness or wrongness of actions usually is not difficult.

This does not mean that ethical decisions are always clear. Some ethical issues are difficult because although basic ethical standards apply, there are conflicts among them that defy resolution.

> Lockheed Aircraft Corp. made large campaign contributions to Japanese officials intended to influence the Japanese to buy airplanes. This saved jobs for American workers. But even though such contributions were not an unusual practice in Japan and for the international aerospace industry in general, they violated domestic business norms. Lockheed's actions are still debated over twenty years later.

Some ethical issues are hidden, at least initially, and hard to recognize.

> The A. H. Robins Co. began to market its Dalkon Shield intrauterine device through general practitioners while competitors continued to sell them primarily through obstetricians and gynecologists. This strategy was wildly successful in gaining market share and did not, initially, appear to raise an ethical issue but, when dangerous health problems with the Shield began to surface, general practitioners were slower to recognize them than specialists. Robin's failure to make extra efforts to track the safety of the device then emerged as an ethical shortcoming.

And some ethical issues are very subtle, submerged in everyday workplace behavior. Managers must often work in a world of uncertainty and act or pass judgment without complete knowledge of facts. The following case involves a commitment, a promise.

> A regional manager says that replacement equipment for a factory with production problems that are due to breakdowns will be ordered from this year's budget.

---

[3]George C. S. Benson, *Business Ethics in America*, Lexington, Mass.: Heath, 1982, p. xvi.

At the end of the year, however, the equipment has not been ordered because, as the regional manager explains, "there just wasn't enough money left to do it." Is the plant manager entitled to expect the budget to be managed so that the commitment could be kept? Why was the commitment not kept? Poor planning? Disguised withdrawal of cooperation? Another reason?

Two Theories of Business Ethics

There is a debate about whether ethics in business may be more permissive than general societal or personal ethics. There are two basic views.

The first, the *theory of amorality*, is that business should be amoral, that is, conducted without reference to the full range of society's ethical ideals. Managers may act selfishly because the market mechanism distills their actions into benefits for stakeholders and society at large. Adam Smith noted that the "invisible hand" of the market assures that "by pursuing his own interest [a merchant] frequently promotes that of the society more effectively than when he really intends to promote it."[4] In this way, capitalism provides moral justification for the pursuit of profit through behavior that is not purposefully ethical.

The apex of this view came during the latter half of the nineteenth century when doctrines of laissez-faire economics and social Darwinism were popular. It was widely believed that business and personal ethics existed in separate compartments, that business was an ethical sanctuary in which less idealistic ethics were permissible.[5] Dan Drew, a builder of churches and the founder of Drew Theological Seminary, summed up the nineteenth-century compartmentalization of business decision making in these words:

> Sentiment is all right up in the part of the city where your home is. But downtown, no. Down there the dog that snaps the quickest gets the bone. Friendship is very nice for a Sunday afternoon when you're sitting around the dinner table with your relations, talking about the sermon that morning. But nine o'clock Monday morning, notions should be brushed aside like cobwebs from a machine. I never took

---

[4]Adam Smith, *The Wealth of Nations,* ed. Edwin Cannan, New York: Modern Library, 1937, p. 423. Originally published in 1776. Smith also believed that merchants must abide by prevailing societal ethics.

[5]This view was encouraged in the writings of the social Darwinist Herbert Spencer, who believed in two sets of ethics. *Family ethics* were based on the principle of charity and benefits were apportioned without relation to merit. *State ethics* were based on a competitive justice and benefits were apportioned on the basis of strict merit. Family ethics interjected into business or government by well-meaning people were an inappropriate interference with the laws of nature and would slowly corrupt the workings of Darwinian natural selection. See "The Sins of Legislators," in *The Man versus the State,* London: Watts, 1940. Originally published in 1884. Dual ethical perspectives have developed in other cultures such as Slavic cultures that assert one set of ethical standards for personal relationships and a second set that justifies less perfection for business matters. See Sheila M. Puffer, "Understanding the Bear: A Portrait of Russian Business Leaders," *Academy of Management Executive,* February 1994, p. 47.

any stock in a man who mixed up business with anything else. He can go into other things outside of business hours, but when he's in the office, he ought not to have a relation in the world—and least of all a poor relation.[6]

The theory of amorality now has far less public acceptance and luster, but it quietly lives on. For many managers, competitive pressures still justify behavior that would be wrong in private life; the theory of amorality continues to release these managers from a burden of guilt that they otherwise might feel.

The second basic ethical orientation is the *theory of moral unity*, in which business actions are judged by the general ethical standards of society, not by a special set of more permissive standards. Only one basic ethical standard exists, so principled behavior and business decisions can be harmonized.

Many managers take this position today, and some did even in the nineteenth century. An example is James Cash Penney. We remember Penney for building a famous chain of retail stores, but his first enterprise was a butcher shop. As a young man, Penney went to Denver and, finding the shop for sale, wired his mother for $300 (his life savings) and bought it. The departing butcher advised that Penney's success would depend heavily on orders from a nearby hotel. "To keep the hotel for a customer," the butcher explained, "all you have to do is buy the chef a bottle of whiskey a week." Penney regularly made the gift, and business was good, but he began to have second thoughts. He resolved not to make profits in such a manner, stopped giving the bribe, lost the hotel's business, and at the age of 23 went broke when the shop failed. Penney later started the Golden Rule Department Store in Denver and argued that his principles of honesty contributed to its ultimate success.

To J. C. Penney, and other exemplars of the theory of moral unity, the market is never a reason or excuse to neglect principled behavior. Profit-making is not the only or the highest standard. Although many managers continue to practice the theory of amorality, the theory of moral unity better spells out the expectations of society today.[7] Ethical conflicts cannot be avoided simply because they occur in business.

We turn now to this question: Are there any factors that excuse or diminish ethical responsibility in business? The answer is yes. More than 2,000 years ago, Aristotle recognized that being ethical requires voluntary choice. A person must be able to choose between alternatives to act unethically. If there is no choice, the behavior is involuntary and can be excused. According to Aristotle, two factors lead to involuntary behavior—*ignorance* and *incapacity.*

A person may be ignorant of facts or the consequences of an act. The South African government at one time used Polaroid film and cameras for the pictures on racial identity papers. Black employees of Polaroid Corporation in

---

[6]Quoted in Robert Bartels, ed., *Ethics in Business,* Columbus: Bureau of Business Research, Ohio State University, 1963, p. 35.

[7]This conclusion is reinforced in a discussion of the history of these two ideas. See Jon M. Shepard, Jon Shepard, James C. Wimbush, and Carroll U. Stephens, "The Place of Ethics in Business: Shifting Paradigms?" *Business Ethics Quarterly,* July 1995.

the United States raised the issue of its complicity with racists, so it prohibited sales to the government while continuing to sell to the South African public. For six years this policy continued, but Polaroid's South African distributor secretly continued sales to the government. On the day that it learned this was going on, Polaroid completely withdrew from South Africa.[8] In this case, Polaroid cannot be condemned; ignorance absolved management from any blame for violation of its policy. Of course, in all such cases, negligence in getting facts or intentional ignorance increases culpability.

Incapacity arises from four circumstances that render actions involuntary. First, an action may impose unrealistically high costs—for example, an auto manufacturer cannot be expected to prevent all traffic deaths since the costs of a completely safe vehicle in materials, design, and production would be staggering. Second, there may be no power to influence an outcome—for example, a manager of an oil company doing business in the Middle East cannot end religious intolerance. Third, no alternative may exist. In prewar Germany, Nazi officials allocated raw materials and controlled import-export licenses and other permissions necessary to do business. They demanded bribes and businesses could not function without paying them. And fourth, external forces may compel action. For example, a manager may pay excessive and unjust taxes in a foreign country because a corrupt ruler demands them.

Aristotle cautions, however, that "[t]here are some things such that a man cannot be compelled to do them—that he must sooner die than do, though he suffer the most dreadful fate."[9] Unlike cases of ignorance, unethical behavior involving coercion is not completely involuntary if a manager can simply refuse to comply with the external force. Those who argue that the market is an irresistible force overriding individual choice give too little credit to the strength of human will.

Major Sources of Ethical Values in Business

Managers in every society are influenced by four great repositories of ethical values: religion, philosophy, cultural experience, and law. These repositories contain sets of values that exert varying degrees of control over managers. A common theme, the idea of *reciprocity,* or mutual help, is found in all these value systems. This idea reflects the central purpose of ethics, which is to bind individuals into a cooperative social whole. Ethical values are a mechanism that controls behavior in business and in other areas of life. Ethical restraint is more efficient with society's resources than are cruder controls such as police,

---

[8]Tom L. Beauchamp, *Case Studies in Business, Society, and Ethics,* Upper Saddle River, NJ: Prentice Hall, 1998, pp. 275–81. Polaroid stayed out of South Africa for 17 years until the apartheid system ended.

[9]*The Nicomachean Ethics,* trans. J. A. K. Thomson, New York: Penguin, 1953, p. 112. Originally written c. 334–323 B.C.

lawsuits, or economic incentives. Ethical values channel individual energy into pursuits that are benign to others and beneficial to society.

Religion

One of the oldest sources of ethical inspiration is religion. Despite doctrinal differences, the major religions, including the Judeo-Christian tradition prominent in American life, converge in the belief that a divine will reveals the nature of right and wrong behavior in all areas of life, including business. The world's great religions are also in agreement on ideas that form the basic building blocks of ethics in every society. For example, the principle of reciprocity is found, encapsulated in variations of the Golden Rule, in Buddhism, Confucianism, Hinduism, Islam, Judaism, and Christianity. These religions also converge in emphasizing traits such as honesty, fairness, charity, and responsibility to the community.

Christian managers often seek guidance in the Bible. Donald V. Seibert, former chairman of J. C. Penney Company, advocated daily Bible reading for executives. He believed that two books are particularly relevant. "Proverbs," he wrote, "is replete with references to the proper approach to business transactions, such as 'A wicked man earns deceptive wages, but one who sows righteousness gets a sure reward.' [11:18]. And Jesus's teachings and parables in Matthew have enough practical wisdom in them to provide a blueprint for almost an entire working experience."[10]

The Bible, like the source books and writings of other main religions, was written in an agricultural society and many of its ethical teachings require interpretation before they can be applied to problems of industrial life. The parable of the prodigal son (Luke 15:11–32) sets forth an image of an unconditionally merciful father—a model applicable to ethical conflicts in modern superior–subordinate relationships in corporations. The story of the rich man and Lazarus (Luke 16:19–31) teaches concern for the poor and challenges Christian managers to improve living conditions of the less privileged.[11] In Islam the Koran is a source of ethical inspiration. The Prophet Muhammad says that "Every one of you is a shepherd and everyone is responsible for what he is shepherd of."[12] In a modern context, the Muslim business executive may be seen as analogous to a shepherd.

In the Jewish tradition, managers can turn to rabbinic moral commentary in the Talmud and the books of Moses in the Torah. Here again, ancient teachings are regarded as analogies. For example, a Talmudic ruling holds that a

---

[10]Donald V. Seibert and William Proctor, *The Ethical Executive*, New York: Simon & Schuster, 1984, pp. 119–20.

[11]See Oliver F. Williams and John W. Houck, *Full Value: Cases in Christian Business Ethics*, New York: Harper & Row, 1978, for discussion of these and other biblical sources of inspiration for managers.

[12]Quoted in Tanri Abeng, "Business Ethics in Islamic Context: Perspectives of a Muslim Business Leader," *Business Ethics Quarterly*, July 1997, p. 52.

person who sets a force in motion bears responsibility for any resulting harm, even if natural forces intervene. This is discussed in the context of an agricultural society in which a person who starts a fire is responsible for damage from flying sparks, even if nature intervenes with high winds. In an industrial context, the moral lesson is that polluting corporations are responsible for problems caused by their waste.[13]

A recent survey of executives from the largest 100 corporations found that 65 percent regularly attend churches or synagogues.[14] Across the United States, many firms try to incorporate religious teachings in their operations. The founders of the motel chain Days Inns of America, Inc., for example, adopted Christian-based policies of not serving alcohol, of giving away Bibles, and of catering to families. Until the chain was sold by the founders, four full-time roving chaplains were available to employees. A Christian fast-food chain based in Atlanta, Chick-fil-A Inc., refuses to open on Sunday, a long-standing policy that has excluded it from some desirable mall locations. Allou Health and Beauty Care, Inc., a company owned by Orthodox Jews, closes one hour before sunset on Fridays and all employees—even those who are not Jewish—must leave.

Philosophical Systems

A Western manager can look back on over 2,000 years of philosophical inquiry into ethics. This rich, complex, classical tradition is the source of a variety of notions about what is ethical in business. Every age has added new ideas, but it would be a mistake to regard the history of ethical philosophy as a single debate that, over centuries, has matured to bear the fruit of growing wisdom and clear, precise standards of conduct. Even after two millennia, there remains considerable dispute among ethical thinkers about the nature of right action. If anything, standards of ethical behavior were arguably clearer in ancient Greek civilization than they are now.

In a brief circuit of milestones in ethical thinking, we turn first to the Greek philosophers. Greek ethics, from Homeric times onward, were embodied in the discharge of duties related to social roles such as shepherd, warrior, merchant, citizen, or king. Expectations of the occupants of these roles were clearer than in contemporary America, where social roles such as those of business manager or employee are more vague, overlapping, and marked by conflict.[15] Socrates (469–399 B.C.) asserted that virtue and ethical behavior were associated with wisdom and taught that insight into life would naturally lead to right conduct. He also introduced the idea of a moral law higher than

---

[13]Moses L. Pava, *Business Ethics: A Jewish Perspective,* New York: Yeshiva University Press, 1997, pp. 72–73.

[14]Evan Gahr, "Spirited Enterprise," *The American Heritage,* July/August 1997, p. 54.

[15]Alasdair MacIntyre, *After Virtue: A Study in Moral Theory,* South Bend, Ind.: University of Notre Dame Press, 1981, p. 115.

human law, an idea that protesters have used to demand supralegal behavior from modern corporations. Plato (428–348 B.C.), the gifted student of Socrates, carried his doctrine of virtue as knowledge further by elaborating the theory that absolute justice exists independently of individuals and that its nature can be discovered by intellectual effort. In *The Republic,* Plato set up a fifty-year program to train rulers to rule in harmony with the ideal of Justice.[16] Plato's most apt pupil, Aristotle, spelled out virtues of character in *The Nicomachean Ethics* and advocated study to develop knowledge of ethical behavior.[17] A lasting contribution of Aristotle is the doctrine of the mean (or golden mean), which is that people can achieve the good life and happiness by developing virtues of moderation. To illustrate, courage was the mean between cowardice and rashness, modesty the mean between shyness and shamelessness.

The Stoic school of ethics, which spans four centuries from the death of Alexander to the rise of Christianity in Rome, furthered the trend toward character development in Greek ethics. Epictetus (A.D. 50–100), for instance, taught that virtue was found solely within and should be valued for its own sake, arguing that virtue was a greater reward than external riches or outward success.

In business, the ethical legacy of the Greeks and Romans remains a conviction that virtues such as truth telling, charity, obeying the law, good citizenship, justice, courage, friendship, and the correct use of power are important ethical qualities. Today when a manager trades integrity for profit, we condemn this, in part, because of the teachings of the Greeks.

Ethical thinking after the rise of Christianity was dominated by the influence of the great Catholic theologians St. Augustine (354–430) and St. Thomas Aquinas (1225–1274). Both believed that humanity should follow God's will; correct behavior in business dealings and all worldly activity was necessary to achieve salvation and life after death. Christianity was the source of ethical expectations as revealed in specific rules such as the Ten Commandments. Christian theology created a lasting reservoir of ethical doctrine, but its domination of ethical thinking declined during the historical period of intellectual and industrial expansion in Europe called the Enlightenment. Secular philosophers such as Baruch Spinoza (1632–1677) tried to demonstrate ethical principles with logical analysis rather than ordain them by reference to God's will. So also Immanuel Kant (1724–1804) tried to find universal and objective ethical rules in logic. Kant and Spinoza, and others who followed, created a great estrangement with moral theology by believing that humanity could discover the nature of good behavior without reference to God. To this day, there is a deep divide between Christian managers who look to the Bible for divine guidance and other managers who look to worldly writings for ethical wisdom.

Other milestones of secular thinking followed. Jeremy Bentham (1748–1832) developed the idea of utilitarianism as a guide to ethics. Bentham observed that an ethical action was the one among all alternatives that

---

[16]Trans. F. M. Cornford, New York: Oxford University Press, 1945.
[17]*The Nicomachean Ethics,* trans. Thomson, p. 51.

brought pleasure to the largest number of persons and pain to the fewest. The impact of this ethical philosophy is almost impossible to overestimate. The legitimacy of majority rule in democratic governments rests in large part on Bentham's theory of utility as refined later by John Stuart Mill (1806–1873). Utilitarianism also sanctified industrial development by legitimizing the notion that economic growth benefits the majority; thus the pain and dislocation it brings to a few may be ethically permitted.

John Locke (1632–1704) developed and refined doctrines of human rights and left an ethical legacy supporting belief in the inalienable rights of human beings, including the right to pursue life, liberty, and happiness, and the right to freedom from tyranny. Our leaders, including business leaders, continue to be restrained by these beliefs.

A "realist" school of ethics also developed alongside the "idealistic" thinking of philosophers such as Spinoza, Kant, the utilitarians, and Locke. The "realists" believed that both good and evil were naturally present in human nature; human behavior inevitably would reflect this mixture. Since good and evil occurred naturally, it was futile to try to teach ideals. Ideals could never be realized because evil was permanent in human nature. The realist school, then, developed ethical theories that shrugged off the idea of perfect goodness. Niccolò Machiavelli (1469–1526) argued that important ends justified expedient means. Herbert Spencer (1820–1903) wrote prolifically of a harsh ethic that justified vicious competition among companies because it furthered evolution—a process in which humanity improved as the unfit fell down. Friedrich Nietzsche (1844–1900) rejected the ideals of earlier "nice" ethics, saying they were prescriptions of the timid, designed to fetter the actions of great men whose irresistible power and will were regarded as dangerous by the common herd of ordinary mortals.

Nietzsche believed in the existence of a "master morality" in which great men made their own ethical rules according to their convenience and without respect for the general good of average people. In reaction to this "master morality," the mass of ordinary people developed a "slave morality" that shackled the great men. For example, according to Nietzsche, the great mass of ordinary men celebrated the Christian virtue of turning the other cheek because they did not have the power to revenge themselves on great men. He felt that prominent ethical ideals of his day were recipes for timidity and once said of utilitarianism that it made him want to vomit.[18] The influence of realists on managers has been strong. Spencer was wildly popular among the business class in the nineteenth century. Machiavelli is still read for inspiration today. The lasting appeal of the realist school is that many managers, deep down, do not believe that ideals can be achieved in business life.

In conclusion, the legacy of more than 2,000 years of recorded ethical debate in Western societies is such that no single approach or principle has been

---

[18]His exact words were: ". . . 'the general welfare' is no ideal, no goal, no remotely intelligible concept, but only an emetic . . ." In *Beyond Good and Evil,* New York: Vintage Books, 1966, p. 157. Originally published in 1886.

found that precisely clarifies the nature of right conduct in business. Indeed, guidelines may be less clear today than they were in the age of Pericles. Eastern philosophy has also studied the question of how to do good and avoid evil, but as in the West, no definitive answers have emerged.

Cultural Experience

Every culture transmits between generations a set of traditional values, rules, and standards that define acceptable behavior. In this way, individuals channel their conduct in socially approved directions. Civilization itself is a cumulative cultural experience consisting of three stages; in each, economic and social arrangements have dictated a distinct moral code.[19]

For millions of generations in the *hunting and gathering stage* of human development, ethics were adapted to conditions in which our ancestors had to be ready to fight, face brutal foes, and suffer hostile forces of nature. Under such circumstances, a premium was placed on pugnacity, appetite, greed, and sexual readiness, since it was often the strongest who survived. Trade ethics in early civilizations were probably deceitful and dishonest by our standards, and economic transactions were frequently conducted by brute force and violence.

Civilization passed into an *agricultural stage* approximately 10,000 years ago, beginning a time when industriousness was more important than ferocity, thrift paid greater dividends than violence, monogamy became the prevailing sexual custom because of the relatively equal numbers of the sexes, and peace came to be valued over wars, which destroyed crops and animals. These new values were codified into ethical systems by philosophers and founders of religions. So the great ethical philosophies and theologies that guide managers today are largely products of the agricultural revolution.

Two centuries ago, society entered an *industrial stage* of cultural experience, and ethical systems began to reflect an evolving institutional, intellectual, and ecological environment. Powerful forces such as global corporations, population growth, the capitalist ideology, constitutional democracy, new technology, and ecological damage have appeared. Industrialism has not yet created a distinct ethic, but it has put stress on old, agriculture-based ethical systems. It is changing ethical values by altering people's judgments about good and evil. For example, the copious outpouring of material goods from factories encourages materialism and consumption at the expense of older virtues such as moderation and thrift. The old truism that nature exists for human exploitation seems less compelling when reexamined in a cloud of industrial pollution.

---

[19]Will Durant and Ariel Durant, *The Lessons of History,* New York: Simon & Schuster, 1968, pp. 37–42.

The Legal System

Laws are rules of conduct established by governmental authority. They codify ethical expectations and change over time as new evils emerge. It is impossible for law to anticipate and prohibit every possible wrong action; new laws always lag behind opportunities for corporate expediency.

Over the past thirty years, the reach of law has grown as new regulations, statutes, common law rulings, and litigation theories have imposed more conduct standards on business. Three main types of sanctions for illegal acts are fines, court-ordered compensation, and prosecution of individual managers. Though each can effectively punish and deter corporate lawbreaking, none is unflawed.

Fines often do not hurt large firms. In 1998 the Environmental Protection Agency threatened to impose a fine of $27,500 per day on General Electric if it refused to clean up toxic waste at a former factory site. For a company with more than $90 billion in annual revenue, this is the equivalent of threatening a person with a $1 million annual salary with a fine of three cents a day. When GE recently paid the government $1.84 million in fines to settle a billing fraud case, it was the equivalent of a $25 parking ticket for a person with a $50,000 annual income.

Sometimes fines do hurt. In 1996 Archer-Daniels-Midland Co. paid $100 million, the largest criminal antitrust fine ever, to settle charges of price fixing. The fine was 7 percent of gross profits, led to a $0.31 per share charge against earnings, and reduced funds available for operating expenditures. The effects rippled throughout the company. In the past, regulators and courts have hesitated to impose devastating fines because the burden would fall partly on innocent bystanders—shareholders, workers, suppliers, and others who had no knowledge of or control over the corporation's deviant behavior but whose livelihood depends on its benefactions. At Archer-Daniels-Midland, the fine resulted from the actions of three top executives, but the effects were felt by many stakeholders.

In 1991 the United States Sentencing Commission, a judicial agency that standardizes penalties for federal crimes, released guidelines for sentencing corporations.[20] The guidelines require corporations to reimburse injured parties, if possible. Beyond this, they set fines based on type of crime, amount of monetary gain to the company or loss to its victims, company size, past criminal convictions, cooperation with law enforcement, and the presence or absence of programs designed to prevent and detect illegal acts.[21]

Courts may assess damages, or payments for harm that has come to an injured party. These include compensatory damages, or payments to restore actual losses of injured parties, and punitive damages, or monetary payments in

---

[20]United States Sentencing Commission, *Guidelines Manual,* Washington, D.C.: Government Printing Office, November 1, 1991, pp. 347–79.

[21]Based on these factors, corporations are subject to a range of fines from $5,000 to $290 million.

excess of a wronged party's actual losses. Punitive damages may be awarded only if malicious and willful misconduct exists. In one case, a regional manager for Browning-Ferris Industries ordered a district manager to drive a small competitor in Vermont out of business using predatory pricing. His instructions were: "Do whatever it takes. Squish him like a bug."[22] Subsequently a jury awarded the competitor $51,146 in actual damages, then added $6 million in punitive damages. In another case, an insurance agent pocketed a woman's premium payments, absconded, and left her with $3,500 in uncovered medical bills. A jury awarded her $840,000 in punitive damages.[23]

The purpose of punitive damages is to punish and deter crime, so they must be large enough to be painful. But they raise many questions about fairness. Given similar offenses, juries often assess higher damages against a big corporation than against a smaller one simply to make certain the penalty hurts. And sometimes the awards are so far in excess of actual damages that they cross the line from punishing a company to destroying it.

The Supreme Court finally decided to rein in punitive damages in the case of an Alabama physician, Dr. Ira Gore Jr., who bought a BMW automobile for $40,751 and drove it for nine months without noticing any problem. After an auto detailer told him that part of the car had been repainted, the owner found out that BMW North America had been secretly repainting cars with shipping damage and selling them as new. Gore estimated his damages at $4,000, or 10 percent of the value of the new car, and sued, charging BMW with gross, oppressive, and malicious fraud. An Alabama jury awarded him $4 million in punitive damages—one thousand times his actual loss. On appeal the Supreme Court held that the award was unconstitutionally excessive.[24] But the Court did not set up any formula for calculating punitive damages, so the definition of excessive is still imprecise. Subsequently, the Alabama Supreme Court reconsidered the case and awarded Gore only $50,000.[25]

A third type of sanction for corporate crime is prosecution of individual managers. Judges are reluctant to sentence managers to jail for fraud, embezzlement, illegal toxic waste disposal, and other so-called white-collar crimes. Managers ordinarily do not violently endanger society and would further crowd prisons. In federal courts, 96 percent of those convicted for robbery, but only 52 percent of those convicted for fraud and 44 percent of those convicted for bribery, go to prison. An offense against the environment leads to prison just 16 percent of the time.[26]

Investigating corporate crime is difficult for prosecuting attorneys, who face a thicket of corporate documents to review, a network of subtle organizational

---

[22]*Browning-Ferris Industries* v. *Kelco Disposal,* 57 LW 4986 (1989).

[23]*Pacific Mutual Life Insurance Company* v. *Cleopatra Haslip,* 59 LW 4157 (1991).

[24]*BMW of North America, Inc.* v. *Gore,* 116 S. Ct. 1589 (1996).

[25]"Alabama Court Slashes Punitive Award in Case Involving Repainted BMW Car," *Wall Street Journal,* May 12, 1997, p. B10.

[26]United States Sentencing Commission, *1997 Sourcebook of Federal Sentencing Statistics,* Washington, D.C.: USSC, undated, Table 4.

relationships to sort out, and the conflicting priority of violent street crime to compete for their attention. Corporations hire stellar defense lawyers; the state's case is often championed by less-experienced attorneys with thin staff support. For these reasons, U.S. and state attorneys find it easier to pursue indictments of street criminals and shy away from the complex corporate cases.

Other methods for punishing corporate crime exist. One guideline for applying them is that they should not cripple or render inefficient legitimate corporate activity. Courts have required advertisements and speeches to show contrition for wrongdoing. Some corporations have paid their fines to charities, and executives have been ordered to do community service.

Federal sentencing guidelines provide for corporate probation periods during which steps can be taken to build controls and reform unethical cultures. When Consolidated Edison Co. pled guilty to hiding asbestos releases, a federal judge gave it three years' probation to eradicate a culture in which employees feared retaliation for reporting pollution problems. One supervisor who reported a mercury leak later found a shovel by his desk, which he took to mean that fellow workers wanted to "bury" him.[27] The court appointed an environmental lawyer to monitor the company's reform efforts. The monitor has extensive oversight powers, including the right to surprise inspections.

Business Ethics in Other Countries

Business practices differ between countries and regions because environmental factors shape ethical values. Here are some simple illustrations of how these factors work.

Historical experience shapes business environments that are radically different from that in the United States. A series of devastating natural disasters—volcanic eruption, flooding, earthquakes, and famine—punctuate the history of Italy. The caprice of these events has led Italians to temporize with chance and live for the moment. An Italian manager may be more carefree than an American one about keeping a promise or fulfilling a contract because of this attitude about the future.[28] As a result, levels of trust between parties in business deals are low in some parts of Italy, and this opens the door for corruption and organized crime. According to one observer, a function of the Mafia is its ability to "enforce" business dealings where law and custom cannot.[29]

Russia has a long history of autocratic, oppressive rule lasting for centuries under the Orthodox Church and czarism and culminating in this

---

[27]Dean Starkman, "Corporate Monitors Form a New Industry," *Wall Street Journal*, December 1, 1997, p. B12.

[28]Stephen J. Carroll and Martin J. Gannon, *Ethical Dimensions of International Management*, Thousand Oaks, CA: Sage Publications, 1997, p. 9.

[29]Amartya Sen, "Economics, Business Principles and Moral Sentiments," *Business Ethics Quarterly*, July 1997, p. 9.

century with Communist rule. This history shapes the ethical environment in many ways.[30] High ethical standards were always right with friends and family, but deception and intrigue in dealing with tyrannical officials became accepted. This ethical split carried over into business life, where it remains today.

Authoritarian rule has created a system of *blat,* or the custom of informal, sometimes corrupt, use of favors to get official action. Under Communism, party officials planned business activity in intricate detail, promulgating blizzards of laws, rules, and orders affecting every industry. It was impossible to comply with all these dictates and be efficient in business, so Soviet managers routinely broke rules, manipulated production data, and fabricated accounts to accomplish business goals. The use of *blat* to get ministers to act was widespread and fostered a climate of corruption.

With the downfall of the Soviet regime, an entrepreneurial, free enterprise system sprouted in Russia. But the ethics of this new business system are low by American standards. Under Communist ideology, entrepreneurship was unethical because people were supposed to work for the collective good of the state. The Communist regime taught Russians a stereotyped image of "wild capitalism" that conformed to Karl Marx's worst nightmare. Now, not only are most Russians hostile toward people who start private companies, but the image of capitalism gone wild has become the template that shapes the behavior of the new capitalists. As a result, free enterprise in Russia is chaotic, characterized by corruption, lack of trust, and unpredictability.[31] If history can be viewed as an experiment, Russia is an example of how not to create a climate of decorous ethics.

The *culture* of a nation is a wellspring of many ethical differences. One remarkable variation in business ethics arises from the emphasis on individualism in U.S. culture as opposed to the emphasis on groups in many other cultures. Individualism in American social philosophy makes individual conscience the source of ethical control; the individual sin concept in Christianity makes personal guilt the penalty for bad conduct. But in other countries, a combination of the underlying factors discussed above has created far different ethical values.

The Japanese, for instance, have a strong ethic of fidelity to work groups and corporations. Beginning in about the sixth century, Japan, like other Asian societies, began to borrow and adapt Chinese culture. Traditional values in China stressed that an individual's primary obligation was not to self but to others, including family, clan, and government. The Japanese also built a strong ethic of loyalty to superiors from the emphasis on fidelity in Chinese Confucianism. In medieval times, the extreme of loyalty was seen in samurai,

---

[30]Detelin S. Elenkov, "Can American Management Concepts Work in Russia?" *California Management Review,* Summer 1998, p. 134.

[31]Sheila M. Puffer and Daniel J. McCarthy, "Finding the Common Ground in Russian and American Business Ethics," *California Management Review,* Winter 1995.

who gave their lives for feudal lords. Today it is seen in corporate employees who do ordinary jobs with life-or-death urgency. The concept of sin is foreign to Eastern religion and philosophy, so the Japanese are not controlled by guilty consciences. Rather, they are shamed by group disapproval.

The collectivist ethic in Japan has many consequences. Japanese employees do not blow the whistle on their companies in the face of wrongdoing; they are restrained by loyalty to employers. A Japanese corporation will fire an employee for the breach of simply interviewing with another firm. Loyalty is so strong that if a company does wrong, all employees feel shame. In one case a number of Japanese working for a camera firm in Tokyo grew ashen-faced, left their desks, and started milling in the halls when they heard that the firm was being sued by a German camera company for design imitation. They were close to bolting from the building and had difficulty understanding that lawsuits are a competitive tactic for European firms. In Japan, where group norms control behavior, resort to legal sanctions is reserved for the most heinous crimes, crimes for which the Japanese would feel strong collective guilt. In another instance, reporters from Japan visited Lockheed headquarters in Burbank, California, during the time when the Lockheed payoff scandals were disgracing a Japanese prime minister and his government. They were amazed to see Lockheed employees walking around, looking happy, and behaving normally. They wrote that the Lockheed workers "had no sense of shame."[32]

Philosophy and *religion* may have a deep impact on ethical values. Asian countries are influenced by lines of thought that originated in ancient China. Asian managers, who are inclined to philosophy, read Bing Fa, a form of strategic thinking developed in Chinese military doctrine beginning around 700 B.C.[33] Bing Fa is based on the study of historic warfare. Asians believe that all parts of human existence are interconnected and that universal principles discovered in one area are at work in all areas of life. So ancient battles and strategies are tirelessly studied to find universal truths that can be applied in business. For Asian managers, then, the conduct of business shades into warfare. A greater range of action is seen as legitimate than is the case in the West.

In Bing Fa texts, the most popular of which is Sun Tzu's *Art of War*, deception is a highly valued tactic.[34] Western managers are sometimes angered in business negotiations with Chinese, Japanese, or Korean managers when the Asians hide their purpose through indirection or distraction that to the Westerner is deceitful. Chinese, Japanese, and Koreans directly pry into trade secrets

---

[32]Jack Seward and Howard Van Zandt, *Japan: The Hungry Guest*, rev. ed., Tokyo: Yohan Publications, 1987, pp. 277–78.

[33]*Bing* literally means "soldier" and *Fa* means "doctrine." Both may be translated into "the art of war." Min Chen, *Asian Management Systems*, New York: Routledge, 1995, p. 39. See also Chin-Ning Chu, *The Asian Mind Game*, New York: Rawson Associates, 1991, pp. 10–82.

[34]Sun Tzu, *The Art of War*, trans. Samuel B. Griffith, London: Oxford University Press, 1963. Originally written c. 500 B.C. Another popular text studied by Asian managers is Miyamoto Musashi, *A Book of Five Rings* (Go Rin No Sho), trans. Victor Harris, Woodstock, N.Y.: Overlook Press, 1994. Originally written in 1645.

and delight in snooping on competitors. They may infringe on patents in part because they see the marketplace as a battlefield where manipulations considered unethical in America are seen as elegant by the standards of Bing Fa.

Finally, the *stage of economic development* in a country is a factor. In countries where economic activity is not supported by institutions and values the way it is in developed economies, basic trust may be missing. In many undeveloped and impoverished countries, including many African nations, the structure of civil institutions fails to support high ethical standards. Such nations lack democratic institutions and rule by law. Citizens have low levels of literacy and civic participation. In this situation, consumers, workers, and others injured by unethical business conduct have neither the opportunity nor the experience to work through groups and governments for improved behavior.

In some countries, various pathologies of government create climates of corruption. If the government is highly bureaucratic, as in Venezuela or Italy, there are so many rules and restrictions that bribery, corruption, and personal favoritism are rampant. Red tape is avoided by bribes and friends are given favors in preference to strangers. In both nations, officials can paralyze businesses by strictly applying laws until they get payoffs. Ethics in such countries sink to accommodate forces in the business environment.

As this discussion shows, ethical behavior in business varies considerably around the world. Are some cultures correct about what constitutes proper business ethics and others wrong? There are two ways to answer this question.

The school of *ethical universalism* holds that in terms of biological and psychological needs, human nature is everywhere the same. So ethical rules are transcultural because behavior that fulfills basic needs should be the same everywhere—for example, basic rules of justice must be followed. Basic justice might be achieved, however, through emphasis on group or individual ethics, leaving room for varying cultural tastes.

The school of *ethical relativism* holds that although human biology is everywhere similar, cultural experience creates widely diverging values, including ethical values. Ethical values are subjective. There is no objective way to prove them right or wrong as with scientific facts. A society cannot know that its ethics are superior, so it is wrong for one nation to impose standards on another.

We cannot settle this debate. With the growth of international economic activity in recent years, nations, groups, and trading blocs have more frequently tried to apply formal codes of business ethics across national boundaries. These efforts have had limited success. National culture continues to be the strongest influence over behavior in business dealings. Some scholars argue that at a high level of abstraction, the ethical ideals of all cultures converge to a basic sameness. Thomas Donaldson believes that within the ethical traditions of Western and non-Western civilizations, there is an "overlapping consensus" about three fundamental principles. First, humans have dignity and are not things to be manipulated. Second, humans have basic rights. And third, there is a duty to support the institutions and bonds of a community.[35] At a less abstract level, some research suggests that ethical reasoning is different from country to country, but that even so, attitudes toward questionable business practices such as bribery, pollution, deception, and lying are very similar.[36]

Factors that Influence Managerial Ethics

Many managers have high ethical standards and in surveys say that honesty is highly valued in business. Yet dishonest behavior not only occurs, it is widespread and frequent. A 1981 survey found that about one-third of American managers from the supervisory to the top executive level believed that their bosses sometimes acted unethically. When the survey was repeated ten years later, there was little change. More recently, 30 percent of respondents in a similar survey believed that managers sometimes ignored ethics and broke the law.[37] These surveys are not unusual; they are typical of others over many years. While they do not define an exact quantity of unethical behavior, they do show that perception of unethical behavior has stayed at the same level for more than two decades.

Why do many managers who, if asked, say that they place a high value on honesty sometimes act unethically? The answer is that there are strong forces at work in the business environment that can, depending on how they are managed, push people toward higher or lower ethics. We discuss here four prominent and interrelated forces that shape conduct.

Leadership

The behavior and example of leaders are the most significant influences on ethical standards in a company. Not only do leaders set formal rules, but by their example they show the importance of right behavior or they undermine it. Subordinates are keen observers and quickly notice if standards are, in practice, being upheld or evaded. At companies such as Correct Craft and J. C. Penney, the high aims of founders supported virtuous people, but at some companies, managers communicate by their actions that there is a difference between formal policies and how things actually work. If a sales manager instructs subordinates to deceive customers, a powerful message is sent about

---

[35]Thomas Donaldson, "Values in Tension: Ethics Away from Home," *Harvard Business Review,* September/October 1996, pp. 53–54.

[36]Bryan W. Husted et al., "The Impact of Cross-National Carriers of Business Ethics on Attitudes about Questionable Practices and Form of Moral Reasoning," *Journal of International Business Studies,* Second Quarter 1996, p. 406.

[37]Louisa Wah, "Workplace Conscience Needs a Boost," *American Management Association International,* July/August 1998, p. 6.

accepted behavior. Diverting blame for mistakes, placing self-interest above company goals, or intentionally failing to support colleagues sends a similar message. Consider the teaching by example implied in the following story.

> Ed was a fast-track manager assigned to run a bottling plant in a highly competitive beverage container market. By observing past promotion practices in the company he concluded that he would probably be in the position no longer than two years before reassignment. Knowing that he would be judged on short-term results and wishing to ensure his next promotion Ed took steps to produce a high return on assets (ROA). He did this by reducing costs relative to plant assets. He cut maintenance and repair budgets, deferred major capital expenditures, and cut inventories. Work force costs were reduced by not replacing retirements, stretching work loads for those remaining, and cutting annual raises from the usual 10 percent to 8 percent. After 18 months Ed had increased ROA by 21 percent and was reassigned to a larger plant.[38]

Strategy and Performance

A critical function of managers is to create strong competitive strategies that enable the company to meet financial goals without encouraging ethical compromise. In companies with deteriorating positions, managers have great difficulty meeting performance targets and may feel pressure to compromise ethical standards to do so. Even excellent overall strategies need to be implemented with policies that support honest achievement. Managers can be pressured by unrealistic performance goals or compromised by unwise reward or compensation systems. Such factors are considerations in the following story.

> George L. Ball, chairman and CEO of Prudential-Bache Securities, set out to build an empire. Over a two-year period he increased the number of branch offices by a third and he hired 3,600 new brokers. This growth strategy created huge overhead costs and for its success demanded the generation of enormous revenues. To get them the company sold $8 billion in rickety limited partnerships between 1980 and 1990 to investors who were misled by exaggerated marketing claims about their safety, returns, and tax consequences. To encourage sales, brokers who sold the partnerships were given commissions of 7 or 8 percent, compared to about 1 percent on a stock sale. Additionally, Pru-Bache took a 3.5 percent management fee and a 4 percent charge for organizing the partnership in the first place. Investors, therefore, went into the investment with an immediate 15 percent loss—and most never recovered. Brokers who questioned orders to push sales, or "jam the product," were fired. Ultimately Pru-Bache customers suffered huge losses. A lawsuit by 137,000 investors created major financial and image problems for Pru-Bache and its parent, Prudential Insurance Co. of America.[39]

---

[38]This case is based on events described by Robert Jackell in *Moral Mazes,* New York: Oxford University Press, 1988, chap. 4.

[39]For the full story, see Kathleen Sharp, *In Good Faith,* New York: St. Martin's, 1995.

Corporate Culture

Corporate culture refers to a set of values, norms, rituals, and behavior patterns that characterize a company. Every corporate culture has an ethical dimension that is enforced not primarily by formal policies, but by daily habit and widespread beliefs about which behaviors are rewarded and which are penalized.

Recent graduates of the Harvard MBA program who were interviewed about ethical climates in their organizations revealed the strong presence of four informal but powerful "commandments" that were communicated to them early in their careers.

> First, performance is what really counts, so make your numbers. Second, be loyal and show us that you're a team player. Third, don't break the law. Fourth, don't overinvest in ethical behavior.[40]

The young managers believed, in the face of these informal norms, that if questionable behavior was accompanied by achievement, it advanced careers. They were in fear of taking ethical stands or blowing the whistle, and not without reason. When one manager persisted in challenging false figures that her superior used, she discovered that she was in trouble.

> He started treating other people better. He wasn't on my side anymore, and you needed him on your side to do things. He wasn't my buddy anymore . . . there were other cases of this. He did it by acting like you weren't that smart anymore. It made it really difficult to get the kind of support you needed to be a really top performer.[41]

One factor that contributes to lowered ethical climates in corporations is the inability to raise and discuss ethical issues among managers. This phenomenon, which was studied by Bird and Waters and labeled "moral muteness," is widespread. In their study, Bird and Waters found that "managers seldom discuss with their colleagues the ethical problems they routinely encounter.[42] Indeed, of 300 cases of ethical issues they discovered through interviews with managers, only 12 percent were every openly discussed. There are a number of reasons for this inability to talk about ethical issues. Some managers believe that making ethical judgments of others is confrontational; it involves placing blame and creates anger or grudges. In organizations where formal standards are not followed and deceit is rewarded, ethical arguments have little legitimacy and lack force. In addition, people in business have a sophisticated vocabulary and logic for discussing business issues but lack these assets in the moral realm, and so have a tendency to redefine ethical issues into business

---

[40]Joseph L. Badaracco Jr. and Allen P. Webb, "Business Ethics: A View from the Trenches," *California Management Review,* Winter 1995, p. 11.

[41]Ibid.

[42]See Frederick B. Bird and James A. Waters, "The Moral Muteness of Managers," *California Management Review,* Fall 1989, p. 74.

matters. For example, if someone lays out a fraudulent ad in a committee meeting, those in attendance will not react by accusing the person of dishonesty, but will discuss possible losses of sales and revenue if the misrepresentation is discovered—even if their primary motive for opposing the ad is a desire to be honest. The tendency toward "moral muteness" may be present to some degree in every company.

Individual Characteristics

It is important to have honest people in an organization. Unethical managers may create costly operating or image problems. They may also demoralize good people who see standards undermined.

Ethical behavior is motivated by a mixture of internal disposition and situational incentives. In a corporation with a poor ethical climate, corrupt leaders, and high pressure to achieve numbers, otherwise honest individuals may behave unethically. But all things being equal, it is better to have employees who are internally disposed to act ethically. People differ greatly in their drives, ambitions, neuroses, and penchants for ethical behavior.

Many statistical studies have attempted to discover what characteristics of people are associated with ethical behavior. Recent scholarly reviews of these studies conclude that their findings are too limited to say much with great confidence.[43] Often the studies are not comparable, disagree in result, or are too few to confirm early indications. Still, some findings are established. High ethical behavior is clearly associated with strong religious conviction. There are indications that higher ethics come with advancing age, longer work experience, and more education. Although some studies find differences in the way men and women regard ethical issues, there is no evidence that one sex behaves more ethically in business than the other.[44] Managers give more ethical responses on surveys about questionable practices than do business students.[45] There is considerable evidence that the company environment influences conduct.[46] Individuals seem to act less ethically as corporations increase in size, but tend to be more ethical where companies have codes of conduct.

At lower levels, dishonest job applicants can be weeded out by paper-and-pencil honesty tests that ask questions about past theft, criminal habits, drug use, and fighting. But at managerial levels, there is no test or standard interview procedure to detect an unethical person. Much depends on how managers are

[43]David J. Fritzsche, *Business Ethics: A Global Managerial Perspective,* New York: McGraw-Hill, 1997, chap. 4.

[44]Donald Robin and Laurie Babin, "Making Sense of the Research on Gender and Ethics in Business: A Critical Analysis and Extension," *Journal of Business Ethics,* October 1997, pp. 79–81.

[45]James R. Glenn Jr. and M. Frances Van Loo, "Business Students' and Practitioners' Ethical Decisions Over Time," *Journal of Business Ethics,* November 1993, p. 844.

[46]See, for example, Linda Klebe Trevino, Kenneth D. Butterfield, and Donald L. McCabe, "The Ethical Context in Organizations: Influences on Employee Attitudes and Behaviors," *Journal of Business Ethics,* July 1998.

evaluated and rewarded once hired. Jack Welch, CEO of General Electric, describes how critical choices about a corporation's values are part of evaluating managers.

> In our view, leaders, whether on the shop floor or at the tops of our businesses, can be characterized in at least four ways.
>
> The first is one who delivers on commitments—financial or otherwise—and shares the values of our company. His or her future is an easy call. Onward and upward.
>
> The second type of leader is one who does not meet commitments and does not share our values. Not as pleasant a call, but equally easy.
>
> The third is someone who misses commitments but shares the values. He or she usually gets a second chance, preferably in a different environment.
>
> Then there's the fourth type—the most difficult for many of us to deal with. That leader delivers on commitments, makes all the numbers, but doesn't share the values we must have. This is the individual who typically forces performance out of people rather than inspires it: the autocrat, the big shot, the tyrant. Too often all of us have looked the other way—tolerated these "Type 4" managers because "they always deliver—at least in the short term."[47]

Interrelatedness

The factors that influence ethical behavior in organizations are interrelated. Leadership, particularly, is important in all four. In the next section we examine how some companies have set up comprehensive management systems to mold these factors and encourage higher ethics.

How Corporations Manage Ethics

In the past it was assumed in most companies that ethics are a matter of individual conscience. A few pioneers tried to manage companywide ethics. In 1913, for example, James Cash Penney introduced a conduct code for employees in his department stores. But his effort was unrepresentative; until recently, most companies made no specific effort to manage ethics.

Today, however, many corporations actively encourage higher ethics. In some cases, companies have set up what are called *ethics programs* that use a wide range of techniques to raise standards. These are sometimes called "compliance programs" if their primary focus is on ensuring compliance with laws. Whatever they are called, they operate similarly.

Two factors have encouraged such programs. The first is scandal in industries that depend on the government as a major customer. In 1986 the defense industry, beset by contract billing frauds and cost overruns, launched the Defense Industry Initiative, a program that required contractors to adopt codes of

---

[47]Quoted in Francis J. Aguilar, *Managing Corporate Ethics,* New York: Oxford University Press, 1994, p. 115.

ethics, train employees to comply with laws, create an atmosphere in which employees could discuss violations, and monitor compliance. Now forty-four of the largest defense contractors have broad ethics programs. A decade later, ethics programs spread through companies in the health care services industry because of a federal crackdown on Medicare billing fraud.[48] A second, and related, factor is that since 1991, federal sentencing guidelines for corporations allow dramatic reductions in fines and penalties for companies that have set up internal programs to prevent and report criminal behavior.[49]

The General Dynamics Program

One of the earliest, broadest, and most widely followed ethics programs is that of General Dynamics Corporation. This program has confronted some difficulties inherent in trying to elevate corporate ethics, and the results are instructive. The program began because the company got in trouble.

In 1985 the Secretary of the Navy suspended Navy contracts with General Dynamics worth more than $1 billion, citing a "pervasive corporate attitude" that mocked the public trust. The company had been caught in a series of illegal acts. Managers shifted costs from fixed-price contracts to contracts that permitted cost overruns. Executives charged country club dues to military contracts. The chairman billed the government for flights to his farm. In return for resumption of work on Navy contracts, General Dynamics agreed to start a corporate ethics program.

It set up an expansive program immediately. The objectives were twofold, to make secure government contracts by ending illegal behavior and to improve the company's image. The implied goals were broader, and included achieving an ethical organization, promoting open discussion of ethical issues, and improving trust in relationships with customers, suppliers, and employees.[50]

As the program began, a twenty-page booklet, *General Dynamics Standards of Business Ethics and Conduct,* was distributed to all employees. The chairman personally handed it to people reporting directly to him. In turn, these managers gave the book in person to their subordinates, and so forth, until the *Standards* had cascaded to the lowest organizational level. More than 60,000 suppliers and subcontractors also received the *Standards* and were asked to abide by the contents.

To oversee the program, General Dynamics set up a board committee on corporate responsibility and hired a staff vice president of business ethics who

---

[48]See Deanna Bellandi, "Rolling Out the Red Carpet: As the Government Turns Up the Heat to Wipe Out Healthcare Fraud, Providers Give Compliance Experts the Royal Treatment," *Modern Healthcare,* September 29, 1997, and Greg Radinsky, "Making Sense of the Federal Sentencing Guidelines: How Health Care Corporations Can Manage Risk by Adopting Corporate Compliance Programs," *Journal of Health and Hospital Law,* June 1997.

[49]You start with a five-point culpability score, and can subtract three points if the company has an ethics program. United States Sentencing Commission, *Guidelines Manual,* footnote 40, p. 360.

[50]Richard A. Barker, "An Evaluation of the Ethics Program at General Dynamics," *Journal of Business Ethics,* March 1993, pp. 166, 171.

reported to the chief executive and supervised ethics program directors at each company facility. All employees were required to attend an ethics training workshop led by a General Dynamics manager, and by 1986 all 103,000 had gone to one. Many employees reacted defensively and negatively to discussions of ethics. Some resented the training, sensing an implication that their personal integrity was deficient.

New communications channels opened to air ethical concerns. All managers were instructed to maintain an atmosphere in which ethical issues could be frankly discussed without fear of reprisal. Annual bonuses were based in part on ethical leadership. The company also set up ethics hotlines, special numbers answered by the ethics directors, which could be used by employees or suppliers to ask questions, seek advice, or report wrongdoing. Callers could remain anonymous. In the first six years of the program, employees made almost 30,000 contacts with ethics directors at a rate of about six contacts per 100 employees per year.

When violations of the *Standards* were discovered, company policy made punishment mandatory. After six years, 1,419 sanctions had been made. Most were warnings (508) or reprimands (432), but 165 employees were discharged.[51]

The early results of the General Dynamics program were mixed. It achieved its main objective, which was to end illegal behavior so that government contracts continued. By 1991 the company was not under investigation by the Pentagon for any illegal activity, despite a record number of ongoing criminal investigations in the defense industry. But it fell short of achieving its broader goal of creating new ethical norms and building trust between superiors and subordinates. After four years of operation, surveys in one division found that only 27 percent of employees thought that the company was genuinely interested in their welfare, about one-third believed that they were not treated with dignity, and two-thirds feared reprisals for using the ethics hotline. Eighty percent of a panel of professional and hourly workers interviewed thought that the program was a "sham" and "simply a whitewash scheme to present a false front to [the government]."[52]

These attitudes reflected less success for the program than had been anticipated. An underlying problem was cutbacks in defense spending. By the early 1990s, General Dynamics had nearly halved its workforce from what it had been when the ethics program began. Building trust with employees was difficult while so many were being laid off.

Guidelines for Managing Ethics Programs

The General Dynamics program exemplifies a state-of-the-art effort to create an ethical corporation. Its mixed results show the formidable resistance in

---

[51]*Standards of Business Ethics and Conduct: The First Six Years,* St. Louis: General Dynamics Corporation, November 1991.

[52]Barker, "An Evaluation of the Ethics Program at General Dynamics," p. 172.

large companies to elevating standards and also the results that can be achieved. The company maintains the program and continues to update the *Standards* to reflect changes in laws and conditions.[53] The following elements, all of which have been important at General Dynamics, are critical to the success of ethics programs if they are to overcome factors that tend to depress ethical behavior.

Top Management Leadership.   The chief executive officer should initiate the ethics program and clearly state the importance of correct behavior. A vivid illustration of how this can be done is seen in the actions of Robert Cushman, CEO of the Norton Company, an abrasives manufacturer with plants in twenty-seven countries. After introducing a strong ethics code, Cushman presented it at a conference for his international managers. A vice president in attendance that day remembers how he was challenged.

> During a panel discussion, some of the key Europeans were particularly animated in objecting to the code's stringent rules on certain kinds of payments which were standard in their countries. Cushman acknowledged their difference of opinion openly and then reiterated what "the Company" expected them to do. He was decidedly unapologetic about taking an authoritarian stance: "I've had to live by certain rules, and so do you." [Some were] taken aback by Cushman's words, but found the session to be a real eye opener about just how strongly top management meant the code to be enforced.[54]

In addition, management must avoid adopting business strategies, time lines, and reward systems that place unreasonable pressure on employees.

Codes of Ethics.   Codes of ethics are written statements of aspirations and rules. They vary from book length to succinct statements that express a company philosophy in one or two pages. One of the simplest on record was that of the Samsonite Company, which issued to its sales force small marbles printed with the Golden Rule. More than 90 percent of large American firms have an ethics code.[55] Smaller companies and non-American ones are less likely to have them.

Effective codes have a number of characteristics. They go beyond generalities. Many codes contain platitudes about honesty, integrity, respect, teamwork, and fairness. But the best ones also give concrete direction on specific ethical conflicts employees are going to face. An example is the Sears code, which asks employees to "deal fairly, honestly, and responsibly with all customers," then defines specific actions that achieve this; for example, sales agents must "never misrepresent a competitor's merchandise or services."

---

[53]*Standards of Business Ethics and Conduct,* 4th ed., Falls Church, VA: General Dynamics Corporation, January 1998.

[54]Laura Nash, "The Norton Company's Ethics Program," in *Corporate Ethics: A Prime Business Asset,* New York: The Business Roundtable, February 1988, p. 120.

[55]Patrick E. Murphy, *Eighty Exemplary Ethics Statements,* Notre Dame, IN: University of Notre Dame Press, 1998, p. 3.

Effective codes are written in an open process that involves employees. They are revised so that they can evolve—when Northern Telecom revised its code, thirty-six employee focus groups were convened to tell the company about practical ethics problems they faced. They are well-communicated—the United Technologies Corporation code is reprinted in twenty-two languages. And they should be well-enforced; if they are not, there may be a double standard in the company culture.

Changes in Organization Structure.   General Dynamics anchors responsibility for its ethics program in two powerful committees, one of board-of-directors members and the other of senior managers. It established a vice president of ethics to run the program and put ethics program directors in major locations around the world. It also involved functional areas and the internal auditing staff in code enforcement. Hotlines were set up to open communications between workers and higher management. In theory, opening such channels facilitates the venting of allegations, since employees can fear speaking to immediate supervisors. In practice, however, employees were suspicious of hotlines and feared retaliation. Other companies have faced similar problems, and multinationals find that some cultures consider hotlines offensive. Northern Telecom got few calls from employees in Asia, where there is no cultural support for disloyalty even toward unethical colleagues.[56]

Training.   A key element of an ethics program is training. At General Dynamics, workers attend half-day workshops where they learn about the ethics program, watch videotapes, and discuss case studies. There are many approaches to training. At Citicorp, workshop attendees play a game called Work Ethic. Players draw cards printed with brief ethical dilemmas and multiple-choice answers. They can then earn points or even be "discharged" depending on the answers they pick. Generally, ethics training is most effective when it is done by company managers, not by outsiders, and when it steers away from abstract philosophy to focus directly on the work lives of those attending.

Enforcement.   A number of approaches are used to get compliance with ethics policies. At many companies, employees must sign statements that they have received and read policies and then sign annual compliance affidavits. At Chemical Bank, internal auditors establish controls to enforce ethical practice. These extend down to levels that in some companies would not have much ethical significance. For example, there is a requirement that records show whether letters expressing regret are sent to rejected job applicants within thirty days.[57] At Boeing, managers are told that a scandal in their plant

---

[56]Nigel Richardson and Megan Barry, "Minding Your Ps and Qs at Nortel," *CMA*, May 1997, p. 20.
[57]"How Chemical Bank Audits Compliance with a Code of Conduct," *Ethikos*, January/February 1993, p. 12.

or program will lead to a severe pay cut—even if they are not guilty of personal wrongdoing.

Violators of standards must be dealt with. Their treatment enters company folklore and conveys by example whether top management is serious or winks at violations. Recently, Lockheed Martin printed the disposition of cases representative of the 4,000 cases handled by its Office of Ethics and Business Conduct over a three-year period. Examples show that the typical violator is not trapped in a convoluted dilemma, the escape from which requires airy philosophical reasoning. Rather, he or she is engaged in worldly wrongdoing, much of it petty.

Case #1: Conflict of Interest

A supplier offered a large sum of cash in an envelope (believed to be several thousand dollars) to a manager at a remote facility. The manager, recognizing the impropriety, declined the offer and promptly reported the incident.

Action: Reported to federal officials as potential kickback. Supplier terminated.

Case #2: Misuse or Abuse of Assets

While seeking necessary business files from an employee's unlocked disk while he was on vacation, a coworker discovered obscene photos, magazines, diskettes, and other material inappropriate to the workplace (some potentially illegal under state and federal law). It was subsequently determined that data were downloaded through the Internet, that company equipment stored the images, and copies of the images were made on company printers.

Action: Employee discharged. Appropriate authorities notified.

Case #3: Gift, Gratuities, and Other Courtesies

A manager reported that a subordinate had accepted tickets to an outside event from a supplier for whom the employee had written a letter of justification to select the supplier over the low bidder. The subordinate's job duties included evaluating the quality of the supplier's work and approving payment.

Action: Employee discharged. Supplier removed from bidders list for a one-year period. A report was made to appropriate authorities regarding potential kickback.[58]

While punishment is often necessary, there is a need to encourage aspiration rather than focus only on bad behavior. When, in the past, General Dynamics published yearly statistical summaries of violations and punishments, some workers were frightened; their feelings that ethics were only about wrongdoing, not uplifting, were reinforced.

Other Measures.   There are many other steps that can be taken. Some companies use ombudsmen to resolve disputes. At Texas Instruments, a weekly electronic newspaper carries information on ethics and cases about which employees around the world can send in comments. Some companies use paper-and-pencil honesty tests to weed out less-ethical job applicants.

---

[58]Adapted from Carol Marshall, "Ethics: The Merger 'Glue,' " *Lockheed Martin Today,* September 1997.

Overall, ethics programs require a set of reinforcing actions. If such actions are taken, lawbreaking can be reduced and a more elevated ethical culture can be nurtured. But problems, including employee cynicism, resistance, and fear, are difficult to overcome.

Concluding Observations

The business environment is rich in sources of ethical values. Yet strong forces in competitive markets and within companies work to depress behavior. Managers can use a range of methods to discourage lawbreaking and encourage higher ethics in their companies. These methods have had some success, but there is no evidence that, overall, behavior is more ethical today than in the past. In the next chapter, we take a close look at ethical decisions to explain why they can be difficult.

DOW CORNING AND BREAST IMPLANTS

In 1943 Dow Chemical Company and Corning Incorporated in partnership started a new company to develop and market a unique material called silicone. This new company was Dow Corning Corporation. It grew into a major corporation in its own right with 9,100 employees, manufacturing locations on five continents, and annual revenues of more than $2 billion. For most of its life, it made a lot of money for its two corporate parents, each of which held 50 percent of its stock (which, in fact, is still the case).

Dow Corning also succeeded as an incubator for new uses of silicone. The company holds more than 6,000 active patents and sells more than 10,000 silicone-based products. One product it pioneered was breast implants made of silicone. In the years that it made them, sales of these implants were never more than one-tenth of 1 percent of its annual revenues.[1] Yet they drove the company into bankruptcy. What follows is the story of how honest, well-intentioned managers muddled their way into a quicksand of lawsuits and bankruptcy.

Development of Breast Implants

Before the advent of silicone, doctors had used other substances to enlarge women's breasts, including stainless steel, rubber, and plastic sponges. The body rejected these materials or the aesthetic results were poor. When silicone became available after World War II, doctors tried injecting it directly into the breast, with results that were often disfiguring when loose silicone migrated in the chest.

In 1959 two physicians at Baylor University had the idea of making better implants by filling silicone bags with saline solution. They turned to Dow Corning for help and the company applied its expertise with silicone to the

---

[1]"Dow Corning Restructures Medical Materials Product Line," *Corporate News,* Dow Corning Corporation, December 8, 1992, p. 2.

231

task. No reliable, nonleaking valve to contain a saltwater solution was available, so the company's chemists recommended filling a silicone bag with a semiliquid silicone gel that would feel much like natural breast tissue.

As the chemists bent themselves to the task of making a prototype, the two doctors put silicone implants in a few dogs for eighteen months. This would be the only testing done to check for biological reactions before the first implants were marketed. Dow Corning did no animal studies of its own but believed, based on experience with other silicone products such as shunts and catheters, that silicone was biologically inert and harmless in the human body. Neither did it do any clinical trials with human subjects. These weren't required because of a gaping loophole in the Food, Drug, and Cosmetic Act of 1938. This law required drug companies to do rigorous animal and human studies before selling a prescription drug. But it allowed "medical devices," even those put into the human body, to be sold without any testing. If Dow Corning had invented a pill to enlarge women's breasts, years of expensive animal tests and clinical trials would have been required to prove its safety. Yet a device to be put in breast tissue required no testing. Therefore, when Dow Corning put the first silicone-gel breast implant on the market in 1963, no testing had proved it safe.

A Closer Look at Silicone

Silicones are long, heavy molecules based on a repeating chain of silicon and oxygen atoms. Silicon is the second most abundant elemental substance, comprising 28 percent of the earth's crust. It is the building block for the silica compounds in sand. To make silicone products, Dow Corning purchases large amounts of silicon from suppliers that refine it from sand.

Silicones do not exist in nature, but are created in a high-temperature process during which chemists can manipulate them by adding organic molecules like methyl or phenyl and raising or lowering the heat. This is how silicone powders, liquids, semiliquid gels (as in breast implants), and solids are made. A child's Silly Putty is a silicone molecule containing a methyl group cooked in a 5 percent boric acid solution for many hours at a temperature above 300° F.

Until the 1940s, silicones were experimental curiosities, but their practical properties were eventually recognized. It was the military value of silicones that led to the formation of Dow Corning. For example, the company made gaskets for searchlights on antiaircraft guns. The gaskets retained their shape and shock absorbency within a temperature range of −55 to +570° F, so they could absorb recoil and withstand heat from the electric arc in the lights. Silicone fluids were made for the hydraulic systems of airplanes, where they retained viscosity over a broader temperature range than motor oils and were less flammable. In those days, silicones were seen as wondrous substances with boundless potential.

The useful properties of silicones also brought them into consumer products. They are inert and do not react chemically at normal temperatures, so in paints and coatings they resist oxidation. They are heat and flame resistant and do not conduct electricity, making them fine insulators. Their low surface tension makes them slippery, so they ease the application of waxes, polishes, hand lotions, and roll-on antiperspirants. Because of antifoaming qualities, they are added to fruit juices, molasses, soft drinks, shampoos, varnishes, and detergents.

A New Generation of Implants

Dow Corning's silicone-gel implants were thought to be completely safe, and demand surged as women took advantage of them. However, in the early 1970s, competitors hired away Dow Corning's scientists and attacked its market monopoly with new, superior, silicone-gel implants. These implants had thinner envelopes and more flexible gel. They felt more like natural breast tissue than the firmer, stiffer Dow Corning implants. By 1975 these competitors had reduced Dow Corning to a one-third market share.

To counter competitors' implants, Dow Corning created a new, thinner, silicone gel of its own called flo-gel (polydimethylsiloxane). The company projected sales of over 50,000 a year and wanted to rush flo-gel to market. A deadline of June 1975 was set and great urgency was attached to meeting it. In January 1975, a mammary task force was set up to guide product development and to oversee medical testing. It was led by Arthur H. Rathjen, a hard-driving manager whose memos featured a countdown to the June deadline. A January 31 memo began: "17 weeks, 121 days, 2,904 hours, 174,240 minutes."[2]

Although members of the task force shared the strong belief that silicone was safe in the human body, it was decided that it was important to see if "gel-bleed" would be a medical problem with the new implants. Gel-bleed occurred when silicone molecules migrated through the thin plastic envelope that encased the new liquid gel. The thinner formulation in flo-gel contained smaller molecules, which is why it was more flexible and felt more natural.

But these smaller molecules slipped through the larger molecular structure of the outer silicone envelope. This was so pronounced that the implants had a greasy, slippery feel in the hand. Sales managers found molecular bleeding to be a nuisance. A memo written on May 12, 1975, said that the implants on display at a trade show "became oily" and "were bleeding on the velvet in the showcase."[3] Some task force members were concerned that gel-bleed might cause adverse reactions in humans.

Dow Corning decided to do some testing on animals and humans. Early in February 1975, implants were inserted in rabbits. Before the rabbit test

---

[2]Marlene Cimons, "Implant Firm's Memos Linked to Full FDA Ban," *Los Angeles Times,* January 17, 1992, p. A32.
[3]Ibid.

ended, eight women in Canada received the new implants in experimental surgery. When the rabbit test report came in four days later, it indicated significant inflammatory reactions in the animals, but stated that these might be related to the implant surgery rather than bleeding gel. In another test the implants were put in dogs and found to have migrated in their bodies. Weeks later the rabbits showed persistent inflammation.

Nevertheless, Dow Corning marketed its new implants on schedule without more testing. A consensus existed in the company that the gel was not a new material, only another formulation of biologically inert silicone. This sanguine view was not unanimous. Thomas Talcott, a product engineer on the implant team, believed that if the implant sac ruptured, the fluid gel would spread to surrounding tissue, posing unknown risks. He urged more study. When it was not forthcoming he resigned. The company attributed his resignation to poor performance reviews.

The new flo-gel implants went on the market in the fall of 1975. Soon, Dow Corning's sales force ran into inquiries and complaints from plastic surgeons about noticeable gel-bleed, migration of leaking gel, and ruptured implants. Sales representatives were angry. "To put a questionable lot of mammaries on the market is inexcusable," wrote one in a memo to his boss. "I don't know who is responsible for this decision but it has to rank right up there with the Pinto gas tank."[4]

When physicians noticed severe inflammatory reactions in some women, Rathjen wrote an internal memorandum raising questions. "We are engulfed in unqualified speculation . . . Is there something in the implant that migrates out of or off the prosthesis? Yes or no!"[5] The scientists in the company concluded that the case reports were medical anomalies and their faith in the safety of silicone was unshaken. So no clinical studies were initiated.

Despite this rocky start, the new flo-gel implants restored Dow Corning's market dominance. Over the next fifteen years, the popularity of breast augmentation soared and plastic surgeons bought hundreds of thousands of them. Most women were pleased with their implants. Reports of problems continued, but they were not frequent or compelling enough to shake the company's belief that silicone was safe.

Breast Implant Surgery

Breast implants are used for reconstruction by women who have accidental or surgical disfiguration. But the vast majority—about 70 percent—are used for cosmetic reasons.

---

[4]Quoted in John A. Byrne, *Informed Consent,* New York: McGraw-Hill, 1996, p. 78.
[5]Philip J. Hilts, "Maker of Implants Balked at Testing, Its Records Show," *New York Times,* January 13, 1992, p. B1.

Mammograph showing a silicone-gel breast implant.

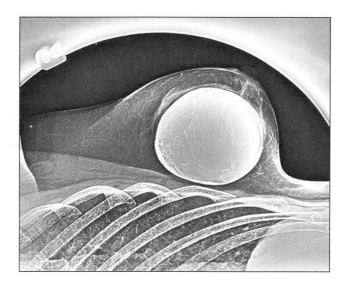

There are three basic types. *Gel-filled* implants contain viscous silicones held in place by a flexible silicone envelope. *Saline* implants contain sterile saline solution inside a silicone envelope. They are like balloons filled with salt water. Saline implants can be inserted in collapsed form through a small incision and then filled in place. If the capsule ruptures, the salt water is harmlessly absorbed by the body within hours. The woman will, of course, wake up in the morning with a deflated breast. (Dow Corning never made saline implants.) *Double-lumen* implants contain a gel capsule surrounded by an envelope of saline (or sometimes the reverse). This design is thought to create a more natural-looking breast.

Most implant surgeries are performed as outpatient procedures. Either local or general anesthesia may be used. Incisions are usually made under the breast where the implant is inserted in a pocket cut out by the surgeon. It takes about two hours and there can be pain afterward. For plastic surgeons, the procedure is simple: "like changing a tire," in the words of one.[6] The current cost of breast implantation is $4,000 to $8,000.

Women who get implants risk complications. After insertion the body forms scar tissue around them. As this tissue hardens it contracts, squeezing the implant into a round shape. The breast may feel hard and be painful. Capsular contracture, as this is called, occurs in about half of the recipients. Another common problem is loss of nipple sensation immediately following

---

[6]Quoted in Susan M. Zimmermann, *Silicone Survivors*, Philadelphia: Temple University Press, 1998, p. 57.

surgery. This also affects about half of all patients. In some cases full or partial sensation returns in six to nine months. Less frequently, women may suffer a range of postsurgical complications such as skin necrosis from inadequate blood circulation when skin stretches to accommodate the implant, asymmetrical breasts, and palpable wrinkling of the implant's surface.[7]

Implants may rupture. With saline implants, the saltwater solution is harmlessly absorbed by the body. With gel-filled implants, however, the gel is no longer confined and can migrate to form disfiguring lumps in the chest, shoulder, or arm. Some ruptured implants are asymptomatic; the gel remains in place and the woman never knows.

Besides these well-known problems, implants are accused of causing autoimmune diseases. Some women with implants have developed connective tissue disorders of an autoimmune origin such as scleroderma, a disfiguring hardening of tissue beneath the skin; lupus erythematosus, a debilitating inflammatory disease of the skin and internal organs; and rheumatoid arthritis, a painful inflammation of the joints. The theory is that silicone molecules leak from implants and trigger the formation of antibodies, which, in turn, cause an autoimmune reaction. This theory remains unproven.

Controversy Rises

In 1977 a Houston jury awarded a woman $170,000 for pain and suffering caused by a ruptured Dow Corning implant. In 1985 a San Francisco jury awarded another woman $1.7 million based on her claim that silicone migrating from a ruptured implant had caused a painful immune system response. During the trial, her lawyers discovered old Dow Corning internal memos questioning the safety of the flo-gel implants and reports on the animal studies in which dogs and rabbits had suffered inflammation. The jury found the company guilty of fraud for its failure to disclose to women the risks alluded to in these documents. It was also found guilty of selling a defective product and breaching its written warranty that the implants would last a lifetime. The company's response was to change the wording on package inserts to disclose more risks.

There were no more lawsuits during the 1980s, but controversy over implants slowly grew. Discussions about them appeared in the media. Activists emerged and campaigned for more investigation and regulation of implants. Their efforts soon bore fruit.

In 1976 Congress passed the Medical Device Amendments to the Federal Food, Drug, and Cosmetic Act of 1938. This new law finally gave the Food and Drug Administration (FDA) authority to require premarket safety testing of

---

[7]Package insert for "Silastic MSI Brand Mammary Implant H.P. Gel-Filled Design by Dow Corning Wright," Rev. 3, June 1991, pp. 4–8.

medical devices. The law was not inspired by breast implants, though it would soon snare them. Rather, it was passed in response to scandals with other medical devices, particularly the Dalkon Shield, an intrauterine device that was untested before its sale. It had caused twenty deaths and thousands of serious infections in women.

Unfortunately, the new law failed to close the devices' loophole completely. About 100 devices that had been on the market before its passage, including silicone breast implants, were exempted. However, if the FDA believed that an exempted device was dangerous, it could require that manufacturers prove its safety. The FDA's medical devices staff did, in fact, believe that silicone-gel implants were dangerous and set out to reclassify them. It took twelve years, but in 1988, over the persistent opposition of Dow Corning, the exemption was ended. Breast implant manufacturers were given thirty months to submit evidence that silicone breast implants were safe.[8]

In 1991 Dow Corning turned over 10,000 pages of data intended to prove safety. The FDA assembled an advisory panel to review the evidence and after several months, the panel concluded that while the data on gel-filled implants were insufficient to prove their safety, the data also were not alarming enough to warrant banning them. Dow Corning was given more time to collect and submit further proof of safety.

The Hopkins Case Leads to an FDA Moratorium

By this time, a hostile media environment had developed in which many emotional and sensational stories about breast implants dominated coverage. Then a San Francisco jury awarded $7.3 million to a woman named Marianne Hopkins who claimed that silicone molecules spreading from a ruptured Dow Corning implant into her lymph nodes had harmed her immune system. She suffered extreme fatigue and swollen, painful joints, and had been diagnosed with irreversible mixed connective tissue disorder. Dow Corning's lawyers argued that there was no scientific evidence that silicone exposure caused immune reactions. Hopkin's attorneys introduced into evidence the internal memos used in the 1985 case. The jury held that the company had marketed a defective design and negligently failed to warn women of risks.

This verdict stunned Dow Corning, which immediately issued a press release calling it "outrageous" and "an affront to the more than 8,000 Dow Corning employees worldwide."[9] After the trial, the internal documents were sealed by court order, but one of Hopkin's attorneys leaked them to FDA Commissioner David Kessler. The documents so alarmed Kessler that on January 6, 1992,

---

[8]53 FR 23856, June 24, 1988.

[9]Dow Corning, *Corporate News,* "Dow Corning and Its Employees Call San Francisco Jury Award Regarding Breast Implants 'Outrageous' . . . ," December 13, 1991, pp. 1, 2.

three days after getting them, he announced a forty-five-day moratorium on the sale of silicone-gel breast implants.

The FDA moratorium, following closely on the heels of the Hopkins decision, was an unmitigated disaster for Dow Corning and all other implant manufacturers. It set the companies on a collision course with a mass of lawsuits. Attorneys around the country who specialize in products liability cases noted Hopkin's $7.3 million award, of which $6.5 million was punitive damages, and the FDA's action, which suggested serious defects. Within a week the sharks were circling. Two Houston attorneys filed seventy-eight implant lawsuits in Texas. Other attorneys set up toll-free numbers and took out newspaper ads seeking plaintiffs. By the end of the month, the number of cases had grown to about 1,000, and this was just the beginning.[10]

In February 1992, the FDA advisory panel met again. It concluded that there was not yet enough evidence to establish a causal connection between silicone-gel implants and the symptoms and diseases they were alleged to cause. But it also said that manufacturers still had not proved the devices safe. It recommended restrictions on their use. So Commissioner Kessler extended his moratorium indefinitely until the safety of the silicone-gel implants was borne out by medical research. Saline implants would remain available. "The legal standard is not that devices must be proved unsafe before the FDA can protect patients against their use," Kessler explained. "Rather, the law requires a positive demonstration of safety—and the burden of proof rests squarely with the manufacturer."[11] After Kessler's announcement, Dow Corning ceased making silicone breast implants and never resumed.

Lawsuits Drive Dow Corning into Bankruptcy

Lawsuits against Dow Corning and its competitors accumulated. One attorney, Stanley Chesley, requested a federal court to certify women with breast implants as a "class" so that an unlimited number of cases could be combined into one action. This would create a class action suit, which is used when a large number of parties seek to redress similar injuries. All the cases are assigned to one court where the judge appoints a committee of lawyers to negotiate a settlement with manufacturers or take the case to trial for all injured plaintiffs. The attorneys receive a percentage of any monetary settlement or trial award. By collecting many cases, plaintiffs' lawyers put extreme pressure on a corporation to settle, and the larger the settlement, the greater their own compensation.

A class certification was given in 1992 and many breast implant cases were consolidated and assigned to federal judge Sam C. Pointer Jr. in Birmingham, Alabama.[12] Lawyers around the country could and did bring their cases

---

[10]Joseph Nocera, "Fatal Litigation," *Fortune,* October 16, 1995, p. 74.

[11]David A. Kessler, "The Basis of the FDA's Decision on Breast Implants," *New England Journal of Medicine,* June 18, 1992, p. 1713.

[12]*In re Silicone Gel Breast Implants Products Liability Litigation,* U.S.D.C., N. Dist., Ala., 92-P-10000-S.

into the class action, which quickly grew to about 10,000 women plaintiffs. Judge Pointer set up a committee of the women's attorneys to negotiate with Dow Corning and other manufacturers.

Other attorneys purposely kept their clients out of the class action. In particular, two Houston attorneys lined up cases for 2,000 women and planned to bring them to trial one by one, running them through the courts "like quarters in a slot machine," and forcing implant manufacturers to face one large verdict or pretrial settlement after another.[13] When they brought their first case to trial, the jury awarded $25 million against another implant maker, Bristol-Myers Squibb. Subsequently, as the Texas attorneys prepared new cases for trial, Dow Corning and other manufacturers, terrified of the potential cost of a jury award, settled with them for up to $1 million per case. Attorney fees were reported to be 40 percent of these settlements.

Dow Corning and the other firms were caught in the vise-like grip of two reinforcing legal strategies. Although the companies won many cases they brought to trial by focusing on the dearth of scientific evidence that implants were harmful, they lost others when women's attorneys convinced juries that women were inadequately warned of risks and that danger signals had been covered up. The sheer mass of cases threatened astronomical legal costs if they went to trial one-by-one, even if the manufacturers prevailed in the majority. The success of the Texas lawyers raised the potential costs of settling the class action. If women in it did not feel that they were getting enough money, they would opt out and have their cases tried individually. Why should they accept a settlement of tens of thousands of dollars when they could go to Texas and get hundreds of thousands?

A Failed Settlement Leads to Bankruptcy

In April 1994, Judge Pointer announced that a $4.25 billion settlement agreement had been reached between women's attorneys and breast implant manufacturers. Under the agreement, women who alleged a wide range of injuries from their implants, either currently or over the next thirty years, would be compensated. Women were to receive 75 percent of the money; the rest, or a little more than $1 billion, would be divided among a few attorneys. But the settlement fell apart. It was very generous—women with autoimmune disease could get up to $1.4 million—and any woman with implants could register to participate in it. Whereas 10,000 women had been enrolled in the class action, more women materialized to sign up for the settlement, until there were almost 400,000 in all, including 137,000 claiming current symptoms. There were so many women that the payment to each would have been less than 5 percent of original estimates. The plan collapsed.

With the class action settlement falling apart and attorneys in Texas prepared to take more cases to trial, Dow Corning faced a debilitating financial

---

[13]Nocera, "Fatal Litigation," p. 78.

gauntlet. If nothing was done, it would eventually run out of cash to conduct normal business operations. On May 15, 1995, the company filed a Chapter 11 bankruptcy petition. This froze all claims against it, including lawsuits, until a committee of creditors could be set up to resolve its financial problems. All implant claims against Dow Corning were moved to a federal bankruptcy court in Michigan where the bankruptcy proceedings would take place.[14]

Later in the year, the other manufacturers that were being sued went ahead without Dow Corning and settled more than 80 percent of the cases against them in an agreement of between $2 and $3 billion (depending on how many women filed claims).[15] For women who settled, payments have ranged from $10,000 to $250,000, with the average being $26,000. Even so, the morass of litigation has continued for these companies as 11,041 women opted not to settle and continued to pursue the class action in Judge Pointer's court or their own individual cases outside the class.

Medical Evidence About Implants

While Dow Corning and the other manufacturers struggled with lawsuits, medical researchers began to publish the results of studies that shed more light on health risks. The most awaited of these studies were the ones initiated to examine the possibility that silicone implants caused serious diseases. There was no question that some women suffered inflammation, infection, capsular contracture, and implant rupture. But claims that implants were responsible for cancer and immune diseases were the ones that led to multimillion-dollar jury awards and placed a high cost on settling the class actions.

Before 1995, evidence of the risks of implants had been largely anecdotal, that is, based on single cases or small numbers of cases. About one percent of American women have implants and another one percent have autoimmune disease. By coincidence then, a small number of women have both. So the individual cases written up in medical journals did not prove that immune disorders were caused by implants. What was needed were studies that compared a large group of women with implants to a large group of women without them to see if disease was more prevalent in the implant group. Work on such studies had begun in the early 1990s when the FDA called for evidence on the safety of the devices.

Uniformly, the studies as they came in failed to show that silicone-gel implants increased the risk of serious disease in women. The first major study to be published came early in 1995. It compared connective tissue disease in

---

[14]*In re Dow Corning Corporation, Debtor,* USBC (E. Dist. Mich., N. Div.), 95-20512-11-AJS.

[15]These companies were Baxter International, Bristol-Myers Squibb Company, McGhan Medical Corporation, Minnesota Mining & Manufacturing Company, and Union Carbide Corporation. The latter two companies were sued as producers of silicone used in breast implants sold by other companies.

1,183 women with silicone-gel implants and 86,381 women without implants. The authors found no association between implants and disease.[16] The next study, published in 1996, looked at connective tissue disease in 10,830 women with implants and 384,713 women without implants. This study found a statistically significant, but very minor, increased risk of connective tissue disease among women with implants. The authors believed that this could have been because women in the study were allowed to self-report a diagnosis of disease. They concluded that "women with breast implants should be reassured that there is no large risk of connective tissue disease."[17] Soon additional large-scale studies were published, and not one showed any statistical connection between implants and a wide range of autoimmune disorders.

Cancer studies also failed to show evidence that women with implants are more likely to have cancer. A 1992 study, for example, found that 11,676 women with silicone implants experienced only about half the number of breast cancers that would be expected in the general population.[18]

The women's attorneys attacked the studies.[19] They argued that the numbers of women in the group studies were too small to detect rare connective tissue disorders. For instance, in the 1995 study discussed above, out of 87,501 women, only 516 had a connective tissue disorder and of these only three had implants.[20] One group of researchers estimated that for a study to have sufficient statistical power to rule out any increased risk of connective tissue disorder, it would be necessary to have 64,000 women with implants in the study group, but organizing this number of women and verifying their medical conditions is an impossible research task.[21] Therefore, the studies do not provide definitive, scientific proof of total safety. They only rule out large risks, so the individual women in court could still be legitimate victims.

Women's lawyers also argued that the studies focused on classic symptoms of connective tissue disease; therefore, the researchers might have missed a new silicone-gel-related disorder. Such a disorder has never been identified and remains an unproven, theoretical possibility. Finally, some of the studies had been funded by Dow Corning, and physicians wrote to medical journals questioning the objectivity of these efforts. Yet the researchers

---

[16]J. Sanchez-Guerrero et al., "Silicone Breast Implants and the Risk of Connective-Tissue Diseases and Symptoms," *New England Journal of Medicine,* June 22, 1995, pp. 1666–70.

[17]C. H. Hennekens et al., "Self-Reported Breast Implants and Connective-Tissue Diseases in Female Health Professionals: A Retrospective Cohort Study," *Journal of the American Medical Association,* February 28, 1996, p. 616.

[18]Hans Berkel, Dale C. Birdsell, and Heather Jenkins, "Breast Augmentation: A Risk Factor for Breast Cancer?" *New England Journal of Medicine,* June 18, 1992, pp. 1649–53.

[19]See "Statement of Sidney M. Wolfe, M.D., Public Citizen's Health Research Group, to the Institute of Medicine Committee on the Safety of Silicone Breast Implants," July 24, 1998, http://www.citizen.org/hrg/PUBLICATIONS/1448.htm.

[20]Sanchez-Guerrero, "Silicone Breast Implants and the Risk of Connective-Tissue Diseases and Symptoms," p. 1666.

[21]S. E. Gabriel et al., "Risk of Connective Tissue Diseases and Other Disorders after Breast Implantation," *New England Journal of Medicine,* June 16, 1994, pp. 1697–1702.

made available their methods and data for others to analyze. Sometimes they had established advisory committees of respected experts to monitor their efforts.[22] Never did evidence emerge that Dow Corning had influenced the conduct of research after making a grant. And findings of studies done without industry funding reinforced the industry-funded studies.

By 1999 more than 1,000 studies of silicone-gel breast implants had been published. Studies of capsular contracture report rates of 4 percent to 50 percent.[23] Most studies show rupture rates of less than 1 percent for silicone-gel implants, though some show rates as high as 6 percent for all kinds of breast implants.[24] A recent, exhaustive review of medical research on cancer in women with implants concluded that "there is currently little evidence to support the notion that breast implants increase the risk of subsequent breast cancer."[25] And a similarly exhaustive review of evidence on all risks by a special panel of seven experts convened by the British government concluded that there was no evidence of harm from silicone-gel implants beyond local complications.[26] Both these reviews said that more research is still needed to prove by scientific standards the complete safety of implants, but viewed results so far as failing to point in the direction of danger.

Dow Corning in Bankruptcy

In a Chapter 11 bankruptcy such as Dow Corning's, all lawsuits and financial claims against the company are frozen. Unlike a Chapter 7 bankruptcy filing, the company is not liquidated. Instead, it continues to operate and, under the supervision of a bankruptcy court, it must produce a debt-restructuring plan. Once the company gets approval of the plan from its creditors, it can emerge from Chapter 11 protection and begin paying its debts.

In 1996 Dow Corning prepared the first of what would be three reorganization plans. It proposed a $2 billion fund to settle the 19,000 breast implant lawsuits.[27] Women who settled immediately would divide $600 million. Another

---

[22]See the letter from Hennekens et al. in reply to criticism in the *Journal of the American Medical Association*, July 10, 1996, pp. 101–103.

[23]See N. Handel et al., "Comparative Experience with Smooth and Polyurethane Breast Implants Using the Daplan-Meier Method of Survival Analysis," *Plastic and Reconstructive Surgery* 88, 1991, pp. 475–81, and L. Gylbert et al., "Preoperative Antibiotics and Capsular Contracture in Augmentation Mammaplasty," *Plastic and Reconstructive Surgery* 86, no. 2, 1990, pp. 260–67.

[24]See S. E. Gabriel et al., "Complications Leading to Surgery after Breast Implantation," *New England Journal of Medicine* 336, no. 10, 1997, pp. 677–82, and A. J. Park et al., "The Detection of Breast Implant Rupture Using Ultrasound," *British Journal of Plastic Surgery* 49, no. 5, 1996, pp. 299–301.

[25]Louise A. Brinton and S. Lori Brown, "Breast Implants and Cancer," *Journal of the National Cancer Institute*, September 1997, p. 1349.

[26]*Silicone Gel Breast Implants: The Report of the Independent Review Group,* Cambridge: Jill Rogers Associates, July 1998. At http://www.silicone.review.gov.uk.

[27]Barnaby J. Feder, "Dow Corning Offers Plan to End Suits," *New York Times,* December 3, 1996, p. C1.

$1.4 billion would be set aside for other women who agreed to be bound by the results of a "causation" trial. In this trial, testimony would be presented to a panel of medical experts that would then decide if there was reasonable scientific evidence that Dow Corning's implants had caused the serious diseases the women claimed. If Dow Corning lost, the women would share the $1.4 billion; if it won, they would get nothing. The women's attorneys refused to accept this gamble.

In 1997 Dow Corning made a second proposal. This time, it offered to put $2.4 billion into two trust funds.[28] One fund would be divided among women who agreed to settle their cases. A second fund would be set up for women to sue if they refused to settle. A "causation" trial would be held. If the plaintiffs prevailed, only then could individual women bring their lawsuits against the trust fund. Again, the women's lawyers refused to accept Dow Corning's plan.

Meanwhile, the class action against other manufacturers continued in Judge Pointer's court. Pointer decided to set up his own science trial. He appointed a panel of four doctors and late in 1997, this panel heard three days of testimony from researchers on both sides. A year later, the panel reported back that it could find no evidence that silicone breast implants cause immune disorders or other health problems.

As time passed and more medical studies were forthcoming, it was becoming harder for women who went to trial to win. In 1993 the U.S. Supreme Court had given federal judges the power to exclude so-called junk science testimony in trials.[29] Since research coming from establishment science consistently failed to find any risk of serious illness from silicone exposure, women's attorneys began relying on testimony by eccentrics with nonmainstream theories about silicone's risks. In some implant cases that came to trial, judges had refused to permit testimony by plaintiff's experts that failed to meet standards of scientific validity.[30]

In 1998, before the expert panel set up by Judge Pointer announced its findings, Dow Corning made a third offer to settle the 177,000 implant claims pending against it worldwide and emerge from bankruptcy. This time it put up $3.2 billion for women who settled.[31] It offered $5,000 to women for implant removal, $20,000 for repair of rupture damage, and up to $250,000 for more serious illness. Payments would average $31,000. In making the offer, Dow Corning did not admit any guilt or accept the validity of theories that implants caused debilitating illness, but agreed to compensate women anyway. Women who did not accept could still sue the company, but only $400 million

---

[28]James P. Miller, "Dow Corning Offers Revised Reorganization Plan," *The Wall Street Journal,* August 26, 1997, p. A3.

[29]*Daubert* v. *Merrell Dow Pharmaceuticals, Inc.,* 509 U.S. 579 (1993).

[30]For example, *Hall* v. *Baxter Healthcare Corp.,* 947 F. Supp. 1387 (Dist. Ore. 1996), and *Kelly* v. *American Heyer-Schulte,* 957 F. Supp. 873 (W.Dist. Tex. 1997).

[31]Jeff Leeds, "Dow Corning Agrees to Pay $3.2 Billion in Breast Implant Case," *Los Angeles Times,* November 10, 1998, p. C1. Other information about the settlement, lawsuits, and medical research is available on the Chapter 11 Web site set up by Dow Corning at http://www.implantclaims.com.

of the $3.2 billion was set aside for litigants to fight over. Tentative agreement was reached on this plan.

Why did Dow Corning still offer to settle when the tide of scientific evidence ran so much in its favor? There are several reasons. First, the cost of defending lawsuits averaged about $1 million per case even when the company won. Second, women's lawyers kept trying to find legal theories that would enable them to crack open the bank accounts of the company's two shareholders, Dow Chemical and Corning. There was fear that some novel legal theory might succeed in bankrupting these companies too. And finally, the implant controversy had been draining in many ways and there was a strong desire to resolve the issues and refocus the company on business opportunities.

Dow Corning: An Ethical Company?

Dow Corning is a company with a history of concern for ethics. In the early 1970s, scandals emerged involving overseas payoffs by American companies. Since one-third of its employees worked in other countries, the company decided to set up a conduct code to guard against payoffs and promote integrity. In 1977, two years after the new flo-gel implants went on sale, an ethics code was written and sent by the CEO to the home of every employee. It was translated into foreign languages, posted in lobbies and hallways, and emphasized in training. A six-member business conduct committee, which reported to a board of directors committee, enforced it.

In 1977 this committee began ethical audits of Dow Corning facilities worldwide. In the audits, small groups of employees met face-to-face with two committee members to discuss code-related issues. These audits were not superficial; sessions lasted up to a full day. Overall, Dow Corning's ethics program was an early, precedent-setting effort. It set up procedures to smoke out and manage ethical concerns about any product.

Many people wonder if the program worked. Did it pick up danger signals about the implants? One section of the code stated: "We will continually strive to insure that our products and services are safe, efficacious and accurately represented for their intended use."[32] In fact, ethical concerns did receive a hearing. Years later, Richard A. Hazelton, Dow Corning's CEO, explained thinking within the company just before the FDA moratorium.

> . . . [W]e found no convincing evidence . . . and we looked—hard . . . that these allegations were scientifically valid . . . But as I've also discussed, we did not then have enough evidence to completely refute the allegations, and we knew it would be several years before we would have the data to absolutely confirm our own confidence, much less satisfy our adversaries.
>
> In that environment, the conventional wisdom would be to play it safe and withdraw the product. But in examining that choice, I think we need to remember

---

[32]Dow Corning Corporation, *A Code of Business Conduct*, 5th rev. ed., 1993, p. 3.

that the moral, business, and 'conventional wisdom' dimensions of an issue are not always completely congruent.

The position that will be immediately most favorably received is not by definition the most ethical one. Certainly withdrawing would have been the best short-term way to placate our critics, and maybe—in hindsight—the best business decision. But I don't think the moral dimension is quite that simple. For what about the woman who has just learned that she has breast cancer and who desperately wants the option of reconstructive surgery as part of her lifeline to hope? What was our moral responsibility to her . . . ?

And what about the hundreds of thousands of women with implants who had no problems? . . . What impact would a decision to pull implants off the market have on the fears of these women, and thus, what was our moral responsibility to them?[33]

Hazelton's remarks indicate that ethical questions were raised and considered at Dow Corning. The conviction that silicone was safe, supported by both the scientific community and by the internal culture of the company, became the foundation for its moral reasoning.

Postscript

Today between one and two million women have breast implants. At the height of their popularity in the late 1980s, approximately 150,000 women per year had augmentation surgery. The number plummeted to 30,607 in 1992 following the FDA moratorium, but it has been rising again and in 1997 more than 122,285 women underwent the procedure. Another 50,337 women received implants for breast reconstruction.[34]

Women who augment their figures are sometimes criticized. Feminists believe that these women have been manipulated by male-defined cultural values. Others see them as cynical opportunists who know what is rewarded in American society and seek to gain every advantage that they can. Most women like their implants and say that they have the surgery to please themselves, not to please husbands and boyfriends.

Recent studies of women who get cosmetic implants, as compared with all women, show that they drink more, have more sexual partners, have children at a younger age, are more likely to have had an abortion, and are more likely to use oral contraceptives and hair dyes.[35] Some of these differences may be independent risk factors that could complicate proof if implants are ever statistically associated with a specific disease.

[33]Richard A. Hazelton, "The Breast Implant Controversy: Threats and Lessons for All of Us," *Vital Speeches of the Day,* December 1, 1998, p. 117.

[34]Press Release, "Rate of Breast Augmentation More Than Triples over Five-Year Span, According to Study by the American Society of Plastic and Reconstructive Surgeons," American Society of Plastic and Reconstructive Surgeons, http://www.plasticsurgery.org/mediactr.breast-sta.htm.

[35]Linda S. Cook et al., "Characteristics of Women With and Without Breast Augmentation," *Journal of the American Medical Association,* May 28, 1997, p. 1612.

Questions

1. Were Dow Corning's current problems avoidable? What actions could it have taken to avoid the lawsuits and bankruptcy?

2. In the years between 1975 and 1992, when Dow Corning marketed silicone-gel implants, were any of its actions irresponsible? If so, which ones?

3. Were Dow Corning's ethics audits flawed because they failed to detect issues related to breast implants? What changes, if any, should be made now in the ethics program and in other management activities?

4. Is the compensation in the company's latest settlement offer fair to women? If women cannot prove using scientific fact that their serious illnesses were caused by implants, should they receive any compensation at all?

5. Based on the story of the products liability lawsuits against Dow Corning and other manufacturers, do you believe that the legal system has worked well to resolve the question of whether breast implants are defective and the issue of how much compensation is due women who have been injured or become ill?

Making Ethical Decisions in Business

Dave Conant, the co-owner and manager of Norm Reeves Honda, a dealership in Cerritos, California, was notified by Dennis Josleyn, the new zone sales manager for American Honda Motor Company, to bid on the right to sell 64 used company cars to the public. Company policy required zone sales managers periodically to set up an auction so that all dealers in the area could bid on company cars driven by Honda executives or used to train Honda mechanics. Josleyn asked Conant to submit bids on each car $2,000 below the wholesale market value. He was targeting him for a kickback.

Conant dutifully inspected the 64 cars and submitted the asked-for bids. Meanwhile, Josleyn busied himself creating fake papers that showed other Honda dealers had bid less than Conant. On completion of this fiction, Josleyn announced the winner. Then the next day, before the cars had been loaded on trucks and delivered to Norm Reeves Honda, Josleyn appeared at the dealership and handed Conant an envelope, saying, "I have a little invoice for you." Conant went to his office, opened the envelope, and found an invoice for $64,000 payable to an advertising agency co-owned by Josleyn and his brother. The message was clear.

Josleyn wanted a 50-50 split with the dealer on the $2,000 windfall each car would bring, so he was billing Conant for half the extra $128,000 the dealer would make from selling the entire batch.

Conant faced a decision. If the invoice was paid, the 64 cars would be delivered and the dealership would make $64,000. If the invoice was not paid, the cars would go to a dealer who was a "player" and future shipments of new Hondas might be slower. He decided to pay the invoice. In his own words: "I believed I had no choice. If I hadn't paid the amount, I would have incurred the wrath of Dennis Josleyn and possibly some of the other Honda gods, and I believe they would have taken our store down."[1]

Conant was not alone, Honda dealers around the country faced an ethical dilemma. After investing large sums to build new showrooms and facilities, they would suddenly find themselves having to choose between two paths. If they gave bribes and kickbacks to Honda executives, they could secure a free flow of cars and make a fortune. On average, in the 1980s, a favored dealer would make $800,000 annually in personal income. If they stayed clean, no matter how well-trained their sales forces or how high their customer satisfaction ratings, they would receive fewer cars and less-profitable models. If they went bankrupt, the Honda executives would arrange for less scrupulous owners to take over their dealer-

ships. Many a clean dealer short on cars drove across town to see a rival's lot packed with fast-selling models in popular colors.

Beginning in the late 1970s, the sales organization of American Honda Motor Company, a subsidiary of Honda Motor Company in Japan, developed a culture of widespread corruption. It started with gift-giving, an ordinary industry practice, but the gifts grew when Honda automobiles became wildly popular and the company could not keep up with consumer demand. In 1981 the Voluntary Restraint Agreement between the United States and the Japanese auto makers limited the number of Hondas available and each car became a small gold mine. Dealers could sell them for thousands of dollars over the sticker price.

A corrupt hierarchy formed within Honda's sales division. Dealers bribed district sales managers for a better mix of cars. They bribed zone sales managers to get more car shipments. And they paid off regional sales managers for new dealer franchises. The graft came in many forms. At lower levels, sales managers were given cash in envelopes and fruit baskets stuffed with $100 bills. Higher-level managers received gifts of Mercedes-Benz and BMW automobiles and secretly held part-ownership of the franchises they granted.

A certain etiquette accompanied the bribes. Managers were instructed to take only cash and never to make direct promises. Most gifts were sent unsolicited. Vans pulled up outside Honda executives' homes and unloaded new furniture, big screen TVs, and hot tubs. Dealers offered to pay

---

[1]Quoted in Steve Lynch, *Arrogance and Accords: The Inside Story of the Honda Scandal*, Dallas: Pecos Press, 1997, p. 106.

for the weddings and college tuition of the executives' children. One manager's wife bought $45,000 of clothing on a dealer's credit card.

The players in the Honda sales division had their own insider's lexicon. "How is Christmas in your zone?" they would ask. In deference to the official company policy that forbade accepting gifts over $50, they complimented each other by saying, "That's a nice $49 suit you have there."

Like the dealers, people in the sales division had an ethical decision to make. Early on they learned that careers stalled for those who did not join the club. An entry-level accomplishment was for an assistant district sales manager to receive a Rolex watch from a dealer. Young managers signaled their eagerness to join the inner circle by showing up at the national sales meeting wearing the least-expensive Rolex, a $2,000 stainless steel "starter" watch. Sometimes they had bought it themselves.

A few managers remained outside the conspiracy. Their careers stagnated and they had nowhere to turn, since the highest-ranking sales executives openly socialized new participants into the system. Top Japanese officials at Honda were warned repeatedly about the corruption, but remained aloof and secretive. Their silence protected the gang of Americans.

After fifteen years of rampant dishonesty, American Honda in 1992 finally began to root out the crooked managers. Depositions in pending lawsuits against the company by some dealers threatened to make public a wide range of graft and fraud. Twelve managers were forced

to resign. In 1995 the Department of Justice brought two top sales division managers to trial who were convicted by a jury of conspiracy, mail fraud, and false testimony.[2] It was the tip of the iceberg. Eventually, forty-nine managers, about one-fourth of the sales division's employees, were fired by Honda, most to be criminally indicted by the government and plead guilty. Their sentences ranged from eighteen months to seven years. Fines of up to $250,000 were levied.

Today, American Honda faces lawsuits of several billion dollars by 30 of its 1,300 dealers who felt cheated during the years of crooked management.[3] Managers who made the hard decision to be honest have not fared well. A new sales management team recruited from outside is wielding the broom of reform and there is great distrust of former insiders. Managers who stayed clean over the years now find that instead of being rewarded, they are tainted by association with the old order. Promotions go to newcomers from outside. Other car companies are suspicious of résumés from ex-Honda sales staff, so switching employers is next to impossible. The Japanese president of American Honda remains. Apparently, the largest criminal bribery prosecution in American history was not sufficient in the eyes of his Japanese superiors to discredit him.

---

[2]*United States* v. *John W. Billmyer, Dennis R. Josleyn,* Criminal Nos. 94-029-01, 94-029-04-JD (USDC, New Hamp.), September 26, 1995.

[3]John O'Dell, "U. S. Honda Unit Sues Dealers in Bribery Case," *Los Angeles Times,* January 16, 1997, p. D3.

Over many years, individual Honda managers and dealers caught in the web of corruption faced career-changing decisions. Should they become complicit? Stay and remain silent? Speak out? Resign? How should they have analyzed their options? Is there any knowledge or method that could have saved many from moral collapse? This chapter contains philosophical and practical guides for making decisions about ethical problems both in business life and in case studies such as those in this book. The principles and methods it contains can help individuals see more clearly the issues and consequences they face.

Principles of Ethical Conduct

We begin with a compendium of ethical principles—some ancient, some modern. There are dozens, if not hundreds, of such principles in the philosophical and religious traditions of East and West.

From a larger universe, we set forth fourteen principles that every manager should know and think about. The fourteen principles here are fundamental guides or rules for behavior. Each of them has strengths and weaknesses. Some were created to be universal tests of conduct. Others have a more limited reach and apply only in a certain sphere of human relations. Some are ideals. Others accommodate balancing of interests where perfection is impossible. A few invite compromise and can be used to rationalize flawed behavior. One principle, might equals right, is a time-honored justification for ignoble acts, but we include it here because it has been the subject of discussion since time immemorial.

These principles distill basic wisdom that spans 2,000 years of ethical thought. To the extent that they offer ideas for thinking about and resolving ethical dilemmas, they are not vague abstractions but useful, living guides to analysis and conduct.[4] We present them alphabetically.

The Categorical Imperative

The categorical imperative (meaning, literally, a command that admits no exception) is a guide for ethical behavior set forth by the German philosopher Immanuel Kant in his *Foundations of the Metaphysics of Morals*, a tract published in 1785. In Kant's words: "Act only according to that maxim by which you can at the same time will that it should become a universal law."[5]

---

[4]Empirical studies show that managers find most of these principles helpful. See Phillip V. Lewis, "Ethical Principles for Decision Makers: A Longitudinal Survey," *Journal of Business Ethics,* April 1989; T. K. Das, "Ethical Principles in Business: An Empirical Study of Preferential Rankings," *International Journal of Management,* December 1992; and Scott K. Jones and Kenneth M. Hiltebeitel, "Organizational Influence in a Model of the Moral Decision Process of Accountants," *Journal of Business Ethics,* July 1995.

[5]Immanuel Kant, *Foundations of the Metaphysics of Morals,* trans. Lewis White Beck, Indianapolis: Bobbs-Merrill, 1969, p. 44. Originally written in 1785.

In other words, one should not adopt principles of action unless they can, without inconsistency, be adopted by everyone. Lying, stealing, and breaking promises, for example, are ruled out because society would disintegrate if they replaced truth telling, property rights, and vow keeping. Using this guideline, a manager faced with a moral choice must act in a way that he or she believes is right and just for any person in a similar situation. Each action should be judged by asking: "Could this act be turned into a universal code of behavior?" This quick *test of universalizability* has achieved great popularity.

Kant was an extreme perfectionist in his personal life. He walked the same route each day at the same time, appearing at places along the route so punctually that neighbors set their clocks by him. Before leaving his house he attached strings to the top of his socks and connected them to a string apparatus held by his belt. As he walked the contraption would pull the slack out of his socks. To no one's surprise, his ethical philosophies are perfectionist also, and that is their weakness. Kant's categorical imperative is dogmatic and inflexible. It is a general rule that must be applied in every specific situation; there are no exceptions. But real life challenges the simple, single ethical law. If a competitor asks whether your company is planning to sell shirts in Texas next year, must you answer the question with the truth?

The Conventionalist Ethic

This is the view that business is analogous to a game and special, lower ethics are permissible. In business, people may act to further their self-interest so long as they do not violate the law. This ethic, which has a long history, was popularized some years ago by Albert Z. Carr in *Business as a Game*[6] "If an executive allows himself to be torn between a decision based on business considerations and one based on his private ethical code," explained Carr, "he exposes himself to a grave psychological strain."[7]

Business may be regarded as a game, such as poker, in which the rules are different from those we adopt in personal life. Assuming game ethics, managers are allowed to bluff (a euphemism for lie) and to take advantage of all legal opportunities and widespread practices or customs. Carr used two examples to illustrate situations where game ethics were permissible. In the first, an out-of-work salesman with a good employment record feared discrimination because of his age—58. He dyed his hair and stated on his résumé that he was 45. In the second, a job applicant was asked to check off magazines that he read and felt justified in not placing check marks by *Playboy*, *The Nation*, or *The New Republic*. Even though he read them, he feared being labeled controversial or politically extreme. He checked conservative magazines such as *Reader's Digest*.[8]

---

[6]Albert Z. Carr, *Business as a Game*, New York: New American Library, 1968.

[7]"Is Business Bluffing Ethical," *Harvard Business Review,* January–February 1968, p. 149.

[8]Carr, *Business as a Game*, p. 142.

The conventionalist ethic has been criticized by those who make no distinction between private ethics and business ethics. They argue that industrial activity defines the life chances of millions and is not a game to be taken lightly. As a principle, the conventionalist ethic is a thin justification for deceptive behavior in business situations.

The Disclosure Rule

This rule has been popular in recent years and is found in many company ethics codes. The way it is stated in IBM's *Business Conduct Guidelines* is, "Ask yourself: If the full glare of examination by associates, friends, even family were to focus on your decision, would you remain comfortable with it? If you think you would, it probably is the right decision."[9]

When faced with an ethical dilemma, a manager asks how it would feel to explain the decision to a wide audience. Sometimes newspaper readers or television viewers are substituted for acquaintances as the disclosure audience. This approach grounds the decision in the values of a surrounding culture. It is particularly useful in consensus and group-oriented cultures. In 1995, a commission was formed in Hong Kong to fight corruption and it led to the development of a model ethics code recommended to companies. At its conclusion, the model code recommends a disclosure test for employees considering an action about which they have a concern: "When in doubt, *the test is whether or not it would survive disclosure and critical public scrutiny.*"[10]

This rule screens out base motivations such as greed and jealousy, which are unacceptable if disclosed, but does not always provide clear guidance for ethical dilemmas in which strong arguments can be made for several alternatives. Also, an action that sounds acceptable if disclosed may not, upon reflection, always be the most ethical.

The Doctrine of the Mean

This ethic, set forth by Aristotle in *The Nicomachean Ethics* and sometimes called the "golden mean," because of subsequent but un-Aristotelian embellishment, calls for virtue through moderation.[11] Right actions are located between extreme behaviors, which represent excess on the one hand and deficiency on the other. When faced with a decision, a decision maker first identifies the ethical virtue involved (such as truthfulness) and then seeks the mean or moderate course of action between an excess of that virtue (boastfulness) and a deficiency

---

[9]International Business Machines Corp., *Business Conduct Guidelines,* Armonk, N.Y.: IBM, undated, p. 6.

[10]Quoted in Patrick E. Murphy, *Eighty Exemplary Ethics Statements,* Notre Dame, IN: University of Notre Dame Press, 1997, p. 117. Emphasis in original.

[11]*The Nicomachean Ethics,* trans. J. A. K. Thomson, New York: Penguin Books, 1982, Book II, chap. 6.

of it (understatement). At ITT, Harold Geneen pushed managers to extraordinary personal sacrifice. Their time, energy, loyalty, and will were bent to corporate purposes. Obsessive work led to remarkable business successes, but also to personal difficulties such as marital problems. While specific operations of ITT, taken one-by-one, were constructive and ethical, immoderation led some to sacrifice a balanced life.[12]

The doctrine of the mean is today little recognized, but the notion of moderation as a virtue remains strong. The doctrine itself is inexact. To observe it is simply to act conservatively, not extremely. The moderate course and specific virtues such as honesty, however, are defined only in terms of what they are not. What they are is open to differing interpretation.

The Ends-Means Ethic

This principle is age-old, appearing as an ancient Roman proverb, *existus acta probat*, or "the result validates the deeds."[13] It is often associated with the Italian political philosopher Niccolò Machiavelli, who wrote interpretive essays about Roman history. In *The Prince* (1513), Machiavelli argued that worthwhile ends justify efficient means, that when ends are of overriding importance or virtue, unscrupulous means may be employed to reach them.[14] When confronted with a decision involving an ethically questionable course of action, a decision maker should ask whether some overall good—as the survival of a country or business—justifies corner cutting.

In the 1980s, Oracle Corporation grew rapidly. To get this growth, founder and CEO Lawrence J. Ellison pushed his sales managers to double revenues each year. The methods of the company's frenzied sales force were scrutinized less closely than its ability to hit targets. In 1993 the Securities and Exchange Commission charged Oracle with double-billing customers, invoicing companies for products that were never sold, and violating accounting standards by recording sales revenue before it was received.[15] But by then Oracle had crushed its competition in the relational database market. Today, Ellison is a multibillionaire. Oracle employs 36,802 people and has made many of them millionaires. Its software makes governments, businesses, and universities more productive. It pays taxes in 60 countries. It conducts a wide range of social responsibility programs. Does this end result justify the competitive tactics used earlier in the company's history?

By using unscrupulous means, a manager concedes the highest virtue and accepts the necessity of ethical compromise. In solving ethical problems,

---

[12]Manuel Velasquez and Neil Brady, "Catholic Natural Law and Business Ethics," *Business Ethics Quarterly*, March 1997, p. 95.

[13]Eugene Ehrlich, *Amo, Amas, Amat and More*, New York: Harper & Row, 1985, p. 123.

[14]Niccolò Machiavelli, *The Prince*, trans. T. G. Bergin, ed., New York: Appleton-Century-Crofts, 1947. Written in 1513 and first published in 1532.

[15]Mike Wilson, *The Difference between God and Larry Ellison*, New York: William Morrow and Company, 1997, p. 239.

means may be as important, or more so, than ends. In addition, the process of ethical character development can never be served by the use of expedient means.

The Golden Rule

An ideal found in both the great religions and works of philosophy, the golden rule has been a popular guide for centuries. Simply put, it is: "Do unto others as you would have them do unto you." It includes not knowingly doing harm to others. A manager trying to solve an ethical problem places himself or herself in the position of another party affected by the decision and tries to figure out what action is most fair to that person.

A related principle called the *practical imperative* was set forward by Immanuel Kant. It is: "Act so that you treat humanity, whether in your own person or in that of another, always as an end and never as a means only."[16] This principle admonishes a manager to treat other persons as ends in themselves. No person should manipulate others for selfish ends. A manager may comply with both the practical imperative and the golden rule by using the *test of reversibility*, that is, by asking if he or she would change places with the person affected by the contemplated policy or action.

A problem with the golden rule is that people's ethical values differ, and they may mistakenly assume that their preferences coincide with others'. It is primarily a perfectionist rule for interpersonal relations. It is sometimes hard to apply in corporations where the interests of individuals are subordinated to the needs of the firm and where competitive activities demand selfish behavior. Marketing strategies, for example, do not treat competitors with kindness, but are based on self-interest.

The Intuition Ethic

This ethic, as defined by philosophers such as G. E. Moore in his *Principia Ethica* (1903), holds that what is good is simply understood.[17] That is, people are endowed with a moral sense by which they intuitively know what is right or wrong. The solution to an ethical problem lies simply in what you feel or understand to be right in a situation.

Most people, when faced with an ethical conflict in their lives, have an emotional, gut-level reaction. A situation bothers them. If they act and what they have done continues to bother them, there is something wrong. Ethical intuition is not entirely subjective. A person's ethical instincts are the product of socialization, role expectations, relationships, and character development. The moral lessons of a lifetime that each person carries are felt emotionally and instinctively. Though fallible, intuition is usually accurate.

---

[16]*Foundations of the Metaphysics of Morals,* trans. Beck, p. 54.
[17]*Principia Ethica*, New York: Cambridge University Press, 1948 (reprint).

Some corporations recognize the intuition ethic in their conduct codes and offer it as a general guideline for employees. At Cummins Engine Company, Inc., for example, employees are told: "If . . . you are uncomfortable with a particular action . . . then DON'T DO IT."[18]

Drawbacks exist. The approach is subjective. Self-interest may be confused with ethical insight. No standard of validation outside the individual is used. It is unpersuasive to others for a manager to say, "It's wrong because I just think it is." Also, intuition may fail to give clear answers.[19]

The Might-Equals-Right Ethic

This ethic defines justice as the interest of the stronger. It is represented by Friedrich Nietzsche's "master-morality," by Marx's theories of the dominance of the ruling class, and in the practiced ethics of drug cartels. The rationale for some competitive strategies and marketing tactics reflects this thinking. What is ethical is what an individual or company has the strength and power to accomplish. When faced with an ethical decision, individuals using this ethic seize what advantage they are strong enough to take, without regard for lofty sentiments.

In the 1860s Ben Holladay, owner of the Overland Stage Line, perfected a competitive strategy based on this thinking. He entered new routes with low-ball coach fares and subsidized his stages with profits from monopoly service elsewhere until local competitors went bankrupt. In 1863 a small stage line between Denver and Central City in Colorado, for example, was charging $6 per run. Holladay put a lavish new-model stage, a Concord Coach with a leather interior, on the line and charged only $2. The competing line soon folded, whereupon Holladay replaced the new Concord Coach with primitive stages resembling freight wagons and raised the fare to $12.

The weakness of the might-equals-right ethic lies in its confusion of ethics with force or physical power. Exerting such force or power is not the same as acting from ethical duty. An ethical principle that can be invalidated by its foundation (e.g., physical force) is not a consistent, logical, or valid principle. The might-equals-right ethic is not seen as legitimate in civilized settings. Its observance invites retaliation and condemnation, and it is not to be used for long-term advantage. Seizure by power violates established rules of cooperation and reciprocity on which societies are based, and the social fabric would be torn apart by widespread use of this principle.

The might equals right ethic is different from other principles in this section in that it endorses base motives. It is a commentary on human nature that it continues to reflect the behavior of some managers.

---

[18]Murphy, *Eighty Exemplary Ethics Statements,* pp. 63–64. Emphasis in original.

[19]For an excellent discussion of intuition in managerial decisions, see Joseph L. Badaracco Jr., *Defining Moments,* Boston: Harvard Business School Press, 1997, chapter 4, "Sleep-Test Ethics."

> You are sailing to Rome (you tell me) to obtain the post of Governor of Cnossus. You are not content to stay at home with the honours you had before; you want something on a larger scale, and more conspicuous. But when did you ever undertake a voyage for the purpose of reviewing your own principles and getting rid of any of them that proved unsound?
>
> *Source:* Epictetus, *The Discourses* (c. A.D. 120).

The Organization Ethic

Simply put, this principle is: "Be loyal to the organization." It implies that the wills and needs of individuals should be subordinated to the greater good of the organization (be it a church, government, corporation, university, or army). A member should act in a way that is consistent with the organization's goals. This ethic helps organizations endure and promotes trust among their members.

Many employees have such deep loyalty to an organization that it transcends self-interest. Some people in American firms jeopardize their health and work excessively long hours without pay out of devotion to the employer. In Asian societies, which have strong collectivist values, identification with and commitment to companies is exceptionally strong. In Japan, workers are so afraid of letting down their work group or employer that they come to work despite broken limbs and serious ailments. This behavior is so common that a word for death from overwork, *karoshi,* has entered the Japanese language.

The ethical boundary of this principle is crossed when duty to the organization is used to rationalize misbehavior. The Nuremberg trials, which tried Nazis for war crimes, taught that Western society expects members of organizations to follow their conscience. Just as no Nazi war criminal argued successfully that he was forced to follow an order in an impersonal military chain of command, so no business manager may claim to be the helpless prisoner of corporate loyalties that crush free will and justify wrongdoing.

The Principle of Equal Freedom

This principle was set forth by the philosopher Herbert Spencer in his 1850 book *Social Statics.* "Every man may claim the fullest liberty to exercise his faculties," said Spencer, "compatible with the possession of like liberty by every other man."[20] Thus, a person has the right to freedom of action unless such action deprives another person of a proper freedom. Spencer believed that this was the first principle of ethical action in society. He thought it essential to protect individual liberty from infringement by others; his deep faith that human progress was based on such free action was unshakable.

---

[20]Herbert Spencer, *Social Statics,* New York: Robert Schalkenbach Foundation, 1970, p. 69. First published in 1850.

In applying this principle, a decision maker asks if a contemplated action will restrict others from actions that they have a legitimate right to undertake. This principle is still well known. One version is "Your right to swing your fist ends where my nose begins."

A problem with this principle is that it does not provide a tie breaker for situations in which two rights or interests conflict. Such situations require invocation of an additional principle to decide which right or freedom is more important. Another difficulty is that some ethically permissible management decisions may circumscribe the rights of some for the benefit of others. For example, all employees have broad privacy rights, but management may abridge them when it hires undercover detectives to investigate thefts.

The Proportionality Ethic

Proportionality, a concept incubated in medieval Catholic theology, is an ethical doctrine designed to evaluate actions that have both good and evil consequences. For example, the manufacture of small-caliber, short-barreled, low-priced handguns that are irreverently called Saturday Night Specials has a dual impact on society. It makes cheap, easily concealable weapons available to criminals. But it also creates a supply of inexpensive self-defense weapons for poor people in high-crime areas who cannot afford large-caliber, expensive handguns costing as much as $500. In this and similar cases, where a manager's action results in an important good effect but also entails an inevitable harmful effect, the concept of proportionality may be useful.

A classic formulation is that of Thomas M. Garrett, a Jesuit priest who wrote about business ethics. Garrett developed a "principle of proportionality" that stated that managers are ethically responsible for their actions in situations where both good and evil effects might occur. They are ethically permitted to risk predictable, but unwilled, negative impacts on people or society (for example, innocent people being shot by handguns) if they carefully consider and balance five factors. First, according to Garrett, managers must assess the type of good and evil involved, distinguishing between major and minor forms. Second, they should calculate the urgency of the situation. For example, would the firm go out of business unless stockholder dividends were cut? Third, they must assess the probability that both good and evil effects will occur. If good effects are certain and risks of serious harm are small or remote, the situation is favorable. Fourth, the intensity of influence over effects must be considered. In assessing handgun injuries, for instance, manufacturers might assume that criminal action was an intervening force over which they had little control. And finally, the availability of alternative methods must be considered. If, for instance, an advertisement subtly encourages product misuse, a more ethical action might be to change the ad. Garrett believed that an overall assessment that took all these factors into consideration would bring out fully the ethical dimension in any decision.[21]

---

[21]Thomas M. Garrett, *Business Ethics,* New York: Appleton-Century-Crofts, 1966, p. 8.

A simpler ethical principle derived from the concept of proportionality is the *principle of double effect*. It states that in a situation from which both good and evil consequences are bound to result, a manager will act ethically if: (1) the good effects outweigh the evil, (2) the manager's intention is to achieve the good effects, and (3) examination reveals that no better alternative is available.

These are complex principles, involving a wide range of considerations. Their complexity is a strength if it forces fuller consideration of relevant factors. But proportionality may be used disingenuously to justify harmful acts. What kind of otherwise questionable acts, for instance, may a failing firm take that are justified by the potential harmful effects of the impending evil of bankruptcy?

The Rights Ethic

Rights protect people against abuses and entitle them to important liberties. A strong philosophical movement defining *natural rights,* or rights that can be inferred by reason from the study of human nature, grew in Enlightenment Western Europe as a reaction against medieval religious persecutions. Over time many "natural" rights were given legal status and became legal rights. Basic rights that are today widely accepted and protected in Western nations include the right to life; personal liberties such as expression, conscience, religious worship, and privacy; freedom from arbitrary, unjust police actions or unequal application of laws; and political liberties such as voting and lobbying. In Eastern societies, especially those transfused by the collectivist values of ancient Chinese culture, there is far less recognition of individual rights. This has led to serious ethical clashes and misunderstandings in the global economy.

Rights imply duties. Because individuals have rights, many protected by law, other people have clear duties to respect them. For example, management should not permit operation of an unsafe machine because this would deprive workers of the right to a safe workplace. This right is based on the natural right to protection from harm by negligent actions of others and is legally established in common law and the Occupational Safety and Health Act. If some risk in operating a machine is unavoidable, workers have the right to be given an accurate risk assessment.

Theories of rights have great importance in American ethical debates. A problem caused by our reverence for rights is that they are sometimes wrongly expanded into selfish demands or entitlements. Rights are not absolute and their limits may be hard to define. For example, every person has a right to life, but industry daily exposes people to risk of death by releasing carcinogens into the environment. An absolute right to life would require cessation of much manufacturing activity (for example, petroleum refining). Rights, such as the right to life, are commonly abridged for compelling reasons of benefit to the overall public welfare.

The Theory of Justice

A theory of justice defines what individuals must do for the common good of society. Maintaining the community is important because natural rights, such as the right to life, are reasonably protected only in an orderly, civil society. A basic principle of justice, then, is to act in such a way that the orderly bonds of community are maintained. In broad terms, this means acting fairly toward others and establishing institutions in which people are subject to rules of fair treatment. In business life, justice requires fair relationships within the corporate community and establishment of policies that treat its members fairly.

In society, a person's chances for justice are determined by basic economic and political arrangements. The design of institutions such as business corporations and political constitutions has a profound effect on the welfare and life chances of individuals. A contemporary philosopher, John Rawls, has developed an influential set of principles for the design of a just society. Rawls speculates that rational persons situated behind a hypothetical "veil of ignorance" and not knowing their place in a society (i.e., their social status, class position, economic fortune, intelligence, appearance, or the like) but knowing general facts about human society (such as political, economic, sociological, and psychological theory) would deliberate and choose two rules to ensure fairness in any society they created. First, "each person is to have an equal right to the most extensive basic liberty compatible with a similar liberty for others," and second, "social and economic inequalities are to be arranged so that they are both (a) reasonably expected to be to everyone's advantage, and (b) attached to positions and offices open to all."[22] In general, inequality would only be allowed if it would make better the lot of the most disadvantaged members of the society.

The impartiality and equal treatment called for in Rawls's principles are resplendent in theory and may even inspire some business decisions, but they are best applied to an analysis of broad societal issues. Acting justly in daily business life, on the other hand, requires the application of maxims that more concretely define fairness. Managers can find such guidelines in three basic spheres of justice.

Distributive justice requires that the benefits and burdens of company life be distributed using impartial criteria. Awarding pay raises based on friendship rather than performance criteria is unfair. All laws, rules, and procedures should apply equally to each employee. *Retributive justice* requires punishment to be evenhanded and proportionate to transgressions. A cashier should not be fired for stealing $5 if an executive who embezzled $10,000 is allowed to stay on the job and pay it back. And *compensatory justice* requires fair compensation to victims. A corporation that damages nearby property must restore it to its original state; one that hurts a customer must pay damages. The general idea of fairness in such maxims of justice supports orderly communities and organizations in which people secure human rights and meet human needs.

The Utilitarian Ethic

The utilitarian ethic was developed between the late eighteenth century and the mid nineteenth century by a line of English philosophers including Jeremy

---

[22]John Rawls, *A Theory of Justice,* Cambridge, MA: Harvard University Press, 1971, pp. 60–71.

Bentham and John Stuart Mill. The principle of utility, on which this ethic is based, is that actions that promote happiness are right and actions that cause unhappiness are wrong. The utilitarians advocated choosing alternatives that led to the greatest sum of happiness or, as we express the thought today, "the greatest good for the greatest number."

In making a decision using this principle, one must determine whether the harm in an action is outweighed by the good. If the action maximizes benefit, then it is the optimum choice over other alternatives that provide less benefit. Decision makers should try to maximize pleasure and reduce pain, not simply for themselves but for everyone affected by their decision. Utilitarianism facilitates the comparison of the ethical consequences of various alternatives in a decision. It is a popular principle. Cost-benefit studies embody its logic and its spirit.

The major problem with utilitarianism is that in practice it has led to self-interested reasoning. Its importance in rationalizing the social ills of capitalism can hardly be overestimated. Since the 1850s, it has been used to argue that the overall benefits of manufacturing and commerce are greater than the social costs. Since the exact definition of the "greatest good" is subjective, its calculation has often been a matter of expediency. A related problem is that because decisions are to be made for the greatest good of all, utilitarian thinking has led to decisions that permit the abridgment of individual or minority group rights. Utilitarianism does not properly relate individual and community ends in a way that protects both.[23]

Do Men and Women Reason Differently about Ethics?

Professor Lawrence J. Kohlberg of Harvard University became famous for research showing that from childhood on people pass through six stages of moral development.[24] These stages begin with utter selfishness and rise to the use of ethical principles. According to Kohlberg, not everyone gets to the highest, or principled-reasoning, stage—the moral development of most people is arrested at a middle stage.

To create and test his theory, Kohlberg had measured changes over more than twenty years in the ethical thinking of eighty-four boys. Others who built on his work soon discovered that women, in particular, were unlikely to get to the higher stages. What was the reason? Were women demonstrably less ethical than men? Professor Carol Gilligan, a colleague of Kohlberg's at Harvard, tried to answer these questions by studying the moral thinking of 144 men and women ranging in age from six to sixty.[25]

---

[23]See, for example, Mortimer Adler, *Desires: Right and Wrong*, New York: Macmillan, 1991, p. 61. John Stuart Mill's famous essay "Utilitarianism" deals directly and brilliantly with these and other criticisms. It is reprinted in Mary Warnock, ed., *Utilitarianism and Other Writings*, New York: New American Library, 1962, pp. 251–321.

[24]See, for example, Lawrence Kohlberg, "The Cognitive-Developmental Approach to Moral Education, in Peter Scharf, ed., *Readings in Moral Education*, Minneapolis: Winston Press, 1978.

[25]Carol Gilligan, *In a Different Voice*, Cambridge: Harvard University Press, 1982.

Gilligan learned that men and women approached ethical reasoning from different perspectives. The men in her studies grew to see themselves as autonomous, separate individuals in a competitive, hierarchical world of superior–subordinate relationships. As a result, male ethical thinking stressed protection of individual rights and enforcement of principled rules to channel and control aggression. The women, on the other hand, tended to see a world of relationships rather than individuals, a world in which people were interconnected in webs rather than arrayed in dominance hierarchies. Women did not think using abstract rules and principles that set sharp boundaries on individual behavior; they focused on the importance of compassion, care, and responsibility in relations with others. They were not ethically stunted; they just thought differently than men.

Kohlberg built his stages on the development of male ethical reasoning. Nevertheless, Gilligan argued persuasively for the existence of a different development process in females, one that is equally valid but cannot be measured on the same scale. Based on her research, a *care ethic* exists, that is, that a person should have compassion for others, avoid hurt in relationships, alleviate suffering, and respect the dignity of others. The care ethic would be violated in business by, for example, cruelty toward subordinates, exploitation of consumers, deceit in relationships, or focus on individual performance coupled with indifference toward colleagues or the welfare of one's company.

Research by others reinforces the idea that men and women have gender-based orientations to ethical dilemmas. Men emphasize rules, individual rights, and duties that can be fixed impartially; women emphasize caring and accept an intuitive, emotional instinct as a valid criterion for behavior.[26] But this marked contrast to ethics disappears in business. Studies of managers, as opposed to studies of young adults and students, fail to show gender differences in ethical decision making.[27]

The Application of Ethical Principles

The use of ethical principles can harmonize ethical decisions with a long tradition of cultural experience. Much ethical common sense—such as be honest, help others, avoid harm, tell the truth, be fair, and respect the life and property of others—can be derived from them. For example, the categorical imperative requires that individuals tell the truth because truth-telling can be made universal, unlike lying, the universalization of which would cause chaos. Standards created by individual managers or companies might lack consistency or might bear the impress of self-interest. The great principles transcend parochialism and contain enduring wisdom. Years ago, J. Irwin Miller of Cummins Engine Company noted that "the tenor of all the major religions of the world, and of all the great philosophers, is that the rules of behavior are

---

[26]Candice Fredrick and Camille Atkinson, *Women, Ethics and the Workplace,* Westport, CN: Praeger, 1998, pp. 32–36.

[27]Donald Robin and Laurie Babin, "Making Sense of the Research on Gender and Ethics in Business: A Critical Analysis and Extension," *Business Ethics Quarterly,* October 1997.

about as inexorable as the laws of mathematics or physics. You violate them at your peril."[28]

A Specific Case

The use of ethical principles, as opposed to the intuitive use of ethical common sense, may improve reasoning, especially in complex situations. Say a bank teller pockets $20 at the end of the day. The person's supervisor strongly feels that stealing is wrong and fires the teller. Ethical common sense is all that is needed in this situation, but the following situation defies a simple solution.

> I was working as a manager in a division that was going to be closed. The secret clock was ticking away to the surprise mass layoff. Then a co-worker approached. He was thinking of buying a house. Did I think it was a good time to get into real estate?
>
> The man's job was doomed and I knew it. But spilling the secret, I believed, would violate my integrity as a corporate officer and doom the company to a firestorm of fear and rumor. There was no way to win and no way out.
>
> I considered it my fiduciary responsibility to the business to keep my mouth shut, and yet here was this person coming for advice as a friend and a business acquaintance and I had material information that would affect him. For someone with a sense of empathy and sympathy, which I like to think I have some of, it was very, very hard.
>
> In the end I swallowed my anguish and kept silent. The man bought the house and lost his job. The secret held. But now 10 years later I have many times relived the story and second-guessed what I did that day.[29]

This is a vexing situation, and one created by the complexities of modern organizational life. The last paragraph finds the narrator alerted by the intuition ethic to the presence of an ethical conflict. Something in the situation causes anguish. In this predicament, however, simple moral homilies such as "tell the truth" or "be fair" are insufficient to resolve conflicts. Let us apply to this case three ethical principles, each of which offers a distinct perspective—utilitarianism, the rights ethic, and the theory of justice.

The utilitarian ethic requires the manager to calculate which course of action, among alternatives, will result in the greatest benefit for the company and all workers. A frank response here will disrupt operations. People would resign, take days off, work less efficiently, and engage in sabotage. Keeping the secret will cause hardship for a single employee about to buy a house and perhaps others in a similar situation. On balance, the manager must protect the broader welfare of customers, stockholders, and remaining employees.

From the standpoint of rights, the employee is entitled to the truth and the manager has a duty to speak honestly. On the other hand, rights are not absolute.

---

[28]From a 1964 speech quoted in David Bollier, *Servant Leadership: The Story of J. Irwin Miller,* Stanford, CA: Business Enterprise Trust, 1992, p. 29.

[29]Paraphrased and quoted from Kirk Johnson, "In the Class of 70, Wounded Winners," *New York Times,* March 7, 1996, p. A12.

The corporation has the competing right to protect its property, and this right must be balanced against the right of an employee to straight talk. In addition, the manager, in effect, promised to keep the layoff confidential and has a duty of promise keeping.

In justice, corporations are required to promote fair, evenhanded treatment of employees. Distributive justice demands the impartial distribution of benefits and burdens. It would be partial to signal the layoff to one worker and not others.

Based on the application of utility, rights, and justice, the manager's decision to remain silent is acceptable. Some judgment is required in balancing rights, but the combined weight of reasoning with all three principles supports the manager's decision. Yet the manager's intuition was not wrongly aroused. The situation required, by commission or omission, a lie, and it violated the practical imperative by treating the employee as expendable while achieving a corporate goal. So both good and evil result from the resolution of this situation. In such cases, application of the principle of double effect is appropriate. Here, the welfare of the company outweighs the welfare of one employee, the manager's intention is not to hurt the employee but to help the company, and no better alternative presents itself (it is possible that the manager could be wishy-washy and evasive; however, this raises suspicion in the employee and, in any case, avoids resolution of the ethical dilemma). So the principle of double effect reconfirms the manager's action.

Character Development

Principled reasoning is a powerful method for defining ethical issues and analyzing them. But it has drawbacks. Principles sometimes contradict. There is no agreement about which ones are best. And, as John Dewey once wrote, they are "not a catalogue of acts nor a set of rules to be applied like drugstore prescriptions or cookbook recipes."[30] Their use demands interpretive thought. And such thinking is learned only in the process of character development. Character development is a source of ethical behavior separate from the use of principles. The theory that character development rather than principled reasoning is the most effective source of ethical behavior might be called the *virtue ethic.* It originates in Aristotle.

Aristotle wrote that moral virtue is the result of habit.[31] Ethical decisions by their nature require choice, and we build virtue, or character, by habitually making ethical choices. Ethical choices are those that accord with appropriate, natural human needs and do not give in to wrong desires for false pleasures.

Application of the virtue ethic requires conscious effort to develop a good disposition by making right decisions over time. Actions are not judged by

---

[30]John Dewey, *Reconstruction in Philosophy,* New York: Holt, 1920, pp. 169–70.
[31]*The Nichomachean Ethics,* trans. Thomson, p. 91.

supreme rules such as the categorical imperative or the principle of utility. Such overarching rules may apply poorly to the multitude of specific, concrete situations they purport to judge. Rather, acts are judged by whether they reflect the disposition of virtuous character, acquired by habitual use of common sense. An act stemming from this character is ethical; an act that is out of character and unguided by correct motives is unethical.

The attractive logic of the virtuous character does not require rejection of the ethical principles presented earlier in the chapter. Virtuous individuals might be more sophisticated in their principled reasoning than less virtuous individuals who have less insight about principles or situations.

Practical Suggestions for Making Ethical Decisions

People in business can take some very practical steps to define better and resolve ethical problems.

First, learn to think about ethics in rational terms using ideas such as universalizability, reversibility, utility, proportionality, or other guidelines from philosophical ethics and religion. Such ideas enhance the ability to see ethical problems clearly and to discover or create solutions.

Second, consider using some simple decision-making tactics to illuminate alternatives. The philosopher Bertrand Russell advocated imaginary conversation with a hypothetical opponent as an antidote for certitude. Write an essay in favor of a position and then a second opposed to it. Seek out a more experienced, ethically sensitive person in the company as an advisor. This person can be of great value in revealing the ethical climate of a company or industry.

Use a two-column balance sheet to enter pros and cons for various alternatives, crossing out roughly equal considerations until a preponderance is left on one side or the other. Balance sheets organize information and may reduce disorganized, emotional thinking. The discipline of entering all relevant considerations can also bring new or unconscious considerations to light.

Another tactic is the "critical questions approach." Here, issues and problems emerge in answer to a list of questions. John Leys surveyed the systems of the great philosophers and derived thirty-six critical questions for the decision maker.[32] The following are a few examples: What are the authoritative rules and precedents, the agreements, and accepted practices? If there is a conflict of principles, can you find a more abstract statement, a "third principle," that will reconcile the conflicting principles? What is not within our power? What are the undesirable extremes in human dispositions? A shorter, more pointed list of leading questions is used at Texas Instruments. The list is shown in Table 8-1.

---

[32]In *Ethics for Policy Decisions*, Englewood Cliffs, N.J.: Prentice-Hall, 1952. For still another list of questions, see Laura L. Nash, "Ethics without the Sermon," *Harvard Business Review*, November/December 1981.

TABLE 8-1 **The Ethics Quick Test at Texas Instruments**

Quick Test
The Ethics Quick Test provides checks to examine the ethical implications of your decisions. Failing any of these tests probably means you should back away from the anticipated action, or at least give it another careful reconsideration. However, passing all of these tests still does not mean that the action is acceptable. There may be other unique circumstances. But these should lead you to a more complete evaluation of the issues.

Ethics Is the Cornerstone of TI.
- ❏ Is the action **legal?**
- ❏ Does it comply with our **values?**
- ❏ If you do it, will you feel **bad?**
- ❏ How will it look in the **newspaper?**
- ❏ If you know it's **wrong,** don't do it!
- ❏ If you're not sure, **ask.**
- ❏ Keep asking until you get an **answer.**

This ethics tests is given to employees of Texas Instruments Inc. on a small pamphlet the size of a business card. When they have a problem, they are asked to consult it. The questions are shorthand for specific approaches to ethical reasoning. Some invoke simple maxims such as "obey the law" and "never knowingly do harm." Others summon up the disclosure ethic and the intuition ethic. The TI Quick Test is backed by a more detailed ethics code. Both are elements of a broad program conducted by the firm's Ethics Office.

Source: http://www.ti.com/corp/docs/ethics/brochure/qtest.htm.

Third, sort out ethical priorities before problems arise. Contemplating personal values when not under stress is beneficial. Clear ethical values reduce stress by reducing temptation and deflating conscience as a source of anxiety. When being ethical is not profitable, it helps to decide in advance that ethics are more important than money.

Fourth, be publicly committed on ethical issues. Examine the workplace and find potential ethical troubles. Then state to coworkers your opposition to the padding of expense accounts, stealing of company supplies, race discrimination, price fixing, or pollution. They will be less inclined to approach you with corrupt intentions, and your public commitment will force you to maintain your standards or risk shame.

Fifth, set a good personal example for employees. This is one of the basic managerial functions. An ethical manager can create a morally uplifting workplace. An unethical manager may make money, but he or she and the company pay the price—and the price is one's integrity. Employees who see unethical behavior by their supervisor always wonder when that behavior will be directed at them.

Sixth, thoughts must be translated into action, and displaying courage in an ethical decision is often necessary. Reaching a judgment is easier than acting on it. Taking an ethical stand may create anger in others or cost a company profits, and there can be personal risks such as loss of a job.

Seventh, cultivate sympathy and charity toward others. The question "What is ethical?" is one on which well-intentioned people may differ. Marcus Aurelius wrote: "When thou art offended by any man's fault, forthwith turn to thyself and reflect in what like manner thou dost err thyself; for example, in thinking that money is a good thing, or pleasure, or a bit of reputation, and the like."[33] Reasonable managers differ with respect to the rightness of factory closings, genetic testing of workers, levels of executive compensation, and other nettlesome ethical questions.

Ethical perfection is illusory. We live in a morally complex civilization with profuse rules, norms, obligations, and duties existing like road signs that generally point in the same direction, but sometimes do not. No method of decision making ends conflicts, no principle penetrates unerringly to the Good, no manager achieves an ethical ideal. There is an old story about the inauguration of James Canfield as president of Ohio State University. With him on the inaugural platform was Charles W. Eliot, president of Harvard University for twenty years. After receiving the mace of office, Canfield sat next to Eliot, who leaned over and whispered, "Now son, you are president, and your faculty will call you a liar." "Surely," said Canfield, "your faculty have not accused you of lying, Dr. Eliot." Replied Eliot, "Not only that, son, they've proved it!"

Why Ethical Decisions Are Difficult

Why are ethical problems refractory even in the presence of principles and methods to guide resolution? In this section we list nine reasons.

First, managers confront a distinction between facts and values when making ethical decisions. Facts are statements about what *is,* and we can observe and confirm them. Ethical values, on the other hand, are statements about what *ought* to be and are held by individuals independently of facts. For example, some years ago, Burroughs Wellcome Co., a British firm, was accused of overcharging for azidothymidine (AZT), the drug that slows replication of the AIDS virus. A capsule that cost $.30 to manufacture had a retail price of $1.60 to $1.80. For AIDS victims the annual cost was $10,000. AZT was expensive to research and develop and the company felt a high price was justified. Was Burroughs Wellcome exploiting desperate AIDS patients, or was it entitled to retrieve AZT's high cost of research and development and earn a profit above that? Facts, such as prices, do not logically dictate values about what is ethical in such a situation. What *is* never defines what *ought* to be. Pressure from gay activists led to price cuts. But yielding to political force does not answer the question "What ought to be?" either.

Second, it is often the case that good and evil exist simultaneously, in tandem and interlocked. Nestlé's sales of infant formula in countries such as Kenya and Zambia have led to infant deaths as mothers mixed the powdered food with contaminated local water and their babies died of dysentery. But evidence also shows that infant formula has saved other infants' lives when the mother is

---

[33]*The Meditations of Marcus Aurelius Antoninus,* trans. George Long, Danbury, Conn.: Grolier Enterprises, 1980, p. 281. Originally written circa A.D. 180.

not available, the infant will not breast-feed, or dietary supplements are needed. Evil should be minimized, but in some cases, it cannot be eliminated.

Third, knowledge of consequences is limited. Many ethical theories, for instance the utilitarian theory of the greatest good for the greatest number, assume that the consequences of a decision are knowable. But the impact of business policy is uncertain in a complex world. In 1977, for example, General Motors substituted Chevrolet engines in Pontiacs, Oldsmobiles, and Buicks, with a policy that extended an old industry practice of parts switching to entire engines. The intention of the policy was to achieve the salutary effects of making more large-block engines available over a wider range of automobiles to satisfy consumer demand. Unpredictably (for General Motors), consumers looked on the engine switching as an attempt to manipulate buyers and rob owners of status—an ethical implication perhaps entirely at odds with corporate motivations.

Fourth, the existence of multiple stakeholders exposes managers to conflicting ethical claims. To illustrate, tobacco firms are in a crossfire of competing ethical claims. Customers assert their right to smoke and demand cigarettes. Tobacco farmers, representing over 275,000 farming families, give ethical priority to maintenance of the tobacco economy in southern states. Stockholders urge the priority of profits. Many third world governments encourage sales of tobacco products; they provide sorely needed economic benefits. On the other hand, the surgeon general's office and doctors condemn smoking for harming health. Feminist and minority groups condemn advertising that targets women and minorities. The Food and Drug Administration has denounced ads that appeal to children. Of course, companies in many industries also suffer the crossfire of clashing stakeholder values.

Fifth, antagonistic interests frequently use incompatible ethical arguments to justify their intentions. Thus, the ethical stand of a corporation is often based on entirely different premises from the ethical stand of critics or constituent groups. Many members of the Animal Liberation Front believe that animals are entitled to rights similar to those enjoyed by humans, including the right to life. The group raided a northern California turkey farm, causing $12,000 in damage and freeing about 100 turkeys, which were taken to "safe homes." Later, members broke into a Delaware poultry farm, taking twenty-five hens and drawing an analogy between Nazi death camps and factory farms in the scrawled message they left behind: "ANIMAL AUSCHWITZ." Poultry growers, on the other hand, accept the utilitarian argument that raising food animals brings benefits to society. A publicist for the industry stated that the group's viewpoint was "an insult to victims of the Holocaust."[34]

Sixth, some ethical standards are variable; they may change with time and place. In the 1950s, American corporations overseas routinely made payoffs to foreign officials, but managers had to curtail this practice after public expectations changed and a new law, the Foreign Corrupt Practices Act of 1977, prohibited most such expenditures. Certain bribes and payments are accepted practice in

---

[34]Quoted in Kevin Thompson, "Meat Is Murder?" *Meat and Poultry,* September 1987, p. 39.

Asian, African, and Latin American countries but are not regarded as ethical in the United States. Doing business with close friends and family is standard practice in the Arab world, but in the United States or Western Europe the same actions are seen as nepotism.

Seventh, ethical behavior is molded from the clay of human imperfection. Even well-intentioned managers may be mistaken in their judgment or motivation. Dennis Levine was an ambitious Wall Street executive who worked hard. He rose from humble origins to make over $1 million a year honestly at Drexel Burnham Lambert. Yet for seven years he also traded on insider information through a bank account in Switzerland. He was prosecuted and jailed. He had never intended to be a criminal, but temptation gradually eroded his honesty. "My ambition was so strong," he later wrote, "that it went beyond rationality, and I gradually lost sight of what constitutes ethical behavior."[35]

Eighth, the late twentieth century presents managers with newly emerged ethical problems that are not solved easily with traditional ethical guidelines. For example, modern ethical theory has not yet developed an adequate principle for weighing human life against economic factors in a decision. Cancer studies may predict that workers exposed to chemicals will become ill in small numbers far in the future. How should this information be balanced against costs of regulation, capital investment, or job loss? Other examples of tough new ethical problems exist. By using gas chromatography to chemically analyze a perfume's ingredients, entrepreneurs are now able to make nearly exact copies of expensive designer perfumes such as Ralph Lauren's Polo and Calvin Klein's Obsession. Because a scent cannot be trademarked like a brand name, the imitations are legal and can be sold cheaply enough to undercut the established brand and piggyback on the expensive advertising that built the foundation of its popularity. Of course, product imitation is an ancient problem. But here the technology has outraced legal remedy and ethical consensus.

Finally, growth of large-scale organizations in the twentieth century gives new significance to ethical problems such as committee decision making that masks individual responsibility, organizational loyalty versus loyalty to the public interest, and preferential hiring of affirmative action candidates. These are ethical complexities peculiar to large organizations.

Concluding Observations

There are many paths to ethical behavior. Not all managers may appreciate the repertoire of principles and ideas available to help resolve problems of business ethics. By studying the principles and guidelines presented here, a person can become more sensitive to the presence of ethical issues and more resolute in correcting deficiencies. In addition, these principles and guidelines are applicable to ethical issues that arise in the case studies in this book. We encourage students to refer to this chapter for conceptual tools.

---

[35]Dennis Levine, "The Inside Story of an Inside Trader," *Fortune,* May 21, 1990, p. 82.

COLUMBIA/HCA HEALTHCARE CORPORATION

This is the story of the world's largest health care company, a remarkable corporation that has led the health services industry in bringing market discipline to the delivery of medical care. Most hospitals in the United States are still tax-exempt, charitable institutions owned by religious orders and local communities. Yet Columbia/HCA Healthcare Corporation runs 318 hospitals for profit. Each year almost two million Americans spend an average of five days in one of the company's 65,184 hospital beds. Millions more use one of its other facilities that include 145 outpatient surgery centers and 18 psychiatric hospitals. When the company treats these patients, it tries to make money on each.

In 1997, Columbia/HCA had $18.8 billion in revenues, equal to Coca Cola and more than Eastman Kodak, Delta Airlines, or Time Warner. It was the nation's sixty-ninth largest company and seventh largest employer. The company has been, at least until recently, a financial success, making its founders and many of its managers wealthy.

Columbia/HCA prospered by using competitive strategies in an industry unaccustomed to this. Its methods brought needed efficiencies and were copied by others, but they also created incentives for unethical and illegal behavior and met with resistance from regulators, politicians, and guardians of traditional values in medicine. As a result, the company has been hindered by criminal investigations, lawsuits, and regulatory proceedings.

Rising Costs Force Changes in the Health Care Industry

The story of Columbia/HCA is best understood against the backdrop of long-term changes in the health services industry. The driving force behind these changes is rising costs. Health care is expensive. The cost of it rose from 4.4 percent of gross domestic product in 1950 to 13.6 percent in 1997, and it continues to rise.[1] Costs are

---

[1] William B. Schwartz, *Life without Disease,* Berkeley: University of California Press, 1998, pp. 8 and 27. By comparison, Japan spends only 7 percent and Great Britain just 6 percent of national income. See Clive Crook, "A Bill of Rights, or a Bill of Goods?" *National Journal,* August 1, 1998, p. 1797.

rising so rapidly and steadily that there is great pressure to hold them down. The origins of these rising costs are found in the post–World War II era.

Shortly after the end of the war, the federal government began to subsidize medical research heavily. This, along with research in companies, resulted in a steady stream of new machines, drugs, and treatment methods that increased the range and expense of medical intervention. As medical care began to cost more, demand for health insurance rose, and in the 1960s, the great majority of Americans enrolled in health plans, most of which were paid for by employers. These plans usually allowed people unlimited access to doctors and hospitals so long as they met small annual deductibles and copayments. Insurers paid claims one-by-one on a fee-for-service basis. Financial incentives to limit treatment costs that had existed when individuals themselves paid vanished when insurance became widespread.

In 1965 the federal government set up Medicare to pay hospitalization and other expenses for persons over 65 years old and, sharing expenses with the states, set up the Medicaid program to finance medical care for the poor. The two programs covered most people who were not in employer-sponsored plans. In effect, government gave every citizen access to medical treatment, and health care soon came to be seen as an entitlement. Later, Congress added kidney dialysis, an extremely expensive treatment, to Medicare. These government programs increased demand for health care services and expenditures climbed.

As costs rose, so did pressures to reduce them. In the early 1980s, government budgets were being strained by Medicare and Medicaid payments. Private employers and insurance companies began to complain loudly that paying for employee health care was sapping productivity and holding down wages. Hospital expenses were the primary reason; it was in hospitals that an array of dazzling new machines and procedures was escalating costs out of control.

Medicare Changes Its Billing Procedure

To combat rising hospital costs, Medicare in 1983 changed its reimbursement method. Instead of paying one-by-one for each in-patient treatment and procedure, it now gave the hospital a lump sum based on one of 470 categories, or "codes," into which patients' illnesses were classified. The single payment that Medicare would make was based on the underlying costs of each hospital and the average severity of specific maladies. This coding system was designed to lower Medicare payouts by giving hospitals an incentive to cut the costs of treatment, and they did so.

When the 470 illness categories—or "diagnosis-related groups" (DRGs)—were introduced, the average length of hospitalizations around the nation dropped. There were cost savings in this method, but within two years, hospital costs began to rise again. The incentive for hospitals was to spend less on patients and cut short their stays. Shorter hospital stays led to a big rise in outpatient procedures and follow-up care, as many Medicare patients walked from hospital rooms to outpatient clinics for treatments. The DRG system, which still functions, is also terribly complex. A small industry of consultants exists to help hospitals understand it, and specialized software is used to ensure that Medicare is billed maximum rates. The coding system lends itself to fraud in a number of ways, and dishonesty in billing is so endemic that the Department of Justice makes Medicare fraud a top enforcement priority.

The Rise of Managed Care

Meanwhile, insurance companies and employers tried to hold down costs by implementing a philosophy of health care delivery that has come to be called managed care. Managed care reduces nonessential and marginally beneficial medical treatment by limiting reimbursement for it, causing it to be rationed.

Although managed care takes many forms, the primary form is the health management organization, or HMO. An HMO is an organization that includes an insurer and a network of physicians, hospitals, and services such as labs. Corporations enter into contracts with HMOs under which they pay a fixed monthly or annual fee per employee in return for a full range of medical care. To compete for the business of employers, HMOs must control their costs, and they do so by limiting access to expensive specialists and treatments.

The idea of managed care swiftly carried the day. As recently as the late 1980s, about 70 percent of insured employees were in older fee-for-service plans, but by the late 1990s, about 85 percent of them were in some kind of managed care plan.[2]

Competition Increases

The rise of managed care and the imposition of DRGs by Medicare forced physicians and hospitals to cut costs and discount their services. This led to dramatic changes in the medical services industry. The role of physicians changed. They have been forced into HMOs to maintain full waiting rooms. Their traditional authority and the sanctity of the doctor–patient relationship are circumscribed in managed care organizations where their treatment decisions can be second-guessed by insurance bureaucrats who approve payments.

Competition to cut costs has become a driving force. Employers and insurance companies want to minimize their health care outlays, so they seek out low-cost providers. To compete for patients, HMOs in turn pry cost concessions from the hospitals and physicians groups that are in their networks. Another path to lower costs is to achieve economies of scale. Merger waves have swept through all parts of the industry including insurers, managed care organizations such as HMOs, and hospitals. These mergers are based on the

---

[2]Brian O'Reilly, "What Really Goes on in Your Doctor's Office?" *Fortune,* August 17, 1998, p. 166, and Mindy Charski, "A Healthy Trend Ends," *U.S. News & World Report,* September 28, 1998, p. 60.

conviction that the larger an entity becomes, the greater the market share it can control and the more leverage it will have in getting patients and revenue.

Competitive forces are felt by both the profit and the not-for-profit entities that provide health care, and both are forced to respond. Even the tax-exempt hospitals must now reduce their costs or risk catastrophic loss of the paying patients who subsidize their charitable work.[3] These competitive forces in the health services industry nurtured Columbia/HCA.

The Rise of Columbia/HCA

Columbia/HCA was the inspiration of a brilliant and hard-working entrepreneur named Richard L. Scott. In 1977, Scott received a law degree from Southern Methodist University and joined a Dallas law firm, where he worked on acquisitions and initial public offerings for large health care corporations. After ten years of this, Scott decided that he wanted to run his own company and startled the industry by lining up financing from Citicorp and Drexel Burnham Lambert and making a $3.9 billion offer to buy Hospital Corporation of America, then the largest hospital corporation in the country. Its directors laughed off Scott's proposal. Here was a suitor, a relative unknown in the industry, whose only direct business experience was working at a donut shop in college, stepping up to take charge of a huge, complex company.

Scott's bid failed, but late in 1987 he was contacted by a Texas investor who agreed to back him in starting a new hospital company. At the time, the hospital industry was ailing. Due to the introduction of DRGs by Medicare and the rise of managed care organizations, the number and length of hospital stays had been reduced. There was an oversupply of hospital beds and many hospitals were failing to cover costs and faced bankruptcy. Scott, however, had a vision of the industry in which he saw opportunity, and he got off to a running start. He set up an office in Dallas and named the new company Columbia Hospital Corporation. Immediately, he wrote 1,000 letters to hospitals around the country asking if he could buy them. Mostly, the answer was no, but eventually he bought two hospitals in El Paso from a large hospital corporation that was unloading weak performers in its chain.

With these two hospitals in hand, Scott began to introduce the strategies that he would use to revolutionize the hospital industry. First, he gave local physicians part ownership of the hospitals. Physicians are the source of patients for a hospital: no patient can be admitted without a doctor's signature. When physicians have an equity interest in a local hospital, they have a financial incentive to refer patients there. Second, he soon moved to consolidate the El Paso market by buying a third hospital in the area and closing it. This reduced the number of beds available and raised demand for the remaining beds in Scott's two other hospitals. And third, he used the hospitals he owned as hubs to which he began attaching a range of other health care services, including a psychiatric

---

[3]Nancy Cybulski, Jo-anne Marr, Isabel Milton, and Dalton Truthwaite, *Reinventing Hospitals*, Toronto: McLeod Publishing, 1997, see chapter 1.

hospital, outpatient diagnostic centers, and a cancer-treatment center. It was his plan to raise revenues by referring insured persons back and forth within a network of services owned by Columbia.[4]

After this start, Scott bought more and more hospitals. Across the country, many independent hospitals were floundering under the twin strains of an oversupply of beds and capped payments from insurers and Medicare. Sometimes their boards of trustees were open to Scott's approach. Scott would fly into town and meet with the trustees, promising to take the stand-alone hospitals and make them run more efficiently as pieces of his Columbia system.

Many hospitals Scott wanted were not-for-profits that had been set up by local communities or religious orders. Their charters gave them tax-exempt status and, in return for that, the Internal Revenue Service required them to provide large amounts of charity care in the local community. When Columbia bought them and converted them to profit-making institutions, it was legally required to set up and endow a charitable foundation to compensate for the value of years of tax exemption. The foundation would continue to do good deeds, while Scott ran the hospital to make money, although there was no legal requirement that the new foundation foster charity health care. Indeed, one such foundation, endowed with $80 million by Columbia, devoted itself to flight-training for high school students and spent nothing on medical causes.

Often, Scott closed deals after promising that top administrators and trustees of charity hospitals would get lucrative positions in the new foundations. For example, when Columbia bought the Miami Heart Institute, its chief executive became the head of a charitable heart research institute created after the sale and received a yearly salary of $135,000.[5]

As Scott rapidly bought hospitals, Columbia also expanded by acquiring other companies. In 1990, Columbia went public, and its successful offering and rising share price gave Scott more capital with which to finance these acquisitions. Columbia absorbed HCI Corp. with three hospitals in 1990; Basic American Medical with eight hospitals in 1992; Galen Healthcare with seventy-one hospitals in 1993; Medical Care America with ninety-six surgery centers in 1994; and Hospital Corporation of America (HCA), the company whose directors had laughed at Scott's proposal seven years earlier, also in 1994 with its 117 hospitals.[6] After the HCA merger, the company's name was changed to Columbia/HCA.

How Columbia Worked

As Scott took over hospitals, he wrung money from them by applying a hard-nosed business discipline exceeding anything ever before seen in hospital

---

[4]Sandy Lutz and E. Preston Gee, *Columbia/HCA—Healthcare on Overdrive,* New York: McGraw-Hill, 1998, pp. 70–73.

[5]Tamar Lewin with Martin Gottlieb, "Health Care Dividend: A Special Report," *New York Times,* April 27, 1997, Sec. 1, p. 1.

[6]Robert Kuttner, "Columbia/HCA and the Resurgence of the For-Profit Hospital Business," *New England Journal of Medicine,* August 1, 1996, p. 362.

management. He was a genius at coaxing efficiencies from a corporate structure, better than his for-profit and not-for-profit competitors alike. Some of his methods were praiseworthy; others danced near ethical boundaries; all of them gamed the incentives in the industry environment to maximum advantage.

Because of Columbia's size and strong balance sheet, when it took over a hospital, it refinanced that institution's debt with cheaper capital. With the savings on debt service that this created, Columbia would make the hospital more attractive by making cosmetic appearance changes, modernizing equipment, and installing a sophisticated information system. Rigorous cost-cutting then took place. Since the hospital was now part of the larger Columbia system, it could take advantage of discounts that Scott demanded from suppliers. Columbia/HCA became the world's largest buyer of medical supplies, and Scott was an expert at squeezing vendors. Often, however, the staff was required to use lower quality items that cost less. At Good Samaritan Hospitals in Santa Clara County, California, nurses complained that the gloves Columbia bought were weaker and more likely to tear than those they had used previously and that the valves for chest tubes lacked open/shut indicators.[7] Just-in-time inventory systems were imposed.

Staff cuts also trimmed costs, and after Columbia takeovers, there were fewer nurses and administrators and more part-time workers. This sometimes led to deteriorating patient care. At Columbia Sunrise Hospital in Las Vegas, the ratio of staff to patients fell 20 percent.[8] Nurses in critical-care units reported that it took more than six hours to get the results of urgent blood tests that should have been reported in minutes. In a poll of workers at the hospital, 44 percent believed that staffing cuts had increased medication errors and 4 percent attributed one or more patient deaths to understaffing.[9]

Scott moved in his own managers and pushed them to perform. Hospital administrators were focused on quarterly earnings and given ambitious targets, typically revenue growth of 15 percent to 40 percent per year. He used a system of "scorecards" that showed the performance of each hospital in multiple areas. For example, part of each scorecard had a "case-mix index" to track the relative proportion of patients with illnesses that were highly reimbursed under Medicare's coding system. Administrators were supposed to raise the index number.[10] Much of a hospital manager's pay was based on a salary bonus plan, and 90 percent of the bonus came from meeting short-term financial goals. In the mid-1990s, a typical hospital manager had an annual salary of $150,000, but could earn up to $1 million with bonus and stock options.[11] This far exceeded the compensation of managers in not-for-profit hospitals.

---

[7]Ibid.

[8]David R. Olmos, "Do Profits Come First at Vegas Hospital?" *Los Angeles Times,* September 26, 1997, p. A1.

[9]Diane Sosne, "The Truth about Hospitals that Exist to Make Money," *Seattle Times,* July 11, 1997, p. B5.

[10]Lucette Lagnado, "Blowing the Whistle on Columbia/HCA: An Interview with Marc Gardner," *Multinational Monitor,* April 1998, p. 18.

[11]Michele Bitoun Blecher, "Rough Crossings," *Hospitals & Health Networks,* October 5, 1997, p. 40.

The Columbia system included unsparing discipline—managers who missed their targets were abruptly replaced. Some hospitals had three or four new heads in a year. Many managers resigned when the pressure became too much or when they felt that their values were being compromised. One chief administrator who left a Columbia hospital in Orlando, Florida, was asked to put a sign in the emergency room saying that patients' green cards would be inspected. Under federal law, no patient can be released from an emergency room until his or her condition is stabilized and so anyone who comes in must be treated. The sign was an effort to reduce expenses by scaring away to some competing hospital illegal immigrants with no health insurance or ability to pay.[12]

Columbia tried to increase revenues as well as cut costs. One way was by creating incentives for physicians. Giving them equity in the hospitals was an important tactic, and many Columbia hospitals were 15 to 20 percent physician-owned. A *New York Times* investigation in 1997 examined referral patterns of sixty-two physicians in two Columbia/HCA hospitals in Florida and found that after investing in these facilities, the doctors as a group referred more patients to them and fewer to competitors.[13] Sometimes Columbia also owned the physician's practices. During its expansion, it purchased 1,400 practices and provider networks that funneled patients in. There were other incentives. On slow weekends at Sunrise Medical Center in Las Vegas, doctors who admitted the most patients won Caribbean cruises.[14]

Another method of raising revenues was aggressive billing of Medicare. As it grew, Columbia got more than 30 percent of its revenues from Medicare and became Medicare's largest single claimant. A team of *New York Times* investigative reporters studied the results of such billing at Cedars Medical Center in Miami.[15] Because Medicare pays a fixed amount for any patient in a given disease category, a hospital gets more if patients are coded in high-reimbursement categories. For example, in DRG 79, which is the code for upper respiratory treatments, there are four categories of pneumonia. The highest-paid category is complex respiratory infection, for which Cedars would be reimbursed $6,800 per case by the government. The lowest-paid category is simple pneumonia, which was reimbursed at $3,150 per case.

Studying records, the *Times* reporters learned that before being taken over by Columbia in 1992, Cedars billed 31 percent of pneumonia cases as complex respiratory infections. After Columbia took over, complex respiratory infections rose to 93 percent of pneumonia cases. Meanwhile, a county hospital across the street billed only 28 percent of its cases as complex respiratory infection. Years later, when the company was accused of illegally "upcoding," or increasing payments by billing in higher categories than justified, it would

---

[12]Ibid.

[13]Martin Gottlieb and Kurt Eichenwald, "High Stakes Investments: Health-Care Giant Offers Its Doctors a Share of Hospitals," *Sun-Sentinel,* April 13, 1997, p. 1G.

[14]Olmos, "Do Profits Come First at Vegas Hospital?" p. 1G.

[15]Martin Gottlieb, Kurt Eichenwald, and Josh Barbanel, "Health Care's Giant: Powerhouse under Scrutiny," *New York Times*, March 28, 1997, p. A1.

argue that the billing at Cedars and other hospitals was not fraudulent; it simply reflected greater mastery of Medicare's complex coding procedures than competitors could develop.

Scott also introduced bold marketing. Alone among hospital chains, Columbia had a sales force that prospected for new business. In 1997 he started a nationwide brand-recognition campaign with television commercials and print ads designed to fix the Columbia/HCA name in the public mind so that when Americans needed to go to the hospital, they would want a Columbia/HCA hospital, just as when they wanted a hamburger, they looked for a McDonald's restaurant.

Resistance and Crisis

As time went on and Columbia's strategies became well known, resistance to new acquisitions grew. If not for this resistance, Columbia/HCA would have expanded even more rapidly. In 1995 alone, it had to back out of thirty pending hospital deals when state regulators and civic groups rose in opposition. Consequently, Columbia tried to avoid public debate and made hospital boards agree to secrecy during negotiations.[16] This did not always work. In 1996, Columbia/HCA reached an agreement to buy its first hospital in Rhode Island, a medical center in Providence, but when Rep. Patrick J. Kennedy (D-R.I.) found out, he organized public forums to air criticisms of the company. The deal was soon put on hold by state regulators. The attorney general of Michigan, a state in which there are no for-profit hospitals, rejected a Columbia/HCA hospital deal there. Regulators in Ohio refused to allow a Columbia/HCA buyout of Ohio Blue Cross.

Nevertheless, the company prospered. Its growth showed in the rise of annual revenues from $4.9 billion in 1990 to $20 billion in 1996. Over this period, net profits averaged 7 percent a year, an excellent return that was 15 to 20 percent higher than at competing companies. By now, Columbia/HCA was not only the largest hospital chain in the United States, but the largest home-care operation as well, with 590 facilities in thirty states. Home care was a critical part of Scott's strategy to develop a continuum of services. One factor that made it attractive was that Medicare payments for home care were more generous than were payments for hospital stays. However, when Scott set a goal for hospital administrators to capture for Columbia/HCA facilities 85 percent of discharged patients who needed home care, it angered Medicare regulators, who had set a figure of 62 percent referrals as the maximum permitted.[17]

---

[16]Kuttner, "Columbia/HCA and the Resurgence of the For-Profit Hospital Business," pp. 446–51.

[17]Lucette Lagnado, Anita Sharpe, and Greg Jaffe, "How Columbia/HCA Changed Health Care, for Better or Worse," *The Wall Street Journal*, August 1, 1997, p. A4.

As Columbia grew, Scott became wealthy. He held 9.4 million shares worth $376 million and by 1996 received an annual salary of more than $2 million. The end for him was, however, near. Entering 1997, he was driving Columbia/HCA hard. He rose early in the morning for 5:00 AM workouts and 6:00 AM strategy sessions. He worked frenetically and pushed people around him to do the same. Initiatives, policies, and programs spewed from him in a rapid-fire manner, and others in the organization were not only fatigued by the demands of Columbia/HCA's growth, but confused as well by frequent priority changes emanating from Scott.

Then in March, federal authorities initiated a widespread investigation into Medicare billing fraud at Columbia/HCA. Agents armed with search warrants raided its hospitals in El Paso and removed Medicare billing documents. Three high-level executives were indicted by a federal grand jury in Florida for submitting false cost reports and claims to Medicare. Soon, the agents returned, serving search warrants at thirty-five facilities in seven states. Subpoenas were issued for records of laboratory billings, DRG coding, and home-care operations.

These investigations drove down Columbia/HCA's stock price, increased resistance to acquisitions, foreshadowed friction with regulators, and threatened crippling fines. But Scott seemed unaware of the danger. On the day the FBI raided thirty-five facilities and the company's shares tumbled 12 percent, Scott appeared on CNN and reassured listeners that "government investigations are matter-of-fact in healthcare."[18]

The investigations unleashed a media obsession with Columbia/HCA. Investigative reports appeared in newspapers and on television news magazines, and they included plenty of horror stories about the effects of market incentives in Columbia hospitals. Neither the company nor Scott responded to the allegations. Scott refused to put together a crisis response; indeed, he seemed not to sense a crisis. But members of the Columbia/HCA board of directors did, and in late July they summoned Scott to a board meeting and forced his resignation. He was given a severance package worth $10 million.

A New Course in a Sea of Troubles

Another board member, Thomas Frist Jr., was picked to succeed Scott. Frist was the founder of HCA and had come on board in 1994 when that firm merged with Columbia. To save Columbia/HCA, Frist quickly announced a series of steps that redefined the company's approach to doing business. These were:

> . . . elimination of annual cash incentive compensation for the Company's employees, divestiture of the home health care business, the unwinding of physician

---

[18]Lutz and Gee, *Columbia/HCA—Healthcare on Overdrive,* p. 135.

interests in hospitals, significant expansion of compliance programs, increased disclosures in medicare cost reports, changes in laboratory billing procedures, increased reviews of Medicare coding and further guidelines on any transactions with physicians.[19]

Frist said that he would refocus the company on strengthening existing operations and putting patient care first. To emphasize compliance with the law and ethical standards, he created the post of senior vice president of corporate ethics, compliance, and corporate responsibility and hired Alan Yuspeh to fill it. Yuspeh had run the successful Defense Industry Initiative set up in the 1980s to reduce criminality and fraud in defense companies. Yuspeh developed a strong companywide compliance program that included a new ethics code.[20] Altogether, Frist's changes amounted to a repudiation of the hard edge of Scott's policies, but not of his basic strategic direction, which was to assemble an efficient market-driven, integrated care network.

Despite Frist's efforts, the company was viciously punished. The investigations scared patients away. With Frist's approval, 40 hospitals dropped Columbia/HCA from their name. Net income fell 80 percent for 1997 and continued falling in 1998. Columbia's share price plummeted. More federal and state regulators announced investigations. The Federal Trade Commission levied a $2.5 million fine for antitrust violations in the Utah hospital market. The Internal Revenue Service assessed $267 million in back taxes for wrongful deductions in 1993 and 1994.

The existence of federal fraud charges spurred angry patients to sue, and numerous individual suits and class actions arose.[21] The battered share price opened the door to investor lawsuits. In one of these, a group of pension funds sued Scott, Frist, and nine other directors as individuals for negligence and intentional breach of fiduciary duties stemming from failure to prevent fraud in the company's operations.[22] Also, former employees now became whistle blowers and said that they had knowledge of hundreds of millions of dollars of false Medicare billings.[23] Under the federal False Claims Act, they would be entitled to pocket 25 percent of any money recovered by the government, so if their allegations were correct, they could become wealthy. Because of these suits, on top of the investigations, corporate legal expenses rose rapidly.

---

[19]Columbia/HCA Healthcare Corporation, *Form 10-K,* for the fiscal year ended December 31, 1997, p. 1.

[20]Andy Pasztor and Lucette Lagnado, "Ethics Czar Aims to Heal Columbia," *The Wall Street Journal,* November 26, 1997, p. D11. See also "Columbia/HCA Ethics and Compliance Program," on the company's Web site at http://www.columbia-hca.com.

[21]For example, *Hoop* v. *Columbia/HCA,* No. 249-171-97 (D.C. Johnson Co., Texas) seeking to certify a class action of persons who paid padded or fraudulent bills or had their illnesses exaggerated for billing purposes.

[22]*McCall* v. *Scott,* No. 3-97-0838 (U.S.D.C., M.D. Tenn.)

[23]For example, *United States ex rel. James Thompson* v. *Columbia/HCA,* No. C-95-110 (U.S.D.C., S.D. Tex., Corpus Christi Div.)

Columbia/HCA also began to shrink. Bad publicity emboldened critics of for-profit hospital conversions, and seven of ten pending takeovers were shelved. Ten construction projects were canceled. Columbia/HCA typically financed acquisitions with its stock, but with share prices falling, the pending acquisition of another health care company was canceled. By mid-1998, Frist had kept his word and sold off home-care operations. He had sold twenty-two hospitals and planned to sell another sixty-five.[24]

The company started negotiating a monetary settlement with federal agencies so that it could get out from under the cloud of suspicion and uncertainty. It may have to pay a fine of as much as $1 billion. When the investigations and lawsuits are settled, the company will move on, but it will be smaller and presumably less combative than it was in the Scott era.

Columbia/HCA as an Agent of Change

The fast-paced era of Rick Scott at Columbia/HCA is over. Many are critical of Scott's strategies that, in the end, brought grief to the company. But were the strategies inherently bad ones for health care delivery, or were they appropriate strategies that were simply mismanaged?

What Scott attempted to do was apply market solutions to intractable problems that had been growing in the health care system for half a century.[25] One problem is that costs of health care are becoming prohibitively high. Scott imposed the for-profit corporate form on health care delivery and worked it to every advantage, ruthlessly seeking cost savings and efficiencies wherever they could be found. Often, the formula succeeded in elevating hospital performance to the advantage of a range of stakeholders beyond Columbia's stockholders. For example, when Columbia converted the tax-exempt Cape Fear Memorial Hospital in Wilmington, North Carolina, in 1995, it made $1 million in improvements. A year later, admissions were up 6 percent, babies delivered up 40 percent, unpaid care to charity patients up 12 percent, and staffing up almost 25 percent.[26] Situations like this were not as newsworthy as claims that Columbia was killing patients with its miserly ways, and so the public mostly heard and read about scandal, not achievement.

Before the rise of for-profit hospital chains, particularly Columbia, the nation relied on not-for-profit, tax-exempt hospitals.[27] At a time when changes were necessary in health care delivery, these old-model institutions had little incentive to streamline and embrace managed care. But when Columbia/HCA

---

[24]Patricia B. Limbacher, "Columbia: Year in Review," *Modern Healthcare,* July 27, 1998, p. 26.

[25]J. D. Kleinke, "Deconstructing the Columbia/HCA Investigation," *Health Affairs,* March–April 1998.

[26]Blecher, "Rough Crossings," p. 40.

[27]See Charles E. Rosenberg, *The Care of Strangers: The Rise of America's Hospital System,* Baltimore: Johns Hopkins University Press, 1987.

moved into a market, the not-for-profits in the area had to discipline themselves or face being underbid by Scott for the business of local employers and HMOs.

Another problem is the market-distorting effects of heavy, ponderous government regulation of the health care industry. Medicare, for example, imposes an arcane and imprecise billing process designed to minimize reimbursement. The system invites fraud and "aggressive billing," and Scott played the game, not a game he invented, but one that the government had set up. There is no evidence of a systematic effort inside Columbia/HCA to bilk the government, but corporate incentives surely tempted some managers to cheat.

Government regulation also stifles health care markets in other ways. Laws that require regulatory approval to build or shut down tax-exempt hospitals led to a nationwide oversupply of beds because politicians never wanted to close hospitals. This oversupply increased competition and made it harder to earn adequate revenues. Scott entered local markets, bought hospitals, and closed some of them. This seemed antisocial, but it brought supply and demand into equilibrium and all hospitals in the area benefitted, not just Columbia's. State and federal laws are also unclear about exactly what financial relationships are permitted between doctors and hospitals, and this has created an arm's-length and sometimes untrusting relationship between the two parties. Scott took advantage of gray areas in the law to bring doctors more closely into the hospital orbit. This brought in more patients. It also gave doctors a stronger voice in hospital operation and an incentive to hold down patient-care costs.

Scott was opposed by nurses' unions that stood to lose members. He was opposed by federal and state regulators who stood to lose their power. He was opposed by many in the American public who wanted to believe that unlimited, universal health care delivered by physicians in the mold of Marcus Welby was a realistic, affordable option. And he was opposed by critics with traditional values about health care who were suspicious of business methods in an industry that dealt with life and death. Not the least among these was Pope John Paul II, who, after the El Paso raids, issued a statement, intended for the ears of trustees at Catholic hospitals, in which he said that "the centrality and dignity of the human person are ignored and trampled on . . . when healthcare is regarded in terms of profit and not as a generous service."[28]

Questions

1. Is a market-driven approach valid for the health care industry? Do you support or oppose tradeoffs between care quality and efficiency? For example, is it wrong for a hospital manager to work for a bonus by cutting the nursing staff to the borderline where care may begin to suffer?

---

[28]"News at Deadline," *Modern Healthcare*, July 7, 1997, p. 4.

2. How should the strategies behind Columbia/HCA's rise to prominence be assessed? Were they fundamentally flawed, wrong, and unworkable? Or were they appropriate and necessary for the industry environment but failed to work because of insensitive application by Scott?

3. Did Columbia/HCA use health care resources more efficiently than its for-profit and not-for-profit competitors? Or did it compromise care, shift costs to various stakeholders, and move savings to salaries, dividends, and acquisitions?

4. Is health care a basic right? Can it be limited if the cost of providing unlimited treatment is prohibitive? If so, should it be regarded as a commodity and limited by market mechanisms or should it be rationed by government regulation? If not, how can the nation pay for it?

AN APPLICATION
OF ETHICAL PRINCIPLES

The following situations raise ethical conflicts for some readers. If you believe that an ethical problem exists in an incident, be specific in stating its nature. Then apply ideas, principles, and methods from the previous chapter to help with the solution.

1. The CEO of a midwestern manufacturing company tells the following story.

   "I was looking over recent performance reviews in the household products division and one thing that struck me was the review of a star sales rep named Al. I know Al because he handles our Wal-Mart account. Al had the highest annual sales for the past five years and last year nearly doubled the next highest reps' total. The sales manager's written evaluation was highly laudatory as expected, but cautioned Al to adhere strictly to discount policy, shipping protocol, and billing protocol. I got curious.

   "A conversation with the division manager revealed that Al ingratiated himself with workers on the loading dock, socializing with them, sending them birthday cards, and giving them small gifts such as tickets to minor-league ball games. The loading dock supervisor complained that Al was requesting and sometimes getting priority loading of trucks for his customers despite the formal first-in, first-out rules for shipping orders. Second, Al had given several customers slightly deeper discounts than authorized, although the resulting orders were highly profitable for the company. And finally, late in December, Al had informally requested that one big account delay payment on an order by a week so that the commission would be counted in the next year. This would have gotten him off to a running start had not an accountant for the purchaser paid promptly and written to Al's manager in refusing the request.

   "The division head stuck up for Al. I didn't press or request that any action be taken. Did I do the right thing?"

   How would you answer the CEO's question?

2. A sales representative for a large manufacturer of consumer electronics equipment headquartered in Los Angeles, California, has courted a buyer from a nationwide chain of 319 retail stores for over a year. At company expense the buyer was flown to Los Angeles from Trenton, New Jersey, with his spouse, for a three-day sales presentation. The company is paying all expenses for this trip and for the couple to attend a Los Angeles Dodgers baseball game and dine at fine restaurants.

   During the second day of meetings, the buyer discusses a one-year, $40 million order. The chain that the buyer represents has not sold the company's products before, but once it starts, reorders are likely. At dinner that evening, the buyer mentions that he and his wife have always wanted to visit Sea World in San Diego. While they are in southern California and so close, they would like to fly down. It is clear that he expects the company to pay for this trip and that he will delay making a commitment for the $40 million order until he gets a response.

   The company has already spent $2,200 for the buyer's trip to Los Angeles. The San Diego excursion would cost about $500. The marketing manager estimates that the company can make a 9 percent gross profit on the sale. The sales representative stands to receive a 0.125 percent commission over base salary.

   What should the sales representative do?

3. Charles Whitcomb managed the Capital Reserve Fund. This fund engaged in options and futures trading. Participation in the fund was limited to those individuals who could advance $5,000,000 or more. During the past eight years, the participants were rewarded with an average annual appreciation of their capital contribution of 38 percent. In recent years, Whitcomb concentrated on foreign exchange market trends. At the moment he was watching events in Logost, a small country in Africa. This nation had a substantial unbalanced budget due to overspending and also difficulty in collecting taxes. Banks were borrowing excessive capital from abroad with short-term maturities. This money was loaned to political cronies who used it to speculate in mining adventures. Many borrowers were having difficulty paying interest on their bank loans. Indeed, a few had defaulted. Foreign lenders were beginning to withdraw their money. There was a large foreign trade deficit and exports were declining. Clearly the currency, the ristat, was overvalued. Yet, the Logost central bank supported the fixed exchange rate for the ristat.

   Whitcomb had a skilled staff that analyzed the economies of foreign countries, especially those appearing to be in some trouble. He and his staff believed that Logost was in deep trouble and could not for long maintain the fixed exchange rate for the ristat. In such a situation Whitcomb would wager billions of dollars to sell short the currency.

His usual practice was to sell futures on a ninety-day contract to deliver a currency at a fixed price. If he was correct and the fixed price of the currency could not be maintained, he would make millions on the transaction.

In the case of Logost he believed the ristat was due to fall significantly as borrowers withdrew their money and the shaky financial situation deteriorated. He also knew that if he did short the ristat and it collapsed for this and other reasons, he would be blamed for any economic disaster. There would be an economic disaster even if he was not involved and thousands of people would be impoverished.

Whitcomb was puzzled about what to do. On the one hand, if he sold the ristat short, he would make a lot of money for participants in his fund. On the other hand, he might contribute to the collapse of a small country's economy and bring hardship to its citizens.

Should he undertake this transaction or pass it up and seek other opportunities?

4. As chairman of an accounting firm in a large city, you were prepared to promote one of your vice chairmen to the position of managing partner. Your decision was based on a record of outstanding performance by this person over the eight years she has been with the firm. A new personnel director recently insisted on implementing a policy of résumé checks for hirees and current employees receiving promotions who had not been through such checks. Unfortunately, it was discovered that although the vice chairman claimed to have an M.B.A. from the University of Michigan, she dropped out before completing her last twenty units of course work. Would you proceed with the promotion, retain the vice chairman but not promote her, or fire her?

5. When Admiral Thomas Westfall took command of the Portsmouth Naval Shipyard, theft of supplies was endemic. It was a standing joke that homes in the area were painted gray with paint stolen from the Navy. Admiral Westfall issued an order that rules related to supply practices and forbidding theft would be strictly enforced. Within a few days, two career petty officers were apprehended carrying a piece of Plexiglas worth $25 out of the base. Westfall immediately fired both of them and also a civilian storeroom clerk with thirty years' service, who lost both his job and his pension. According to Westfall, "the fact that I did it made a lot of honest citizens real quick." Did the admiral act ethically?

6. Sam, Sally, and Hector have been laid off from middle-management positions. Sam and Hector are deeply upset by their misfortune. They are nervous, inarticulate, and docile at an exit meeting in the personnel department and accept the severance package offered by the company (two weeks' pay plus continuation of health benefits for two weeks) without questioning its provisions. Sally, on the other hand, manifests her anxiety about job loss by becoming angry. In the exit meeting, she complains about the inadequacy of the severance package, threatens a

lawsuit, and tries to negotiate more compensation. She receives an extra week of pay that the others did not get. Has the company been fair in its treatment of these employees?

7. The Tokyo Bay Steamship Company operated a tourist ship between Tokyo and the volcanic island of Oshima 50 miles offshore. It also had a restaurant on the island. It was a modest business until February 1933, when Kiyoko Matsumoto, a 19-year-old college student, committed suicide by jumping into the crater of the volcano, which bubbled with molten lava. Ms. Matsumoto left a poetic suicide note and, through newspaper stories, the Japanese public became obsessed with her story.

   Soon other Japanese emulated Ms. Matsumoto. In the next ten months, 143 people threw themselves into the crater. Many more came to watch. One Sunday in April, for example, thirty-one persons tried to jump. Twenty-five were restrained, but six succeeded. People crowded around the edge of the crater waiting for jumpers. Shouts of "Who's next?" and "Step right up, there's plenty of room in front" could be heard.

   The Tokyo Bay Steamship Company capitalized on the volcano's popularity. It increased its fleet to thirty ships and added nineteen more restaurants. Meanwhile, the Oshima police chief met the boat and tried to weed out potential suicides using a crude behavioral profile (was someone too happy or too sad?). A police officer stood at the rim of the volcano. The Japanese government made purchase of a one-way ticket to Oshima a crime. Many suicides were prevented; others succeeded. Twenty-nine people who were stopped at the volcano killed themselves by jumping into the ocean on the return boat to Tokyo.

   In the meantime, Tokyo Bay Steamship company prospered. Its shares rose on the Tokoyo exchange. But did it meet basic standards of ethics?

8. You are asked by a potential employer to take a psychological profile test. A sample segment includes these items.

	Yes	No	Can't Say
It is difficult to sleep at night.			
I worry about sexual matters.			
Sometimes my hands feel disjointed from my body.			
I sometimes smell strange odors.			
I enjoyed dancing classes in junior high school.			
Not all of my friends really like me.			
Work is often a source of stress.			

Because you have read that it is best to fit into a "normal" range and pattern of behavior, and because it is your hunch that the personnel office will weed out unusual personalities, you try to guess which answers are most appropriate for a conservative or average response and write them in. Is this ethical?

9. In 1809 a lawyer informed John Jacob Astor of an unusual situation. In 1776, at the start of the Revolutionary War, the State of New York had confiscated 51,102 acres of land in Putnam County from Roger Morris and his wife because they supported the British. The state then sold this land to farmers, and by 1809 about 700 families made their homes on it and had made improvements that greatly increased its value.

   However, the lawyer told Astor, simply because the Morris's were Tories, the state had not had proper authority to seize the land and the land was not legally owned by New York or the farmers on it, but by the Morris's children. Astor sought out the children and talked them into selling their legal claim for $100,000.

   Then Astor notified the 700 families who, for thirty-three years, had believed they had proper ownership of their farms that they were trespassing on his land. The farmers appealed to the legislature and public opinion was aroused against Astor, so he offered to sell the land to the state for $667,000. His offer was rejected as outrageous and from there the matter went to court. Astor waited patiently and after many years his legal claim was upheld. Finally, in 1827, the state gave Astor $500,000 to purchase title to the property for the farmers. In this way, Astor made a 500 percent profit off the taxpayers of New York.

   Were Astor's actions ethical?

10. Mary P., an aerospace engineer, tells about a difficult career experience in which her friend Tom plays a central role.

   "My friend Tom and I are employed by Republic Systems Corporation. We started about the same time after graduating from engineering school five years ago. The company does a lot of defense work, mostly for the Air Force, and it's big. Tom and I worked on project teams doing tests to make sure that electronics shipped to customers met specifications. We have very similar backgrounds and job records and there has always been a little competition between us. But neither one of us pulled ahead of the other on the corporate ladder. That is until last winter.

   "At that time, we were assigned a special project to modify the testing protocol on certain radar components. The success of the project was critical; it had to be done before Republic bid for two more years on its big radar systems contract. About 40 percent of our people work radar.

   "We rolled up our sleeves and put in long hours. After a month, though, Tom volunteered to be on a companywide task force developing a new employee privacy policy. Privacy is a big deal to Al Manchester, our CEO.

   "Tom continued to work with me, but he gradually put more and more of his energy into the privacy project. I had to start taking up some of the slack. He enjoyed the task force meetings. They met in the dining room at the Kenthill Country Club and he could hobnob with Al and some of the other big shots. He worked overtime to impress them.

"We finally finished the testing project and it was a success. But towards the end I did the lion's share of it. One day Tom made me angry by ending a capacitor test at 94 hours instead of the 100 hours you really have to have for validity. He did it because he was late for a privacy task force meeting. Overall, I guess Tom helped a lot, but he didn't do his share all the way through.

"Last month the assistant manager of the radar project left the company and Tom and I both applied for the position. It was a pay raise of several grades and meant getting a lot of recognition. They chose Tom. The announcement in the company newsletter said that he was a 'strong team player' and mentioned both the testing project and the privacy task force as major accomplishments.

"I don't think it was fair."

Was Tom fair to Mary? Was Tom's promotion fair to Mary? Was the company wrong to promote Tom?

11. You are the president of a company that manufactures chain saws. A chain saw is a dangerous but necessary tool. Each year some workers are injured while using your saws and the saws made by your competitors. You comply with all pertinent federal safety standards, but there are expensive design alterations you could incorporate into your product that would prevent some injuries. These alterations would raise production costs considerably in a very competitive industry. It is probable your competitors would not follow suit. Are you ethically remiss if you do not change your design?

PART 4

Business and Government

The Government–Business Relationship: An Overview

One of the most secretive production facilities in the United States, the "Skunk Works," produced some of the most spectacular airplanes ever built. The Skunk Works was a nondescript-looking facility located at the Lockheed Airport in Burbank, California.* Among the major aircraft built there were the following: the highly respected P-38 fighter of World War II; the P-80, the first jet fighter of the United States; the F-104, the first supersonic jet fighter; and more recently the U-2, the SR-71, and the F-117A. In building all these airplanes, the Skunk Works leapfrogged existing technology and did so in astonishingly low time and cost from contract to prototype. All were built under the most restrictive national security conditions.

The U-2 was built in 1955 to fly high-altitude surveillance missions. It broke all altitude records because it could fly at almost 75,000 feet and for

_____
*Relocated to Palmdale, CA, in 1995.

ten hours on one tank of fuel. It was the famous plane shot down by the Russians in 1960. The SR-71, built in 1965, was the first surveillance plane that flew at three times the speed of sound and broke all speed records, many of which still stand. The F-117A, built in 1981, is the stealth tactical fighter that performed so spectacularly in Desert Storm.

Clarence "Kelly" Johnson was the founder of the Skunk Works and was given a good bit of leeway from federal regulations until he turned over the management of the organization in 1975 to Ben R. Rich. Rich faced management frustrations that Johnson avoided because of new social, in contrast to military, regulations. Many of the problems he faced are chronicled in the book *Skunk Works,*[1] by Rich and Leo Janos. For instance, he was forced by law to purchase 2 percent of his materials from minority or disadvantaged businesses, but many of them, he complained, could not meet his high-security requirements. He also was required by the Equal Employment Opportunity Commission (EEOC) to employ a certain number of the disadvantaged. "I was challenged," he said, "as to why I didn't employ any Latino engineers. 'Because they didn't go to engineering school' was my reply. If I didn't comply I could lose my contract, its high priority notwithstanding. And it did no good to argue that I needed highly skilled people to do very specialized work, regardless of race, creed, or color. I tried to get a waiver

on our stealth production, but it was almost impossible."[2]

Rich said that on the later airplanes, especially the F-117A, he had to work with exotic materials on the plane's outer skin. "The radar-absorbing ferrite sheeting and paints required special precautions for workers. OSHA demanded sixty-five different masks and dozens of types of work shoes on stealth alone. I was told by OSHA that no worker with a beard was allowed to use a mask while spray coating. Imagine if I told a union rep that the Skunk Works would not hire bearded employees—they'd have hung me in effigy."[3]

OSHA created other problems for Rich. He tells how an OSHA inspector visited the old facilities of the Skunk Works, many of them dating to World War II days. Ladders were everywhere, lots of wires, a few oil slicks, inadequate ventilation, and other disarray characteristic of a highly talented organization that knew how to avoid hazards and to produce high quality under pressure. An inspector from OSHA came, at the invitation of Rich, and fined the company $2 million for no fewer than 7,000 OSHA violations. "He socked it to me," Rich said, "for doors blocked, improper ventilation, no backup emergency lighting in a workspace, no OSHA warning label on a bottle of commercial alcohol. That latter violation cost me three grand. I felt half a victim, half a slumlord."[4]

---

[1]Ben R. Rich and Leo Janos, *Skunk Works,* Boston: Little, Brown, 1994.

[2]Ibid., p. 75.
[3]Ibid., pp. 75–76.
[4]Ibid., p. 78.

The story of the Skunk Works illustrates a serious problem with intrusive regulations that complicate business activity, sometimes unnecessarily. Experiences such as this are not unusual and are increasingly pervasive in business. In this and the following chapter, we discuss the nature and significance of federal regulations to business and society. (State and local rules are very important in this relationship, but we do not have space to deal with them except in an incidental way.)

Specifically in this chapter we discuss the legal basis of government actions toward business, the underlying reasons for them, how regulatory patterns have changed in our history, how regulations originate and are administered, the impact of regulations on society, and how U.S. regulations compare with those in other countries.

Legal Basis of Government Regulation of Business

The fundamental authority for federal regulation of business is the Constitution of the United States. In the Constitution, most of the economic powers exercised by the federal government are contained in Article 1, Section 8. This section gives Congress wide powers. Included is the power "to regulate commerce." This has been called the "commerce clause," and upon its authority the federal government has extended its reach widely over business. There are, however, other powers in Article 1, Section 8, that also provide a base for the exercise of business regulatory powers. Included, for example, is the power to levy and collect taxes, to provide for the common defense and general welfare, to borrow money, to establish bankruptcy laws, to promote science and useful arts by granting patents and exclusive rights over writings and discoveries, and "[t]o make all Laws which shall be necessary and proper for carrying into Execution the foregoing Powers, and all other Powers vested by this Constitution in the Government of the United States, or in any Department or Officer thereof."

The Constitution also is designed to "promote the general Welfare." Broadly interpreted, this clause plus the powers granted in Article 1, Section 8, now provides a broad legal authority for advancing government regulation of economic and social affairs. In contemplating this significant grant of power to the federal government, it must be kept in mind that the convention drafting the Constitution was specifically convened to give power to the central government, not to take it away.

The federal government's ability to exercise these powers to regulate business depends on the interpretation of them by the Supreme Court of the United States. As a result of current liberal interpretations by the Court, the federal government today is able to impose on business just about any regulation that can be passed through the congressional law-making machinery.

Supreme Court Interpretations of Constitutional Powers

Chief Justice Hughes is reported to have observed (when governor of New York), "we are under a Constitution, but the Constitution is what the judges say it is." This is true. Therefore it is important to look briefly at the major themes of Court decisions about government regulation of business.

Early History

For a century and a half, the Court took two major paths so far as legal authority over business is concerned. On the one hand, it protected business from government regulation, both federal and state. On the other hand, it opened the door to new regulations. We briefly look at landmarks in these paths.

For example, in 1819 the Supreme Court gave business a strong protective shield against arbitrary state power in the *Dartmouth College* case. The New Hampshire legislature amended the charter of Dartmouth College, a private institution, to make it a public institution. The Supreme Court ruled that state legislatures could not impair a contract, and that the charter "is a contract, the obligation of which cannot be impaired without violating the Constitution of the United States.[5]

In other cases, the Supreme Court firmly established the legal foundation for the supremacy of federal law over state law. In *McCulloch* v. *Maryland,* also in 1819, the Court outlawed a tax levied by Maryland on The Bank of the United States, a federally chartered bank.[6] In another famous case in this period, the Court expanded federal legal power to control interstate commerce. The state of New York sought to regulate steamboats on the Hudson River. In *Gibbons* v. *Ogden,* the Court struck down such laws on the grounds that they interfered with federal powers over commerce granted in the Constitution.[7]

But then, in 1837, the Supreme Court entered the second path in the *Charles River Bridge* case. The Charles River Bridge Corporation was chartered by the Massachusetts legislature in 1785 to build and operate for seventy-five years a bridge across the Charles River between Charleston and Boston. In 1828, the legislature authorized another company to build a bridge a few yards from the first span. The property was to be surrendered to the state and be free of tolls after a period of time not exceeding six years. The Charles River Bridge Corporation sued, charging it had been granted exclusive rights for seventy-five years. The Supreme Court ruled that the state had a right to exercise its power over private property unless it said in "plain words" that it intended to surrender its power.[8]

Milestone Decisions: Post-Civil War to 1911

The progressive movement, as described in Chapter 4, led to state laws regulating railroads after the Civil War. The Supreme Court said these laws were constitutional in *Munn* v. *Illinois* (1877) and declared that "When private property

---

[5]*Dartmouth College* v. *Woodward,* 4 Wheaton 519 (1819).
[6]*McCulloch* v. *Maryland,* 4 Wheaton 316 (1819).
[7]*Gibbons* v. *Ogden,* 9 Wheaton 316 (1819).
[8]*Charles River Bridge* v. *Warren Bridge,* 11 Peters 420 (1837).

is devoted to a public use, it is subject to public regulation."[9] It becomes "affected with a public interest." This case provided a new foundation for broad regulation of industry. It supported the creation of the Interstate Commerce Commission in 1887 to control railroads, the Sherman Antitrust Act in 1890, the Food and Drug Act of 1905, the Meat Inspection Act of 1905, and other major pieces of legislation. The thrust of new laws was to curb the abuses of an ebullient, aggressive, and often irresponsible business world.

There were, however, some positive developments for business. The Supreme Court said in the *Santa Clara* case in 1886 that corporations are cloaked in the mantle of the Fourteenth Amendment to the Constitution.[10] This amendment had been passed in 1868 to protect blacks and forbade states to abridge the privileges and immunities of citizens; to deprive any person of life, liberty, or property without due process of law; or to "deny to any person within its jurisdiction the equal protection of the laws." The Court upheld the idea that a corporation is a person and that therefore the benefits of the amendment extend to it. In effect, states could regulate corporations, but the regulations had to be developed through accepted legal procedures and be nondiscriminatory as compared with those covering individual citizens. This armor proved to be highly protective to business in the legal jungles of regulation.

Efforts by federal, state, and local governments to introduce social reforms, such as permitting workers to strike and improving working conditions, met with repeated rebuffs by the Supreme Court. For example, the state of New York attempted to reduce the hours of work in bakeries to ten a day. But this attempt, said the Court in *Lockner* v. *New York* in 1905, was an unreasonable, unnecessary, arbitrary, illegal, and "meddlesome interference with the rights of the individual" and contrary to the Fourteenth Amendment.[11]

On the other hand, the Court did permit state and local regulations over business for certain purposes falling within state powers. Generally, the Court permitted state regulations where they were believed to promote the morals, peace and good order, or health and safety of the public. For example, a Minnesota law prohibiting the sale of habit-forming drugs was permitted in *Hodge* v. *Muscatine Co.* (1905).[12]

The ruling of the Supreme Court in the first antitrust case brought by the federal government under the Sherman Antitrust Act of 1890 was not promising for those interested in breaking up monopolies. In *U.S.* v. *Knight* (1895),[13] the Court decided that a sugar-refining company that controlled 98 percent of the market had not violated the act. In a series of later cases, the

---

[9]*Munn* v. *Illinois,* 297, 299, 317 (1877).

[10]*Santa Clara County* v. *Southern Pac. RR,* 118 U.S. 394 (1886).

[11]*Lockner* v. *New York,* 198 U.S. 45 (1905).

[12]*Hodge* v. *Muscatine Co.,* 196 U.S. (1905). For more details about Supreme Court decisions regarding state laws, see Paul Kens, "The Source of a Myth: Police Powers of the States and Laissez-Faire Constitutionalism, 1900–1937," *The American Journal of Legal History,* 36, no. 1, January 1991.

[13]*U.S.* v. *E. C. Knight Co.,* 156 U.S. 1 (1895).

Court reversed itself. Illustrative were *U.S.* v. *Standard Oil* (1909),[14] and *U.S.* v. *American Tobacco* (1911).[15] Both companies controlled about 95 percent of their respective markets, and the Court declared this percentage contrary to the law.

The Court Invalidates New Deal Laws

When President Franklin Roosevelt was elected in 1932, he faced the most devastating economic depression the country had ever suffered. A few statistics reveal the extraordinary tragedy. For instance, the gross national product (GNP) dropped (in current dollars) from $103.1 billion in 1929 to $58 billion in 1932. Industrial production was almost halved between these two dates. Durable goods production in 1932 was one-third the 1929 level. Steel production in 1932 was at 20 percent capacity. The unemployment rate rose in 1933 to 25 percent of the labor force and stayed at that level for months. Thousands of businesses and farmers went bankrupt, and millions of investors lost their life savings.

To deal with this economic catastrophe, President Roosevelt's "New Deal" broke new federal regulatory ground. The federal government for the first time assumed responsibility for stimulating business activity out of an economic depression. It undertook to correct a wide range of abuses in the economic machinery of the nation, particularly business, and amassed more far-reaching laws to this end in a shorter period of time than ever before or since. It assumed responsibility on a large scale for relieving the distress of businesses, farmers, workers, homeowners, consumers, investors, and others.

The new laws were quickly challenged in the courts and received harsh treatment. In one day, May 27, 1935, the Court declared three laws to be unconstitutional! The most celebrated was the *Schechter* case, which struck down the National Industrial Recovery Act (NIRA). The NIRA was a major enactment that established "codes of fair competition" for all industries. The codes included minimum wage scales, maximum hours of work, collective bargaining by labor unions, prohibitions against employing child labor, fair prices, and boycotts for nonsigners of each code. The codes were agreements hammered out by trade associations and organized labor. When federal officials approved the codes, they became law.

The Schechter Poultry Corporation was a New York City firm that slaughtered chickens and resold them to local retail dealers. The government said the company violated several provisions of the Live Poultry Code, including a ban on the sale of sick chickens. The government argued that the chickens sold in New York City were from out of state and substantially affected the stream of interstate commerce. This, said the government, fell within the powers granted by the commerce clause to regulate interstate commerce: the NIRA was therefore constitutional, argued the government.

---

[14]*U.S.* v. *Standard Oil Co.*, 156 U.S. 1 (1909).
[15]*U.S.* v. *American Tobacco Co.*, 211 U.S. 106 (1911).

In a unanimous decision, the Supreme Court declared the NIRA to be unconstitutional. First, it stated that Congress could not delegate so much power to the president. Second, the chickens became commingled with the mass of property within the state of New York and the flow of commerce stopped. Thus, the commerce clause did not apply to federal regulatory powers and the chicken transaction fell within the domain of state power. To conclude otherwise, said the Court, "there would be virtually no limit to federal power, and for all practical purposes we should have a completely centralized government."[16]

The Court Reverses Itself

President Roosevelt was outraged and tried, but was repulsed by the Senate, to "pack" the Court by adding six new justices to the existing nine so that he could get a majority to approve the constitutionality of his legislation. Four days after President Roosevelt submitted his court-packing plan to Congress, the Supreme Court began consideration of a few other cases, especially the constitutionality and powers of the National Labor Relations Act. One year after Roosevelt's attack, the Court, in a 5–4 decision, reversed itself in the *Jones and Laughlin* case.[17] In this case, the federal government had ordered the Jones and Laughlin Steel Corporation, the fourth largest steel company in the United States at the time, to cease and desist engaging in unfair labor practices at its Aliquippa, Pennsylvania, plant. The complaint was about the company firing union leaders for trivial violations of company rules and refusing to bargain collectively with the labor union. The corporation said the government had no power to issue such an order because the corporation was engaged in production at a local facility and not interstate commerce.

The Court found that since the company shipped steel out of state, the case fell within the commerce clause. Therefore, Congress had the power to delegate authority to the president and the NLRB was acting upon legitimate constitutional authority.

Significance of the Decision

The complete reversal in the *Jones and Laughlin* decision from the *Schechter* case opened wide the door for federal regulation of individual businesses.

With other contemporary cases, it constituted one of the most important legal foundations supporting the flood of federal regulation that has been enacted since then. It also illustrates that the Supreme Court's interpretation of the Constitution reflects changes in its environment.

We now turn to the major specific reasons underlying government regulation.

---

[16] *Schechter Poultry Corp.* v. *United States*, 225 U.S. 495 (1935).
[17] *National Labor Relations Board* v. *Jones and Laughlin Steel Corp.*, 201 U.S. 1 (1937).

Underlying Reasons for Government Regulation of the Private Sector

Federal justifications for regulating the private sector occur in two circumstances: when flaws appear in the marketplace that produce undesirable consequences; and where adequate social, political, and other reasons for government regulation exist. For the first century and a half of U.S. history, regulations were introduced mostly in response to flaws in the market mechanism; thereafter, regulations were increasingly introduced for broad social reasons.

Flaws in the Market

When functioning perfectly, the competitive market mechanism determines which of society's resources can be used most efficiently in producing the goods and services that people want. It yields the "best" answer to the questions of what should be produced and when and how the product will be distributed. The market mechanism has great appeal in democratic societies because, through it, social welfare can be advanced without central government control. Although highly efficient, the free market competitive model is not flawless. Some of the more important market failures that have justified government action are as follows.

Natural Monopoly.   When a firm can supply the entire market for a good or service more cheaply than any combination of smaller firms, it is said to have a natural monopoly. Under such circumstances, competition would be wasteful of resources. The typical examples of such monopolies are local public utilities, and state commissions have long regulated them. Today, however, many local utilities have been deregulated and face competition.

Natural Resource Regulation.   Exploitation of a natural resource can result in monopolistic practices that should be regulated. For example, the total volume of oil that can be produced in a single field is a function of the number of wells drilled and the rate of pumping. Too many wells and too rapid pumping reduce the field pressure and the quality of recoverable oil. That is avoided by government regulation. Government allocation of limited wavelengths in the electromagnetic spectrum is another example of natural resource regulation.

Destructive Competition.   When companies dominate an industry, they may engage in unfair or destructive competition. For example, they may cut prices enough to force competitors from the market and then raise prices. Several large firms may conspire to fix prices. To illustrate, in 1995 the Department of Justice began an investigation of the giant food processor ADM for allegations that it conspired with others to fix the price of lysine (an amino acid derived from corn that promotes muscle growth). The antitrust laws are designed to stop such practices.

Externalities.   Externalities are costs of production that are borne not by the enterprise that causes them but by society. For example, a factory that dumps toxic waste into a river may pollute it. It costs the factory nothing, but the community may have to pay dearly to clean up the mess. Why does the factory not invest in equipment to avoid the waste? Competition inhibits it. Suppose one steel mill tries to eliminate water pollution, but competing mills avoid the expense. Costs of the first mill will rise and, if high enough, could bankrupt the company. So society either pays for cleanup or forces all factories to bear the costs. The principle applies to industrial safety practices, health hazards, and jet noise, to give just a few examples.

Inadequate Information.   Competitive markets operate more efficiently when everyone associated with them has enough information to make informed choices. To the extent that such information is not available, government finds justification for regulating the knowledge in question. This category covers a very wide range of information, including information for consumers about product quality, warranty, content, and so on; information to workers about work hazards; disclosure of financial information for investors; disclosure of costs of capital to investors; and so on.

Social, Political, and Other Reasons for Regulation

During the past four decades, a number of structural and value changes have taken place in our society that have resulted in increasing pressure on government to interfere in the market mechanism. Here are a few.

Quality-of-Life Demands.   Pressures on government and business to meet new quality-of-life demands are significant causes of new government regulations. Clean air, clear water, and toxic waste disposal are examples.

Protecting Individual Rights.   This concern has always been a cause of federal regulation. Unethical and immoral actions of business are, of course, a subject for regulations that aim to prevent their occurrence. The very first Congress passed legislation to help poor and indigent sailors. Help to individuals has expanded to include programs for safe working conditions, better and safer products for consumers, elimination of discrimination in employment, provision for improved health care, and investor protection from misinformation and fraud.

Resolution of National and Global Problems.   As we have grown, the federal government has taken on more and more responsibilities to resolve national problems not effectively resolvable by state and local government or individuals—for example, regulation of railroads, banks, pollution, discrimination, foods, and so on. We are now part of a global economy in which we encounter fierce and competent competitors for our goods and services. The

Figure 9-1

Historical waves of government regulation of business.

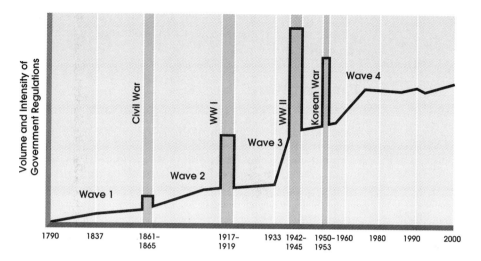

federal government is stepping in to help our companies compete more effectively in that market.

Regulation to Benefit Special Groups.   It is possible for regulations to be passed largely as a result of pressures on the legislative process by individuals or groups to pass measures for their own benefit. The expressed justification for such legislation, however, is not based on that objective but on more lofty goals. Nevertheless, much regulation does protect the interests of special groups, such as manufacturers of steel and producers of peanuts.

Conservation of Resources.   Federal regulations seek to conserve our natural resources, such as agricultural land, pristine forests, lakes and mountains, clean air, and endangered species.

Historical Patterns of Federal Regulations of Business

The volume of government regulations historically has moved in a wave-like pattern, as shown in Figure 9-1. Each wave has been triggered by the rise of popular demand for government to solve particular problems. After each burst of activity, the rate of new regulation has leveled off or declined. Except after wartime, the declines have been minimal. Generally, each new wave has brought more regulatory activities than existed previously; the exception has been the controls imposed during wartime, most of which were lifted following the end of hostilities.

The scale to the left of Figure 9-1 is our estimate of relative volume and impact of federal regulation on business. Though it is a qualitative estimate with all the limitations of such a measure, we offer it to sharpen the reader's perspective on regulatory growth. Following are highlights of a few major events in each wave.

The First Wave

This wave of government regulation took place from 1790 to 1837. During this period, regulations were predominantly promotional for business. The government gave vast financial subsidies and huge grants of land (to be sold) to private interests for the building of turnpikes, canals, and railroads. Through these actions, the federal government facilitated the building of a much-needed infrastructure.

The Second Wave

This era of regulation was dominated by demands of the progressives and Supreme Court decisions giving the federal government power to act. However, states were restrained by the court in regulating business.

The Third Wave

This burst of activity was the result, as noted above, of the many New Deal laws designed to deal with the ravages of the Great Depression of the 1930s.

The Fourth Wave

A groundswell of interest in improving the quality of life in the 1960s and 1970s led to the fourth wave of government regulations. The result was the development of new controls that involved government ever more deeply in managerial decision making, enormously increased the volume of regulation, and tightened government's control over business—precisely the topics that make up the subject of much of this book. Government regulatory agencies are involved in decisions in every major functional and operational area of a typical large corporation.

War Blips

As Figure 9-1 shows, wars have brought sudden increases in government controls. During the Civil War, there was very little control over production and prices, but the North created the National Banking System to help finance the war, and this had lasting impact on our financial system. World War I witnessed the introduction of substantial controls over industry, but the war ended before the controls began to "bite." The federal government exercised complete control over the economic system during World War II and to a lesser but still substantial extent during the Korean War. After both wars, the wartime controls were completely abandoned. There were no comparable regulations of business during the Vietnam War or the Gulf War.

The Second Managerial Revolution

The massive accumulation of regulatory powers has brought a virtual revolution in the way corporations are managed. We contrast it with the first managerial revolution, when the old entrepreneurial class of managers was replaced by corporate professional managers. This change took place over a long period of time, but gained public attention in the classic study of Berle and Means called *The Modern Corporation and Private Property*, published in 1932.[18] The second managerial revolution is characterized by a massive transfer of power from the managerial class to a new class of public servants in the federal, state, and local governments, armed with authority to make decisions formerly reserved for managers in privately owned businesses.

Traditional Industry versus Functional Regulation

The fourth wave of regulation introduced a "new model" of regulation that contrasts with the "old model." The old style of regulation was concerned with one industry, such as railroads, airlines, or pharmaceuticals. The principal purposes of the older-type regulations (of agencies such as the ICC, FTC, and FCC) (see Table 9-1 for agency titles) were to prevent monopoly; to increase competition; to establish uniform standards of safety, security, communications, and financial practice; and to prevent abuses of managerial power.

The main focus of the newer model is on functions that cut across all industries. The principal purposes of the newer agencies (e.g., CPSC, OSHA, EEOC, EPA) are to improve the quality of life by securing cleaner air and clearer water, protecting consumers from shoddy products, ensuring more information to consumers, preventing discrimination in the workplace, and so on.

Older agency policies and regulations generally applied to entire companies in an industry. The newer agencies limit rules to specific business functions to implement their policies. For example, automobile seat belt rules established by NHTSA are directed at design engineers, OSHA worker safety rules are focused on safety engineers, and the EEOC sets standards for hiring and firing workers that concern directors of human resources. Regulators of these agencies are concerned with their particular functional area and not the total company. Indeed, in pursuit of their narrow mandate, they may even insist on regulations that adversely affect other areas. This is in contrast to older agencies that, like the ICC, were more concerned about a whole company and industry.

---

[18]Adolf A. Berle Jr. and Gardner C. Means, *The Modern Corporation and Private Property*, New York: Macmillan, 1932.

TABLE 9-1   Major Federal Regulatory Agencies Classified
              by Dominant Orientation

Agency	Date Established
Predominantly Industry	
Food and Drug Administration (FDA)	1906
Federal Reserve Board (FRB)	1913
Federal Trade Commission (FTC)	1914
Federal Home Loan Bank Board (FHLBB)	1932
Federal Deposit Insurance Corporation (FDIC)	1933
Federal Communications Commission (FCC)	1934
Federal Aviation Administration (FAA)	1958
Federal Maritime Commission (FMC)	1961
Nuclear Regulatory Commission (NRC)	1975
Federal Energy Regulatory Commission (FERC)	1977
Predominantly Functional	
Securities and Exchange Commission (SEC)	1934
National Labor Relations Board (NLRB)	1935
Equal Employment Opportunity Commission (EEOC)	1964
Environmental Protection Agency (EPA)	1970
National Highway Traffic Safety Administration (NHTSA)	1970
Occupational Safety and Health Administration (OSHA)	1971
Consumer Product Safety Commission (CPSC)	1972
Mine Safety and Health Administration (MSHA)	1977

These are broad generalizations to make a point. In fact, many regulatory agencies are mixtures of both models. The SEC, for example, regulates the securities industry but also sets rules concerning content of financial statements prepared by corporations and how securities will be traded. The FTC, an older agency, is concerned with ensuring fair competition but also specifies rules for a company's advertising.

As late as the 1950s, aside from World War II, the federal government assumed major regulatory responsibility in only four areas: antitrust, financial institutions, transportation, and communications. Today, at least one federal agency regulates something in virtually every department of an individual business.[19]

Impact of Newer Regulations on Managerial Decisions

The patterns of newer regulations make government officials active managerial partners with business executives. Government has always been a partner with business, but has never been so directly active in management as it is

---

[19]Murray L. Weidenbaum, *Business and Government in the Global Marketplace,* 6th ed., Upper Saddle River, N.J.: Prentice Hall, 1999, p. 38–39.

today. It is involved from the highest corporate managers, through the specific ways in which products are made and distributed, to what takes place between producer and customer after products are sold. Many managers today in fact act as agents of the government without being under contract.

How Are Government Regulations Made?

The preceding discussion outlined the vast increase in federal regulations. Now we describe briefly how government regulations originate.

Rules, Rule Making, and Regulation

Rules are decisions made by agencies of government to implement laws enacted by Congress. The process by which they are made is called *rule making,* and the result is a specific *regulation.* This is the most important function of government regulatory agencies. These regulations are laws with the same power as congressional legislation, presidential executive orders, or decisions of the Supreme Court.

There are many different types of rules. For example, some rules command a business to do something or stop doing something, some rules ask only for information, some set prices, some set specific standards for business to meet, some license business to do something, some establish procedures for business to follow, some prescribe how standards set by government shall be met, and some subsidize business.

Many believe that federal regulations are made by bureaucrats in isolated offices. Politicians run campaigns against the "mindless" and autocratic bureaucracy blindly exceeding authority to burden industry with unnecessary regulations. That is far from reality. All rules are based on statutes passed by Congress with powers delegated to executive branch agencies.

In implementing statutes, agencies may have narrow or broad grants of authority. Here are a few broad grants of authority. The Federal Reserve Board has complete authority to set interest rates. The Federal Trade Commission has authority to determine what is and what is not unfair advertising. The EPA can set standards that limit polluting discharges in air, in water, and on land.

On the other hand, some legislation contains specific instructions to agencies. The Clean Air Act Amendments of 1990 charge the EPA with establishing standards for 189 of the most prevalent and hazardous air pollutants. The Pollution Prevention Act of 1990 requires that each manufacturing facility that uses one or more of 300 listed chemicals must prepare an annual report.

The trend in recent years has been for the Congress to be more specific in its legislative enactments. However, the great bulk of federal regulations today are established by staffs in executive agencies of government based on broad grants of authority in many statutes passed over the years.

The fundamental process of rule making is established by the Administrative Procedures Act (APA) passed in 1946. This act sets forth in detail how the process must operate. The APA identifies two different ways in which federal agencies formulate and then enforce their regulations. The first is *rule making.* In this approach, the agency writes a rule to be followed by companies. This is a *legislative* function and the result is a law. The second is *adjudication.* This is a judicial function that deals with specific disputes with companies; the agency follows quasi-judicial procedures to settle the dispute.

There are two types of adjudication procedures. One is formal, where the agency holds hearings before an administrative law judge, evidence is presented, witnesses called, and a decision reached. Formal records are kept and the decision may be appealed to a federal court. The second type is informal, where an agency will determine the rights or duties of parties in question in less formal proceedings. Most adjudicatory procedures are informal. Both processes result in an *order.*

Steps in Rule Making

The APA still stands as the fundamental guide to rule making. Since its passage, however, many laws have been enacted to add additional screens to rule making. For example, the Office of Management and Budget (OMB) was created by President Nixon in 1970 and given the power to coordinate executive branch budgets. Later the agency was given authority to approve or disapprove of specific agency-proposed regulations. For example, Executive Order 12606 directs federal agencies to determine whether proposed regulations will have a significant impact on family formation, the stability of the family, or marital commitment. Executive Order 12611 says that agencies must determine if regulatory actions will have a significant impact on the distribution of power and responsibilities among various levels of state and federal governments. Other executive orders direct agencies to be concerned about ensuring that if private property is taken and a loss incurred by the owner, the proposed regulation is justified by the public safety protected. Other orders concern potential impacts on the environment, public health, economic activity, and so on. The Congress also has required specific screens before regulations are implemented. For example, the Regulatory Flexibility Act of 1980 directs that agencies certify that a new rule will not have a significant adverse impact on small business. This act, together with the Unfunded Mandates Reform Act (1995) and Executive Order 12866, directs agencies to assess costs and benefits of regulatory alternatives and then to select regulations that will maximize benefits. Agencies must also examine a reasonable number of alternatives. These requirements are imposed for all expenditures over $100 million likely to be incurred by the regulations. Thus, agencies must go through a thicket of thorns before entering the process of implementation.

No single path is followed in all agencies for all regulations. The following sequence of activities is adapted from Cornelius M. Kerwin and James O'Reilly.[20]

1. *Origin of Authority.* The basic fundamental authority derives from Congress, as noted above.

2. *Origin of Individual Rules.* Although all rules can be traced to statutes, the origin of specific rules may arise in many sources. The head of the agency may have ideas from his or her policy agenda. Some agencies have organized systems for analyzing legislation to determine the details of rules needed to implement the statute. Some agencies have advisory committees composed of the legal counsel, technical experts, and others in the agency who can contribute to the rule-making process. Agency staff in the field who are administering rules also are sources of ideas for new regulations or modification of old ones. Agency staff often follow legislation as it weaves through Congress to determine what specific rules are needed to implement the final enactment. There are also many outside sources of ideas for rules. This includes other interested agencies, the OMB, the White House, and individuals in the private sector. Any citizen may petition an agency to make a rule.

3. *Drafting the Regulation.* The agency administering the statute must prepare the content of the new rule and show that it follows congressional authority. Extensive consultation within and outside an agency may be used in this process. This step may be done in a few days for a very simple rule, or it can take years if it is extremely complex and controversial. A few waste disposal rules of the EPA have taken a decade to prepare and issue.

4. *OMB Review.* The draft regulation may be reviewed by people within and outside the agency, but the most important review is that of the OMB. The OMB has broad oversight responsibilities and can return draft rules to agencies for revision.

5. *Public Response.* When the draft is completed, it must be published in the *Federal Register.* This is the official government means of communicating proposed and completed rules and regulations to the public. Public comments are invited. Agencies can and do, of course, prepare other documents for public information and to solicit comments. The agency may conduct hearings, meet with members of Congress interested in the rule, or discuss the regulation with other interested agencies.

---

[20]Cornelius M. Kerwin, *Rulemaking: How Government Agencies Write Law and Make Policy,* Washington, D.C.: CQ Press, 1994; and James O'Reilly, *Administrative Rulemaking,* Colorado Springs: Shepard's/McGraw-Hill, 1983, pp. 90, 131.

6. *Action on the Draft Regulation.* When the draft rule has been evaluated and revised, it is submitted to the OMB for final clearance and then again published in the *Federal Register.* If the agency decides to modify or drop the proposed rule, that decision will also be published.

7. *Post–Rule Making.* If the regulation works well and there is no difficulty with it, there is no need to tinker further with it. If there is great controversy, the agency may prepare for litigation. It may meet with business managers who are puzzled about precisely what to do, or are unhappy with the rule. The agency may issue explanations or technical corrections.

If an appeal is made to the courts by a company dissatisfied with a ruling, the Supreme Court has long recognized that if Congress is very clear and precise in its intent, that governs. If, however, a statute leaves a gap to be filled by a regulatory agency, the Court will not intervene unless the agency's rule is arbitrary, capricious, or manifestly contrary to the statute. This judgment was strongly expressed in a well-known case involving Chevron and is recognized today as *the Chevron doctrine.*

The Scope of Government Relations with Business

Following, briefly, are the many ways in which the federal government is involved with business.

Government prescribes rules of the game. Government sets broad rules of business behavior within which individuals are comparatively free to act in conformity with their self-interest. The regulations vary in the extent to which they restrain an individual business, but they serve to establish the "rules of the game."

Government is a major purchaser of the output of business. Out of a gross domestic product (GDP) of $8.9 trillion in 1999, the federal government is expected to spend $542 billion. State and local governments are expected to spend $1 billion.[21] Few companies do not benefit directly or indirectly from such procurement.

Government uses its contracting power to get business to do things the government wants. Businesses that want government contracts must subcontract to minority businesses, pay prevailing minimum wages, comply with safety and sanitary work regulations, refrain from discrimination in hiring, and meet pollution standards. It is a case of "no compliance, no contract."

Government promotes and subsidizes business. The government has a complex and powerful network of programs to aid business. Promotion ranges from tariff protections to loans, loan guarantees, maintenance of high levels of economic activity, and direct subsidies.

Government owns vast quantities of productive equipment and wealth. The government is an important producer of goods and services, such as ammunition, guns,

---

[21]*The UCLA Business Forecast for the Nation and California,* Los Angeles: The Anderson School at UCLA, June 1998.

ships, atomic energy, postal services, weather-reporting services, and dams. The federal government owns vast stockpiles of raw materials and most of the land in many western states.

Government is an architect of economic growth. It has assumed responsibility for achieving an acceptable rate of stable economic growth, as set forth in the Employment Act of 1946.

Government protects interests in society against business exploitation. For instance, many laws protect the interests of investors, customers, employees, and the competitors of a business.

Government directly manages large areas of private business. "Manages" here means that government dictates certain decisions through regulation and joint decision making.

Government is the repository of the social conscience and redistributes resources to meet social ends. Government increasingly redirects resources by transfer payments, research and development expenditures, tax incentives, and subsidies. In mind here, among other things, are Social Security, Medicare, and Medicaid. The government also exerts moral pressure on business to conform with generally accepted social goals.

Government is our national security protector. This includes, of course, maintenance of our national military forces.

Government is the arbiter of disputes. This function cuts across a number of those noted above. In mind, for example, are laws governing labor disputes in which the government can step in to either decide an issue or determine how it can be resolved. Many laws enacted by Congress grow out of disputes among interest groups. Current pending legislation dealing with health management organizations (HMOs) is directly related to disputes among patients, administrators, and insurers.

Attempts to Stem the Tide

For the past fifty years, major efforts have been made to restrain the growth of federal regulations, reverse the trend, and reform the system. The first was the Hoover Commission, chaired by former President Hoover and completed in 1949. Since then, each president has campaigned against excessive regulation (some established commissions like the Hoover Commission) and, like King Canute, tried in vain to stem the tidal wave. Each succeeded in creating some reforms, but the trend of expansion has proceeded.

Here are a few highlights of such efforts in recent years. In the Carter administration (1976–1980), there was important deregulation of many industries. The most widely known effort was the airline industry following passage of the Airline Deregulation Act of 1978. The Natural Gas Policy Act of 1978 provided partial decontrol of natural gas by 1987. Partial decontrol of railroads (Staggers Rail Act of 1980) and trucking (Motor Carrier Act of 1980) also occurred.

President Reagan (1980–1988), upon taking office, named Vice President Bush to head a new Task Force on Regulatory Relief, and issued Executive Order

No. 12291, which gave the OMB strong powers and set up in the OMB a new agency, the Office of Information and Regulatory Affairs (OIRA), with authority to review regulation. This executive order mandated that agencies make cost–benefit analyses of their proposed new rules and gave the OMB and OIRA power to ensure that benefits were greater than costs before issuances. Thus, cost–benefit screening became a new and important strategy in federal regulation.

There was a sharp decline in the imposition of new regulations in the early Reagan years. However, by the end of Reagan's second term, the trend of regulatory growth resumed.

The record of the Bush administration (1988–1992) was mixed. On the one hand, the administration tried to control the imposition of new regulations. For example, President Bush appointed Vice President Quayle to head a new Council on Competitiveness. This council had overall authority to review new proposed regulations and was successful in stopping many that were perceived by business to be "unfair" or too costly. On the other hand, two new regulations were passed that have had significant impacts on industry: the Clean Air Act Amendments of 1990 and the Americans with Disabilities Act of 1990. Both have required substantial new business spending for compliance.

President Clinton in September 1993 issued Executive Order No. 12866, "Regulatory Planning and Review." This order reinforced President Reagan's order for cost and benefit analysis, as noted above. It also established a new planning process that required agencies to prepare plans each year for the most important actions they anticipate. These are then reviewed by OIRA, circulated among affected agencies, and returned to the originating agency for revision or action.[22]

President Clinton also asked Vice President Gore to head a commission called the National Performance Review. The commission set out "to make government *work better* and *cost less*." The final report made hundreds of specific suggestions for cutting red tape and costs, and many of them were implemented.[23]

Although presidents have failed to stem the increase in regulations, their efforts have significantly reformed the regulatory process. On the other hand, comparatively little has been done to modify existing statutes that authorize regulations.

Costs and Benefits of Complying with Federal Regulations

The sheer volume of federal regulations of business is a growing burden and of increasing concern to managers. Each year thousands of new rules are written and their accumulation has significant impact on everyone,

---

[22]For details of this Executive Order, see Susan E. Dudley and Angela Antonelli, "Congress and the Clinton OMB," *Regulation,* Fall 1997.

[23]Vice President Al Gore, *Creating a Government that Works Better & Costs Less,* Report of the National Performance Review, Washington, D.C.: U.S. Government Printing Office, 1993.

especially business, that would be hard to exaggerate. Reliable data are not available to measure this impact, so we must rely on a few indicators and anecdotes to help understand complaints about regulatory burden and costs. It must be kept in mind that added to federal regulations are thousands of state and local laws with which business must comply. Since space does not permit discussion of them, the following relates only to the federal government.

Costs of Complying with Regulations

A number of measures are used to show the burden of regulations, but all are flawed. Some analysts count the number of pages in the *Federal Register*. The more pages there are, the greater the cost and burden of regulations are presumed to be. The total has been going up in recent years and reached 68,530 in 1997. This publication is a fine-print, three-columns-per-page, mind-numbing, detailed publication that is printed every working day and sets forth new proposed and final regulations of all federal agencies. We chose at random January 17, 1997, as an example of content.

On that day, the *Federal Register* was 341 pages and totaled about 429,660 words, equal to 781 pages of this textbook. Just one amendment to a final rule by the Environmental Protection Agency took up 106 pages. The technically worded title itself was 34 words—"National Emission Standards for Hazardous Air Pollutants for Source Categories: Organic Hazardous Air Pollutants from the Synthetic Organic Chemical Manufacturing Industry and Other Processes Subject to the Negotiated Regulation for Equipment Leaks: Rule Clarifications," In the same issue, the Department of Agriculture issued "Amendments to the Peanut Poundage Quota Requirements," and the Federal Aviation Administration issued an "Airworthiness Directive for Fairchild SA26 Series Planes Regarding the Pitch Bearing Attaching Nuts on Elevator Control Rod End Bearing Assemblies at the Walking Beam."

The number of employees of regulatory agencies is another measure often used. Figure 9-2 presents data for this standard. Two points stand out. First, the upward trend continues. Second, staff of agencies concerned with social programs have increased substantially relative to those engaged in economic regulations.

Calculations of the total cost burden of regulations on the private sector have been made by analysts. Their estimates range from $600 to $700 billion. While the figures are imprecise, given the nature of the subject, the totals are sobering, around 8 percent of GDP.

The present volume of regulations is so large that no corporation can faithfully comply with all the laws and rules to which it is subject. This generalization is supported by the results of a 1996 General Accounting Office study. The agency sought to learn the costs of regulations on individual companies, but not one of the 15 companies it studied could provide

FIGURE 9-2

Summary of staffing of federal regulatory activity (fiscal years, full-time-equivalent employment).

Note: Social regulations include those for consumer safety and health, job safety and other working conditions, environment and energy. The economic regulations include those for finance and banking, industry-specific regulation, and general business. Source: Melinda Warren and William F. Lauber, *Regulatory Changes and Trends: An Analysis of the 1999 Federal Budget,* Center for the Study of American Business, Washington University, Regulatory Budget Report 21, November 1998, p. 5.

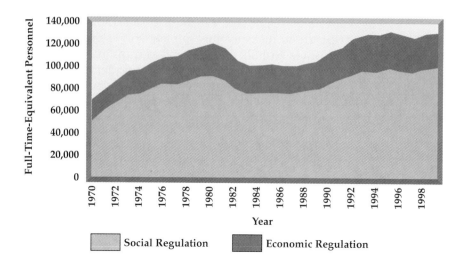

comprehensive cost data or identify all the regulations with which they were supposed to comply.[24] Here are a few responses.

An official of a tank car company said that the Department of Transportation's requirement that all its employees receive hazardous materials training was unnecessary since only 1 percent actually handled such materials. A hospital said it was very difficult to keep pace with frequently changing Medicare and Medicaid billing rules. A paper company said compliance with a ruling by the Occupational Safety and Health Administration to install guards for machines would require costs out of proportion to any benefits. A fish farm manager said that the company was thinking of creating a pension system but has not because the Employee Retirement Income Security Act required so much detailed reporting that the cost of the retirement system would be made prohibitive.

These are direct costs. There are also indirect costs that the participants in the GAO study said were substantial. Among them were "lost productivity, decreased competitiveness, lost business opportunities, delays in the expansion of new products or businesses, misallocation of resources, and delays in construction of new plants and/or equipment."[25] There are many other complaints of business, such as the costs of time diverted from other company business, restraints on more efficient alternative methods to achieve desired goals, and inability to keep track of all regulations applicable to the business.

Benefits of Government Regulations

In assessing the burden of regulations on business, it is necessary to measure benefits. Such measurement is far more difficult than calculating costs.

---

[24]General Accounting Office, *Regulatory Burden: Measurement Challenges and Concerns Raised by Selected Companies,* Washington, D.C.: General Accounting Office, November 1996.

[25]Ibid., p. 52.

At an aggregate level, business could not operate and society could not prosper without certain types of regulation. Regulation has helped improve the position of minorities, clean the air, clean our waters, prevent monopoly, strengthen free competition, reduce industrial accidents, provide resources for the elderly, ensure health services not otherwise available, control communicable diseases, and so on.

The GAO said that most of the companies surveyed recognized that regulations provide benefits to society as a whole, to their industries, and even to them. For example, a paper company said federal regulations helped to improve its manufacturing process. A hospital said that OSHA's blood-borne pathogens standards helped reduce needlestick injuries. Others commented that regulations benefitted them by ensuring a level playing field of uniform requirements for all businesses.[26]

Generous subsidies also benefit specific companies and industries. The American Enterprise Institute has identified more than 125 subsidy programs for private business.[27] For example, the federal government subsidizes loans to small business (e.g., restaurants, builders), provides subsidies to companies to make international sales and purchases, provides insurance to multinational companies for foreign investment risks, provides loans and subsidies for agricultural sales, subsidizes road construction for timber removal by private companies, subsidizes minority businesses, aids the United States shipping industry, and so on. Peanut farmers receive tariff protection that elevates their profits. This is also true of sugar producers.

These are substantial benefits. Unfortunately, the costs and benefits on one individual or company may not coincide. But for the nation as a whole, there is a much more even balance than when costs alone are considered.

Growing Demands for New Regulations

Potential sources of new regulations are numerous. For example, the accelerated pace of new technologies, deteriorating parts of the environment, public health, education, global competition, and pressures to deal with acute social and economic problems inevitably will result in demands for more regulation.

In each of these areas, there are specific demands. Take, for example, the environment. Trends toward global warming, disposal of nuclear and other toxic wastes, and introduction of new genetically engineered microbes, plants, and animal strains undoubtedly will bring demands for new regulations.

Business interests will exert great pressure for federal help in reducing costs of regulation. But individual businesses will also pressure the federal government to throw hand grenades at their competitors, both domestic and foreign. For example, for years butter producers lobbied the Congress to tax oleomargarine, a

---

[26]Ibid., p. 54.
[27]"Business Welfare," *The American Enterprise*, July–August 1995.

competitive product to butter. Congress did eventually pass a law taxing margarine in response to these pressures, but it was subsequently repealed due to other pressure groups. Businesses have petitioned the federal government to set uniform standards in some areas to avoid having to deal with fifty individual state regulatory laws and bodies. For example, pesticide manufacturers and trade groups have asked Congress to amend the Federal Insecticide, Fungicide and Rodenticide Act to preempt states from getting involved in pesticide residues in food. Manufacturers want uniform product liability laws. Automobile companies have asked the Federal Trade Commission to overturn procedures required in forty-four states under so-called lemon laws.

The Mixed Economy

Regulation has evolved to the point that virtually no aspect of economic activity is closed to government action. Despite this comparative open door to intervention, the remarkable fact about the American economy is not how much of economic life the government controls but how much it does not. Although the federal government directly controls or indirectly influences economic activity to a significant degree, the economy is in no way centrally administered or controlled. People are rather free to pursue their economic interests as they see fit. Ours is a mixed economy in which individuals enjoy much economic freedom and the free market mechanism is still a powerful allocator of resources, but governments, especially the federal government, exercise pervasive and strong controls.

A Note on Regulation in Other Countries

Among other major countries of the world, there are different patterns of specific types of control than in the United States, but, overall, the United States is economically the freest in the world. Here are a few examples of foreign regulations.

In European countries, businesses are much more constrained than in the United States, especially with respect to relationships with labor. For example, in Germany, regulations inhibit labor mobility and raise unit labor costs to the point where wage rates are among the highest in the world. This has led companies like BMW and Mercedes to locate plants in the United States, where wage rates are lower. It is difficult to discharge unneeded workers in France and Italy. German air pollution controls cover fewer substances and processes than in the United States, but the standards of those controlled are comparable to ours.

Japan is a nation with massive regulations but implementation differs from that in the United States. Government agencies, for example, have substantial direct influence over business operations, but there is also close collaboration between business and government agencies. Regulations are focused more on helping business than consumers. Laws concerning insider trading are weak. Companies are not required to report as much information about their financial condition as in the United States. The United States has exerted strong pressure on Japan to reduce its extensive import controls with only limited success.

There is a proposal at this writing before the European Commission to adopt a cost–benefit requirement for all new regulations. China has highly centralized economic controls, but there are a number of free enterprise zones permitted by the government. Mexico has stringent antipollution laws, but in practice there is little enforcement.

A broad overview of regulations in major foreign countries shows trends to privatize government operations and to loosen some government controls. The trends, however, differ greatly among these countries. We will refer to some of them later in the book.

Concluding Observations

In this chapter, we describe how federal regulation of business has expanded over time. There have been ups and downs in the trend of regulations, but the basic direction has been up, with respect to both total volume and complexity. Successive efforts of presidents during the past fifty years have not succeeded in slowing the expansion despite the fact that some of them ran their campaigns on the promise that, if elected, they would reduce the size of government. J. M. Clark, one of the great economists of the twentieth century, astutely observed in 1932:

> The frontiers of control . . . are expanding . . . they are expanding in the range of things covered and the minuteness of regulation . . . Whether one believes government control to be desirable or undesirable, it appears fairly obvious that the increasing interdependence of all parts of the economic system . . . will force more control in the future than has been attempted in normal times in the past.[28]

As we have seen, the cost of federal regulations is huge, but the cost is offset in significant degree by the many benefits of regulation to society as a whole, individuals, companies, and industries. Analysis of both costs and benefits suggests that costs can be reduced and benefits increased by reforms in the regulatory system. That is the subject of the next chapter.

---

[28]J. M. Clark, "Government Regulation of Industry," *Encyclopedia of the Social Sciences,* New York: The Macmillan Company, 1932, vol. 3, p. 129.

AIRLINE DEREGULATION

In 1978, after forty years of federal regulation, the Airline Deregulation Act (ADA) was passed and a major industry was relieved of most, but not all, federal regulations. A massive and dramatic transformation of the airline industry began immediately and continues to this day. Changes in the industry since deregulation have benefitted consumers but have also raised issues that need attention. This case summarizes these issues and discusses some recommendations for dealing with them.

The Overall Result of Deregulation Is Positive

The Department of Transportation (DOT) points out that since 1978, average airfares have dropped 35 percent and continue to decline. Passenger air traffic has grown from 260 million in 1978 to 600 million in 1997. The percentage of Americans flying has risen from 64 in 1978 to 80 in 1997. Consumers have welcomed lower fares and more choice but have complained about service and fare differentials.

Overall, the system exhibits superior competitive service. In a number of markets, however, the DOT says that major airlines use their power to extract unfairly high ticket prices. When this occurs, the DOT says it will take action to redress the situation.

Authority of the Department of Transportation

Prior to the ADA, the Civil Aeronautics Board (CAB) regulated airline fares and service. This it did in massive detail. Its rules covered allowable rates of return, price of fares, routes traveled, schedules, mergers, and safety. The ADA phased out the CAB, which finally closed its doors in 1981. However, the Federal Aviation Administration, located today in the DOT, continued to have responsibility for regulating safety standards covering all aspects of civil aviation. DOT, together with the Department of Justice, was given broad responsibility to prohibit unfair methods of competition.

The Hub-and-Spoke System

One important factor in the success of the airline industry after deregulation has been the hub-and-spoke system. It also has been the source of major airline competitive power in some hub areas. The system was created as a strategy of major airlines to deal with the vigorous competition that followed deregulation. Here is how it works.

At major airports, larger airlines began acquiring gates in close proximity. These airports were called hubs. There are two distinct types of traffic that use hubs. One is local traffic, or passengers that are destined to or from the hub city. The other is connecting traffic, or passengers that are entering the hub city as a means of traveling to a different city on the same airline. Before deregulation, the CAB assigned routes to carriers. This forced them to fly turnabout service between city A and city B. Usually there were no intermediate stops.

When the requirement for direct nonstop flights between two points is eliminated, a hub can increase geometrically the number of cities and towns connected (see Exhibit 1). The hub aggregates commuter traffic from smaller

EXHIBIT 1

Route multiplication through a hub. Top: Point-to-point service without hub; Bottom: Service via hub connections.

Source: Melvin A. Brenner, James O. Leet, and Elihu Schott, *Airline Deregulation*, Westport, CN: Eno Foundation for Transportation, Inc., 1985, p. 83.

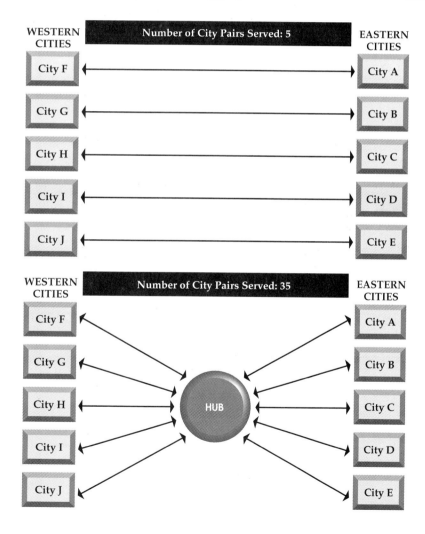

communities and feeds it back into the route system, making it worthwhile to maintain service to small communities. Flights can be more frequent, and the traveler need not change airlines (indeed, passengers are locked into an efficient system of coordinated baggage transfer, flight times, and gates in close proximity).

The DOT calculates that there are 60 cities that may be classified as major hubs. This system permits large airlines to dominate competition at their hubs. They control the number of gates through long-term leases with the airports. New entries are thus effectively blocked. Even established carriers have difficulty penetrating markets when rivals have established hubs. Thus, the hub-and-spoke system has effectively consolidated the hold of major airlines on the industry, a hold not likely to weaken without airport expansion and new rules for airport gate allocation to promote competition.

Competitive Concerns of the DOT

Statistics about fares raise concerns about the state of competition in some areas. Where low-cost, low-fare airlines are absent, major airlines tend to charge premium fares. Where low-cost, low-fare airlines exist, the rates are lower.

Exhibit 2 shows that in routes under 750 miles where low-cost and low-fare airlines exist, real average fares dropped by 41 percent between 1979 and 1997. Where the low-fare airlines have not operated, air fares have risen 23 percent. In contrast, in long-haul routes where there is competition from both low-fare airlines and major airlines, average fares have dropped.

EXHIBIT 2

U.S. domestic airline industry: change in real average fares, 1979 versus 1997.

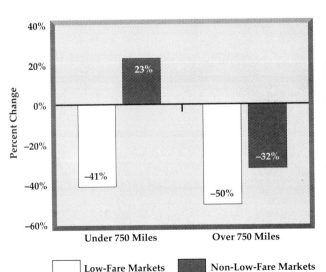

Since deregulation, inflation adjusted average fares are up 23% in short-distance markets without low-fare competition. These markets account for almost one-fourth of total domestic passengers.

Where there has been low-fare competition in short-haul markets, passengers quadrupled between 1979 and 1997, or grew by 59 million. In other short-haul markets, the number of passengers grew by only 68 percent, or 28 million.[1]

The number of passengers in markets with low-fare competition expanded rapidly up to 1996. Thereafter there was a recorded decline. If continued, this decline also indicates a potential for weakened competition.

The DOT study shows that almost 500 city pairs were served by only network airlines in the first quarter of 1997. The lack of competition, says the DOT, leaves a large part of consumer demand untapped. If these markets were opened to low-cost, low-fair airline competition, the resulting consumer benefits would be similar to those shown above.

When there is low-fare competition in both short- and long-haul markets, fares are much lower. Often fares are less than one-half those in similar markets without such competition.

Where hub airports are dominated by a major carrier, fares can be 50 to 60 percent higher than those in comparable competitive markets. Furthermore, fare premiums are higher than ten years ago and are growing. This is shown in Exhibit 3.

Table 1 on the following page also shows the beneficial impact on fares when low-fare competition exists. In every major hub city shown in Table 1, fares for the approximately same distance traveled are much higher in the absence of low-fare competition.

EXHIBIT 3

Fare premiums at dominated hubs.

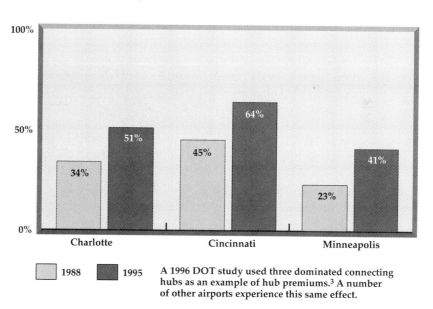

A 1996 DOT study used three dominated connecting hubs as an example of hub premiums.[3] A number of other airports experience this same effect.

___

[1]Except where otherwise noted, these data and others in the following analysis are from "Competition in the U.S. Domestic Airline Industry: The Need for a Policy to Prevent Unfair Practices," Washington, D.C., Department of Transportation, undated; and Federico Pena, "Statement of the Secretary of Transportation: The Low Cost Airline Service Revolution," Department of Transportation, undated.

TABLE 1   **Examples of Low-Fare Carrier Price Discipline, Fourth Quarter 1997**

City Pair	Nonstop Distance	Daily Passengers	Average One-Way Fare	Participants with Greater than Five Percent Market Share
Atlanta–Greensboro	306	325	$224	Delta 91%
Atlanta–Mobile	302	290	110	Delta 81%, Airtran 18%
Chicago–Cincinnati	264	618	259	American 5%, Delta 59%, United 34%
Chicago–Louisville	271	904	72	Air Wisconsin 12%, Southwest 70%, United 12%
Denver–Des Moines	590	106	255	United 92%
Denver–Kansas City	532	979	104	United 60%, Vanguard 29%
Detroit–Philadelphia	453	705	226	Northwest 58%, US Airways 38%
Detroit–St. Louis	440	982	81	Northwest 41%, Southwest 33%, TWA 24%
Houston–Memphis	485	173	206	Northwest 43%, Continental Express 38%
Houston–Lubbock	472	400	86	Continental 33%, Southwest 62%

Decline in New Low-Cost Carriers

There is no competition at hub sites if only one airline provides service. Where low-cost, low-fare airlines are absent or dominated by major airlines, competition is weak. A worrisome trend to the DOT is the decline and then demise of new low-cost airlines commencing service.

Southwest was the only low-cost airline of note at the beginning of 1992, but in that year six new airlines began business, then there were four in 1993, six in 1994, three in 1995, four in 1996, and none in 1997 and 1998. Most of the new entrants as well as some older airlines have disappeared.

The Air Transport Association reports that in 1997, there were thirteen airlines with revenues over $1 billion. There were thirty-four national lines with revenues from $100 million to $1 billion, and fifty-two regional lines with revenues under $100 million.[2] With so many airlines, the system appears to be competitive. There is, however, concentration in the industry. The five largest carriers accounted for about 64 percent of the industry's $110 billion revenues in 1997.

Prospective New Entrants Face Daunting Barriers

New entrants face difficult obstacles. Many observers believe that the major source of these is the chilling effect of large airline exclusionary practices. But

---

[2]Air Transport Association, *Annual Report*, New York: Air Transport Association, 1998.

there are other deterrents, including (1) computer reservation systems, (2) code sharing, (3) frequent flier programs, (4) price competition, and (5) alliances.

Unfair Exclusionary Conduct

Exclusionary conduct, says the DOT, is major airline behavior toward low-cost carriers that goes beyond normal vigorous competitive responses. A proposed policy by the DOT to deal with this situation was placed in the *Federal Register* on April 6, 1998. The DOT said it will "begin an investigation if there exists evidence that a major airline has taken extreme measures to eliminate low-fare competition at its hub. If the major airline adds seat capacity on a route and floods the market with low fares to such an extent that its own revenues actually decline—a business strategy that makes sense only if it results in the elimination of the new competitor so that fares at or above pre-competition levels can be reinstated—DOT will act."[3]

The DOT presented several examples of precisely what practices will be considered unfair. For example, suppose a dominant airline cuts fares and increases available seats to the point where the local low-cost airline finds its revenues so drastically reduced that it goes out of business. Revenues of the dominant carrier decline despite the increase in traffic. Then the dominant airline raises rates well above those prevailing before its predatory action. That is an unfair exclusionary practice, says the DOT, and it will act to remedy it.

The response of Northwest Airlines to Pro Air Inc. in early 1998 is a case in point. Pro Air Inc., one of the newest commuter lines at the time, offered fares as much as 85 percent less than Northwest Airlines on comparable routes from Detroit's City Airport. Northwest, which dominated traffic out of Detroit, responded promptly. The airline cut prices and added seats to Pro Air destinations such as Milwaukee. Pro Air offered a $69 one-way trip to Milwaukee that was promptly abandoned. Shortly thereafter, Northwest offered the same trip for $200.[4]

Computerized Reservation Systems (CRSs)

Practically all airline bookings are made through one of four airline-owned computer reservation systems. These systems cost millions of dollars to develop and provide information to airline reservation agents about available flights, rates, fare restrictions, and schedules.

These systems have significant advantages for the airlines that own them. First, they earn money for the airlines since fees are charged for their use. Second, airlines can use information about bookings to make constant adjustments

---

[3]"Competition in the U.S. Domestic Airline Industry: The Need for a Policy to Prevent Unfair Practices," U.S. Department of Transportation, undated. The detailed policy is in the *Federal Register* (Friday, April 10, 1998), entitled "Enforcement Policy Regarding Unfair Exclusionary Conduct in the Air Transportation Industry," pp. 17919–22.

[4]Adam Zoglin, "Hunting the Predators," *Time,* April 20, 1998.

in fares to optimize use of available seat capacity. Third, the major airlines can tie into their system feeder lines with which they are affiliated. Fourth, airlines can easily determine the total bookings of reservation agents and use that information to offer cash incentives. Finally, the flight schedules of the airlines owning the CRS will be listed first on the computer. This advantage yields what is sometimes called the "halo effect," or a preference by the travel agent for the airline schedule listed first.

Smaller airlines, of course, have neither the CRSs nor the volume of business needed to take advantage of the full capabilities of a CRS. It is one important way that the major airlines seized an advantage over frail competitors.

Critics say the CRSs give the owners unfair advantages. Not only do they earn money, but they use the systems to improve their scheduling and encourage travel agents to make decisions in their favor. In their defense, it can be said, the systems provide a significant technology to improve efficiency in airline operations, and that may be of benefit to consumers.

Code Sharing

Code sharing refers to arrangements between a major airline and feeder lines in which the computer reservation system uses the same code for both the major and the feeder when they jointly serve a particular route. Until 1992 most code-sharing arrangements were made by major airlines with commuter lines in the United States. After 1992, these arrangements expanded greatly between U.S. and foreign airlines, a point discussed later.

Critics say code sharing is used to mask anticompetitive arrangements between actual or potential competitors. For example, a major and a low-fare airline may so cooperate through the code system that a potential rival is unable to compete with them. Proponents argue that code sharing is procompetitive because it lowers costs and improves efficient scheduling.

Frequent-Flier Programs

American Airlines introduced the first frequent-flier program in 1981 as a marketing strategy to secure brand loyalty. These programs were never intended to last, but they have become such a powerful loyalty-building tool that airlines cannot now get rid of them.

Very simply, these programs credit passengers with mileage traveled on the sponsoring airline. Additional credit or bonus points may be earned by flying first-class, leasing cars from specified rental agencies, staying at hotels affiliated with the airline, or flying on new routes promoted by the airline. When enough mileage has been flown and credits have been accumulated, the airlines give free trips to those earning them. So popular are these programs that some fliers take roundabout routes to a destination to gain free mileage credits. Any airline without such a program risks losing passengers to those that have one. Small airlines or new-entry carriers are at a disadvantage with a major airline with extensive routes.

The use of frequent-flier programs raises ethical issues. Should employees whose companies have paid for their tickets use the mileage credits for their personal use? Companies have tried to prevent such usage, but airlines steadfastly refuse to report the names of free-trip winners to employers, citing an unacceptable paperwork burden. Some employers complain that in order to gain credits, employees will take inconvenient flights that cost their company both money and employee time. One observer of the plans noted that "in essence, there is a kickback built into the price of every $150-a-night hotel room and every full-fare airplane ticket. What we are witnessing is a massive, open, and wildly successful campaign to corrupt the morals of the corporate class."[5] A comparable ethical question is raised with legislative representatives. For example, the House Committee on Administration of the U.S. Congress "encourages" members to use travel awards earned on official trips for subsequent official business, "whenever practicable," which of course is a loophole for members to use the rewards for personal travel if they choose.

So popular have frequent-flier programs become that airlines are now loaded with credits for free travel. In recent years they have sought to put some restraints on credit redemption, such as confining passengers using free tickets to a small percentage of seats. But the plans are such a potent marketing tool that they are certain to continue in use.

These programs give an airline important competitive advantages quite unrelated to any efficiency or service characteristics of the airline using them. For example, an airline serving important vacation cities has an advantage over one that does not fly to such places or has no frequent-flier program. A research study by the Brookings Institution concluded that market shares would change considerably if these programs were eliminated by all airlines. In this case, for example, American Airlines would lose 17.8 percent of its domestic market. If American gave up its program and other airlines continued theirs, it would lose over 50 percent of its domestic market.[6]

Cost-cutting and Fare Discounting

The airline industry has several major types of competitive strategies. One already discussed is the exclusionary behavior at hubs. A second is that of small low-cost airlines. A third is fare discounting.

Low-Cost Airlines.   New commuter airlines have a cost advantage over the major airlines. Their capital cost is far lower. They can, for example, begin with small second-hand or leased airplanes. They usually can employ people at somewhat lower rates than the majors. The workforce, as at Southwest

---

[5]Michael Kinsely, "Greed Gets Most Mileage out of Airline Credits," *The Wall Street Journal,* October 10, 1985.

[6]Steven A. Morrison and Clifford Winston, *The Evolution of the Airline Industry,* Washington, D.C.: Brookings Institution, 1995, pp. 58–60.

Airlines, does what is required irrespective of job classification. For instance, on occasion pilots will help with the luggage.

Their lower costs permit them, of course, to make a profit with lower fares. However, when they attract competition from the majors, their low fares may not save them. Southwest Airlines was the most notable small airline in 1992 and it has been profitable since then. But, in the meantime, more than 100 smaller, new airlines disappeared. Small lines that survive fill uncompetitive niches, serve thin markets, and cut costs. Large airlines blame failure of small ones not on the major's actions but on poor management, unrealistic planning, lack of financial backing, public doubts about reliability, or bad pricing policy.

Fare Discounting.   Freed to compete, airlines have engaged in a series of price wars to gain competitive advantage and to fill empty seats. For years, the pricing system has been extremely erratic and complex. Thousands of fares change on a daily basis. A major reason for this situation is the structure of the industry. The fixed costs of airlines—for planes, facilities, and fuel—are a relatively high part of total costs. Employee costs, which can vary, are about 35 percent of the total. The marginal cost of adding a passenger to a partly filled flight is very small. It involves paying only for a can of soda, pretzels, or peanuts and minimal costs for ticketing. As a consequence, airlines are constantly seeking ways to fill flights and one way, of course, is to attract customers with low prices. An airline can justify selling an unfilled seat for a very low price. With the magic of computers, they are in a position to calculate where and under what circumstances a particular flight on a particular route will justify fare discounting. Such discounting raises an interesting ethical question. On most flights, the fares vary significantly among passengers. Sitting side by side, one may pay as much as five times that of the neighbor. Is that ethical?

Alliances

Airlines have extended their competitive prowess by alliances. One method is through code sharing, noted above. Code sharing often involves cooperation in ticketing, baggage transfer, facilities, frequent flier programs, schedule coordination, marketing, and equity investments.

Recently, many alliances have been formed with foreign carriers. The advantages are substantial. For example, Northwest Airlines has alliances with KLM that increase its access to more than thirty cities in Europe and the Middle East. These cities are served by connecting flights with KLM. Northwest flies its own planes only to four cities but it can advertise that it serves thirty-four cities. The same arrangements exist between other U.S. and foreign airlines. Prior to an alliance with U.S. Air, British Airways flights between London and the United States reached fifteen cities. After the alliance, many more cities were covered.[7]

---

[7]Kenneth M. Mead, "International Aviation: Airline Alliances Produce Benefits, But Effect on Competition Is Uncertain," Washington, D.C.: General Accounting Office, April 1995.

The results of alliances on competition in the industry are a mixture of good and bad. They have had a positive impact on revenues of the allied airlines. Consumers have benefitted through schedule coordination, shorter layovers between connections, and lower fares. On the other hand, alliances have concentrated power in major airlines and have sometimes led to less competition and higher fares.

Service

Customer service has been one of the casualties of deregulation. One flier observes that "the mix of large planes, small seats, and computer technology has yielded the air-travel equivalent of wearing shoes three sizes too small."[8]

Consumers have many complaints including cramped space, poor or no food, snacks instead of a hot meal or sandwiches, crowded airports, lost luggage, less frequent flights, and discount fare requirements. Businesspeople who cannot schedule flights far in advance are at a particular disadvantage because their fares are generally far above discount rates. Business complains bitterly about this, but the practice still exists. Everyone who flies has experienced some of these irritating problems.

Cost-Cutting and Employee Welfare

Prior to deregulation, employees of the major airlines enjoyed compensation in wages and benefits well above the national average for all industries. Following deregulation, as intense competition swept the industry, the position of employees deteriorated.

New entries into the airline market, many of them nonunion, paid lower wages and in other ways cut costs and offered reduced rates to travelers. Since wages and salaries are about the only sizeable costs that can be cut when an airline is in financial difficulty, the pressure to do so is intense. A classic illustration of the battle to cut wages is that of Eastern Airlines under former astronaut Frank Borman. He tried desperately to reduce labor costs and succeeded until he asked too many times and for too deep a cut. He finally tangled with the Machinists Union and the embroglio led eventually to the firing of Borman and the demise of Eastern Airlines. It was bought on the cheap by Frank Lorenzo, who had made a reputation as a wage cutter, but he too failed and Eastern disappeared.[9]

American Airlines was the first carrier to introduce a two-tier wage structure. This plan paid newly hired workers lower wages for doing the same job

---

[8]Bill Saporito, "Going Nowhere Fast," *Fortune*, April 3, 1995, p. 59.

[9]For an excellent account of this and other stories about the development of the airline industry, see Thomas Petzinger Jr., *Hard Landing*, New York: Random House, Times Business, 1995.

as workers who had been employed before wage cutting occurred. It was applied to pilots as well as flight attendants. This system raises questions about equity. The issue has been raised in labor negotiations, and in some airlines the two-tier systems have been abandoned. The practice still exists, however, among some airlines.

The Financial Situation in the Industry

The airline industry has a history of earnings volatility, and over the years its return on investment has been below the average for all industries. There were modest profits reported in the years following deregulation until disaster struck in the 1990s. In the five years from 1990 through 1994, there were substantial losses totaling $13 billion. The picture brightened thereafter and profits totaled $5.2 billion in 1997.

Huge losses in the 1990s were due largely to severe fare wars stimulated by what one airline executive called the "virus" of suicidal price cutting. This was initiated by companies in or about to go into bankruptcy that were desperate for cash.

The impact of the heavy losses of the 1990s was devastating. A number of famous airlines disappeared in bankruptcy—Pan American Airways, Braniff, and Eastern Airlines. Many others went through bankruptcy and survived. Thousands of employees lost their jobs, not only in the airlines but among airplane builders and their suppliers as well. While customers enjoyed lower fares, services suffered.

Safety in the Skies

Air travel today is far safer than before deregulation. Industry analysts feared that following deregulation, the heightened competitive conditions could affect airline safety. Some speculated that unregulated competition would lead to lower profits and skipped maintenance. Some thought that the expected growth in commuter carriers might increase accidents. None of these fears were realized. The National Transportation Safety Board reports that air travel safety for both commuter and larger airlines combined has improved. As two Brookings Institution analysts concluded: "Safety . . . should be the least controversial concern about air transportation. Regardless of how it is measured, only one conclusion can be reached: the chance of dying in an airplane crash continues to diminish."[10]

Despite the statistics, the public is still concerned about safety. It reads almost daily about the need for upgrading the air traffic control system, and periodically it is traumatized by a major accident.

---

[10]Morrison and Winston, *The Evolution of the Airline Industry*, pp. 32–33.

Do We Need to Reregulate the Airline Industry?

Alfred E. Kahn, the primary architect of airline deregulation when he headed the CAB, is emphatic that it would be a grave mistake to reregulate by returning the industry to the system that existed prior to 1978. He is joined by most other authorities on the subject. For example, John E. Robson, former chairman of the CAB, writes that there are many ways to address problems in the industry other than reregulation and still preserve the system that today is the envy of all the world.[11]

There are others who disagree. Richard D. Cudahy, circuit judge, U.S. Court of Appeals for the Seventh Circuit, wrote: "Competition in this industry has been destructive because on balance wealth has been destroyed and both tangible and intangible values have been undermined. Competition itself has been awakened, and for that reason a return to some form of regulation is likely."[12] Several dozen bills have been introduced in Congress to remedy one or more airline industry problems. They range from subsidizing new aircraft for small airlines, to allocating slots at airports, to reregulating the entire industry. Robson comments that it would be wrong to take even a small step in the direction of regulation. We have a troubling history, he says, of planting small regulatory seeds that grow into weeds and choke industries.[13]

If not reregulation, what should be done to fix some of the serious problems in the industry? Neil Goldschmidt, former secretary of DOT, says problems of the system can be addressed in one of two ways—investment or reregulation. The latter would be a grave mistake he says.

> Invest and we can obliterate the frustrations of slots, an outdated air traffic control system and legitimate concerns about public safety. These improvements, combined with the marketplace demanding better commuter jet equipment and beginning to force competition in hubs . . . will keep in place the benefits we have while extending them to places we would like to see them go. Regulate, and we backtrack on an American economic success and divert the one agency with the charge and visibility to get the problem solved.[14]

Questions

1. The ADA was passed in 1978 to ensure fair and efficient competition in the airline industry. Has this objective been achieved?

---

[11]John E. Robson, "Airline Deregulation: Twenty Years of Success and Counting," *Regulation,* Spring 1998.

[12]Richard D. Cudahy, "The Coming Demise of Deregulation," *Yale Journal on Regulation,* Winter 1993.

[13]Robson, "Airline Deregulation," p. 17.

[14]Neil Goldschmidt, "Don't Resume Airline Regulation, Expand the System," *Aviation Week and Space Technology,* October 5, 1998.

2. Has deregulation been a net gain or net loss to the major stakeholders of the airlines?

3. Should the federal government reregulate the airline industry to improve competition? If so, why? If not, why not? Precisely, what actions should the government take?

4. Do frequent-flier plans encourage a subtle larceny among business travelers?

5. Are two-tier wage plans fundamentally unjust in unequally compensating individuals with identical jobs?

6. Are common notions of equality violated when seats in the same flight are sold by the airlines for different fares?

7. Is it ethical to lower fares on one route to drive out a smaller competitor who cannot cross-subsidize the route by charging higher prices elsewhere?

Reforming the Regulatory Process

Monsanto Company
www.monsanto.com

Monsanto began in St. Louis in 1901 as the Monsanto Chemical Works. Its first product was saccharin. In the years since, the company became one of the dominant chemical firms in the world. In 1997 the company spun off its chemical business and moved aggressively into agricultural biotechnology. In 1997 total revenues of the firm were $7.5 billion, net income was $294 million, and it had 21,900 employees.

The first genetically modified food crops moved into the European market in 1996, and Monsanto was among the first with its genetically engineered Roundup Ready soybean. The result was an immediate firestorm of rejections by the public, farmers, food processors, retailers,

politicians, and even some scientists. However, in 1996 European Union authorities approved the product. Directive 90/220 said it did not pose a risk to the environment or human health.

Roundup Ready soybeans allow growers to use Monsanto's powerful Roundup herbicide, and other herbicides, without disturbing the plant. This was accomplished by inserting genes into the plant that make it resistant to herbicides. Weed control is therefore possible without affecting crop performance. Roundup Ready soybeans are but one of many genetically engineered products of Monsanto.

The use of such plants will significantly increase agricultural output. Proponents stress that this new biotechnology will help feed the growing world population.

European Resistance

Europeans are much less tolerant of new agricultural products than people in the United States. A number of reasons for this have been suggested. To begin with, there is far more skepticism of regulatory bodies than in the United States. This is partly a result of regulatory failures in the so-called mad cow fiasco in which regulators permitted livestock feeds that caused a brain damaging disease in cattle that, it was believed, moved from cattle to humans. Many farmers take the position that "what was good enough for my forebearers is good enough for me." Some ask: "Does it make sense to interfere with nature to produce a firmer tomato or sweeter corn?" Consumers believe that these new products amount to tampering with food and they do not like the idea.

As a result, Norway no longer allows imports of American soybeans because a sizeable percentage are genetically engineered. Austria and Luxembourg prohibit all genetically modified food. The government of France established a commission to study the subject. The result was an ambiguous report that the government said it would consider in its policies. In Great Britain, there have been violent demonstrations at sites where genetically modified products are being tested.[1]

Powerful critics fan the flames of concern. The Prince of Wales, for example, alleges the new herbicide-resistant plants will kill other plants and strip fields of all plant life. He is reported to have said that crop biotechnology "takes mankind into realms that belong to God, and to God alone."[2] Greenpeace has held demonstrations in many European cities. Such views reflect criticisms voiced in the United States years earlier. Critics raise many questions. Will fields become barren of weeds and lead to loss of wildlife? Will changing a plant's genes affect its allergenic properties? Could the modified plants cross-pollinate to produce new superweeds resistant to herbicides? Will these plants throw particles into the air that create new problems?

Monsanto's Response

Monsanto decided to launch a $5 million advertising campaign in Europe in 1998 to promote genetic engineering products for crops. These ads not only speak of the benefits of genetic engineering but invite readers to seek opinions from critics. The ads give the addresses of Web sites for these critics such as Greenpeace and Friends of the Earth. In addition, Monsanto has set up its own Web site (www.monsanto.com.uk) to answer questions about its products.

What Is Biotechnology?

According to the Office of Technology Assessment, biotechnology includes any technique "that uses

---

[1]Michael Specter, "Europe, Bucking Trend in U.S., Blocks Genetically Altered Food," *New York Times,* July 20, 1998.

[2]Scott Kilman, "Monsanto Brings 'Genetic' Ads to Europe," *The Wall Street Journal,* June 16, 1998.

living organisms (or parts of organisms) to make or modify products, to improve plants and animals, or to develop microorganisms for specific uses." Biotechnology is an old science. For example, the fermentation process in making wine uses microorganisms to convert sugar into alcohol. What is new and dramatic in the field today is the ability of scientists to alter the structure of cells to affect the growth characteristics of microorganisms. These alterations promise a new class of products as exciting as those based upon the microelectronic computer chip that ushered in the information revolution. New medicines to cure human and animal diseases, new seeds that will grow disease-resistant and larger plants, new insecticides to kill bugs, new products to produce larger and healthier animals in a shorter period of time, cheaper and more nutritious foods, and new enzymes to absorb toxic wastes are but a few of the possibilities.

The Climate for Biotechnology in the United States

The environment for biotechnology innovations has been more congenial in the United States than anywhere else. In early experiments in the 1980s with plant genetic engineering, however, there were serious criticisms and restraints about the experiments. There have been critics, and they are still vocal, but that has not restrained developments. Indeed, the federal government has had a powerful role in funding the biomedical and other fundamental research in biology, biochemistry, and genetics that has formed the basis for the new biotechnology.

The first genetics firm founded for commercial purposes was Genentech, Inc., in 1977. Growth of private commercial firms was slow until the Supreme Court ruled in 1980 that microorganisms could be patented under existing law.[3] General Electric became the first company to get such a patent. After that, the creation of new companies to do research in the field was explosive and the results were widely employed in the United States.

Examples of Issues Raised about Biotechnology

Three principal agencies are involved in regulation in this area: the U.S. Department of Agriculture (USDA), the Food and Drug Administration (FDA), and the Environmental Protection Agency (EPA). The USDA is responsible for plant technology. It has been generally supportive of new technology and has sought to inform the public about it. The FDA is concerned with genetic engineering for new drugs. The EPA is concerned with outdoor plant experiments. Both the FDA and the EPA have many restrictive regulations in their areas of authority. Many unresolved questions exist, however, for this new technology. For example:

- Are new laws needed? If so, what are they?
- Should regulatory agencies here and abroad coordinate their actions to avoid impeding progress in the field?
- Do the potential benefits of biotechnology justify the risks?

---

[3]*Diamond* v. *Chakrabarty*, 100 S.Ct. 2204 (1980).

How and by whom should risks be determined?

- Are there ethical problems in tampering with genes used in treating human diseases? If so, what are they?

The case for federal regulatory reform was established in the last chapter. In this chapter, we discuss major reform recommendations. First, we set forth a few outstanding principles that should govern reform. Then the rec-

ommendations are divided into two major categories: statutory reforms by Congress and administrative reforms. This is followed with a discussion of reform of the antitrust laws. We close the chapter with a few comments comparing regulatory reform in the United States with that in selected foreign countries. The reader may be reminded of the dynamic forces model (Figure 1-3) in considering the many forces at play in virtually all the issues discussed in this chapter.

Congressional and Executive Branch Reforms

Vice President Gore wrote in his massive study of ways to improve the regulatory process: "It is almost as if federal programs were *designed* not to work. In truth, few are 'designed' at all; the legislative process simply churns them out, one after another, year after year. It's little wonder that when asked if 'government always manages to mess things up,' two-thirds of Americans say 'yes.' "[4] As noted in the previous chapter, significant reform efforts have been made over the years, with some successes. However, there is much more to be accomplished.

Shortcomings of federal regulation are rooted in many causes. Among them are

- Poorly drafted basic legislation.
- Insufficient budgets for proper implementation.
- Legislative excess (e.g., the Congress has overloaded agencies with impossible tasks and denied them money to even try to comply with the law).
- Contradictory laws and regulations.
- Lax administration and incompetent managers.
- The concentration of special interests on regulatory matters in both Congress and executive agencies.

There is general agreement among analysts of the regulatory process that most of these shortcomings spring from congressional legislation rather than deficiencies in the administration of these laws in the executive branch. The chapter emphasizes, proposed reforms for Congress as well as the executive branch. Before discussing these reforms, we present two important principles

---

[4]Al Gore, *Creating a Government that Works Better & Costs Less*, Washington, D.C.: U.S. Government Printing Office, 1993, p. 1.

governing regulatory reforms, namely, to stress the comparative advantages of government and business and to rely more on the free market. At the end of the chapter, we examine reforms that have been made in administering the antitrust laws.

Stress the Comparative Advantages of Government and Business

An effort should always be made to determine whether business or government can best perform an activity that is needed by society. Each has strengths and weaknesses. There clearly are certain activities that government can perform more efficiently than individuals in the private sector. For example, Mobil Corporation once argued that only government can perform the following significant functions:

- Only government can set forth national goals and work out the necessary compromises to reconcile conflicting regional and other interests and to recognize the priorities among various energy sources.
- Only government can develop the ground rules under which private industry must work.
- Only government can formulate a national policy on environmental tradeoffs that will strike a sensible and workable balance between unacceptable environmental risks and unacceptable economic risks.
- Only government can hammer out the sort of balanced policy that is necessary for environmental protection.[5]

These are not the only functions best performed by government. For example, national security policy, foreign policy, and taxation for social purposes are functions that only government can perform.

Business has many advantages over government in the performance of other functions necessary in this society. For example, costs of government management of productive facilities are likely to be higher than those of the private sector because of a requirement for accounting for "the last penny," because equal attention must be given to unimportant and important elements of the activity, because in government personal loyalty is often more valued than efficiency, and because any activity assumed by government becomes part of a huge bureaucracy with inherent inefficiencies. Furthermore, the motives of those in the public sector are more likely to be driven by political considerations at odds with objectivity. Finally, when compared with government, business generally enjoys an advantage in flexibility and adaptability.

---

[5]Mobile Corporation, *Energy Solutions and Nonstarters: Where a Government Role Is Needed: Accent on Achievement*, New York: Mobil, 1978.

For such reasons as these, it seems sensible to assign to governments and business the production of those goods and services that clearly are their responsibility and that each can produce at the lowest cost and highest benefits, using those terms broadly. The principle is more easily stated than implemented. It is often difficult to determine precisely where government rather than private enterprise should act. For example, how much should government get into production of military hardware and how much should be assigned to private enterprise? Should government or business, or both, operate the space shuttle?

Rely More on the Free Market

In recent years, there has been a worldwide movement for governments to rely more on market forces and less on regulations. It has many dimensions, ranging from almost complete deregulation of industries to the application of antitrust laws to ensure free competition. Here we discuss briefly privatization, deregulation, and regulations that stimulate business innovation. Later in the chapter, we discuss antitrust laws.

Privatize Government-Owned Property and Services

"Privatization is commonly defined as any process aimed at shifting functions and responsibilities, in whole or in part, from the government to the private sector."[6] Reprivatization jokingly has been called "a little yard sale" of excess government assets. But it is much more than that.

Much has been done at the federal level. For example, many military bases have been returned to private ownership. The private United Space Alliance was awarded a contract by NASA to operate the space shuttle, prepare shuttles for flight, conduct astronaut training, aid in Mission Control operations, maintain some of its bases, and launch satellites. The Elk Hills Naval Petroleum Reserve and a small Helium Reserve have been sold to private companies.

Some of the federal impetus toward reprivatization arises from the widespread policy of state and municipal governments to contract out public services to private firms. A number of states are contracting with private enterprise to do much of the work of the welfare system. States are also contracting with private companies to run prisons. Municipal governments have led the way to privatization since they have been doing it for many years. The mayor of Indianapolis, Indiana, for example, said that since 1992, his administration has opened more than seventy services to competitive bidding. Local governments have contracted vehicle towing, legal services, streetlight operations, solid waste disposal, street repair, hospital operations, ambulance service,

---

[6]General Accounting Office, *Privatization: Lessons Learned by State and Local Governments,* Washington, D.C.: General Accounting Office, March 1997.

data processing, zoos, firefighting, and many others.[7] The claim is made that private enterprise can do these things more cheaply and efficiently than local governments. In some cases this is valid. In others it is not.[8]

Privatization in foreign countries is proceeding rapidly. Under the leadership of Margaret Thatcher, Great Britain deregulated virtually all the industries that had been government-owned and operated under previous administrations. In Europe today, privatization is rapid. An outstanding example, of course, is Russia, where privatization has been accomplished on a massive and often corruptive scale. To meet deadlines established by the European Union for competition in the telecommunications industry by the year 2003, European countries are selling stakes in their state-owned telephone monopolies. This ownership transfer is especially rapid in Greece, Portugal, Spain, and Ireland.

Deregulate Selected Industries

Deregulation, as the term implies, refers to the removal or substantial reduction of government regulations. Beginning in the 1970s, the United States has deregulated one major industry after another. Examples are trucking, banking, airlines, railroads, shipping, telecommunications, and electricity. This development is a reversal of the previous century of growing regulations. Deregulation represents a major regulatory reform, but at the same time, as noted in the preceding chapter, the trend for the total volume of new regulations is up.

Deregulation has produced significant benefits to society, but it has also created problems. On balance, however, there seems little doubt about the fact that deregulation has produced a significant net advantage to the United States.

Deregulation today is a worldwide movement. In Germany, for instance, much is happening in banking, the labor market, and price competition (e.g., insurance, air fares, machine tools, retailing).[9] The European Commission, the executive body of the European Union, has issued orders for competition in telecommunications, financial services, and transportation. This has created a flurry of action throughout Europe, which, among other forces, has produced a wave of mergers.

The Japanese in 1996 undertook moderate deregulation of their banking system as a part of Prime Minister Hashimoto's effort to revive the economy. However, the result has been modest and the Japanese economy is still highly regulated.

Reduce Command Controls in Favor of Incentive Controls

Another significant route to harnessing the benefits of the free market is to replace command controls with incentives. Command controls require firms

---

[7]Stephen Goldsmith, "Can Business Really Do Business with Government?" *Harvard Business Review,* May–June 1997, p. 110.

[8]"Privatization on a Roll," *The American Enterprise,* November/December 1997.

[9]Greg Steinmetz, "German Consumers Are Seeing Prices Cut in Deregulation Push," *The Wall Street Journal,* August 15, 1997.

and individuals to meet specific standards or behaviors and are enforced by civil and, in some cases, criminal penalties or loss of government contracts. Incentive controls seek to achieve desired regulatory ends by permitting affected firms or individuals flexibility in choosing methods to meet goals. If this is done, the presumption is that innovation will be inspired in technology, service, pricing, management, or organization. In turn this will lead to more efficiency, government standards will be met, and consumers will benefit.

Government agencies increasingly are looking for ways to replace command-and-control regulations with those that harness the power of private interests. For example, the EPA issues permits for allowable emission levels to specific companies. A firm that has created more effective and cheaper pollution control measures can sell not only its unused permits but the new technology. In another area, the government has exempted automobile companies from the antitrust laws so that they can form a consortium to develop new engines. These and other efforts to replace command controls with incentive regulations are helpful. However, the net reduction to the total pyramid of command controls built over the past quarter century is not large.

Statutory Reform

The most important type of regulatory reform is statutory reform by Congress because it is Congress that grants authority to regulatory agencies. "The underlying statutes," editorialized *The Washington Post*, "are not a coherent body of law but a kind of archeological pile, each layer a reflection of the headlines and political impulses of its day."[10] Congress passes statutes with admirable goals and broad grants of authority, then denounces agencies for aggressive and costly regulations to implement them. Some statutes mandate or forbid very specific actions by regulatory agencies. For example, the basic OSHA legislation prohibits the use of cost–benefit analysis in regulation, said the Supreme Court in a decision made when the agency wanted to use the cost–benefit tool.[11] Congress directed the Consumer Product Safety Commission, in the Child Safety Protection Act (1994), to require labeling on toys intended for children aged three to six.

Recent Statutory Reforms

It was anticipated that the Republican-controlled Congresses following the 1994 election would significantly reform the regulatory process. That did not happen. There were, however, a few important reforms in new laws passed.

---

[10]*The Washington Post*, Weekly Edition, April 3–9, 1995.
[11]*American Textile Manufacturers Institute* v. *Donovan*, 452 U.S. (1981).

The Unfunded Mandates Reform Act of 1995, for example, requires agencies to make a cost–benefit analysis of costs imposed on state, local, and tribal governments. The agencies must select "the least costly, most cost-effective, or least burdensome alternative" for achieving the objective sought.

The Food Quality Protection Act of 1996 partly rescinded the Delaney clause in the Food, Drug, and Cosmetic Act of 1938. This law, which will be discussed more fully in Chapter 16, mandated a zero-standard for any carcinogenic food additive. The new law, applied only to the agricultural pesticide residues in processed foods, permits the establishment of a tolerance level to ensure "a reasonable certainty that no harm will result from aggregate exposure." For other food additives, the old law still applies.

The Government Performance and Results Act of 1993 requires agencies to prepare five-year strategic plans for the OMB, which reviews them and passes summaries on to Congress. This law has the potential for facilitating congressional policy decisions and agency reform. More will be said about this law later in the chapter.

Other Recommendations for Congressional Regulatory Reform

Many other suggestions have been made for congressional reform of business regulations. A few of the most important are these:

- Review major *existing* legislation in the areas of environment, consumer safety, and workplace to require cost–benefit analysis of new rules.
- Require all major *new* regulations of agencies costing more than $100 million annually to pass a broadly defined cost–benefit analysis.
- Require all agencies to report annually to the public on the quantifiable and nonquantifiable costs and benefits of their new rules.
- Legislate more authority and more funds to the OMB to review new rules. This was partly done in the Food Quality Protection Act of 1996.
- Attempt some rough determination of costs versus benefits for all new legislation. It is difficult to make a convincing cost–benefit analysis of new legislation in a new field, but the discipline involved might prevent ill-conceived regulations.
- Encourage courts to use cost–benefit analysis in judicial review of regulatory cases.
- Direct the OMB and each regulatory agency to review ten major existing regulations to evaluate whether they are being implemented with the least cost and maximum benefit.[12]

---

[12]These were drafted from recommendations of Robert W. Crandall, Christopher DeMuth, Robert W. Hahn, Robert E. Litan, Pietro S. Nivola, and Paul R. Portney, *An Agenda for Federal Regulatory Reform,* Washington, D.C.: American Enterprise Institute for Public Policy Research and The Brookings Institution, 1997; and Christopher H. Foreman Jr., "Congress & Regulatory Reform," *Brookings Review,* Winter 1998.

Improve Administration of the Regulatory Process

As previously noted, many management problems in regulatory agencies are rooted in shortcomings of basic legislation. For example, under the 1872 Mining Act, it is possible to buy public lands for $2.50 to $5.00 an acre when ore is discovered. Secretary of the Interior Bruce Babbitt in September 1995 signed over title to federal land containing more than $1 billion in minerals to a Danish mining company for $275 under the terms of this law. He called the signing a "tawdry process" and a "flagrant abuse of the public interest," but the law mandated his action. In 1994 he signed title over land containing about $10 billion in gold to a Canadian firm for about $10,000 and called it "the biggest gold heist since the days of Butch Cassidy."

President Clinton and Secretary Babbitt have tried to convince Congress of the need for revising this law as well as granting the administration permission to lift the grazing fees on lands across sixteen western states. Congress has refused and is likely to continue to do so. However, in 1997 Congress legislated a moratorium on new grants. The old ones are still valid and the basic legislation still stands. Table 10-1 shows some of the major "giveaways."

Aside from laws leading to these types of management problems is the simple fact that an agency such as the Bureau of Land Management in the Department of Interior does not have the staff to administer properly the vast resources placed under its jurisdiction. For example, these resources include timber, minerals, oil and gas, geothermal energy, range land, wild horses, wilderness areas, and other resources in millions of acres of public lands.[13]

Another case is that of the EPA. Even its strongest supporters agree it is poorly managed. How can it be otherwise in light of the massive, often ambiguous, and complex statutory obligations Congress has charged it with implementing? The agency is told to administer over ten major pieces of legislation and several dozen lesser statutes covering air and water pollution, hazardous waste, carcinogens of all types, chemicals, pesticides, and drinking water. It has jurisdiction over millions of pollution emitters, including every car and truck, thousands of factories, and so on. And, while its tasks have escalated, the current Congress wants to make major cuts in its allocations. Unfortunately, there are other agencies with comparable problems.

Mismanagement is not solely due to congressional shortcomings. Vice President Gore in his report referred to above said, "With their rigid preoccupation with standard operating procedure, their vertical chains of command, and their standardized services, these bureaucracies (are) . . . slow and cumbersome. . . . Many federal organizations are also monopolies, with few incentives to innovate or improve. Employees have virtual lifetime tenure, regardless of their performance. Success offers few rewards; failure, few penalties."[14] He said further that politics intensifies the problem and creates a

---

[13]Jeanne McDowell and David Seideman, "The Land Lord," *Time,* March 8, 1993.
[14]Gore, *Creating a Government that Works Better & Costs Less,* p. 3.

TABLE 10-1   Examples of Mining Patents Issued Since 1994

Location of Patent	Date	Mineral	Mineral Value	Paid to United States
Eureka and Elko Counties, Nevada	5/1994	Gold	$10,000,000,000	$9,765
Clark County, Idaho	9/1995	Travertine limestone	1,000,000,000	275
Humboldt County, Nevada: Imperial County, California	3–6/1995	Gold	1,200,000,000	3,585
Pima County, Arizona	12/1995	Copper and silver	2,900,000,000	1,745
Eureka County, Nevada	9/1995	Gold	68,000,000	540
Mohave County, Arizona	4/1996	Gypsum	85,000,000	100
Seward Peninsula, Alaska	9/1996	Gold	38,600,000	2,680
Pinal County, Arizona	9/1996	Copper	56,000,000	500
Total			15,348,000,000	19,190

Source: Department of the Interior and *Economic Report of the President,* Washington, D.C.: U.S. Government Printing Office, 1997, p. 218.

climate of fear of failure. The entire system, he concludes, is antiquated and needs major reform to serve the American people better. Gore's report made over 1,000 specific recommendations of reform, but most of them have not yet been adopted.[15] When President Clinton signed the Paperwork Reduction Act of 1995, which passed Congress without a dissenting vote, he pledged that the EPA would cut its paperwork hours by 25 percent the first year. Actually, the EPA's paperwork hours increased 4.5 million annually.[16]

Remove Flapdoodle Standards and Specifications

One significant dimension of federal regulations is the growth of nonsense regulations. Classic examples are found in early OSHA regulations, many of which now have been expunged. For example, "Jacks which are out of order shall be tagged accordingly, and shall not be used until repairs are made." OSHA has had difficulty in erasing such trivia from the minds of critics, partly because there are still instances (sometimes myths and often real cases) of such nonsense. Anyway, such trivia has little to do with the really important causes of industrial accidents and worker illness.

Other regulatory agencies are just as guilty of similar shortcomings. For instance, in March 1995, the EEOC issued a rule expanding the definition of mental disability to include an inability to perform functions such as "thinking, concentrating, and interacting with other people."[17] The American Psychiatric

---

[15]Ibid.

[16]John Shanahan, "Regulating the Regulators," *Regulation,* Winter 1997.

[17]James Bovard, "The Disabilities Act's Parade of Absurdities," *The Wall Street Journal,* June 22, 1995.

Association's diagnostic manual lists 374 mental disorders that potentially could fall under this definition. A worker's absenteeism, lateness, rudeness, or slovenliness might oblige a company to accommodate the worker under the act if the behavior could be linked to a mental disorder.[18]

AMOCO believed it had a better and cheaper way to reduce benzene emissions in a Virginia refinery than spending $30 million to upgrade its wastewater treatment system. It wanted to improve the way it loads gasoline into barges at a cost of $6 million to achieve the same pollution control. But because the EPA rules focused on sewage systems and ignored barges, EPA would not approve the alternative.[19] Under the Clean Air Act, a person can wind up in jail for violating its provisions, even though he or she has complied with an identical state law. In early 1991, the Department of Agriculture, under pressure from the Pickle Packers International Inc., a trade group, defined standards for making the perfect pickle in eight mind-numbing pages of fine print. Included were two pages of pickle definitions such as this: "The diameter in whole style means the shortest diameter measured transversely to the longitudinal axis at the greatest circumference of the pickle."[20] It is easy to understand the frustrations of people in business when encountering such definitions and rules as these.

Reduce Conflicts among Agencies and Regulations

The regulatory structure is loaded with conflicts—some amusing, some benign, some creating puzzling dilemmas for business and government, and some having serious consequences for business and individuals. Problems of overlapping jurisdictions plague the government's handling of issues of trade, health and safety, child welfare, food inspection, financial institutions, and federal–state relationships. Conflicts in policies among agencies are endemic. Restrictive trade policies conflict with free trade policy. Export controls over weapons and advanced technologies (for national security purposes) may conflict with promoting global competitiveness.

Much of the regulatory system seems to be out of sync with new challenges. A classic current example concerns tobacco. On the one hand, several government agencies seek to curb smoking, which, of course, would affect tobacco growers. The FDA seeks to control tobacco use as a drug, which nicotine is. The White House wants to stop advertising that may influence youths. On the other hand, the Department of Agricultural extension service is helping tobacco growers to improve their tobacco production. And the IRS allows tobacco ads to be tax deductible.

---

[18]Margaret A. Haven, "Giving People License to Behave Badly on the Job," *Los Angeles Times,* July 22, 1997.

[19]Ann Reilly Dowd, "Environmentalists Are on the Run," *Fortune,* September 19, 1994, pp. 98–99.

[20]Bridget O'Brian, "Government Sets New Standards for Ways to Get Properly Pickled," *The Wall Street Journal,* September 25, 1991.

The General Accounting Office has identified fourteen government agencies that issue regulations over food.[21] With so many agencies concerned with the same subject, although with different aspects of it, there is bound to be conflict. Management of a meat-packing firm was visited by an OSHA safety inspector who said it was contrary to regulations for the floors to be wet and slippery. Employees could fall and be injured. But Department of Agriculture rules require that floors be hosed down for sanitary reasons. Agencies have set up interagency coordinating committees to deal with conflicts. That has helped, but only marginally.

Federal–state jurisdictional conflict is a different dimension. There have always been disputes between these government bodies. However, the Supreme Court has been consistently clear that federal preemption by statutes establishes authority over the states when Congress explicitly says the states cannot act. States are currently active in regulating business in such areas as food labeling, pollution control, automobile safety, insurance, advertising, employee medical problems, and antitrust. This has prompted business groups to seek federal legislation to preempt state regulation. As one business official said, "I would rather deal with one federal gorilla than 50 state monkeys."[22] Some managers who fought for federal deregulation in the past now fight for reregulation. A critical issue here is not so much whether federal regulation is good and state controls are bad. Rather, it is whether it makes sense for both the federal government and the states to regulate the same business behavior.

Increase Speed of Decisions

The process of decision making in regulatory agencies is often slow. Managers have complained for years about excessive delays about decisions concerning vital matters. Delays in acquiring patents have plagued the biotechnology industry. Pharmaceutical firms complain bitterly about delays in FDA approval for selling new drugs. They assert, among other things, that their patent protection period is so shortened that they have difficulty using the protection to recoup their investment. To introduce a new drug in the United States and meet all FDA requirements may take up to ten or more years and cost $50 million or more. The FDA has stepped up to the problem and has much improved the drug approval process. One thing it has done is to charge user fees that have increased the agency's resources to permit hiring some 600 additional investigators. As a result, some review times have been cut in half. In the FDA as well as in many other agencies, more can be done to speed the regulatory process, although budget limitations clearly restrain such efforts. It must be conceded, however, that agencies such as the FDA face a difficult

---

[21]General Accounting Office, *Maze of Food Regulations,* Washington, D.C.: General Accounting Office, 1980.

[22]W. John Moore, "Stopping the States," *National Journal,* July 21, 1990, p. 178.

problem balancing the benefits of speed to industry and consumers with public vulnerability to potentially dangerous medicines and medical equipment.

Improve Performance-Based Management

Of key significance in improving regulatory management is the Government Performance and Results Act of 1993. This law requires federal agencies to prepare five-year strategic plans. The plans are to describe the agency's mission, performance goals, strategies and resources needed to achieve them, and measures of performance. The plans are also to include key external factors that could preclude achievement of the goals. As noted previously, annual reports must be prepared and sent to the OMB where an aggregate plan must be presented to Congress. The first cycle of planning began in September 1997.[23]

Patterns of Change in the Antitrust Laws[24]

Fundamental in the effective operation of the individual enterprise system is the idea of competing economic units. From the beginning of this nation this idea was written into law. To restrain excess prices of grain mills having a local monopoly, colonial governments controlled the prices charged by mills. During the nineteenth century, the states regulated local monopolistic practices but ran into difficulty in exercising control over the giant companies formed during that period.

The Standard Oil Trust formed by John D. Rockefeller and many of its imitators in the 1880s provoked formidable opposition among small-business owners, farmers, and the public. So widespread and strong was the opposition to the trust movement that the Sherman Act of 1890, designed to curb the trusts, passed the Senate with but one dissenting vote and passed the House without opposition. This law is still the key statute of antitrust enforcement today.

The Sherman Antitrust Act

The two most significant sections of the Sherman Act are 1 and 2. Section 1 reads: "Every contract, combination in the form of trust or otherwise, or conspiracy, in restraint of trade or commerce . . . is hereby declared to be illegal." Section 2 says: "Every person who shall monopolize, or attempt to monopolize . . . trade or commerce . . . shall be deemed guilty . . ."

---

[23]Susan S. Weston and J. Christopher Mihm, *The Results Act: An Evaluator's Guide to Assessing Agency Annual Performance Plans,* Washington, D.C.: General Accounting Office, April 1998.

[24]The antitrust laws were so named because of the method of corporate consolidation in the late nineteenth century. Briefly, owners of stock of competing organizations transferred legal title to a group of trustees and received certificates in return. The trustees then exercised control of the firms as a single company.

Dissatisfaction with the operation of the Sherman Act created by adverse Supreme Court decisions and lax administration raised demands for more precise definitions of illegal monopolistic practices. Congress responded in 1914 by passing the Clayton Act and the Federal Trade Commission Act.

The Clayton Act

The Clayton Act named specific monopolistic practices prohibited by law. For example, price discrimination, exclusive and tying contracts, and interlocking directorates are illegal when the effects might be to substantially lessen competition or tend to create a monopoly.

The Federal Trade Commission Act

This act established an agency, the Federal Trade Commission, to continuously supervise and administer the antitrust laws, to stop "unfair methods of competition in commerce, and unfair or deceptive acts or practices in commerce . . ." The act was amended in 1938 by the Wheeler-Lea Act, which gave the FTC power to regulate deceptive advertising.

The Department of Justice has authority to enforce the Sherman Act and shares jurisdiction with the FTC in Clayton Act cases. The Supreme Court, of course, has the final word in interpreting both laws and various statutes reinforcing them.

Through the years, exceptions to the antitrust laws have been granted. For example, excepted are labor unions, agricultural cooperatives, the insurance industry, baseball, certain joint export trading activities, and certain joint research efforts in some industries.

Theories of Antitrust Enforcement

Much has been written about the purpose of the antitrust laws. One of the best statements is that given in a Supreme Court opinion made in a Sherman Act case, as follows:

> The Sherman Act was designed to be a comprehensive charter of economic liberty aimed at preserving free and unfettered competition as the rule of trade. It rests on the premise that the unrestrained interaction of competitive forces will yield the best allocation of our economic resources, the lowest prices, the highest quality, and the greatest material progress, while at the same time providing an environment conducive to the preservation of our democratic political and social institutions. But even were that premise open to question, the policy unequivocally laid down by the Act is competition.[25]

This is not solely an economic policy but has social as well as political implications. Socially it means greater welfare for individuals. Politically it

---

[25]*U.S.* v. *Northern Pacific R.R. Co.,* 356 U.S. 1 (1958).

supports democracy by preventing concentrated economic power able to distort democratic impulses.

In seeking to achieve this fundamental objective, two major theories of enforcement have developed, namely the *structure* and the *performance* theories. Until recently, the Supreme Court, as well as government regulators and academic economists, leaned toward the structure theory in deciding antitrust cases, as supported by most of the scholarly studies on concentration and merger. In the late 1960s, however, an increasing body of impressive evidence emerged that contradicted this view and supported the performance theory.

The Structure Theory.   Until recently, the main view of the Court was that corporate size and large market share are a reliable index of monopoly power. The typical measure of power is concentration of assets or sales of one or a few companies in an industry. (Concentration is calculated as the ratio of sales and/or assets of one or a few companies in an industry to total sales and/or assets of the entire industry.) The structure theory argues that excessive concentration of market power gives corporate managers discretionary power to fix prices, determine which products come to market and in what volume, and make huge profits. Extraordinary market power produces price inflation, inefficiencies in production, and, of course, a decline in competition. Adherents of this theory argue that the way to ensure competitive markets is to break up concentrations of economic power and/or prevent such concentration from developing. This is the essence of the structure theory. It was supported for decades by economists and expounded in their scholarly research.[26]

The Performance Theory.   This theory argues that public policy should seek appropriate market structures as well as efficient business performance. Efficient performance ensures product and process innovation, reduced costs that benefit consumers with lower prices, productive capacity in balance with product demand, profits not out of line with other industries, and emphasis on service to consumers. Furthermore, any assertion that concentration inhibits competition is seriously challenged when world markets are considered. Today more than ever, American industry is faced with powerful global competitors. The concentration numbers tend to shrink substantially when foreign competition is considered. For example, there is high concentration in the United States in jet engine production, but when sales of foreign producers are considered, the ratio drops significantly.[27]

Research Findings.   These assertions have been supported by more and more economists and scholarly research. For example, studies show a lack of

---

[26]For example, see John M. Blair, *Economic Concentration, Structure, Behavior and Public Policy,* New York: Harcourt Brace, 1973.

[27]J. Fred Weston, *Concentration and Efficiency: The Other Side of the Monopoly Issue,* Croton-on-Hudson, N.Y.: Hudson Institute, 1978.

correlation between measures of concentration and excessive profits.[28] Research concludes that substantial price flexibility exists in concentrated industries and that price increases during inflationary periods have been lower in industries dominated by "super concentrations" than in those less concentrated. Productivity also has risen faster in industries that are concentrated than in other industries. If high profits are found in large firms, say performance theorists, this may be due more to efficacy than to any market power they possess.[29]

Such research findings do not refute completely every assertion by structural theorists. Some concentrations at some times and places may result in excessive profits, price inflexibility, inhibitions to innovation, and so forth. They do show, however, that for most cases of concentration, structure theory describes the opposite of reality.

The Theories in Practice.   Up to the 1970s, decisions of the Supreme Court and Department of Justice concerning monopolistic practices were based largely on the structure theory. In 1974 the Supreme Court held that the calculation of the effects of a merger should not rely exclusively on structural tests, but should take into account a much broader range of economic information.[30] In 1986 a decision of a lower court based strictly on the structure theory was rejected by the Supreme Court in a decision reflecting the performance theory.[31]

The Supreme Court and the Department of Justice have not abandoned the structure theory. Rather, there has been a noticeable shift in theory and policy toward favoring efficiencies in markets over formal criteria of structure. Antitrust decisions, therefore, face a major challenge in balancing the two theories.

Challenges to Antitrust Enforcement Agencies

New major challenges to the enforcement agencies spring from the current merger movement, high-technology industries, and globalization.

Mergers

Proposed and actual mergers have achieved levels of numbers and assets never before reached. Figure 10-1 shows the growth of numbers of recent mergers. The explosive growth of numbers is evident. The asset value of the mergers has shown a more rapid growth. In 1991 the total value of assets of mergers was less than $200 billion. By the end of 1997 it was over

---

[28]Ibid.
[29]Ibid.
[30]*U.S.* v. *General Dynamics Corp.*, 415 U.S. 486 (1974).
[31]*Cargill, Inc., and Excell Corporation* v. *Montford of Colorado, Inc.*, 55 L.W. 4027 (1986).

FIGURE 10-1

Mergers filed with the antitrust agencies. Large mergers must be filed with the U.S. antitrust enforcement agencies. Fiscal 1997 was the second consecutive year of record filings.

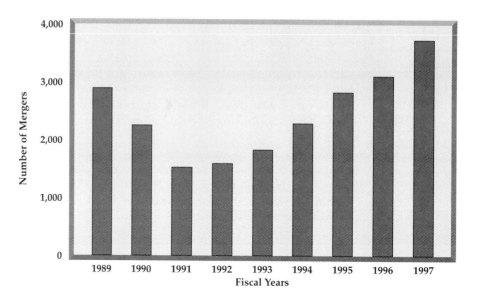

Sources: Department of Justice (Antitrust Division), Federal Trade Commission, and *The Economic Report of the President,* Washington, D.C.: U.S. Government Printing Office, 1998, p. 197.

$1 trillion. The largest deal in 1997 was the $36.5 billion acquisition of MCI Communications by Worldcom Inc.

In evaluating proposed mergers and deciding which ones to challenge, the enforcement agencies face difficult choices. For example, a merger may yield significant cost savings by eliminating duplications and creating other efficiencies. However, at the same time, the merger may leave fewer companies in the industry, which increases concentration and could lead later to price increases as a result of collusion among the remaining companies.

Guidelines for Antitrust Action.   To facilitate meeting this type of challenge, the Department of Justice jointly with the FTC in 1992 established "Horizontal Merger Guidelines" to facilitate evaluation of mergers. The guidelines have been modified periodically since then. The most important are as follows:

- define the relevant market and calculate its concentration before and after the merger,
- assess whether the merger raises concerns about adverse competitive effects,
- determine whether entry by other firms into the market would counteract those effects, and
- consider any expected efficiency gains.[32]

---

[32]*Economic Report of the President,* Washington, D.C.: U.S. Government Printing Office, 1998, p. 98.

Market Definition.   The first step is to define the market where the merger is to take place. Then the impact on concentration is evaluated. The relevant market is generally specific products and geographic areas where a merger is likely to raise prices significantly, taking into account the reduction in demand caused by consumers reducing their purchases because of the higher price.

For example, the FTC challenged the proposed merger of Staples Inc. and Office Depot Inc. in 1997 on these grounds. It said the relevant market was "the sale of consumable office supplies through office superstores," and these were the largest firms in that market. Staples countered that the combined firms would account for less than 6 percent of the broad market for office products, including sales by discount stores, drug stores, and wholesale clubs. The FTC said the products of the two stores were much less inclusive of products in these other stores and, in the relevant market of the two stores, the merger would significantly increase concentration and be anticompetitive.

In another case, the Georgia-Pacific Corp. wanted to buy plants from Domtar Inc. The company claimed its product (gypsum drywall) was only a small percentage of the total market. The FTC said, however, that the relevant market was the Northeastern states where most of its plants were located. There the merger would likely lead to price increases and it was challenged.

In determining the impact of concentration created by a merger, the agencies apply a formula. The formula (the Herfindahl-Hirschman Index) measures the competitive impact of concentration by taking account of both the total number of firms in a market and the relative power wielded. Proportionate weight is given to larger firms.[33]

Competitive Effects.   The guidelines recognize that two merged firms can so concentrate an industry that collusion among the firms will result in price increases and other anticompetitive practices. Analysis of such effects is a major step in evaluation. Sometimes the antitrust authorities will permit a merger to proceed if the merged companies agree to divest certain divisions and products or agree to another arrangement to prevent anticompetitive behavior. For example, in the merger of Time Warner Inc. and Turner Broadcasting System Inc. in 1995, the FTC would agree to the merger only if the two companies separated their cable operations.

Entry.   If other firms can enter a market, it will be more difficult for merged companies to engage in anticompetitive practices. The guidelines say entry must be timely and able to counter any potential merger anticompetitive practices.

Expected Efficiency Gains.   Potential merger partners usually exaggerate the efficiencies to be gained through the merger and also the savings that will be passed on to consumers in lower prices and better service. The guidelines suggest that such claims should be carefully scrutinized. Even though savings may

---

[33]For an explanation of this index, see J. Fred Weston, Kwang S. Chung, and Juan A. Siu, *Takeovers, Restructuring, and Corporate Governance,* Upper Saddle River, N.J.: Prentice Hall, 1998.

be verifiable, a remaining question is whether they will be passed on to consumers. The Staples and Office Depot case was partly challenged on the grounds that while there undoubtedly would be savings, there remained a serious question as to whether they would be passed on to consumers in lower prices.

Nonhorizontal Mergers.   Most mergers are of the horizontal type and are more likely to create competitive problems than other types. However, the above guidelines are completely applicable to nonhorizontal mergers.[34] But there are special features of the nonhorizontal type of merger for which other guidelines are prepared. For example, the FTC stopped a proposed merger of a small company by a large firm because, said the agency, the large company could be a "deep pocket" or a "rich parent" that could open all sorts of possibilities for the small company to undersell or otherwise "ravage the less affluent competition."[35]

High-Technology Industries

Many of the fastest-growing companies are found in high-technology industries such as computer hardware and software, telecommunications, and aerospace. These industries create special problems for antitrust enforcement. At the end of this chapter, some of these problems are illustrated in a case the Department of Justice is bringing against Microsoft.

The Global Market and Antitrust

Expansion of global markets raises new issues for the antitrust agencies. For example, prosecuting price-fixing agreements becomes much more difficult when foreigners are involved. Currently, the Department of Justice has indicted the Japan-based Nippon Paper Industries Co., a United States firm, and five other Japanese companies on price-fixing charges. The charge is that these companies plotted in Tokyo to raise the price of fax paper by 10 percent in the

---

[34]A *horizontal merger* is one that combines the activities of companies within the same industry, such as two steel mills. A *vertical merger* takes place when a company acquires other firms, either back in the production chain, toward raw materials, or forward, toward consumers of final products and services. For example, a merger of a company producing fabricated steel shapes and forms with one mining iron ore and one building steel bridges is a vertical merger. A *conglomerate merger* is neither horizontal nor vertical and involves two firms that are engaged in unrelated lines of business. A simple illustration would be the merger of a producer of wooden office furniture with a company owning and mining coal. Conglomerate mergers can be of different varieties. For example, the acquired firms may be completely unrelated, or they may associate with a basic company purpose. Conglomerates may merge with firms that are not directly competitive, such as those with common production or distribution characteristics, or companies in the same general product line but making sales in different geographic regions.

[35]*FTC* v. *Reynolds Metal Company,* TRADE CASES ¶ 70, 741 (U.S. S.Ct. 1962).

United States.[36] Critics, especially in foreign countries, say that in cases such as this, the reach of the U.S. antitrust laws is stretched too far and interferes too much in the sovereignty of other countries. The Department of Justice has collected fines in judgments against many large international price-fixing conspiracies. But the Nippon case is the first time a foreign company has been tried for price fixing conducted on foreign soil.

The courts have held that when an alleged violation of antitrust laws has an intended and significant impact in the United States, the laws apply. However, it may be difficult to bring a case against individuals or firms located in foreign countries. To deal with this situation, Congress in 1994 passed the International Antitrust Enforcement Assistance Act. This law authorizes U.S. enforcement agencies to make agreements with foreign antitrust officials to coordinate actions.

In a different legal direction, the European Commission's Minister for Competition, Karel van Miert, has complained about the potential competitive impacts of mergers between other U.S. companies. For example, he bitterly objected to the merger in 1997 of the two commercial aircraft manufacturers Boeing and McDonnell Douglas. He was, of course, concerned about the effect of their domination of the commercial jet market on Airbus Industrie, the European aircraft consortium based in Paris. This raises a question, say the critics, of whether the European Union is stretching too far its antitrust reach.

Mr. Miert has also complained about mergers of U.S. companies with European firms. For instance, he sought to stop the merger of British Airways with American Airlines. He argued that the two would control a majority of landing slots for flights between the United States and Heathrow Airport in London.

European merger regulations do not have guidelines similar to those of the United States. They focus more on market share and less on broader questions of competition. However, the Commission is moving in the direction of the United States. It recently published a draft guide similar to the guidelines used in the United States.[37]

Concluding Observations

It seems likely that the current backlash against actual and perceived excesses in federal regulations will result in substantial reductions in regulations. In the reform process, there are two important considerations that must not be neglected. First, do not throw out the baby with the dirty bath water. Second, we probably should not expect too much. We comment on each of these.

---

[36]*United States* v. *Nippon Paper,* 109 F.3d 1 (1997).
[37]*The Economist,* August 2, 1997, p. 61.

Regulatory Reform Should Not Neglect Benefits

The Tolchins remind us in the following words that no right-minded person wants to get rid of *all* regulations.

> Regulation is the connective tissue, the price we pay for an industrialized society. It is our major protection against the excesses of technology, whose rapid advances threaten man's genes, privacy, air, water, bloodstream, lifestyle, and virtual existence. It is a guard against the callous entrepreneur, who would have his workers breathe coal dust and cotton dust, who would send children into the mines and factories, who would offer jobs in exchange for health and safety, and leave the victims as public charges in hospitals and on welfare lines . . . Regulations provide protection against the avarice of the marketplace, against shoddy products and unscrupulous marketing practices from Wall Street to Main Street.[38]

Regulatory Reform Will Meet with Resistance

We should expect Congress to continue its deregulatory thrust in major industries. There are also laudable efforts being made today, both in Congress and in the executive branch, to get rid of trivial, nonsensical, and ineffective regulations.

We are mindful, however, that there are elements in society demanding further regulation of business. Despite all the clamor, reform has a weak political base. One reason for this is that the public is not excited about reform. Aside from business, the ultimate beneficiaries are generally unaware of their stake in reform. Because the benefits of reform to one person are very small in relation to the costs involved in bringing it about, there is a lack of initiative by individuals, except those in business. The result is a coalition of congressional committees, bureaucrats who administer the laws, and interest groups, constituting political power that resists quick and substantial regulatory reform. There are no comparable opposing political powers.[39]

---

[38]Susan J. Tolchin and Martin Tolchin, *Dismantling America: The Risk to Deregulation*, New York: Oxford University Press, 1983.

[39]James Q. Wilson, ed., *The Politics of Regulation*, New York: Basic Books, 1980.

MICROSOFT CORPORATION AND ANTITRUST

The rapid growth and dominance of Microsoft in the computer industry is one of the most, if not the most, spectacular success stories in the history of American business. From a two-man shoestring operation in 1975 revenues of the small firm leaped to almost $14.48 billion in 1998 and employed over 28,000 people.

Microsoft transformed the personal computer (PC) from a toy in the early 1970s to a machine that has changed the way people live, work, and think. The great contribution of Bill Gates and Paul Allen (the cofounders of Microsoft) was to develop a set of commands that transformed the microprocessor into the PC we know today. Now, the company is hoping to lead the world into new forms of communications networking.

This brief case tells the story of the extraordinary growth of Microsoft and its domination of computer operating systems and the software market. This domination drew the attention of the Antitrust Division of the Department of Justice and developed antitrust problems for Microsoft. That is the main focus of this case.

In analyzing this case, it is necessary to have a rudimentary understanding of the computer. Central in the computer is the *microprocessor,* a chip that is the "brain" of the computer. Microprocessors manufactured by Intel and several small competitors run the IBM PCs and IBM-clone PCs. The *operating system* is software that links the memory, keyboard, display screen, printer, and other components in the computer. Computers are usually sold with the chips and operating systems installed. *Applications* software is then designed to function with the operating system to permit the computer to perform specific tasks, such as word processing, data management, and so on.

It is essential that applications be compatible with the operating systems. Otherwise the computer will not operate. The compatibility struggle has shaped the industry and is at the core of the antitrust litigation of Microsoft. Before getting into the litigation, it is useful to present a brief history of the company.

349

Origins and Growth of the Company

William Henry Gates III was born in Bremerton, Washington, in 1955. His parents sent him to Lakeside School, an exclusive independent institution, where he said "it all began" when the mothers of students put a computer terminal in the school in 1968. He and Paul Allen, another student three years older, were fascinated with the computer and spent as much time as they could playing with this new "toy." Gates wrote his first software program (for playing tic-tac-toe) when he was 13 years old. He and Paul Allen were so knowledgeable that they got entry-level programming jobs while in high school.

Following high school, Gates and Allen organized their first company, called Traf-O-Data. They used the newly invented Intel 8008 microprocessor chip to count traffic flows. Then Gates entered Harvard University and Allen came east for a job with Honeywell. In the autumn of 1974, Allen saw an ad in *Popular Electronics* for the "World's First Minicomputer Kit to Rival Commercial Models." It was called the Altair 8080 since it was built around Intel's new 8080 microprocessor. This machine had neither a keyboard nor a screen and had limited memory (only 256 bytes). The Altair obviously had to be programmed if it was to be useful and Gates and Allen saw the opportunity to do just that. They developed a program called BASIC (Beginner's All-purpose Symbolic Instruction Code) to operate the 8080 microprocessor and licensed it to the small company called MIT in Albuquerque, New Mexico, which had created and advertised the Altair.

The two entrepreneurs left Boston for Albuquerque to work out any bugs in adapting their software to the Altair. Allen quit his programming job with Honeywell and Gates dropped out of Harvard. In Albuquerque in 1975, they formed Microsoft (an abbreviation for microcomputer software), the world's first microcomputer software company. Revenues for 1975 were $16,000 with Gates and Allen the only employees. The little firm soon prospered and revenues for the year 1978 were $1.4 million. They had thirteen employees.[1] As Intel was adding more transistors to its chips, Gates and Allen foresaw a continued rapid multiplication of microprocessor capacity and unimaginable opportunities for improved operating systems for new computers. In January 1975 they decided to relocate to a suburb in Seattle, Washington.

The company prospered, reaching revenues of $8 million by 1980. Then, in that year, luck plus Gates's marketing skills provided the base for the remarkable success of Microsoft. The giant computer company, IBM, had been focusing too intently on its highly successful mainframe computers and had been neglecting the PC. Given time the company could have chosen a suitable microprocessor and developed its own program for it, but it did not have the time. It chose Intel's 8088 for the microprocessor and Microsoft's MS-DOS (which stands for Microsoft Disk Operating System) for the operating system.

---

[1]Michael A. Cusumano and Richard W. Selby, *Microsoft Secrets: How the World's Most Powerful Company Creates Technology, Shapes Markets, and Manages People,* New York: Free Press, 1995.

Since the Microsoft license to IBM for the MS-DOS system was not exclusive, Microsoft licensed it to manufacturers of clones of the IBM PC. The IBM PC, together with the Intel chips and MS-DOS, became the computer operating standards for the PC industry.

Gates recognized that the success of an operating system depended on the popularity of applications software that used the system. He thereby set forth to produce his own software for the MS-DOS and to induce other software firms to do likewise. In this he was successful and the popularity of the MS-DOS operation system benefited from the development of hundreds of new applications.

Today Microsoft is the largest software producer in the world with over 200 products. The product line is wide, ranging from books (*Encarta* is the largest-selling encyclopedia in the world), to music, movies, new services, maps, financial services, and paintings. In the 1980s, Microsoft developed Windows, which enables computer users to add graphic display [called graphical user interface (GUI)] and to run more than one program at the same time. Subsequent versions of Windows have met with great success.

Bill Gates will be evaluated in history not only as a gifted entrepreneur (along with Paul Allen, who left the company in 1983 because of illness) but also as an exceptional manager. Most small companies fail after a few years but Microsoft has boomed every year since its founding. In commenting on Microsoft's success, Gates said that ". . . there is no simple answer, and luck played a role, but I think the most important element was our original vision."[2] The vision was "a computer on every desk and in every home, all running Microsoft software."[3]

Significant in Microsoft's success has been the single-mindedness of Gates in the achievement of that vision. He has been characterized by both friends and competitors as a man obsessed with competing hard and aggressively to win his vision.[4] This hard-driving behavior has been buttressed by formulating and implementing a few major managerial strategies. These are set forth by Cusumano and Selby in a book called *Microsoft Secrets*, which devotes a chapter to each strategy.[5]

Joel Klein and Bill Gates Joined in Combat

On October 20, 1998, Joel I. Klein, Assistant Attorney General in charge of the Department of Justice (DOJ) Antitrust Division; twenty state's Attorneys General; and Bill Gates, chairman and chief executive officer of the Microsoft Corporation, joined in an epic struggle before Judge Thomas Penfield Jackson in the U.S. District Court for the District of Columbia. The issues before the court

---

[2]Bill Gates, *The Road Ahead,* New York: Viking Penguin, 1995, p. 18.
[3]Brent Schlender, "Bill Gates and Paul Allen Talk," *Fortune,* October 2, 1995, p. 86.
[4]See James Wallace and Jim Erickson, *Hard Drive: Bill Gates and the Making of the Microsoft Empire,* New York: HarperCollins, 1992.
[5]Cusumano and Selby, *Microsoft Secrets.*

were serious charges against the Microsoft Corporation set forth in briefs presented to the court. Attorney General of the United States Janet Reno, in a press release announcing the action, said:

> The Justice Department today charged Microsoft with engaging in anticompetitive and exclusionary practices designed to maintain its monopoly in personal computer operating systems and to extend that monopoly to internet browsing software.

Microsoft denied the charges.

The following discussion sets forth briefly the main arguments of the government and Microsoft and raises the question: who is right? Is Microsoft a monopolistic predator that uses illegal means to stifle competition? Or is Microsoft acting as companies do in a rapidly changing technical market?

DOJ and States Attorneys General Charges

The complaints of the DOJ and Attorneys General are similar and, except as noted, the following will be attributed to the DOJ.[6]

Microsoft Has Monopoly Powers

Microsoft has a monopoly in its PC Windows operating system, which enjoys 90 percent of the market. It uses that monopoly power to engage in unfair competitive practices. The exercise of this power inhibits innovation, restricts consumer and manufacturer's choices, and restrains new entry into the market. The Attorneys General add that the anticompetitive practices of Microsoft threaten loss or damage to the general welfare and economies of the states.

To protect its Windows monopoly against potential competitive threats, the company has engaged in a pattern of anticompetitive activities. Included are

> agreements tying other Microsoft software products to Microsoft's Windows operating system; exclusionary agreements precluding companies from distributing, promoting, buying or using products of Microsoft's software competitors or potential competitors; and exclusionary agreements restricting the right of companies to provide services or resources to Microsoft's software competitors or potential competitors.

The prosecution says that attempting to maintain its monopoly in the market, unreasonably restraining trade, and unfairly competing are all in violation of Sections 1 and 2 of the Sherman Antitrust Act.

---

[6]*United States of America* v. *Microsoft Corporation,* Civil Action No. 98–1232, Complaint filed in the United States District Court for the District of Columbia, May 18, 1998; and *Attorneys General, States of New York, California, Connecticut, District of Columbia, Florida, Illinois, Iowa, Kansas, Kentucky, Louisiana, Maryland, Massachusetts, Michigan, Minnesota, New Mexico, North Carolina, Ohio, South Carolina, Utah, West Virginia, Wisconsin* v. *Microsoft Corporation,* No. 1:98CVO12333, Complaint filed in the United States District Court for the District of Columbia, May 18, 1998. The Department of Justice press release and complaint can be found at http://www.usdoj.gov/atr.

Franklin M. Fisher, an MIT economist, both in his written and oral testimony at the trial, strongly supported the DOJs allegations that Microsoft had monopoly power and used it.[7] A number of executives from firms such as Intel, IBM, and Sun Microsystems portrayed Microsoft in their testimony as a bullying monopolist.[8]

Microsoft and Netscape Communications Corporation

Both the DOJ and Attorneys General said that Microsoft's response to Internet browsers is a prominent and immediate example of the pattern of anticompetitive behavior taken to maintain and extend its monopoly. In May 1995 Gates said the Internet was "the most important single development to come along since the IBM PC was introduced in 1981." At that time, Netscape had developed an Internet browser that had 70 percent of the market. Gates saw in the Internet browser, and specifically Netscape's browser, a significant competitive threat to his Windows operating system. On January 5, 1996, he said: "Winning Internet browser share is a very, very important goal for us." On August 20, 1996, he directed: "Internet Explorer (IE) (the Microsoft browser) will be distributed every way we can . . . Bundled with Windows 95 upgrade and included by OEMs (Original Equipment Manufacturers)." In September 1996, Microsoft's General Manager for the Windows PC Platform noted that "Browser share is job 1 at this company." The government produced a number of other memoranda that emphasized in clear terms that Microsoft had used the leverage of its Windows (meaning its domination of the market for operating systems). For example, Senior Vice President James Allchin wrote on December 20, 1996, that unless Microsoft were to "leverage Windows . . . I don't understand how IE is going to win . . ."

What is the threat of Netscape's browser? The browser is software for viewing and navigating the Internet. It has the potential of offering consumers an alternative platform for software applications in competition with Windows. Java (described later) is a program language used in developing software applications. When connected with an Internet browser such as Netscape's, the two can be a serious threat to the Windows monopoly.

In May 1995, not long before Microsoft introduced its first version of IE, the company's executives visited with Netscape executives. The governments charge that at this meeting Microsoft attempted to persuade Netscape not to compete with Microsoft but to divide the browser market, with Microsoft the sole supplier of the browser for use with Windows 95 operating systems. This proposition, said the DOJ, "was a blatant and illegal attempt to monopolize the Internet browser market." Netscape declined the offer.

---

[7]Declaration of Franklin M. Fisher, In the United States District Court for the District of Columbia, *United States of American, Plaintiff,* v. *Microsoft Corporation, Defendant,* Civil Action No: 98–1232, Filed May 18, 1998.

[8]Steve Lohr, "The Prosecution Almost Rests: Government Paints Microsoft as Monopolist and Bully," *New York Times,* January 8, 1999.

The Netscape browser continued to serve all computer users that worked on Windows 95 as well as other operating systems. It continued to have potential to become an alternative platform to Windows and, of course, a major threat to Microsoft. So Microsoft embarked on a series of moves aimed at eliminating the threat. The company developed and introduced its own browser, the IE, and used its monopoly power to drive competing Internet browsers from the market. Here are some of the actions Microsoft took that the government said were illegal and anticompetitive practices.

Bundling

This is a marketing strategy by which a weaker product is attached to a more popular one. Microsoft bundled its IE in its Windows operating system and said it was free to consumers, as a strategy to induce consumers to use it in favor of any other browser. Once incorporated in Windows, it could not easily be separated. This was confirmed by Professor David Farber of the University of Pennsylvania, a long-time expert in Internet technology, in testimony at the trial.[9] This was an attempt, said the DOJ, to exclude Netscape in favor of IE.

Exclusionary Agreements with Internet Service Providers (ISPs) and On-Line Services (OLSs)

Microsoft entered into anticompetitive agreements with virtually all the major and most popular ISPs and OLSs. These firms (such as AT&T Worldnet, MCI, and Earthlink) provide communications links between PC users and the Internet. They are sometimes called Internet Access Providers. The agreements with these firms commit them to offer Microsoft's IE primarily or exclusively through all the channels they employ to distribute their services. They cannot promote or mention to their subscribers the existence of competing browsers. They must eliminate links on their Web sites by means of which subscribers can download a competing browser. They are to use the Internet sites in such a way as to ensure that Microsoft's browser is more effective than any competing system when using the service.

Why did these companies agree to do this? Microsoft agreed to place icons (notices of services) on the Windows desktop (the computer screen first seen when the computer is turned on) in a prominent place. This is an important advantage because once the desktop position is established, it will remain because original equipment manufacturers (OEMs) are obliged to use the screen designed by Microsoft and not modify it without permission. As a result, these service providers are assured a position in the location where users first look when they make a decision about which service to use. If the agree-

---

[9]Reported by Times Wire Service, "Software Expert Criticizes Microsoft," *Los Angeles Times,* December 9, 1998.

ments are not met, the contracts permit Microsoft to delete the mention of the service on the desktop.

Exclusionary Agreements with Internet Content Providers (ICPs)

Firms such as Disney, Hollywood Online, and CBS Sportsline are ICPs that provide news, entertainment, and other information from sites on the Web. Microsoft also made exclusionary agreements with them similar to but not the same as those noted. When the computer is turned on, there appears on the right side of the desktop screen "channels" that display various services. For an agreement with Microsoft, the ICP may receive a preferred position on this screen with the same advantages as noted for the ICPs and ISPs. For this position, the ICP is committed to specific actions. For example, it is not to promote any other browser. It is to design its Web site so it looks better with IE than with other browsers.

Modification of Agreements

In late April 1998, just prior to scheduled hearings before the U.S. Senate Judiciary Committee, and following the issuance of civil subpoenas to ISPs about agreements with Microsoft, the company said it was modifying the contractual agreements with certain ISPs. However, says the DOJ, Microsoft has not changed its agreements with the largest ISPs.

The government says these modifications, made on the eve of congressional inquiry and under threat of litigation, do not absolve the company of its anticompetitive practices. Nor do the modifications ensure that the company will not continue such exclusionary practices in the future. Furthermore, by its own admission, these modifications do not apply to all existing restrictions nor to all Internet servers.

Restrictions on Original Equipment Manufacturers (OEMs)

Around August 1996, Microsoft imposed restrictions on OEMs that were anticompetitive and illegal. They were enjoined from modifying or obscuring the sequence of any desktop screen displays unless the user initiated action to change the sequence. They cannot include any display, sound, or welcome screens until after the Windows desktop screen first appears.

With such restrictions, Microsoft, among other things, can reward firms with whom it has agreements with preferred positions on the desktop screen. The restrictions provide Microsoft leverage to ensure that Microsoft-designed applications or other software reach Windows users. For example, it ensures a preferred position on the desktop screen for its IE and a more obscure placement for competitors.

OEMs have objected to these restrictions, but Microsoft has refused to change them and threatened to deny Windows licenses to those who violated the agreement.

America Online Inc. (AOL)

Stephen M. Case, chairman of AOL, testified that he was approached in the spring of 1996 to make Microsoft's IE the main browser for his subscribers, which at the time were in the millions. For this Microsoft agreed to give AOL a prominent position on the Windows desktop. However, Case complained to the DOJ that Microsoft planned to introduce its own online server in August 1996 and place it in a prominent position on the desktop of Windows. He argued that this "bundling" of Microsoft's online service to its operating system gave the company an unfair competitive advantage over AOL.

Java

Java is a programming language developed by Sun Microsystems Inc. that produces programs capable of running on almost any computer or operating system. Functioning through browsers, it can link on the Internet many computers at the same time. For example, it permits a person to play a game of poker with others on separated computers, or collect sales figures from many sources simultaneously.

The government charges that Microsoft executives saw in Java a serious threat to its operating system and took action to "neutralize" it. At the trial, the government presented e-mail and other documents purportedly showing how concerned Microsoft was. For example, in September 1996, Gates wrote an e-mail saying: "This scares the hell out of me," and called on Microsoft staff to make it a top priority to stop Java.

Sun made an agreement in March 1997 whereby it would license Java technology to Microsoft in exchange for Microsoft's ability to distribute the technology. In October 1997 Sun filed a lawsuit against Microsoft for breach of contract. Sun alleged that Microsoft was "polluting" the technology to weaken Java's use and developing its own technology to replace it. In March 1998 Judge Whyte of the U.S. District Court in San Jose, California, granted Sun an injunction enforcing the provision of the agreement that prevented Microsoft from altering Java. A trial was scheduled for 1999.

Spyglass Inc.

Spyglass was a small company selected by the National Center for Supercomputing at the University of Illinois as the commercial licensee for browser technology it had developed. In December 1994 it licensed its technology to Microsoft. Spyglass had licensed its technology to eighty-two other companies, including IBM and Digital, for use in their software products. The company's revenues from this source amounted to $20 million. But on December 7, 1995, Microsoft announced it was giving its browser technology for free. Spyglass lost its sales for this product and moved into other software areas. Mr. Colbath, chairman of Spyglass, lamented: "Whenever you license technology to

Microsoft, you have to understand it can someday build it itself, drop it into the operating system and put you out of that business."[10]

Browser Market Shares

Netscape's Navigator browser was introduced in December 1994. Within two months, it captured 60 percent of the market and reached 90 percent in early 1996. Then it began to decline and reached less than 50 percent by mid-1998. In the meantime, Microsoft's IE share rose from 5 percent after its introduction to almost 50 percent in mid-1998. There were many practitioners who asserted that Netscape's browser was superior to Microsoft's. Why, therefore, did these market shares move as they did? The primary cause, said the government, was Microsoft's anticompetitive behavior.

Microsoft's Response

Microsoft replied point by point to the charges of both the DOJ and the states' Attorneys General.[11] The company denied it was a monopoly and had engaged in uncompetitive practices. It said, "computer software is one of the fastest moving, most innovative and most competitive businesses in history." At the trial, Microsoft's lead attorney, John Warden, said, ". . . everything Microsoft has done is standard competitive behavior; its actions don't even come close to violating antitrust law."[12]

Warden caustically assailed the government's case. He said the case was "not really an antitrust case, but a return of the Luddites, the nineteenth century reactionaries who . . . went around smashing machines with sledgehammers." Admittedly, Microsoft is a tough competitor, he said, but such behavior is legal: ". . . the antitrust laws are not a code of civility."[13]

Competition in the Computer Industry

In a comprehensive "white paper," Microsoft described in detail why it was not a monopoly and why it was not in violation of the antitrust laws. "Antitrust

---

[10]Steve Lohr and John Markoff, "How Software's Giant Played Hardball Game," *New York Times,* October 8, 1998.

[11]*Defendant Microsoft Corporation's Answer to the Complaint Filed by the U.S. Department of Justice, United States of America* v. *Microsoft Corporation,* United States District Court for the District of Columbia, No. 98–1232 (TPJ), July 28, 1998; and *Defendant Microsoft Corporation's Answer to Plaintiff States' First Amended Complaint and Counterclaim, State of New York ex. rel.* v. *Microsoft Corporation,* United States District Court for the District Court of Columbia, No. 98–1232 (TPJ), July 28, 1998.

[12]Quoted in Joseph Nocera, "High Noon," *Fortune,* November 23, 1998, p. 166.

[13]Quoted in John R. Wilke, "Microsoft Blasts Prosecution as 'Return of the Luddites,'" *The Wall Street Journal,* October 21, 1998.

policy," said the company, "seeks to promote low prices, high output, and rapid innovation. On all three measures, the personal computer software industry generally—and Microsoft in particular—is a model of competitiveness."[14]

In the "white paper," the company claimed it accounted for less than 1 percent of the industry revenues, which totaled $1 trillion in 1996. While the company is dominant as a software producer, it is but one of more than 10,000 software companies in the United States and thousands overseas. The top twenty independent software publishers, including Microsoft, account for only 42 percent of total software revenues. While Microsoft is best known for its computer operating systems, such as Windows, it faces intense competition from many companies, such as IBM, Hewlett-Packard, Sun Microsystems, Apple, AOL, and other major companies. The high market share of Microsoft in operating systems today may easily be gone tomorrow, said the company in these words:

> In the software industry . . . the significance of a high market share in any particular segment is quite limited because the figure represents only a snapshot of current software shipments. Market share numbers do not reflect the highly dynamic nature of the software industry, where entire business segments can disappear virtually overnight as new technologies are developed.[15]

Microsoft claims that personal computer hardware and software prices are constantly falling and that, in important degree, is due to Microsoft's development of its standard operating system. Furthermore, Microsoft has substantially reduced prices on its own products.

Innovation in the computer industry has been dazzling. Product life cycles are very short, typically twelve to eighteen months. Microsoft and other software producers are shipping products that were nonexistent a few years ago. Microsoft has been a major catalyst in innovation and this will continue. Its research budget for 1998 amounts to $2.6 billion. The rapidity of innovation, of course, contributes to the intense competition in the industry. There is always the threat of new technology completely obsoleting existing products.

In a 320 page written testimony Richard L. Schmalensee, an MIT economist and former student of Franklin Fisher, supported these defenses. He wrote:

> Microsoft does not have monopoly power over the PC operating system software category. Microsoft cannot, and has not, excluded competition from this category. Microsoft cannot control prices in this category because it is constrained by competition from its own installed base, piracy, competition from other operating systems, and, most importantly, the long-run considerations that drive all pricing and innovation in the microcomputer software industry.[16]

---

[14]Microsoft PressPass, "Competition in the Software Industry," January 1998, http://www.microsoft.com/presspass/doj/1–98whitepaper.htm, July 25, 1998.

[15]Ibid.

[16]Richard L. Schmalensee, Direct Testimony, in the United States District Court for the District of Columbia, *United States of America Plaintiffs* v. *Microsoft Corporation Defendant*, Civil Action No. 98–1232 (TPJ), January 13, 1999, p. E-2–3.

The government at the trial produced memoranda, e-mail, and other documents to support its charges. Microsoft accuses the government of selecting snippets from this huge volume of information and using it out of context. Here are some of the facts, says Microsoft. Unless otherwise specified, the following is from Microsoft's response to the government's charges.

Relations with Netscape

The first meeting with Netscape was the result of an invitation by James Clark, one of the co-founders of Netscape. Clark sent Microsoft an e-mail on December 29, 1994, six months before the meeting of June 21, 1995, with a plea to do business with Microsoft. "We never planned to compete with you," Clark wrote. "We'd like you to work with us . . . Depending on the interest level, you might take an equity position to divide the market."[17]

> Microsoft has consistently said that the 1995 meeting was a . . . standard meeting between two companies exploring the possibility of forging a strategic partnership in some areas of their businesses, while continuing to compete in many others—the same kind of relationship Sun Microsystems and IBM and many other companies have with each other. The facts support this.[18]

One of the reasons Netscape lost market share is because consumers believed Microsoft's IE was a superior product. At the beginning, Microsoft admits Netscape's Navigator was a better product than IE. When IE was developed, however, many reviewers said the IE was the superior product. Actually, it was only after IE began beating Navigator on its merits that it started gaining users. Microsoft admits, however, that Netscape continues as a vigorous competitor to Microsoft with new successful versions of its Navigator.

Bundling

Microsoft has often used free software as a competitive strategy. Wrapping IE into Windows is just another application of that strategy. Not only is Microsoft giving consumers what they want, but it benefits them in terms of price. If consumers do not want to use IE, they can delete it from the operating system. Furthermore, consumers can use Netscape if they choose because it can be introduced into Windows. So they have a choice. "It takes no more than a few mouse-clicks or keystrokes to install, say, Netscape's browser and display it prominently on the PC desktop. Given that Netscape's share of browser usage remains at more than 50 percent, many Windows users clearly do just that."[19]

---

[17]Quoted in Nocera, "High Noon."

[18]Microsoft PressPass, "Fact vs. Fiction," http://www.microsoft.com/presspass/fvsf.htm, December 18, 1998, p. 3.

[19]Ibid, p. 4.

The government wants Microsoft to include Netscape's browser with Windows. Microsoft says that Netscape has consistently said it plans to use its browser technology as a basis for a new computing platform to make Windows obsolete. The DOJ, therefore, is asking Microsoft to incorporate a competitor's product that is intended to undermine and destroy Windows. That is unprecedented and unreasonable. Microsoft should not be asked to distribute its competitor's products along with its own.

> Coca-Cola is not forced to distribute Pepsi. McDonald's is not forced to sell Burger King or Wendy's hamburgers. Sears is not forced to allocate floor space in its stores to Wal-Mart. By the same token, Microsoft should not be required to build competing—and duplicative—browser technology into its operating system. Netscape is free to have its product running on Windows, included on new machines from computer manufacturers or available in many other ways. It should not be forced in as part of Windows.[20]

In response to allegations that Microsoft bundled its browser into Windows to thwart competition, James E. Allchin, senior vice president for Microsoft personal and business sytems, testified that the decision to give away free the IE "was a straightforward product-design decision that benefits consumers."[21]

Schmalensee testified also that "Microsoft did not, in fact, foreclose Netscape from distributing its Web-browsing software." Netscape's share of the browser market, he said, was due to the superiority of IE.[22]

Contracts with OEMs

The licensing agreements Microsoft has made with OEMs have been standard in the industry. It is common practice that these contracts contain a provision not to modify or delete any part of Microsoft's copyrighted Windows software without license from the company to do so. Microsoft rightfully insists that the first time an end user turns on the computer, the system is permitted to go through the sequence as designed. OEMs, as well as users, can add icons on Windows desktop. Such agreements are widespread in industry and are both legal and pro-competitive.

Contracts with ISPs and ICPs

Microsoft responded as follows to the government's charges that these contracts included unfair competitive practices:

---

[20]Ibid, p. 6.
[21]Steve Lohr and Amy Harmon, "Microsoft Executive Defends Folding Browser Into Windows," *New York Times,* January 28, 1999.
[22]Richard L. Schmalensee, Direct Testimony, op. cit., p. 322.

In attacking Microsoft's cross-marketing agreements with other firms, the Complaint seeks to deny to Microsoft the use of ordinary competitive arrangements. The challenged contracts (i) foreclose no one from full and complete access to the many available channels for the distribution of software providing web browsing functionality and (ii) are contracts for the promotion of commerce.

These contracts are commonplace in the industry and work to the mutual benefit of both parties. Microsoft helps to promote and distribute their products and they help to promote and distribute Microsoft's. There is nothing wrong with that. It is legal and pro-competitive.

Java

Microsoft claimed its "tweaking" of Java was within the contractual agreement. At the trial, Microsoft's lawyers said many consumers were frustrated with Java's shortcomings and Microsoft was trying to improve the language. In the meantime, the company said, it had developed its own technology that was much faster than Java and better designed. Industry reviewers, said the lawyers, found the Microsoft system superior to Sun's. *PC Magazine,* said Microsoft, "named Microsoft's Java implementation its Editor's Choice, stating that Microsoft's implementation was more compatible than even Sun Microsystems' own Java implementation . . ."[23]

Who Was Harmed?

A reporter at the trial observed that Microsoft's defense "boils down to one question: Where's the harm?"[24] While Warden never used these words, the question was put in hundreds of ways to the witnesses. As noted above, the DOJ and some of its witnesses claim that Microsoft's monopoly and behavior have harmed consumers. Franklin Fisher, in his written testimony said: "There is substantial probability that these anti-competitive actions will permit MS to retain its power over price in operating systems and will inhibit development of MS-independent innovations. Both would harm consumer welfare."[25]

Microsoft has repeatedly taken the position that consumers have benefited. Richard Schmalensee in his written testimony concluded: "Consumers have benefited from lower prices, greater output, better software and higher rates of innovation as a result of the actions taken by Microsoft that Plaintiffs seek to enjoin."[26]

---

[23]Microsoft PressPass, "Fact vs. Fiction," op. cit., p. 6.
[24]Steve Lohr, "Microsoft Refrain: Who Was Harmed?" *New York Times,* October 26, 1998.
[25]Franklin M. Fisher, Direct Testimony, op. cit., p. 11.
[26]Richard L. Schmalensee, Direct Testimony, op. cit., p. E-2.

Expert Opinions

In a high profile case such as this, experts are called upon to testify and others gratuitously offer their comments. Here are a few examples.

For the Government

Robert H. Bork, author of an authoritative book on antitrust,[27] former judge, currently a scholar at the American Enterprise Institute, and representing Netscape, strongly supports the government's charges. He says the company has a monopoly and "will do whatever it takes to keep that monopoly . . . Microsoft employs a minefield of restrictive agreements that make it hard for rivals to attack, coupled with direct assaults upon Netscape and Sun."[28]

James F. Rill, former assistant attorney general in the Antitrust Division of DOJ, wrote: " . . . abuse of the operating-system monopoly could give Microsoft control over Internet access and enable it to exact a consumer toll on every electronic transaction."[29]

Bob Dole, past Senate majority leader and presidential candidate, observed: "This case, despite the company's protests, is not about one man, Gates, or one company, Microsoft. It is about a fundamental principle of our economic system: open and free competition. When a dominant company artificially dictates how, where and even if consumers have choice in the online marketplace, it is time for the government to step in and enforce the antitrust laws."[30]

In Defense of Microsoft

William F. Bacter, a former Assistant U.S. Attorney General in charge of the Antitrust Division of DOJ, and a consultant to Microsoft, writes that the case simply is to prevent Microsoft from designing its own software. The integration of IE into Windows is legal and creates advantages for the consumer. "Microsoft's practices, neither separately nor collectively, have not foreclosed Netscape from the market."[31] He also adds that " . . . [of] independent technical reviewers who have compared the two, Internet Explorer today is superior to Netscape's web browsing software."[32]

Gary S. Becker, Nobel laureate, professor at the University of Chicago, and a fellow of the Hoover Institution, writes that ". . . we should resist proposals for greater government oversight of computing and other network industries with rapid progress. Competitors that develop superior technologies are far

---

[27]Robert H. Bork, *The Antitrust Paradox*, New York: Basic Books, Inc., 1978.
[28]Robert H. Bork, "The Most Misunderstood Antitrust Case," *The Wall Street Journal*, May 22, 1998.
[29]James F. Rill, "Why Bill Gates Is Wrong," *The Wall Street Journal*, November 20, 1997.
[30]Bob Dole, "Microsoft Must Obey the Law," *Los Angeles Times*, November 24, 1997.
[31]William F. Baxter, "Microsoft is Wrongly Targeted," *Los Angeles Times*, October 19, 1998.
[32]Ibid.

better protectors of consumers than government officials and bureaucrats who march to the beat of political popularity."[33]

He says that computer operating systems involve what economists call "network externalities." This is a phenomenon that describes a situation where a company attains a decisive lead in an industry and consumers are strongly drawn to it. In the case of computers, the lead of Microsoft influences software producers to design only for Microsoft because that is where sales are. Consumers then find advantages in having access to more choices. Under such circumstances, it is difficult for new entrants. But the situation is legal.

Robert J. Barro, professor of economics at Harvard University, and a fellow of the Hoover Institution, writes that the usual rationale for government action is to promote competition and thus lower prices and quicken innovation. That is precisely what has been going on in the computer industry. "The bottom line is that the best policy for the government in the computer industry is to stay out of it."[34]

The Changed Industry Structure

In December 1998, America Online Inc. announced a $4.2 billion bid to acquire Netscape Communications Corp. and to form an alliance with Sun Microsystems Inc. The announcement prompted Charles Condon, Attorney General of South Carolina, to pull out of the case. He said the merger proves that "competition is alive and well" in the technology industry.[35] Microsoft also said the merger and alliance show clearly that it faces strong competition. Spokesmen for the DOJ said the action made no difference at all in its case against Microsoft.

Bill Gates Looks Ahead

In his book *The Road Ahead*, Bill Gates describes the potential of what he then called the new developing information highway. Currently it is loaded with technological wonders, he said, and there undoubtedly will be many more to come. It will be a world filled with aggressive competitors. In this world, he expressed concern about the ability of Microsoft to maintain its dominant position. He wrote:

> It's a little scary that as computer technology has moved ahead there's never been a leader from one era who was also a leader in the next. Microsoft has been a

---

[33]Gary S. Becker, "Let the Marketplace Judge Microsoft," *Business Week*, April 6, 1998.

[34]Robert J. Barro, "Why the Antitrust Cops Should Lay Off High Tech," *Business Week*, August 17, 1998.

[35]Jube Shiver Jr., "United Front Cracks in Case against Microsoft," *Los Angeles Times*, December 8, 1998.

leader in the PC era. So from a historical perspective, I guess Microsoft is disqualified from leading in the highway era of the Information Age. But I want to defy historical tradition.[36]

Questions

1. Why do you think Microsoft was so successful up to the time of the DOJ–Microsoft trial?
2. Do you believe Microsoft has a monopoly as defined by the DOJ, or does its power derive only from what economists call "network externalities"?
3. When Microsoft and Netscape executives first met, the DOJ claims Microsoft sought to divide the market illegally. Microsoft says the meeting merely sought to develop common industry working relationships. What do you think happened?
4. Argue pro and con that Microsoft used anticompetitive power in arranging agreements with ISPs, ICPs, and OEMs.
5. Does the merger of AOL and Netscape and the partnership with Sun Microsystems prove there is strong competition in the PC operating systems market?
6. If you were the judge in this case, would you rule for the DOJ or Microsoft? Explain your position.

---

[36]Gates, *The Road Ahead,* p. 18.

11

Business in the Political Process

Archer Daniels Midland Company, often called simply ADM, is a giant food and agricultural products firm. It has a reputation for working quietly and effectively behind the scenes in Washington, D.C. The story of ethanol is illustrative.

Ethanol is methyl alcohol, the ingredient added to alcoholic beverages. It is made from corn by adding yeast to ferment sugars and starches. Ethanol is one of a number of so-called oxygenates, or oxygen-containing substances, that can be combined with gasoline, usually at about 10 percent of the mixture, to create a "reformulated" fuel for ordinary cars and trucks. The presence of additional oxygen reduces polluting emissions. Since it comes from corn, it saves oil and is a renewable resource. ADM produces more ethanol than any other company.

MTBE, or methyl tertiary butyl ether, is an oxygenate derived from natural gas that competes with ethanol. ADM does not make MTBE; big oil companies do. Both ethanol and MTBE improve combustion and reduce smog-producing emissions. Just which one is better is a matter of opinion. Various studies claim more environmental benefits for one over the other. There is no body of evidence that ethanol is superior. However, policy in Washington, D.C., is not always based on scientific merit.

Over the years, Congress has given ethanol a series of subsidies, incentives, and boosts not given to MTBE. The cost of making ethanol is so high that gasoline reformulated with it could not compete at the gas pump. In 1990 lobbyists for ADM managed to get Congress to subsidize ethanol by passing a federal tax credit of 5.4 cents per gallon for gasoline that contains it. This means that the federal gasoline tax of 18.3 cents per gallon is reduced to 12.9 cents, which lowers the purchase price. Congress also enacted a tax credit for companies that blended ethanol and gasoline. Together, these tax incentives made ethanol about 30 percent less expensive than MTBE. In addition, beginning in 1995, Congress required that nine cities with the worst smog use gasoline containing an oxygenate. This created a huge market for both ethanol and MTBE.

Reformers attack the ethanol subsidy as an example of corporate welfare at its worst. The 5.4-cent-per-gallon tax credit has meant more than $7 billion in lost tax revenue to the federal government since 1990, money that could have been used on highway construction and repair. In effect, much of this money has been transferred to employees and stockholders of ADM. Showing any benefit to the American public from using ethanol is difficult. In addition to seeing tax dollars siphoned away, the public pays more for corn. Demand for corn to convert to fuel raises the price of each bushel that goes to feed beef or into food products for the grocery store.

To make a case for the ethanol, its advocates claim that it reduces dependence on imported oil, is environmentally friendly, and is based on a renewable resource—corn. "Tankers will not spill ethanol into our oceans," Senator Carol Moseley-Braun (D-Ill.) once assured a grateful nation.[1] Braun had received at least $16,000 in campaign contributions from ADM and its executives in the three years preceding this statement. But ethanol constitutes no more than 1 percent of the nation's gasoline volume and studies conclude that there is no extra environmental benefit from using it instead of MTBE. If the market were allowed to take its course without government interference, ethanol would disappear from gasoline. But opponents of the subsidy are unable to end it.

One reason is that ADM and its executives are generous contributors to both parties. In the decade between 1987 and 1997, the company and its chairman, Dwayne Andreas, gave soft money contributions of $3 million and its political action committee gave another $1.2 million.[2] ADM's contribution strategy is to give to the party in power. In the late 1980s, the company and its executives ladled money to President Bush and the Republican party, but with the election of President Clinton in 1992, the biggest donations flowed to the Democrats. After the Republicans gained majorities in both houses of Congress in 1994, ADM tipped the scales of giving back toward them. Andreas has denied that these contributions are intended to elicit specific favors.

---

[1]*Congressional Record,* March 11, 1998, p. S1754.

[2]These figures are based on a study by Common Cause. See "Fuel's Gold," *Common Cause News,* http://www.commoncause.org/publications/fuelsgold_toc.htm.

The most recent attempt to slay the ethanol tax break came in 1998. In the House of Representatives, lawmakers friendly to ADM tried to amend a transportation spending bill to extend the subsidy, but the Ways and Means Committee, whose chairman Bill Archer (R-Tex.) called the subsidy "highway robbery," rejected the amendment by a vote of 22-to-11. The Senate, however, passed a bill giving the subsidy life until 2007. Speaker of the House Newt Gingrich (R-Ga.) then clinched the victory for ADM by naming ethanol supporters to the joint House–Senate conference committee that met to reconcile the two versions of the bill. These appointments were a rebuke to Archer, who would normally have selected the members from the House side. On the House floor, Archer called the ethanol measure an "outdated and reckless subsidy" and said that he would vote against the entire $215 billion spending bill for that reason.[3] Archer had received no campaign contributions from ADM for at least several years. The bill passed and the subsidy is entrenched until 2007.

The ADM story illustrates how corporations can achieve tangible benefits by being politically active. In this chapter we discuss in more detail a range of tactics that business uses to influence government. We begin, however, with a brief discussion of the nature of American government and a short history of business's role in politics.

How the Structure of American Government Affects Businesses

Throughout American history, business has sought and exercised political power in a government that is extraordinarily open to influence. This power, whether used for good or ill, is exercised on constitutional terrain created by the Founding Fathers over 200 years ago. The Constitution of the United States, as elaborated by judicial interpretation since its adoption in 1789, establishes the formal structure and broad rules of political activity. Its formal provisions predispose a certain pragmatic, freewheeling political culture in day-to-day political life.

Several basic features of the Constitution shape the political system. Each stands as a barrier to the concentrated power that the Founders feared would lead to tyranny. Each has consequences for corporate political activity.

First, the Constitution sets up a *federal* system, or a government in which powers are divided between a national government and fifty state governments. This structure has great significance for business, particularly for large corporations with national operations. These corporations are affected by political actions at different levels and in many places.

---

[3]*Congressional Record,* May 22, 1998, p. H3962.

The *supremacy clause* in the Constitution stipulates that when the federal government passes a law, it preempts, or takes precedence over, state laws on the same subject. Sometimes business prefers federal regulation. It has to follow one law instead of as many as fifty different state laws. In the 1960s, for example, New York and some other states tried to pass laws requiring health warning labels on cigarette packages. If states had been allowed one-by-one to require labels, the tobacco companies would have had to print specially worded cigarette packs for sale in each state. Therefore, they supported legislation in Congress that, when passed, preempted that area of law and required a uniform warning label across the country. The insurance industry, on the other hand, fights federal regulation of its activities, preferring instead oversight by state insurance commissions. Insurance companies, which are big employers and heavy campaign contributors in many states, receive gentle treatment from these commissions. In 1992 a bill was introduced in Congress to set up a federal agency to regulate insurers, but the industry mobilized and defeated federal preemption of state agencies.

Second, the Constitution establishes a system of *separation of powers*, whereby the three branches of the federal government—legislative, executive, and judicial—have checks and balances over each other. The states mimic these power-sharing arrangements in their governments. For business, this means that the actions of one branch do not fully define public policy. For example, after Congress passes a law, corporations lobby regulatory agencies in the executive branch to get favorable implementation of its provisions.

Third, the Constitution provides for *judicial review*. This is the power of judges, ultimately those of the Supreme Court, to review actions of government officials and to refuse to uphold those that conflict with their interpretation of the Constitution. A classic example of judicial review occurred in the spring of 1952 when U.S. military forces in Korea were hard-pressed and a strike by the steelworkers' union threatened to shut down steel production. President Harry Truman ordered his Secretary of Commerce to take possession of and run the steel industry. However, the Supreme Court held that Truman had exceeded his constitutional powers and the steel companies were returned to private hands.[4] This case is also an example of the relative independence of business from government authority that is permitted in the American system. In addition to reviewing government actions, the Supreme Court also defines and redefines the great clauses of the Constitution.

The government structure created by the Constitution is open. It diffuses power, creates many points of access, and invites business and other interests to attempt influence. Because no single, central authority exists, significant government action often requires widespread cooperation among levels and branches of government that share power. The system also is particularly vulnerable to

---

[4]*Youngstown Sheet & Tube Co.* v. *Sawyer,* 343 U.S. 579. The basis for the Court's ruling was that Congress had once considered giving presidents the power to seize industries in similar circumstances but had not done so.

blockage and delay. Because significant actions require the combined authority of several elements in the political arena, special interests can block action by getting a favorable hearing at only one juncture. To get action, on the other hand, an interest like business must successfully pressure many actors in the political equation. Thus, there has developed a style in the American system, in which interests are willing to bargain, compromise, and form temporary alliances to achieve their goals rather than stand firm on rigid ideological positions.

The First Amendment is an additional feature of the Constitution critical to business. It protects the right of business to organize and press its agenda on government. In its elegantly archaic language is stated the right "to petition the Government for a redress of grievances." The First Amendment also protects rights of free speech, freedom of the press, and freedom of assembly—all critical for pressuring government. Without these guarantees, the letter-writing campaigns, speeches, newspaper editorials, and advertisements that business orchestrates might be banned. Imagine how undesirably different our system would be if the public, angered by "windfall" profits, pressured Congress to restrict the lobbying rights of some industry. While the corporate right of free speech is expansive, it is restricted in one area. The Supreme Court has defined monetary campaign contributions as a form of speech[5] and, as will be explained later in this chapter, these contributions are restricted because of fears that corporate money will corrupt elections.

A History of Political Dominance by Business

Though not ordained in the Constitution, the preeminence of business interests in the political pressure equation has been an enduring fact in America. Some historians believe that the Revolutionary War of 1775–1783 was fought to free colonial business interests from smothering British mercantile policies.[6] The Founders who later drafted the Constitution were an economic elite. John Jay and Robert Morris, for example, were among the wealthiest men in the colonies. It comes as no surprise that the government arrangements they fabricated were conducive to domination by business interests. The prominent historian Charles Beard argued that the Constitution was an "economic document" drawn up and ratified by propertied interests, for their own benefit.[7] His thesis was and remains controversial, in part because it trivializes the importance of philosophical, social, and cultural forces in the politics of constitutional

---

[5]In *Buckley* v. *Valeo*, 424 U.S. 1 (1976).

[6]See, for example, Clarence L. Ver Steeg, "The American Revolution Considered as an Economic Movement," *Huntington Library Quarterly*, August 1957.

[7]Charles Beard, *An Economic Interpretation of the Constitution of the United States*, New York: Macmillan, 1913.

adoption.[8] Yet the record of business in American politics subsequent to the adoption of the Constitution is one of virtually unbroken predominance.

The Groundwork Is Laid

Business interests were important in the new nation but did not dominate to the extent that they would later. There were few large companies. The economy was 90 percent agricultural, so farmers and planters were a major part of the political elite. Their interests balanced and checked those of infant industry. The fledgling government was a tiny presence. Economic regulation was virtually nonexistent. Nevertheless, under the leadership of the first Secretary of the Treasury, Alexander Hamilton, the new central government was soon turned toward the promotion of industry. Hamilton mistrusted the common citizen, having once said that "the people is a great beast"; he advocated rule by an economic elite.[9] Over the objections of Thomas Jefferson and others, and with the support of business leaders, Hamilton implemented a visionary program to stimulate the economy. His actions laid essential groundwork for the unexampled industrial growth that came in the next century.

Economic development was rapid. Although Jefferson served as president from 1800 to 1808, it was already too late to reverse Hamilton's commitment of government machinery to the promotion of industry. As the economy expanded, so also did the political power of business.

Ascendance, Corruption, and Reform

Throughout the nineteenth century, business interests grew in strength. When the Civil War decimated the power base of southern agriculture, a major counterweight to the power of northern industry vanished. In the period following the Civil War, big business dominated state governments and the federal government in a way never seen before or since. It was a time of great imbalance, in which economic interests faced only frail obstacles. It was commonplace for corporations to manipulate the politics of whole states. West Virginia and Kentucky were dominated by coal companies. New York, a number of midwestern states, and California were dominated by railroads. Montana politics was controlled by the Anaconda Copper Mining Company. In Ohio, Texas, and Pennsylvania, oil companies were predominant; the great critic of Standard Oil, Henry Demarest Lloyd, wrote that "the Standard has done everything with the Pennsylvania legislature, except refine it."[10] Business was also

---

[8]See, for example, Robert E. Brown, *Charles Beard and the Constitution,* Princeton: Princeton University Press, 1956; and Forrest McDonald, *We the People: The Economic Origins of the Constitution,* Chicago: University of Chicago Press, 1963.

[9]Quoted in Vernon Louis Parrington, *Main Currents in American Thought,* vol. 1, New York: Harcourt, Brace, 1958, p. 300. Originally published in 1927.

[10]"The Story of a Great Monopoly," *The Atlantic,* March 1881, p. 322.

Nineteenth century political cartoonist Joseph Keppler (1838–1894) was a critic of big business who particularly resented the ascendancy of moneyed interests in politics. This cartoon, which appeared in the magazine Puck *on January 23, 1889, reflected his exasperation with the situation in that period.*

THE BOSSES OF THE SENATE.

predominant in Washington, D.C. Through ascendancy in the Republican party, corporations had decisive influence over the nomination and election of a string of pro-business Republican presidents from Ulysses S. Grant in 1868 to William McKinley in 1900.[11] In the Congress, senators were suborned by business money; some even openly represented companies and industries. One observer noted that in 1889,

> a United States senator . . . represented something more than a state, more even than a region. He represented principalities and powers in business. One senator, for instance, represented the Union Pacific Railway System, another the New York Central, still another the insurance interests of New York and New Jersey . . . Coal and iron owned a coterie from the Middle and Eastern seaport states. Cotton had half a dozen senators. And so it went.[12]

---

[11]The exception was the election of the Democrat and reformer Grover Cleveland in 1884. But even Cleveland had strong supporters from the business community, Andrew Carnegie and James J. Hill among them. His administration never threatened business interests.

[12]William Allen White, *Masks in a Pageant*, New York: Macmillan, 1928, p. 79.

Under these circumstances, corruption was rampant. Grant's first term, for example, was stained by the famous "whiskey ring" scandals in which liquor companies cheated in paying taxes and a member of Grant's cabinet solicited bribes in exchange for licenses to sell liquor to Indian tribes. In Grant's second term, the Crédit Mobilier Company gave away shares of stock to members of Congress to avoid investigation of its fraudulent railroad construction work.

The soaring political fortunes of businesses in the post–Civil War era invited reaction. A counterbalancing of corporate power began that continues to this day. Late in the century, farmers sought to reassert agrarian values with the Populist party. They floundered, but not before wresting control of a number of state legislatures from corporations. Two other formidable adversaries emerged. One was organized labor. The other was the powerful Anti-Saloon League, which advocated prohibition of alcoholic beverages. Like labor, the Anti-Saloon League became a strong national foe of business. Brewers and distillers were not its only adversaries. Big corporations in many industries worked against prohibition because they opposed the principle and onset of more government regulation.

After 1900, reforms of the progressive movement curtailed overweening corporate power. For example, the Seventeenth Amendment in 1913 instituted the direct election of senators by voters in each state. Corporations fought the amendment. Before, senators had been chosen by state legislatures, a procedure that invited corrupting influence by big corporations. For example, in 1884, representatives of Standard Oil called members of the Ohio legislature one by one into a back room where $65,000 in bribes were handed out to obtain the election of Henry B. Payne to the Senate. One witness saw "canvas bags and coin bags and cases for greenbacks littered and scattered around the room and on the table and on the floor . . . with something green sticking out."[13] Corporations also fought suffrage for women. The battle was led by liquor companies, which feared that women would vote for prohibition. But there was broader fear of women voters. It was widely believed by businessmen that women would vote for radical and socialist measures. The powerful Women's Christian Temperance Union, which had as many as 10,000 local chapters by 1890, frightened business by standing against liquor, child labor, and income inequality. But after adoption of the Nineteenth Amendment in 1920, the women's vote brought no special change in national politics.

The great political reforms of the progressive era were reactions to corruption in a political system dominated by business. It would be a mistake, however, to conclude that because of reforms and newly emerged opponents, the primacy of economic interests had been eclipsed. While business was more often checked after the turn of the century, it remained preeminent. Corruption continued. In 1920 Warren G. Harding, a back-room candidate selected by powerful business interests at a deadlocked Republican party convention, was

---

[13]Quoted in Henry Demarest Lloyd, *Wealth Against Commonwealth,* New York: Harper, 1898, pp. 377–78.

elected president. His vice president was Calvin Coolidge, the rabidly antilabor ex-governor of Massachusetts. Harding's administration was so beset by scandals in which officials accepted money for granting favors to corporations that Congress was considering impeaching him when he died of a stroke in 1923. The worst scandal involved Secretary of the Interior Albert B. Fall, who accepted bribes from oil company executives in return for the right to pump oil from government reserves in Teapot Dome, Wyoming. The Teapot Dome affair came to light only after Harding's death, but so besmirched his reputation that it was eight years before his grand tomb in Marion, Ohio, could be dedicated.

A Step Backwards under the New Deal

By the time that Harding had been officially laid to rest, the stock market had crashed and catastrophic economic depression racked the country. Conservative business executives argued that the depression would correct itself without government action. After the election of Franklin D. Roosevelt in 1932, corporations fought his efforts to regulate banking and industry, strengthen labor unions, and enact social security. Du Pont, General Motors, and other firms supported the anti-Roosevelt Liberty Lobby, which opposed New Deal measures. Against social security, for example, business lobbyists argued that children would no longer support aging parents, that the required payroll tax would discourage workers and they would quit their jobs, and that its protection would remove the "romance of life."

Many executives hated Roosevelt. They said that he was bringing communism to the United States and called him names such as "Stalin Delano Roosevelt."[14] But business had lost its way. Corporate opposition to New Deal measures ran counter to public sentiment. It became ineffective and was sometimes disgraceful. In 1935, for example, utility lobbyists sent Congress 250,000 fake letters and telegrams in a losing effort to stop a bill. Subsequently they ran a whispering campaign saying Roosevelt was insane.

Much New Deal legislation was profoundly egalitarian and humanitarian and reasserted the tradition of agrarian idealism. Because business lacked a positive philosophy for change, its political power was greatly diminished. According to Edwin M. Epstein, "corporate political influence reached its nadir during the New Deal."[15] Roosevelt was hurt by all the hate and felt that through his major New Deal programs, he had saved capitalism in spite of the capitalists.

The New Deal was a political sea change born out of the Great Depression. One lasting legacy of the era was the philosophy that government should be used to correct the flaws of capitalism and control the economy so that prosperity would no longer depend solely on unbridled market forces.[16]

---

[14]William Manchester, *The Glory and the Dream,* vol. 1, Boston: Little, Brown, 1973, p. 126.

[15]*The Corporation in American Politics*, Englewood Cliffs, N.J.: Prentice Hall, 1969, p. 31.

[16]For the story of how this philosophy developed during the New Deal years, see Alan Brinkley, *The End of Reform: New Deal Liberalism in Recession and War*, New York: Knopf, 1995.

Government would also be used to create a "welfare state" to protect citizens from want. Whereas, in the past, government had kept its hands off corporations, now it would actively use interest rates, regulation, taxes, subsidies, and other policy instruments to control them. Whereas, in the past, most domestic spending had been for infrastructure programs that promoted business, spending would increasingly focus on social programs such as social security. These changes laid the groundwork for an increasingly large, powerful, and activist federal government.

Postwar Politics and Winds of Change

In the 1940s, industry's patriotic World War II production record and subsequent postwar prosperity quieted lingering public restiveness about corporate political activity. During the 1950s, corporations once again predominated in a very hospitable political environment. In the years between 1952 and 1960, Dwight D. Eisenhower was a pro-business president with a cabinet dominated by political appointees from business. A pro-business conservative coalition of southern Democrats and Republicans in Congress ensured legislative support. Corporations could promote their policy agendas by influencing a small number of leaders. Charls E. Walker, an official in the Eisenhower administration and currently a business lobbyist, recalls how only four men shaped economic policy.

> These four officials were President Eisenhower, Treasury Secretary Robert Anderson, Speaker of the House Sam Rayburn, and Senate majority leader Lyndon B. Johnson. These four men would get together every week over a drink at the White House and the President would say, "I think we ought to do this or that." Then Mr. Sam or LBJ might say, "Well, that's a real good idea; send it up and we'll get it through." And they would. They could deliver because at that time they had great influence in Congress, partly because of the seniority system."[17]

But changing political trends soon forced business into more aggressive and sophisticated forms of political intervention. During the 1960s and 1970s, national politics became dominated by a liberal reform agenda. New groups arose to challenge business, reforms in Congress made that institution more openly democratic and responsive to business's foes, business was bridled with massive new regulatory programs, and the government dramatically increased the scope of its activities.[18] During this period, the business agenda suffered defeats at the hands of public interest groups and increasingly powerful agency heads in government. These defeats encouraged corporations to become more aggressive and sophisticated in their political activity.

---

[17]Quoted in Gene E. Bradley, "How to Work in Washington: Building Understanding for Your Business," *Columbia Journal of World Business*, Spring 1994, p. 53.

[18]These factors are analyzed by David Vogel in *Fluctuating Fortunes: The Political Power of Business in America*, New York: Basic Books, 1989, chaps. 3–6.

The Rise of Antagonistic Groups

During the late 1960s, the climate of pressure politics changed with the rise of new groups focused on consumer, environmental, taxpayer, civil rights, and other issues. Some, including Ralph Nader's Public Citizen, the Natural Resources Defense Council, and the Consumer Federation of America, grew to have many members and enough power to push an agenda of restricting and regulating corporations.

The presence of these groups changed the political arena for business. A decade earlier, corporations had dominated Washington politics with quiet, behind-the-scenes influence over key leaders. Now they faced an array of hostile groups that used a favorable climate of public opinion to wrest control of the policy agenda away from business. The result was a remarkable period, lasting roughly from the late 1960s to the late 1970s, during which the antagonists of business pressured Congress to enact one massive regulatory program after another.

The rise of groups hostile to business is part of a broader trend in which new groups of all kinds, including business groups, have been stimulated by growth of government. Government growth is reflected by fast-rising federal spending. In 1960 the federal budget was $92 billion. By 1980 it reached $591 billion, an increase of over 600 percent, and by 1997 it was $1.5 trillion.[19] As government grows, interest groups proliferate around policy areas. One estimate is that there are 23,000 organized interest groups, roughly 400 percent more than in the 1950s.[20]

The heyday of the public interest movement was short-lived. Citizen lobbies have some advantages. They can focus on dramatic, emotional, or confrontational issues and get media coverage. They also get the support of public opinion by identifying themselves with the lofty ideal of a public interest in opposition to the so-called special interests of business. GM, Ford, and Chrysler and their suppliers employ 1.5 million workers and big oil companies have tens of millions of shareholders. But public interest groups, even those with small memberships, often succeed in painting such corporations and industries as selfish entities seeking special favors in politics.

However, citizen lobbies are unable to match the financial resources of business. They cannot make as large political contributions and cannot afford to hire as many lobbyists. By the late 1970s, business interests had mobilized to fight the public interest movement in more sophisticated ways, and never again would the movement win great victories, although it remains as an institutionalized foe of business. The decline of the movement is shown in a recent

---

[19]Bureau of the Census, *Statistical Abstract of the United States: 1997*, Washington, D.C.: Government Printing Office, October 1997, table 515.

[20]Burdett A. Loomis and Allan J. Cigler, "Introduction: The Changing Nature of Interest Group Politics," in Cigler and Loomis, *Interest Group Politics*, 5th ed., Washington, D.C.: Congressional Quarterly Press, 1998, p. 11.

ranking by experts of 120 interest groups in order of their perceived power on Capitol Hill. Public interest/environmental/reform groups ranked low. The highest was the Sierra Club at No. 37, but the other major environmental groups ranked in the seventies and eighties. Common Cause was ranked No. 91 and Ralph Nader's Public Citizen was No. 111. The Nader-associated Center for Science in the Public Interest ranked last at No. 120.[21] A number of business groups are ranked among the most powerful.

When business and public interest groups collide today, it is often an uneven contest. For example, trucking firms are regulated by the Office of Motor Carriers (OMC), an agency located in the Federal Highway Administration. The OMC is not as active in policing the industry as safety advocates believe it should be, and in 1998 language was inserted in a 2,500-page appropriations bill in the House to make it part of the National Highway Traffic Safety Administration, a more activist and public-safety-oriented agency. This change in the location of the OMC within the federal bureaucracy was not trivial to the American Trucking Associations. Since the Republicans won a majority in Congress in 1994, the truckers had given more than $500,000 to Republican members. They lobbied to get the change removed from the bill. Highway safety advocates lobbied to keep it in, but could not match the trucker's influence and lost.

Diffusion of Power in Government

A second change in the climate of politics, in addition to new groups, has been the diffusion and decentralization of power in Washington, D.C. Three major reasons for this are (1) reforms in Congress, (2) the decline of political parties, and (3) increased complexity of government.

Traditionally, both the House and Senate were run autocratically by a few party leaders and powerful committee chairs. But the stubborn resistance of southern Democrats to civil rights legislation in the 1960s eventually led in 1974 to an uprising of junior members of Congress, who passed procedural reforms that democratized Congress by taking power from a few party leaders and spreading it widely. After 1974 subcommittees could hold hearings on any subject they wished; they developed large staffs and often became small fiefdoms of independent action. Instead of an institution dominated by a few leaders, Congress was described by one observer as "like a log floating down a river with 535 giant ants aboard, and each one thinks he or she is steering."[22]

After the reforms, business lobbyists had to contact nearly every member of a committee or subcommittee to get support for a measure, rather than just

---

[21]Jeffrey H. Birnbaum, "Washington's Power 25," *Fortune*, December 8, 1997, p. 147. Rankings were based on a survey of members of Congress, congressional and White House staff, lobbyists, academics, and pollsters.

[22]Bradley, "How to Work in Washington," p. 55.

the chair. Veteran lobbyist Charls E. Walker muses about the old days. "On a tax issue if you had the agreement of the chairman of Ways and Means, you could go out and play golf," but "these days you can't rest easy unless you've worked all the members."[23]

Changes outside Congress further undermined party leaders. One change was the rise of political action committees (PACs) formed by interest groups and corporations to contribute campaign money. Previously, Senate and House members who were loyal to party leaders could count on substantial campaign funds from the Republican and Democratic parties. After 1974, however, special-interest PACs began contributing such large amounts that legislators could act more independently of party leaders and still raise enough money to be reelected.

Other factors also eroded party authority. The media, particularly television, have replaced to some extent the parties as a source of information about candidates. Using television, politicians can bypass their parties and speak directly to voters. Also, the electorate is more highly educated and independent than it was in past eras and many voters identify only weakly with parties. Increasingly, they split their ballots and use decision cues other than party labels. Recent changes in campaign finance laws that allow party committees to raise large amounts of soft money that can be used to help elect candidates have restored some of the luster to parties, but they have not recovered their former importance by any means.

An additional cause of power diffusion is the growth in size and complexity of the federal government. Washington today is a maze of competing power centers, including elected officials, congressional committees, cabinet departments, regulatory agencies, political parties, courts, and interest groups. Relations among these power centers continuously shift as partisan tides, personal ambitions, power struggles, and emerging issues glide across the political landscape.

The sum total of government activity has a much greater impact on business than in the past and, because of this, corporations are far more politically active than in past eras. The expanded size and scope of government mean that its actions can be critical to company operations. Government action affects taxes, interest rates, import/export rules, antitrust policy, defense spending, regulatory compliance costs, health care costs, the dollar exchange rate, research and development, technology transfer, and other factors.

Many bills passed by Congress, such as tax, trade, and appropriations laws, directly affect earnings. At the urging of the National Association of Broadcasters, Congress in 1996 passed a law giving a free second frequency for digital picture signals to every television station in the country. These channels were estimated to be worth $30 billion. Another example is the situation faced by Walt Disney Corp. By the late 1990s, copyrights taken out by

---

[23]Quoted in Jill Abramson, "The Business of Persuasion Thrives in Nation's Capital," *New York Times*, September 29, 1998, p. A23.

founder Walt Disney in the 1920s and 1930s on Mickey Mouse, Donald Duck, Pluto, and other cartoon characters were about to expire under existing copyright laws that protected them for only 75 years. Walt Disney Corp. led a lobbying campaign that resulted in passage of the Copyright Term Extension Act in 1998, a statute that added 20 more years of life to the copyrights.

The Universe of Organized Business Interests

There are literally thousands of groups that represent business. What follows is a summary of this universe.

The most prominent groups are *peak associations* that represent many different companies and industries. The largest is the U.S. Chamber of Commerce, which was founded in 1912. The Chamber is a federation of 3,000 local and state chapters, 1,200 trade associations, and 215,000 companies. The next largest is the National Association of Manufacturers, founded in 1895, which, as the name suggests, represents manufacturers. It has a membership of 13,500 companies. Both the Chamber and the NAM have staffs of lobbyists who carry a conservative business agenda to Congress. These two groups are among the most powerful in Washington. But because they have large memberships of mostly smaller companies, when issues divide big and small firms, they are frequently unable to take the position of large corporations. Hence, several entities have arisen to represent the views of the largest corporations.

The Business Council was started in 1933 in response to Franklin D. Roosevelt's desire to have a business advisory body for the Department of Commerce. Its membership is limited to about 100 chief executives of blue-chip corporations who are picked to represent geographic regions and major industries. The Council does not take positions on policy issues or lobby in the traditional sense. Its members meet in forums with high government officials several times a year to exchange ideas. The Council's influence is very low key. A second group, the Committee for Economic Development (CED), is directed by approximately 250 trustees, most of whom are chief executives of the biggest corporations. Subcommittees of trustees focus on a few key policy areas, and their members commit themselves to speak out and lobby on behalf of CED positions. A third group, the Business Roundtable, was founded in 1972. Its membership consists of 200 CEOs of the largest corporations. Like the CED, the Business Roundtable focuses on a limited number of issues critical to big business and the member-CEOs personally lobby members of Congress. These three organizations are not noted for powerful arm-twisting. They take strong policy positions only on the few occasions when big corporations are united, and their style of direct lobbying by CEOs had more force years ago when Congress was dominated by a few autocrats.

In addition to these peak associations, more than 6,000 *trade associations* represent companies grouped by industry. Virtually every industry has one or more such associations. Illustrative are the American Boiler Manufacturers Association, the Compressed Gas Association, the Oxygenated Fuels Association, the National Turkey Federation, and the Institute of Makers of Explosives. In addition to lobbying for the industries they represent, trade groups also act as early warning systems in Washington for companies, hold training conferences, and publish data. Trade associations such as the American Petroleum Institute have large staffs and deep financial resources and are among the most powerful players in Washington.

About 700 corporations now have staffs of government relations experts in Washington. These *Washington offices* are set up mainly by big companies. General Electric, for example, has a staff of twelve lobbyists organized into teams that specialize in lobbying on government activity that affects the company's separate business lines. Some specialize in contacting Republicans; others work more with Democrats. The office also gives GE managers information about how events in Washington may affect their operations. Although a few smaller firms have Washington outposts, they are expensive, and small companies tend to rely on trade associations or hired lobbyists.

Business interests also form *coalitions* to create broader support. There are dozens of business interest coalitions in Washington at any given time. These coalitions of instant allies can be ephemeral. Many form around specific policy issues and break up when those issues pass. Not infrequently, coalition allies on one issue find themselves opposing each other on another issue.

Business gains strength when it is united, but there is frequent disunity. Skirmishes occur, for example, between domestic and foreign firms, truckers and railroads, manufacturers and retailers, banks and insurance companies, and raw material producers and end-product manufacturers. To illustrate, for many years the American Sugar Alliance, which represents sugar growers and refiners, has fought to preserve federal price supports on sugar in opposition to big corporations such as RJR Nabisco and Coca-Cola, which argue that higher sugar prices raise the cost of manufacturing cookies, candy, and soft drinks.

A powerful Coalition for Sugar Reform has tried for years to repeal price supports. Members include trade groups such as the Chocolate Manufacturers Association and the National Soft Drink Association, public interest groups including the Consumer Federation of America and Citizens for a Sound Economy, and several environmental groups that think the subsidies encourage cane-growing in the Florida everglades. The coalition hires top Washington lobbyists to work on Congress. Sometimes its tactics are theatrical, as when it sent lollipops to congressional staff with a note saying, "it's time to lick big sugar," and hired child actors dressed as newsboys of the 1800s to hand out a paper called *Bittersweet Times* containing its policy views.[24] But so far, the sugar growers have prevailed and subsidies continue.

---

[24]Jerry Hagstrom, "From the K Street Corridor," *National Journal,* May 3, 1997, p. 880.

The Government Relations Process

There are two basic areas of business involvement in politics. The first is government relations, or lobbying, in which business influences policy by contacting government officials. The second is the electoral process, in which business contributes money to political campaigns. Naturally, these areas are closely related.

Lobbying

Lobbying is advocating a viewpoint to government. A lobbyist is a person who presents the position of a corporation, interest group, or trade association to a government official. The word "lobbyist" entered the language in the nineteenth century to describe people who stood in the lobbies of legislative halls trying to buttonhole lawmakers.

Lobbying has negative connotations for many people, and business lobbyists are caricatured as pleading selfish interests, ignoring the public interest, and corrupting officials. However, lobbyists perform two valuable functions. First, they give lawmakers useful technical information about bills, and second, they give them politically relevant information about how constituents and special interests stand. These briefings are valuable to busy legislators who cannot possibly investigate every issue and provision in the roughly 12,000 bills before Congress each year. Each industry has quirks and problems, about which that industry's lobbyists have special knowledge. Says former Representative Bob S. Bergland:

> Lobbyists perform a useful function. For example, I served on two committees of the House, but there were dozens of bills on the floor from committees [of] which I was not a member. I oftentimes would not know how they would affect my district. I would call lobbyists and ask them. If they level with you it's terribly important.[25]

Lobbyists can mislead a lawmaker with bias and falsehood, but this is counterproductive. Lawmakers shut out lobbyists who mislead them. A lobbyist who lacks integrity loses access to the very people he or she earns a living from influencing. In addition, effective business lobbyists must defend their proposals on the basis of public benefit since legislators and regulators, as a rule, cannot justify acting simply to promote corporate self-interest.

Legislators sometimes recruit lobbyists to further their own agendas. Prior to the 1998 elections, Senate Majority Leader Trent Lott (R-Miss.) and House Speaker Newt Gingrich (R-Ga.) invited dozens of prominent lobbyists to a meeting at the offices of the National Republican Senatorial Committee. The guests were asked to raise $10 million from corporations they represented.

---

[25]In Myron Struck, "Deaver Probe Revives Doubts about 'Revolving Door' Ethics," *Insight*, June 9, 1986, p. 17.

The money was used for issue advertising to help Republican congressional candidates in close races.[26]

Lobbyists are loosely regulated. It is hard to restrict them because political advocacy is speech protected by the First Amendment. The House prohibits them from giving gifts of any size to members, including, for example, meals and travel. The Senate prohibits any gift of $50 or any series of gifts over $10 that add up to $100 per year. Beyond antibribery laws and these limits on the value of gifts, there are few legal restrictions on lobbying.[27]

How Business Lobbies Government

Business uses many lobbying techniques. In-person contact with officials is important, and lobbyists cultivate friendly relations. They telephone, write letters, and visit. They attend committee meetings in the House and Senate, and it is common practice for them to catch a representative's eye and give a thumbs-up or thumbs-down signal as various provisions come to a vote. Unless they are former senators or representatives, they are not allowed on the floor of either chamber, but they can stand in hallways and confer with lawmakers. Lobbyists in hallways with laptops draft debating points and legislative language that they send to lawmakers on the floor.

Direct contact with legislators, however critical, occupies only a minor portion of the typical lobbyist's day. Legislators are too busy to be available often or for long meetings. So most personal contacts are with staff rather than with lawmakers. Lobbyists do research and write promotional material. They organize and attend parties and fund-raisers. They serve in political campaigns for the advantage it gives them in working with elected officials later. Corporations and trade associations also set up charity events, seminars, and speaking engagements for members of Congress and regulatory agencies.

Corporations may employ in-house lobbyists. They may also hire advocacy firms, where top lobbyists make as much as $550 an hour to press their cases. The most prominent of these firms employ former administration officials, ex-legislators, and knowledgeable insiders of both political parties to offer a potent mix of access, influence, and advice. Lobbying firms may serve many clients at once, some with interests that seem antithetical. One of the largest and most prestigious law and lobbying firms in Washington, Patton Boggs, represents 180 clients, and two of the largest are the Smokeless Tobacco Council and New York Life Insurance Co.[28] In the pragmatic culture of Washington, such conflicts in principle are reconciled.

---

[26]Peter H. Stone, "Money-Meisters," *National Journal*, March 21, 1998, p. 624.

[27]The Lobbying Disclosure Act of 1995 law requires lobbyists to register with Congress if, over a six-month period, they spend more than one-fifth of their time and more than $5,000 on influence efforts. Corporations must register if they spend over $20,000 in six months. Registration requires disclosure of which policies lobbyists are trying to influence, who employs them, and how much they spend. There were 17,000 lobby registrations in 1997.

[28]Louis Jacobson, "Makeover on M Street," *National Journal*, October 31, 1998, p. 2552.

Many business lobbyists are former elected officials, congressional staffers, or employees of regulatory agencies. Experience and contacts inside government are valuable to companies seeking to influence decisions. For example, Kenneth J. Kies earned $132,000 a year as chief of staff of the Joint Committee on Taxation. Kies decided to leave his congressional post and was hired by PricewaterhouseCoopers at $1 million a year to lobby tax matters on behalf of its clients. In 1998 Kies showed that he was worth this salary. He ran a lobbying campaign for General Electric and other large corporations and stopped the Treasury Department from issuing a ruling, a ruling that would have ended tax breaks the companies enjoyed worth $180 million per year. The law prohibits former government employees from lobbying the agencies where they worked for one year after they leave, so while Kies himself went to see Treasury officials, he had others on the lobbying team meet with members of Congress.[29]

There are many styles of direct lobbying. The Motion Picture Association of America capitalizes on the glamour of Hollywood with a private theater in Washington, D.C., in which senators and representatives view films prior to public release. The Methyl Bromide Working Group, on the other hand, has far less potential for dazzle but is effective in its own way. This trade group speaks for companies that make a soil fumigant used on crops such as strawberries and grapes to kill pests. Methyl bromide is highly toxic and its use is being phased out in the United States. Peter Sparber, a lobbyist for the group, works up and down the halls of Congress explaining to legislators that since methyl bromide is still used in foreign countries, American farmers will be less competitive. When asked if there are safer alternatives to methyl bromide, he gives out big green flyswatters printed with the words "OFFICIAL EPA-APPROVED METHYL BROMIDE ALTERNATIVE."[30]

Lobbyists for corporations and trade associations may also try to influence a decision by having customers, employees, or other constituents, including the general public, pressure government officials for action. These efforts are given a variety of names, including grassroots lobbying, outside lobbying, and national campaigns. A classic grassroots effort occurred in 1983 when Congress required banks to withhold income taxes on the interest earned by customers' savings accounts. The banking industry generated 22 million postcards and letters against the new law and Congress repealed it.

There are many ways to create grassroots support. Mass mail, phone calls, faxes, and e-mail to a lawmaker are sometimes generated by lobbyists who keep databases of interested parties. Issue-oriented advertising is run to shape public opinion.[31] Some lobbying firms specialize in creating grassroots pres-

---

[29]Jill Abramson, "The Business of Persuasion Thrives in Nation's Capital," *New York Times,* September 29, 1998, p. A22.

[30]Sheila Kaplan, "The Art of the Hard Sell," *George,* April 1998, pp. 82–83.

[31]Ken Kollman, *Outside Lobbying: Public Opinion & Interest Group Strategies,* Princeton, N.J.: Princeton University Press, 1998, pp. 28–57.

sure for corporate clients and can generate contacts for a fee. For about $40,000, one of these firms will conduct a campaign to change the vote of a single legislator; it can cost millions to fund a grassroots lobby for an entire congressional committee. Some of this kind of lobbying is directed at getting just a few influential friends of a representative to call him or her and ask for support on an issue—in the vernacular of Washington, this is "grasstops" lobbying. Defense companies generate grassroots support for major weapons systems by using suppliers in many states and congressional districts. Lockheed Martin has spread out the subcontracting for its F-22 advanced tactical fighter to 1,150 companies in forty-five states.

Grassroots lobbying is increasingly prominent today for several reasons. First, recent advances in communication technology such as e-mail, computerized mail lists, and fax machines have made it easier to quickly target and contact large numbers of people. Second, the 1995 restrictions on gift-giving and meal-buying have led to less reliance on inside lobbying. And third, polling, media, and public relations firms that specialize in generating support for politicians during elections have tried to build revenues by selling their skills to corporations.

The Corporate Role in Elections

In the first presidential campaign, George Washington did little campaigning and spent nothing to get elected. Since then, the length and cost of campaigns for federal offices—president, vice president, senator, and representative—have soared. In 1996 total campaign expenditures were about $2.7 billion. This is a large sum, but should be kept in perspective: it is only five one-hundredths of our gross domestic product, less than the cost of one nuclear-powered aircraft carrier, and less than Americans spend on potato chips or perfume each year. What is the role of corporations in elections?

Throughout the nineteenth century, companies made direct contributions from their treasuries to candidates, a practice that reached its zenith in William McKinley's campaigns. The election of 1896 matched the pro-business Republican McKinley against the radical Populist William Jennings Bryan. Bryan, a spellbinder on the stump, scared the eastern financial community by advocating the silver standard, a radical and unwelcome change in the currency system. Marcus Hanna, campaign manager for McKinley, capitalized on this fear. He systematically assessed 0.25 percent of the assets of each bank from the trembling financiers and raised about $3.5 million.[32] This doubled the amount raised in previous elections and was sufficient to elect McKinley. In 1900 Bryan opposed McKinley again, this time on a platform attacking trusts. So Hanna

---

[32]See Herbert Croly, *Marcus Alonzo Hanna: His Life and Work*, New York: Macmillan, 1912, p. 220. A grateful McKinley engineered the appointment of Hanna to the U.S. Senate.

assessed giant trusts such as Standard Oil and U.S. Steel, based on their assets. A new record sum was raised, and McKinley won by an even larger margin. Hanna believed his system had elevated the ethics of campaign finance above the borderline bribery and petty extortion that had long characterized it, but progressive reformers sought to derail the business juggernaut. In 1907, they passed the Tillman Act to prohibit banks and corporations from making direct contributions to federal candidates, and this remains the law today.

American political culture is heavily influenced by egalitarian ideals. Huge campaign contributions by business strain popular belief in a rough equality among interests. The Tillman Act was the first of many efforts to protect the electoral system from lopsided contributions by business. But money, and especially corporate money, plays an essential role in funding elections. It is a resource that may be converted to power. Candidates use it to reach and persuade voters. Contributors use it to buy access, influence, and favors. Because money is elemental in electoral politics, new sources and methods of giving arise whenever federal laws limit unsuitable contribution methods.

After 1907 the Tillman Act, a well-intentioned reform, was quickly and continuously circumvented. Companies found numerous indirect ways to funnel money into elections. These included giving salary bonuses to managers for use as campaign contributions, loaning money to candidates and later forgiving the loans, paying for expensive postage-stamp-size ads in political party booklets, loaning employees to campaigns, and providing free services such as air travel or rental cars. Also, since individual contributions were not limited by the Tillman Act, wealthy donors stepped in. These "fat cats," who included many corporate executives, legally gave unlimited sums.

In response to growing appearances of impropriety, Congress passed the Federal Election Campaign Act (FECA) in 1971, which required full public disclosure of campaign contributions and expenditures. But immediately after its passage, the election of 1972 once again made corporate money in politics a major reform issue. It was in 1972 that the record among known contributions was set when W. Clement Stone, an insurance company executive, gave $2 million to the Nixon campaign. Then, investigations related to the Watergate scandals revealed that twenty-one corporations had violated the Tillman Act by making direct contributions totaling $842,000, also to the Nixon campaign.

In reaction to this illegality and to the appearance of influence buying that was created by large fat-cat contributions, Congress extensively amended the FECA in 1974 (the first of five amending acts over a decade). This revised FECA attempted to curb wealthy donors by placing ceilings on both campaign contributions and expenditures. Congress also established public financing for presidential candidates and created the Federal Election Commission to enforce the law.

The 1974 additional FECA amendments set up a regulatory framework designed to limit large contributions by business interests. However, more than twenty years later, it is now evident that federal election law, which occupies 254 double-columned, small-print pages in the *Code of Federal Regulations* and has an eighty-seven-page index, has failed to control as intended large corporate, special-interest, and individual contributions. The reason is that the new FECA regulations were, after 1974, quickly undermined by three unanticipated developments.

First, in 1976 the Supreme Court severely compromised the FECA's design for controlling campaign money. In *Buckley* v. *Valeo,* the Court held that giving and spending money in political campaigns are a form of expression protected by the guarantee of free speech in the First Amendment.[33] The Court upheld the FECA's *contribution* limits, saying that the government had a legitimate interest in avoiding corruption and the appearance of corruption that was invited by unlimited contributions. But it invalidated *expenditure* limits, and with them the act's ability to control campaign spending.

The Federal Election Campaign Act, as it now stands, attempts to limit contributions from wealthy contributors and special interests by restricting contributions to candidates for federal office. For example, individuals may contribute $1,000 per election per candidate, $5,000 per year to PACs, $20,000 per year to national party committees, and $25,000 per year to all sources. Contributions by political action committees and party committees are also limited (see Figure 11-1). Direct contributions from corporations remain illegal. These dollar limits have never been raised. Inflation over the intervening years has reduced the value of what individuals can contribute to less than a third of what it was in 1974. In the meantime, the growing size of the electorate and the increasing use of television have made campaigns much more expensive. This has encouraged efforts to circumvent legal giving limits.

Presidential campaigns are heavily funded by the U.S. Treasury using money raised from the checkoff feature on federal income tax forms that allows taxpayers to earmark $3 of their taxes for a presidential election fund. In the primaries, presidential candidates may accept individual, PAC, and party contributions that comply with the legal limits in Figure 11-1, and these are then matched by U.S. Treasury funds. In the general election, presidential candidates who accept public funding cannot accept other contributions from any source.

Second, the proliferation of interest groups in the 1960s and 1970s created more organized interests to fund campaigns. Because the FECA—even after the *Buckley* decision—limited individual contributions, the era of fat cats seemed to be over, though, as we shall see, only temporarily. So interest groups and corporations raced to set up political action committees (PACs), which could legally contribute to candidates. The number of PACs grew rapidly, and with them the amount of money entering elections.

And third, corporations and lobbyists adapted to the new FECA regime by learning how to exploit, circumvent, and live with its regulations. Their machinations paralleled those that followed the reforms of the Tillman Act in 1907 and showed once again that political money is like water in a stream: dammed up in one place, it flows around and over in another.

---

[33]421 U.S. 1.

Figure 11-1

Federal campaign contribution and expenditure limits.

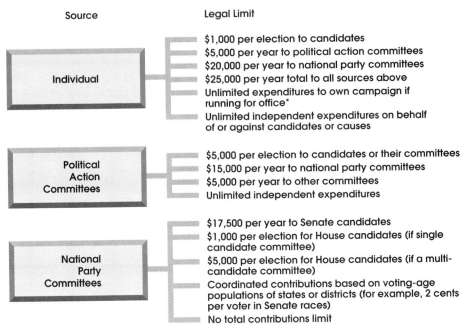

Source

Legal Limit

Individual

- $1,000 per election to candidates
- $5,000 per year to political action committees
- $20,000 per year to national party committees
- $25,000 per year total to all sources above
- Unlimited expenditures to own campaign if running for office*
- Unlimited independent expenditures on behalf of or against candidates or causes

Political Action Committees

- $5,000 per election to candidates or their committees
- $15,000 per year to national party committees
- $5,000 per year to other committees
- Unlimited independent expenditures

National Party Committees

- $17,500 per year to Senate candidates
- $1,000 per election for House candidates (if single candidate committee)
- $5,000 per election for House candidates (if a multi-candidate committee)
- Coordinated contributions based on voting-age populations of states or districts (for example, 2 cents per voter in Senate races)
- No total contributions limit

*Presidential and vice presidential candidates are limited to $50,000 if federal funding is accepted.

What follows is a discussion of some of the ways that corporations now funnel money to politicians and government officials.

Political Action Committees

When Congress limited individual contributions, it left open a loophole permitting organizations to establish political action committees (PACs), or committees composed of organization members who receive money from other members and contribute it to candidates. Corporations previously had not formed PACs, although unions had used them since the 1940s, but when individual contributions by executives were strictly limited by the FECA, they emerged as a new conduit through which business money could reach candidates. After the new FECA amendments went into effect in 1974, companies rushed to form PACs; by 1980 there were 1,204 corporate PACS and in 1988 the number peaked at 2,008. Since then it has declined slightly, and in 1998 there were 1,745 business PACs. Leveling off and decline came as corporations' experience with PACs diminished expectations of what they could accomplish. Other interests also use PACs, and in 1998 there were 4,486 PACs altogether, including 345 labor union and 891 trade association and other membership-group PACs.[34]

---

[34]Federal Election Commission news release, "FEC Releases 18-Month Summary on Political Action Committees," September 24, 1998. This news release and other FEC data cited in this chapter can be found on the FEC Web site at http://www.fec.gov.

How PACs Work

To start a PAC, a corporation must set up an account for contributions, a "separate segregated fund" to which it cannot legally donate 1 cent (because of the prohibition since 1907 of direct corporate giving). The money in the PAC is disbursed to candidates based on decisions made by PAC officers, who must be corporate employees. Corporations may, and typically do, pay the administrative costs of PACs.

Corporate PACs must get their funds from contributions by employees and others. The law spells out the solicitation procedure and divides those eligible to contribute into two groups. Group 1, or stockholders, executives, managers, and their families, can be solicited as often as desired in person or by mail. They can contribute by check or through monthly payroll deductions. Many corporations suggest amounts based on a percentage of salary, usually about 1/4 to 1 percent of annual salary. Group 2, or hourly paid employees and their families, can be solicited only twice a year by a corporate PAC, and then only by mail to the home. It is illegal for companies to require or apply pressure for PAC contributions, but many employees resent the solicitations and feel subtle pressure to contribute.

Foreign nationals may not legally contribute to PACs because they are barred from making contributions to candidates. Some U.S. subsidiaries of foreign corporations have PACs, but in them all PAC officers and contributors are U.S. citizens. There are no dollar limits to the overall total of PAC contributions each year, though each individual PAC contribution must comply with FECA limits.

The majority of corporate PACs raise and contribute less than $50,000, although a few large ones give much more, as Table 11-1 indicates. Corporate PACs coordinate their contributions with company lobbyists, who know that PAC contributions create an expectation of access, or a hearing of the corporation's position, after the candidate is elected. Some access-buying is formalized. In 1998, a corporate PAC contribution of $25,000 to the Republican party entitled corporate officers to have dinner with senior GOP senators, and $15,000 bought an invitation to have monthly breakfasts with Democratic senators.[35]

Big corporate PACs usually pursue a strategy of giving contributions of $1,000 or $2,000 to a large number of House and Senate candidates, favoring incumbents (who tend to be reelected), but often giving to their opponents too. This pattern of giving, designed to ensure access to office holders of both parties, is another sign that in Washington pragmatism outweighs ideology. Contributions of this size are relatively small. In 1998, a $2,000 contribution was less than one-hundredth of 1 percent of the $3,765,000 cost of an average Senate race and less than one-tenth of 1 percent of the $675,000 cost of an average House race.

Some corporations elect not to have PACs. Of the largest 544 companies in the United States, only 239 have one.[36] Some very large companies that have no PAC

---

[35]Jeffrey H. Birnbaum, "Capitol Clout: A Buyer's Guide," *Fortune,* October 26, 1998, pp. 180–81.
[36]Ralph Vartabedian, "Many Top Firms Say No to Political Contributions," *Los Angeles Times,* September 22, 1997, p. A1.

TABLE 11-1   The Five Largest Corporate PAC Contributors to Federal Elections, January 1, 1997–June 30, 1998

1. United Parcel Service of America Inc. Political Action Committee	$1,094,120
2. Lockheed Martin Employees Political Action Committee	907,487
3. Federal Express Corporation Political Action Committee	642,750
4. AT&T Corp. Political Action Committee	633,107
5. Ernst & Young Political Action Committee	596,978

Source: Federal Election Commission news release, September 24, 1998.

include IBM, Kimberly-Clark, and Colgate-Palmolive, but most PAC-less firms are among the smallest of the 544. The main reason that companies forgo a PAC is to avoid incessant pressure from candidates for contributions. A recent survey of corporate PACs found that 70 percent of their contributions were made due to candidate requests.[37] Public perception is that corporations hold out offers of money to politicians, but politicians are also persistent and systematic in asking for it. For instance, some staff members of congressional committees, as part of their duties, find corporations that are affected by provisions in pending bills so that committee members can request contributions from them.[38] This kind of solicitation disgusts many business executives, who are repelled by the implications.

Circumventing Contributions Limits

Although federal law prohibits corporate contributions and imposes strict contribution limits on individuals, PACs, and national party committees, there are ways to circumvent it.

A time-honored fund-raising technique that is unregulated by the FECA is *brokering.* Brokering takes place when a lobbyist, corporate executive, or group representative acts as an intermediary between candidates and contributors. For example, a Washington lobbying firm might sponsor a $1,000-a-plate dinner for a senator. Buying such a dinner is a campaign contribution under the law. If 400 people attend, the firm has brokered a $400,000 contribution (minus expenses) to the senator.

A second technique for circumventing legal contribution limits is *bundling.* It is legal for any individual (even a nonemployee) to contribute to a corporate PAC and to earmark the contribution, or stipulate which candidate is to receive it. The PAC then acts as a conduit for these earmarked funds, which do *not* count against contribution limits. Bundling is used to pass on a collection

---

[37]Eliza Newlin Carney, "Donor Fatigue," *National Journal,* February 22, 1997, p. 366.

[38]Robert Kuttner, "What Ails Campaign Finance," *Washington Post National Weekly Edition,* February 17, 1997, p. 5.

of checks "bundled" together and given to a politician. A PAC may legally give only $10,000 per election cycle to a congressional candidate ($5,000 in the primary and $5,000 in the general election), but there is no limit to the amount of earmarked contributions for which a PAC may act as a conduit.

A third channel for business money entering politics is *soft money,* or money that is given to political parties and unregulated under federal law. Because soft money can be given in unlimited amounts by individuals, corporations, and PACs, it evades the spirit of the strict contribution and spending limits under the FECA. It arose after a 1979 amendment to the FECA placed contributions for the purpose of state and local party-building activities outside federal law. This money was supposed to be used for such things as yard signs, posters, brochures, party newsletters, and mailings. Soon, however, the national parties began to collect large sums and transfer them to state parties where they were used in inventive ways, not to buy lawn signs, but to further the election of federal candidates.

Although corporations are prohibited from contributing to federal campaigns, a series of advisory opinions by the Federal Election Commission opened the door for them to give soft-money contributions to national party committees. As a result, corporations and executives now give colossal sums to the Democratic and Republican parties. For example, in the four months preceding the midterm congressional elections in 1994, the Republican party got $300,000 from Federal Express; $290,000 from Philip Morris; $250,000 from Burlington Northern & Santa Fe Rail Corp.; $150,000 from Donald Fisher, CEO of The Gap; and $100,000 from James Barksdale, CEO of Netscape. The Democratic party received similar contributions, including some from the same corporations. Federal Express, for example, also gave the Democrats $200,000.[39]

In 1996 the Supreme Court permitted the use of soft money for political ads.[40] The Court made a distinction between "issue advocacy," which presents a political view or comment on an electoral race, and "express advocacy," which specifically suggests the election or defeat of a candidate using words such as "vote for," "defeat," or "support." Soft money, therefore, can be used for issue advertising that tiptoes around direct electioneering by avoiding the use of certain phrases, even though the intent to support or oppose a candidate for federal office is clear.

For example, in 1998, Representative Vince Snowbarger (R-Kan.) was supported for reelection by big corporations because of his views on international trade. Some of these corporations gave contributions of $100,000 to the National Republican Congressional Committee, which ran issue ads in his Kansas district attacking the stands of his opponent for, among other things, being soft on crime.[41] Since the ads did not expressly ask for Snowbarger's election, it was legal to use soft money from corporations to pay for them.

---

[39]Common Cause News, "National Parties Raise $162 Million in Soft Money through October 14," November 2, 1998, http://commoncause.org/publications/raise_chart1.html-chart2.html.

[40]*Colorado Republican Federal Campaign Committee* v. *FEC,* 116 S.Ct. 2390 (1996).

[41]Peter H. Stone, "Issue Ads, the Weapons of Choice," *National Journal,* October 31, 1998, p. 2570.

The amount of soft money raised by the national parties is growing, and it makes a mockery of the post-Watergate campaign spending limits. During the 1998 midterm elections, the two parties raised more than $173 million in soft-money contributions, most of it from corporations.[42] The key to understanding soft-money contributions is that although they are ostensibly made for state and local party-building, their real purpose is to help elect and influence federal candidates.

Fourth, individuals and PACs may make unlimited *independent expenditures* for or against candidates in addition to direct contributions. An independent expenditure is money spent to promote the election of a candidate, buying a radio ad or billboard for example, that is not coordinated in any way with the candidate. So while it is illegal for a corporate PAC to give more than $5,000 to Jones, a candidate for Congress, the PAC can spend an unlimited amount buying media ads to "elect Jones," provided that the Jones campaign is not informed or consulted. The Supreme Court, in the *Buckley* decision, protected independent expenditures as free speech that cannot be limited. In practice, corporate PACs do not make significant independent expenditures, but the potential exists. If reformers seeking to limit the amount of business money in politics succeed in banning corporate soft-money contributions, then independent expenditures might increase to compensate.

There are more legal methods for channeling money into politics in excess of FECA contribution limits. For example, lobbyists frequently pay honoraria, typically about $2,000, to members of Congress for brief speeches at breakfasts or luncheons.[43] Corporations are also allowed to give directly to help pay for presidential party-nominating conventions.

Using a variety of tactics, a corporation can contribute much more than the nominal legal limits set forth in Figure 11-1. A PAC wishing to influence a Senate candidate, for example, can give $5,000 in the primary, $5,000 in the general election, and $5,000 to a trade association PAC that might be supporting the candidate. In addition, the PAC can make unlimited independent expenditures and unlimited soft-money contributions to the candidate's party.

The Influence Process

In America, there is a historic fear that business money will corrupt legislators and officials. Because of this fear, even where business's influence efforts are legal, the large sums involved raise apprehensions.

Critics believe that corporate money creates unwholesome obligations to special interests. Contributions from executives and PACs are blatant efforts

---

[42]Federal Election Commission news release, "Fundraising Escalates for Political Party Committees," October 27, 1998.

[43]House members may keep honoraria up to 27 percent of their salary; senators cannot accept them but may donate them to charity.

to buy votes; they are investments from which donors expect a return. Charles Keating, the owner of Lincoln Savings and Loan and a large campaign donor, once confirmed the critics' worst fears when he said, "One question, among many, has had to do with whether my financial support in any way influenced several political figures to take up my cause. I want to say in the most forceful way I can: I certainly hope so."[44] Keating's remark was ingenuous. The reality of influence is more subtle.

Bribery is illegal. If lawmakers or regulators accept money as a condition for official action, they commit a crime. This does not mean that contributions associated with lobbying efforts are made without the expectation of a return. Large contributions create a debt on the part of legislators who receive them. But because of bribery laws, the etiquette of legislator–lobbyist relations requires that collection of the debt be discrete. To avoid suspicion of bribery, financial contributions are not mentioned in connection with requests for action. Former Senator Tom Eagleton (D-Mo.) explains:

> I've never had . . . a guy come into this office or over the phone say, "Tom, such-and-such vote's coming up next week. You remember I gave X in your last campaign, and I'm certainly expecting you to vote that way." I've never had anything that direct, blunt, or obscene. However, let's change the phraseology to this: "Tom, this is so-and-so. You know next week an important vote's coming up on such-and-such. I just want to remind you, Tom, I feel very strongly about that issue. Okay, my friend, good to hear from you." Now a senator receives "gentle" calls of that sort.[45]

It is difficult to prove or measure business influence in the political process. Often there is a correlation between contribution and action, that is, one occurs followed by the other. Did the contribution cause a lawmaker to vote a certain way? Or did the contribution reward earlier support by a like-thinking representative? There are other strong influences on representatives aside from money, including in particular party loyalty, ideological disposition, and the opinions of voters back home. What, then, caused the vote or action to occur?

Sometimes the influence of business money is barely visible to researchers. A lobbyist is alleged to have once said that figuring out political influence is like finding a black cat in the coal bin at midnight. Former U.S. Senator William Proxmire (D-Wis.), who throughout his career declined to accept campaign contributions, once said this:

> The payoff may be as obvious and overt as a floor vote in favor of a contributor's desired tax loophole or appropriation. Or it may be subtle . . . a floor speech not delivered . . . a bill pigeonholed in subcommittee . . . an amendment not offered . . . Or the payoff can come in a private conversation with four or five key colleagues in the privacy of the cloakroom.[46]

---

[44] In Herbert E. Alexander, *Financing Politics,* 4th ed., Washington, D.C.: Congressional Quarterly Press, 1992, p. 68.

[45] Quoted in Hedrick Smith, *The Power Game,* New York: Ballantine Books, 1988, p. 255.

[46] Center for Responsive Politics, *Ten Myths about Money in Politics,* in Anthony Corrado et al., *Campaign Finance Reform: A Sourcebook,* Washington, D.C.: Brookings Institution Press, 1997, p. 155.

There is a perennial debate over whether there is too much corporate money in politics. Corporations are prohibited from directly contributing to campaigns. This silencing of corporate speech goes against the grain in a political system that regards unlimited debate and free expression as supreme virtues. Corporations have important interests to voice just as farmers and consumers do. Why should government step in to limit and censure the opinions of these large voluntary organizations that employ millions of workers and affect the lives of every citizen?

The Supreme Court has held that speech restrictions on corporations are justified for two reasons. First, the corporate form, which allows the accumulation of immense wealth based on success in economic markets, is an unfair advantage in the political arena.

> [T]he resources in the treasury of a business corporation . . . are not an indication of popular support for the corporation's political ideas. They reflect instead the economically motivated decisions of investors and customers. The availability of these resources may make a corporation a formidable political presence, even though the power of the corporation may be no reflection of the power of its ideas.[47]

Second, the Court has recognized a "compelling governmental interest" in preventing corruption or the appearance of corruption in elections.[48] That is, it has tried to balance the right of free speech against the importance of corruption-free elections and has found the latter more important.

Not everyone agrees. Justice Antonin Scalia argues that corporations should have the right to unlimited free speech, that they should be able to make campaign contributions and spend as much money as they wish, just like any other group. Prohibiting corporate funds in elections is, he writes, "incompatible with the absolutely central truth of the First Amendment: that government cannot be trusted to assure, through censorship, the 'fairness' of political debate."[49] He trusts the ability of the public to judge the validity of corporate arguments and to withdraw support from politicians who succumb to corporate influence and sell out the public interest.

The pervasive and sinuous presence of money in politics that is characteristic of the American system is a concern in every industrialized country. Some nations, for example France, have laws that prohibit corporate political contributions. Others restrict the amount that corporations can give, for example Italy ($13,700 per candidate) and Japan ($410 per candidate). Political corruption has pronounced, negative effects wherever it occurs. In South Korea, the Hanbo Iron & Steel Co. made large payments to political party officials, who then pressured banks to make loans to Hanbo even though it was faltering. Hanbo's subsequent bankruptcy endangered the solvency of

[47]*Federal Election Commission* v. *Massachusetts Citizens for Life,* 479 U.S. 257 (1986), from the opinion by Justice William J. Brennan, Jr.

[48]*Austin* v. *Michigan Chamber of Commerce,* 58 LW 4373 (1990).

[49]Dissenting in *Austin,* 58 LW 4379.

the banks. Such corrupt dealings eventually cause scandal, which in turn can lead to the enactment of reform, as has occurred in Korea recently and in other nations periodically.

Concluding Observations

Government continues to grow in size, and its actions more and more affect the operations of companies. This makes the corporate political environment important, challenging, and sometimes uncertain. Still, business retains its historically dominant position among interests.

Business dominance is not new. The power of business in politics today is typical of its power in the past, but in some ways less threatening to egalitarian ideals. There is a great imbalance of resources between corporate interests and other interests such as poor people, small farmers, environmentalists, and consumer advocates. Labor unions can sometimes match the political muscle of business, but often not. However, a similar or greater imbalance has existed since the end of the colonial era, and business is today forced to deal with more, and stronger, opposing interests than in the past. Similarly, corporations and executives are today circumventing the spirit of election laws with large contributions. But they have been doing so since early in the century and disclosure requirements in the FECA create more openness than in the past.

The challenge for American society is to balance the First Amendment right of corporations to political expression against the societal interest of maintaining corruption-free elections and government decisions. So far, our society has been successful in maintaining a rough balance.

FEDERAL EXPRESS
AND CONGRESS

Late in the second session of the 104th Congress, a heated, partisan debate took place over an amendment to an aviation bill. The amendment had been attached at the request of Federal Express Corp., a unit of FDX Corp. Republicans argued that it was a minor correction for a mistake in a previous bill. Prolabor Democrats tried to portray it as an all-out corporate and Republican assault on the working people of America.

What follows is the story of this amendment as best we can tell it. Tracing the exercise of influence in Washington, D.C., is difficult. Companies and politicians do not step forward to volunteer their motivations or the nonpublic actions that can shape outcomes. Some parts of the story remain hidden and may never be known. It requires patience to penetrate the arcana of law and bureaucracy to see the practical consequences of federal activity on the operations of a company. Yet the story is worth telling to illustrate why corporations need to be active in politics and how they flex political muscle.

Federal Express

Federal Express Corp., sometimes called FedEx, was started in 1971 by an entrepreneur named Frederick W. Smith. Since then, Smith has built it into a company that is familiar to almost every American. Federal Express offers rapid transport and delivery of documents, packages, and freight in 211 countries. To move its daily average of three million items, it operates large fleets of airplanes and trucks. It owns 619 aircraft, making it the world's sixth largest air carrier, and in 1998 it had 110 more planes on order. The truck fleet consists of 41,500 vehicles ranging from panel trucks to big tractor-trailer rigs, and drivers put in more than 2.5 million miles each day. In 1998 Federal Express ranked 134 on the *Fortune* 500 list and had revenues of $11.2 billion.[1]

---

[1]Figures in this paragraph are from the Federal Express Web site at http://www.fedex.com/us/about/facts.html; the company's Form 10K405, filed on August 21, 1998, with the Securities and Exchange Commission; and "1998 Fortune Five Hundred," *Fortune*, April 27, 1998, pp. F5–F6. Since 1998, Federal Express has been a wholly owned subsidiary of FDX Corporation, a holding company formed with the acquisition of Caliber System, Inc.

The mail, package, and freight delivery industry is highly competitive in terms of price and service. FedEx battles for customers with firms such as Airborne Express, passenger airlines that carry freight, airfreight companies, and the U.S. Postal Service, but its strongest competitor is United Parcel Service of America, Inc. (UPS). UPS, with $22.5 billion in revenues in 1998, is twice the size of Federal Express and its operations are similar. It delivers in 200 countries, about the same number as FedEx; it operates 555 aircraft, slightly fewer than FedEx; and it runs 169,000 trucks, four times as many as FedEx.[2]

One big difference between these two rivals is that UPS's employees are unionized, while FedEx's are not. Although 3,000 FedEx pilots are in a pilot's union, its remaining 140,000 employees are nonunion. At UPS, on the other hand, the International Brotherhood of Teamsters represents 104,000 full-time and 151,000 part-time employees, and 2,000 pilots are in a pilot's union. Both the Teamsters and the United Automobile Workers of America have been trying for many years to organize Federal Express, but unsuccessfully.

Management at Federal Express does not want unions and has used a range of tactics to keep organizers at bay. Some FedEx employees want a union.[3] In 1997, UPS drivers made an average $4 per hour more than FedEx drivers. But many others are satisfied with the pay and working conditions. The company has a number of employee-friendly policies, including a Guaranteed Fair Treatment program in which any worker can appeal a supervisor's decision all the way up to CEO Smith.[4] Smith allocates four hours a week to acting on these appeals. In spite of strenuous efforts, unions have failed to make inroads into the FedEx labor force. This gives it a labor cost advantage over UPS.

Two Labor Laws, Two Approaches to Labor Relations

The success that Federal Express has had in preventing unionization of its employees, besides the pilots, is due in large part to the way union activity is regulated by the federal government. Two main laws guide organizing, and they are very different in philosophy.

The Railway Labor Act

The first law is the Railway Labor Act of 1923. Early in this century, labor law favored managers of companies and discouraged union activity. The Railway Labor Act was the first major statute to encourage and protect unions. In it Congress required that railroad managers bargain in good faith with workers

---

[2]Form 10K, United Parcel Service, Inc., March 27, 1998, pp. 1–5.

[3]"Fed Up" is a Web site set up to air complaints on labor issues by Federal Express employees and communicate news about organizing efforts. It is at http://ourworld.compuserve.com/homepages/kevin_osiowy/.

[4]For a description of employee-friendly practices at Federal Express, see James C. Wetherbe, *The World on Time: The 11 Management Principles that Made FedEx an Overnight Sensation,* Santa Monica, Calif.: Knowledge Exchange, 1996.

about union contracts and created an agency called the Labor Mediation Board to settle union–management disputes. The law applied only to railroads but, unlike today, these were among the largest and most visible businesses of that era, and so it was very significant.

With the growth of the airline industry, the law was extended to include air carriers. It was then further extended to cover express companies. However, there was only one express company in existence, Railway Express Agency (REA), which was a unique company. The story of this firm begins during World War I when the government nationalized all the railroads, including four express companies that shipped packages by railroad. After the war, the assets of all four companies were transferred to a newly created entity named Railway Express Agency, which was owned by 86 railroad companies in proportion to the amount of express business carried over their tracks.[5] Since REA was an outgrowth of existing railroads, the Railway Labor Act was extended to cover its employees. In the 1950s, REA began using trucks, and in the 1960s, it also began using planes, but as rail traffic dropped, its revenues declined and it was liquidated in 1975.

At this time, however, Federal Express came into existence with a novel method of express service that relied on the idea of bringing packages to a central hub and then flying them out to customers. Under Smith, FedEx created a new express market that combined the speed of air travel and the convenience of pick-up and delivery at the customer's business or home.[6] FedEx started with a fleet of Falcon 20 aircraft and soon bought DC-8s and DC-10s. From the beginning, it was classified as an "air carrier" under the Railroad Labor Act.

The National Labor Relations Act

A second law that oversees management–union interactions is the National Labor Relations Act (NLRA) of 1935. The NLRA gives much more extensive protection to workers and unions than did the Railway Labor Act. It prohibited tactics that companies commonly used to stop unions, including, for example, firing union members and refusing to bargain, and it set up a powerful new agency, the National Labor Relations Board (NLRB), with strong powers to remedy unfair practices. The NLRB has jurisdiction over employees at all companies other than railroads, airlines, and express companies covered in the less stringent Railway Labor Act.[7]

It is much more difficult for a union to organize employees under the Railway Labor Act than under the NLRA. The fundamental purposes of the laws are different. The main goal of the former is to protect against labor disharmony that could disrupt the flow of interstate commerce. Thus, enforcement

---

[5]George Drury, "Yesterday's FedEx: Railway Express Agency," *Trains Magazine,* August 1996, p. 75.

[6]Allan Ditter, "Express Carriers Took Off after Regulation," *Air Cargo World,* March 1992.

[7]In addition to employees of rail, air, and express companies, the NLRA also excludes agricultural and government workers.

focuses on mediating disputes and avoiding strikes. Bargaining agreements are not allowed to expire and negotiations simply continue until a new agreement is reached. The goal of the NLRA, on the other hand, is to protect the rights of workers to organize and bargain. It is aggressively enforced to protect unions from management plots and abuses. One other key difference between the two laws is that the Railway Labor Act only allows workers to organize a national union, whereas the NLRA permits organization of local unions on a facility-by-facility basis.

Although UPS and FedEx have similar operations today, UPS began as a trucking and courier company. This means that its workers fall under the NLRA and explains why UPS workers are unionized and Federal Express workers are not.

Union Efforts to Organize FedEx

Labor union membership in the United States is declining. In 1983, 20 percent of all wage and salary workers were union members, but that fell to 14.5 percent in 1996.[8] The decline has been steep for the two unions that have tried hardest to organize FedEx workers. In the late 1960s, the United Auto Workers (UAW) had 1.5 million members; today it has only a little more than half that number. The Teamsters, which had more than two million members in the 1970s, were badly hurt by trucking deregulation and today have about 1.4 million members.[9] So it would be a welcome gain for either one to grab the 93,000 hourly wage earners at Federal Express. Both unions have tried. FedEx CEO Smith once wrote in the company newsletter that if all the company's hourly workers were unionized, they would pay $20 million in annual dues to one union or the other.[10]

In 1990 the United Auto Workers started a big campaign to organize FedEx workers on the East Coast. It sponsored rallies and organizing drives in Pennsylvania, New Jersey, and Delaware, but it faced a stiff task. Under the Railway Labor Act, the union had to get 35 percent of all FedEx workers nationwide to sign organizing petitions or no election could be held. It would be much easier if the workers could be organized city by city under the NLRA.

Since FedEx had far more truck drivers than pilots, the UAW petitioned the National Labor Relations Board to place the drivers under the NLRA. It argued that although FedEx was classified as an "air carrier" subject to the Railway Labor Act, most of its workers had nothing to do with airplanes. Instead, they worked at pick-up counters, sorted packages, and dispatched and drove

---

[8]Bureau of the Census, *Statistical Abstract of the United States: 1997,* 117th ed., Washington, D.C., 1997, table 688.

[9]Figures are from John H. White and Brian Jackson, "Rival Unions Vie for FedEx," *Chicago Sun-Times,* May 13, 1997, p. 43.

[10]Ibid.

trucks and, therefore, they should be reclassified as covered under the National Labor Relations Act.

In July 1995, after a hearing on the union's petition, the National Labor Relations Board decided that the case was ambiguous and elected to submit the arguments of both FedEx and the UAW to the National Mediation Board, the body that resolves disputes under the Railway Labor Act, for an advisory opinion.[11] One board member, William B. Gould IV, the chairman of the NLRB, wrote a dissenting opinion in which he agreed with the union and stated that FedEx workers outside its air operations should fall under NLRA jurisdiction. His dissent was unsettling for Federal Express.

In November 1995, however, the National Mediation Board issued its opinion, holding that all Federal Express employees were covered under the Railway Labor Act and stating in part:

> . . . Federal Express is an air express delivery service which holds itself out for hire to transport packages, both domestically and internationally . . . [T]here is no dispute over whether Federal Express is a common carrier by air . . . The [Railway Labor] Act's definition of an employee of an air carrier includes, "every air pilot or other person who performs any work as an employee or subordinate official of such carrier or carriers, subject to its or their continuing authority to supervise and direct the manner of rendition of his service." The Railway Labor Act does not limit its coverage to air carrier employees who fly or maintain aircraft. Rather, its coverage extends to virtually all employees engaged in performing a service for the carrier so that the carrier may transport passengers or freight.
>
> Employees working in the . . . positions sought by the UAW perform functions equally crucial to Federal Express' mission as an integrated air express delivery service. As the record demonstrates, without the functions performed by the employees at issue, Federal Express could not provide the on-time express delivery required of an air express delivery service.[12]

The board suggested that ruling otherwise would break off parts of labor forces at railroads and airlines around the country and "drastically alter labor relations" at all these companies. Even if some employees do not work with airplanes, if a company is classified as an "air carrier," all its workers should be covered by the Railway Labor Act, not just some of them.

The National Mediation Board opinion was sent to the National Labor Relations Board, which took it under consideration and continued to deliberate. The situation now was that the NLRB could still reject the National Mediation Board's opinion to allow the UAW to organize FedEx employees under the NLRA. This was a threat to the anti-union stance of FedEx management.

---

[11]*Federal Express Corp.*, 317 NLRB 1155 (1995).
[12]*Federal Express Corporation*, 23 NMB 32, November 22, 1995.

Deleted Wording

Quickly, another threat arose for Federal Express when, a month later, Congress passed the Interstate Commerce Commission Termination Act of 1995. This law ended the existence of the nation's first independent regulatory commission 108 years after its creation. The Interstate Commerce Commission (ICC) was set up in 1887 to regulate railroads, and over the years its authority had been expanded so that it also regulated trucking companies, bus lines, moving companies, freight forwarders, and coal slurry pipelines. In the 1970s and 1980s, the duties of the ICC had been considerably reduced as Congress mandated deregulation in these industries and agency appropriations were cut by more than half. Eventually, the agency had withered so much that Congress passed an act to move its remaining powers to the Surface Transportation Board, a small entity in the Department of Transportation.

The termination of the ICC was a complex legislative process because, over the years, Congress had passed twenty-two major statutes for the agency to administer and, in addition, had repeatedly amended the original Interstate Commerce Act. A bill had to be written in which all these laws were rescinded, rewritten, or amended.

The intricate process of drafting the ICC termination bill went forward and, in due course, both the House and Senate passed it. Then, during the House–Senate conference committee proceedings that take place to reconcile different versions of bills passed in each chamber, ICC staff members recommended dropping the words "express company" from the Interstate Commerce Act because they thought that the language was obsolete. After all, the only company that had ever been classified as an express company was the defunct Railway Express Agency.

When the ICC Termination Act was sent back to both chambers and passed in 1995, it struck the words "express company" from the original ICC Act and, in a conforming amendment, dropped those words from the Railway Labor Act as well. Legislators paid little attention to the change and Federal Express seems not to have noticed it. Republicans would later claim that it was a mistake to be corrected with a technical amendment. Democrats would argue that reinserting the language was a substantive change for the benefit of a special interest.

Once alerted, Federal Express badly wanted the language put back in the law because the words "express company" represented added assurance that its truck drivers were covered by the Railway Labor Act.[13] If the National Labor Relations Board, in its pending decision, ruled that some employees were not protected from union-friendly organizing because they worked for an "air carrier," then FedEx could argue for reclassification as an "express company."

---

[13]Frank Swoboda, "Labor Wants to End FedEx's Railway Act Protection," *The Washington Post*, October 2, 1996, p. C1.

For many years, FedEx had been arguing to the National Mediation Board that it was both an "air carrier" and an "express company." The Board had never accepted this argument, but it might in the future. The company resolved to get the words back into the law when Congress reconvened early in 1996.

Federal Express Mobilizes

Federal Express is exceptionally skillful at exerting political influence in Washington, D.C. It does not shrink from pressing for government actions that benefit its operations. For example, in 1990 it got Congress to exempt its aircraft from local noise abatement requirements. In 1994 it supported an amendment to an aviation bill that ended the authority of states to regulate the routes and services of its planes and trucks. In 1995 it succeeded in eliminating federal safety requirements for trucks in the 10,001-to-26,000-pound range, the kind of trucks driven by most of its employees.[14]

Federal Express lobbyists approached Republican congressional leaders at the start of the second session of the 104th Congress in 1996 and requested amendment of the Railway Labor Act to restore the words "express company." They argued that omission of these words was just a mistake because elsewhere the ICC Act stated that "the enactment of the ICC Termination Act of 1995 shall neither expand or contract coverage of the employees and employers by the Railway Labor Act." Therefore, reinsertion of the words was a harmless correction with no effect on the status quo.

When organized labor discovered what Federal Express was up to, its lobbyists called on labor-friendly House members of both parties to fight the change. It did not see the change as a minor technical amendment; rather, it saw a potential roadblock to organizing FedEx employees.

Five attempts to reinsert the words during the session failed. The Republicans never sent the amendment to a standing committee for discussion and never held any hearings. Instead, they tried to hook it on as a rider to unrelated legislation. In the House, they attached it to the fiscal year 1996 omnibus appropriations bill and it was voted down. They attached it to the National Transportation Safety Board reauthorization bill and it failed. They attached it to a bill amending the Railroad Unemployment Act and it failed. They attached it to the Department of Transportation appropriation bill and it failed. In the Senate, they attached it to a Department of Labor appropriations bill and it failed again.

Five defeats might have discouraged another company, but not Federal Express. The company knows how to orchestrate a range of tactics to sway politicians. It uses its fleet of corporate jets to fly members of the House and

---

[14]Public Citizen press release of October 2, 1996, cited in the *Congressional Record*, October 2, 1996, p. S12189.

Senate to fundraising dinners around the country. Under the rules of Congress, the lawmakers have to pay the equivalent of first-class fare on a scheduled airline when they fly on a FedEx plane, but they are nonetheless grateful. Two former senators sit on the company's board of directors, former Republican leader Howard H. Baker Jr. and former Democratic leader George J. Mitchell.

Federal Express lobbies aggressively. Chief executive Frederick W. Smith visits Capitol Hill to see members of Congress in person. The company has a Washington office and also hires lobbyists in Washington law firms for special jobs. In just the first six months of 1996, it had spent $1,149,150 on lobbying activity, and $367,000 of this went to nine outside firms, some of which were hired to help with the Railway Labor Act amendment.[15]

Washington Law Firms Hired by Federal Express

Here is a list of the firms hired by Federal Express in the first six months of 1996 and the fees paid to them. Firms hired to work on the Railway Labor Act are shown with an asterisk.

Oldsker, Ryan, Phillips & Utrecht	$80,000
The Dutko Group*	60,000
O'Brien Calio	60,000
Cassidy & Associates	42,000
Aun Eppard Associates	40,000
Washington Counsel, P.C.	40,000
Cliff Madison Government Relations*	20,000
Bill Simpson & Associates	15,000
James E. Boland*	10,000

Source: Public Citizen from Senate records and printed in Neil A. Lewis, "This Mr. Smith Gets His Way in Washington," *New York Times,* October 12, 1996, p. B1.

Federal Express is also a very large campaign contributor. Among corporations, it has one of the largest political action committees. In 1995 and 1996, its PAC gave $948,000 to senators and representatives of both parties, and the company itself gave $400,000 in soft money to the Republican National Committee and $250,000 to the Democratic Senatorial Campaign Committee.[16]

---

[15]Neil A. Lewis, "This Mr. Smith Gets His Way in Washington," *New York Times,* October 12, 1996, p. B1.

[16]Contribution figures are from Federal Election Commission, Political Action Committee Report, 1995–1996 Cycle, Contributions, FEPAC; and Bob Woodward and Ann Devroy, "When Mr. Smith Came to Washington," *Washington Post National Weekly Edition,* August 25, 1997, p. 12.

The Final Push

As the end of the second session of the 104th Congress approached, another effort was made to restore "express company" to the Railway Labor Act. Both the House and the Senate had passed a Federal Aviation Authorization bill with broad, bipartisan support. In addition to $19 billion in funding for Federal Aviation Administration (FAA) programs and increased airport security, the bills also mandated $4.6 billion in grants for airport construction projects in the districts of representatives and senators. This meant more jobs and votes back home.

When separate bills are passed by the House and Senate, a conference committee composed of the principal sponsors from each chamber meets to iron out differences in wording. The committee then reports one uniform version of the bill back to each chamber for final approval.

In the September 1996 conference committee meeting on the aviation bill, Senator Earnest Hollings (D-S.C.) added an amendment that reinserted "express company" in the Railway Labor Act. Sen. Hollings was indebted to Federal Express because, when a drought had hit South Carolina, FedEx planes flew in loads of hay to prevent cattle from starving. The company's PAC had also made two $2,000 campaign contributions to Hollings in the two previous months.[17] The conference committee approved Hollings' amendment by a vote of 8–6. Thus, when this enormously popular bill was reported back to the House and Senate for enactment, it contained the Hollings amendment.

Laws Bearing on the FedEx Amendment

Railway Labor Act of 1926. The law that contains labor relations rules for employees of railroads, air carriers, and express companies. Federal Express is classified as an air carrier under this law.

National Labor Relations Act of 1935. This law contains labor relations rules for all workers not covered by the Railway Labor Act (except those in agriculture and government). It goes further in protecting workers' rights and makes it easier to organize unions.

Interstate Commerce Commission Termination Act of 1995. This act abolished the Interstate Commerce Commission and transferred its remaining powers elsewhere. A passage in it took out the words "express company" from the original ICC Act and, through a conforming amendment, from the Railway Labor Act as well.

Federal Aviation Reauthorization Act of 1996. This act authorized funds for airport construction and aviation safety. For Federal Express, Senator Earnest Hollings attached an amendment to the conference report of this bill to reinsert the words "express company" in the Railway Labor Act.

---

[17]Hollings received $2,000 on August 22, 1996, and $2,000 on July 17, 1996.

A Scorecard of Federal Agencies

National Mediation Board. This agency mediates disputes over wages, hours, and working conditions that arise under the Railway Labor Act. It is a small entity with three board members and a handful of employees.

National Labor Relations Board. This is an independent agency given responsibility to enforce the National Labor Relations Act. It conducts union elections and is empowered to investigate and remedy a wide range of unfair labor practices.

Interstate Commerce Commission. This was the first independent regulatory agency in American history. It had extensive powers to regulate railroads and other forms of surface transportation. Its existence ended in 1995.

Surface Transportation Board. The agency Congress created to receive residual powers once exercised by the Interstate Commerce Commission. It is in the Federal Highway Administration, which is, in turn, part of the Department of Transportation.

Federal Aviation Administration. This is another agency within the Department of Transportation. It sets and enforces rules for airline safety and operation.

Debate in the House of Representatives

On September 27, the conference report came up in the House for consideration. Representative John Linder (R-Ga.) introduced the Federal Aviation Authorization Act of 1996 and urged passage of the conference version, saying that it closely resembled the bill originally passed by the House. Immediately, objections to the Hollings amendment were heard from prolabor Democrats who were primed for combat. Rep. Joe Moakley (D-Mass.) took the lead.

> This bill contains a direct attack on working Americans. This bill contains a provision that was not part of either the House or Senate bill. This provision will resurrect the term "express carrier" solely on behalf of the Federal Express Co . . . [T]his bill pulls that term out of the trash heap, and in doing so will effectively prohibit the employees of Federal Express from unionizing.
>
> The supporters of this provision, this blatant attack on American workers, call it a technical correction. The person testifying before the committee said it was inadvertently left out of the House bill. It was inadvertently left out of the Senate bill. But somehow it showed up in the conference committee report.
>
> I would argue that for the 130,000 employees of Federal Express this change is hardly a correction, it is more like a misdirection.
>
> If Federal Express employees cannot unionize locally, Mr. Speaker, they cannot unionize at all, and the powerful people at the top of Federal Express know it.

So I urge my colleagues to stand up for those 130,000 employees of this company and defeat . . . the bill. Despite all of the progress this bill will make towards improving air travel and airline safety, it should be defeated because of that one provision.[18]

One by one other Democrats rose to fight the amendment. Rep. William O. Lipinski (D-Ill.) called it a "horrible extraneous provision" designed "to aid and assist one giant corporation against the American middle class."[19] Rep. Peter A. DeFazio (D-Ore.) remarked that "the working people of this country are going to be screwed by a large corporation, screwed behind the closed doors of a conference committee."[20] Rep. Jerrold Nadler (D-N.Y.) called the change "a union-busting provision, pure and simple."[21] Others rose as well; perhaps the most colorful rhetoric was that of Rep. Harold L. Volkmer (D-Mo.):

> . . . I love flowers and flowers are very beautiful, and what I saw developing as this bill passed through the House, passed through the Senate, started in the conference up to Wednesday was a beautiful bouquet of flowers that smelled just beautifully. And then Wednesday night, something happened. Wednesday night, a skunk snuck in a beautiful flower garden and smelled up the whole thing, and this bill now just smells, smells, smells terribly.
>
> Why? Because of one special interest provision that was put in there for Federal Express . . .
>
> I think somebody should take a look at the Federal Election Commission reports and let us see where FedEx money is going to. How much is the Republican National Committee getting from FedEx? How much are the members of the leadership on that side getting from FedEx?
>
> I think there is our answer right there, Members. That is what this is all about. It is a payoff; that is all it is, a payoff.[22]

Republican leaders spoke to defend the amendment. They argued that it was indeed a "technical" correction. They pointed out that there had been no intent to expand or contract coverage of workers under the Railway Labor Act. In the end, they prevailed and, in a vote that hewed closely to party lines, the Federal Aviation Authorization Act of 1996 passed the House.

Filibuster in the Senate

Three days later, on September 30, the conference report came to the floor in the Senate. At the time, the Senate was ready to adjourn so that members could get home to campaign before the November elections. However, Democrats were primed for a fight. Sen. Ted Kennedy (D-Mass.) led the charge by starting a filibuster on Monday, September 30, when the conference report came to the Senate floor.

---

[18]*Congressional Record,* September 27, 1996, p. H11453.
[19]Ibid.
[20]Ibid. p. 11457.
[21]Ibid. p. 11458.
[22]Ibid. pp. 11460–61.

Unlike the House, the rules of the Senate permit each senator unlimited time to speak unless he or she voluntarily yields. A senator who is opposed to legislation can tie up the Senate and prevent it from acting by keeping the floor and refusing to yield. This is called a filibuster. The only way to get the agenda moving again when a filibuster is in progress is to invoke Rule XXII of the Senate. Under Rule XXII, a senator can be forced to give up the floor if sixteen other senators sign a petition calling for a vote of cloture (KLO-choor). Then, if two-thirds plus one of the senators present vote in favor of cloture, the motion passes and the filibuster is ended. Absent a successful cloture motion, Senator Kennedy could hold the floor and the Senate could not finish its business and adjourn.

Kennedy strongly condemned both Federal Express and the Republican majority for "denying some fundamental justice to scores of American workers who have been playing by the rules."[23] He said that FedEx truck drivers were angry because they had not had a raise in seven years. He read letters from FedEx employees who had been trying to start a union. One complained about safety issues. FedEx drivers are required to deliver one package every three minutes, and FedEx policy guarantees that some deliveries will occur by 10:30 AM. They are forced to rush and sometimes drive unsafely. One driver in Chicago trying to meet the 10:30 AM deadline hit a 70-year-old woman at 10:28 or 10:29 while looking for an address. Other workers complained that the company would not give them time off when they needed to care for sick family members.

Then Kennedy attacked the Republicans.

> Few things more vividly illustrate the antiworker bias of the Republican Congress than this shameful antiworker rider. Republicans say, "Who cares about a handful of truck drivers in Pennsylvania?"
>
> We reply, "We do. Democrats do. Democrats are on their side."
>
> It has placed a spotlight on a cynical Republican attempt to help one of their corporate friends at the expense of that company's employees.
>
> They had hoped to carry out their scheme in the shadows, so that no one would recognize the injustice that was being done. That part of the Republican plan has already failed. The entire country now knows that the Republican Congress is ending as it began, with an assault on working men and women and their families. Key Republicans in Congress have conspired with Federal Express to . . . deprive Federal Express workers of their right to form a local union.[24]

Senator Hollings soon rose to defend the amendment that he had put in the aviation bill. It was, he said, simply a technical correction that did not change coverage of FedEx employees under the Railway Labor Act. He accused Kennedy of grandstanding and making a partisan issue of the matter in order to hurt Republicans in the upcoming 1996 elections.

---

[23]*Congressional Record,* October 2, 1996, p. S12178.
[24]*Congressional Record,* October 3, 1996, pp. S12219 and S12182.

> . . . [I]t is not a question of one company succeeds. It is the question of one Congress can succeed. Congress made the error, not Federal Express. Federal Express had nothing to do with the dropping of the language when we passed the ICC termination bill last December. We made a mistake. We are on trial. And this distortion: coming in here and flyblowing a wonderful company—"antiworker," "a Republican attack" . . .—none of that has anything to do with it.
>
> . . . I have been a Democrat since 1948. I think you were just learning to drive at that time. So you can't define who is a Democrat, we will see how the Democrats vote.
>
> We know this is a partisan onslaught. We know this [is] nonsense about working people and working families . . .[25]

Senator Kennedy's filibuster continued for three days. Finally, a petition signed by sixteen senators forced a roll-call vote on a motion for cloture, which passed 66-to-31. In the majority, forty-nine Republicans were joined by seventeen Democrats. Many of these Democrats would have voted with Kennedy, but they believed that the aviation bill was too important to kill because of this rider. Voting against were twenty-nine Democrats and two Republicans. This was a very close vote. If only two senators had switched sides, the motion would have failed, Kennedy's opponents would have had to concede defeat, and Federal Express would have lost.

Now, however, there was no way for prolabor forces to stop the Federal Aviation Authorization Act, and it passed with ninety-two "yeas" and only two "nays." The two no votes were cast by Sen. Arlen Specter (R-Pa.) and Senator Paul Simon (D-Ill.), both of whom dissented in principle because of the Hollings amendment. Surprisingly, they were not joined by Senator Kennedy, who, having failed in his primary objective, decided to vote for the rest of the act, which everyone agreed had great merit.

Postscript

President Clinton signed the aviation act into law five days after it passed the Senate. For a short time after the Senate debate, John Sweeney, president of the AFL-CIO, refused to take phone calls from Senate Democrats and threatened to cut off campaign contributions to the Democratic party. He relented after a visit from an apologetic Ted Kennedy.[26]

The term "express company" remains in Section 151 of the Railway Labor Act. Eight months after the battle in Congress, the National Labor Relations Board denied the UAW's request to reclassify trucking employees at Federal Express under the National Labor Relations Act. Its decision was based largely on the fact that more than 85 percent of FedEx shipments travel by air at some

---

[25]Ibid., pp. S12221 and 12223.

[26]Robert Novak, "Senate Democrats' Betrayal of Labor Is Telling Tale of How Washington Works," *Buffalo News*, October 17, 1996, p. 3B.

point and that trucking employees who handle them are an integral part of the air operation. But it also noted that the Hollings amendment to the aviation act showed a congressional intent that Federal Express employees were to fall under the Railway Labor Act.[27] While congressional intent is not the letter of the law, it gives Federal Express an additional, commanding argument to support its labor-law position.

In August 1997, the Teamsters struck at UPS. During the strike, the nonunion workers and drivers at FedEx put in long hours picking up the business of UPS customers. FedEx made an extra $600 million in revenue and UPS estimated that it might permanently lose about 5 percent of its business.[28] After the strike ended, FedEx gave a 10 percent bonus to all employees in appreciation for their hard work. Labor leaders called the bonus an effort to derail union organizing. Later in the year, Federal Express spent $2.4 billion buying a large trucking company, Caliber System, Inc., another UPS competitor that specializes in transporting packages between businesses. Since buying Caliber, Federal Express continues to expand its trucking operations. Its drivers have not been unionized.

Federal Express also continues to make large contributions to both parties. Because of its reputation as a big money-giver, it is often solicited by politicians and party leaders. CEO Smith recently told two *Washington Post* reporters that it would not be smart for a company with $13 billion in revenues to refuse these requests. "Sure, you're darn right, you better be responsive," said Smith. "Whether you use the language of the street and call it a shakedown or whether you just call it our system, however you put it, it's a messy system."[29] Smith seemed to be saying that with as much influence as Federal Express has, he believes that it is also a victim.

Questions

1. Was the FedEx amendment a technical fix or a substantive change in the Railway Labor Act?
2. Do you agree with Federal Express? Based on your knowledge of its business and the way it operates, is there a logical argument for classifying it as an "express company"?
3. Do you agree with the United Auto Workers? Should trucking employees of Federal Express be reclassified as non–air carrier employees, so that they can organize and bargain collectively under the National Labor Relations Act?

---

[27]*Federal Express Corporation and International Union, United Automobile, Aerospace and Agricultural Implement Workers of America, UAW, Petitioner,* 33 NLRB No. 157, May 30, 1997.

[28]Donna Rosato, "FedEx Delivers Strong Earnings on UPS Strike," *USA Today,* September 16, 1997, p. 3B.

[29]Woodward and Devroy, "When Mr. Smith Came to Washington," p. 12.

4. Was the decision in Congress on the amendment based on merit or politics or both? Were Republicans doing an unwarranted favor for Federal Express? Were Democrats unfairly using the amendment as a pretext for painting Republicans as anti-labor?

5. Did Federal Express buy the victory with money spent on lobbying and campaign contributions? Would the result have been the same without this effort?

6. What is the lesson of this story? Does it teach that the public should be cynical about the political process in Washington, D.C., because it favors special interests with money? Or does it illustrate a political process open to many interests that produced a reasonable outcome in a situation where no party had a monopoly on truth and logic?

PART 5

Global Management Issues

Multinational Corporations and Government Relationships

British Petroleum Company
www.bp.com

The British Petroleum Company, based in London, is the third largest oil company in the world after Royal Dutch/Shell and Exxon. In 1997 its revenues were $71.2 billion and its profits were $4 billion. It has operations in over 70 countries and employs 56,450 people.

In 1995 BP shocked the people of Lima, Ohio (population 50,000), with the announcement that it would close its refinery in the town at the end of two years, despite the fact that the plant was operating profitably. (BP did not publish profits of the plant, but it was estimated that in 1996 profits amounted to more than $45 million.)[1] Managers and workers believed the plant was efficient and capable of producing thousands of gallons of automobile fuel a day to meet the demands of

---

[1] The following account is derived principally from Paulette Thomas, "A Town Is Buffeted by Global Crosswinds," *The Wall Street Journal,* March 30, 1997; and Marc Cooper, "A Town Betrayed," *The Nation,* July 14, 1997.

BP stations throughout the United States. The plant employed about 455 workers, and many more local jobs were supported by expenditures of the refinery. One estimate was that closure would cost the town $100 million and an additional 1,000 to 2,000 jobs outside the refinery. This would be a serious blow to a town that had lost 8,000 jobs through downsizing, the closure of an army base, and shutdown of industrial plants during the preceding decade. A Refinery Task Force of politicians, unionists, and businesspeople was formed to help find a buyer for the refinery.

Several bidders appeared, including Marathon and Ashland oil companies, but BP rejected all bids. Townspeople believed BP peremptorily rejected the offers. Said the Mayor, "I don't believe for one moment that London ever seriously considered the bids. We were patronized and not dealt with honestly. BP had simply made a global strategic decision to not manufacture oil products beyond what they can sell."[2]

BP claimed the bidders did not have the economic clout to withstand the volatility of the refining market and could not guarantee the necessary supply of gasoline and other products of the refinery that BP said it needed. Furthermore, said BP, the refinery could not process the heavy sour crude oils required for a refinery to be profitable in the future. The Lima plant could process only the light sweet crude. BP said that while

the refinery was profitable, the return on investment was insufficient. There were other opportunities in the global market for better use of the invested funds, said the company, and any refinery not "world class" and with a net margin of 25 percent would be closed or sold. The Lima plant fell short of these standards. In January 1998, BP announced that no more bids would be accepted and the plant would close at the end of 1998.

However, BP did accept a bid in April 1998 submitted by Clark, USA, Inc. This company is owned jointly by the Blackstone Group, a New York investment firm that owns 68 percent of Clark, and Occidental Petroleum, which owns 31 percent. Clark bought the plant from BP for $2.5 million. The company promised to continue hiring existing employees.

Like so many companies with laudable policies of social responsibility, BP faced a difficult choice. Its basic policy concerning social performance is as follows:

> We see active support for the people and communities where we operate as a fundamental part of our contribution; an expression of belonging, but also of a wider responsibility.
>
> A responsibility to:
>
> - be aware of the social impact of our activities
> - engage positively with governments, community leaders and others to manage our impact on the basis of dialogue and partnership
> - ensure that our overall impact is beneficial to the communities affected by our presence

---

[2]Cooper, "A Town Betrayed."

- bring positive energy to social and community development needs.[3]

This statement of policy had to be balanced with BP's commitment to advance stockholder interests, and the Lima plant and community did not weigh equally with shareholders. The story of BP in Lima, Ohio, illustrates two significant points as an introduction to this chapter. First, large multinational companies have enormous economic power over small governments and communities. Here was a company, with headquarters in London some 3,000 miles from Lima, making decisions that could have seriously affected the lives of thousands of people in a small community. Sec-ond, corporations face difficult choices in balancing the competing forces in their achievement of basic company social purposes. The reality is that all companies that profess social responsibilities face this difficult question of balance. Unfortunately, there are no quantitative formulas to determine the balance. The result is always a judgment of top executives.

In this chapter we first define the meaning of multinational corporations (MNCs). Then we examine the relationships between MNCs and governments. Special attention is given in this discussion to foreign payoffs. The chapter concludes with a discussion of free trade versus protectionism.

The MNC Defined

There are many definitions of the MNC. We accept one used by the United Nations, that MNCs are "enterprises which own or control production or service facilities outside the country in which they are used."[4] The MNC is an agency of direct, as opposed to portfolio, investment in foreign countries. It is not always incorporated or private. It can be a cooperative or state-owned entity. Almost every large business organization has some direct or indirect involvement with foreign countries, but only when an enterprise confronts one or more of the problems of designing, producing, marketing, or financing its products or services within and among foreign nations does it become truly multinational. Many MNCs progress through the following stages:

1. Export products to foreign countries.
2. Establish sales organizations abroad.
3. License use of patents and know-how to foreign firms that make and sell the MNC's products.

---

[3]British Petroleum Company, "BP Social Report 1997," www/bp.com/commun/report/main2/main2.htm.

[4]United Nations Economic and Social Council, Special Intercessional Committee, *The Impact of Transnational Corporations on the Development Process and on International Relations,* New York: United Nations, 1975. For other definitions, see Ricky W. Griffin and Michael W. Pustay, *International Business: A Managerial Perspective,* Reading, Mass.: Addison-Wesley, 1995, pp. 13–16.

4. Establish foreign manufacturing facilities.
5. Multinationalize management from top to bottom.
6. Multinationalize corporate stock ownership.
7. Coordinate global operations.

To simplify, MNCs can be divided into two categories. First are those that operate in foreign countries on the basis of policies and controls administered by home-country headquarters. Companies in stages 1 through 3, noted above, are in this category. In some instances, however, foreign subsidies exercise a good bit of autonomy.

Second are those that operate on a global basis. These companies have an executive group somewhere in the world responsible for integrating and planning for a product line and allocating company resources accordingly. The decisions of what to sell, where to sell, where to manufacture, and where to buy raw materials and components are determined on a worldwide basis. These corporations have been given a number of names, such as transnational, global, international, multinational, and worldwide. Robert J. Eaton, Chrysler Corp., chairman, said after his company merged with Daimler-Benz Ag (a German company) that the combined firm would be "a transglobal company." There is no consensus on the meaning of any of these terms. We use these words and MNC interchangeably.[5]

The Ford Motor Company is a good example of an MNC. Ford has manufacturing and assembly plants in countries around the world. It has a network of dealers in over 200 countries. IBM is another example. It imports electronic components from many countries and sells computers throughout the world. Foreign companies such as Seimens of Germany, Phillips of the Netherlands, Nestlé of Switzerland, the European Airbus Corporation, and Toyota of Japan also are examples of MNCs.

Some MNCs are said to be stateless or borderless, meaning that if they choose, they can, with impunity, locate their world headquarters anywhere. This distinction, however, is more theoretical than operational. They are national firms with international operations. Even a company such as Switzerland's Nestlé, despite the fact that 98 percent of its sales and 89 percent of its assets are outside the home country, is not likely to move its headquarters for many cogent reasons.

For example, the common-stock ownership and control for the typical MNC remains national rather than international. Except for a few companies like Nestlé, most employees are nationals of the home nation. The global company maintains its records in the home currency and is subject to its tax and other laws. These ties are part of the culture of the company, which is not easily modified.[6]

---

[5]Michael Porter views the multinational firm as one having business activities in many nations but it makes no effort to link them. Global companies, he says, also have activities in many countries but seek to coordinate them. Michael Porter, *The Competitive Advantage of Nations*, New York: Macmillan/Free Press, 1990.

[6]Yai-Su, "Global Corporations Are National Firms with International Operations," *California Management Review*, Winter 1992.

Steve Burow, president of the Anheuser-Busch Companies' international operation, put this perspective colorfully. He said: "It would be difficult to disassociate ourselves from America, even if we wanted to do so . . . Our packaging is even red, white and blue, and the American eagle is part of our image."[7]

Objectives of MNCs and Host Governments

The fundamental motive of going abroad is, of course, profit. MNCs in stages 1 through 3 seek to profit in obvious ways. The process is more complicated when a company gets to stage 4. Theoretically, in this stage management would like to manufacture in those countries where it finds the greatest competitive advantage; would like to buy and sell anywhere in the world to take advantage of the most favorable price to the company; would like to take advantage throughout the world of changes in labor costs, productivity, trade agreements, and currency fluctuations; and would like to expand or contract on the basis of worldwide comparative advantages. Its objectives are to obtain a high and rising return on invested capital, achieve greater sales, keep financial risk within reasonable limits in relations to profits, and maintain its technological and other proprietary strengths.

Generally speaking, dominant goals of most countries around the world, developed and less developed, would embrace the following: economic growth, full employment of people and resources; raising of workers' skills; price stability; a favorable balance of payments; more equitable distribution of income; a fair share of the profits made by MNCs; improvement of technology in and productivity of domestic business firms; national hegemony over the economic system; control over national security; social stability; and advancement of the quality of life.

MNCs have been and can be of enormous help to governments in their efforts to achieve most of these goals, especially the economic ones. At the same time, it is clear that conflicts between the two sets of goals and decision-making processes are inevitable.

The Power of MNCs: An Overview of Defenders and Critics

The large global companies exert enormous economic as well as technological, environmental, political, and cultural power in the world. This was illustrated in the BP story. Table 12-1 shows the top 15 largest MNCs in 1997 in order of their total revenues. The revenues of each of these companies are greater than the gross domestic products of most other nations of the world.

---

[7]Louis Uchitelle, "Global Tug, National Tether," *New York Times,* April 30, 1998.

TABLE 12-1   **The World's Largest Corporations in 1997**
Ranked in Order of Revenues

			$ mil.
1	General Motors	U.S.	178,174.0
2	Ford Motor	U.S.	153,627.0
3	Mitsui	Japan	142,688.3
4	Mitsubishi	Japan	128,922.3
5	Royal Dutch/Shell Group	Brit./Neth.	128,141.7
6	Itochu	Japan	126,631.9
7	Exxon	U.S.	122,379.0
8	Wal-Mart Stores	U.S.	119,299.0
9	Marubeni	Japan	111,121.2
10	Sumitomo	Japan	102,395.2
11	Toyota Motor	Japan	95,137.0
12	General Electric	U.S.	90,840.0
13	Nissho Iwai	Japan	81,893.8
14	Intl. Business Machines	U.S.	78,508.0
15	Nippon Telegraph & Telephone	Japan	76,983.7

Source: *Fortune,* August 3, 1998.

These and many other MNCs have huge sums of money, access to the latest technology, and, through their operations, political power. Professor Thomas Donaldson of Georgetown University correctly observes that "with the exception of a handful of nation-states, multinationals are alone in possessing the size, technology, and economic reach necessary to influence human affairs on a global basis."[8]

Supporters of the MNCs see them as engines that bring to poorer nations new technology, new products at low cost, new jobs and income, and financial investments. Critics have a very different view.

Critics of the MNCs—The Activists

While the subject of this chapter is about the MNCs and government relationships, it is relevant to consider the criticisms of what might be called professional MNC critics. These are organized activist groups that have their own agendas but often act as self-appointed protectors of third-world countries. To name a few, there are Ralph Nader's Public Citizen and its magazine *Multinational Monitor;* Greenpeace; the Sierra Club; and Friends of the Earth. They have worldwide influence. Greenpeace, for instance, has offices in 33 countries. These organizations often form coalitions across national boundaries to pressure MNCs for a special purpose, such as ending reliance on child labor. They tend to focus on environmental and human rights issues.

---

[8]Thomas Donaldson, *The Ethics of International Business,* New York: Oxford University Press, 1989, p. 31.

For example, activists have pressured corporations to get out of Myanmar because of the human rights abuses of the government. Many companies have responded and left the country. RTZ-CRA, the largest mining group in Great Britain, and Freeport-McMoRan, a United States company, have been attacked by environmentalists for their operations in Indonesia. In Malaysia, a $5.5 billion hydroelectric dam to be built by Asea Brown Boveri, a Swiss-based company, and other associated companies is being accused of destroying rainforest.[9]

Critics see MNCs as powerful despoilers of the ecological, political, and social systems where they choose to operate. One critic observes that: "In effect, what has taken place is a massive shift in power, out of the hands of nation-states and democratic governments and into the hands of TNCs (transnational corporations) and banks. It is now the TNCs that effectively govern the lives of the vast majority of the people on Earth."[10] Critics see the MNCs as greedy global bullies interested only in profits and detached from human interests.

These groups can hurt MNCs by publicizing alleged shortcomings, organizing consumer boycotts, bringing lawsuits, and pressuring legislators to enact laws to achieve the objectives of critics. These tactics have paid dividends. Many companies have responded by acceding to pressures for developing new policies on social and community responsibilities.

The MNCs and Lesser-Developed Countries (LDCs)

Relationships between MNCs and LDCs have changed dramatically during the past two decades. Former resentments and deep suspicion have given way to the welcome mat as the LDCs have seen the benefits that the infusion of MNC capital and technology has brought to their countries. Indeed, LDCs have offered generous inducements to MNCs to locate plants in their countries. For example, they offer tax holidays, exemptions from import duties, construction of infrastructure, low-interest loans, cheap labor, and relaxation of environmental restrictions.

Although the critical rhetoric is at a lower pitch today and the welcome mat is down, the inherent tensions between the MNCs and LDCs persist. The global financial crisis of 1997–98, discussed in the next chapter, devastated many developing countries and reignited old flames of discontent with MNCs. While the cause of the crisis cannot be lodged against the MNCs, they became a target. Here are some of the more important older and persistent complaints.

1. *Challenge to Nation-State Sovereignty.* They want control of their economies and want to achieve their economic, political, and social objectives. The power of the MNC can influence each of these objectives

---

[9]"The Fun of Being a Multinational," *The Economist*, July 20, 1996.

[10]Tony Clark, "Mechanisms of Corporate Rule," Chapter 26 in Jerry Mander and Edward Goldsmith, eds., *The Case Against the Global Economy*, San Francisco: Sierra Club Books, 1996. This book presents a detailed statement of the many specific criticisms leveled at MNCs.

and in so doing may challenge the sovereignty, or the supreme political power, of the government. A country may be obliged to give up some power and independence in exchange for the wealth an MNC may bring.

2. *Inequities.* One of the most enduring and persistent complaints about alleged inequities by LDCs is that prices of raw materials extracted from their countries are falling, while prices of imported manufactured goods from industrialized countries are rising. This, they say, creates a growing inequity. Other perceived inequities include avoidance of taxes and giving the best management jobs to MNC home-country citizens.

3. *Interference with Economic Objectives.* Interference can occur in many ways. For example, an MNC may wish to locate a plant in an area of prosperity when the host country would prefer its location in an underdeveloped region. MNC demands for local support can add to host-country expenditures for infrastructure. Since MNCs typically do their research and development at home, host countries become technologically dependent on the MNCs for innovation and invention. The MNCs have the strength to attract bank loans that otherwise might be available for local businesses.

4. *Social Disruption.* The introduction of different mores, habits, behavior, and ethical values, plus new products, management styles, distribution systems, more money, and technology, do affect local ways of thinking and doing things. The introduction of blue jeans, movies, Western attitudes toward women, work habits, or automobiles shifts cultures toward Western values. Some locals may applaud the changes, while others deplore them.

5. *Environmental Degradation.* Many nations are becoming more concerned about the impact of MNCs on their environment. Environmental concerns are rapidly moving higher in the chain of priorities throughout the world, including in most of the LDCs.

6. *Imperialism.* Many of the awakening nations look on foreign managers with fear and distrust as the embodiment of an old, not easily forgotten, exploitative colonialism. Many LDCs feel relegated to the role of supplying raw materials and cheap labor because they are denied the technology to develop into industrialized nations.

7. *Symbol of Frustration and Antipathy.* The LDCs have grievances about their position in the world that have nothing to do with the MNC but the MNC is a convenient visible target for their anger. Many of the LDCs are governed by some form of dictatorship that is antagonistic to the free market mechanism governing decision making of the MNCs.

The MNCs and Industrialized Nations

LDCs are not alone in seeking advantages offered by MNCs. For example, France offered lucrative enticements to get the Mercedes-Benz Swatchmobile factory to locate in France in 1995. In the United States, South Carolina brought a BMW plant to Spartanburg partly with inducements. California, Tennessee, and other states brought Japanese automobile plants to their areas with various inducements. European countries offer inducements to U.S. semiconductor companies to locate there. This phenomenon is not new. It has existed for years.

On the other hand, industrialized countries may impose barriers of various types to impede foreign direct investments. For example, foreign company investments are restricted in the United States in national defense, nuclear energy, coastal shipping, and broadcasting, to name a few. Industrial countries also impose barriers to imports, an issue that will be discussed later in the chapter.

Response of the MNCs to Host-Government Criticisms

Naturally, MNC managers and their defenders respond that many of the criticisms of their behavior are only partially true at best and outright false at worst. Despite their alleged shortcomings, they say, MNCs significantly help host governments achieve their national aims. The most frequently expressed claims of how MNCs benefit host nations, in no particular order of priority, are as follows:

- Provide employment.
- Train managers.
- Provide products and services that raise the standard of living.
- Introduce and develop new technical skills.
- Introduce new managerial techniques.
- Provide greater access to international markets.
- Raise the gross national product.
- Increase productivity.
- Help build foreign exchange reserves.
- Encourage the development and spin-off of new industries.
- Assume investment risk that might not otherwise be undertaken.

MNC managers have their own litany of complaints. The flip side of virtually all host-country grievances noted above is an MNC complaint. For example, MNCs dislike restrictions on what they produce, how they produce it, the pricing of products, product distribution, and repatriation of profits.

These are general responses. But what is the MNC response when specific demands are made? For example, what happens when an LDC demands an MNC hire only native managers, give local citizens a 51 percent control interest in the company, or bring new advanced technology to its operations? The response of an MNC will vary, of course, depending upon such factors as bargaining power of the host country, importance of the plant to the host country, or the ability of the country to replace the plant. A study of reactions of MNCs in China showed that among all the possible strategic responses, the most often used by far was compromise.[11]

Despite the great power that large MNCs can exert over LDCs, the fact remains that LDCs have the sovereign power to decide what MNCs can and cannot do in their countries. Each party wants something from the other and each wants to exercise control over the other. Each, therefore, must balance conflicting interests.

Codes of Conduct

In the past decade, MNCs have been awash in codes of behavior prepared by international organizations, governments, companies in their industries, and themselves. A multiplicity of forces have converged to bring this about. For instance, increasing pressure is exerted on corporations to respect human rights, act ethically, and be socially responsible. Activist groups persist in their efforts to have corporations meet their standards of conduct. There is a growing perception among business managers that good community relations and attention to corporate social responsibilities pay off in higher profits. Governments are enacting more laws concerning ethical behavior in business operations. Finally, widespread attention is given in the media to allegations of corporate conduct, which, of course, puts pressure on business to respond.

In the United States, there has been widespread publicity given to allegations that American companies are exploiting child labor in foreign lands for profit. Kathie Lee Gifford, a well-known television personality and wife of a football star, for example, was accused of lending her name to a line of discount women's clothing that had been produced by child labor in foreign lands. But there were many other targets, especially Nike and Reebok. In immediate response, apparel manufacturers and their contractors agreed to form an Apparel Industry Partnership that adopted a code of conduct concerning working conditions and limits on child labor in apparel factories.

European companies also have been the focus of activist attention. Ikea, a Swedish company, and Vellon S.A., a Swiss company, for example, were accused of selling oriental rugs made by children. They, together with other oriental rug sellers, responded by forming the Foundation for a Just Trade in Oriental Rugs. This group agreed to contribute money for the elimination of child labor.[12]

Three major religious groups published an eighty-page magazine-size pamphlet that contains twenty-three codes prepared by organizations around the

---

[11]Ingmar Bjorkman and Gregory E. Osland, "Multinational Corporations in China: Responding to Government Pressures," *Long Range Planning*, June 1998.

[12]John Tagliabue, "Europe Fights Child Labor in Rug Making," *New York Times*, November 19, 1996.

world.[13] For instance, included are the CERES Principles on the Environment, which grew out of the *Exxon Valdez* oil spill in Prince William Sound, Alaska; the International Code of Ethics for Canadian Business; the International Covenant on Economic, Social & Cultural Rights, ratified by the United Nations General Assembly; the Beijing Declaration, prepared by representatives of governments participating in the Fourth World Conference on Women in Beijing, China; and the White House Apparel Industry Partnership Workplace Code of Conduct & Principles of Monitoring.

This by no means exhausts the list of important codes. Noteworthy is the Caux Round Table Principles for Business. The Round Table was formed by executives from global companies meeting in Caux, Switzerland, to formulate a code of behavior for the conduct of international business. The group plans a series of meetings with businesspeople from around the world to discuss the code.

Added to this list, of course, are the specific codes adopted by individual companies, illustrated by Johnson and Johnson in Chapter 5, Royal/Dutch Shell in Chapter 6, and Caterpillar in the case after Chapter 13.

This new emphasis on codes has focused the attention of MNCs on improving their behavior in foreign lands. Debora L. Spar correctly observes that "the available evidence indicates that the presence of U.S. multinationals usually corresponds to an improvement in human rights."[14] Beyond human rights, these codes have resulted in more concern for all aspects of company behavior.

Issues of Ethics and Social Responsibility

U.S. MNCs face a question about selling abroad pesticides that are banned in the United States. Also, questions arise about how to ensure that pesticides and chemicals that are approved in the United States are used properly in underdeveloped countries. The same issues apply to pharmaceuticals. Additional questions arise when U.S.-banned pesticides may be exported back to the United States in foreign-produced foods. Importing such products is illegal, but often the illegality may be difficult to detect.

What are the responsibilities of a company producing foods that may be misused in foreign lands, such as infant milk formula? What should policy be with respect to toys that are considered dangerous in the United States but acceptable abroad? What responsibilities do MNCs have to operate with due concern for problems in the world environment, such as global warming, ocean contamination, and air pollution? How far can and should an MNC go to protect human rights in a host country?

---

[13]The Interfaith Center on Corporate Responsibility, The Ecumenical Council for Corporate Responsibility, and The Taskforce on the Churches and Corporate Responsibility, *Principles for Global Corporate Responsibility: Bench Marks for Measuring Business Performance,* New York: Interfaith Center on Corporate Responsibility, 1998.

[14]Debora L. Spar, "The Spotlight and the Bottom Line," *Foreign Affairs,* March/April 1998.

In dealing with issues such as these, intertwined in executive decision making is the question of whether a proposed action is ethical even though it may be legal. How about dumping toxic waste in an underdeveloped country that is hungry for the cash paid for permission to dump, though this may endanger the health of citizens of that country? How far can and should a company go in applying the standards of the home country to LDC operations? What about illicit payments made to get something legitimate done?

Or consider a situation such as this: You are doing business in Mexico and pay workers the same wages as local companies. Critics in the United States denounce you for exploiting Mexican workers. You respond to the criticism by raising wages in your Mexican plant. The local businesses then accuse you of trying to steal their best workers by paying the higher wages. They say you are fomenting labor unrest and competing unfairly with local companies. What should you do?

In the final analysis, it is the individual nation-state and the international community acting in unison that will determine the conduct of multinational operations. But this is a weak reed to depend on. While international codes are probably helpful in drawing attention to acceptable standards of behavior, there is no world organization to enforce them. Many host countries are too weak economically and politically to force upon MNCs the type of standards, say, that are applicable to companies doing business in more advanced industrial nations such as the United States.

Hopefully, over time, there will be a gradual improvement in the social and ethical standards of MNCs as new laws are passed, and as MNCs voluntarily assume more social responsibilities and inject more ethical values in their decision making. We agree with David Vogel of the University of California, Berkeley, that "those who make decisions for global enterprises need to be encouraged, pressured, and even inspired to make decisions that show as much sensitivity as possible to human rights, social justice, and world peace."[15]

Foreign Payoffs

Cultural differences around the world sometimes create extremely difficult moral and ethical problems for American MNCs. The ways in which business is conducted sometimes entangle U.S. companies in a complex web of rewards for influence, intricate interplay with political forces in a foreign country, customs, and subtle business arrangements. Companies have often found in some highly industrialized countries as well as in the LDCs that, in order to do business, it is necessary to make some sort of payment.

Many types of payoffs raise questions of ethics and legality. At one end of a spectrum are lubrication bribes involving relatively small amounts of money.

---

[15]David Vogel, "The Responsibilities of Multinational Corporations," in Reed Moyer, *International Business Issues and Concepts,* New York: Wiley, 1984, p. 399.

These range from tips for services rendered to "requests" for money to get someone to perform, such as getting packaged machinery off ports of entry to a purchaser. These are often called "honest graft," "tokens of appreciation," or "contributions." The practice is universally accepted as legitimate for services rendered. The payments are often justified as offsets to low salaries.

At the other extreme of the spectrum are extortion and clear bribery. This is a situation in which, for example, the head of Gulf Oil Corporation found himself when South Korea's Republican party threatened the company's $300 million investment (mostly in refining and petrochemicals) if the company did not make a $10 million contribution to the party. Bob Dorsey, chairman of Gulf, eventually haggled the amount down to $3 million.[16] This, of course, was blackmail. But many other U.S. companies were found guilty of making payments to foreign nationals to gain contracts.

As a result of such payoff disclosures Congress passed the Foreign Corrupt Practices Act of 1977 (FCPA) (amended in 1988). This act makes it a criminal offense to offer a bribe to a foreign government official. For unlawful acts companies may be fined $1 million and individuals may face fines of $10,000 and five years in jail. The law does not apply to facilitating or "grease" payments that are intended only to expedite normal business affairs. The law prohibits offering money or anything of value to any person (foreign or domestic) if it is known that any or all of the money or value offered will be used to influence a foreign official, politician, or political party. This means, of course, that a corporation and an individual manager may run afoul of the law if it is known that commission payments are used to induce government officials to do something on behalf of the company.

Since 1977 the Department of Justice has not been too diligent in prosecuting cases under the FCPA but currently it has more than 40 alleged violations under investigation.[17]

American companies have complained for years that they have lost contracts to MNCs from countries that tolerate bribes. Indeed in some European countries bribes are tax deductible. The U.S. Commerce Department said that firms willing to pay bribes win 80 percent of the contracts up for bid.[18] As a result, the United States has been putting pressure on other countries to enact measures to control bribery. This attempt succeeded in November 1997 when the world's large industrial countries agreed to a treaty that would outlaw the practice of bribing foreign government officials. Following a bruising and acrimonious series of meetings, the twenty-nine European and Asian members of

---

[16]Peter Nehemkis, "Business Payoffs Abroad: Rhetoric and Reality," *California Management Review,* Winter 1975. See also Neil H. Jacoby, Peter Nehemkis, and Richard Eells, *Bribery and Extortion in World Business,* New York: Macmillan, 1977.

[17]Nelson, "29 OECD Nations Commit to Pact Penalizing Bribery"; and "$24.8 Million Penalty Paid by Lockheed," *New York Times,* January 28, 1995.

[18]Jack Nelson, "29 OECD Nations Commit to Pact Penalizing Bribery," *Los Angeles Times,* November 21, 1997.

the Organization for Economic Cooperation and Development (OECD) agreed to present the treaty to their respective parliaments.

While the treaty clearly is a major victory for the United States in stopping payoffs, some controversial issues are unsettled. For example, the treaty specifies payoff crimes but leaves the MNC home government to "consider" them in controlling bribery. The question of whether payoffs are tax deductible has not been settled by all governments. There is also a question of who is a "public official" to whom bribes will be illegal. These and other issues arise partly because payoffs have long been accepted in many countries and attitudes and laws vary greatly among nations. An unanswered question at this time is whether all twenty-nine member nations will approve the treaty. Finally, there is a question of how seriously various countries will prosecute offenses.[19]

The law and the codes highlight ethical and legal questions in foreign sales, especially of expensive items having large sales in one country. It appears that the global trend of higher ethical standards in foreign transactions is moving in the right direction.

MNC–Government Relations in Home Countries: An Overview

The United States

A policy of the United States for many decades has been, and still is, to foster worldwide economic progress. The government has always viewed the MNC as an instrument of global economic progress. Sometimes, however, the goals of MNCs and United States foreign policy conflict.

While the basic business–government relationship can be adversarial, there is still plenty of cooperation between MNCs and government agencies. Remember, too, there are thousands of lobbyists in Washington and state capitals who pressure government on behalf of their companies and industries.

Examples of specific aids to the MNCs provided by our government abound. Substantial subsidies are made to encourage agricultural exports and special measures are available to companies that explore for scarce resources abroad, such as oil. The government provides abundant information about foreign business opportunities without cost to business. The Export-Import Bank, created in 1934, is a government-owned corporation that promotes U.S. foreign trade in the form of direct and guaranteed loans to foreign buyers of U.S. export products.

The federal government, on the other hand, has sometimes restrained MNCs. For instance, the Clinton administration, because of strains with China over human rights, recently told the Export-Import Bank it should not help

---

[19]Edmund L. Andrews, "29 Nations Agree to Outlaw Bribing Foreign Officials," *New York Times*, November 21, 1997.

American MNCs participate in China's mammoth $30 billion Three Gorges dam project. U.S. manufacturers of sophisticated electronics equipment have been prevented from selling abroad in the interests of national security. According to the National Association of Manufacturers, the United States has invoked economic sanctions seventy times against more than thirty-five countries from 1993 through 1996. The major purposes, in order of numbers of sanctions, have concerned human rights and democratization, anti-terrorism, nuclear nonproliferation, anti-narcotics, political stability, worker rights, use of prison labor, and environmental protection.[20]

Raymond Vernon, a prominent scholar of the MNCs and professor at Harvard University, sees increasing conflict in the future between MNCs and their base governments. He writes: "My concern . . . is that some of the most important political struggles which multinational enterprises face in the future will originate within the home countries of the multinationals . . . "[21] He believes the conflict will heighten between those who advocate free markets and those who feel disadvantaged by the MNCs. That is happening now. For instance, labor unions attack the MNCs for exporting jobs. Critics, such as Ralph Nader, denounce the MNCs, alleging that in their foreign operations, they fail to resist human rights abuses, exploit low-paid workers, pollute the environment, and in general fail to assume community social responsibilities. On the other hand are those groups that believe the world will benefit from free markets that are left to operate unfettered.

Other Countries

The United States is not alone among the nations of the world in encouraging or inhibiting home-based MNCs. A good illustration is Europe's Airbus Industries four-nation consortium. Since 1970 this group has received billions of dollars (some estimates are as high as $25 billion) in government aid to finance the development of commercial jet airliners. The consortium was formed and supported by France, Great Britain, Germany, and Spain as a direct challenge to American dominance in the civilian jet airliner business. It has worked. A decade ago three U.S. companies—Boeing, McDonnell Douglas, and Lockheed—commanded the world market for large commercial jet airplanes. Today, Airbus has captured about one-third of the market. In reply to our complaints about these subsidies, the Europeans say we subsidize our aircraft manufacturers with defense contracts, which is partly correct.

The interrelationships between business and government among the European countries are much more cooperative than in the United States, with the exception of Great Britain, where the linkage now is more comparable to that in

---

[20]Found in Evelyn Iritani, "U.S. Learns How to Anger Friends While Failing to Influence Enemies," *Los Angeles Times*, March 24, 1997.

[21]Raymond Vernon, *In the Hurricane's Eye*, Cambridge, Mass.: Harvard University Press, 1998, p. 109.

this country. Business and government are much more closely related in Germany and especially in France. A number of large companies are owned by the French government: for instance, France Telecom, Air France, and a number of aerospace firms such as Thomson. The French MNC–government relationship is more similar to that of Japan than the United States. In countries such as the Netherlands, Norway, Sweden, and Denmark, there are close relationships between government and large companies. In Japan, as noted in several places in this book, there is a very close relationship among large companies and the government. The government is deeply involved in helping Japanese companies penetrate foreign markets and protects their turf at home from foreign competition. In China, South Korea, and in many countries in Southeast Asia, the relationship is very close with companies owned and operated by officers in the military (as in China) or by family members (as in Indonesia).

Free Trade versus Protectionism

From the beginning of our history, we have, on the one hand, maintained a free trade policy but, on the other hand, protected our industries from foreign competition. In recent years, the United States has taken the lead in creating international agencies to advance free trade throughout the world. At the same time, protectionist pressures have increased in the United States. Why free trade? And why protectionism?

Why Free Trade?

The case for free trade is comparatively simple. By virtue of climate, labor conditions, raw materials, capital, management, or other considerations, some nations have an advantage over others in the production of particular goods. For example, Brazil can produce coffee beans at a much lower cost than the United States. Coffee beans could be grown in hothouses in the United States, but not at a price equal to that which Brazilians can charge and make a profit. But the United States has a distinct advantage over Brazil in producing computers. Resources will be used most efficiently when each country produces that for which it enjoys a cost advantage. Gain will be maximized when each nation specializes in producing those products for which it has the greatest economic edge. This is what economists call the *law of comparative advantage*. It follows that maximum gain on a worldwide basis will be realized if there are no impediments to trade, if there is free competition in pricing, and if capital flows are unrestricted.

It is not always easy, however, to see just where a nation has a comparative advantage. At the extremes the case is clear, but not in the middle range. Differences in monetary units, rates of productivity of capital and labor, changes in markets, or elasticities of demand, for instance, obscure the degree of advantage one nation may have over another at any time. Nevertheless, it is

FIGURE 12-1

Index of world trade and gross domestic product.

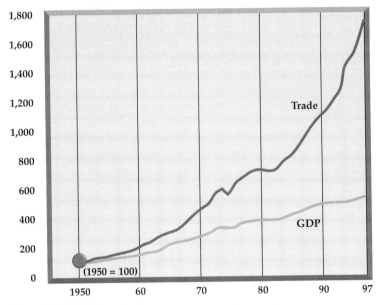

Source: World Trade Organization.

argued that free trade will stimulate competition, reward individual initiative, increase productivity, and improve national well-being. It will enlarge job opportunities and produce for consumers a wider variety of goods and services at minimum prices and with higher quality.

This is the theory. In practice, all countries have erected restraints on imports to protect their industries. We now discuss pressures for and against free trade around the world.

The United States Moves toward Free Trade

Since World War II, the United States has taken the lead in sponsoring liberalized trade and open markets. As a result of worldwide negotiations, trade in the global economy is far freer and more open and efficient than in prior years. One result has been an extraordinary leap in trade, as shown in Figure 12-1, and the generation of wealth for both developed and less-developed nations of the world.

A significant milestone in world trade was the ratification of the General Agreement on Tariffs and Trade (GATT) in Morocco in March 1994 among 125 nations of the world. This negotiation began in Uruguay in September 1986 and is known as the Uruguay Round, the eighth in a series that began in 1947 when GATT was started. Each round resulted in a general lowering of tariff and nontariff barriers around the world. The last round reduced tariff barriers by over 30 percent overall and by a higher percentage among highly industrialized countries. For some items (e.g., some pharmaceuticals, construction equipment, and paper), tariffs were completely eliminated.

FIGURE 12-2

U.S. merchandise trade (billions of 1992 dollars)

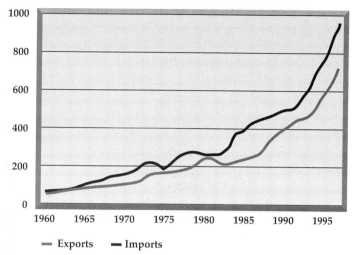

— Exports   — Imports

Source: U.S. Department of Commerce.

The participants in the Uruguay Round agreed that a faster method of tariff negotiation than GATT was essential and, as a result, they approved a new dispute settlement process in the World Trade Organization (WTO) located in Geneva, Switzerland. Since 1995 the United States has used the WTO dispute settlement procedure to resolve trade questions.

Another milestone was the Canada–United States Free Trade Agreement (CFTA), signed in 1987. This was followed in 1992 when the United States, Canada, and Mexico signed the North American Free Trade Agreement (NAFTA). Area free trade agreements are being formed around the world. The most important, in terms of scope, is the European Union.

These powerful initiatives for free trade have been partly offset by deviations from free trade among nations of the world, including the United States.

Pressures for Protectionism

Most domestic businesses, whether engaged in foreign trade or not, feel pressures from foreign competitors with better products and lower prices. Many seek and get protection from government. This is protectionism, and it has existed in the trade history of all nations.

In the early history of the United States, the motivation for protectionism was to "protect infant industries." Recently, there have been powerful pressures on government to protect some mature industries (e.g., automobiles, steel, textiles) from foreign competition. Politicians have responded affirmatively and legislated protection, despite a basic policy of free trade. Here are three justifications often given for this trend.

First, there are large trade deficits that need to be reduced (see Figure 12-2). In 1975, the United States enjoyed a small trade surplus (the difference between total exports and total imports of goods and services). Since then we have had large annual deficits each year. The deficit reached a peak of $152 billion in 1987 but dropped to $110 billion in 1997. Protectionists are concerned about the persistence and size of these deficits and believe they are detrimental to the United States and should be corrected. One way, they assert, is to discourage excessive imports.

Second, protectionists want to shield industries from "unfair" foreign competition. For example, foreign competitors have penetrated the U.S. market for textiles, steel, shoes, motorcycles, dolls, luggage, automobiles, and television sets. The result, say protectionists, is loss of jobs and other injuries to the economy.

Third, unfair trade barriers in foreign countries restrict American imports. Examples are nontariff barriers such as excessive and delayed inspection of imported products; unreasonable technical standards for product characteristics, such as size, quality, health, and safety; customs practices that inhibit consumer purchases of foreign goods and services; and quotas. These practices cost American jobs and should be stopped or retaliated against.

A leading exponent of protectionism in the United States today is Patrick J. Buchanan, who is a candidate for president of the United States in the forthcoming election of 2000. One major plank in his platform is prevention of loss of jobs from global competition by protecting our industries and workers through government action. His position is clarified in a book with the title *The Great Betrayal: How American Sovereignty and Social Justice Are Being Sacrificed to the Gods of the Global Economy.*[22] He wants tax and trade policies "that put America before the Global Economy, and the well-being of our own people before what is best for 'mankind.'"[23] According to Buchanan, "Efficiency does not come first. The good society, a decent income for all our families, the good life for all our people, come first."[24] More specifically, this means preservation of jobs, diminished dependence on foreign trade for the necessities of life, and restoration of America's lost sovereignty. He says our sovereignty is being surrendered by agreements such as NAFTA, GATT, and the WTO, and they should be abolished.

Free Trader Responses to Protectionists

Laura D'Andrea Tyson, a former chair of the White House Council of Economic Advisors, says that the implications of the large deficits are overstated. While large, they represent only a little over 1 percent of our gross domestic product. Furthermore, about 40 percent of our imports are intracompany transactions of American MNCs. She points out also that low-wage jobs may be lost because of imports of such items as toys from China. However, our exports of high-technology products such as jet aircraft benefit high-wage jobs.[25]

---

[22]Boston: Little, Brown and Company, 1998.
[23]Ibid., p. 288.
[24]Ibid., p. 289.
[25]Laura D'Andrea Tyson, "Trade Deficits Won't Ruin Us," *New York Times*, November 24, 1997.

Free traders point out that one of the reasons for the significant increase in world trade and gross domestic product, shown in Figure 12-1 was the success of GATT in lowering world tariff barriers. To eliminate the GATT and WTO would mean a return to an old system of negotiating every trade issue with each country involved, a path to sluggish growth of world trade.

Free trade advocates might accept the goals of protectionists as set forth by Buchanan but not the means. Senator Phil Gramm, for example, says that impediments or hindrances to free trade are "immoral." "They limit my freedom," he says. "If I want to buy a shirt in China, who has the right to tell me as a free person that I can't do it?"[26]

United States Deviation from Free Trade Policy

Despite strong free trade rhetoric and the steady lowering of tariff and other barriers to imports, the United States has protected industry from foreign competition. Over the years, we have raised tariffs, imposed quotas, and prohibited the import of various products. Beginning in 1981, Japan, under intense pressure from the federal government, imposed quotas on its export of cars and trucks to the United States. The quotas were voluntary and exist to this day. In 1988 quotas were placed on cotton diapers from China. We have erected high tariffs on many products over the years—certain specifications of motorcycles, textiles, tableware, and glassware, for example. We restrict foreign ownership of companies in certain industries, such as defense, airline, and radio broadcasting.

Trade records are marbled with "buy American" laws. The Federal Buy American Act of 1933, still in force, requires federal agencies to pay up to a 6 percent differential for domestically produced goods. Many states have similar laws covering a wide range of products. The Merchant Marine Act prohibits foreign vessels from plying domestic waterways.

But relative to the total trade of the United States, such restraints are not significant. Barriers imposed on U.S. imports by major trading partners are relatively much more important. Briefly, here are illustrative barriers on imports in Japan, Europe, and China.

Japanese Trade Barriers[27]

Japan is the third largest export market for our products. Our merchandise exports to Japan in 1997 were $65.7 billion and our imports were $121.4 billion, creating a deficit of $55.7 billion.

Contrary to popular notions, Japan has significantly reduced tariffs and quotas on manufactured goods. However, there are still high tariffs on many

---

[26]Gerald F. Seib and John Harwood, "Disparate Groups on Right Join Forces to Make Opposition to China's Trade Status a Key Issue," *The Wall Street Journal*, June 10, 1997, p. A20.

[27]The following on trade barriers in Japan, the European Union, and the People's Republic of China were derived from the U.S. Trade Representative, http://www.ustr.gov, 1998.

items, such as foods. The basic criticism is that Japanese trade practices and policies create barriers to U.S. exports, whereas our country has few restrictions on Japanese imports, and the result is not only a substantial trade deficit with Japan but loss of jobs in the United States.

A good example of the nontariff barriers confronting many American companies in Japan is the problem of Guardian Industries Corporation, of Auburn Hills, Michigan, in trying to sell flat glass in Japan. In testimony before Congress, Peter S. Walters, Group Vice President of the company, said:

> From the outset, we met a stone wall in Japan. With minor exceptions, neither glass distributors nor glass fabricators would handle our products, even though we were able to provide prices at least 30 to 50 percent below domestic prices. It soon became clear that the problem centered on Japan's distribution system. Each of the three Japanese flat glass companies—Asahi Glass Company, Nippon Sheet Glass Company, and Central Glass Company—maintained an exclusive network of distributors. Moreover, the three operate as a cartel, maintaining steady market shares of 50, 30, and 20 percent respectively since the early 1950s. In order to avoid what the Japanese call "confusion," no salesman for one Japanese flat glass manufacturer calls on another manufacturer's customer. Foreign suppliers clearly are not part of the club. Any distributors tempted to purchase imported glass are pressured in a variety of ways, including threats that their domestic sources of supply would be cut off.[28]

Guardian created a sales subsidiary in Japan and set up a network of warehouses to ensure quick delivery. In 1995 U.S. Trade Representative Mickey Kantor concluded a trade agreement with MITI Minister Ryutaro Hashimoto that opened the market to foreign glass producers. Mr. Peters told the House Subcommittee that despite these efforts "fully 80 percent of Japanese distributors say that they are not going to buy more foreign glass."[29] Guardian typically enjoys a market share of 10 to 20 percent in most major markets, but not in Japan, where its share is less than 1 percent.

There are other formidable nontariff barriers in Japan. Some U.S. food products are totally banned due to concerns over the entry of pests. In this category are eggplants, potatoes, and plums. Restrictions exist on imports of fresh fruits, vegetables, and other horticultural products. Imports of produce are hampered by burdensome on-site inspection requirements. Strict quotas exist for many fish, such as pollack surimi, pollack roe, herring, cod, and squid. Rice not only is imported under quota, but Japan has established a system that allows importers to set quality and other requirements. The United States has complained about this and also objected to the fact that our rice exports are put into stock and thus prevented from reaching Japanese consumers.

Currently there is a gradual relaxation of trade and nontrade barriers in Japan. Under intense recessionary pressures, Japanese companies and people

---

[28]Testimony of Peter S. Walters before the House Ways and Means Trade Subcommittee, U.S. House of Representatives, July 15, 1998.

[29]Ibid.

are seeking avenues to cost and price reduction. Nevertheless, the wall of barriers to free trade in Japan is still high and is likely to remain so.

European Union

The European Union (EU) is our largest trading partner. Our merchandise exports to the EU in 1997 were $140.8 billion and our imports were $157.5 billion, leaving a deficit of $16.7 billion. Importers into the EU face many restrictions. For example, fur and fur products of certain species are banned from countries that permit leghold traps or do not conform with trapping practices set forth in international standards. Regulations permit only importation of those wines produced with oenological practices authorized for the production of EU wines. As noted in the story of Monsanto at the beginning of Chapter 10, food products that contain genetically modified organisms are viewed with disfavor in Europe. The approval of such products is under review and final decisions will not likely be made for several years. Meanwhile, imports are subject to unexplained delays, procedural reviews, and other harassing tactics.

Exporters often face differing requirements among individual European states. While the European Commission has forged common standards for hundreds of items, it permits individual countries to prohibit imports of products that threaten "public security." The Dormont Manufacturing Company, which makes hoses that hook up deep-fat fryers and other appliances that use gas connections, has sold hoses throughout Europe without any safety problems. Now the company finds that inspectors are rejecting the hoses in favor of products made by local manufacturers. The reason given is that the connections are not tight and therefore the hoses are a hazard.[30]

States have their own standards for testing, labeling, and certifying products. In France, pet food must be accompanied by a veterinary certificate. Greece has its own standards for imported wheat. Italy has its own standards for processed meat, wood products, poultry, and seafood. Member states differ concerning intellectual property protection.

People's Republic of China

U.S. merchandise exports to China in 1997 were $12.8 billion and imports from that country were $62.6 billion, leaving a deficit of $49.7 billion. China's total imports in 1996 increased 5.1 percent while imports from the United States rose only 0.2 percent. China retains far more stringent controls over its foreign trade than Japan.

China has been lowering average tariff rates: from over 42 percent in 1996 to 17 percent in 1997. However, the country has used prohibitively high tariffs amounting to 100 percent on some products, (e.g., vehicles) to protect domestic industry. On the other hand, China wants high-technology items and tariffs

---

[30]Timothy Aeppel, "Europe's 'Unity' Undoes a U.S. Exporter," *The Wall Street Journal*, April 1, 1996.

on them are significantly lower. Indeed, some products are exempted from tariffs. Businesses complain that tariff rates on the same item differ among ports of entry. Added to the tariff rates are value-added taxes of 17 percent and consumption taxes also at 17 percent. Some importers, however, are able to negotiate exemption from these rates.

Some nontariff barriers such as licenses and quotas are centrally controlled. Government officials evaluate needs for particular products and allocate quotas accordingly. Quotas are administered only by government approved entities. In addition, products of great interest to China, such as grains, cotton, vegetable oils, and petroleum, may be imported only through state trading enterprises. Since the demand for such products usually exceeds the allowed supply by a wide margin, rampant smuggling and corruption exist.

China has inspection standards on hundreds of items. Unfortunately for businesses, there is great difficulty in learning what the standards are. Standards vary for imports from different countries. They also are different from those for the same type of domestic products. They differ from international standards. Quality licenses are required for manufactured goods before they can be imported. China does not accept U.S. certification, so businesses must go through a time-consuming and expensive process to obtain licenses. Import quarantine standards are arbitrarily applied. For example, the possible presence of the Mediterranean fruit fly has been used as a reason for banning entry of citrus fruit from certain areas in the United States.

Classical Free Trade Theory versus Reality

The reality is that the global economy is a mixture of free trade and protectionism. It always has been. Furthermore, classical free trade theory based on comparative advantage, explained above, has lost much validity for a large part of world trade. Many of the assumptions of the seventeenth and eighteenth centuries, upon which the theory is based, no longer are valid in today's world.

Professor Michael Porter of the Harvard Business School has formulated a major modification to classical theory to fit the modern world. He calls it *competitive advantage of nations.* Porter asks: Why does a nation achieve global superiority in one industry? He answers that it is because "industrial clusters" are formed in the nation. These clusters are composed of firms and industries that are mutually supporting, innovative, competitive, low-cost producers, and committed to meeting demanding consumer tastes.

Why is it, he asks, that Switzerland, a land-locked country with few natural resources, is a world leader in the production of chocolates? Why is it that Italy is a world leader in producing quality shoes? Why is it that Japan, a country whose economy was in shambles after World War II, is a global leader in making low-cost, mass-produced, quality, high-technology products?

Porter's answer lies in a congeries of factors that go beyond natural resources. Among the factors are a sizable demand from sophisticated consumers, an educated and skilled workforce, intense competition in the industry, and the existence of related and supporting suppliers. Government plays a part, but not a major one. Porter's theory is convincingly and amply illustrated in a major research project on the subject.[31] Classical theory is still valid for many products. However, Porter's work modernizes it to better fit the current reality of trade among nations in a vast range of products.

Classical economic doctrine postulates that when industries are granted relief from foreign competition, they fail to make needed capital investments, grow lazy, forget product quality, lose incentives, fail to innovate, raise prices, and enjoy excess profits from captive markets. Recent experiences in five protected industries in the United States contradict this theory. Indeed, relief from predatory foreign trade practices in the automobile, steel, textile, semiconductor, and machine tool industries has produced just the reverse results. In each of these industries, foreign competitive practices have had serious adverse impacts. But in each case federal protective measures from foreign imports have had remarkably beneficial results.[32]

The experience in these industries does not mean, of course, that protectionism is a good policy. It means, rather, that a government can help an industry recover from predatory foreign trade when it chooses the appropriate means, on a limited scale, for a limited period of time, for a few industries, and for the right reasons. Free trade should be the policy, but with some exceptions.

Concluding Observations

When corporations engage in international trade, new and complex problems of corporate social responsibility, ethics, and relationships with host governments as well as with the home government appear. While we have discussed international BGS relationships in other chapters, nowhere else is the focus so concentrated on a wide range of relationships as in this chapter. We continue the discussion in the next chapter.

---

[31]Michael E. Porter, *The Competitive Advantage of Nations,* New York: Free Press, 1990.
[32]Alan Tonelson, "Beating Back Predatory Trade," *Foreign Affairs,* July/August 1994.

NORTH AMERICAN FREE TRADE AGREEMENT (NAFTA)

N AFTA created a free trade block consisting of the United States, Canada, and Mexico. The first step in its formation was taken in 1987, when the United States and Canada signed the Canada–United States Free Trade Agreement (CFTA). In 1994 the agreement was extended to Mexico. By linking the United States, Canada, and Mexico, NAFTA creates the largest trading bloc in the world with 400 million customers in countries with a combined annual gross domestic product (GDP) over $8 trillion.

Supporters of NAFTA see it as an important benefit to the peoples of these countries. In the United States, however, it has powerful opponents who consider NAFTA to be a mortal blow to workers and some companies. The agreement raises significant political, social, and economic issues.

The present case relates primarily to issues associated with the United States and Mexico, and mostly the United States. The reason for this focus is that these issues are the core of the controversy surrounding NAFTA. When CFTA was signed in 1987, there was very little argument, nor was there concern about relationships with Canada when NAFTA was signed in 1994.

What Are the Major Provisions of NAFTA?

NAFTA is a massive, detailed, mind-numbing, nearly 2,000-page treaty of thousands of specific agreements. Here are a few highlights.

- One-half of the products the United States exports to Mexico became duty-free the day after NAFTA was implemented. Other tariffs will be completely eliminated, in phases, within ten years, although a few import-sensitive products (principally agricultural products and textiles) will have a fifteen-year transition.

Tariffs and Other Agreements

- Major nontariff barriers, such as quotas (on pharmaceuticals, for example), and some other types of restrictions (for instance, insisting on Mexican ownership of companies in certain industries) are removed.
- U.S. trucking firms were free to carry international cargo to Mexican states contiguous to the United States and to all of Mexico by the end of 1999.
- Restrictions on foreign investment in Mexico are removed except for oil exploration.
- Protections are to be enforced for investments, intellectual property, and trade secrets.
- U.S. and Canadian banks could acquire Mexican banks up to 8 percent of the industry's capital, and could have complete ownership by the year 2000.
- Environmental laws in the treaty are to be enforced on both sides of the border, and a panel is created to monitor how well the countries are implementing them. Sanctions can be applied if this panel finds that any of the three NAFTA members are violating environmental laws.
- If a domestic industry is suddenly seriously damaged by a surge of imports, there is a mechanism to revert back to pre-NAFTA duties as a safeguard.
- The Transitional Adjustment Assistance (TAA) program has been created for American workers who lose jobs or are threatened with job loss by Mexican imports. The program includes training, job search allowances, and relocation allowances.

Administrative Structure

A large infrastructure has been established to monitor the many NAFTA agreements. It includes about twenty new commissions. For example:

- NAFTA International Coordinating Secretariat. Supports and coordinates efforts of trade ministers of the three countries.
- Border Environment Cooperation Commission. Deals with environmental problems in the border region.
- North American Development Bank. Helps financing and development of NAFTA-related environmental and structural projects.
- North American Bank Community Adjustment Office. Helps administer government loans to small businesses affected by NAFTA.
- Commission for Labor Cooperation. Implements and monitors labor provisions of NAFTA.
- North American Commission for Environmental Cooperation. Implements and monitors environmental provisions of NAFTA.

In addition there are many committees and working groups: for example, Committee on Agricultural Trade, Committee on Private Commercial Disputes Regarding Agricultural Goods, Working Group on Agricultural Subsidies, and Working Group on Trade and Competition.[1]

The General Accounting Office observed that this bureaucracy is likely to be daunting to business since a company has to determine which agency can deal with a particular problem. On the other hand, it is difficult to see how a large and complicated treaty like NAFTA can be properly implemented without creating many coordinating and adjudicating groups.

Why Does the United States Want NAFTA?

Here are a few of the outstanding benefits claimed by supporters of NAFTA.

- Mexico is a large market for U.S. products and will grow into a larger one.
- U.S. business expansion into Mexico will enhance our global competitiveness, principally because of lower labor costs.
- NAFTA will generate more high-paying jobs for U.S. workers as Mexico imports more of our finished products.
- Economic growth of Mexico will support the reforms of the Mexican government and ensure greater political and social stability in that country.
- NAFTA is a model for further economic trade agreements with other Latin American countries. That will benefit our consumers, improve global competitiveness of American industry, and enhance the geopolitical leadership of the United States.

What Does Mexico Want from NAFTA?

- The Mexican government realizes that Mexico must change from an inward-focused economy to an outward-looking one to accommodate the rapidly growing demand for jobs caused by its swelling population. Closer economic linkage with the United States will help lock in the reforms of the Mexican government and growing trade will stimulate the economy.

---

[1]*North American Free Trade Agreement between the Government of the United States of America, the Government of Canada and the Government of the United Mexican States,* Washington, D.C.: U.S. Government Printing Office, 1993. For a general discussion, see Larry Brookhart et al., *Potential Impact on the U.S. Economy and Selected Industries of the North American Free-Trade Agreement* (Publication 2596), Washington, D.C.: United States International Trade Commission, January 1993; and Terry Wu and Neil Longley, "The U.S.-Canada Free Trade Agreement," *Journal of World Business,* Summer 1991.

- NAFTA will attract foreign investment as well as repatriation of investment by Mexican nationals, to the benefit of workers, business, and consumers.
- Mexico is concerned about growing U.S. purchases from Canada of products for which Mexico claims to have a comparative advantage, such as automobile parts.
- Mexico has a huge foreign debt, and growing export earnings as a result of NAFTA will help pay interest and principal.

NAFTA Incites Sharp Controversy

NAFTA is the most far-reaching trade agreement ever adopted by the three nations. It is unprecedented in its scope and depth. We now have four years of experience with the treaty and sharp division of opinion still exists with respect to NAFTA's benefits. Some think NAFTA has been beneficial to the three countries. Others are highly critical of what has happened.

Evaluation of the impact of NAFTA on the three countries is a complex undertaking. To begin, a number of its provisions are phased in over many years—some up to fifteen years. Also the financial crisis of Mexico in 1995 complicates analysis. Then, too, factual data on trade have many shortcomings. It is very difficult to disentangle NAFTA's economic impacts from the many other important forces affecting the economy. With these reservations, we summarize the basic arguments made for and against NAFTA.

What Are the Major Arguments against NAFTA?

Opposition to NAFTA has been strong and vocal, especially from labor and environmental groups. Except as noted, most of the following is derived from a joint statement by six labor and public interest organizations with the title *The Failed Experiment*.[2]

Jobs and Trade Will Be Adversely Affected

The essence of the argument concerning jobs was made by Ross Perot, the billionaire businessperson and presidential nominee, in these words: ". . . you'll hear a loud sucking noise" as jobs across the country are vacuumed up and sent to low-wage, low-benefit Mexico. Thomas Donahue, a vice president of the AFL-CIO, voiced an equally strong warning: "Among those who would suffer

---

[2]Economic Policy Institute, Institute for Policy Studies, International Labor Rights Fund, Public Citizen's Global Trade Watch, Sierra Club, and U.S. Business and Industrial Council Educational Foundation, *The Failed Experiment: NAFTA at Three Years,* June 26, 1997.

the most from NAFTA are industrial workers in the United States. It would pave the way for tens of thousands of their jobs to be exported to Mexico . . ."[3]

Critics claim that NAFTA turned a trade surplus the United States enjoyed with Mexico into a series of deficits. A surplus of $1.7 billion in 1993 turned into a deficit of $17 billion in 1996. While U.S. exports to Mexico expanded, imports from Mexico increased. The result, say critics, was a loss of 420,000 jobs in the United States.

Critics point to many disastrous incidents for workers and the U.S. economy. For example, in June 1998, workers at the General Motors Delphi East factory in Flint, Michigan, struck. The strike forced the closing of other GM plants when they could not get parts made at the Delphi plant. Behind this strike was the attempt by the United Auto Workers Union to stem the movement of jobs to Mexico. GM planned to shift production from the Delphi and other plants to a GM plant in Matamoros, Mexico. Workers at the Mexican plant earned $1 to $2 an hour while at the Flint plant workers were earning close to $22 an hour. The proposed movement was part of a long-term trend. Since 1978, GM had built over fifty parts factories in Mexico with 72,000 employees.[4] Hundreds of U.S. companies have reduced in size or shut down plants as management moved work to Mexico. Furthermore, managers have threatened downsizing to gain concessions from unions and workers. This point is made anecdotally but supported by an academic study by Kate Bronfenbrenner. She studied companies between 1993 and 1995 and concluded that one-half of them threatened to close the plant and move to Mexico as an anti-union strategy.[5]

Opponents of NAFTA say that jobs moved to Mexico are lost forever to U.S. unskilled workers. Jeff Faux and Thea Lee of the Economic Policy Institute observe that ". . . our past experience . . . show(s) that U.S. workers displaced by trade are more likely to move *down* the job ladder, to lower-paying jobs, to move *off* the ladder to permanent unemployment, not up the ladder to better jobs than they started with."[6]

We should note here that prominent politicians are highly critical of NAFTA. Patrick Buchanan, a current presidential candidate, wants to scrap NAFTA because he says the treaty costs Americans jobs and infringes significantly on national sovereignty. Another influential critic is Richard Gephart, minority leader in the U.S. House of Representatives. He is highly critical of what he says is a major loss of American jobs because of NAFTA.

---

[3]Thomas R. Donahue, "The Case against a North American Free Trade Agreement," *Columbia Journal of World Business,* Summer 1991, p. 93.

[4]Sam Dillon, "A 20-Year G.M. Parts Migration to Mexico," *New York Times,* June 24, 1998.

[5]Kate Bronfenbrenner, "Final Report: The Effects of Plant Closing or Threat of Plant Closing on the Right of Workers to Organize," Cornell University. Submitted to the Labor Secretariat of the North American Commission for Labor Cooperation, 1996. See also Kate Bronfenbrenner, "We'll Close! Plant Closings, Plant-Closing Threats, Union Organizing and NAFTA," *Multinational Monitor,* March 1997.

[6]Jeff Faux and Thea Lee, *The Effect of George Bush's NAFTA on American Workers: Ladder Up or Ladder Down?* Briefing Paper, Washington, D.C.: Economic Policy Institute, 1993, p. 4.

Wages

Real wages and compensation of American blue-collar workers have been declining. A major reason for this trend, say critics, is that low-wage jobs are lost in the United States as American companies move production to foreign low-wage countries. Also, as the American market is flooded with imports from low-wage foreign producers, jobs are lost in the United States. Workers who lose their jobs for these reasons flood the labor pool for low-wage jobs and further depress wages. Also, the outward flow of investment has a chilling effect on workers' collective bargaining climate. Increased immigration also adds to this pool. As the pool grows, managers have increased leverage over wage rates.

Mexico, say critics, has been a major force in these trends as a result of NAFTA. In addition, as a result of the peso crisis, discussed later, lower wage rates in Mexico have widened the gap between U.S. and Mexican workers. The differential increased from roughly a 7:1 ratio when NAFTA was signed to 11:1 today.[7]

Worker Rights

NAFTA is weak on mandatory worker rights and benefits. Both Kirkland and Donahue pointed out that the European Union has a charter that is stronger in protecting worker rights than NAFTA.[8] Critics complain that the labor agreement in the treaty provides no means to change the traditional record in Mexico of weak enforcement of its labor laws. Worker rights, they fear, will remain unprotected by NAFTA.

Degradation of the Environment

NAFTA has exacerbated environmental degradation near the so-called *maquiladoras.* Maquiladoras are located in industrial areas in communities like Tijuana, Juárez, Reynosa, and Matamoros, just across the border from the United States. In 1965 the Mexican government created a free trade zone, a strip of land 130 miles wide and extending 2,100 miles from the Pacific Ocean to the Gulf of Mexico, to encourage foreign corporations to build factories and create jobs for Mexicans. Companies can send components to be produced or assembled there that are then returned, duty-free, to the United States for final assembly, except for a tariff based on value added by the Mexican plants. About 3,000 plants have been erected there, employing close to 1,000,000 and exporting goods valued at $36.8 billion in 1996. Well over half the plants are owned by U.S. companies.

Critics say that the number of workers in maquiladoras increased 50 percent during the first three years of NAFTA. That intensified the appalling

---

[7]Robert Blecker, "NAFTA and the Peso Collapse: Not Just a Coincidence," Briefing Paper, Washington, D.C.: Economic Policy Institute, 1997.

[8]Lane Kirkland, "U.S.-Mexico Trade Pact: A Disaster Worthy of Stalin's Worst," *The Wall Street Journal,* April 18, 1991; and Donahue, "The Case against a North American Free Trade Agreement."

environmental conditions existing in the border towns, especially on the Mexican side. Border towns have been unable to improve infrastructure to keep pace with the growing numbers of people working there. Many of the areas have become sinkholes of abysmal living conditions and environmental degradation. Many ramshackle "homes" have no running water or toilets. Waterways are polluted with industrial and human waste.[9] The incidence of diseases transmitted through water and food contaminated by untreated sewage has grown. Hepatitis-A, for example, rose in the border region to between two and five times the U.S. national average.

The treaty contains provisions for enforcing environmental laws that are as strict in Mexico as in the United States. The problem, say critics, is lack of the means and will for enforcement.

Major Arguments in Support of NAFTA

Supporters of NAFTA reject these arguments. They advance a fundamental economic axiom that free competition and free trade are necessary for economic growth and that will raise the well-being of nations. They claim history is on their side when they argue that free trade will expand trade. This has been the experience with CFTA. After some experience with NAFTA, they point to the results in support of their defense of the treaty.

They also point to the fact that Mexico's economy and trade are such a small proportion of U.S. GDP and trade that it cannot have a significant impact on the U.S. economy. Mexico's GDP is less than 5 percent of U.S. GDP and its nonoil trade is much less than 1 percent of the U.S. GDP. We turn to a brief account of what has happened.

There are a number of reputable studies of the impact of NAFTA.[10] Every analysis and all data are subject to questions that complicate evaluation and conclusions. For instance, as noted above, some of the provisions of NAFTA are phased in over time. Also, data for 1997 and beyond are not complete. Trade and employment data are affected by many influences other than

---

[9]Frank Clifford and Mary Beth Sheridan, "Borderline Effects on Pollution: Swath of Pollution Links U.S., Mexico," *Los Angeles Times*, June 30, 1997.

[10]The president of the United States is required by law to submit each year a report to Congress on the operation of NAFTA. The latest is his *Study on the Operation and Effects of the North American Free Trade Agreement*, submitted to Congress July 1997. This report cites a number of studies. Three important studies are summarized in JayEtta Z. Hecker, *North American Free Trade Agreement: Impacts and Implementation*, Testimony before the Subcommittee on Trade, Committee on Ways and Means, House of Representatives, reproduced in United States General Accounting Office, GAO/T-NSIAD-97-256, Washington, D.C., September 11, 1997. The most comprehensive study of industrial sectors is Raul Hinojosa Ojeda, Curt Dowds, Robert McCleery, Sherman Robinson, David Runsten, Craig Wolff, and Goetz Wolff, *North American Integration Three Years after NAFTA: A Framework for Tracking, Modeling and Internet Accessing the National and Regional Labor Market Impacts*, North American Integration & Development Center, Los Angeles: UCLA, December 1996.

NAFTA. Then, too, each major analysis has been done with its own method-ological approach. Finally, the peso crisis of 1995 skews the data.

The Peso Crisis

During the 1980s, Mexico negotiated a debt-reduction package with its credi-tors that went into effect in 1990. The result was a substantial boost in confi-dence of investors, who prior to the debt negotiation had withheld invest-ment, and money began to flow in large quantities to Mexico. The Mexican government held the foreign exchange rate for the peso at too high a level in light of prices in Mexico and the result was overvaluation of the peso, which stimulated a boom in imports. Exports rose, but not nearly as rapidly as im-ports and a large trade deficit resulted. To finance the deficit, the government increased foreign borrowing, principally with short-term instruments. At the same time, investor confidence began to erode because of the large trade deficit, political unrest in the State of Chiapas in 1994, and the assassination of the ruling party's presidential candidate.

These events led to a sharp decline in the flow of capital and the govern-ment found it difficult to maintain the high exchange rate for the peso. In De-cember 1995, the government decided to let the market determine the value of the peso and it immediately plummeted in value.[11] (Prior to devaluation, the peso was 3.5 to the U.S. dollar.) The U.S. government stepped in with a $20 billion loan and arranged for an equal amount from other sources, such as the World Bank, to help Mexico pay off its debts and stabilize the peso. The peso became stabilized at a lower rate at around 7.5 to the dollar.

It is important to note that NAFTA did not contribute to this crisis. Rather, the crisis was a major disruption in the implementation of NAFTA and thwarted reaching the benefits claimed for the treaty.

Jobs

The president's report calculated that the goods exported to Canada supported about 1.56 million jobs in the United States in 1996. In the same year, the total number of U.S. jobs supported by exports to Mexico amounted to 749,000.[12] These numbers are, of course, important but not large relative to the approxi-mately 10 million total jobs added in the United States in the past decade.

Estimating the number of jobs lost because of NAFTA is very difficult for reasons noted above. One measure is the certification requests for help of those displaced. This information is reported by the Department of Labor (DOL) from requests for help under the Transitional Adjustment Assistance Program (TAA) set up by NAFTA. This program provides training and other assistance

---

[11]For a brief account, see Paul Krugman, "Dutch Tulips and Emerging Markets," *Foreign Affairs*, July/August 1995; and *Economic Report of the President,* Transmitted to the Congress, February 1995, Washington, D.C.: U.S. Government Printing Office, 1995.

[12]*Study on the Operations and Effects of the NAFTA*, p. 2.

Exhibit 1

Trade with Mexico and Canada (in billions of dollars)

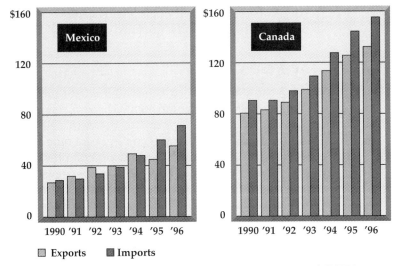

Exports   Imports

Source: U.S. Department of Commerce, in Helene Cooper, "Experts' View of NAFTA's Economic Impact: It's a Wash," *The Wall Street Journal,* June 17, 1997.

for workers certified as being dislocated because of NAFTA. From the beginning of NAFTA until mid-1997, 220,000 workers petitioned the DOL for adjustment assistance. The DOL certified 136,000 as eligible for assistance. These numbers are not large relative to total U.S. employment of approximately 130 million in 1937 and an annual labor turnover of about 2 million workers.[13]

Trade

NAFTA reduced tariff barriers in both the United States and Mexico. Prior to NAFTA, the average tariff level was 10 percent in Mexico; it dropped to 2.9 percent in 1996. In the United States the average tariff was 2.07 percent; it dropped to 0.65 percent in 1996. The result was a significant increase in trade, but it only accelerated a trend that had begun in 1988. During the 1980s, trade virtually stagnated. After 1988 both exports and imports sharply increased. By 1996 U.S. exports to Mexico had risen to $57 billion while imports totaled $74 billion. The deficit of $17 billion continued a long trend of deficits with Mexico. These trends are shown in Exhibit 1 and compared with Canada. Canada is the largest trading partner of the United States, and Mexico is the second largest export market.

A major criticism of NAFTA is that it incurred significant trade deficits with Mexico. The president's report included this assertion: "Generally, the facts do not support the view that trade surpluses increase employment levels or that trade deficits necessarily result in reduced employment. Over the last

---

[13]Gary Burtless, Robert Z. Lawrence, Robert E. Litan, and Robert J. Shapiro, *Globaphobia: Confronting Fears about Open Trade,* Washington, D.C.: Brookings Institution, Progressive Policy Institute, and Twentieth Century Fund, 1998.

40 years, U.S. employment generally grew more and the unemployment rate was lower during periods when the U.S. trade balance was deteriorating."[14]

Some U.S. Companies Will Be Hurt

A number of U.S. companies in industries now enjoying tariff protections may be unable to withstand competition from Mexican companies. U.S companies having labor-intensive production will, as noted above, find their competitive position weakened by Mexico's comparative advantage in this regard. In addition, some capital-intensive companies may find that some Mexican companies have high-skilled workers and will compete favorably with U.S. companies. This is likely, for example, in automobile parts, where Mexican companies today match productivity of some American parts makers.

There will be structural changes among U.S. industries, but the net impact of NAFTA will be positive. For example, labor-intensive companies will tend to reduce their low-skill labor force in favor of lower-wage foreign operations. Tuna canaries in California, for example, will lose their comparative advantage, as will sugar beet growers, and producers of brooms, some textiles, and frozen orange juice. Capital-intensive companies will gain. Caterpillar, for example, says it will not move to Mexico because its higher worker productivity gives it a comparative advantage over low-wage Mexico. The company noted that the removal of Mexican import duties on Caterpillar machines will increase enormously its competitive position.

Wage Rates

The logic of critics who claim NAFTA has some responsibility for declining wage and compensation growth in the United States seems creditable at first glance. Deeper analysis, however, rejects this conclusion, say proponents. The president's report calculated that in a study of sixty-seven of eighty-six industry sectors, NAFTA imports had no effect on wages.[15] Four economists from the Brookings Institution examined this issue and concluded there are several reasons why the impact of U.S. trade with low-wage countries has had only minimal impact on declining wages and compensation in the United States. For example, they say, "compensation growth fell because productivity growth declined at virtually the same rate. The trends in trade played only a small role, at best, in the trend toward lower productivity growth."[16] They add that imports from low-wage countries are such a small part of total U.S. trade that the impact is very small. So far as NAFTA is concerned, say proponents, very few U.S. workers are in direct competition with Mexican workers.

---

[14]*Study on the Operations and Effects of the NAFTA,* p. 19.

[15]Ibid., p. 28.

[16]Burtless, Lawrence, Litan, and Shapiro, *Globaphobia,* p. 64.

Impact on Environment

There is no question about the fact that industrial growth causes environmental damage. The issue is whether the damage can be contained so that growth takes place with minimum harm to the environment.

Accompanying the NAFTA treaty was the North American Agreement on Environmental Cooperation, which went into effect at the same time as NAFTA. This agreement aims to protect, conserve, and improve environments through cooperation with the three governments.

The NAFTA Commission for Environmental Cooperation (CEC) was created to administer the agreement. It reported a 72 percent reduction in serious environmental violations in the maquiladora industry since NAFTA. It also reported a 43 percent increase in maquiladora facilities in complete compliance. Some pesticides are no longer used and several water treatment facilities have been constructed.[17] However, a report by the General Accounting Office confirms that substantial infrastructure needs in the U.S.-Mexican border region remain unmet.[18]

Worker Rights

The North American Agreement on Labor Cooperation, like the above agreement, went into effect with NAFTA. It aims to improve working conditions and living standards in each country. The agreement created the Commission for Labor Cooperation to administer the agreement.

Steps have been taken in Mexico to enforce compliance with child labor laws, reduce the number of workplace injuries, and enforce occupational health and safety regulations. An important decision was made by the Mexican Supreme Court that will protect the freedom of association and right to organize. The court said state laws that prohibit more than one union per government entity were unconstitutional.

Like the environmental agreement, implementation has been minimal. Enforcement of the agreement has been weak because of budget problems and bureaucratic inertia.

What Are the Long-Range Benefits of NAFTA?

There is no consensus on the answer to this question. The president's report says there are long-run benefits to the three countries. The report cites studies of independent scholars who conclude that NAFTA will lift the GDP of the United States. The estimates vary from 0.1 percent to 0.5 percent annually.[19] These are not relatively large gains, but they are positive.

---

[17]Ibid., p. 112.

[18]General Accounting Office, *International Environment: Environmental Infrastructure Needs in the U.S.-Mexican Border Region Remain Unmet,* Washington, D.C.: General Accounting Office, July 1996.

[19]*Study on the Operations and Effects of the NAFTA,* p. 17.

The reduction of trade barriers will also permit more companies to take advantage of low wages in Mexico and thus reduce prices in world markets, making products more competitive. Increased trade should benefit Mexico. It should enhance economic growth, and that means more jobs there. It should also help stabilize the country politically, and that will be a plus for both nations. Many people in Mexico are pleased that their struggling economy is linked to the gigantic consumer market of the United States. On the negative side, labor unions in the United States are convinced that NAFTA will mean the loss of thousands of jobs in the United States and the displaced workers will be unable to find other jobs paying them as much as those they lost. Many people in both Mexico and the United States believe that NAFTA will result in further pollution of the environment of Mexico, especially in the maquiladora regions.[20] The *Multinational Monitor*, a Ralph Nader publication, argues that NAFTA will result in the spread of the maquiladora's environmental impoverishment throughout Mexico.

Should NAFTA Be Expanded to Include Other Countries?

Advocates of NAFTA believe that it establishes a platform for expansion of the free trade area to include other Latin American countries. The treaty specifies that the members can admit additional members. At this writing, negotiations are under way concerning the admission of Chile, and other South American countries have expressed interest in joining. Opponents view such an expansion with misgivings.

Ralph Nader's Public Citizen, Inc., has declared its opposition to expansion, a position joined by labor unions. Their concerns are the same as noted above—environmental degradation, loss of jobs in the United States, and so on. In favor of further widening are business groups such as the U.S. Chamber of Commerce. However, some economists who are free trade advocates also are reluctant to see a widening of NAFTA, at least soon. They fear that liberalization of trade will come at the expense of higher barriers for products of countries not in the free trade zone. They fear that companies in the free trade zone will meet outside competition with charges of "dumping." They also fear that the development of free trade zones around the world will result in economic and political clashes among them.[21]

In a thoughtful, readable discussion of the question about NAFTA expansion, Professor Sidney Weintraub, of the University of Texas at Austin, argues that before a widening of NAFTA, there should be a deepening, especially with Mexico. He points out that it is by no means a forgone conclusion that NAFTA will be a roaring success. A successful NAFTA would be a sound basis for further expansion, but a NAFTA failure would not be.

By deepening he means further reducing nontariff barriers; resolving all issues relating to investments, intellectual property, and agriculture; solving

---

[20]See, for example, "NAFTA: Trashing the Border," *Multinational Monitor*, May 1993.
[21]Ben Wildavsky, "On the Outside Looking In," *National Journal*, July 8, 1995.

environmental problems; solving problems concerned with standardization of products; building a stronger infrastructure in Mexico; and developing an effective functioning of the administrative structure. Only when an acceptable level of performance is achieved in these areas, says Weintraub, should NAFTA be expanded.[22]

Questions

1. What is NAFTA and what are the objectives sought for it?
2. What are the arguments of those who are opposed to NAFTA?
3. What are the arguments of those who support NAFTA?
4. On balance, is NAFTA a major factor in the American economy? How about the Mexican economy?
5. Do you believe political and social advantages claimed for NAFTA equal or outweigh the potential economic impacts on the United States?
6. Do you believe NAFTA should be extended to other nations?
7. Is a company acting irresponsibly when it decides to move a plant to Mexico to take advantage of lower wage rates there?

[22]Sidney Weintraub, *NAFTA: What Comes Next? (The Washington Papers/166)*, Washington, D.C.: The Center for Strategic and International Studies, Westport, Conn.: Praeger, 1994.

13

Global Trends Affecting the BGS Relationship

Nestlé
www.nestle.com

Nestlé is the world's largest food company, with 1997 sales of $48 billion. This was almost twice the sales of Conagra, the largest American food company. Nestlé employed over 226,000 people in 1997, 97 percent of whom worked outside Switzerland.

Nestlé was founded in Switzerland by Henri Nestlé, a German-born chemist, who decided to make a milk-based food product for infants who could not be nursed. At the time, one baby in five in Switzerland died in the first year of life. In 1867 he began to sell a product composed of milk mixed with meal and it became an instant success because babies thrived with it. At about the same time, Charles A. Page, who came to Switzerland as the American consul, got the idea of making condensed milk. In 1866 he formed the Anglo-Swiss Condensed Milk Company in Cham, Switzerland, to produce and sell his product.

The two companies were bitter rivals through the remaining years of the century. Finally, in 1905 they merged into the Nestlé and Anglo-Swiss Condensed Milk Company. By that time, Nestlé had grown to the point where it had seven factories in Switzerland and eleven in five other countries.[1] It was an early multinational.

Most people associate Nestlé with chocolate. Actually, it was not until 1904 that the firm got into the chocolate business, when it agreed to market abroad chocolate made by the Swiss General Chocolate Company. In 1929 Nestlé bought that company.

In 1997 Nestlé operated 495 factories in 70 countries. One half its sales were in Europe, and 25 percent came from North America. The company produces hundreds of products including coffees, cereals, milk, chocolates and confectioneries, frozen foods, and pharmaceuticals.

The company has been extremely successful in its global operations. Among the strategies it has implemented to achieve this are the following. Through aggressive acquisitions it has expanded its sales with new, high-margin, sophisticated products. Paralleling this is the strategy of acquiring and/or developing widely known brands. Another important strategy is to continuously improve traditional products. For instance, Nestlé produces over 200 types of instant coffee, all tailored to meet the requirements of specific countries. One final strategy we mention here is that the company has given local managers substantial autonomy. However, basic strategy, brand pol-

icy, and financial decisions are controlled at company headquarters in Vevey, Switzerland.

In the early 1970s Nestlé was faced with worldwide criticism of its aggressive advertising and distribution of powdered infant formula in less developed countries (LDCs) as an alternative to breast feeding. Critics claimed that infant mortality increased as a result. The main reason was that mothers in poor countries diluted the formula with water that was often contaminated, did not refrigerate the milk, and added water to the powder to the point where it had no nutrition. "Nestlé made profits, but babies died," was the cry. Several organizations launched a world-wide boycott of Nestlé products. At first Nestlé refused to discuss the issue with critics and groups that sought to boycott its products. However, in 1981 when Helmut O. Maucher, a new CEO, took charge, this attitude swiftly changed. He met with critics and established as company policy a new stringent code of ethics for advertising and distributing the infant formula that had been prepared by the World Health Organization in 1981. He also established a commission and asked Edmund Muskie, a highly respected former U.S. Secretary of State and U.S. Senator, to chair it. The responsibility of the commission was to monitor the company's compliance with its code of ethics. These measures went a long way to satisfy critics. Today, without consumer advertising, Nestlé has maintained a large share of the infant formula market in the LDCs.

---

[1]Milton Moskowitz, Michael Katz, and Robert Levering, eds. *Everybody's Business: An Almanac*, San Francisco: Harper and Row, 1980, pp. 59–61.

Nestlé has an enviable worldwide reputation for superior performance. It is a model of how to succeed in the global market and provides a fitting story to begin this chapter.

In this chapter we discuss major trends of globalization: the growth of globalization, increasing competition and how American companies are dealing with it, the creation of regional trade agreements, destabilization of the international financial system, the spread of capitalism and free markets around the world, the erosion of nation-state sovereignty, and the spreading of certain values around the world.

Expanding Globalization

Globalization is a term used to identify a new phenomenon of worldwide integration of consumer markets, production, labor, technology, investments, and cultures. So rapid has this integration been during the last three decades that many observers rightly speak of it as a revolution. It has created enormous riches, wealth, and higher living standards for millions of people. It has also been associated with a severe worldwide financial crisis, insecurity, and turmoil in the lives of millions of people.

A major force in the rise of globalization has been world trade. Total world trade, as shown in Figure 12–2, has grown impressively, especially in the period following the end of the Cold War in 1989. As also shown in Figure 12–2, the GDP of the world expanded rapidly, but not as fast as trade. Until the financial crises of 1997, the countries of Asia recorded exceptionally fast expansion of per capita GDP. In China the figure was 8.1 percent a year, in Malaysia it was 4 percent a year, in the so-called four tigers (Hong Kong, Singapore, Taiwan, and Korea) it was 6 percent or more a year, and in Japan it was even higher.[2]

This growth of GDP represented important gains in well-being for millions around the world. In Southeastern Asia, for example, prior to the financial crisis of 1997–98, tens of millions of people were lifted from the ranks of poverty into the middle classes.

There have been many powerful forces behind globalization. These are the major ones:

- The number of MNCs has grown significantly and their actions have accentuated globalization. They seek to exploit growing global wealth. They have been pressured to find outlets for their enlarged productive capacity. In this attempt they not only have sought increased sales in foreign lands but have established more plants there.

---

[2] *Economic Report of the President*, Washington, D.C.: U.S. Government Printing Office, February 1997, p. 239.

- There has been an explosive growth of money floating around the world to finance expanding trade and facilities. Banks have increased their lending activity. Speculative money has been abundant.
- Many nations have been receptive to free-market ideas and implemented them.
- Costs of communications by air and ocean transport have been sharply reduced.
- The speed of electronic communications is accelerating. The following is an illustration of how much communications have changed: Queen Isabella learned of Columbus's discovery after five months. Europe learned of Lincoln's assassination in two weeks. But the world learned of Neil Armstrong's first step on the moon in 0.3 second.
- Standardized products of similar quality, such as cameras, soft drinks, watches, computers, chemicals, and drugs, have become popular around the world with but minor modifications to fit local situations.
- Relative peace has existed in the world following the Vietnam War.

The great benefits of globalization have not blinded critics to some of its adverse impacts. We noted Patrick Buchanan's criticisms in the last chapter. William Greider asserts that the global economy is sowing "creative destruction" everywhere.[3] Daniel Yergin says the forces of globalization are wresting control from governments.[4] This is a position taken also by Dani Rodrik.[5] This by no means exhausts the list of influential critics. We will return later in the chapter to discuss these assertions.

Increasing Global Competition

The pace and intensity of economic competition have accelerated with globalization. Prior to the 1980s, foreign trade was such a small part of total United States' output that it received little attention. Then, increasingly, foreign producers successfully challenged American corporations both at home and abroad. This awakened the nation and its corporations to the comparatively weak competitive position of a number of industries.

---

[3]William Greider, *One World Ready or Not,* New York: Simon and Schuster, 1997.
[4]Daniel Yergin and Joseph Stanislaw, *Commanding Heights,* New York: Simon & Schuster, 1998.
[5]Dani Rodrik, *Has Globalization Gone Too Far?,* Washington, D.C.: The Institute for International Economics, 1997.

American Industries' Competitive Position in the 1980s

What was the competitive position of American companies in the 1980s and how did they respond to the new threat?

Weaknesses.   A prestigious 1989 study by the Massachusetts Institute of Technology (MIT) Commission on Industrial Productivity concluded that "American industry indeed shows worrisome signs of weakness. In many important sectors of the economy, U.S. firms are losing ground to their competitors abroad."[6]

These conclusions were based on clearly identified deficiencies throughout many core technologies and industries. For example, large consumer product industries such as consumer electronics virtually disappeared in the United States. Radios and television sets were clear examples. By the end of the 1980s, only one company, Zenith, was making TV sets in the United States and that company stopped production in 1995. Semiconductors, invented in the United States, seemed to be dominated by Japanese companies. In steel, automobiles, machine tools, and other industries, statistics of decline were compelling. We used to be the world leader in robotics, structural ceramics, and flexible manufacturing, but lost that position to foreign businesses.

Shocked by the danger of losing the competitive race with foreign companies, American firms reorganized to improve management decision making and respond appropriately to the unique requirements of successfully doing business in foreign cultures. Before discussing the strategies employed, it is necessary to point out that despite problems, some U.S. industries enjoyed significant competitive strengths.

Strengths.   The 1980s industrial landscape, as described by the MIT study, was not completely bleak. In many critical areas the competitive position was strong. Then, as now, the United States was the world leader in supercomputers, software engineering, artificial intelligence, computer-aided design and engineering, telecommunications, genetic engineering, and rocket propulsion. Many products were the finest in the world. Examples include desktop computers, satellite navigation systems, fiber optics, communications satellites, artificial sweeteners, razors, instant film, artificial heart valves, pacemakers, oil drill bits, laser angioplasty catheter heads, motion pictures, locomotives, and brain electrical mapping systems.[7] Many U.S. corporations were expanding sales abroad, including IBM, Ford, Coca-Cola, General Electric, Merck, and Procter & Gamble.

---

[6]Michael Dertouzos et al., *Made in America: Regaining the Productive Edge,* Cambridge, Mass: MIT Press, 1989, p. 8.

[7]For a long list of products in which the United States excels, see "What America Makes Best," *Fortune,* March 28, 1988.

U.S. Corporate Strategies to Become More Competitive

Important objectives of the strategic response have been to reduce costs, improve product quality, stay ahead of competition technically, exploit new markets, raise market share, and, of course, enhance profits. A few of the important strategies employed to achieve these objectives are as follows.

Partnerships with Suppliers

An important objective of the strategic response has been to reduce costs. Assuming a partnership relationship with suppliers has been one approach to achieving this goal. This contrasts with the old system where companies negotiated adversarially (often under severe pressure) with the lowest-cost suppliers. At Chrysler, now merged into Daimler-Chrysler, the company arranges long-term relationships with suppliers, cooperates in engineering design with them, and gives them a voice in quality improvement. Chrysler and its suppliers arrange so-called just-in-time (JIT) delivery schedules. The JIT system integrates the flow of components from suppliers into production schedules so that the part is delivered at the precise moment it is needed in production. This eliminates the need for inventories and lowers production cost. Experience of many companies has shown that closer relationships with suppliers will unleash more innovation, quality improvement, and lower cost production.

Coordinating Functional Departments

Functional departments in the past often acted independently of other departments. Now there is more integration of basic functions such as product development, research, product design, manufacturing, communications, human resources, and marketing. Top priority is given to product quality control and flexible manufacturing. The end result is a reduction in product development time, lower costs, and quicker accommodation to changes in consumer demand.

Outsourcing

Outsourcing is another cost-cutting strategy. It occurs when a company moves work out of the enterprise. Companies do this both at home and abroad. Nike, for example, uses low-cost workers in foreign countries to produce sneakers. The practice is used by companies making electronics, automobiles, airplanes, and garments, to mention a few items. Foreign companies do the same. Japanese firms, for example, have outsourced in Southeast Asia. German companies have gone to lower-wage areas in Poland.

This practice has given rise to severe criticism of many companies, alleging that they are exploiting foreign workers. Sometimes there is truth to these allegations, but many responsible companies seek to avoid exploitation. (See the case of Levi Strauss at the end of Chapter 6.) A positive result of outsourcing to low-wage countries is not only that jobs are provided, but manufacturing technology moves there and workers are trained in new skills.

One troubling question is whether outsourcing to foreign countries costs jobs in the United States. That question is partly addressed in the last chapter and in the NAFTA case that followed that chapter.

Expanding Foreign Direct Investments (FDIs)

FDI refers to investments for building a plant, purchasing all stock of a company, or acquiring a controlling interest in a company. There has been a surge in FDIs during the past decade. The total value of U.S. direct investment assets in foreign countries rose from $2 trillion in 1988 to $4.3 trillion in 1996.[8] Most of the U.S. FDIs are in Europe, but an increasing share in recent years has been in LDCs.

There are many motives for FDIs: for example, to meet foreign demands most efficiently by cutting production and distribution cost, to employ lower-cost workers, to achieve a presence in a foreign land, or to satisfy a demand of a foreign government for capital investment.

FDIs also aid in the economic development of LDCs by introducing new technology, managerial styles, worker skills, market access to other countries, and competition. As noted in Chapter 12, these are among the reasons why LDCs welcome MNCs.

Improving Productivity

Productivity, the index of production output per unit of labor input, is an important measure of the economic strength of a country, its competitive advantage, and its standard of living. For example, if productivity is expanding, business can and does raise wages without increasing prices. When it is rising, the goods and services available to consumers are increasing. Unfortunately, despite a massive effort on the part of the U.S. Bureau of Labor Statistics to develop accurate measures of productivity, the numbers are by no means precise. This is not so much a fault of experts who calculate the subject but of the complexity of the measurement problem.[9]

---

[8]*Economic Report of the President*, Washington, D.C.: U.S. Government Printing Office, February 1998.

[9]For a discussion of the problems of measuring productivity, see "Expanding the Nation's Productive Capacity," *Economic Report of the President*, Washington, D.C.: U.S. Government Printing Office, 1995, chap. 3. Total productivity is measured by labor input compared with output of goods and services. Labor input is heavily dependent on capital investment, efficiency of machinery and tools, education of workers, skill of workers, commitment of workers, hours worked, research and development expenditures, and managerial talent. Output is measured by the volume of goods and services produced. The impact on productivity of each of these elements in the equation is extremely difficult to measure. Furthermore, different things are used to measure productivity in different industries. For example, output in banking is assumed to be equal to the increase in hours worked. In railroads the key measure is tonnage shipped.

Efforts of American companies discussed above presumably led to increases in national productivity. But that is not clear. Between 1985 and 1997, the annual rate of productivity growth for both goods and services was about the same as the long-term rate of 1.1 percent. The historic rate in the United States was less than that of other major industrial countries such as Japan, Germany, France, and the United Kingdom. But productivity gains in manufacturing have been much better, growing at an annual rate of about 3 percent from 1985 to 1997. It is noteworthy that Alan Greenspan, chairman of the Federal Reserve Board, believes the official rate of productivity given here is much too low. He is joined in this view by a number of economists. Actually, in 1997 the average gain was 1.8 percent. In the second quarter of 1998, it was 3.7 percent.

Forming Combinations with Other Companies

The growth of foreign operations of American companies has been facilitated by arranging combinations with other companies through mergers, acquisitions, and alliances. Mergers take place when one company is formed from one or more other companies. Acquisitions take place when one firm acquires a controlling interest in another, generally with an offer to buy enough shares of stock to gain control. An alliance is a cooperative arrangement between two or more companies to achieve a specific purpose.

Mergers and Acquisitions (M&As).   Globalization has stimulated M&As both in the United States and in foreign countries. The fundamental reason for this trend, of course, is the assumption that merged companies will be more efficient and more competitive. Since 1980 there has been a significant growth of mergers among U.S. companies. In that year there were 1,889 reported. By 1997 the number was 7,800. The total dollar value of the mergers rose from $44.3 billion in 1980 to $657.1 billion in 1997.[10]

U.S. companies have been increasingly active in foreign countries. In 1983 there were 146 mergers reported, and that grew to 1,107 in 1997. Their total value rose from $2.5 billion in 1983 to $79.4 billion in 1997. Most of the M&As took place in Europe, with the greatest number in the United Kingdom. To illustrate, General Electric invested over $2 billion in Germany in 1997–1998 by acquiring medical technology, credit card services, and telecommunications companies.[11] Recently there have been mergers of large European and American companies. For example, the Daimler-Chrysler Corp. joined two major car companies. Another was between Siemens, a German company, and Westinghouse Electric Corp.

---

[10]These data and those following are from *Mergerstat Review 1998,* Los Angeles: Mergerstat, 1998.
[11]Mary Williams Walsh, "German, U.S. Firms Tie Transatlantic Knot," *Los Angeles Times,* May 16, 1998.

Alliances.   Companies used to grow essentially by internal expansion or acquisition, or both. Today more companies are expanding through alliances. John R. Harbison and Peter Pekar Jr. estimate that more than 20,000 new alliances were formed worldwide between 1987 and 1992, compared with only 750 in the 1970s.[12]

Among all types of alliances, joint ventures are most prominent. These are partnerships by which two or more firms create an organization to achieve specific objectives. Joint ventures are much less expensive than building new factories or buying companies. They make it possible for a company to meet new market demands quicker than by building new marketing and distribution systems. Through joint ventures, companies can share risks as well as costs in developing new technologies or new products. They can defend strategic positions against forces too strong for one firm to resist. They can penetrate trade barriers. They help a company coordinate resources in a global market system, accumulate more capital, and pool technical skills in developing a new technology. Jack Welch, chairman and CEO of General Electric, expressed the necessity of joint ventures this way: "If you think you can go it alone in today's global economy, you are highly mistaken."[13]

American companies have formed alliances for years with foreign partners. For instance, Ford formed one with Mazda in 1978 that still exists. The original arrangement was Ford's purchase of 25 percent of Mazda stock. In 1996 Ford raised its share to 33.4 percent of the total and introduced new Ford management to help Mazda strengthen its weak financial condition. Fuji Photo and Xerox formed a joint venture more than a quarter century ago with twelve employees; it now has thousands of employees. Hewlett-Packard formed a joint venture with Yokogawa over twenty-five years ago.

A different type of alliance is a consortium. In 1984 Congress passed the National Cooperative Research Act, which permitted the alliance of two or more competing companies to form a consortium to achieve a specific purpose. An outstanding example is SEMATECH (Semiconductor Manufacturing Technology). It was formed at a time when American companies were losing world market share for computer chips because of the superiority of Japanese producers. The mission of the consortium was to develop new technologies to achieve world leadership. SEMATECH developed low-cost methods to manufacture specialized high-value computer chips. This gave the industry new competitive power in the global market, not only in selling sophisticated chips but also in exporting the chip-making machines. Other industries have taken advantage of the National Cooperative Research Act. For example, General Motors announced in May 1997 that it was teaming with Arco and Exxon to develop a fuel cell system that would convert gasoline to hydrogen for electric-powered automobiles.

---

[12]John R. Harbison and Peter Pekar Jr., *A Practical Guide to Alliances: Leapfrogging the Learning Curve*, Los Angeles: Booz Allen & Hamilton, Inc., circa 1997.

[13]Ibid., p. 1.

While popular, alliances are risky. Conflicts of corporate cultures typically result in failure. No one knows the exact failure rate, but for American companies the number is high, as much as 50 percent, according to one study.[14] Harbison and Pekar found that only 17 percent of American manager's think alliances are effective. Japanese managers are much more enthusiastic and in that country alliance failures are much lower.[15]

Other Competitive Strategies to Gain Competitiveness

The above by no means exhausts the list of important strategies employed by U.S. companies to gain and maintain global competitive strength. To improve manufacturing efficiency, for example, companies have employed new technologies, such as computer-designed engineering, computer-assisted production, robotics, faster technology transfer, and better management.

Strategies other than M&As and alliances to penetrate foreign markets include making contractual arrangements for buying and selling, licensing, and franchising; employing foreign nationals; improving internal communications; decentralizing decisions; and redesigning work structures. Sometimes patience and making an effort to understand foreign cultures and institutions are important. Many U.S. companies now successful in Japan started years ago becoming more involved there. For example, AFLAC, a Georgia-based insurance firm, began in a small way years ago to sell insurance in Japan. Today, the company is Japan's fourth largest insurer.

Other Competitive Strengths of American Industry

Other competitive strengths exist. American companies have access to a huge pool of liquid capital from banks, securities markets, and venture capitalists willing to risk financing new product innovations. The United States has unexcelled research and development laboratories in universities, businesses, and government. American universities are strong, especially graduate technical schools, and are generally considered the best in the world. Foreign nations send thousands of students to attend them for technical training. We have more engineers and scientists than any other nation. This all builds the knowledge base that is a fundamental strength.

Threats to the U.S. Corporate Global Competitive Position

There are, however, serious threats to the global competitive position of American companies. Here are a few of them.

---

[14]Kathryn Rudie Harrigan, "Making Joint Ventures," part 1, *Management Review,* February 1987; *Managing for Joint Venture Success,* Lexington, Mass.: Lexington Books, 1986.
[15]Harbison and Pekar, *A Practical Guide to Alliances.*

Foreign companies, for a variety of reasons, are establishing productive facilities in this country. Well known are the Japanese automobile companies—Toyota, Honda, Nissan, and Mazda—that have built assembly plants here. European auto companies including Volkswagen, Mercedes-Benz, and BMW also have been producing in the United States. European companies have U.S. production plants in other industries, such as Siemens in electronics, Hoechst AG in pharmaceuticals, and Nestlé in food processing.

The rapid diffusion of worldwide communication makes possible new major competition from any country. With the ease of technology transfer, the education of foreign executives in American universities and businesses, and the availability of capital, it is not difficult to envision the appearance of a strong global competitor from any corner of the globe.

A study made for the Council on Competitiveness (before the 1997–1998 financial crisis in Southeastern Asia) surveyed American executives about their competition. Nearly 50 percent saw their stiffest foreign competition coming in the future from emerging nations rather than the major industrial countries. However, most of them also believed that these emerging countries provided great selling opportunities.[16]

In a later report prepared by the Council based on analysis of 120 managers in corporate research and development, universities, and national laboratories, this conclusion was strongly supported with respect to innovation. The managers said that developing countries learned a fundamental lesson—use the model that works in the United States. That model teaches that "Investment in people, research, and technology, along with an innovation-friendly environment, pays off in economic growth and higher-wage jobs."[17] Following this model, some developing countries have already made the transition from imitator to innovator.

Expanding Global Trading Agreements

Coinciding with globalization has been a rapid increase in regional trading arrangements. So numerous have they become that virtually all countries now belong to at least one club.[18] These agreements, of course, will add to increasing global competition. They will also expand trade and give further impetus to globalization. The four largest are the European Union(EU), the North American Free Trade Agreement (NAFTA), Mercosur, and the Association of

---

[16]Council on Competitiveness, *Competitiveness Index 1996: A Ten-Year Strategic Assessment*, Washington, D.C.: Council on Competitiveness, 1996.

[17]Council on Competitiveness, *Going Global: The New Shape of American Innovation*, Washington, D.C.: Council on Competitiveness, 1998, p. 9.

[18]See Jeffrey A. Frankel, *Regional Trading Blocs in the World Economic System*, Washington, D.C.: Institute for International Economics, October 1997.

Southeast Asia Nations (ASEAN). We will discuss briefly these areas except NAFTA, which is the case at the end of the last chapter.

Arrangements vary significantly among trading blocs. Some are simply agreements to begin talking further about a more formal trade arrangement. At the other extreme are those having well-established structures, free trade with partners, few barriers, and common tariffs with countries outside the bloc.

The European Union (EU)

On January 1, 1993, the EU became a new expanded world market. On that date a long list of customs, tariffs, and nontariff barriers were removed between the twelve European nations comprising the union at that time. Also removed were many national laws and policies affecting trade. They were replaced with hundreds of new rules and regulations concerning such matters as health, environment, and quality standards that are to be consistent among member states. Since 1993, three more nations have joined, making fifteen in all (see Figure 13-1).

Today the EU offers great opportunities for American companies, but it also poses serious competitive threats. This vast market of over 350 million people with a gross domestic product over $7 trillion, about equal to that of the United States, is a lucrative market. It is the largest purchaser of U.S.-produced goods and services and is the biggest foreign investor in this country. There are in Europe today companies clearly the equal in competitiveness with our best companies.

The fundamental objective of the EU is to form an economic and political union among member nations. A milestone step in this direction took place on January 1, 1999, when the European Monetary Union (EMU) was formed with a uniform currency—the euro.[19] The European Central Bank (ECB), established in 1998, began functioning, and those countries in the EMU began to prepare for the conversion of their currencies to the euro. Euro coins and notes are to go into circulation January 1, 2002, and national currencies will be withdrawn on July 1, 2002. Jeffrey E. Garten, dean of the Yale School of Management and former Under Secretary of Commerce for International Trade, predicts that the euro "will be the most important change in the global economy well into the next century."[20]

Thoughtful analysts predict an important restructuring of industry in Europe and more competitive companies. For example, firms will consolidate to achieve economies of scale, seek lower-cost countries within Europe for production, and press governments for favorable tax and labor policies. The EMU will be a catalyst for greater labor mobility and more harmonization of

---

[19]Eleven of the fifteen members of EU joined the EMU. They are Austria, Belgium, Finland, France, Germany, Ireland, Italy, Luxembourg, the Netherlands, Portugal, and Spain.

[20]Jeffrey E. Garten, "The Euro Will Turn Europe into a Superpower," *Business Week*, May 4, 1998, p. 30.

FIGURE 13-1

European Union Countries

European policies that affect business. Globalization pressures will force European companies to push aggressively to become more efficient. European companies, therefore, are expected to challenge American companies more directly in global markets.

There are immediate costs of conversion. For example, French banks estimate their conversion costs will be $3.3 billion. But avoiding in the future the necessity of dealing with multiple currencies and different exchange rates will save them money.[21] How about U.S. companies? Alessandro Profili, Honeywell Europe's director of public affairs, says: "We're dealing with 20-plus currencies now, so one more won't make a world of difference."[22] In the meantime, as noted above, U.S. companies have been anticipating the EMU by more aggressive moves to merge, acquire, and make alliances with European companies.

There are skeptics who think the EMU will not hold together. For example, they believe that a tight money policy of the ECB demanded by Germany will be unacceptable to some countries (e.g., Italy and Spain) and force them to leave the union. They also predict that individual countries will become frustrated at the loss of financial sovereignty that comes with the creation of the ECB. Some think that countries will be so pressured by business to change policies concerning working conditions, hours of work, and social contributions that the result will be political turmoil. Some observers think the EMU can exist in the long term only with complete political union, and they are skeptical that European nationalists will accept the necessary loss of sovereignty such a union entails. Henry Kissinger believes that the EMU faces a dilemma. "It is difficult to see how the European Monetary Union can succeed," he writes. "It is even more difficult to imagine that it will be permitted to fail. How to navigate between these perplexities increasingly will challenge U.S. foreign policy."[23]

Mercosur

In March 1991, Argentina, Brazil, Paraguay, and Uruguay signed the Mercosur Accord to establish a preferential trading area. This is a large trading area with approximately 240 million people and a combined GDP over $1 trillion, which is half that of all Latin America. The objective of the agreement is eventually to install a common currency. Today, however, the accord is far from this goal. Tariffs for many products have been mostly eliminated among the members, but there are significant exceptions, notably automobiles and sugar. This accord represents the most ambitious plan after the EU, but it is well behind the EU in development.

Mercosur is not the only trade agreement involving Latin American countries. The United Nations Economic Commission for Latin American and the Caribbean reports thirty-one international agreements in Latin America since 1990.[24] For example, Mexico has agreements with Venezuela and Colombia and is working on an agreement with five Central American neighbors.

---

[21]John Thor Dahlburg, "Euro: Continent Gears Up for Momentous Shift in How It Does Business," *Los Angeles Times,* May 3, 1998.

[22]Michael Hickins, "U.S. Business Blinks at the Euro," *Management Review,* April 1998, pp. 33–34.

[23]Henry A. Kissinger, "Monetary Union May Spur Political Trouble," *Los Angeles Times,* May 10, 1998.

[24]"Mercosur," *The Economist,* October 12, 1996.

ASEAN

ASEAN was formed in 1967 with six nations but has expanded and now includes Brunei, Indonesia, Laos, Malaysia, Myanmar, the Philippines, Singapore, Thailand, and Vietnam. It has reached a few trade agreements, but they cover only a small portion of total trade in the area. Japan and China, the largest economies in the region, are not in the organization. All the nations in ASEAN depend heavily on exports, especially to Japan. There is also great disparity in economic strength among these nations. For example, the per capita GDP of Singapore is ten times that of Indonesia. If Japan were to enter the group, the difference between total national GDP of any of these countries and Japan would be much greater. In sum, ASEAN has not reached the degree of maturity of the other major trading areas.

Globalization Produces Financial Instability

The forces of globalization have made the world's financial system crisis-prone. The most serious manifestation of this began with a financial crisis in Thailand in 1997 and spread almost immediately to Indonesia, Malaysia, the Philippines, and South Korea. In 1998 the Russian financial system collapsed and countries in Latin America came under intense pressure. For a decade, the Southeast Asian countries had been increasing their GDPs at 6 percent or more a year. They brought millions of people from poverty to middle-income levels. Now these millions once again face poverty. What happened?

Forces at play in these crises differed among the nations. But there is general agreement on the most important factors. Of great significance was the enormous volume of money moving around the world. No one knows the total volume nor all that was invested in the countries affected. We do know that it was in the trillions of dollars. It is estimated that $1.5 trillion were involved in daily foreign exchange dealings. This was ten times greater than a decade before. In addition, foreign banks loaned generously to LDCs, and domestic banks in these countries freely used the money to make loans. Billions if not trillions of dollars generated by speculators in foreign currencies and securities added to the volume. Hundreds of billions of dollars of this money could be transferred instantly by the touch of a keyboard.

The banking systems of many countries lagged the expansion of financial transactions. There was insufficient bank regulation and weak supervision. Banks borrowed money with short-term maturities and loaned it with long maturities to borrowers with political connections who often employed it unwisely. Important information about banks and private corporations was not available to investors, so they could not make appropriate risk assessments. Both foreign banks and investors understood the situation but made loans anyway. This was partly because investors believed the safety of their money was guaranteed by governments. Such practices led to excessive construction of factories and office buildings, a real estate boom with accompanying inflated prices, and soaring stock markets.

Laws, ideas, and institutions needed to accompany vibrant capitalism were weak or absent. In mind, for example, are laws concerning antitrust and corruption, bankruptcy courts, social security nets, laws pertaining to the governance of private companies, and modern information systems.

A policy of some countries to maintain a fixed exchange rate when the currency was overvalued was hurtful. Currency reserves were exhausted in an attempt to maintain the artificial rate.

This was a volatile mixture that, without proper control, could and did lead to disaster. Eventually, borrowers were unable to repay loans, export markets weakened, and a few banks and companies became insolvent. Foreign investors and speculators lost confidence and withdrew their funds. The foreign exchange value of the currency dropped sharply, which made the repayment of called loans more difficult because many of them had been made in dollars. This was a pattern started in Thailand that developed in other countries.

Thailand asked the International Monetary Fund (IMF) for help in July 1997, and that agency came to the rescue in August with $17.2 billion. In October 1997 the IMF provided a $43 billion rescue package for Indonesia. Then in December 1997, $58 billion was arranged for South Korea. In the same month, the IMF resumed lending to Russia and in July 1998 arranged an additional $22.6 billion. In late 1998 the IMF and the World Bank came to the rescue of Brazil with a $42 billion package.

Some people argue that the requirements laid down by the IMF for its help actually made the situation worse. In Thailand, for instance, the IMF prescribed raising interest rates to stem exchange rate depreciation, supporting the foreign exchange value of the baht (the Thai currency), closing insolvent banks, and introducing a variety of structural reforms such as closer supervision of financial institutions. This medicine did not cure the patient. Indeed, the situation in Thailand got worse. Similar IMF actions in other Southeast Asian countries did not provide the recovery intended.

Martin Feldstein, former chairman of the President's Council of Economic Advisers and professor of economics at Harvard, was one of a number of economists highly critical of the IMF.[25] Feldstein made several points. First, the IMF publicly criticized the Southeast Asian countries as having inept leadership and fundamentally unsound economies. This encouraged further withdrawals by investors and discouraged new investments. Second, the problem in these countries was illiquidity, not insolvency. It was insolvency that the IMF mostly addressed. With but moderate adjustments the countries could have acquired the necessary foreign exchange to repay debts. The IMF, rather than insisting on tough financial actions, should have brought creditors and

---

[25]Martin Feldstein, "Focus on Crisis Management," *The Wall Street Journal,* October 6, 1998.

debtors together to work out rescheduling of loans. Third, IMF policies were contradictory. Its prescription of higher interest rates (to attract foreign capital and protect the value of the currency) and tax increases (to reduce consumer demand to cut imports) restrained rather than stimulated economic recovery. The IMF later eased its requirements for loans.

The IMF vigorously defended its loan requirements. Stanley Fischer, deputy managing director, said that the fiscal constraints and other requirements were designed to restore macroeconomic stability and growth and to remedy structural weaknesses in each country.[26] They did not work as planned because of environmental changes that reduced the demand for exported goods. Japan, for example, by far the largest economy in the area, was in economic recession and other countries were experiencing financial difficulties. Trade and investment declined in the region. Fischer conceded that had the IMF known at the time that consumer demand in the area would fall, less fiscal contraction would have been recommended. He also said that another problem arose from the fact that the governments did not implement the reform recommendations.

Lawrence Summers, Deputy Secretary of the Treasury, came to the defense of the IMF with these words:

> To be sure, important policy challenges remain, particularly in the uncertain environment of Indonesia. But without the support the IMF provides in these situations, we would probably now be dealing with a great deal worse: debt moratoriums in some countries, a generalized withdrawal of capital from the developing world, and potentially large consequences for our export industries and our financial markets.[27]

Feldstein, as well as most other informed critics, does not want to abolish the IMF, which has accomplished much for the world. As Summers points out, for example, it has been a major supporter of Russia, it has supported stabilization in Poland and other Central European countries, and it has helped to advance trade liberalization around the world. It has done all this, points out Summers, at no cost to the U.S. taxpayer. The IMF has not had a major default in 50 years. "So," says Summers, "the IMF is indispensable and without expense."[28] Few informed observers wish to abolish it, but they recommend changes in policies.

Finally, much more is needed than a few adjustments in IMF policies to stabilize global financial markets. As President Clinton pointed out at a 1998 joint meeting of the IMF and the World Bank in Washington, D.C., what is needed are methods to temper the volatile swings of the international marketplace. There need to be global financial regulations, methods to stabilize

---

[26]Stanley Fischer, "Reforming World Finance: Lessons from a Crisis," http://www.imf.org/external/np/replies/100398.htm, October 7, 1998, reproduced from *The Economist,* October 1998.

[27]Lawrence Summers, "Why America Needs the IMF," *The Wall Street Journal,* March 27, 1998.

[28]Ibid.

exchange rates, controls over speculative funds, and systems to make the public better informed about financial conditions and risks.

Such recommendations, at best, would take decades to develop. In the meantime, what happens to those people forced into poverty? James Wolfensohn, World Bank president, admonished his fellow financiers by saying that in the rush to protect currencies, they were paying too little attention to the growing ranks of unemployed. "The poor cannot wait on our deliberations," he said.[29]

Spreading Capitalism

The global spread of capitalism is one of most significant trends in recent history. This development resulted from many forces. Highly important was the defeat of authoritarian governments in World War II and the imposition by the victorious powers of democratic free-market principles and institutions. The model was American capitalism. Following the war, a major foreign policy of the United States was to foster democracy and free-market economies throughout the world. The rapid economic growth of the United States after the war also attracted admirers. The heady burst of economic activity confirmed the notion that the American model of capitalism was the best approach to wealth and national power. The extraordinary rise of Japan to become the world's second largest economy was seen as a striking illustration of this dogma.

Deviations from the American Capitalistic Model

The classical capitalism model has been the foundation of the free-market economy of the United States. As amply illustrated throughout this book, there have been substantial deviations from this model in the United States. So, too, have there been variations of the model throughout the world. There is no country today with the same democratic free-market structure as the United States.

To oversimplify, for example, while the Japanese economy fundamentally is free market, it is dominated by an interlacing of companies in massive aggregations called *keiretsu*, discussed in Chapter 3. So dominant a feature of the Japanese economy is the keiretsu that one author calls it *alliance capitalism*.[30] South Korea has adopted the Japanese model of gigantic alliances of companies in comparatively few conglomerates, called *chaebols*. In some Southeastern Asian countries, popular leaders give close friends and family members

---

[29]Quoted in David E. Sanger, "Dissension Erupts at Talks on World Financial Crisis," *New York Times,* October 7, 1998.

[30]Michael L. Gerlach, *Alliance Capitalism: The Social Organization of Japanese Business,* Berkeley, Calif.: University of California Press, 1992.

control of state enterprises. In Indonesia, for example, former President Suharto, who held power for three decades, named members of his family to operate state-owned enterprises. This has been called *crony capitalism.*

China is governed by the Communist Party, which exercises central planning and control over the economy. However, it has established free-market zones, loosened the reins over banking, and ended the control of military leaders over state enterprises. It is toe deep into capitalism and slowly moving deeper. Most other countries of the world have embraced free markets and other forms of capitalism, but each has adopted variations in political controls, state ownership of productive enterprises, government relationships with corporate enterprises (both public and private), protectionism, and financial structures. There are obviously many different brands of capitalism around the world.

Critics of Modern Capitalism

Jeffrey E. Garten wrote an article entitled "Can the World Survive the Triumph of Capitalism?[31] It was a review of a book by William Greider, a leading, thoughtful, and incisive critic of global capitalism. Garten answers his question in the affirmative, but, he says, we must take seriously the critics of global capitalism.

Greider points out in his book that the global economy has made possible the accumulation of great wealth but at the same time has serious flaws.[32] Among them, first, is that global capitalism is repeating some of the shortcomings of capitalism that were experienced 100 years ago in the United States; for example, exploitation of workers, including children, and inequality of income distribution. Second, uncontrolled investments lead to excessive productive capacity and overproduction of many products. Third, the exuberant growth of global capitalism leads to degradation of the environment. Fourth, the extraordinary growth of money and its free flow inevitably will result in destabilizing the world's financial systems. Greider wrote his book before the 1997–1998 world financial crisis. He was, therefore, prescient.

In addition, Greider and other critics see fallacies in some fundamental assumptions of capitalism.[33] One is that the free market will be self-regulating. That is, for example, if there is excessive production, then demand will be generated to take up the supply. History does not bear out the validity of this assumption, say critics. They point to the present global surplus capacity in automobiles, steel, chemicals, and aircraft, to mention only a few industries.

---

[31]Jeffrey E. Garten, "Can the World Survive the Triumph of Capitalism?" *Harvard Business Review*, January–February 1997.

[32]William Greider, *One World, Ready or Not: The Manic Logic of Global Capitalism*, New York: Simon & Schuster, 1997.

[33]See, for example, David C. Korten, "The Mythic Victory of Market Capitalism," Chapter 15 in Jerry Mander and Edward Goldsmith, *The Case Against the Global Economy*, San Francisco: Sierra Club Books, 1996.

A second is that the free market can be depended upon to solve fundamental problems of society and, therefore, government intervention is not needed. Currently, say critics, while many of the industrialized countries have improved safety nets, such as social security, pensions, unemployment compensation, and health insurance, these benefits are either meager or absent in many LDCs. Third, free markets and economic growth in a nation with authoritarian rule will eventually lead to political democracy. This is the assumption that free markets and political democracy go together and that without democracy, free markets will wither and fade away. There are many nations where this has not happened. In the fascist societies of Italy, Germany, and Spain in the 1940s, for instance, there were free markets but no democracy. Today in China, as noted above, there are a few free-market areas, and they are growing, but there is no political democracy. Indeed, the Chinese government has been diligent in stifling pleas for democracy. The free market has thrived under authoritarian rule in Singapore.

Finally, rising incomes created by vigorous global capitalism will raise all boats. That demonstrably has not happened. Throughout the world, including the major industrial nations such as the United States, the income gap between the rich and poor has widened. In the United States during the economic boom of the 1990s, real wages declined, except at the end of the decade, while the percentage of total income received by the top 10 percent increased.

Critics like Greider do not want to abolish capitalism, only to reform it to make it more efficient in achieving a maximum of human welfare.

Rethinking Capitalism in the Developing Countries

In many countries, there is a continued belief in the benefits and inevitability of capitalism, but the weaknesses of global capitalism that resulted in the global financial crisis of 1997–1998 caused developing nations to rethink and modify their approach to free markets. Many countries rejected the fundamental tenet of capitalism that money should be free to flow anywhere in the world where it appears to the lender it can be most efficiently employed. Malaysian Prime Minister Mahathir Mohamad, for example, in September 1998 imposed stringent currency controls in his country. At that time, many proponents of capitalism accepted the idea of currency controls, at least temporarily, to halt sudden outflows of capital in financially troubled countries.

This is a backlash and not a rejection of global capitalism. The leaders of the developing countries know that if their nations are to thrive, they must have capital and technology from outside, and only free markets can deliver them. However, they believe they should modify capitalism to fit their particular needs. Indonesian economist Mari Pangestu said that "Developing countries can't just be given a global template for a financial architecture and told to take it or leave it . . . They have to be part of the process."[34]

---

[34]Pete Engardio, "Crisis of Faith for the Free Market," *Business Week*, October 19, 1998, p. 38.

The Infrastructure of Capitalism

There are many institutional arrangements and ideas that must be in place and perfected for capitalism to work effectively, including a trustworthy financial system, bankruptcy courts, antitrust laws, a minimum social security net, limited government regulation, an efficient tax system, an acceptance of private property and the profit motive, and an assumption by private enterprises of responsibilities to workers and communities. These institutions and ideas cannot be installed overnight. One of the problems of Russia today is the absence or imperfect development of many of them. Most of these institutions and ideas are either absent or slowly evolving in many developing countries.

Globalization Erodes Nation-State Sovereignty

Market forces have eroded the sovereignty of nations and yet the nation-state still retains unlimited authority within its own borders. How is this paradox explained?

As demonstrated in the above discussion of the financial crisis in Southeast Asia, governments felt helpless to prevent the wreckage created by abrupt and voluminous capital withdrawals. To make their industries competitive in global markets, governments must attract capital and technology. This cannot be done, they know, if too much restraint is placed on the free flow of money.

Another infringement on sovereignty flows from agreements of governments with certain international institutions that supplant decisions heretofore made by governments. The agreements of members of GATT and its successor agency, the WTO, bind members to the collective decisions of those organizations. Similarly, NAFTA ties Canada, the United States, and Mexico to its provisions. The European Commission has issued hundreds of trade rules that bind its members. We explained how the IMF imposes decisions on countries receiving its financial aid. The new ECB makes important monetary decisions heretofore decided by central banks of individual countries.

At a different level, governments in both industrialized as well as developing countries are often held hostage to the power of large multinational corporations. A case in point is Daimler-Chrysler. This fifth largest carmaker in the world, and the biggest industrial company in Europe after Royal/Dutch Shell, has exceptional clout. The German government will be receptive to its pressures for tax and social reforms that improve its competitive position. If costs of production in Germany are prohibitively expensive, the company can move its headquarters to the United States, close plants in Germany, and build assembly plants elsewhere. LDCs can be expected to respond faster to pressures of giant MNCs than large industrial states.

Daniel Yergin and Joseph Stanislaw point out that free markets are wresting control from government of the "commanding heights."[35] This expression, they explain, was first used by Ilyich Lenin to mean the dominant power of the government over the marketplace. To Lenin it was the state that would control the most important elements of the economy. The idea was carried to an extreme in Russia under Stalinism with the total elimination of private markets.[36] Today, however, not only in Russia, but around the world, the balance is tipping toward market power.

While yielding some powers to the market, governments have exercised more control over social affairs. Free markets have not been particularly effective in protecting the social net for people, environmental quality, or human rights. Governments remain the solution of last resort to meet these needs. In some cases, France and Germany for example, market forces have forced moderate retrenchment in social programs. However, worldwide the trend is toward more rather than less government concern about social demands.

Yergin and Stanislaw observe that despite the erosion of government power by globalization, this by no means signals the end of government. Governments are still major forces in the economy and, if they choose, can sit astride "the commanding heights."

Globalization Influences Cultures

In July 1998 officials of nineteen countries met in Ottawa, Canada, to discuss the growing impact throughout the world of U.S.-produced movies, television shows, music, and other entertainment. Their purpose was to decide what to do to protect their cultures from this infusion. In Canada, for instance, the vast majority of movies, CDs, and magazines are American. This led the government to propose regulations limiting television time devoted to U.S.-made programs. "Market forces, left to their own devices," said Sheila Copps, the minister of Canadian heritage, "would have made the entire Canadian broadcasting system a U.S. subsidiary."[37] This raises a question, of course, whether the issue is alteration of culture or commercial self-interest.

The rapid and explosive spread of American culture throughout the world is one of the significant trends of globalization. For example, Coca-Cola is consumed worldwide. American movies are shown in remote corners of the world in preference to other films. Baseball caps of American teams and American blue jeans are worn by teenagers worldwide. English is used universally, and children in many foreign lands are taught it as a second language.

---

[35]Daniel Yergin and Joseph Stanislaw, *The Commanding Heights,* New York: Simon & Schuster, 1998.
[36]Ibid, p. 12.
[37]Roge Ricklefs, "Canada Fights to Fend Off American Tastes and Tunes," *The Wall Street Journal,* September 24, 1998.

However, throughout the world, there is resentment about the transmission of certain Western cultural values. The French for years have sought to reject entry of English words into their language. Members of the French Académie Française cringe at the use by the general population of such expressions as *le hotdog*. Icelanders cherish and protect a language that is virtually identical to that used by the Vikings who settled the land in the ninth century. The clerics in the Islamic world are strongly opposed to many American values, such as the equality of women in society, the pleasures of alcohol, individualism, human rights, and democracy.

Communications and the sale of American products are not the only forces spreading new cultural values around the world. Economic forces of globalization have stimulated massive migrations of peoples. In Germany, for example, the demand for workers stimulated the influx of Turkish people, who brought with them their cultures, some aspects of which infiltrated into German society. In the United States, recent Latin American and Asian immigrants have influenced American language and music.

A major question, of course, is: how much of the spread of cultures around the world really changes the core value of peoples? This question was addressed by Samuel P. Huntington in his seminal book on civilizations.[38] He points out that much of the cultural diffusion may be faddish and does not alter underlying values. There are core cultural values in societies that are not easily changed. For example, he says, use of the English language in the world is more a convenient means of intercultural communication than a force to change core values.

There seems little doubt that globalization has significantly influenced the flow of values. Some of the forces, such as types of entertainment, may have temporary impact. Other forces, such as technological innovations (e.g., computers, biotechnology, pharmaceutical, motor vehicles) may have more lasting impact. However, it is difficult to reject the thesis of Huntington and others that the core cultures of peoples are not easily and significantly changed.

Concluding Observations

Globalization has been a revolutionary force. It has created enormous wealth for peoples. It has also brought severe suffering to many. It has changed business–government–society relationships in fundamental ways. On balance, there seems little question that the forces of globalization have been beneficial to the peoples of the world and give promise of even greater benefits in the future. To achieve this promise, however, important reforms will be necessary.

---

[38]Samuel P. Huntington, *The Clash of Civilizations and the Remaking of World Order*, New York: Simon & Schuster, 1996.

CATERPILLAR INC. IN THE GLOBAL MARKET

Caterpillar Inc. is the world's largest manufacturer of earth-moving, construction, and materials-handling equipment. It is also the world's largest producer of natural gas engines, induction gas turbines, and diesel engines. Since World War II, it has dominated the global market, but not without strong challengers. Caterpillar was named the most admired company in the industrial and farm equipment industry in 1998 by executives in the industry.[1]

Today, the company has thirty-eight manufacturing locations in the United States and thirty-six in other nations. Its products are sold and serviced through a worldwide network of 197 independently owned dealers who operate in 200 countries.

In addition to its manufacturing plants and dealer network, the company has subsidiaries to buttress its operations. For example, the Caterpillar Financial Services Corporation, founded in 1983, provides various types of insurance for dealers. The Caterpillar World Trading Corporation, formed in 1984, expedites sales in countries having foreign exchange shortages. A half dozen other subsidiaries deal with special concerns, such as investing in new products with profit potential, meeting specific customer and market needs, and designing new products.

Total sales of Caterpillar in 1998 were $20.8 billion and profits were $1.51 billion. One-half the sales were from outside the United States and the company employed about 66,000 people worldwide.

Donald V. Fites, Caterpillar chairman and chief executive officer, said, "One of our chief strengths as a corporation has been our ability to deal with change—to meet the challenges of an evolving world."[2] This case demonstrates that. It describes the company's entrance into the global market, how forces in the global market devastated the company in the 1980s, and the strategies devised to achieve its superior global competitive position. The case also describes the company's code of ethics and its social responsibility policies.

---

[1]Eryn Brown, "America's Most Admired Companies," *Fortune*, March 1, 1999.

[2]"Caterpillar Inc. Again Named One of the 'World's Most Admired Companies," News Corporate, http://www.cat.com/cgi-bin/pr/dissplaypr. . ./corporate.html&init_section= newscorp&origindoc, November 28, 1998.

History of Caterpillar

Farmers in the grainfields of California were having trouble plowing at the turn of the century. They were using large, heavy, steam-driven tractors, the wheels of which sank into the fine, moist earth of the delta lands in the Sacramento Valley. Benjamin Holt, whose company had been building combines for years, decided to try the idea of a "treadmill" machine, one that laid its own roadbed, to solve the problem. He made the first track out of wood and tested it successfully in 1904. Later he acquired the trademarks "Caterpillar" and "Cat" for his equipment.

By 1915, Holt sold his machines in twenty countries. They became the standard artillery and supply tractor during World War I for the United States, Great Britain, and France. During World War II and subsequent wars, they became standard heavy earth-moving and construction machines for the U.S. military services. The famous Seabees of World War II relied heavily on them.

In 1925, the Holt Manufacturing Company merged with the C. I. Best Tractor Company to form the Caterpillar Tractor Company (later it became Caterpillar Inc.) with headquarters in Peoria, Illinois, where it remains. Production of agricultural equipment was abandoned in favor of construction equipment when that market appeared to have greater growth potential. Understanding the financial losses of "downtime" for expensive construction equipment, the company early adopted a priority strategy of making only high-quality machines and providing superior services for them. These strategies have been dominant in company policy ever since. Throughout the years, Caterpillar has been undisputed worldwide champion of quality earth-moving equipment.

Caterpillar Begins To Build A Global Network

Prior to the 1950s, Caterpillar assembled its machines and then shipped them abroad. In the mid-1950s, the company launched its first production venture outside the United States. Caterpillar Tractor Co., Ltd., was established in Great Britain to work with British manufacturers to produce parts that met the company's worldwide standards of quality. Shortly thereafter, the company built manufacturing plants in Canada and France. In the mid-1960s, other manufacturing plants were built in Australia, Belgium, and Brazil. A joint venture was started in Mexico. In 1963, the firm entered the Japanese market in a joint venture with Mitsubishi. Caterpillar preferred 100 percent ownership of its overseas plants and agreed to joint ventures only when host governments required that arrangement.

Realities of Global Competition

Caterpillar's strategy of producing abroad and working with other companies in alliances and joint ventures was successful in giving the company dominance in global markets. Komatsu Limited of Japan, however, was determined to outdo Caterpillar. Komatsu management made very clear early in the rivalry that its main objective was to end Caterpillar's dominance. Its rallying cry was "Maru-C," which means "encircle Caterpillar."[3] At first, Komatsu specialized in small machines for the Japanese market but later moved into mining machinery and other specialized machines. The challenge of Komatsu became strong in the 1980s. In 1981, it had a 15 percent price advantage over Caterpillar through its efficient manufacturing and its policy of sacrificing profits to gain market share. With the rise of the value of the dollar, the advantage rose to about 40 percent in 1982 and held through 1984. In addition, Komatsu extended liberal free tryouts to attract prospective customers and kept its engineers on constant alert to deal with equipment problems. Like Caterpillar, it expanded its product line and emphasized quality. Its weakest link was and still is a dealer network inferior to that of Caterpillar.

Caterpillar's Wake-up Call in the 1980s

In 1982, for the first time in fifty years, the firm registered a deficit. In three years, sales dropped almost in half and deficits totaled over $1 billion. Ten plants were closed, 30,000 employees lost their jobs, and the value of the company's stock fell 57 percent by late 1984. What happened?

A number of powerful forces hit the company. There was a global recession. An overvalued dollar made Caterpillar's exports progressively more costly for foreign customers. Komatsu of Japan took this opportunity to increase substantially its global market share and become a major competitor of Caterpillar. Such foreign competition forced the company to slash prices, but that did not overcome the cost advantage of foreign companies from the currency over-valuation. A long and bitter strike by the United Automobile Workers (UAW) virtually shut down U.S. operations. The acquisition of Turbines International in 1981 drained profits. Finally, an overconfident, conservative, highly inbred, and stodgy management weakened the company in many ways. "Quite frankly, our long years of success made us complacent, even arrogant," said Pierre C. Guerindon, an executive vice president of the company.[4]

From this experience there evolved a number of major strategies that have strengthened the company. They are basic to the company's posture today and will likely continue to improve the enviable position of Caterpillar in the future.

---

[3]U. Scrinivasa Rangan, in Christopher A. Bartlett and Sumantra Ghoshal, *Transnational Management* (Homewood, Ill.: Irwin, 1992), p. 326.

[4]Quoted in Kathleen Deveny, "For Caterpillar, the Metamorphosis Isn't Over," *Business Week,* August 31, 1987.

Caterpillar's Strategies

Management was energized to take the most obvious immediate steps of reducing costs, discounting prices, and closing plants. In addition, it introduced significant new strategies and reemphasized some old ones. Here are the main ones.

New Top Management

George A. Schaefer was named CEO in 1985 and formed a new top-management team. As so frequently happens when top management is changed, the company took on a new vigor. Schaefer developed the turn-around strategies that were continued by Donald V. Fites, who became CEO in 1990. Fites also formulated and implemented some new strategies.

Plant Modernization

One of the most important strategies was the development of a major plant modernization program in 1986 called "Plant With a Future" (PWAF). The intent was to increase the efficiency of plants and reduce production costs. The firm committed $1 billion to the project, but eventually the total reached $2 billion.

The project produced significant results. Caterpillar prides itself on being a leader in the design, installation, and operation of large, multimillion–dollar metal-cutting systems, flexible manufacturing systems, and automated production lines. The PWAF adds a new dimension by installing robots, laser technology, CAD/CAM numerical control machine tools, automated factory systems, and other automated equipment. Production today is state-of-the-art. Manufacturing times have been cut by as much as 75 percent. For example, it used to take 6,000 workers twenty-five days to produce a back-loader. Now, it is done with 3,000 workers in six days. In the past, it would typically take up to ten years to design and introduce a new machine. Now it takes twenty-seven months.[5] Caterpillar can build twenty different machines from the same basic design. Production levels can be changed with a week's notice, compared with as much as six months only a few years ago.[6] This type of efficiency has helped the company reduce inventories by 60 percent.

Foreign Expansion

Fites has made global diversification a top priority and has said he hopes foreign sales will produce 75 percent of Caterpillar's revenues by 2008. The number of foreign plants has doubled over the past five years. Foreign expansion serves a number of objectives, such as jumping over trade barriers, reducing

---

[5]"Caterpillar's Comeback," *The Economist,* June 20, 1998.
[6]De'Ann Weimer,"A New Cat on the Hot Seat," *Business Week,* March 9, 1998.

costs, getting close to markets, filling holes in the product line, and challenging competitors in the same market. Overall, it is much cheaper for a company to acquire another plant than to build it.

Caterpillar has manufacturing plants located in both hemispheres. They are in many European countries, Canada, Russia, India, Indonesia, China, Japan, and Australia. During the past few years, Caterpillar has spent over $2 billion acquiring engine plants, such as MaK Motoren in Germany and Perkins Engines in the United Kingdom. The former adds to Caterpillar's full line of engine products (from 5 to 15,000 horsepower), and the latter produces small engines. The company also has joint ventures and alliances throughout the world. Its partners include Skogsjan, a Swedish company producing forestry machines; Claas, a German company making agricultural machinery; and Shin Caterpillar Mitsubishi (SCM), a Japanese company. SCM has aspirations of beating Komatsu to become the leading producer of construction equipment in the Japanese market.[7]

Product Quality

Caterpillar has a worldwide reputation for producing high-quality, high-technology products. Ensuring quality products has been a strategy from the company's very beginning, and it still permeates all aspects of its operations. William Newman, past chair of Caterpillar, said that "We adopted a policy that a Caterpillar product or component—no matter where it was built—would be equal in quality or performance to the same product or component built at any other location whether in this country or abroad."[8]

Focus on Core Business

Fites underscored this strategy in these words: "We are not going to diversify in the classic sense. . .even though we are number one, there's a lot of market share that we aren't getting. Rather than worrying about getting into some other business, we need to worry about doing even better in the businesses we're in."[9]

A Full Product Line

A major strategy is to have a full line of machines in each category and continuously create new products. As noted above, many acquisitions and joint ventures have been made to complete a product line.

---

[7]See Caterpillar, "Global Japan," http://www.cat.com/about/global/07_japan/japan.html, November 28, 1998.

[8]Quoted in Thomas J. Peters and Robert H. Waterman, *In Search of Excellence: Lessons from America's Best-Run Companies* (New York: Harper, 1982,) p. 55.

[9]Donald V. Fites, "An Interview with Donald V. Fites," *Inter-Business Issues*, December 1992, p. 33.

New Products

In the past five years, 294 new or improved products have been introduced. For example, the company for years has built engines for its construction equipment; recently, it has built the engines for other uses, such as generating electricity, and power for large trucks. The company today sells generators in such different markets as electric power generation in developing countries and standby generators for riverboat casinos. Engineers have also perfected rubber tracks for agricultural equipment that usually run on wheels. Caterpillar's new tractors have advantages over wheeled tractors because they reduce soil compaction and allow farmers to work in adverse weather when ordinary machines cannot.

Customer Service

Caterpillar has always been a customer-driven firm. The emphasis on product quality, continuous research, and maintenance of a full product line illustrate the point. Its attention to a strong dealer network is another facet of this strategy, and the company depends on its dealers for superior service to customers. The company is developing a worldwide communications system to facilitate quickly getting knowledge of customer needs and responding immediately to them.

Strong Dealer Network

Caterpillar's dealers are solidly established in their markets and are loyal to the company, partly because the company carefully selects them and supports them in times of financial difficulty. The company sees its dealers as partners (although most are privately owned) and has subsidiaries to give them special assistance. Dealers are financially strong and turnover is very low.

Organizational Reform

In 1990, Fites announced a major reorganization, the central feature of which was the creation of thirteen profit centers (later increased to twenty-six). Managers of the centers are given much autonomy and authority. The idea is to push decisions down the organization, focus closer attention on customers, cut costs, enhance product quality, and increase the center's return on assets.

Relations with Unions

In 1991, The United Automobile Workers (UAW) struck over wages and working conditions. The dispute lasted for 6 1/2 years until settled in early 1998. While the strike at first affected the productive efficiency of the company, by 1998 new levels of sales and profits had been reached. This was in no small measure attributable to the strategies employed by the company as noted above, and to the fact that some 4,000 union workers crossed the picket lines, managers and officer workers joined the production lines, and several thousand new workers were hired.

Key provisions of the new contract were an immediate wage increase, improved pension fund benefits, a moratorium on plant closings, reinstatement of disputed grievance procedures, reinstatement of union members fired by the company, and increased sickness and disability benefits. In return, the union agreed to drop 443 unfair labor practice complaints filed with the National Labor Relations Board; grant amnesty to about 4,000 union members expelled from the union for crossing picket lines; and accept two-tier wage levels, the use of temporary employees, and the institution of more flexible work schedules.[10]

Caterpillar's Competition

The company continues to face aggressive competition by powerful companies at home and abroad. In the United States, Deere & Co. and Case Corp. are waging a forceful battle with Caterpillar in sales of agricultural equipment. Cummins Engine Co. is trying to achieve dominance in diesel engine production, both in the United States and abroad. Cummins Engine Co., although less than one-third the size of Caterpillar, is a formidable foe with a long history of diesel engine production. Its 1998 sales were $6.3 billion and it employed 26,300 people. Like Caterpillar, it has formed alliances and joint ventures around the world.

Perhaps the most formidable competitor is Komatsu. This company began in 1917 as Tokeuchi Mining Co. and today has plants around the world, including the United States. Its sales in 1998 were $8.3 billion and it employed 27,917 people. It produces a wide range of construction and mining equipment comparable to Caterpillar's. Unlike Caterpillar, Komatsu is involved in many other industries, such as electronics (e.g., silicon wafers, control systems, etc.), industrial machinery (e.g., sheet metal presses, laser cutting machines, robots, etc.), civil engineering, and architecture.

Komatsu's entrance into the United States was in 1961 when it signed a technology-sharing agreement with Cummins Engine Co. In 1970, it established Komatsu America Corp., and since then has formed a number of other companies.

In April 1997, the company announced a four-year management strategy called "G" 2000. The G stands for global growth into the year 2000. Its slogan is "Together We Sow, Together We Reap." Its mission, says management, is to prepare the foundation for our dreams to come true in the next century.[11] One dream is to accomplish "Maru-C."

---

[10]For a history of the dispute and its settlement, see Michael H. Cimini, "Caterpillar's Prolonged Dispute Ends," *Compensation and Working Conditions,* Fall 1998.

[11]Komatsu, http://www2.komatsu.co.jp/kmfactb. . ./ 50e2d5ec757492564670003c91c?OpenDocumen, December 15, 1998.

Caterpillar's Mission Statement

- Provide customers worldwide with differentiated products and services of recognized superior value.
- Pursue businesses in which we can be a leader based on one or more of our strengths.
- Create and maintain a productive work environment in which employee satisfaction is attained with high levels of personal growth and achievement while conforming to our "Code of Worldwide Business Conduct and Operating Principles."
- Achieve growth and provide above-average returns for stockholders resulting from both management of ongoing businesses and a studied awareness and development of new opportunities.[12]

The company says:

Caterpillar is poised to enter the next century as a global leader. We are planning for a 5 to 7 percent average annual real growth. We'll become a $30 billion-plus company before the end of the next decade—adjusted for inflation. We'll manage to operate profitably even during economic downturns. And we'll continue to offer consistently attractive dividends to our shareholders. The strategies to achieve these ambitious goals are already in place. And we're committed to achieving them.[13]

Code of Worldwide Business Conduct and Operating Principles

Of special interest to students of corporate responsibility is this code, first introduced in 1974, but since revised. In issuing the latest revision in August 1992, Fites wrote: "This fourth revision of the Code still has the purpose of guiding Caterpillar people in a broad and ethical sense, in all aspects of our worldwide business activities. Experience has demonstrated the practical utility of this document . . . No document issued by Caterpillar is more important than this one. I ask that you give this Code your strong support as you carry out your daily responsibilities."[14] These words are not mere rhetoric because the company tries to instill its principles in company behavior world-wide.

The code is far too detailed to be reproduced here. It is thirteen printed pages long and sets forth in detail guides to many areas one would expect in

---

[12]*Caterpillar: The Global Competitor 1997 Annual Report: Making Progress Possible*, p. 23.
[13]Ibid, p. 24.
[14]Caterpillar Inc., *Caterpillar Code of Worldwide Business Conduct and Operating Principles*, Peoria, Ill.: Caterpillar Inc., 1992.

EPA Announces One Billion Dollar Settlement with Diesel Engine Industry for Clean Air Violations

On October 22, 1998, the Department of Justice and Environmental Protection Agency announced a settlement with seven manufacturers of heavy-duty diesel engines for clean air violations. Attorney General Janet Reno said: "The diesel engine industry has illegally poured millions of tons of pollution into the air. It's time for the diesel engine industry to clean up its act and clean up our air."[15] The $1 billion settlement included the largest civil penalty ever imposed for violating an environmental law.

The complaint alleges that the companies violated the Clean Air Act by selling diesel engines with "defeat devices"—software that alters an engine's pollution control equipment under normal driving conditions. The devices allowed the engines to meet the EPAs standards during routine tests but disabled the emission controls during normal highway driving. This has resulted in emissions of tons of nitrogen oxide during the years the devices were in the engines. Oxides of nitrogen contribute to urban smog and acid rain.

The settlement involved seven companies: Caterpillar Inc., Cummins Engine Company, Detroit Diesel Corporation, Mack Trucks, Navistar International Transportation Corporation, Renault Vehicles Industries, and Volvo Truck Corporation. The companies agreed to spend at least $850 million to introduce cleaner new engines, rebuild old engines, and recall pickup trucks that have the defeat devices. They also will spend $109 million for emission control research. Finally, the civil penalty was set at $83 million. The agreement is expected to reduce nitrogen oxide emissions from diesel engines by one-third in five years.

The engine makers maintained they did nothing wrong. Caterpillar vice president Sid Banwart said: "Our engines have never employed any type of device to evade EPA guidelines. Our engines have always been in compliance with the Clean Air Act and EPA emissions regulations." Navistar International Corp. said its engines complied with the law. However, the settlement was an acceptable way to avoid controversy with the EPA and settle the issue.[16]

---

[15]Press Release, "DOJ, EPA Announce One Billion Dollar Settlement with Diesel Engine Industry for Clean Air Violations," October 22, 1998, http://www.usdoj.gov/opa/pr/1998/October/499 emr.htm.

[16]News Search, "U.S. Diesel Engine Makers Reach $1 Billion Deal with EPA," http://www.dieselnet.com/news/9810epa.html, October 22, 1998.

such a code. To name a few: business ethics, protection of the environment, relations with suppliers, sharing of technology, differing business practices, competitive conduct, public responsibilities, inside information, observance of local laws, relationships with public officials, and reporting code compliance. Here are selections from sections on business ethics and public responsibilities.

Business Ethics

The company's most valuable asset is a reputation for integrity. If that becomes tarnished, customers, investors, suppliers, employees, and those who sell our products and services will seek affiliation with other, more attractive companies. We intend to hold to a single high standard of integrity everywhere. We will keep our word. We won't promise more than we can reasonably expect to deliver; nor will we make commitments we don't intend to keep.

In our advertising and other public communications, we will avoid not only untruths, but also exaggeration and overstatement.

Caterpillar employees shall not engage in activities that produce, or reasonably appear to produce, conflict between personal interests of an employee and interests of the company.

We seek long-lasting relationships—based on integrity—with all those activities that touch upon our own. The ethical performance of the enterprise is the sum of the ethical performance of the men and women who work here. Thus, we are all expected to adhere to high standards of personal integrity. For example, any illegal act ostensibly taken to "protect" the company is wrong. The end doesn't justify the means.

Public Responsibility

This section is too long to be reproduced here, so we limit the selection to three categories of responsibility set forth in the code.

We believe there are three basic categories of possible social impact by business:

1. First is the straightforward pursuit of daily business affairs. This involves the conventional (but often misunderstood) dynamics of private enterprise: developing desired goods and services, providing jobs and training, investing manufacturing and technical facilities, dealing with suppliers, attracting customers and investors, earning a profit, and paying taxes.

2. The second category has to do with conducting business affairs in a way that is socially responsible. It isn't enough to successfully offer useful products and services. A business should, for example, employ and promote people fairly, see to their job safety and the safety of its products, conserve energy and other valuable resources, and help protect the quality of the environment.

3. The third category relates to initiatives beyond our operations, such as helping solve community problems. To the extent our resources permit— and if a host country or community wishes—we will participate selectively in such matters. Each corporate facility is an integral part of the community

in which it operates. Like an individual, it benefits from character building, health, welfare, and educational and cultural activities. And like an individual, it also has a citizen's responsibility to support such activities.

Concluding Comment

For decades, Caterpillar has had an enviable reputation for high-quality products. It has built an integrated network of companies and dealers around the world that has given it a strong global competitive position. It is an example of a company that can surmount crises and formulate strategies that yield a global competitive advantage.

Questions

1. Briefly trace the history of Caterpillar.
2. What caused Caterpillar's crisis in the early 1990s? Should the company have foreseen it?
3. What strategies did Caterpillar formulate and implement to overcome the crisis?
4. Evaluate the strategies?
5. Appraise Caterpillar's mission statement.
6. Appraise the business ethics section of the code.
7. Appraise the social responsibility section in the code of conduct.
8. Comment on the DOJ-EPA civil penalties in light of Caterpillar's code.
9. What major problems do you see ahead for Caterpillar in competing in the global market?

Pollution and Environment

14

Industrial Pollution and Environmental Policy

Indian Health Service
www.ihs.gov

Daniel Schultz, a surgeon at the Santa Fe Indian Hospital in New Mexico, was puzzled and alarmed when, in an eighteen-month period in 1984 and 1985, he diagnosed three cases of malignant mesothelioma in Indians from a nearby pueblo. An investigation of a state tumor registry revealed two more cases from this pueblo in 1970 and 1982, for a total of five cases over fifteen years. On average, the victims were 65 years old and lived only 3.8 months after diagnosis.[1]

Malignant mesothelioma is an incurable tumor in the lining of the chest cavity that is virtually always caused by exposure to asbestos. It has a latency period of forty to fifty years. Five cases of this unusual cancer in a pueblo of 2,000 Indians was roughly 1,000 times the expected number predicted over fifteen years by standard mortality tables. Normally, five cases could be expected in a city of two million, not such a tiny Indian pueblo. Samples of lung tissue from the three cases in the Indian Hospital revealed the presence of all three types of asbestos used in commerce—chrysotile, amosite, and crocidolite. The Indians had been exposed to airborne asbestos fibers. But how? Schultz called

---

[1]Richard J. Driscoll, Wallace J. Mulligan, Daniel Schultz, and Anthony Candelaria, "Malignant Mesothelioma: A Cluster in a Native American Pueblo," *New England Journal of Medicine*, June 2, 1988, p. 1437.

in Richard J. Driscoll, an environmental health officer with the Indian Health Service (IHS), a small agency in the Department of Health and Human Services. Driscoll, along with colleagues from the IHS, set out to do some detective work to learn how asbestos exposure was occurring.

Immediately the investigators ran into a problem. The Indians were reluctant subjects. They had a superstitious belief that fatal illness was explained by the presence of evil in its victims. They believed that people who discussed disease were wishing it on others and inviting additional sickness. The Indians also disliked attention and interference from outsiders because they wanted to keep their native culture and ways intact. Tribal elders finally agreed to discuss possible causes of asbestos exposure. Here is the story that emerged.

In the 1930s, a brick-manufacturing plant was built in the vicinity of the pueblo. A small private railroad was started to shuttle between the plant and a nearby main line of the Santa Fe Railroad, and a steam locomotive operated on it. When the boiler and pipe insulation on the locomotive needed replacement, workers discarded the old asbestos insulation near the tracks, where it was found by members of the tribe and brought back to the pueblo. It was put to many uses. Asbestos pads were used for worktable insulation by silversmiths making Indian jewelry. Dancers at religious festivals scraped and pounded their deer-hide leggings with crumbling wads of pipe insulation to whiten them, releasing clouds of floating asbestos fibers. Gradually the Indians found more and more uses for

asbestos, and the trackside scrap was supplemented by tribe members in construction work who scavenged at their job sites for more.

The investigators discovered that four of the five mesothelioma victims had been silversmiths, and that all five had been active participants in ceremonial dances. The Indians were reluctant to give up their asbestos; selling it had become a cottage industry in the pueblo. When the investigators went door to door, they found that Indian families were hoarding asbestos in bags, pots, and jars. It was hard to get the Indians to part with it, but they found that by emphasizing the harm it could cause to children, most of it could be removed.

The story of what happened to the Indians in the pueblo is analogous to what has happened to large populations in industrial societies. In both cases, dangerous substances with useful qualities promised better living. In both cases, elevated exposure to these substances predated adequate knowledge of their harmful effects. And in both cases, it was only after substantial exposures had occurred and sickness began to appear that government agencies mobilized to protect public health.

In this chapter we discuss the nature of industrial pollutants and the practices and social philosophies that allowed them to darken skies, poison waters, and despoil land. We then discuss how, in the United States beginning in the 1970s, massive regulatory programs developed to control industrial pollution. We explain the current operation of these programs, how they affect corporations, and how well they work.

Sources of Pollution

Pollution is any substance in the environment that endangers human welfare. It can come from natural sources. Forest fires give off particles causing atmospheric haze. Water picks up trace metals and asbestos as it flows over rocks, gravel, and sand. Uranium ore emits ionizing radiation that breaks chemical bonds in human DNA.

Human activity adds more contaminants to the environment. For millions of years, hunter-gatherer bands generated little pollution. However, a gradual revolution in agricultural methods beginning about 10,000 years ago led to more settled societies in which populations grew and people gathered in cities. The primary pollution problem this created was disposal of human and animal waste in a way that maintains a sanitary water supply. Water treatment plant technology introduced in the nineteenth century eventually protected water supplies. Then the primary pollution problems became contamination from fossil-fuel combustion and manufacturing activity.

Most industrial pollution simply adds to background levels of naturally occurring substances, so that human exposures to metals, carbon compounds, radiation, and other substances reach artificially high levels. It is estimated, for example, that because of environmental exposure, the average American carries a tissue concentration of lead at least 1,000 times greater than prehistoric people.[2] Some industrial pollutants, however, are not found in nature. The rise of synthetic chemical production since the 1940s led to the creation and dispersal of persistent, complex artificial molecules used in plastics, fumigants, and pesticides.

Industrial pollution endangers both the environment and human health. For example, carbon dioxide occurred naturally in the atmosphere in 1850 at 275 parts per million (ppm), but over the years it has risen to 364 ppm because the combustion of wood, coal, oil, and natural gas releases carbon faster than natural sinks absorb it. This increase of 89 ppm is a minuscule change in the total atmosphere, less than one-thousandth of a percent, but atmospheric carbon dioxide absorbs heat radiated from the earth and there is growing evidence that the tiny increase in it is responsible for a rise of 1° F in the mean average global temperature since 1890. The release of other industrial pollutants into the environment, particularly synthetic chemicals, has caused adverse human health effects including induction of cancer (carcinogenesis), genetic changes in cells (mutagenesis), nonhereditary birth defects (teratogenesis), noncancerous disease processes,[3] and behavioral impairment.

---

[2]Joel Schwartz and Ronnie Levin, "Lead: Example of the Job Ahead," *EPA Journal,* March/April 1992, p. 42.

[3]These include damage to the nervous system (neurotoxicity), suppression of host defense mechanisms (immunotoxicity), liver injury (hepatotoxicity), kidney damage (renal toxicity), and hormonal disruption.

Mortality caused by industrial pollutants adds up to an unknown, significant total, but it is far less than mortality from pollution not caused by industry. For example, outdoor air pollution from factories and vehicles, artifacts of the industrial age, causes an estimated 0.4 to 1.1 percent of mortality worldwide each year and has been estimated to cause 2 percent of cancers. On average, it reduces the life span of residents of the most polluted urban areas by between one and two years. It causes higher death rates, 2 to 5 percent, in developing nations where regulatory controls are lax compared with industrialized countries.

Indoor air pollution, on the other hand, is more deadly. Exposure to smoky fuels such as wood and coal smoke used for cooking and heating in less-developed countries causes 6 percent of annual deaths worldwide, far more than outdoor air pollution from autos and factories. When nations make the transition from dirty fuels to cleaner ones such as gasoline and nuclear energy, mortality falls. Greater than either of these airborne dangers is water polluted by feces, which causes 7 percent of annual deaths worldwide, almost all in less-developed nations.[4]

Although industry is a direct cause of environmental damage, there are other underlying causes. One is population growth. Between 1900 and 2000, world population grew from 1.2 billion to 5.9 billion, and it continues to grow. Each birth creates new demands for energy, food, and industrial products. A second cause is urbanization, a worldwide phenomenon that concentrates pollutants in small areas where they are not easily dispersed. The percentage of the world's population living in cities will continue to rise, growing from 39 percent in 1980 to a predicted 57 percent in 2020.[5] A third cause is affluence. In developed societies, it encourages resource consumption, and in poorer countries it is an ideal that makes industrialization a priority over environmental protection.

The operation of these underlying forces is illustrated by the decade 1980 to 1990 in the United States. During these years, the population grew 10 percent and urban areas also grew by 10 percent (since almost all the twenty-two million new people lived in them). The gross domestic product rose 105 percent and real disposable personal income grew by 106 percent. Other statistics reflect the environmental impact of these changes. Solid waste production rose by 29 percent, the number of motor vehicles in use increased 28 percent, production of chemicals rose 71 percent, and industrial production increased 26 percent.[6] This decade was typical, not unusual. These statistics illustrate how efforts to control pollution operate against a backdrop of increase in those factors that cause it. And growth is even more rapid in some developing nations.

---

[4]Figures in this paragraph are from research summarized in a joint publication of the World Resources Institute, the United Nations, and the World Bank, *World Resources: 1998–99,* New York: Oxford University Press, 1998, pp. 1, 33–34, and 63–66.

[5]Ibid., *World Resources: 1998–1999,* p. 274.

[6]These percentages are based on figures in the *Statistical Abstract of the United States,* Washington, D.C.: Government Printing Office, September 1994, various tables.

Industrial Growth and Environmental Pollution

Industrial activity, broadly defined, is the source of enduring pollution problems, yet for most of the period since the early 1800s, when industry began to transform societies, there was little concern for protecting nature or human health. Carelessness abounded. In the United States, great eastern forests were toppled to get wood needed for industry. In the West, hydraulic mining with high-pressure hoses washed away mountainsides to extract ore. By the 1880s, growing use of electricity created an insatiable, global demand for copper to make wire. Copper extraction characterized the ecological carelessness of the period.

The Anaconda Copper Mining Company began operating in 1882 and eventually dug 10,000 miles of passageways in ore-bearing hills surrounding what is now Butte, Montana. Copper ores roasting in open pits belched fumes of sulfur and arsenic and smoke so thick that street lamps burned at midday. The teeth of cows grazing nearby were coated with fugitive copper fallen from the air. Isaac Edinger, a nearby rancher of that time, said:

> I used to carry a few of those gold-colored teeth in my pocket all the time because no one would believe me, and I'd have to show 'em. When they were shown they always wanted to keep the evidence, and I'd have to get a new supply every time I went back to the slaughterhouse.[7]

The mining eventually contaminated the areas' underground aquifer and stunted vegetation for miles. Today, a 600-acre open pit mine filled with 28 billion gallons of poisoned water sits near the city of Butte. The water is so acidic that it liquefies boat propellers. When a flock of snow geese migrating from the Canadian arctic happened to land there a few years back, 342 of them died. Autopsies found burns in their necks and intestines.[8] Today the old mine area is one of the nation's largest Superfund sites.[9]

Industrial take-off eras in other countries were just as destructive. Half a world away from Butte, in the mountains north of Tokyo, the giant Ashio copper-mining complex caused ecological damage equaling or exceeding that in Butte. Mining operations left gaping holes in the landscape. Fallout from smelter emissions blackened hundreds of square miles of forests. In 1883, a sulfurous gas release shriveled the leaves of mulberry trees in a nearby town. Silkworms that fed on the leaves and supported a thriving local silk industry spat out greenish fluid and died. Their livelihood destroyed, the silk farmers abandoned the town. Copper fallout contaminated wide swathes of other farmland, igniting a farmer's political movement to shut down the smelter,

---

[7]C. B. Glasscock, *The War of the Copper Kings: Builders of Butte and Wolves of Wall Street,* New York: Grosset & Dunlap, 1935, p. 86.

[8]Edwin Dobb, "Pennies from Hell," *Harper's Magazine,* October 1996, p. 39.

[9]The old Anaconda Smelter was a separate Superfund site. Its cleanup was completed in 1998 and is described on the Web site of the Environmental Protection Agency, http://www.epa.gov/superfund/accomp/redevel/anaconda.htm.

When Air Pollution Was Held in High Esteem

In the morning light of the industrial era, factory smoke was a sign of prosperity and progress. William McKinley, the Republican presidential candidate in 1896, wanted to raise tariffs to protect American companies from foreign competition. On a campaign poster, he evoked poetically the specter of smokeless chimneys that might result from lower tariffs.

The Smokeless Chimney

Morn after morn the artisan
Has watched with long eye
To see the grimy smoke in wreaths
Swirl up into the sky;
He listens for the whistle shrill—
Its echoes come not back—
And cold and black and desolate
Still stands the chimney stack.

O, Chimney Top! Good Chimney Top!
Put on thy crown of black;
Let life and hope and goodly cheer—
Spout from thy lofty stack!

Source: Poster reprinted in Ralph K. Andrist, ed., *Confident Years: 1865–1916*, New York: American Heritage/Bonanza Books, 1989, p. 293.

---

but the movement was doomed to defeat. The mine had great importance to the government because exported copper brought in foreign currency and strengthened Japan's drive to become a world power.

Half a century later, Joseph Stalin's push for the growth of heavy industry in the Soviet Union again showed the high price of ignoring ecological damage. In the 1930s, Stalin sent prisoners to labor camps in Siberia, where they built a metallurgical complex of smelters and mills producing steel, copper, and nickel. This complex had more than 200 stacks and became the world's largest industrial source of sulfur dioxide emissions. It still operates today, and air pollution is so heavy that local residents are ordered to stay indoors an average of thirty days a year and, for another sixty days, staying in is recommended.

Industrialization has been accompanied by sensational accidents. In recent memory is the gas leak at Union Carbide's Bhopal, India, pesticide plant in 1984 that killed 4,037 people; the release of radionuclides by a Russian reactor at Chernobyl in the Ukraine killing thirty-one people immediately in 1986; and the release of 250,000 gallons of crude oil from the *Exxon Valdez* in 1989. All illustrate catastrophic failures of industrial processes to contain pollutants. These catastrophes vary widely in their consequences. The *Exxon Valdez* grounding killed no one and did little permanent habitat damage. The

Chernobyl radiation release, on the other hand, is clearly the worst industrial accident on record. An estimated 32,000 have died of radiation exposure so far and elevated death rates will continue for many years due to the long latency periods of radiation-induced illnesses.[10]

Spectacular accidents, however, are atypical and account for little industrial pollution, most of which is undramatic, garden-variety degradation. Factories, for example, are inevitably polluting and leave their mark on the environment. Electroplating produces air emissions of chromium, paint factories discharge cadmium in wastewater, petrochemical plants evaporate hydrocarbons, and semiconductor manufacturing releases toxic solvents. Even the best control devices are never 100 percent efficient, often far less, so these industries and others leave their characteristic signatures on air, water, and land. In addition, it is virtually impossible for an industrial plant not to pollute in many small ways. Dust escapes through wall vents. Oil drips from forklift engines in warehouses, later to be washed down drains. Dust from ductwork clean out escapes into the air. Outside, gophers burrow under spill-containment dikes for chemical tanks. Industry is inevitably messy. The sum of this garden-variety pollution imposes a larger burden on the world ecosystem than a few spectacular accidents.

Today there are nations on every continent with ambitious development plans that prioritize industry over environmental protection. Their leaders see industrial growth as the only practical way to increase living standards and national power. According to United Nation's estimates, about 30 percent of the world's population lives in poverty. These poor people are not lucky enough to be citizens of the roughly two dozen industrial nations that account for 81 percent of world GDP. So they, and their governments, aspire to industrialize.

If populous underdeveloped nations were to take the path of the industrial revolution in England, Japan, the United States, and Russia, the pollution and resource depletion that would result might lead to ecological disaster. In the United States, there are about 750 automobiles per 1,000 people; in India, only 8 per 1,000; and in China, only 7 per 1,000. Yet India and China encourage auto factories. In China, for example, production has risen by 50 percent per year in recent years. The world ecosystem is already strained by carbon dioxide build-up, acid rain, and stratospheric ozone depletion. A further magnitude of increase in pollution would aggravate these problems. What would happen if there were 750 autos per 1,000 Indians and Chinese?

Much interest today is focused on the notion of *sustainable development,* that is, nonpolluting economic growth that raises standards of living without depleting the net resources of the earth. However, the modern industrial revolution, as it is currently unfolding in developing nations, bears little resemblance to this ideal. In fact, it promises to exceed by far the old-time industrial revolutions in generating pollution and depleting resources. First, industrialization is

---

[10]James Rupert, "It's Spring, and the Radioactivity Is in Bloom," *Washington Post National Weekly Edition,* May 6–12, 1996, p. 10.

rushed. Economic growth rates in countries such as Korea, Thailand, and China have compressed the transformation into less than two decades rather than the hundred years and more it took in England and the United States. As growth skyrockets, a range of modern industries appears, creating more varied and dangerous pollutants than were typical of eighteenth and nineteenth century factories. Industrial nations have caused this by sending their dirtiest, most dangerous businesses to the developing world. Asbestos manufacturing, virtually nonexistent in the United States, now flourishes as an export industry in Brazil, Pakistan, India, and the Republic of Korea. Moreover, the urban population density in developing countries is typically much higher than it was in the nations of the West when they industrialized, so larger numbers of people are exposed to deadly pollutants.

Although sustainable development is a useful philosophy, and as we will see, some nations and corporations attempt to put it in action, the broad reality in developing economies bears little resemblance to the sustainable ideal. Instead, growth seems predicated on older ideas. In the next section, we discuss the development of these ideas.

Ideas Shape Attitudes toward the Environment

What is the proper relationship between business and nature? Destructive industrial activity has been legitimized by Western values that regard nature as an adversary to be conquered. Ancient Mediterranean society incubated these values and eventually they appeared in biblical text, giving them religious sanction and magnifying their influence. In the story of creation in Genesis, God creates first nature and then man and afterward instructs man on how to relate to nature.

> Be fruitful and multiply, and replenish the earth and subdue it; and have dominion over the fish of the sea, and over the fowl of the air, and over every living thing that moveth upon the earth. (1:28)

This Judeo-Christian view laid the foundation for the conviction in Western civilization that humans were both separate from and superior to the natural world. The Judeo-Christian heritage also incorporated the idea that humans must exercise wise stewardship over their dominion, but until recently the stewardship concept languished as a minor theme.

When Church dogma began to lose its primacy during the Renaissance in Europe, secular philosophers did not reject the doctrine of human superiority to nature but reinforced it with nonbiblical ideas. Within the comparatively short span of 150 years, four new ideas in particular appeared that, combined, determined how nature would be regarded and treated during the coming industrial revolution.

The theory of *dualism* held that humans were separate from nature. The French philosopher René Descartes (1596–1650) believed that nature operated like a machine, according to fixed laws that could be studied and understood by humans. Humans were separate from nature and other living organisms because they alone had the power of reason and, unlike plants and animals, had souls. Descartes's perspective laid the foundation for modern experimental science but also established a dualism that reinforced the Judeo-Christian idea that humans were superior to and apart from nature.

The Renaissance was also marked by improved living conditions, growth of cities, inventions, and the birth of industries. Such experiences kindled great optimism in European intellectuals who wrote of the idea of *progress*, or belief that history was a narrative of improvement in which humanity moved from lower to higher levels on an inevitable march to perfection. This idea rejected the pessimism of previous civilizations that had looked back on past golden eras. The idea of progress was supported in the popular mind by Charles Darwin's theory of evolution. As industry expanded, the conquest of nature and the exploitation of natural resources for human welfare became entwined with the notion of progress.

Then, during the early years of industrial revolution in England, basic doctrines of economics and ethics arose, which in additional ways justified the exploitation of nature. The theory of *capitalism*, based on principles set forth by Adam Smith in 1776, valued nature primarily as a commodity to be used in wealth-creating activity that would increase the power, welfare, and comfort of society. This improved human condition was seen as progress, which justified it and gave it priority over activity based on values that would have sanctified and preserved nature. As a practical matter, early capitalism in action largely ignored environmental damage. This tendency still exists. For example, the gross domestic product, which is the accounting system of capitalism, rises when goods or services are produced, but does not fall when pollution damage occurs. Thus, the GDP rose because of the *Exxon Valdez* oil spill, adding up the miliions of dollars spent by Exxon on the cleanup but not subtracting the costs of dead animals and degraded shoreline.

The doctrine of *utilitarianism*, or "the greatest good for the greatest number," arose in England simultaneously with the rise of capitalism and was used to justify economic activity that destroyed nature. Industry made the utilitarian argument that, although pollution is harmful, the economic benefits of jobs, products, taxes, and growth outweighed the costs of environmental damage and were the "greatest good." Utilitarianism became the moral pillar holding up a worldview that blinded Western societies to alternative, but less exploitive, views of nature.

In Eastern civilization, philosophies such as Buddhism and Taoism placed a greater emphasis on the interconnectedness of people and nature. They portrayed a more humble, less domineering role for humanity. However, their main impact was in interpersonal relations. Industrialism in Asia has been, if anything, more destructive of the environment than in the West.[11]

---

[11]For further discussion, see Clive Ponting, *A Green History of the World*, New York: St. Martin's Press, 1992, chap. 8.

New Ideas Challenge the Legitimacy of Exploiting Nature

In the second half of the twentieth century, concern about the harm done to nature by industry grew and an alternative, non-exploitive environmental ethic began to emerge.

The naturalist Aldo Leopold was a pioneer in thinking about an expanded environmental ethic. His seminal statement of a new "land ethic" in a 1949 book, *A Sand County Almanac*, inspired later generations of ethicists. He wrote:

> All ethics so far evolved rest upon a single premise: that the individual is a member of a community of interdependent parts . . .
>
> The land ethic simply enlarges the boundaries of the community to include soils, waters, plants, and animals, or collectively: the land. . . .
>
> In short, a land ethic changes the role of *Homo sapiens* from conqueror of the land-community to plain member and citizen of it. It implies respect for his fellow members and also respect for the community as such.[12]

For Leopold, the conventional boundaries of ethical duty were too narrow. They should be expanded to include not only duties toward fellow humans, but also duties to nonhuman entities in nature, both living and nonliving.

A more radical form of this "land ethic" was set forth later by a Norwegian philosopher, Arne Naess. Beginning in the early 1970s, Naess argued that even Leopold and mainstream environmentalists were too shallow in their thinking because they accepted the industrial-age worldview and tried to mitigate pollution within the context of a society that promoted material affluence. He said that there were "deeper concerns," and his position came to be called *deep ecology*. Rather than simply suggesting, as Leopold had, that humans had a broad duty to respect nature, Naess said that human domination of nature should cease. Philosophies of domination should be replaced by notions of biospheric egalitarianism in which other species had equal rights to live and blossom. Nature had intrinsic value; its components should not be valued as inputs for factories as in capitalist economics. Naess said that the present level of human interference in nature was excessive and detrimental and that it was the duty of people who agreed with him to take action. Drastic changes were needed.[13]

Naess's work has inspired radical environmental groups such as Earth First! These groups believe that extreme measures, including lawlessness, are warranted by the moral obligation to stop the destruction of nature.

Other new environmental philosophies have generated innovative ideas to justify expanding rights to nonhuman entities. For example, philosopher Peter Singer popularized the concept of *speciesism*, or "a prejudice or attitude

---

[12]Aldo Leopold, *A Sand County Almanac*, New York: Ballantine, 1970, pp. 239–40.

[13]Naess's basic arguments are in "The Shallow and the Deep, Long-Range Ecology Movement: A Summary," *Inquiry*, Spring 1973; and "A Defense of the Deep Ecology Movement," *Environmental Ethics*, Fall 1984.

of bias towards the members of one's own species and against those of members of other species," that is analogous to racism or sexism.[14] The racist and sexist believe that skin color and sex determine people's worth; the speciesist believes that the number of one's legs or whether one lives in trees, the sea, or a condominium determine's one's rights. Traditionally, when *Homo sapiens* compete for rights with plants and animals, the latter have lost. Singer argues that humans, though superior in important ways, are simply one species among many. And the others have intrinsic value independent of any economic usefulness to *Homo sapiens.*

Arguments such as Singer's show that the new environmental ethic is a powerful rights ethic. It challenges the centuries-old view of human dominance and undermines the human-centered morality of industrial development—at least until such development occurs in a way that does not disturb plants and animals. Without a practical technique of sustainable industrial development, therefore, adopting this ethic would call into question most economic activity and would consign hundreds of millions of humans to a condition of permanent poverty. On the other hand, it would prevent further deterioration of oceans, species, rainforests, and the atmosphere.

Environmental Laws and Regulations

The dominant approach to controlling industrial pollution in the United States has been to pass laws that strictly regulate emissions, effluents, and wastes. Before the 1970s, there was little environmental regulation, but, in the 1960s, the public became frightened of pollution and a strong popular mandate for controlling it emerged. Beginning in 1969, and spanning what came to be called the "environmental decade" of the 1970s, Congress passed a remarkable string of new laws, creating a broad statutory base for regulating industry. Table 14-1 lists the major enactments.

Since 1980, additional laws have been passed, but infrequently. The two most notable are the Emergency Planning and Community Right-to-Know Act of 1986, requiring companies to tell nearby residents about toxic chemical risks at their facilities; and the Pollution Prevention Act of 1990, requiring regulators to promote cleaner, less-polluting industrial processes. The laws of the 1970s are still the basis of environmental regulation. Most have been reauthorized and amended, some several times, and some of these revisions, such as the Clean Air Act Amendments of 1990, were so extensive that they fundamentally altered the statute, always by making it more complex and requiring more expensive regulation.

---

[14]Peter Singer, *Animal Liberation,* New York: Avon, 1975, p. 7.

TABLE 14-1   Major Environmental Regulatory Statutes: 1969–1980

National Environmental Policy Act	1969	Declared environmental quality a federal policy goal, required environmental impact studies, and established the Council on Environmental Quality.
Clean Air Act (and amendments in 1977)	1970	Authorized air quality standards, auto emission limits, state implementation plans, air quality regions, monitoring of stationary source pollution, and research.
Occupational Safety and Health Act	1970	Set up the Occupational Safety and Health Administration to enforce health and safety standards and oversee state health and safety programs.
Noise Pollution and Control Act	1972	Directed the EPA and FAA to limit noise from industrial activity and products and from transportation equipment.
Federal Water Pollution Control Act Amendments	1972	Set a national goal of eliminating all pollutant discharges into U.S. waters by 1985. Industry was required to conform to emission technology standards; a massive sewage-treatment construction grant program was authorized; and the EPA was required to set effluent standards and issue discharge permits.
Federal Environmental Pesticide Control Act	1972	Required registration of pesticides by the EPA, required applicants for registration to submit extensive data, authorized the EPA to restrict or ban pesticide uses, and set up labeling requirements.
Marine Protection, Research, and Sanctuaries Act	1972	Required the EPA to set up a permit system for ocean dumping, prohibit dumping of hazardous materials (including radioactive waste, but amended in 1982 to permit dumping of radioactive waste as regulated by the EPA), and preserve marine sanctuaries free from industrial activity and dumping.
Endangered Species Act	1973	Created a comprehensive program to identify animal and plant species on the verge of extinction and protect them. Enforced by agencies in the Department of Interior, Commerce, and Agriculture.
Safe Drinking Water Act	1974	Authorized the EPA to set and enforce national standards for drinking water.
Hazardous Materials Transport Act	1974	Authorized the Department of Transportation to regulate shipment of hazardous materials. Prohibited shipment of radioactive materials in passenger planes.
Resource Conservation and Recovery Act	1976	Established EPA regulation of solid and hazardous waste disposal; authorized the EPA to define hazardous waste materials and to encourage and supervise state programs.
Toxic Substances Control Act	1976	Established a national control policy for chemicals posing a risk to the environment. Authorized the EPA to set chemical testing and licensing procedures, to ban excessively risky chemicals, and to set up record-keeping requirements for chemical manufacture.
Federal Mine Safety and Health Act	1977	Established the Mine Safety and Health Administration in the Department of Labor to regulate mine safety and health, enforce and set standards, and undertake a rigorous inspection schedule for mines.
Surface Mining Control and Reclamation Act	1977	Regulated strip-mining operations and set standards for reclamation of abandoned mines by a newly established Office of Surface Mining Reclamation and Enforcement in the Interior Department.
Department of Energy Organization Act	1977	Created a new cabinet-level Department of Energy to administer national energy policies, including nuclear waste management, energy conservation, and energy impacts on the environment.
Comprehensive Environmental Response, Compensation, and Liability Act	1980	Established a Hazardous Substance Response Trust Fund and taxes on the chemical and oil industries. Required the EPA to identify and remediate dangerous dumpsites of high priority and to establish disposal standards for hazardous substances.

The Environmental Protection Agency

The Environmental Protection Agency, the nation's largest regulatory agency, administers thirty-one major environmental statutes. In 1999, it had more than 22,455 employees and a budget of $5.2 billion, making it larger and better funded than the Department of State.

When Congress passes an environmental law, EPA employees write detailed, specific rules to carry out the more general directives in the statute. The EPA may enforce these rules directly on corporations, but most statutes permit delegating enforcement to the states. For example, the EPA has turned over hazardous waste regulation to state agencies in forty-seven of the fifty states. State regulators, acting with federal funding and following EPA guidelines, now do most of the enforcement of the nation's environmental laws. In 1996, for example, states took 85 percent of all enforcement actions.[15]

The EPA was created in 1970 by President Richard Nixon. At the time, it had a tiny budget and most of the laws it would one day administer had yet to be passed, but it quickly flexed its muscles. During its first two years, it undertook more than 1,000 enforcement actions and meted out $9 million in fines to startled companies. In November 1971, a dramatic demonstration drove home to industry the extent of the EPA's powers. It shut down all factories in heavily industrialized Birmingham, Alabama, for twenty-four hours during a temperature inversion in which air contaminants built up to high levels. To this day, the EPA retains an exceptionally aggressive enforcement philosophy.

Throughout the 1970s, the agency had an excellent reputation for effectiveness, but it soon bogged down. A brief review of the march of laws in Table 14-1 suggests that some indigestion was inevitable. In addition, Congress responded to public pressure by filling some of these laws with unrealistic goals and impossible timetables. For instance, the goal of the Federal Water Pollution Control Act of 1972 to eliminate all polluting discharges into waterways by 1985 was sheer fantasy, because the technology required to purify all effluents did not exist at the time (and still does not exist). By the end of the decade, the agency was being criticized for paperwork backlogs, delays in issuing standards, and inadequate enforcement.

The election of President Ronald Reagan in 1980 worsened the EPA's problems. While campaigning, Reagan called EPA regulators "environmental extremists" and, after his election, the agency's budget was so severely butchered that not until 1992 did it return to its pre-Reagan level. Notwithstanding, during these years, the EPA faced a continuing avalanche of new statutory duties as Congress revamped basic laws, each time expanding them. To illustrate, the Superfund law passed in 1980 was 19 pages long, but when

---

[15]General Accounting Office, *Environmental Protection: EPA's and States' Efforts to Focus State Enforcement Programs on Results,* GAO/RCED-98-113, May 1998, p. 16.

Congress reauthorized it in 1986, it grew to 200 pages. The Clean Air Act was 50 pages long in 1970 and 800 pages after amendments in 1990.[16]

Although the EPA remains an aggressive agency, its work overload is a constant problem. Throughout the 1990s, its budget has been under constant pressure from Republicans in Congress wanting to reduce the regulatory burden it imposes on business.

Assessing the Nation's Environmental Laws

How well have the laws worked? A fair overall assessment is that they have had mixed success.

In a few areas, there is great progress. Public exposure to airborne lead, polychlorinated biphenyls (PCBs) in electrical transformers, and the pesticide DDT has been largely eliminated. Emissions of chlorofluorocarbons implicated in ozone depletion are being rapidly curtailed. The unpermitted discharge of toxic effluents from factories into water bodies has virtually ceased. In other areas, such as emissions that cause urban smog, progress is less rapid, but significant.

Yet in some important areas, there is little progress. No effective program exists to control emission of carbon dioxide and other greenhouse gases. Little headway has been made in controlling agricultural runoff, the major source of water pollution today. And despite billions of dollars in appropriations, the Superfund law is an inefficient, slow device for cleaning toxic waste sites.

Why haven't the laws worked better? There are many reasons. A basic problem is that the laws are inadequate to deal with *transmedia pollution*, or pollution that moves between water, air, and/or land. When pollutants are caught in control devices, they are not destroyed but merely trapped and eventually transferred elsewhere in the environment (one exception is high-temperature incineration that breaks down dangerous molecules into harmless water vapor, oxygen, and simple organic compounds). For example, devices that remove small particles from coal boiler exhaust create a sludge containing impurities found in coal, including mercury, arsenic, and radioactive particles. It must be disposed of in landfills that then become hazardous waste sites. At these landfills, aromatic compounds from the sludge may evaporate back into the atmosphere, and other pollutants can bind with soil particles or enter the groundwater.

Typically, statutes direct that a pollutant be controlled in one medium without full consideration of its migration to another, reflecting the more limited scientific understanding of the 1970s. The EPA and state environmental agencies are organized along media lines, which contributes to a fragmenting of enforcement efforts. In the coal-fired boiler example mentioned above, one

---

[16]Kenneth Chilton, *Environmental Dialogue: Setting Priorities for Environmental Protection,* St. Louis: Center for the Study of American Business, Washington University, Policy Study No. 108, October 1991, p. 19.

group of inspectors would enforce stack gas emission standards on the boiler under authority of the Clean Air Act, other inspectors would issue permits for transporting the sludge from the flue gas cleaning devices to approved disposal sites under authority of the Resource Conservation and Recovery Act, and still others would regulate the waste dumps themselves under one of three other laws.

Environmental protection statutes are sometimes confusing and contradictory. Different laws set different control standards. For example, the Toxic Substances Control Act permits balancing public health benefits against pollution control costs. The Clean Air Act, however, forbids considering costs and requires air quality standards that protect against "any adverse health effects." The definition of terms in the laws is often unclear. The precise meaning of even basic terms such as "health effect" or "hazardous waste" is debatable.

Some enforcement difficulties arise from the sheer complexity of the EPA's standard-setting efforts. The agency must set standards of control for literally thousands of pollutants and thousands of industrial processes. To give one example, pursuant to the Clean Water Act, the EPA wrote standards for companies that form metals by processes such as pouring molten metal into a mold. During these processes water contacts various metals and picks up contaminants. The EPA set contaminant levels for various pollutants, including oil and more than a dozen trace metals, for fourteen separate metal-forming processes. To complicate the project further, the law requires factories to install one of three grades of pollution-control devices depending on the factory's age and the kind of machinery it uses. So the EPA had to set three different compliance standards for each pollutant and each process. This resulted in forty-two complex charts listing parts-per-million standards for a dozen metals, or 504 charts in all! Factory managers puzzled over these charts, and state regulators required extensive training to understand and enforce them.

Space permits only brief mention of several other problems. The EPA has relied mainly on an inflexible, adversarial style of regulation with a heavy emphasis on penalizing violators. This is defensible as necessary to ensure compliance by reluctant companies, but it stifles innovation and diverts corporate resources into legal wrangling.[17] The science used to set standards is often intelligible only to experts in narrow fields and lacks certainty. And emphasis on laws and rules invites lawsuits by both environmentalists wanting more enforcement and corporations seeking delays.

Principal Areas of Environmental Policy

There are three media for pollution: air, water, and land. Here we give a brief overview of regulations that protect each from degradation. In each area, we describe laws, basic problems, central concerns for business, and progress.

---

[17]Jonathan H. Adler, "Bean Counting for a Better Earth," *Regulation,* Spring 1998.

Air

Air pollution is best described as a set of complex interrelated problems, each requiring its own control measures. The Clean Air Act is the primary air quality statute. It was first passed in 1963 as a weak research measure, then amended in 1970 and again in 1990, each time becoming more complex, forceful, and expensive.

Although the Clean Air Act permits the use of some market incentive controls, these provisions are not central and it is basically an inflexible, draconian piece of command-and-control legislation. Since the early 1970s, air pollution abatement expenditures have risen steadily and will continue to rise unless implementation is relaxed. In 1993, these expenditures totaled $30 billion, and 70 percent of this was paid by business. We now discuss regulation of different air pollution problems.

National Air Quality.   The Clean Air Act requires the EPA to curb six *criteria pollutants* emitted in massive quantities by factories, power plants, and vehicles. They are lead, carbon monoxide, volatile organic compounds (substances such as gasoline vapors that react with sunlight to form ozone), sulfur dioxide, particulates (essentially dust), and nitrogen dioxides. All these harm human health, but small particulates are most dangerous. Studies of cities with air pollution show that death rates are strongly associated with high particulate levels but are not clearly associated with elevated levels of other criteria pollutants.[18] Particulates are also associated with sudden infant death syndrome and with overall infant mortality in urban areas having moderate to heavy particle pollution.[19] Overall, particulates are estimated to cause 64,000 deaths annually in the United States.[20]

To suppress criteria pollutants, the Clean Air Act mandates a range of expensive actions including, most importantly, emission controls on factories, power plants, and vehicles. Since emission restrictions began in 1970, significant reductions have been achieved for all but one criteria pollutant and air quality trends are positive. The great success story is reduction of lead emissions, which fell 98 percent between 1970 and 1995, mainly because lead was removed from gasoline in 1979. In the same period, particulates have fallen 77 percent, sulfur dioxide is down 41 percent, carbon monoxide is down 28 percent, and volatile organic compounds are down 25 percent. The one failure is nitrogen dioxide, which is up 6 percent.

---

[18]Douglas W. Dockery et al., "An Association between Air Pollution and Mortality in Six U.S. Cities," *New England Journal of Medicine,* December 9, 1993.

[19]Tracy J. Woodruff et al., "The Relationship between Selected Causes of Postneonatal Infant Mortality and Particulate Air Pollution in the United States," *Environmental Health Perspectives,* June 1997.

[20]Marla Cone, "Grit in L.A. Air Blamed in 6,000 Deaths Yearly," *Los Angeles Times,* May 9, 1996, p. A1.

Despite these reductions, which are impressive because they were achieved in an uphill battle with a growing economy and a rising number of vehicles, criteria pollutants can hardly be said to be under control. Each year, more than 200 million tons of them pour into the nation's air and 70 areas still violate EPA urban air standards. Except for carbon monoxide, 80 percent of which comes from vehicles, industry is the source of most of these emissions.

Toxic Pollutants.   Besides controlling the six criteria pollutants, the Clean Air Act mandates control of *toxic pollutants.* Toxic air pollutants pose health risks in smaller amounts than criteria pollutants. They can cause cancer and lung damage in adults and brain damage or retardation in children. Examples are arsenic, asbestos, chloroform, dioxin, mercury, and vinyl chloride. The EPA has identified 329 air toxics and estimates overall releases total 2.7 billion pounds each year.[21] Industry is the primary source.

The Clean Air Act requires the EPA to set emission standards for 189 air toxics at levels that prevent disease and requires industry to use the "maximum achievable control technology" to comply. This is a complicated process, and the agency is slowly moving forward.[22] Meanwhile, significant reductions have been encouraged by the requirement that corporations publicly reveal the amount of these chemicals they release. Since this disclosure requirement went into effect, corporations have significantly reduced emissions.

Acid Precipitation.   Acid precipitation in the United States is caused mainly by emissions of coal-fired electric utility boilers in the Northeast and Midwest. The combustion of coal releases sulfur dioxide (SO_2) and nitrogen oxides, which undergo chemical reactions in the atmosphere and return to earth as acidic particles that degrade the ecosystem by altering the pH of water. Acid rain is not a public health problem, although in high concentrations its two precursor pollutants—SO_2 and nitrogen oxides—can cause respiratory problems and lung damage.

The Clean Air Act Amendments of 1990 set strict emissions limits on more than 2,600 coal-burning utilities and factories. Nationwide, SO_2 emissions are now permanently capped at 1980 levels. Companies that exceed emission limits can be fined such large amounts that compliance costs would be a relative bargain. Utilities that lower emissions to below what the law requires are allowed to trade the extra increment on an open market.

Indoor Air Pollution.   Indoor air pollution is defined by the EPA as a mixture of eighteen pollutants commonly found indoors, including radon, tobacco smoke, asbestos, chloroform gas released from use of chlorine-containing

[21]John J. Fialka, "EPA Probers Find Big Flaws in Major Clean-Air Effort," *The Wall Street Journal,* December 28, 1998, p. A16.

[22]See, for example, Environmental Protection Agency, "National Emission Standards for Hazardous Air Pollutants for Polyether Polyols Production," 62 FR 46803-46857 (September 4, 1997).

water, and benzene vapors from household cleaners. These pollutants pose serious health problems because Americans spend 90 percent of their time indoors. Radon, a common radioactive gas found in ground under homes, causes up to 21,800 lung cancer deaths yearly.[23] This is more than 10 times the estimated number of cancer deaths from all toxic chemical emissions by industry. Although the EPA regulates some polluting substances, such as insecticides and paints, it has little direct authority over indoor air. Congress has been reluctant to let EPA inspectors invade homes and offices with measuring equipment, forms, and ticket books.

Ozone Destroying Chemicals.   While ozone in urban smog is unwanted, ozone in the upper atmosphere screens out ultraviolet energy harmful to living tissue. In the presence of a chlorine atom, a chain reaction occurs that destroys thousands of ozone molecules. Emissions of long-lived chlorine-containing molecules such as chlorofluorocarbons (CFCs) and several similar compounds pose a threat to the ozone layer.

In 1987, a treaty called the Montreal Protocol was signed by 110 nations to phase out use of these compounds by 2010. Since then, world production of CFCs has dropped by 70 percent and ozone depletion has leveled off. The United States and other developed nations ceased all CFC production by 1996 as required by the treaty, but developing nations such as Brazil, Mexico, India, and China, given until 2010, have raised production. CFC substitutes are more expensive, and many businesses around the world are unwilling to pay the price of conversion.

To overcome this resistance, the United States and 48 other countries contribute to a fund that has paid out $570 million for almost 2,000 conversion projects in developing nations.[24] If all CFC production ends as scheduled in 2010, sometime after 3010, the atmosphere will be free of ozone-destroying chemicals and ozone destruction will cease.

Greenhouse Gases.   Industry activity raises emissions of a half dozen gases—the most important being carbon dioxide, methane, and nitrous oxide—that act to trap solar heat in the atmosphere. The United States, with only 4 percent of the world's population, emits 22 percent of these warming gases and, together, industrialized nations produce 60 percent. In the Kyoto Protocol of 1997, industrialized nations agreed in principle that by 2012 they would cut emissions to an average of 6 percent below 1990 levels. The United States is committed by this accord to cut emissions 7 percent, which would mean dramatic reductions in energy use and altered industrial processes.

---

[23]Susan Baily, "New Report: Radon Blamed for Cancer Deaths," *Nuclear News,* November 1998, p. 61.

[24]General Accounting Office, *Operations of the Montreal Protocol Multilateral Fund,* GAO/T/RCED-97-218, July 30, 1997, pp. 2–4.

One problem with the accord is that most developing nations, including China and India, refused to make significant reductions. This is disappointing because by 2015, developing nations will catch up to the now-industrialized nations in greenhouse gas emissions.[25] The Kyoto Protocol has not yet been ratified by the Senate and so the policies and incentives necessary to cut emissions are not in place in the United States. Strong corporate opposition to it exists. Business fears that large reductions would raise production costs, give competitors in less-developed countries a price advantage, and slow economic growth.

The EPA has twenty programs to encourage voluntary lowering of greenhouse gas emissions by business. One example is Green Lights, a program in which the agency gives information about energy-efficient lighting to companies and tries to remove regulatory impediments that might slow its installation. Green Lights and the other voluntary programs have produced only an infinitesimal reduction in CO_2 emissions. It has thus far eliminated six-tenths of a metric ton of CO_2, less than one-ten-thousandth of one percent of current emissions.[26]

Water

The Federal Water Pollution Control Act of 1972, usually called the Clean Water Act, is the basic law for fighting water pollution. Congress intended it to be a powerful measure that would stop the deterioration of the nation's lakes, rivers, steams, and estuaries. Its goal was to eliminate *all* polluting discharges into these waters by 1985. However, the goal is still unmet and will not be met in the foreseeable future. Currently, the nation spends more than $40 billion a year to comply with the Clean Water Act, and most of this, about 70 percent, is spent by industry.

The Clean Water Act is effective in reducing, but not eliminating, polluted factory outflows, or effluents. Every industrial plant uses water, and sources of pollution are numerous. In production processes, for example, water is used as a washing, scrubbing, cooling, or mixing medium. It becomes contaminated with a variety of particles and dissolved chemicals. Besides threatening human health, industry discharges may harm wildlife. For example, effluents from a USX coking plant on the Black River in Ohio caused liver tumors in catfish.[27] Years ago, untreated effluents were directly discharged into water bodies or sewers, but the Clean Water Act prohibits any polluted factory discharge without a permit.

---

[25]John H. Cushman Jr., "Big Problem, Big Problems: Getting to Work on Global Warming," *New York Times*, December 8, 1998, p. G4.

[26]General Accounting Office, *Global Warming: Information on the Results of Four of EPA's Voluntary Climate Change Programs*, GAO/RCED-97-163, June 1997, pp. 5–7.

[27]Paul C. Bauman and John C. Harshbarger, "Decline in Liver Neoplasms in Wild Brown Bullhead Catfish after Coking Plant Closes and Environmental PAHs Plummet," *Environmental Health Perspectives*, February 1995.

These permits are issued by either the EPA or state regulators and cover three categories of pollutants. *Conventional* pollutants are the contaminants found in household sewage. They are biological oxygen demand,[28] suspended solids, oil and grease, pH, and fecal coliform bacteria. *Toxic* pollutants are 126 industrial wastes that can be dangerous in very small amounts, such as asbestos, organic compounds, pesticides, and metals such as cadmium and zinc. *Nonconventional* pollutants are other pollutants that can be measured, for instance, ammonia, sulfides, phosphorus, and nitrogen.

The EPA sets water quality criteria for pollutants. Usually, there are two standards, one for protecting human health and the other for aquatic life. To give examples, the chloroform standard prohibits chronic exposure of aquatic life to concentrations of more than 1,240 μg/l and exposure of humans to more than 470 μg/l.[29] Although scientific analysis enters standard-setting, most often such limits are simply based on how much pollution the best control devices can remove from wastewater. These devices range from simple screens for large particles to intricate chemical and biological treatment systems. The law requires new factories to install the "best available control technology" (BAT). For a plant making paperboard out of wastepaper, for instance, the EPA has defined BAT as effluent containing no more than 0.87 pound of pentachlorophenol and 0.30 pound of trichlorophenol for each 1 million pounds of paper produced.[30]

Within limits, permits are tailored for each factory effluent source. They may specify the amount, temperature, clarity, and content of discharged wastewater. The permit system, called the National Pollution Discharge Elimination System (NPDES), has cut releases of pollutants dramatically since its start in 1972. Currently, about 50,000 facilities operate under an NPDES permit and about 7,000 of them are classified as major sources.

While the EPA has limited factory discharges, "nonpoint" effluents, or runoff that enters surface waters from diffuse sources, is largely uncontrolled. Runoff from agriculture—animal wastes, pesticides, and fertilizers—is now the primary cause of impaired water bodies. Although general language in the Clean Water Act permits the EPA to act against any source of water pollution, the law avoided specific language aimed at farmers because of their political power. So farms have been relatively immune to regulation. However, growing pollution from big animal feedlots and poultry farms has led the EPA to place about 2,000 factory farms under permits, and the agency is also trying to reduce runoff of agricultural chemicals. These efforts are just beginning.

---

[28]Biological oxygen demand encompasses a variety of organic materials that, when discharged into surface waters, are broken down by protozoa and bacteria. If large quantities of such material are present, the level of dissolved oxygen in the water is lowered, causing odors and threatening the respiration of aquatic life.

[29]General Accounting Office, *Water Pollution: Poor Quality Assurance and Limited Pollutant Coverage Undermine EPA's Control of Toxic Substances,* GAO/PEMD-94-9, February 1994, p. 59.

[30]40 CFR 430.5.

Overall progress in improving the quality of surface waters is disappointing. The last comprehensive audit undertaken by the EPA in 1991 showed that 38 percent of river and stream miles and 46 percent of lake acres failed to meet standards. Polluted agricultural and urban runoff is unabated. Although the NPDES system has ended unpermitted discharges by industry, that does not mean that factory discharges have ended. Permits allow industry to release legally more than 650 million pounds of toxic substances annually, and the permits are not always obeyed. A recent audit of 7,053 major facilities under permits discovered that one out of six "significantly violated the discharge limits in their permits."[31]

Annals of Water Pollution

On February 1, 1993, the cruise ship *Nordic Empress* was returning to its home port of Miami. On deck, crew members and stewards wore buttons reading "Save the Seas" and asked passengers not to carry paper cups or other objects that could blow away and litter the ocean. Below deck, engineers had rigged a pipe under the engine room floor to bypass the oil separator and discharge oily bilge waste directly into the Atlantic.

Bilge water is seepage contaminated with engine oils. To comply with the Clean Water Act, bilge water pumped into United States territorial waters must contain less than 15 parts per million of oil. Therefore, ships are outfitted with devices that separate oil from water so that the water can be discharged and residual oil can be collected and disposed of in port. This equipment can reduce oil in the water to as little as 1 to 3 ppm, but it is expensive to maintain. Royal Caribbean Cruises Ltd., the company that owned the *Nordic Empress*, gave bonuses to engineers for cutting operating costs. Bypassing the oil separator could save more than $300,000 a year and result in a larger bonus. The pipe was unhooked and hidden during Coast Guard inspections, and a required oil record book that required an entry each time the oil separator was run was routinely falsified.

Unknown to the crew, a Coast Guard plane equipped with forward-looking infrared radar, a device that can "see" through clouds and darkness, had filmed an oily discharge from the ship. When it arrived in Miami, it was boarded and the secret bypass pipe was discovered. The Coast Guard turned the matter over to the FBI and the Criminal Investigative Division of the EPA. Together, the three agencies began an investigation of the company and a surveillance of its nine cruise ships.

On October 25, 1994, a Coast Guard plane overflew *Sovereign of the Seas*, a floating garden, trailing an oil slick off the coast of Puerto Rico. On arrival in port, it was boarded by Coast Guard inspectors, who discovered a bypass pipe rigged under the engine room floor. The chief engineer ordered crew members to deny its existence and presented a falsified oil record log. Engine room hands called the book "Eventyrbok," the title of a Norwegian book of fairy tales.

---

[31]General Accounting Office, *Water Pollution: Many Violations Have Not Received Appropriate Enforcement Attention*, GAO/RCED-96-23, March 1996, pp. 1–4.

Subsequently, a grand jury in Puerto Rico brought a ten-count felony indictment against Royal Caribbean Cruise Lines related to oil dumping on *Nordic Empress, Sovereign of the Seas,* and three other ships. A Miami grand jury indicted the company for lying to regulators and falsifying records on the *Nordic Empress.* The company hired Benjamin R. Civilette, a former U. S. attorney general, and fought the indictments with a string of disingenuous legal arguments. Although its headquarters are in Miami, Royal Caribbean is a Liberian company and its ships fly Norwegian flags. The company argued that under international law of the flag, only Norway had legal jurisdiction to prosecute the company. Notwithstanding, it then argued two points of U.S. constitutional law. First, since the Coast Guard had already fined it $4,000, any further penalty would violate the prohibition against double jeopardy in the Fifth Amendment. Second, the Coast Guard had violated the company's Fourth Amendment right to be free of unreasonable searches when it inspected its vessel's engine rooms. A federal court rejected these artful points and in 1998 Royal Caribbean entered guilty pleas and agreed to pay $9 million in fines.[32]

Meanwhile, environmental officers had been placed on each Royal Caribbean ship to ensure compliance with all environmental regulations. Training programs emphasized following environmental policy. A senior vice president position was created to oversee compliance. Yet within a month of the guilty plea, the *Nordic Empress* was caught again dumping oily bilge waste through a bypass pipe. And, as in the early incidents, the ship's engineers presented a false oil log book and lied to investigators. The company fired two engineers, but the incident called into question the efficacy of its reforms.

Land

After Congress passed air and water pollution control laws early in the 1970s, it became apparent that poorly regulated dumping of hazardous waste on land was a mounting problem. Devices that removed air- and water-borne poisons from industrial processes produced tons of hazardous sludges, slimes, and dusts that were being trucked away into landfills. Many of these landfills failed to contain the pollutants that entered them.

In 1976, Congress passed the Resource Conservation and Recovery Act (RCRA) to manage "from cradle to grave" a wide range of hazardous wastes. Firms must now label hazardous waste when it is created, and they are required to get permits to store, treat, or dispose of it. Meticulous records must be kept.

The RCRA is a difficult statute to administer and with which to comply. It requires regulators to keep track of literally all hazardous waste produced anywhere in the country—an exhausting job. It relies on smothering command-and-control regulation and prohibits balancing costs against benefits. One indication

---

[32]*United States* v. *Royal Caribbean,* No. 96-0333, U.S.D.C., Dist. of Puerto Rico, September 19, 1997.

FIGURE 14-1

RCRA landfill groundwater monitoring requirements. The EPA grants permits to all operators of hazardous waste dumps that comply with standards for physical layout, groundwater monitoring, and emergency planning. The drawing is a cross section of ground below a landfill illustrating minimal RCRA monitoring requirements. Water samples drawn from downgradient wells can detect chemical contamination seeping into the groundwater (saturated zone) from the landfill above. Today, approximately 3,700 hazardous waste landfills are in operation.

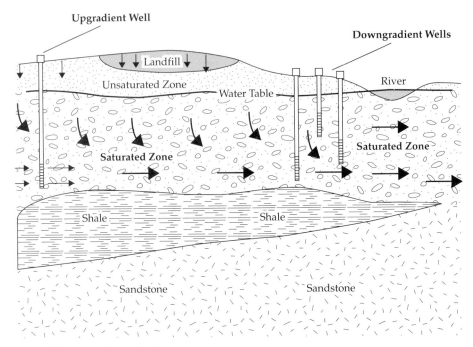

Source: Environmental Protection Agency.

of the heavy regulatory burden it imposes is that when it was first implemented, nearly half the nation's waste disposal facilities elected to close rather than comply with it. Figure 14-1 illustrates a typical installation of wells required to monitor groundwater quality.

RCRA is, in the words of one observer, "an amazingly inflexible law with extraordinarily detailed regulations, demanding controls, and a glacially slow permitting system [that] entails almost astronomically high costs."[33] If, for example, a factory wants to install a treatment tank for waste, it can take up to nine months and cost $80,000 to get the permit. One steel company had to wait seven months for a permit to fence in its waste pit and to use propane-powered cannons for scaring animals away.[34] A permit for a landfill takes more than five years and costs as much as $1 million.[35] Although costs are high, there is no question that hazardous waste is much better handled than before RCRA.

While RCRA ensured that existing facilities would operate at a high standard, it did nothing about the thousands of abandoned toxic waste sites around the country. So Congress passed a law to clean them up. This law is the Comprehensive Environmental Response, Compensation, and Liability

---

[33]Robert J. Smith, "RCRA Lives, Alas," *Regulation*, Summer 1991, p. 14.

[34]General Accounting Office, *Hazardous Waste: Progress under the Corrective Action Program Is Limited*, GAO/RCED-98-3, October 1997, p. 9.

[35]General Accounting Office, *Hazardous Waste: Remediation Waste Requirements Can Increase the Time and Cost of Cleanups*, GAO/RCED-98-4, pp. 8-9.

Figure 14-2

Typical rotary kiln incinerator at a superfund site.

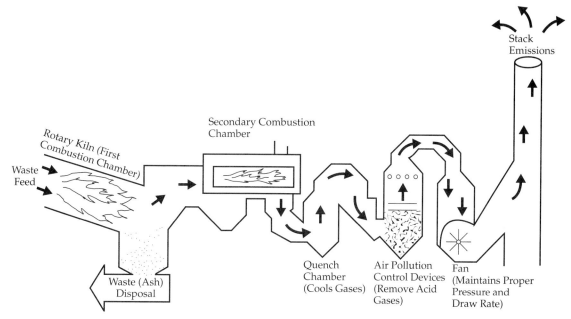

Source: EPA. From: General Accounting Office, Superfund: EPA Could Further Ensure the Safe Operation of On-Site Incinerators, GAO/RCED-97-43, March 1997, p. 4.

Act (CERCLA) of 1980, better known as Superfund, so-named after the large trust fund it sets up to pay for cleanups. This trust fund is generated from congressional appropriations, special taxes on oil and chemical companies, and a small—0.12 percent—addition to the general corporate income tax.

When the Superfund law was passed, Congress intended it to be a temporary supplement to RCRA that would be phased out when toxic sites were all cleaned. But the number of sites is far greater than predicted and the process of cleaning them more difficult and expensive than envisioned in 1980. Currently 30,000 sites need a cleanup and about 1,200 of the worst are on a priority list.

Cleaning up these sites is a slow process. When a new location is discovered, an average of 9.4 years goes by before it is placed on the National Priority List and then another 10.6 years pass before it is cleaned up.[36] By 1998, eighteen years after passage of Superfund, the EPA had finished cleaning only 500 sites, although work is in progress on many others.

Superfund sites are complicated and expensive to restore. Methods of decontamination and containment differ from site to site. One method sometimes used is high-temperature incineration of dirt. Figure 14-2 shows a diagram of

---

[36]General Accounting Office, *Superfund: Times to Complete Site Listing and Cleanup,* GAO/RCED-98-74, February 4, 1998, pp. 1–4.

an incinerator. At a rate of 20 tons per hour and a cost of $1,200 per ton, soil is dug up and placed in a giant revolving kiln and heated to 1,800° F to break down hazardous organic compounds into simple inorganic molecules such as CO_2 and H_2O. Gases from inside the kiln are filtered to remove poisonous air toxics. The dirt is then backfilled.

The entire process must conform to strict RCRA standards. The standard for dioxins and PCBs, for example, requires 99.9999 percent destruction efficiency, that is, for every 1 million molecules entering the incinerator, only 1 can emerge. Waste ash is treated and disposed of as hazardous waste. Incinerators are surrounded by air pollution monitors connected to alarms in case stack emissions fail to meet standards. At many sites, groundwater is also pumped to the surface, flushed of toxic chemicals, and then reinjected. The remediation process at a complex site involving incineration and groundwater treatment can take a decade and require installation of equipment covering the area of a football field.

Who pays for all this? The Superfund law establishes harsh rules of liability for any company that has ever dumped hazardous waste in a Superfund site. In legal terminology, this liability is strict, retroactive, and joint and several. In practical terms, this means that any company that has ever dumped hazardous waste on a site can be held responsible for the full cleanup cost even if it obeyed the law of years past, was not negligent, and dumped only a small percentage of the total waste.

The EPA conducts cleanups using money in the Superfund, then bills "responsible parties" for the cost, which averages between $20 and $30 million per site, but can run higher. For example, in 1998, the EPA billed 680 businesses and cities for a share of the $600 million cost of cleaning a site in Monterey Park, California. Among the businesses were large corporations such as Walt Disney Co. and many smaller ones. Jim Wilson, the owner of a Cadillac dealership in Sherman Oaks, opened his mail one day and found a bill from the EPA for $142,000, his share of the cleanup cost.[37] Years before, Wilson had owned a carwash next to the dealership and grease from the cars that was captured in a holding tank had been trucked to the Monterey Park landfill. Although the carwash had closed down in 1980, prior to the enactment of Superfund, and although all waste-handling laws of its era had been followed, it was still a responsible party. If small businesses do not pay these bills, they are often sued by larger companies trying to ease their financial burden. It is common for Superfund projects to be surrounded by a swarm of lawsuits, and, on average, a third of corporate cleanup costs are for litigation, not remediation.

Other Regulatory Programs

The laws and regulatory programs discussed in this chapter are the most prominent, but there are many others. The EPA administers other programs,

---

[37] Antonio Olivo, "EPA Bills Carwashes for Landfill Cleanup," *Los Angeles Times,* October 19, 1998, p. A1.

and a few programs lie outside its jurisdiction. For example, the Occupational Safety and Health Administration regulates air quality for factory workers and the Department of the Interior protects endangered species. Space prohibits a detailed discussion of these additional programs. Suffice it to say that the complexities and problems in them are similar to those in the programs already discussed.

Concluding Observations

Industrial processes damage the environment and have caused serious local and global deterioration. A first wave of environmental statutes in the United States has reduced pollution and deterioration, primarily through rigid and expensive regulations. Now that experience has been gained with these laws, their high cost, inflexibility, and adversarial nature are seen as shortcomings. There are many suggestions for more cost-effective and flexible regulation. In the next chapter, we discuss methods for determining how regulatory programs can become more efficient and effective and also what corporations are doing to reduce pollution and protect the environment.

OWLS, LOGGERS, AND OLD-GROWTH FORESTS

The secretive northern spotted owl *(Strix occidentalis caurina)* lives in remote sections of coastal forest in Washington, Oregon, and upper California. Since the 1800s, timber harvesting has reduced the owl's habitat by as much as 80 percent, threatening its extinction. Environmentalists trying to save old-growth forests from the ax have focused on the owl's plight, but they face powerful opposition. The health of the Pacific Northwest wood products industry depends on harvesting some old-growth timber to keep sawmills running. We begin the story with a trip into the forest.

Old Growth

An old-growth forest is one that has developed undisturbed through stages. In nature, a forest usually begins when fire destroys the vegetation on an expanse of land. At first, opportunistic plant species such as wildflowers invade the area, their seeds blown in by wind. In a few years, these pioneers are displaced by dense shrubs that create more shade than the wildflowers can tolerate. In turn, shrubs are shaded out by red alders, aspens or other fast-growing deciduous trees. The dominant tree species is the one that can propagate in the shade of these early trees and persist to ultimately supplant all competitors for nutrients. This species is called the climax species. In the conifer forests of Washington and Oregon, it tends to be the Douglas fir; in California, it is the coast redwood.

It may be centuries before the climax species takes over. Some large forest stands in the Pacific Northwest are over 1,000 years old, and a commonly accepted definition of old growth is a stand that has developed without catastrophic disturbance for 175 to 250 years or more. These old-growth forests are unique ecosystems dominated by large, live trees rising 200 to 300 feet through an uneven, multilayered canopy. Dead trees, called snags, stand in place, and the floor is littered with decaying logs. Some snags have fallen in streams, damning and diverting the water flow.

Ancient forests are more structurally and biologically complex than younger forests. Snags and logs, for example, provide habitat niches for a variety of plant and animal life. During the 200 to 500 years it takes a large log to disintegrate, it may nurse an expansive population of bacteria, insects, lichens, plants, and small animals that use the stored moisture and nutrients in the deadwood. First come boring insects that open pathways into the log. Then microorganisms such as fungi invade the wood, followed by mites, spiders, and the beetles that feast on them. Birds come to catch insects. As the wood fragments, ferns and small hemlocks force their roots in and tap stored moisture. Soon mice and wood rats find homes, attracting predators such as the northern spotted owl. Eventually scavengers that feed on dead vegetation and animal feces arrive. Put poetically, in the downed tree "decay is merely a counterpoint, life and death a single process, like a mirror fugue conceived by a composer even better than Bach."[1]

Old-growth forests achieve great natural beauty and inspire comparisons with cathedrals. They have much richer biotic communities than younger forests and are repositories for species that have adapted to ecological niches created only under old-growth conditions. The spotted owl is one such species.

The Northern Spotted Owl

The northern spotted owl is a perch-and-dive predator with a wingspan of 2 feet and a weight of about 1½ pounds. Its body is mottled brown with patches of white, making it nearly invisible as it roosts in the cavities of tall conifers. Its habitat ranges from British Columbia in the north to the redwood stands above San Francisco in the south.

The modern owl family emerged as a separate evolutionary line 70 to 80 million years ago. Since then, owls have developed anatomy and behavior suited for efficient predation of small mammals and reptiles. At one time, owls came into competition with the line of raptors that became hawks, falcons, and eagles. Both phyletic lines hunted small prey by diving upon it and grasping it with sharp talons. But habitat confrontation was avoided in a way that allowed both to exploit the same prey resources. Hawk-like species became diurnal hunters, and owls became nocturnal hunters. Hence, by day the spotted owl roosts in the cavities of standing snags; it emerges to hunt only after sunset. One study of sixty-two pairs found that, on average, they left their roosts fourteen minutes after sunset to forage and returned at twenty-one minutes before sunrise.[2]

---

[1]David Kelly and Gary Braasch, *Secrets of the Old Growth Forest,* Salt Lake City: Peregrine Smith Books, 1988, p. 39.

[2]E. D. Foresman, E. C. Meslow, and H. M. Wight, "Distribution and Biology of the Spotted Owl in Oregon," *Wildlife Monographs,* Monograph No. 87, 1984.

The northern spotted owl, like other owls, is adapted to nighttime activity. It has a large head with a relatively large brain compared to other birds, and big round eyes. "Indeed," notes one biologist, "the heads of owls are basically little more than brains with raptorial beaks and the largest possible eyes and ears attached."[3] Spotted owls' eyes have rod-rich retinas that provide exceptionally acute black-and-white vision in low-light conditions. They can locate and dive on scampering mice in illuminations as much as thirty times below the lowest reported human visual threshold. Their hearing is similarly acute. Without benefit of vision, they can locate tree squirrels or mice that make small rustling noises in frequency ranges inaudible to humans. Their brains calculate time lags of microseconds in the arrival of sounds at each ear, enabling them to fly unerringly to a sound source through dark of night. The northern spotted owl, despite its sedentary daytime roosting, has a high metabolism and hunts actively through the night. Its prey is mainly small mammals such as flying squirrels, wood rats, rabbits, mice, and tree voles. It also eats over twenty species of birds and some reptiles.

Northern spotted owls exhibit a wide range of social behavior. They have courtship rituals, and pairs bond for extended periods. They communicate with postural signals, displays of aggression, and a variety of hoots and calls. They are territorial, and announce their presence with a series of four hoots (described phonetically as "hooo hoo hoo hooo").[4] These low hoots have long wavelengths especially suited for penetrating dense foliage. The territory of a mated pair of northern spotted owls is huge; observation with radiotelemetry has documented foraging ranges from 1,000 acres up to 27,000 acres.[5] Reproduction occurs in spring and summer, when females lay an average of two eggs in a nest. After hatching, the young owls are cared for by the parents for one month before flying away to establish their own territories.

Spotted owls prefer old-growth habitats. The dense vegetation protects them from predators such as the red-tailed hawk. A thick, multilayered forest canopy also provides thermal cover, insulating them from extremes of heat and cold. Owls nest in the cavities of standing snags, and a large number of fallen snags create conditions that support abundant prey to satisfy their voracious appetites. The spotted owl plays a niche role in the old-growth ecosystem by culling small mammal and bird populations.

Early studies of northern spotted owls suggested that they lived only in old-growth forests.[6] Environmentalists claimed that the owl was like the canary

---

[3]Paul A. Johnsgard, *North American Owls: Biology and Natural History*, Washington, D.C.: Smithsonian Institution Press, 1988, p. 42.

[4]This is what ornithologists refer to as its "four-note location call." It has other vocalizations as well, including "barks" and whistles. U.S. Department of the Interior, *Recovery Plan for the Northern Spotted Owl—Draft*, Washington, D.C.: Government Printing Office, April 1992, p. 15.

[5]Ibid., p. 23.

[6]A study in Washington, for example, found that 97 percent of spotted owls lived in old-growth forests, with no known reproductive pairs in second-growth areas. "Proposed Threatened Status for the Northern Spotted Owl," 54 FR 26668 (June 23, 1989).

*The northern
spotted owl.*

Source: U.S. Fish & Wildlife Service.

in the coal mine. If the northern spotted owl at the top of the forest food chain was in danger of extinction, this was a warning that other species and the old-growth habitat itself were also endangered.

Some subsequent studies have shown that northern spotted owls can live and breed in younger forests and forests that have been logged. Occasionally they stray out of the forest completely. In November 1998, a juvenile spotted owl flew into Everett, Washington, and roosted in a downtown maple tree growing between Fitness World and Jimmy Z's bar. People gathered with cameras and binoculars to see it, and a newspaper reporter wrote that it ate a starling.[7] After two days, a wildlife biologist climbed the tree as the owl slept, lassoed it by the neck with a wire noose at the end of a pole, and drove it to an old-growth forest.

Stories such as this seem to cast doubt on the assertion that spotted owls need old-growth to survive. Yet they clearly prefer old-growth, and population densities are highest in mature forests. Where they live in younger forests, they seek out areas that have high structural diversity. The age of the forest is not as critical as is its composition. Some owls do try to nest, roost, and forage in younger, less-diverse forests, but scientists believe that these are juvenile owls dispersing from old-growth stands. Spotted owls are territorial, live 10 to 15 years, and maintain large domains in diminishing stands of old growth. This makes it difficult for juvenile owls to stake out territories in the fewer and fewer remaining stands of high structural complexity. Therefore, young owls leaving nests after breeding season may wind up in younger forests. They forage and breed there, but scientists believe that reproductive success in young forests is insufficient to balance higher death rates from predation.[8]

Loss of Old Growth Imperils the Spotted Owl

The expansion of America came at the expense of forests. When pilgrims landed at Plymouth Rock, the landmass destined to become the continental United States had 850 million acres of forest. By the 1920s, only 138 million acres of virgin forest remained, roughly 16 percent of what had existed.[9] The rest had been burned, grazed, cut, radically disturbed, or converted to other uses. Reduction of forest area stopped in the 1870s and, on balance, regrowth now exceeds destruction.

The northwest coastal forest covered about 94 million acres in the 1860s when settlers and loggers first arrived. Today only about 30 million acres of this coastal forest remain, including just 7.7 million acres of old growth. Much of this old growth is not contiguous; rather, it is a checkerboard of old stands mixed with bare timber-harvest areas, young growth, and tree farms. Of these 7.7 million acres, 2.8 million acres are in national parks or wilderness areas closed forever to timber harvest. By the late 1980s, about 2 percent of the remaining 4.9 million acres of old growth was being cut each year, largely for timber sales on federal lands. At this rate, virtually all remaining old-growth habitat outside national parks would be gone in fifty years.

---

[7]Diane Brooks, "Rare Owl Roosts in Everett," *Seattle Times,* November 19, 1998, p. B1.

[8]See, for example, remarks of ecologist H. Ronald Pullium cited by Paul R. Ehrlich and Anne H. Ehrlich in *Betrayal of Science and Reason,* Washington, D.C.: Island Press, 1998, p. 118.

[9]Figures for forest size are from Michael Williams, *Americans and Their Forests: A Historical Geography,* New York: Cambridge University Press, 1989, pp. 3–4.

Little remaining old growth is on private land; virtually all is on federal land managed by the U.S. Forest Service and the Bureau of Land Management. These agencies are required by law to open forests for "multiple use" activities such as logging, mining, recreation, and geothermal development. Hence, they hold timber auctions in which logging companies bid for the right to fell selected stands of timber. Once the winning bids are picked, timber harvesting proceeds based on precise regulations describing boundaries, logging techniques, and the restoration and replanting that is necessary. In sixty years, a replanted forest can be reharvested; a high-density replanting will yield more timber than the original old growth.

As old-growth forest area dwindles, the northern spotted owl loses its preferred habitat. In 1989, government biologists estimated that there were only 1,550 breeding pairs of the owls in the Pacific Northwest.[10] This low count worried scientists who believed that the owl was on the margin of survival as a species.[11] When species decline to very low numbers, there is great danger that even if human impacts are reduced or removed, events in nature, such as random fluctuations in climate or food supply, cannot be overcome. When numbers fall, the reproductive pattern of the species is critical. Unfortunately, the spotted owl has a very low reproductive efficiency. A mated pair produces an average of 0.50 young per year. Then juvenile owls suffer an 88 percent mortality rate in their first year.[12] This high mortality rate occurs in part because, as patches of old growth are logged, more young owls disperse to a habitat that increases predation by the great horned owl, a natural enemy that inhabits more open areas.

Environmentalists Campaign to Protect the Owl

In the 1980s, environmental groups began to make a cause of the northern spotted owl. They believed that the owl had intrinsic, unlimited value as a species; its extinction would be a permanent loss. Equally important, they knew that the owl's use of old growth as a habitat made saving owls a convenient pretext for saving ancient forests from the logger's ax. Using the owl,

---

[10]"Protection Proposed for the Northern Spotted Owl," *Endangered Species Technical Bulletin,* July 1989, p. 1.

[11]Two subspecies of spotted owl, the northern spotted owl (*Strix occidentalis caurina*) and the California spotted owl (*Strix occidentalis occidentalis*) are separated by only a twelve- to fifteen-mile gap in forest habitat in northern California. A third subspecies, the Mexican spotted owl (*Strix occidentalis lucida*) lives in the forests of northern Arizona, Utah, Colorado, Texas, and parts of Mexico. The Mexican spotted owl has also been classified as a threatened species (see "Final Rule to List the Mexican Spotted Owl as a Threatened Species," 58 FR 14248 (March 16, 1993). Some scientific debate exists about whether the California and northern spotted owls are, in fact, genetically distinct subspecies.

[12]Daniel Simberloff, "The Spotted Owl Fracas: Mixing Academic, Applied, and Political Ecology," *Ecology,* August 1987, p. 768.

they could invoke the Endangered Species Act and elevate the idea of forest preservation above the interests of timber companies, lumber mills, and logging communities.

The Endangered Species Act is an exceptionally strong statute. It is the most powerful law that any nation has to protect plant and animal species from extinction. Passed in 1973, it set forth procedures for designating, or "listing," plants and animals in danger of extinction. The act defines an *endangered* species as one that is "in danger of extinction throughout all or a significant portion of its range." It also permits listing of a *threatened* species that is "likely to become an endangered species within the foreseeable future throughout all or a significant portion of its range."[13] Once a species is listed in either category, it is entitled to a great deal of protection. Under threat of civil or criminal penalties, it is illegal to "take"—that is, "to harass, harm, pursue, hunt, shoot, wound, kill, trap, capture, or collect"—any individual of a listed species on public or private lands.

Subsequent amendments have expanded the law's reach. In 1978, it was amended to protect geographically defined "critical habitat" of listed species. In 1982, it was again amended, this time to require that listings be based solely on scientific evidence about species survival needs; consideration of economic and political consequences was prohibited. Over the years, the government agencies that enforce it further expanded the law's power by zealously turning out strict rules to enforce its provisions and by listing more and more species.[14] At the beginning of 1999, there were 1,177 species, 475 animals and 702 plants, listed as threatened or endangered.

The Endangered Species Act applies not just to government property, but to private land also, so that if a listed species is discovered in a forest owned by a timber company or a small farm owned by an individual, regulators can step in and halt activity that might disturb the plant or animal or alter its habitat. The survival of the species takes precedence over the property rights of the landowner. Economic losses to landowners deprived of the use of their property need not be considered. Such losses can greatly reduce the value of property to owners who get no compensation for land resources locked up for sole use as species habitat.

At first, the Department of the Interior declined to list the northern spotted owl as endangered, stating that biological evidence was insufficient. Angry environmental groups sued the agency. In 1990, bowing to the pressure, it listed the northern spotted owl as a "threatened" species.[15] This set in motion the powerful devices of the Endangered Species Act and soon an entire region of

---

[13]U.S.C., Sec. 1532(20).

[14]The Endangered Species Act is enforced by two agencies. The Fish and Wildlife Service within the Department of the Interior is responsible for plants and animals found on land and in freshwater environments and for migratory birds. The National Marine Fisheries Service within the Department of Commerce enforces the law with respect to marine species.

[15]"Determination of Threatened Status for the Northern Spotted Owl," 55 FR 21623 (June 26, 1990).

the United States felt the consequences. The Department of the Interior adopted protective rules that remain in force today. Logging is banned within 70 acres of a known spotted owl nest and is sharply restricted within a 2,000-acre radius. Even when a nest is found empty, there is a three-year moratorium on logging to ensure that it is abandoned.

In 1991, a federal district court in Seattle issued an injunction virtually halting timber sales in the government-owned old-growth forests of the Pacific Northwest until the Department of the Interior developed a species recovery plan for the owl. This was a boon for the owls, which could sleep during the day without the buzz of chainsaws, but it was a disaster for the forest products industry, which depended on timber harvests, and for loggers and mill workers, who did the work of felling and processing. In 1990, the year before the injunction, 10.6 billion board feet of timber were cut on federal lands. In 1991, only 4.4 billion board feet were harvested before Judge Dwyer's injunction took hold. And the next year only 0.7 billion board feet were sold.[16]

Hard Times in the Pacific Northwest

Halted timber sales caused hardship in timber areas. Hundreds of small-town economies built on jobs created by logging, milling, and related trucking and shipping spiraled downward. The owl injunction came on the heels of a prolonged recession in the Pacific Northwest in the early 1980s. Thousands of loggers and mill workers had already lost jobs as the big forest products corporations moved operations to Southwestern forests and larger high-tech mills replaced older, more labor-intensive facilities. Now, because of the Endangered Species Act, many more would be jobless.

Despair and anger permeated logging towns. In Forks, Washington, where unemployment rose to 20 percent, someone shot a spotted owl and nailed it to a sign (risking a $20,000 fine and one year in prison). In Oregon, loggers had bumper stickers that read: "IF IT'S HOOTIN', I'M SHOOTIN", "SAVE A LOGGER/EAT AN OWL," and "I LIKE SPOTTED OWLS . . . FRIED." In Happy Camp, California, all four sawmills closed and the town collapsed as area timber harvests declined from 50 million board feet to 8 million. The population fell from 2,500 to 1,100, and more than half those remaining were on public assistance.[17] In many areas, taxes from timber sales were used to fund schools. With timber sales nearly halted, school districts were badly hurt.

---

[16]Department of the Interior memorandum in *The Administration's Response to the Spotted Owl Crisis: Joint Oversight Hearing before the Subcommittee on National Parks and Public Lands of the Committee on Interior and Insular Affairs,* U.S. House of Representatives, March 24, 1992, p. 167.

[17]Richard C. Paddock, "Town's Decline Rivals That of the Spotted Owl," *Los Angeles Times,* October 23, 1995, p. A3.

These dislocations were the result of a shift in the social contract between urban America and the rural populations of timber industry workers. Throughout most of American history, forests had been managed for maximum fiber yields. But the new political force of environmentalism succeeded in redefining forests as pristine tree museums. This change angered and puzzled loggers and mill workers whose culture supported the moral imperative of "getting the wood to town." They resented government interference and felt manipulated by distant political forces.[18]

Years of Impasse, Conflict, and Controversy

The court injunction against logging federal lands was based on the lack of a satisfactory recovery plan for the spotted owl population. The Endangered Species Act requires a plan for each listed species to serve as a road map for eventual recovery and delisting. In 1992, the Department of the Interior prepared such a plan, but environmentalists challenged it, and the federal court that had issued the logging injunction ruled that it was inadequate.

In 1993, then newly elected President Clinton fulfilled a campaign promise by presiding over a "timber summit" in Portland, Oregon, and listening to the strong and polarized views of scientists, environmentalists, and timber industry representatives. As a result, early in 1994, the Clinton administration introduced a program designed to resolve controversy and move forward. This program, called Option 9 because it was one of ten options given to the president by a task force, tried to appease both industry and environmentalists. Critical habitat for the spotted owl was protected by a logging ban covering 80 percent of old-growth areas in federal forests. Preservation of wide swaths of old forests would provide dispersal area for young owls and was set forth in Option 9 as a recovery plan for the owl. But to help the timber economy of the Pacific Northwest, Option 9 also permitted logging 1.2 billion board feet of remaining old-growth each year.[19] This harvest level was nearly double that of years since the injunction, but was still almost 90 percent less than the year before the injunction. Option 9 spelled permanent loss of tens of thousands of timber jobs, so it committed $1.2 billion more over five years to retrain workers, help small businesses, and compensate for lost tax revenues in timber towns.[20]

---

[18]Matthew S. Carroll, *Community & the Northwestern Logger,* Boulder, Colo.: Westview Press, 1995, p. 149.

[19]Report of the Forest Ecosystem Management Assessment Team, *Forest Ecosystem Management: An Ecological, Economic, and Social Assessment,* Washington, D.C.: U. S. Department of Agriculture, et al., July 1993.

[20]Congressional Research Service, *The Clinton Administration's Forest Plan for the Pacific Northwest* (by Rose W. Gorte), 93-664 ENR, July 16, 1993, p. CRS-4.

Despite the broad recovery plan and paltry timber harvest authorized by Option 9, environmentalists sued to block it. A federal court upheld it, but even so, for the next year, little timber cutting took place. Delay was caused by convoluted, bureaucratic U.S. Forest Service procedures for setting up timber auctions. These procedures invited litigation, and environmental groups sued the agency at every turn to delay action.

Then the political climate in this battle over the forests abruptly changed. After the midterm elections of 1994, Republicans had a congressional majority and began an attack on environmental laws, including the Endangered Species Act, which they regarded as a prime example of runaway government power. In 1995, Republican majorities put a rider on a budget bill expediting timber sales under Option 9. This rider waived the applicability of environmental laws to timber sales, thus depriving the owl's defenders of grounds for lawsuits.

By this time, a storm of protest swirled around the Endangered Species Act, much of it generated by a rising property rights movement. This movement represented property owners hurt by regulations that reduced the value of their land. Both corporations that owned expanses of timber and small landowners with only a few acres were hurt when they could not fell the trees they owned. They demanded compensation by government when this occurred.

A clause in the Fifth Amendment, known as the takings clause, protects property owners. It reads: "nor shall private property be taken for public use without just compensation." In the past, the takings clause has been interpreted as requiring compensation only when government takes over property through eminent domain or when the owner is wholly deprived of its use. Except in unusual circumstances, it has never been held to require payment for land-use restrictions incidental to enforcement of the nation's environmental laws. But opponents of heavy-handed regulation have seized on the takings clause to argue that landowners must be paid when regulators reduce the value of their property. By 1995, five states had enacted laws requiring compensation of property owners when state regulations decreased the value of their land, and two bills had been introduced in Congress to mandate compensation for federal actions. In addition, the Endangered Species Act was up for reauthorization and Republicans were proposing a range of changes to reduce its scope and power.

Faced with the possibility of a vitiated Endangered Species Act, the Clinton administration "discovered" new flexibility in the law's provisions. A little-used section of the law permitted federal regulators to negotiate *habitat conservation plans* with private landowners. A habitat conservation plan is a binding, voluntary agreement in which a landowner agrees to take conservation measures, sometimes beyond the letter of the law, and in return receives permission to log or otherwise use property, even if it means harming some endangered species or critical habitat in the process. For example, in 1995, the Murray Pacific Company, which owned a 53,000-acre tree farm in Washington populated by spotted owls, agreed to preserve 43 percent of the tree farm as habitat for the owl and four other endangered species. The agreement was detailed and specific; for example, the company was to leave trees outside five cave openings to protect a bat species and had to monitor the temperature of streams and leave more trees standing on their banks to shade them if readings began to rise. In exchange, Murray Pacific received an "incidental take permit" absolving it from blame if, in logging the rest of the property, any members of an endangered species were harassed or killed. A similar plan was negotiated with Weyerhaeuser Co., permitting it to log parts of 209,000 acres of owl habitat it owns in Oregon. In return, Weyerhaeuser agreed to leave corridors of old growth for spotted owls. Previously, both Murray Pacific and Weyerhaeuser probably would have been denied the right to log their land at all.

By 1999, there were more than 240 habitat conservation plans, and hundreds more were in preparation. The size of the areas covered by individual plans is increasing. The plan agreements include a "no-surprises" clause, a guarantee that even if new evidence about an endangered species emerges years later, no additional conservation measures will be required.[21] And they incorporate a "baseline" policy so that if the numbers of an endangered species increase, the landowner is not required to take additional measures to protect them. This removes a strong disincentive that existed in the past to discourage or kill endangered species if they were discovered, for fear their presence would render land useless for harvest or development.

Most environmental groups oppose the use of habitat conservation plans, incidental take permits, and the no-surprises policy, all of which they see as compromising the survival chances of species on the borderline. Incidental take permits allow logging companies to destroy some owl habitat. And the no-surprises policy may turn out to be foolish. Science is just beginning to understand certain species and complex ecosystems. Yet habitat conservation plans are locked into place for decades—some for as long as 100 years. Even if new information about causes of extinction is discovered, landowners cannot be forced to alter their activities. They can volunteer to do so, and government must pick up the cost.

Controversy Continues

There may never be another year of timber harvest in the Pacific Northwest as bountiful as those before listing of the northern spotted owl. Despite the use of habitat conservation plans, enforcement of the Endangered Species Act has held harvests at least two-thirds below what they were. The timber economy continues to fade. In Linn County, Oregon, for example, the forest products industry injected $12.7 million into the economy in 1988, but only $2.1 million in 1996.[22]

The overall cost of protecting the owl is elusive, but it may be great. One study looked at projections of wood prices, consumption and production trends

---

[21]"Habitat Conservation Plan Assurances ('No Surprises') Rule," 63 FR 8859 (February 23, 1998).
[22]"Northern Spotted Owl Impacts Sweet Home, Oregon," http://www.sweet-home.or.us/forest/owl/index.

in the United States, and estimated changes in wood products revenues, incomes, and surplus costs to consumers due to owl protection. The authors concluded that measures to raise the survival odds of the owl to 91 percent would lead to a $33 billion reduction in economic welfare, most of which would come out of the pockets of workers and businesses in the Pacific Northwest. Enforcing the Endangered Species Act in a way that would raise the owl's survival odds to 95 percent would push the economic sacrifice up to $46 billion.[23]

Some sawmills and wood products factories in spotted owl country now manage to stay open only by importing timber from New Zealand and Chile. Logs, planks, and chips arrive by ship at ports such as North Bend, Oregon, and are trucked to the region's small factories. There, within sight of some of the world's great forest expanses, they substitute for locally grown sawtimber and are turned into such things as porch posts, door frames, and garden furniture.[24] The irony would be no greater if gasoline refineries in Saudi Arabia had to depend on oil in tankers arriving from Texas.

Resistance in the Pacific Northwest to the species protection juggernaut is rising. Both giant corporations and small landowners are combating what they perceive as unconstitutional regulatory takings of their property. Heretofore, courts have held that no compensation by government is required when regulatory action reduces property value. But in 1997, an Oregon jury awarded Boise Cascade Corp. more than $2 million for the value of fifty-six acres of timberland that it was unable to harvest because of a spotted owl nest.[25] This was the first case in which a private landowner successfully sued for compensation due to a regulatory taking.

Attention now focuses on a lawsuit by a retired couple in Oregon. In 1987, three years before the spotted owl was listed as a threatened species, Alvin and Marsha Seiber bought 196 acres of forest near Sweet Home. They planned in their retirement years to harvest timber on the land for income. In 1996, the Seibers notified the Department of Forestry that they intended to log on their parcel. However, a pair of spotted owls had been seen, not on the Seiber's land, but on nearby property, and the state forester prohibited logging a seventy-acre corridor containing the owl's roost, including forty-one acres belonging to the Seibers.

Two years later, the Seibers tried again. After high winds toppled large numbers of trees, they submitted a plan to remove blown down timber from the forty-one acres. In the plan, they agreed not to disturb the area between March and September, the months when spotted owls nest and produce offspring. The state forester denied them permission. The Seibers, tired of the State of Oregon using their property as an owl preserve, brought suit, claiming that this was a taking under the Fifth Amendment entitling them to compensation. Said Marsha Seibert:

---

[23]C. Montgomery et al., "The Marginal Cost of Species Preservation: The Northern Spotted Owl," *Journal of Environmental Economics and Management,* 26 (1994), p. 111.

[24]Richard Read, "As Its Timber Dwindles, the Northwest Becomes Just Another Stop in Global Wood Production," *The Oregonian,* March 29, 1998.

[25]Kate Freedlander, "Timber Firm Wins Judgment on State's Logging Limits," *The Oregonian,* November 23, 1997, p. 1.

We have a total of 41+ acres of our land that has been set aside for owl habitat, that we can do nothing with, but still have to pay property taxes on. We were told we could do anything we wanted on the land so long as it does not disturb the owl. I would like to know what this could possibly be, as anything that makes noise disturbs the owl. We have timber on the ground that is now rotten, because we were not allowed to clean it up . . .

I was always raised to believe that if you take care of the land, it will take care of you. Now we are being told we are not allowed to take care of our own land, but still we pay the taxes. We depend on this land to take care of us in our retirement.[26]

So the battle for the timber continues. Government regulators and environmentalists now have the upper hand. But if courts begin to rule that spotted owl protection constitutes a regulatory taking within the meaning of the Fifth Amendment, the federal and state governments might be required to pay landowners, as in the case of Boise Cascade. Such payouts for vast tracts of timberland would transfer the burden of spotted owl protection from the wood products industry and its employees to the broad base of American taxpayers.

The most recent census of the owls was in 1995, when the Fish and Wildlife Service reported 5,431 known forest locations inhabited by either single owls or pairs.[27] This number, though higher than the 1989 count, is insufficient to comfort wildlife biologists.

Questions

1. Is there any way to resolve the conflict between saving the northern spotted owl and allowing enough timber cutting to preserve the economy in logging areas of the Pacific Northwest?

2. Which interest should be given priority—protection of owls or preservation of the timber economy?

3. Should the nation's national forests become exclusively preserves for the protection of wildlife? Or should they continue to have multiple uses such as logging, mining, and recreation?

4. When state and federal agencies prohibit logging near spotted owl nests, does this violate rights given the landowners by the takings clause of the Fifth Amendment? Should owners of private timberland, both corporations and individuals such as the Seibers, be compensated by the government for their losses? Would it be fair to shift the burden of species protection to taxpayers?

5. Should enforcement of the Endangered Species Act continue to become more flexible? Or should it tighten again to protect spotted owls more?

---

[26]Quoted in Ron Schaleger, "Sweet Home Timber Land Owners Sue Oregon Department of Forestry for Lack of 'Just Compensation,'" Sweet Home On-Line, www.sweet-home.or.us/forest/owl/1998-seibersuit1.

[27]"Proposed Special Rule for the Conservation of the Northern Spotted Owl on Non-Federal Lands," 60 FR 9483 (February 17, 1995).

15

Managing Environmental Quality

In 1973, Arthur and Margaret Orjias settled on fifty acres of land in an eastern Colorado valley. They had almost finished building their house in 1984, when a new Louisiana-Pacific Corporation plant started operating nearby. The Olathe Plant, as it was called, turned out waferboard, a type of paneling made by mixing aspen chips in a glue-like resin, pressing them into wafers, and baking them in an oven. The oven was heated by burning wood. Inside it, hot exhaust gases from the fire cured the board. These gases emerged from the oven containing formaldehyde, isocyanates, and tiny wood particles.

Immediately after production began, nearby residents were bothered by smoke so dense that cars going through the valley sometimes turned on their headlights during the day. The Orjias suffered from coughing, headaches, earaches, swollen glands, and nausea. After three years of medical problems and unresolved complaints to the company, the couple abandoned their home and moved.

In 1988, Colorado regulators finally issued a permit to the Olathe Plant mandating the use of air pollution equipment and setting levels of control to be achieved. A continuous monitor that recorded an opacity

521

FIGURE 15-1

An opacity monitor. Factories and power plants are given permits by the EPA or state regulators mandating the use of mechanical or chemical devices to remove gases, particles, and odors. To reduce smoke, the Olathe Plant was required to run exhaust gases through an electrified filter. Positively charged soot particles in the oven exhaust smoke were run through negatively charged filters that attracted and retained them. Filtered exhaust streams at the Olathe plant were to have an opacity reading of 20 percent or less, that is, no more than 20 percent of the light passing through the air in the exhaust stream could be reflected by particles. This 20 percent opacity limit was to be achieved 95 percent of the time. The diagram illustrates how an opacity monitor works. A light beam from the left passes through exhaust gases and any loss of light is measured by the detector at right.

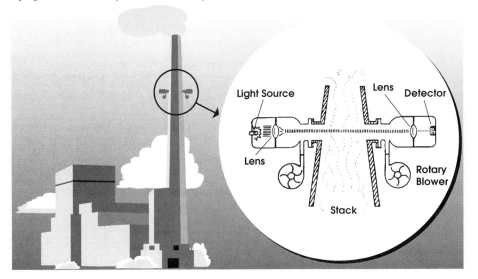

Source: General Accounting Office.

reading on a graph every six minutes was also required (see Figure 15-1).

For the next two years, the plant repeatedly violated its permit and, in 1990, it was fined $80,000 by the Colorado Department of Public Health. A new and more stringent permit was then issued, placing an hourly limit on wood fuel for the oven and limiting the plant to production of 210,000 square board feet of finished panels per 12-hour shift. These limits were intended to improve air quality in the valley.

The plant manager, however, ordered employees to tamper with the opacity monitor. When permit limits were likely to be exceeded, the workers placed adhesive tape with reflective backing near the light beam to trick the device, and they wedged wood chips in the recording pen to prevent it from going over the 20 percent limit. After a fired employee revealed what was going on, the EPA raided the plant, seizing 23 boxes of records. It took investigators three years to figure out how the scheme worked. Meanwhile, the Olathe Plant documents so alarmed the EPA that even before they were fully reviewed, it launched a nationwide investigation of Louisiana-Pacific facilities.

What it found was a corporate culture of complicity. ". . . [I]n the structure of an organization like this you don't need to tell people to violate the law," said one federal prosecutor working on the investigation. "You tell them 'we need so much production' and people know what they're going to have to do."[1] As a preliminary result of the investigation in 1992 the EPA barred Louisiana-Pacific from contracting with the federal government or buying timber from the U.S. Forest Service. In the same year, a court ordered the company to pay $2.3 million to the Orjias and three other families who had abandoned their homes in the valley. Then, in 1993, the EPA culminated its nationwide investigation, fining it $11 million and forcing it to install $70 million worth of new pollution control equipment.

In 1995, the EPA brought a criminal indictment against Louisiana-Pacific and two Olathe Plant employees.[2] Then, the firm's top three executives resigned and a new management team came in, determined to improve environmental performance. The Olathe Plant case was settled in 1998 when the company agreed to a $37 million fine and five years' probation. The plant superintendent was fined $10,000 and given six months' home detention and a supervisor was sentenced to five months in prison, both for criminal conspiracy to violate the Clean Air Act.

Louisiana-Pacific's new CEO Mark A. Suwyn appeared in the Colorado courtroom to apologize for the corporation. He announced that the Olathe Plant would become a "model of environmental compliance."[3]

Louisiana-Pacific is a forest products company with $2.4 billion in 1997 sales. It makes 4.5 billion square feet of waferboard annually in sixteen plants, making it the nation's largest producer of that kind of paneling. It also manufactures lumber, pulp, hardwoods, veneers, and cellulose insulation and it owns 1.4 million forest acres in nine states. It has been a profitable company in recent years, except for a loss in 1997 due to the cost of lawsuits.[4]

Strict enforcement of environmental laws taught the company a lesson and it is now "greening" itself. Top management has prioritized environmental responsibility. Although the company set aside a $29 million reserve fund to pay for environmental fines and lawsuits, CEO Suwyn has a goal of zero violations. Environmental audits of facilities are conducted to ensure that standards are met. An impressive "Corporate Policy on Protection of the Environment" exists.[5] New procedures and training programs reinforce the policy.

The company has spent hundreds of millions of dollars on new pollution control equipment at its ninety-nine

---

[1]Quoted in Mark Eddy, "Judge Fines Timber Firm $37 Million," *Denver Post*, May 28, 1998, p. A1.

[2]*United States* v. *Louisiana Pacific Corp.*, 908 F.Supp. 835 (1995); 925 F.Supp. 1484 (1995); and 106 F.3rd 345 (1997).

[3]Quoted in Nina Siegal, "If I Believed in Hell, This Could Be No Worse," *The Progressive*, December 1998, p. 30.

[4]Louisiana-Pacific Corporation, *Form 10-K,* March 31, 1998, p. 44.

[5]The full policy is at http://www.lpcorp.com/hq/policy.html.

pulp mills and manufacturing plants in the United States, Canada, and Ireland. At its waferboard mills, it installed costly ceramic thermal units that reduce formaldehyde emissions by heating exhaust gases to high temperatures as they rise through stacks. And it is moving beyond pollution control to think more in terms of zero emissions and resource conservation. At waferboard plants, hundreds of tons of tree bark that used to be thrown in landfills are now being made into compost and packaged for sale. The company has also pioneered building insulation made from recycled newspaper.

Command-and-control enforcement is critical in environmental regulation. It forced Louisiana-Pacific to move beyond an obsession with max-imum output and to focus on sustainable production. Yet, as important as strict regulation is, further progress in reducing pollutants requires increasing flexibility and corporate initiative. Strict enforcement will always be necessary, but a more open approach to the rules benefits corporations that are not miscreants.

In this chapter, we will explain the process of assessing and choosing which pollution risks are most important to regulate. We then discuss flexible approaches to regulation. And, finally, we show how companies are adopting management systems that move them beyond legal compliance. Louisiana-Pacific has just begun reaching beyond compliance; many prominent corporations have done this for decades.

Regulating Environmental Risk

Since the 1970s, the cost of pollution abatement has steadily risen, and the EPA estimates total abatement expenditures in the United States of more than $170 billion in 2000.[6] To put this sum in perspective, it is roughly equal to the cost of building twenty-eight new nuclear aircraft carriers and more than the GDP of South Korea. Is this money well spent?

If the nation's environmental budget is to have maximum effect, spending must be focused on the highest risks to human health and the natural environment. *Risk* is a probability existing somewhere between zero and absolute certainty that a harm will occur. The probability of any pollution risk can be studied scientifically; then regulators, politicians, and the public must decide what, if anything, should be done to mitigate it.

Congress, in recent years, has added about thirty provisions in environmental laws requiring that regulatory decisions be based on risk assessments. The goal of these provisions is to better focus spending on the greatest hazards. Two basic types of risk analysis are done by the EPA. The first focuses on human health risks and the second focuses on ecological risks, that is, risks to plants, animals, and natural ecosystems. We briefly explain the basic model for each.

---

[6]*EPA Strategic Plan,* Washington, D.C.: Environmental Protection Agency, EPA/190-R-97-002, September 1997, p 69.

FIGURE 15-2

*Risk analysis
procedure.*

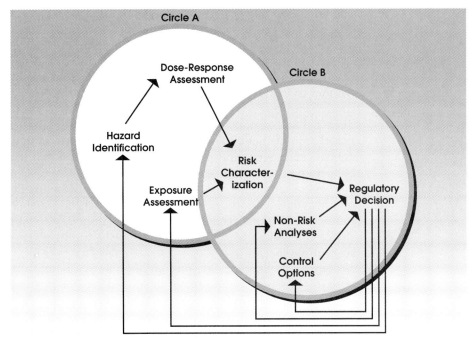

Source: Environmental Protection Agency.

Analysis of Human Health Risks

Risk Assessment

The model for analyzing human health risks is shown in Figure 15-2.[7] It separates risk analysis into two interrelated processes represented by two circles. Circle A shows the elements of *risk assessment,* which is the process, largely scientific and technical, of figuring out how much danger a contaminant poses. Risk assessment is intended to be a quantitative, objective process leading to the unbiased judgments of experts about risk. Its four elements are as follows.

Hazard Identification.   Hazard identification establishes a link between a substance, such as a chemical, and human disease. When a substance is thought to pose a risk, there are two basic methods of proving it dangerous.

---

[7]The model described here is basic to a number of specific health risk analysis procedures used by the EPA. See, for example, "Proposed Guidelines for Carcinogen Risk Assessment," 61 FR 17959 (April 23, 1996); "Reproductive Toxicity Risk Assessment Guidelines," 61 FR 56273 (October 31, 1996); and "Guidelines for Neurotoxicity Assessment," 63 FR 26925 (May 14, 1998). The basic model is also followed in Europe and Japan.

The first is *animal tests,* in which animals such as mice and rats are repeatedly exposed to high levels of the substance through diet, inhalation, or other means for an appreciable part of their life span. In a cancer study, as many as 1,000 animals may be divided into three groups with different exposure levels. One group is exposed to the maximum dose that the animals can tolerate without dying. The second group receives half this dose. The third group is a control group receiving no exposure. At the end of the test, the animals are dissected and tumors and other abnormalities on organs are counted. If the exposed animals have many tumors, the assumption is that the chemical is an animal carcinogen, and regulators tend to assume that it is, therefore, probably a human carcinogen as well.

Several problems cast doubt on the validity of animal tests. First, scientists rely heavily on strains of rats and mice genetically disposed to high rates of tumor production.[8] This predisposition raises doubts about whether a substance is a complete carcinogen or simply a tumor promoter in an otherwise susceptible species.

Second, when animals receive large amounts of a chemical, tumors can arise from tissue irritation rather than normal carcinogenesis. For example, rats forced to breathe extreme concentrations of formaldehyde exhibit nasal inflammation. They develop tumors in their noses, but some or all of these tumors could result more from abnormally rapid cell division that magnifies chromosomal abnormalities than from the carcinogenic properties of formaldehyde. It is scientifically uncertain if a substance that promotes cancer in high doses also promotes it in lower doses. Humans, of course, have lower environmental exposures to chemicals than the prodigious doses given to test animals.

And third, animal physiology may be so different from that of humans that disease processes are unique. For example, gasoline vapor causes kidney tumors in male rats, but the biological mechanism causing these tumors is unique to rats; humans lack one of the proteins involved. Even animals differ in their susceptibility to disease. Inhalation of cadmium dust, to which workers in battery factories are exposed, causes high levels of cancer in rats, but no cancer in mice. Which result is appropriate for assessing risk to workers?

A second method of identifying hazards is the *epidemiological study,* a statistical survey of human mortality (death) and morbidity (sickness) in a sample population. Epidemiological studies can establish a link between industrial pollutants and health problems. To illustrate, recent studies show the following associations:

- Elevated rates of breast cancer in men who worked around electrical equipment.[9]

---

[8]Tracy Lyon, "Carcinogenesis in Transgenic Mouse Models," *Environmental Health Perspectives,* September 1997, pp. 912–13.
[9]Paul A. Demers, "Occupational Exposure to Electromagnetic Fields and Breast Cancer in Men," *American Journal of Epidemiology,* August 15, 1991.

- Elevated risk of loss of color vision among workers exposed to styrene in factories producing fiberglass-reinforced plastics.[10]
- Elevated mortality from lymphatic cancers among workers at synthetic rubber plants.[11]

Epidemiological studies have the advantage of measuring real human illness, but have low statistical power and are riddled with uncertainties. In particular, people are exposed to literally thousands of substances, and individual exposures vary. For example, the study of synthetic rubber plant workers, noted above, found four lymphatic cancers among 364 workers, more in a group that size than the 0.69 expected from standard mortality tables. All 364 workers had been exposed to the chemical butadiene (byoo-ta-DIE-een) by working for at least six months in butadiene production units at three Union Carbide synthetic rubber plants in West Virginia. The four lymphatic cancers are statistically significant but still a small number. Could exposure to another chemical over the thirty-nine-year period covered by the study have caused these cancers?

There are other difficulties with epidemiological studies. Because lung tumors and other cancers have latency periods of up to forty years, these studies may not detect harm done by newly introduced chemicals. Death certificates may be inaccurate, particularly when multiple diseases contributed to death. However, even though their accuracy is subject to doubt, the results of epidemiological tests can be valuable. Arsenic, for instance, does not cause cancer in lab animals; only epidemiological tests show it to be a human carcinogen.

Annals of Epidemiology

In 1958, the Lipari Landfill was opened near housing tracts in Gloucester County, New Jersey. It closed in 1985 after taking in three million gallons of liquid chemical wastes and 12,000 cubic yards of solid wastes from companies including DuPont, Gliddon Co., Hercules Inc., Owens-Illinois Inc., and Rohm & Haas Inc. As the dump grew, it exposed the surrounding population to toxic chemicals.

Organic chemical waste is volatile, and molecules of benzene, toluene, and methyl chloride evaporated quickly and were inhaled by nearby residents, who complained of odors, headaches, nausea, and breathing problems. One day the landfill exploded and twice fires broke out. Heavy metals, including arsenic, chromium, nickel, mercury, lead, and silver, seeped into streams, a nearby lake, and soil. The site once ranked No. 1 on the EPA's Superfund priority list, but it has now been cleaned at a cost of $140 million.

(continued)

---

[10]Fabriziomaria Gobba et al., "Acquired Dyschromatopsia among Styrene-Exposed Workers," *Journal of Occupational Medicine,* July 1991.
[11]Elizabeth Ward et al., "Mortality Study of Workers in 1,3-Butadiene Production Units Identified from a Chemical Workers Cohort," *Environmental Health Perspectives,* June 1995.

Annals of Epidemiology   (concluded)

Researchers did an epidemiological study to see if there was an association between low birth weight and a mother's living near the Lipari Landfill.[12] They divided surrounding residential areas with 36,600 residents into three zones based on proximity to the landfill. Then, from birth records, they recorded the birth weights of 11,579 children born between 1961 and 1985 to women with street addresses in one of these zones. In addition, they recorded the baby's sex, its gestation period, and the mother's race, age, education, and prior pregnancy history. The data were used in statistical tests to check the possibility that other risk factors, besides exposure to dumpsite toxins, were at work.

A look at the data showed that mothers living in the zone closest to the landfill were, on average, older and better educated, factors associated with higher birth weight in the general population. And in fact, in the early years of the dump's operation, babies born in the closest zone—less than one mile from the landfill—were heavier than in the other two zones. But between 1965 and 1975—the dump's busiest years and therefore the time of suspected high exposure to hazardous chemicals—birth weights of infants born to mothers living in the closest zone fell below those of babies in the other two zones.

Previous research has found that low birth weight in animals is associated with exposure to volatile organic compounds and with the metals cadmium and lead. Other studies have found that low birth weight is associated with mothers who work near auto body solvents and chemicals used in electrical transformers. Children born to parents living near the infamous Love Canal toxic waste site in Niagara Falls, New York, have also been found to have below average birth weights.

The Lipari Landfill study adds to this developing body of research on chemical exposure and birth weight. It does not prove, however, that any chemical or combination of chemicals causes low birth weight and it does not document ill health effects in later life for low-birth-weight babies.

Dose-Response Assessment.   Dose-response assessment is the process of determining how toxic a substance is to humans or animals at varying levels of exposure. The potency of carcinogens, for example, varies widely. Formaldehyde is a strong carcinogen that causes cancer in 50 percent of exposed laboratory animals at a dose of 15 parts per million (ppm). Vinyl chloride, on the other hand, is a very weak carcinogen that is benign at less than 50 ppm and, even at the much higher dose of 600 ppm, causes cancer in less than 25 percent of animals.[13]

Workers and the public, even when exposed to elevated levels of toxic substances, receive much lower doses than test animals. So regulators use mathematical models that predict low-dose risks to humans using data gathered in

---

[12]Michael Berry and Frank Bove, "Birth Weight Reduction Associated with Residence Near a Hazardous Waste Landfill," *Environmental Health Perspectives,* August 1997, pp. 856–61.

[13]Louis A. Cox Jr. and Paolo F. Ricci, "Dealing with Uncertainty: From Health Risk Assessment to Environmental Decision Making," *Journal of Energy Engineering,* August 1992, p. 79.

high-dose animal tests. For many years the EPA has used a model that assumes a linear dose-response rate—that is, that there will be a proportional increase in cancers from small exposures to large ones (if, for example, exposure increases by 25 percent, then cancers will increase by 25 percent).

Since the *linear model* predicts more cancer at lower exposures, its use is conservative. It suggests that more needs to be done to protect the public from small exposures and it leads to high expenditures for controlling small releases of carcinogens. Alternatively, regulators could use a *threshold model*, which assumes that carcinogens do not cause cancer at very low doses. In this model, only when exposures rise past a certain point, or threshold, does cancer risk appear. Threshold models suggest that spending limited abatement dollars to control low levels of pollution is extravagant. In the past, the EPA used only the linear model in the risk assessment process. Environmentalists, who favor more regulation and risk reduction, approved of this. But industry, which dislikes the expensive regulations it spawns, favored threshold models that would require less regulation of emissions. The EPA has recently indicated willingness to use threshold models if strong scientific evidence supports their validity.

Exposure Assessment.   Exposure assessment is the study of how much of a substance humans take in through inhalation, ingestion, or skin absorption. For example, gasoline contains five toxic organic compounds that evaporate easily.[14] Pumping gas displaces air in fuel tanks and exposes people to them. To measure this exposure, researchers took blood samples of 60 motorists in Alaska, both before and after they filled their tanks. They found that blood concentrations of all five compounds rose after gas pumping. Benzene, for instance, rose from 0.19 part per billion (ppb) to .54 ppb and toluene from 0.38 ppb to 0.74 ppb. The higher concentrations lasted no longer than 10 minutes. This study confirms that motorists have short-term exposure to carcinogens and suspected carcinogens when they pump gas.

Since widespread blood sampling is impossible, exposures can be difficult to calculate and involve making assumptions. The EPA often calculates them by determining the risk to a hypothetical *maximum-exposed individual.* For air toxics, the EPA assumes that nearby residents stand at a factory's fence and breath the highest recorded emissions around the clock for seventy years. OSHA makes worker exposure estimates by assuming a peak level of inhalation eight hours per day, five days a week, fifty weeks a year, over a forty-five year period. These assumptions obviously exaggerate people's exposures, but regulators are making conservative assumptions that protect public health. The EPA takes the position that "it is appropriate to err on the side of protection of health and the environment in the face of scientific uncertainty."[15]

---

[14]These are benzene, ethylbenzene, *m-/p*-xylene, *o*-xylene, and toluene. Lorraine C. Backer et al., "Exposure to Regular Gasoline and Ethanol Oxyfuel during Refueling in Alaska," *Environmental Health Perspectives,* August 1997, p. 850.

[15]Environmental Protection Agency, "Proposed Guidelines for Carcinogen Risk Assessment," 61 FR 17999 (April 23, 1996).

Risk Characterization.   Risk characterization is an overall conclusion about the danger of a substance. It is a written, nontechnical narrative that summarizes all the evidence about hazard, dose-response, and exposure, and then makes a final risk estimate. This risk estimate then helps to decide what level of abatement should be required of industry.

A full risk characterization is a short essay describing the risk in words and discussing assumptions and uncertainties about it. Sometimes risk characterizations are statistical representations of probability. For example, before regulating releases of vinyl bromide, a gas used in plastics manufacturing, OSHA characterized it as posing a lifetime risk of 155 liver cancers per 1,000 workers exposed.[16]

There is no agreement about how high a risk should be before regulators must act to reduce it. In 1980, the Supreme Court, in a case that required OSHA to establish significant health risks to workers before requiring expensive worker protective measures, addressed the subject of "significant" risk.

> Some risks are plainly acceptable and others are plainly unacceptable. If, for example, the odds are one in a billion that a person will die from cancer by taking a drink of chlorinated water, the risk clearly could not be considered significant. On the other hand, if the odds are one in a thousand that regular inhalation of gasoline vapors that are 2% benzene will be fatal, a reasonable person might well consider the risk significant and take the appropriate steps to decrease or eliminate it.[17]

At the EPA, cancer risks are considered low if they are equal to or less than 1 in 10,000 over a lifetime, but if the risk is greater than 1 in 10,000, it becomes "significant" and may require regulatory action.[18] Policy guidelines such as this that tolerate small risks enrage some agency's critics. Environmental activist Lois Gibbs asks: "Would you let me shoot into a crowd of one hundred thousand people and kill one of them? No? Well, how come Dow Chemical can do it? It's okay for the corporations to do it, but the little guy with a gun goes to jail . . ."[19]

Risk characterizations are built on a series of calculations about toxicity, potency, and exposure that, as we have noted, are done with scientific method but ultimately involve a series of value judgments because of the limits and uncertainty of science in this area. So they may not be very accurate. Nevertheless, they are the basis for many regulatory standards.

Risk Management

Risk management, which is in circle B in Figure 15-2, is the process of regulating dangerous pollutants. It contains several elements. Whereas the risk assessment process in Circle A is based on science, the risk management process is

---

[16]Occupational Safety and Health Administration, "Substances for Which Proposed Limits Are Based on Avoidance of Cancer," 57 FR 26396 (June 12, 1992).

[17]*Industrial Union Department, AFL-CIO* v. *American Petroleum Institute,* 488 U.S. 655 (1989).

[18]See General Accounting Office, *Superfund: EPA's Use of Risk Assessments in Cleanup Decisions,* GAO/T-RCED-95-231, June 22, 1995, p. 3.

[19]Quoted in John A. Hird, *Superfund: The Political Economy of Environmental Risk,* Baltimore: Johns Hopkins University Press, 1994, p. 200.

based on law, politics, economics, and ethics. We briefly discuss the risk management process here.

Non-Risk Analysis.   This kind of analysis involves the use of feasibility studies about control options. Technical data, such as control device engineering, may open or limit options. Public opinion polls or interviews may define politically acceptable options. Cost-benefit studies can illuminate economic consequences of alternative regulatory approaches. Cost-benefit analysis is discussed at greater length later in the chapter.

Control Options.   These are alternative ways to mitigate risk. Many environmental laws are specific about risk reduction required and the methods of achieving it. Some statutes permit balancing risk against control costs; others prohibit such balancing. Some laws set up strict command-and-control regimes; others provide financial incentives for companies or encourage only voluntary programs. Later in this chapter, we discuss more fully a range of control options.

The Regulatory Decision.   This is the action taken. In both this chapter and the last, we give examples of how corporations are affected by agency actions. Decisions can affect future calculations of risk, as is shown by the arrows in Figure 15-2 that connect various elements in circles A and B.

Analysis of Ecological Risks

A second model of risk assessment used by the EPA is the ecological risk assessment model shown in Figure 15-3 in simplified form. This model is used to assess risks to plants, animals, and ecosystems.

During *problem formulation*, scientists and regulators set forth the case that ecosystem damage is being caused by some pollutant or human activity. In the *analysis* stage, scientists study how this "stressor" enters the environment and how it is dispersed and transported to come in contact with biological entities. In one study, pesticides sprayed on fields were ingested by birds. When these birds died, birds of prey and scavenger species devoured their carcasses and the pesticide moved further in a food chain. After studying how exposure occurs, scientists then try to characterize the ecological damage. If, for instance, construction of logging roads releases silt into streams, species that spawn in the tiny spaces between rocks in gravel stream beds may have trouble reproducing when these spaces fill. If such species have long reproductive cycles, the danger to their survival is greater than if they have shorter cycles. Then, in the *risk characterization* stage, a description of overall risk is written, discussing all the evidence and explaining the degree of confidence for risk estimates. This picture of risk forms the basis for decisions made by regulatory agencies, that is, for subsequent *risk management*.[20]

---

[20]Environmental Protection Agency, "Guidelines for Ecological Risk Assessment," 63 FR 26845-924 (May 14, 1998).

Figure 15-3

Ecological risk assessment.

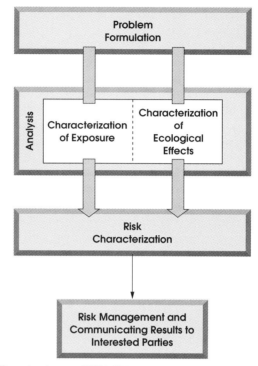

Source: Environmental Protection Agency, 63 FR 26850.

Cost-Benefit Analysis

We now move on to treat at greater length the risk management process, which is the end stage in both models of risk analysis described to this point. We begin with a discussion of cost-benefit analysis.

Cost-benefit analysis, like risk analysis, is used to improve the efficiency of environmental regulation. In it, costs and benefits of a proposed action are systematically compared. If benefits exceed costs, the action is desirable, other things being equal. Rigorous cost-benefit studies assign common values, such as dollar amounts, to all costs and benefits so that they can be compared using a common denominator. The EPA began doing such studies in the 1970s and, during that decade, cost-benefit requirements were built into some, but not all, environmental statutes. A few laws, such as the Endangered Species Act, forbid its use.

The studies themselves typically are several hundred pages long and cost hundreds of thousands of dollars. Although they may lead to more cost-effective decisions, they also complicate regulation and make it more expensive. Cost calculations may include capital costs to industry, inflation, plant closures, and lost jobs. Benefits can include increases in aesthetic appeal, property values, and tourism; reduced medical expenses; and lives saved. The accounting is detailed.

For example, the expected number of cancers avoided by abating pollution is calculated from risk data. They are then described by age distribution, disabilities likely to result, their length, medical costs, lost productivity, foregone wages, and amounts of compensable pain and suffering. The money value of a statistical life can be estimated in several ways, but is usually calculated with a formula based on wage premiums demanded by workers in high-risk occupations.

Advantages of Cost-Benefit Analysis

Cost-benefit analysis has several advantages. First, it forces methodical consideration of each economic impact a policy will have on society. It disciplines thinking, though it does not always result in clear choices. Cost-benefit studies show which alternative is optimal in terms of economic impacts, but they do not show which alternative is best in terms of non-economic criteria such as ethics or public acceptance.

A second advantage is that it can inject rational calculation into emotional arguments. Sometimes, passionate decisions are not the best ones to protect people and nature.

And, third, cost-benefit analysis that reveals marginal abatement costs can help regulators find the most efficient level of regulation. One reason that the bill for pollution control has ballooned is that, as a rule, control costs rise steeply when 100 percent cleanup is approached. Here is an example. The 1990 Clean Air Act Amendments required the EPA to set emissions standards for 189 toxic air pollutants to ensure an "ample margin of safety for public health." Soon the agency was in the middle of a conflict. Environmental groups argued that because airborne carcinogens may cause cancer even at low levels, only a standard that reduced emissions to near zero could guarantee public safety. The chemical industry, however, believed that such a standard would impose staggering control costs far exceeding benefits.

The Chemical Manufacturers Association provided illustrative data, used to construct Figure 15-4, that show an exponential rise in control costs as zero emissions is approached. In the figure, point B is the near-zero emission level advocated by environmentalists. In the past, the Office of Management and Budget has rejected or delayed air emission regulations costing over about $2,200 per ton removed—at about point C. The chemical industry argued that after point A, control costs increased exponentially, with negligible pollution reduction and probably unmeasurable health benefits. Adding roughly $800 to move from point C to point A and spending about $3,000 per ton of emissions removed would remove about 30 percent more. This might be the most cost-effective level of regulation.

In cases such as this, cost-benefit analysis can identify efficient regulatory goals to prevent skyrocketing costs that produce trivial benefits. It provides an artificial but a valuable test of efficient resource allocation for regulators not subject to a market mechanism.

FIGURE 15-4

*Exponential rise
of control costs
nearing 100
percent control.*

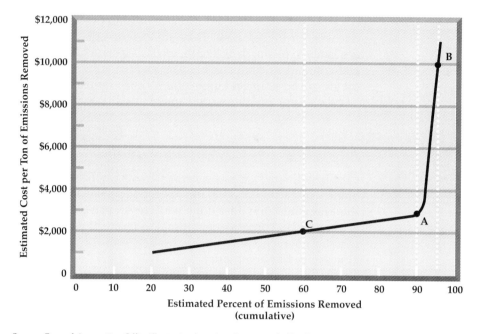

Source: General Accounting Office illustration based on data provided by the Chemical Manufacturers Association.

Criticisms of Cost-Benefit Analysis

As attractive a method as cost-benefit analysis is, it has critics.

First, fixing precise values of costs and benefits is difficult and controversial. Where benefits are measured in dollars, how can the value of a clear sky, fish in a stream, fragrant air, or extra years of life be priced? Their value is subjective. Assigning dollar amounts to untraded goods such as aesthetic beauty or human life invites discord. There are ways to do it, but they require making assumptions on which there is no consensus.

One method of measuring the monetary worth of natural features is *contingent valuation,* a polling process in which individuals are asked to put a dollar amount on nature. The EPA recently required that the gargantuan Navajo Generating Station cut sulfur dioxide emissions by 90 percent at a cost of $89.6 million yearly. The estimated ecological benefit of doing this is a 7 percent improvement of winter visibility in the Grand Canyon. Is this worth $89.6 million annually? Yes, said the EPA, extrapolating from a survey of the public in which it asked how much money households would be willing to pay each year for cleaner Grand Canyon air. The public was willing to pay from $1.30 to $2.50 per year per household, making the visibility improvement worth $90 to $200 million.[21]

---

[21]General Accounting Office, *Navajo Generating Station's Emissions Limit*, GAO/RCED-98-28, January 1998, Appendix III.

Methods of calculating the value of human life are controversial because they clash with public values of fairness and equity. If life value is based on wages earned over a lifetime, an objection is that the lives of workers in low-wage jobs are worth less than the lives of people in high-paying jobs. One critic notes that such calculations run "directly contrary to the egalitarian principle, with origins deep in the Judeo-Christian heritage, that all persons are equal before the law and God."[22] Because of such criticisms, EPA valuations of life are now based on earnings surveys that measure wage premiums paid in dangerous occupations. A problem with this approach, however, is that acceptance of these premiums may not be based on accurate risk assessments. Some critics of life valuation reject all approaches, arguing that the very process of pricing human life mocks its extraordinary, incomparable, and sacred greatness.

Related criticisms come from environmentalists who dislike cost-benefit approaches because they invite trade-off of environmental quality. To them, pristine nature has an intrinsic value transcending money. One critic writes that "there may be many instances where a certain decision might be right even though its benefits do not outweigh its costs" and points out that the Bill of Rights and the Emancipation Proclamation were not subject to cost-benefit study because the moral rights they claimed were absolute.[23] Such objections reject the primacy of efficiency as a decision criterion. For many, maximum efficiency is not the test of the good society. Although cost-benefit analysis seems objective and neutral, it embodies the utilitarian notion that moral rights may be balanced against utilitarian benefits to society.

Another general difficulty with cost-benefit analysis is that the benefits and costs of a program can accrue to separate parties. Purifying factory wastewater raises costs to the business and to consumers of its product. Yet benefits from cleaner water accrue to shoreline property owners, realtors, individuals with lower medical bills, and fish. In such cases, weighing diverse cost-benefit effects raises questions of justice.

In sum, there is truth in criticisms of cost-benefit analysis, but it may nonetheless facilitate more effective regulation. Pricing life evokes a callous image, but it is a hard reality that decisions about where to spend limited dollars on pollution abatement must be made. Zero-discharge standards protect public health and natural ecosystems, but only at an astronomical price. Society cannot afford the infinite expenditures necessary to reduce pollution to the no-risk level. Expenditures below this level suggest policies that compromise between preserving life and maintaining a high standard of living.

----

[22]Thomas O. McGarity, "Health Benefits Analysis for Air Pollution Control: An Overview," in John Blodgett, ed., *Health Benefits of Air Pollution Control: A Discussion,* Washington, D.C.: Library of Congress, Congressional Research Service, February 27, 1989, p. 55.

[23]Steven Kelman, "Cost-Benefit Analysis: An Ethical Critique," *Regulation,* January/February 1981, p. 31.

Options for Managing Environmental Risks

A wide range of options for reducing risks to health and the environment are open to legislators and regulators. The most important of these are the following.

Command-and-Control Regulation

One cause of high pollution-abatement costs is heavy reliance on command-and-control regulation. Most federal statutes ask regulators to set uniform standards across industries, apply rigid standards to individual pollution sources, specify cleanup technology, set strict timetables for action, issue permits, and enforce compliance, all with limited or no consideration of costs. There are advantages to command-and-control regulation. It enforces predictable and uniform standards. There is great equity in applying the same rules to all firms in an industry. The record proves that it produces abatements and it comforts the public to know that the EPA resembles an old-fashion schoolmarm, watching companies like a hawk, slapping wrists, and putting unregenerate polluters in the dunce's chair.

But this kind of regulation can be inefficient and increase costs without commensurate increases in benefits. It generates a large bureaucracy, becomes adversarial, and focuses on activity, not environmental quality. In 1999, for example, the EPA's "performance plan" required 15,000 inspections and 2,600 enforcement actions.[24]

Command-and-control regulation can be unnecessarily expensive when it is inflexible. One example is a study by the EPA and Amoco Corporation of how typical regulation worked at a single Amoco refinery. A key finding was that under the EPA's command-and-control regimen, cuts in air emissions averaged $2,100 per ton, but if the refinery were given more flexibility, 90 percent of reductions would cost only $500 per ton.[25] Because situations such as this are typical, there is great interest in other options for controlling pollution either through the use of market incentives or by making regulation flexible.

Market Incentive Regulation

Market incentives bring flexibility by giving companies financial motives to reduce pollution and then allowing market forces to decide where abatement expenditures are most efficient. There are many market-incentive approaches.

Taxes and fees can be imposed on polluting emissions or products. They are widely used in Europe. France and Germany, for example, tax the discharge of chemicals into water bodies and Sweden taxes air emissions of SO_2.[26] Pollution

---

[24]General Accounting Office, *Environmental Protection: EPA's and States' Efforts to Focus State Enforcement Programs on Results,* GAO/RCED-98-113, May 1998, p. 8.

[25]Caleb Solomon, "What Really Pollutes? Study of a Refinery Proves an Eye-Opener," *The Wall Street Journal,* March 29, 1993, p. A1.

[26]Frank Convery, "The Types and Roles of Market Mechanisms," in Diane Palframan and Andrew Tank, *Using Market Mechanisms in Environmental Regulation,* New York: The Conference Board, 1998, p. 12.

taxes can be effective. An Austrian tax on fertilizers and pesticides reduced their use by 30 percent within two years. But they are unpopular, and politicians hesitate to enact them. In the United States, pollution charges have been a minor control method. There are some examples; for instance, nineteen states charge fees for waste disposal ranging from $0.25 to $4.25 a ton, but, on the whole, taxes are little used.[27] However, the government has generously enacted corporate tax breaks with anti-environmental consequences. For example, corporations can deduct the costs of oil and chemical spills and Superfund cleanups.[28]

Emission trading programs (1) set an overall cap on emissions of a pollutant, (2) divide among companies the total amount of emissions by giving each permits to pollute specific amounts, and then (3) allow trading of these permits. The premier example of this is the sulfur emissions trading program among coal-burning utilities in the United States. National emissions have been capped. On an auction market, or with each other, utilities can now buy and sell permits to release one ton of sulfur. The current price for each permit is a little more than $100. Companies can stay under their limit by running one high-polluting plant and cleaning up another one so that average emissions fall under their share. Or they can buy permits on the open market. To reduce pollution, the EPA is retiring permits, in effect, lowering the nationwide cap and clearing the nation's skies.

Deposit-and-refund laws require consumers of products that degrade the environment to pay an extra charge at the time of purchase that gives them an incentive to recycle the products after use. Only ten states have laws providing redemption values for beverage containers.

There is growing interest in market incentives, but so far they play only a minor role in the United States and in other developed nations. Environmental groups usually oppose them, believing that when government creates a right to buy and sell wastes, it removes the immorality of polluting and turns it into a business transaction. "Suppose there were a $100 fine for throwing a beer can into the Grand Canyon, and a wealthy hiker decided to pay $100 for the convenience," writes one critic of incentives. "Would there be nothing wrong in his treating the fine as if it were simply an expensive dumping charge?"[29]

Flexible Regulation

Market incentive approaches get much attention but little implementation. Meanwhile, the EPA is experimenting with more flexible compliance approaches.

---

[27]Christopher Douglass, *Government's Hand in the Recycling Market: A New Decade,* St. Louis: Center for the Study of American Business, September 1998, p. 7.

[28]Gawain Kripke and Brian Dunkiel, "Taxing the Environment: Corporate Tax Breaks to Promote Environmental Destruction," *Multinational Monitor,* September 1998, p. 9.

[29]Michael J. Sandel, "It's Immoral to Buy the Right to Pollute," *New York Times,* December 15, 1997, p. A19.

Collaboration is illustrated by Project XL (Excellence and Leadership), begun in 1996. In Project XL, the EPA collaborates with a few companies, relaxing command-and-control regulation and allowing them to develop innovative, lower-cost methods of protecting the environment. Participating firms agree to reduce pollution beyond levels set by existing standards. At a Weyerhaeuser pulp mill in Georgia, for example, the EPA agreed to let managers choose the most cost-effective pollution control methods and lessened their paperwork burden by letting them report just once every two years. In return, Weyerhaeuser promised that over a ten-year period, it would achieve a list of specific goals exceeding what it would have done under traditional regulation. It also promised to report progress to the public twice yearly via the Internet.[30]

Project XL is one of several collaborative programs started by the EPA. Its Common Sense Initiative sets up committees of industry representatives and stakeholders to examine how environmental laws are applied and figure out more flexible and cost-effective approaches. Its One Stop Reporting Program is focused on reforming onerous reporting requirements and has a goal of reducing paperwork by 25 percent. Many states are also experimenting with more cooperative enforcement measures.[31]

The EPA has approximately forty *voluntary programs.* For example, WasteWi$e focuses on reducing trash, Green Lights encourages energy-saving lighting, Climate Wise facilitates CO_2 emissions cuts, and the WAVE program aims to reduce water use. When a company signs up for a voluntary program, there are often reporting requirements. The WAVE program, for example, requires firms to identify methods for reduced water use. But no enforcement actions are taken for failure to meet goals. Companies have many motives for participating. They get technical advice from the EPA, the agency freely hands out awards that have public relations value, and there can be cost savings.

Still another flexible approach is *information disclosure.* An example is the Toxic Release Inventory (TRI). The Emergency Planning and Community Right-to-Know Act in 1984 required polluters publicly to report on the amount of 643 dangerous chemicals that they released into the environment. Because of this reporting requirement, release of these chemicals declined by 43 percent over a decade.[32] Primarily, this is because companies regard emissions reductions as good public relations.

---

[30]Kelly H. Ferguson, "EPA Regulatory Reinvention Program Offers Flexibility for Weyco Flint River," *Pulp & Paper,* August 1998, p. 65. See also http://www.weyerhaeuser.com/news/012698.htm.

[31]General Accounting Office, *Environmental Management: An Integrated Approach Could Reduce Pollution and Increase Regulatory Efficiency,* GAO/RCED-96-41, pp. 11–12.

[32]"EPA Says Release of Toxic Chemicals Fell 46% since 1988," *The Wall Street Journal,* May 21, 1997, p. A16. TRI data can be found on the EPA's Web site at http://www.epa.gov/opptintr/tri/.

Managing Environmental Quality

In the 1970s, corporations passed over a great divide, leaving an era of freedom in which they were subject to few environmental constraints and passing into an era of strict rules and limits. At first, many managers saw new rules as cost burdens and took a grudging, reticent approach. Some companies resented regulators, hid problems, and resisted the laws. Most firms found regulation to be expensive, adversarial, and sometimes irrational, but they tried to comply. These two approaches, resistance and compliance, still predominate. Yet many companies have moved beyond compliance and operate in ways that better sustain the earth's resources. The reason is that many forces have gathered in the business environment that encourage improved environmental performance. These forces are briefly explained in Table 15-1.

Environmental Management

The most proactive companies establish *comprehensive environmental management systems.*[33] These systems are usually founded on formal statements of environmental policy. A document entitled "Global Environmental Policy" guides the worldwide Sony Group. It begins with a deceptively simple section titled "Philosophy" that reads in its entirety as follows: "Recognizing that environmental protection is one of the most pressing issues facing mankind today, Sony incorporates a sound respect for nature in all of its business activities."[34] This philosophy is followed by a set of ten specific guidelines; number six, for instance, is: "The Group will make products and develop technologies that minimize environmental impact." Sony implements this guideline by setting very specific targets. By the year 2000 Sony will cut power consumption in its consumer electronics by 50 percent from 1990 levels, reduce by 50 percent the ratio of waste volume to net sales, and cut by 25 percent the ratio of petroleum-equivalent energy consumption to net sales. Most proactive companies have a similar hierarchy of guidelines that flow from general statements about purpose and mission to specific goals and targets.

To support environmental policies, companies make many organizational changes. It is important for top executives to reinforce the importance of policies and to use widespread training and education of employees. To emphasize environmental affairs at DuPont, the chief executive officer also holds the title of chief environmental officer, but simultaneously the company has set a goal that "every employee be able to recognize an unsound environmental practice and correct it or call it to the attention of those who will."[35] At Allied Chemical,

---

[33]W. Gary Wilson and Dennis R. Sasseville, *Sustaining Environmental Management Success: Best Business Practices from Industry Leaders,* New York: John Wiley & Sons, 1999.

[34]Sony Group, *Global Environmental Policy,* at http://www.sony.co.jp/soj/CorporateInfo/EnvironmentalReport97/c2.html.

[35]General Accounting Office, *Environmental Auditing,* GAO/RCED-95-37, April 1995, p. 25.

TABLE 15-1   Incentives to Improve Environmental Performance

Customer demands	Consumers increasingly favor less-polluting, resource-conserving products.
Insurance premiums	Insurers lower premiums for companies when they face less risk of paying for pollution liability.
Disclosure requirements	Government agencies require public disclosure of a range of information about how the company affects the environment. For example, the Securities and Exchange Commission requires disclosure of potential environmental liabilities to investors in Form 10Ks.
International trade	Nations vary in their environmental requirements and sometimes have more stringent product standards than in the United States. In the Netherlands, for example, the government has stringent recycling standards. When AT&T sold telephone equipment to the government, it had to agree to take it back for recycling after 40 years of use.[1]
Industry codes	Many industry associations have created voluntary environmental management codes and systems. An example is the Chemical Manufacturers Association, which requires chemical firms to follow an environmental, health, and safety code as a condition of membership. It has almost 200 members. A growing number of trade associations now have similar codes and either require adherence for membership or offer to audit and certify companies as in compliance.
Regulatory relief	The EPA requires that companies benefitting from new flexible regulation initiatives have excellent past compliance records and show ability to exceed legal requirements in the future.
Legal liabilities	The legal system now has a tight grip on polluters. The EPA fines companies for violating laws. Criminal violations have sent many managers to prison. No company wants to incur future Superfund liability.
U.S. Sentencing Commission Guidelines	When criminal offenses occur, sentencing guidelines reduce penalties for companies and their managers if management controls to ensure compliance with emissions limits were in place.
Profit and cost reduction potential	Many companies find ways to convert former wastes into saleable products or raw material for production processes. Changing production processes to reduce emissions often lowers costs. And some studies show that firms with better environmental performance are more profitable.[2]
Certification to standards	In the last decade there have appeared a number of sets of standards requiring companies to install highly structured management systems that ensure environmental responsibility. Some of these are industrywide standards. For example, the Chemical Manufacturers Association developed a set of standards called Responsible Care that almost 200 chemical firms now follow. On an international level, the Eco-Management and Audit Scheme of the European Union requires continuous environmental performance improvement in companies. A set of standards named ISO-14001, developed by the International Standards Organization, sets up universal standards for managing environmental aspects of manufacturing. To get ISO-14001 certification, companies must go through a rigorous inspection and auditing process. Increasingly, companies and governments around the world are asking suppliers to prove that they have been certified under one or more of these standards. Big firms are going along with this. Matsushita Electric Industrial, for example, set a goal of having all 213 of its industrial plants around the world certified under ISO-14001 by 1999.

[1]Mark Sharfman, Rex T. Ellington, and Mark Meo, "The Next Step in Becoming 'Green': Life-Cycle Oriented Environmental Management," *Business Horizons*, May-June 1997, p. 14.

[2]See, for example, Michael V. Russo and Paul A. Fouts, "A Resource-Based Perspective on Corporate Environmental Performance and Profitability," *Academy of Management Journal*, June 1997.

a corporate environmental affairs department, headed by a vice president, helps Allied's operating units in complying with environmental laws. It sets up regular meetings with managers to probe for problems. A risk assessment committee reviews hazards posed by company products. One-third of some middle-managers' bonuses depend on meeting environmental objectives.

Many companies audit their environmental performance by undertaking systematic reviews of facilities and procedures and regular inspections of equipment. Objectives of these audits include verifying regulatory compliance, assessing risks from operations, evaluating emergency plans, pricing existing and potential legal liabilities, and measuring the performance of management systems. At Union Carbide, environmental audits are carried out by corporate staff that report to the board of directors. Managers who fail to follow up on audit recommendations can be fired, and audit data are used in managers' performance reviews.

Operational Changes

Companies with comprehensive environmental management systems work to change operations in ways that shrink the footprints they leave on the environment. They innovate to reduce pollution and conserve resources and often lower costs or earn revenues doing so. Innovations, by definition, are unique, but they fall mainly into three categories—pollution prevention, product analysis, and product differentiation.

Pollution Prevention

End-of-the pipe control technologies isolate or neutralize pollutants after they are generated by an industrial process. Pollution prevention, on the other hand, occurs when industrial processes themselves are modified to eliminate contaminants. Pollution is prevented because it is not generated. For example, many companies have stopped using solvents to clean production equipment, substituting soap or isopropyl alcohol in their place. This eliminates toxic air and water emissions tied to solvent use and often works just as well and at lower cost. There are many other examples. Olin Corporation discovered a chemical that lowered the surface tension of wastewater from chrome plating. This reduced evaporation and air emissions of solvents.[36]

Frequently, waste streams created by one industrial process can be used as material inputs for other processes. The concept of *industrial ecology* is that production facilities can be connected in a web of materials exchange. At Kalundborg, an industrial park in Denmark, a number of businesses feed off

---

[36]"Innovative Olin Corp. Pollution Prevention Projects Sharply Reduce Reportable Emissions," *Business Wire*, February 5, 1998.

each other in this way. One plant makes plasterboard using surplus gas from a refinery and gypsum from a coal-burning power plant. The power plant also sends excess steam to a pharmaceutical plant and warm water to a fish farm.

Minnesota Mining and Manufacturing (3M) Corporation is a longtime leader in pollution prevention. In 1975, it began a program called Pollution Prevention Pays, which required scrutiny of manufacturing methods to find waste reduction opportunities. By 1998, more than 4,500 projects had been carried out, preventing generation of 739,000 tons of pollution and saving $750 million in costs.[37]

Product Analysis

When companies look closely at products from an environmental standpoint, they find ways to make them more friendly to nature and conserving of resources. The first step is often an analysis of the product as it goes through its life cycle, beginning with production and moving through transportation, sale, consumer use, and disposal or recycling. Products can then be redesigned for easier disassembly and recycling, energy savings, and pollution reduction. Here are some examples.

When Xerox designed its 265 family of copiers, it wanted to make them more environmentally friendly through the product life cycle. The engineers went on trips to deserts, mountains, and a landfill to build an appreciation of nature. They came up with a design that reduced the number of parts from the 2,000 found in some of the company's copiers to 250. Instead of being welded or glued, most parts were screwed together, cutting down disassembly time. And 98 percent of the material in the copier could be recycled.[38]

Soon after SC Johnson Wax adopted an environmental management policy in 1990, a team examining the company's RAID insecticide felt that the product, which was based on a flammable solvent that evaporated volatile organic compounds, could not meet probable regulatory standards of the future. They reformulated RAID with a water-based solvent and cut its emissions in half. Distributors' costs were lowered because they no longer had to store a potentially explosive product. And the company estimated it had prevented 15 million pounds of volatile organic compound emissions annually.[39]

Product Differentiation

Some firms try to position their products to sell based on environmental benefits, but this is not a simple or sure-fire strategy. To succeed, the business must create a distinct product that competitors cannot easily match, successfully

---

[37]Joseph T. Ling, "Industrial Waste Management," *Vital Speeches of the Day,* February 15, 1998, p. 286. Dollar savings of projects are calculated for the first year only; the company does not count savings repeated annually.

[38]Gail Dutton, "The Green Bottom Line," *Management Review,* October 1998, p. 59.

[39]Livio D. DeSimone and Frank Popoff, *Eco-Efficiency: The Business Link to Sustainable Development,* Cambridge, Mass.: MIT Press, 1997, p. 187.

advertise the distinction, and target consumers who are attracted to environmental causes.[40] Patagonia, Inc., which sells high-quality outdoor clothing, developed a reputation for environmentally friendly manufacturing when it decided, largely because of its founder's unique philosophy, that it would operate in a more sustainable manner. It stopped using certain materials such as virgin polyester and began making thermal garments from recycled plastic bottles. For lighter clothing, it switched from commodity cotton to organic cotton. These material changes reduced negative environmental impacts, but they raised production costs markedly. Patagonia advertised to position its clothing as both high quality and environmentally friendly. Customers were willing to pay a premium, and Patagonia had rising sales.

The presence of slime, grasses, and barnacles on a vessel's hull creates drag. Overcoming this drag increases a ship's fuel consumption and raises engine emissions. To control infestations, the shipping industry relies on coatings containing biocides that kill marine organisms. For decades, the standard has been a tin-based poison called tri-butyltin oxide that does not degrade rapidly in water, indiscriminately kills a wide range of sea life, and builds up in the tissues of marine animals. In 1991, Rohm and Haas Co. marketed a less-toxic antifouling agent named Sea-Nine 211. Sea-Nine 211 breaks down rapidly, has a half-life of less than one hour in seawater, and does not accumulate in living tissues or bottom sediment. Tests show that while tin-based antifoulants produce concentrations of up to 0.63 ppb in seawater near hulls, Sea-Nine 211 produces only 0.001 to 0.01 ppb.[41] Since this more benign antifoulant went on the market, both Japan and the United States restricted use of tin-based hull coatings, so most manufacturers of marine paints introduced products containing Sea-Nine 211. Rohm and Haas has built a new $40 million plant to meet demand.

Concluding Observations

A nation that spends $160 billion per year on pollution abatement must try to spend that money wisely. In this chapter, we discussed structured methods that focus regulation on the greatest risks to human health and human habitats. In addition, we explained that regulation is beginning to evolve from a strict command-and-control approach to a more flexible, innovative approach. Finally, we enumerated forces in the business environment that create incentives to build a more environmentally protective, sustainable perspective in industry. The reality, however, is that regulation remains largely inflexible and while corporations are becoming more environmentally proactive, most do not yet see this as a competitive advantage.[42]

---

[40]Forest L. Reinhardt, "Environmental Product Differentiation: Implications for Corporate Strategy," *California Management Review,* Summer 1998.

[41]"Protecting Ships without Fouling the Environment," *Chemical Engineering,* November 1997, p. EC-60.

[42]Warren B. Brown and Necmi Karagozoglu, "Current Practices in Environmental Management," *Business Horizons,* July–August 1998, p. 17.

ASBESTOS LAWSUITS "BANKRUPT" JOHNS MANVILLE CORPORATION

J ohns Manville Corporation was the world's largest asbestos producer until the 1970s, when fear of asbestos-caused disease wilted demand. Then, injured workers sued the company and drove it into bankruptcy. This is the story of Johns Manville and also of the toxic material that was its livelihood. Now out of bankruptcy, it no longer mines or sells any asbestos. Under the umbrella of a court-ordered immunity from asbestos-injury lawsuits, it has reinvented itself, increased sales, and returned to profitability. But it leaves a turbulent wake. Workers with incurable illnesses from exposure to Johns Manville asbestos as long as fifty years ago still struggle to be compensated. And federal regulators have tried but failed to ban asbestos.

Asbestos

Asbestos is the generic term for a family of six fibrous minerals named chrysotile, crocidolite, amosite, anthophyllite, tremolite, and actinolite. The type of asbestos that has been used most widely is chrysotile (KRIS-ah-till); among the others, only amosite (AM-ah-site) and crocidolite (crow-SID-alight) have been used commercially and only in small amounts.[1] Today, chrysotile is the most widely used type of asbestos around the world and constitutes 99 percent of the U.S. market (the other 1 percent is crocidolite).

Underground formations containing asbestos are mined; then the ore is put through a manufacturing process. Rocks are crushed to free tiny asbestos fibers and a blowing process separates them from debris. The fibers are then combined with other materials to make commercial products. For instance, fibers longer than 1 centimeter (about 4/10 inch) can be spun with cotton into yarn for

---

[1]All types of asbestos are inorganic chemical compounds; chrysotile, for example, is composed of magnesium, silicon, oxygen, and hydrogen ($3MgO \cdot 2SiO_2 \cdot 2H_2O$).

fireproof clothing. Shorter lengths can be matted together with wool in a process involving heat and moisture to create felt insulation for boiler pipes. Asbestos easily combines with other materials, has phenomenal strength, does not burn, and resists heat conduction. It is an ideal insulating and fireproofing material.

Over the years, asbestos has brought many benefits to society. Lives have been saved as a result of its fireproofing quality. In brake linings, it has increased motor vehicle safety. And its use in paint, roofing, and insulation has added comfort to living. Today asbestos use is declining. At its high point in 1980, world asbestos production was almost five million tons a year, but has dropped to less than half that and continues to fall.[2] The United States uses less than 1 percent of world asbestos production. Manufacturers have changed products to replace it with other materials.

Workers are exposed to asbestos when they inhale fibers the size of tiny motes of dust. Even the largest chrysotile fibers have a diameter only one-twenty-fifth that of a human hair. They are sharp and tough and, once inhaled, they embed themselves in the lungs. Heavy exposures cause progressive, irreversible scarring of lung tissue, which leads to shortness of breath and an irreversible pulmonary fibrosis called asbestosis. The fibers also irritate bronchial cells and initiate cellular changes that lead to bronchial carcinoma. A rare and fatal cancer of the chest lining called malignant mesothelioma is strongly associated with asbestos exposure and is thought to be caused by fibers that penetrate through lung tissue into a membrane on the chest wall.

Even with heavy or prolonged exposure, these conditions usually take at least ten years to appear. Latency periods for lung cancer and mesothelioma are as long as forty years. Current standards control workplace exposures so that asbestos factories today, if properly managed, are not very dangerous. But exposures that occurred years ago continue to make people sick.

Recently it has been learned that chrysotile is less dangerous than other kinds of asbestos. This is because within weeks to months after inhalation, the lungs expel chrysotile fibers. Amosite and crocidolite fibers, on the other hand, remain embedded for many years. World War II shipyard workers used both chrysotile and amosite. Even though the bulk of their exposure was to chrysotile, when they are examined today their lungs show high amosite counts, but chrysotile counts are no higher than in the general population.[3] Chrysotile fibers, because of a curled shape, do not penetrate as deeply into the lungs and, because of their chemical composition, break up more easily than amosite. Nevertheless, heavy and prolonged exposures to chrysotile dust are injurious and are responsible for most asbestos illness.

Rarely do workers survive to old age unimpaired after working for any length of time in high-fiber concentrations. Asbestos illness is even found

---

[2]Bureau of the Census, *Statistical Abstract of the United States,* 117th ed., Washington, D.C.: Government Printing Office, October 1997, table 1158.

[3]Andrew Churg, "Deposition and Clearance of Chrysotile Asbestos," *The Annals of Occupational Hygiene,* August 1994, p. 626.

An old photograph showing spray application of LIMPET asbestos, a product of the Keasbey and Mattison Company. The two unprotected workmen at right are feeding lumps of asbestos into mixing machines.

Source: David E. Lilienfeld, "The Silence: The Asbestos Industry and Early Occupational Cancer Research—A Case Study." *American Journal of Public Health* 81, no. 6, June 1991, p. 796.

among family members of asbestos workers whose only exposure is the dust that came into the home on the breadwinner's clothes at the end of the day.[4] Years ago, in asbestos towns, where sons followed fathers into dusty plants, the ranks of families were decimated. Because of widespread use, the general population in developed countries has been exposed to asbestos. Autopsy results show that most people have less than fifty asbestos fibers per gram of dry lung, but individuals heavily exposed to asbestos may have more than four million fibers per gram of dry lung.[5]

The Asbestos Giant

The Johns Manville Corporation was created in the merger of two roofing and insulating companies in 1901.[6] Over the years, the company grew until, in the

[4]Henry A. Anderson et al., "Asbestosis among Household Contacts of Asbestos Factory Workers," in Irving J. Selikoff and E. Cuyler Hammond, eds., *Health Hazards of Asbestos Exposure*, New York: New York Academy of Sciences, 1979, p. 387.

[5]Hiroyuki Yamada et al., "Talc and Amosite/Crocidolite Preferentially Deposited in the Lungs of Nonoccupational Female Lung Cancer Cases in Urban Areas of Japan," *Environmental Health Perspectives*, May 1997, pp. 505–6; Andrew Churg et al., Correspondence, *New England Journal of Medicine,* October 1, 1998, p. 999.

[6]The company has had the following names: H. W. Johns-Manville Company (1901), Johns-Manville Corporation (1926), Manville Corporation (1981), Schuller Corporation (1996), and Johns Manville Corporation (1997).

early 1960s, it dominated the industry, having thirty-three plants and mines and turning out 500 asbestos-bearing products. Johns Manville was extremely profitable and, because of this, is thought to have had a somewhat complacent culture in which loyalty and unquestioned acceptance of the system were rewarded. Despite profitability, there was heavy pressure on asbestos plants to make quarterly and yearly performance numbers.

It was known to Johns Manville workers and managers that asbestos dust caused serious illness. As early as the 1940s, the company installed advanced dust collection and filtration machinery to protect workers. But, in many plants where profit pressure existed, operation of this equipment was considered a cost unrelated to productivity, and so repair and maintenance were deferred.

Bill Sells, a Johns Manville manager in the 1960s, told of acquiring a new vocabulary after taking over the Waukegan, Illinois, plant. A worker who had serious asbestosis was "dusted." When the company physician took X-rays and discovered workers with pathological lung changes, these "red cases" had to be assigned to lower exposure areas. Sells installed better ventilation systems and saw improvement in companywide practice, but it came too late. "During the 1970s and 1980s," he writes, "I had to say good-bye to every member of my Waukegan administrative staff. They had become my friends, and now, one by one, they contracted mesothelioma and died."[7]

Sells blames the failure to protect workers on a corporate culture that reinforced an attitude of denial. Managers believed that asbestos was a terrific product and that the company was doing what it could to reduce exposure. In fact, Johns Manville had set an exposure limit of 6 fibers per cubic centimeter (f/cm^3) in its plants, half the standard of 12 f/cm^3 recommended in the 1960s by an industry trade association and well below the probable 100 f/cm^3 exposures that occurred years before in uncontrolled plants. This was commendable, but the company went no further. It did not, for example, aggressively fund research to confirm the safety of any exposure level. Today, the standard set as safe by the Occupational Safety and Health Administration is 0.1 f/cm^3, only 2 percent of Johns Manville's standard in the 1960s.

Asbestos Litigation Swamps Johns Manville

Johns Manville's culture of denial got a rude shock in the 1970s when juries began to give injured workers large awards. These large awards arose because of two important changes in the law. First, workers were permitted by courts to bring tort actions, or lawsuits alleging wrongful acts, against asbestos makers. Previously, workers could only make these allegations through state worker-compensation claims and they received little money. Second, there were major changes in products liability law, or the body of common law that

---

[7]Bill Sells, "What Asbestos Taught Me about Managing Risk," *Harvard Business Review*, March–April 1994, p. 82.

requires manufacturers such as Johns Manville to compensate persons who are injured by their products.

Prior to the 1960s, manufacturer liability was based on the idea of *negligent conduct.* For an injured person to win in court, a manufacturer had to be proven negligent, that is, shown to have acted without reasonable care in making a product. But by the time asbestos cases arose, products liability law had begun to incorporate a theory of *strict liability,* under which manufacturers could be found legally responsible for injuring consumers even if they had not been negligent.[8] The rise of strict liability made it increasingly difficult for Johns Manville to win in court. A landmark defeat for the company came in the *Beshada* case in 1982, when a court accepted the argument that it could be held liable for asbestos injury even without the plaintiff proving that its management knew asbestos was dangerous.[9] This decision turned the tide of litigation against Johns Manville.

In other cases attorneys were able to prove that the firm's executives engaged in a conspiracy to hide the dangers of asbestos. They learned that in the 1920s Raybestos-Manhattan, a brake-lining manufacturer, had requested that Metropolitan Life Insurance Co. undertake health surveys of its workers. Metropolitan reported in 1931 that there was a high incidence of asbestosis among Raybestos-Manhattan workers and issued a strong warning about asbestos illness. The report was discussed at a meeting between top officials of Johns Manville and Raybestos-Manhattan, and those present agreed to keep the information secret to avoid lawsuits. The minutes of this meeting were locked in a vault at Raybestos-Manhattan until the executive keeping them died; then they were given to the man's relatives, who kept them in storage for many years. When asbestos litigation became news, an attorney for asbestos victims was given minutes of this secret meeting by a relative of the deceased executive. The discovery of conspiracy made it possible for Johns Manville to convince juries that its managers had been ignorant of asbestos dangers until the 1960s. Juries began returning record punitive damages when they heard about the secret meeting.

Another breakthrough was the testimony of Dr. Kenneth W. Smith, a former company doctor at a Johns Manville plant in Canada. Smith stated that in 1949 he became concerned about sick employees and sent a report to management showing that out of 708 workers he had X-rayed, only four had normal, healthy lungs. He also said that he had withheld his diagnoses from workers to avoid upsetting them and lowering their productivity. Dr. Smith documented the fact that top company officers—including a future Johns Manville president—had seen his report but did not act on it.

---

[8]See American Law Institute, *Restatement of the Law of Torts, 2d,* Washington D. C.: American Law Institute Publishers, vol. 2, section 402A, 1965, pp. 347–48. Section 402A imposes liability for damages on anyone who sells a product in defective condition unreasonably dangerous to the consumer where the product reaches the consumer without substantial change and causes the consumer injury even though the seller has exercised all possible care in the manufacture and distribution of the product.

[9]*Beshada* v. *Johns-Manville Products Corp.*, 90 N.J. 191, 447 A.2d 539 (1982).

The growth curve in the number of cases against Johns Manville was rapid. The first came in 1968, and by 1973 there were only thirteen; but by 1980 there were 5,000 and by 1982 there were 16,500. Most of the plaintiffs were not Johns Manville employees; rather, they were or had been employed at shipyards, factories, and construction companies using the company's products.

Ultimately, the beleaguered firm could no longer hold back the deluge. Lawsuits were being settled for an average $40,000 a claim; 500 new ones arose each month; and an independent study projected another 36,000 future claims for a total liability by the year 2000 of at least $2 billion and probably much more. In addition, five large claims early in 1982 averaged punitive damage awards of $616,000 each—an unsettling augury. Punitive damages are awarded in excess of due compensation for injury to punish a corporation for flagrant misbehavior.

On August 26, 1982, Johns Manville filed a voluntary petition to reorganize under Chapter 11 of the Bankruptcy Reform Act of 1978.[10] Chapter 11 allows companies that might become bankrupt to restructure their debts before becoming insolvent.

The Bankruptcy Period

In a newspaper advertisement the day after Johns Manville's bankruptcy filing, its chief executive, John A. McKinney, wrote:

> To avoid Chapter 11, we would have had to strangle the Company slowly, by deferring maintenance and postponing capital expenditures. We would also have had to cannibalize our good business just to keep going. If recent trends had continued we would have had to mortgage our plants and properties and new credit would be most difficult and expensive to obtain. This is no way to go forward.

However, the Chapter 11 filing was controversial. An impressionable *Fortune* magazine writer called it "a particularly daring example of the new uses of bankruptcy,"[11] and a Harvard law professor admired it as "pretty creative,"[12] but others were less charitable. A former asbestos worker accused the firm of "cold-hearted profit motives" and "murder." Senator Robert Dole (R-Kan.) said it was "dubious and unusual at best."[13]

After filing for Chapter 11, Johns Manville continued normal business operations but was protected from creditors. Payments to suppliers, banks, and victorious plaintiffs stopped. Lawsuits were frozen. This extraordinary sequestering of the company's assets would last until it negotiated with its creditors a reorganization agreement, or a plan to pay its debts, and had the plan approved by a bankruptcy court.

---

[10]11 U.S.C. Sec. 1101 et seq.

[11]Anna Cifelli, "Management in Bankruptcy," *Fortune,* October 31, 1983, p. 18.

[12]Quoted in Clemens P. Work, "Bankruptcy: An Escape Hatch for Ailing Firms," *U.S. News & World Report,* August 22, 1983, p. 66.

[13]Quoted in Ben Sherwood, "Probe of Bankruptcy Laws Pledged in Manville Case," *Los Angeles Times,* August 28, 1982.

Six years passed while Johns Manville, attorneys of asbestos victims, and creditors negotiated such a plan. During this time, more than 2,000 asbestos claimants died, their lawsuits stalled by bickering in bankruptcy proceedings. A letter from a physician underscored this tragic aspect of the Chapter 11 gambit.

> Death and disease are not held in abeyance for legal writs. The victims are barred from applying for the financial help needed to ease their difficulties. Men are dying of mesothelioma or lung cancer, unable to seek medical care to ease their last days, and others are not able to afford the medical surveillance that could save their lives. Still others, short of breath, with asbestos lung scarring and no longer able to make a living, can't keep their families together.
>
> It is hard to appreciate the terror of a woman whose husband has been sent home from a hospital with a tracheostomy tube in his throat, unable to afford a nurse, resuscitating him at each emergency, until the final episode. Or widows—of shipyard workers, steam-locomotive repairmen, construction workers, power and utility plant personnel, and other craftsmen—having used slowly accumulated retirement dollars for the illness brought on by asbestos.
>
> Some have written me that they come close to begging in the streets. Others get along by visiting the children in rotation. Often, when I write a widow for scientific information, the reply comes from a trailer park: the house sold. After a lifetime of hard work, to die and to have his widow live in penury is a bitter final reward for a worker.[14]

The Reorganization Plan

In November 1988, Johns Manville emerged from Chapter 11 with an approved reorganization plan.[15] The plan required Johns Manville to give $2.5 billion to a trust fund that would be run independently of the company, and from which payments to all present and future victims of the company's asbestos would be made. To put money in the fund, Johns Manville gave the trust 80 percent of its common stock. This was accomplished with a one-for-eight reverse split of common shares. If, for example, you had held 800 shares of Johns Manville before the split, you owned only 100 afterwards. The other 700 went to the trust to pay asbestos victims. Thus, common shareholders—including many former asbestos-plant employees—were the biggest financial losers under the reorganization plan. Ironically, Johns Manville's victims became its new owners because the trust, with a majority of common shares, had effective control of the company.

---

[14]Dr. Irving Selikoff, letter written to the *New York Times* in 1985, reprinted in Paul Brodeur, *Outrageous Misconduct: The Asbestos Industry on Trial,* New York: Pantheon Books, 1985, pp. 302–3.

[15]This complex plan, briefly summarized here, is set forth in a 554-page document filed with the U. S. Bankruptcy Court, Southern District of New York, *In re Johns-Manville Corporation et al., Second Amended Disclosure Statement, Second Amended and Restated Plan of Reorganization, and Related Documents,* December 9, 1988.

A second and much smaller $240 million fund was set up to pay lawsuits by owners of buildings containing asbestos. And a small $5 million charitable fund was started for deserving asbestos victims who technically did not qualify for any money from the trust.

There was more to the reorganization plan. Johns Manville had to pay 20 percent of its adjusted net earnings (a measure of profit) into the trust beginning in 1992 and for as long as needed to pay all injury claims. The plan gave current and former Johns Manville executives permanent immunity from asbestos lawsuits. Sick workers who had waited six years to resolve their cases now could only apply to the trust for compensation. Under the trust fund system, Johns Manville's payout to asbestos victims was limited and far lower than it would have been had the pre-Chapter 11 lawsuits gone forward. This was the key to the company's survival. The trust would pay limited amounts to people with asbestos illness; there would be no more crushing punitive damage awards.

As part of the reorganization, the top-management team that had led the firm into bankruptcy was forced out. The new CEO, W. Thomas Stephens, argued that the arrangements in the reorganization plan were fair and noted that most of the managers who had made mistakes in years past were now dead. "I get a little hot under the collar when people say that [Johns] Manville entered Chapter 11 to evade its legal responsibilities," he said. "Giving up $2.5 billion, 20 percent of your profits and 80 percent of your stock is not exactly walking away from the right solution."[16]

The Rebirth of Johns Manville

During its six years in Chapter 11, Johns Manville ended all asbestos operations. On emerging from bankruptcy, it no longer sold any asbestos-bearing products, but it had other problems. Its reputation had suffered. Eventually, it tried to escape the asbestos stigma with a short-lived name change to Schuller Corporation in 1996. But because the Johns Manville brand name was so well established, a new CEO reversed this decision a year later.

A more important problem faced by Johns Manville was making its common shares attractive to investors once again. The company badly needed additional equity and the trust fund, which owned 80 percent of the shares, would have more money to pay victims if share prices rose. Although Johns Manville showed annual profits throughout the bankruptcy years (with the exception of three years when extraordinary charges related to reorganization occurred) and remained profitable, investors were scared away by its future obligation to pay 20 percent of its profits to the trust. To make the stock more attractive to wary investors, Johns Manville and the trust negotiated an agreement in 1996 in

---

[16]George Melloan, "A Company Held Captive by the Plaintiff Bar," *The Wall Street Journal,* October 4, 1988.

which the company gave the trust an additional 32.5 million shares and, in return, the annual profit payment to the trust was eliminated. This removed some uncertainty from the shares and they spiked upwards in price, although they have since slipped back again.

In 1997, Johns Manville had $1.65 billion in sales and earned a record $131 million in profits.[17] It had 8,300 employees and 50 plants in the United States, Europe, and China. It is organized into three business lines—insulation, roofing, and engineered products (mats, fibers, and filters). These are mature products in highly competitive, cyclical industry segments. Demand for them depends heavily on levels of activity in the construction industry. To increase the value of the company and its share price, Johns Manville has adopted the dual strategy of acquiring new businesses and of emphasizing cost-cutting.

The Trust Is Underfunded

While the company prospers, the Manville Personal Injury Settlement Trust struggles. There are more sick workers than anticipated and there is too little money to settle their claims.

The goal of the trust is to pay adequate and fair compensation to all asbestos victims, both present and future. When it was created in 1988, it was thought that there would be a maximum of 100,000 asbestos-injury claims and that they would be settled for an average of $25,000 each. But both claims and settlements swelled far beyond expectations. By 1990, the trust had settled 23,867 claims at an average $43,231 each and an additional 157,000 claims existed. More were predicted. Based on these numbers, the trust could not pay existing claims, let alone future ones.[18]

When this shortfall became apparent, a federal judge ordered the trust to suspend payments until revised payout guidelines could be set up. It took 4½ years of legal wrangling before the trust resumed operation. During this time, it was estimated that its total future assets to 2049, when asbestos injury claims are expected to fall off, would be $3 billion. But the trust would receive about 520,000 claims, creating total liabilities of $30 billion, or ten times more than assets.[19]

The solution to this deep insolvency was to pay only 10 percent of the value of all current and future claims. This was approved by court order early in 1995 and the trust resumed settlements.[20] It has been paying injured asbestos workers just 10 percent of what they were to have received. And lawyers representing the victims receive 25 percent of their awards

---

[17]More information about the company is available on its Web site at http://www.jm.com.

[18]*Ocsek* v. *Manville Corp. Asbestos Compensation Fund*, 956 F.2d 152 (7th Cir. 1992) at 154.

[19]Manville Personal Injury Settlement Trust, *Highlights of the Trust Distribution Process*, March 7, 1995, pp. 19-20.

[20]*In re Johns-Manville Corporation*, 878 F.Supp. 473 (E. & S. D.N.Y. 1995).

In 1994, the Manville Personal Injury Settlement Trust set up seven claim categories.

The first three categories enumerate clinical stages of progressive lung damage commonly known as asbestosis. The first stage is asymptomatic. The be eligible for payment, injured workers in each category must prove (1) exposure to a Johns Manville asbestos product. (2) exposure sufficiently heavy to cause symptoms, (3) a latency period of at least ten years between exposure and diagnosis, and (4) a physician's diagnosis documented by medical tests and records.

Initially, the trust intended to make settlements for the full amount stipulated in each catefory. But current rules permit the trust to pay only 10 percent of the fixed dollar value in each category to all present and future claimants.

Category	Scheduled Disease	Scheduled Value
1	Bilateral Pleural Disease	$12,000
2	Nondisabling Bilateral Interstitial Lung Disease	$25,000
3	Disabling Bilateral Interstitial Lung Disease	$50,000
4	Other Cancer (Colorectal; Laryngeal; Esophageal; or Pharyngeal)	$40,000
5	Lung Cancer (One)	$60,000
6	Lung Cancer (Two)*	$90,000
7	Malignant Mesothelioma	$200,000

*Category 6 claimants must establish that they are nonsmokers.

plus expenses. So, for example, a former shipyard worker with disabling asbestosis will receive $5,000 instead of $50,000 and may owe a lawyer $1,250 or more; a construction worker with mesothelioma will receive $20,000 instead of $200,000 and may owe a lawyer $5,000 or more.

The court judged this fair on the grounds that all present and future claimants would be equally paid. But victims feel anger and disappointment. By 1998, the trust had paid about $1.7 billion to claimants and had total assets of $2.9 billion. It has received 381,000 claims so far and handles them on a first-in, first-out basis.[21] In an effort to diversify its assets, it has sold several million shares of Johns Manville but still owns 79 percent of the company's shares. It is also suing tobacco companies, because among workers exposed to asbestos those who smoked are more likely to be ill.[22] The trust operates independently of Johns Manville and has four representatives sitting on the company's board of directors.

---

[21]Details about claim processing and finances may be found on the trust's Web site at http://www.mantrust.org.

[22]Frances A. McMorris, "Manville Trust, H. K. Porter Sue Makers of Tobacco to Recoup Asbestos Claims," *The Wall Street Journal,* January 2, 1998, p. A13.

Regulating Exposure to Asbestos Now

In 1989, the Environmental Protection Agency issued a rule to ban all production and sale of asbestos products by 1996.[23] It estimated that the ban would save between 148 and 202 lives over a thirteen-year period at a cost of $450 million to $800 million. This ban was challenged by companies that still use asbestos and was struck down by a federal appeals court two years later.[24] The court held that the astronomical costs of the asbestos ban were unreasonable compared to its small benefits.

For example, the EPA estimated that three lives would be saved over thirteen years by banning asbestos pipe at a cost of $128 to $227 million or $43 to $76 million per life saved. In calling this cost unreasonable, the judge noted that the EPA was asking the nation to spend as much as a quarter of a billion dollars to save fewer lives than would be lost by swallowing toothpicks.[25] The EPA never appealed this decision and has not tried again to ban asbestos. Thus, some asbestos products are still made and used in the United States as in other countries (though none by Johns Manville).

Recent research firmly establishes the danger of high-level asbestos exposure, but also indicates that low-level exposures may not be harmful. Dose-response curves in epidemiological studies of workers in several industries are shallow for all varieties of commercial asbestos, meaning that the incidence of asbestosis and lung cancer rises very slowly as exposures increase and that only heavy exposures over extended periods cause disease. There is growing agreement that a threshold model for lung cancer and mesothelioma is appropriate because no increase in mortality is observed at low exposure levels.[26]

Many buildings still contain asbestos, exposing maintenance and office workers to airborne fibers. These exposures are mostly to short-fibered chrysotile and are not believed to be a significant health risk. One estimate is that they pose an annual death risk of one in ten billion, a risk twenty times less than that of dying from a bee sting.[27] Unfortunately, many work sites where asbestos is torn from buildings are poorly managed and heavy exposure to asbestos has occurred in an unknown but significant number of removal workers. Because of this, a wave of new asbestos illness claims on the trust is expected over the next ten to thirty years. These exposures have led the

---

[23]54 FR 29460 (1989).

[24]*Corrosion Proof Fittings* v. *EPA,* 947 F.2d 1201 (5th Cir. 1991).

[25]Judge Jerry E. Smith cited L. Budnick, "Toothpick-Related Injuries in the United States, 1979 through 1982," *Journal of the American Medical Association,* August 10, 1984, p. 796, a study that showed an average of one toothpick death annually.

[26]See Hans Weill, "Biological Effects: Asbestos-Cement Manufacturing," *The Annals of Occupational Hygiene,* August 1994; and Michel Camus et al., "Nonoccupational Exposure to Chrysotile Asbestos and the Risk of Lung Cancer," *New England Journal of Medicine,* May 28, 1998.

[27]Janet M. Hughes, "Human Evidence: Lung Cancer Mortality Risk from Chrysotile Exposure," *The Annals of Occupational Hygiene,* August 1994, p. 557.

EPA to rescind asbestos removal requirements and recommend that asbestos materials be left in place and sealed where possible.

Questions

1. Did Johns Manville make responsible use of bankruptcy law? What were the advantages and disadvantages of the Chapter 11 filing? What were the advantages and disadvantages of the reorganization plan?

2. Was the reorganization plan fair to asbestos victims, shareholders, and employees? In principle, which method was better for compensating injured asbestos workers: large court awards and settlements or the trust fund set up during reorganization?

3. Was Johns Manville adequately punished for its actions? Should it have been permitted to reorganize and resume normal operations?

4. Pretend for a minute that you develop a serious asbestos disease many years from now. After investigating, you learn that you cannot sue Johns Manville because of a settlement in a bankruptcy case to which you were not a party, a case that enriched lawyers supposedly representing you, a future asbestos victim. Then you learn that the Manville Personal Injury Settlement Trust will provide only trivial compensation for your high medical bills. Have you been fairly treated? Would you favor lifting the injunction that prevents asbestos lawsuits against Johns Manville?

5. Is there a better solution for compensating asbestos victims than the current trust fund arrangement? Are current asbestos victims, who receive only 10 percent of planned settlement amounts, being fairly treated?

6. Should the Environmental Protection Agency do more to regulate asbestos now?

Business and the Consumer

16

Consumerism

Samuel Moore Walton opened a new variety merchandise store in Rogers, Arkansas, on July 2, 1962. A sign across the front said WAL-MART. On one side of the sign was "We Sell For Less." On the other was "Satisfaction Guaranteed." These two cornerstone philosophies still guide the company. Overall, there was and still is complete dedication to the consumer.

This new store began a revolution in retailing as great as that started by J.C. Penney, F.W. Woolworth, and Sears & Roebuck at the beginning of the century. Wal-Mart's sales were about $1 million the first year, compared with $2 million for another variety store in the town. But the underlying philosophies and managerial strategies developed by Sam Walton led to fabulous growth.

In his autobiography Sam Walton succinctly stated the core philosophy of his company:

. . . the secret of successful retailing is to give our customers what they want . . . if you think about it from your point of view as a customer, you want everything: a wide assortment of good quality merchandise; the lowest possible prices; guaranteed satisfaction with what you buy; friendly, knowledgeable service, convenient hours; free parking; a pleasant shopping experience. You love it when you visit a store that somehow exceeds your expectations, and you hate it when a store inconveniences you, or gives you a hard time, or just pretends you're invisible.[1]

By 1997, total sales were $119 billion and net profits were $3.5 billion. The company was the largest private employer in the United States with

---

[1] Sam Walton with John Huey, *Sam Walton: Made in America*, New York: Doubleday, 1992, p. 173.

875,000 workers. It had 3,400 outlets on four continents.

Throughout the development of Wal-Mart, Walton constantly traveled to visit his stores. From the beginning he flew his own airplane so he could more easily visit stores and spot new locations.

He said that because everyone worked hard, there was no reason for them not to have fun, do silly things, and be cheerful. It is a sort of "whistle while you work" philosophy, he said. He and his employees (he called them "associates") did crazy things to attract the attention of customers. In 1984, for example, he promised to do the hula down Wall Street if the profits of the company rose above 8 percent. They rose 8.04 percent and he fulfilled his promise.

Walton believed that everyone should share in profits, and in 1971 set up a profit-sharing plan for all associates. While he believed that profit sharing was important, he realized that much more was needed to motivate people. One of his rules was to think constantly, each day, of ways and means to motivate and challenge his associates. He believed that it was important to communicate with them everything that was important, including most of the numbers about the business. He listened to them because he said they were on the firing line and had much to contribute to making the company a success. He constantly sought to have everyone think small, to avoid creating a huge bureaucracy, to ignore conventional wisdom, to remember always that the associates were small-town merchants and that the company was built store by store. Above all, he wanted everyone to strive to exceed the expectations of the customers.

For years before his death on April 5, 1992, Sam Walton was hailed as a genius, a hero, the epitome of entrepreneurship, who brought good merchandise at low prices to locations neglected by large discounters. President Bush awarded him the nation's highest civil tribute, the Medal of Freedom, for his accomplishments. But he was not universally loved.

James McConkey was forced to close his hardware store in Albany, Missouri, population 2,100. On Christmas eve 1985, he looked at his stock of brand-new bicycles and the appliances filling his shelves. His store and downtown Albany were festooned in Christmas decorations. All was festive except for one thing: there were no customers. They all were at a Wal-Mart store in Maryville, population 9,500, and 34 miles west of Albany.[2]

This is a typical experience for merchants in small towns located near Wal-Mart stores. The only way they can compete is to find a niche not served by Wal-Mart and exploit it. That, however, is very difficult for the typical small-town merchant. Wal-Mart not only has changed the façade of commercial areas in small towns, but in the process has ended a way of life in the towns.

Observers maintain that Wal-Mart cannot be blamed as the sole force diminishing small-town business. Many other factors have been at work and Wal-Mart has merely speeded a process that began in the 1950s.

---

[2]Hugh Sidey, "Stack It Deep, Sell It Cheap, Stack It High and Watch It Fly!" *Time,* April 20, 1992.

Wal-Mart has encountered similar love-hate problems in its efforts to expand abroad. In Seoul, South Korea, for instance, the company was seen "as a fearsome foreign invader that is disrupting a retail landscape long dominated by a small group of powerful conglomerates and a huge network of mom-and-pop stores."[3] However, as in America, the consumers were voting with Wal-Mart by clearing the shelves quickly of merchandise.

Following Sam Walton's death, the culture of Wal-Mart began to fray. The stock of the company fell from a high of $34 per share in 1993 to $19.1 in 1996. This led management to undertake measures to raise stock price that, in addition to other factors, led to employee discontent. Wages were held low. According to Bob Ortega, a *Wall Street Journal* reporter, in 1997 the average hourly wage of a Wal-Mart worker, including benefits, was $10 compared with $44 for a General Motors' employee. The pension plan was based on how well the stock was doing, and, with the drop in stock price, its assets fell substantially. Workers who tried to unionize were

fired. Women who complained of sexual harassment by their supervisors were fired or rebuffed. Employees complained the company was more interested in profits than their concerns. The company also was the subject of adverse publicity for selling products made with cheap and child labor in foreign countries.[4] Despite its problems, the company continued to expand and its sales, profits, and stock price reached record levels in 1999.

This story of Wal-Mart serves as a fitting introduction for this chapter. The consumer movement has undergone great changes in the past twenty-five years, and companies like Wal-Mart had a major role in it.

The menu of important consumer issues is long, but in this chapter we select only a few for discussion. Before examining the issues, we explain the contemporary foundations for the consumer movement. This is followed by a description of the government protective shield for consumers, food safety issues, products liability issues, false and deceptive advertising, food labeling, and the patient's bill of rights for health care.

Foundations of Contemporary Consumerism

Consumerism is a movement to improve the rights and powers of consumers in relation to the sellers of products and services. It is also a protest movement of consumers against what they or their advocates see as unfair, discriminatory, and arbitrary treatment. There is nothing new about the idea of consumerism. It is as old as business. Indeed, many current consumer issues are similar to those that existed in the Civil War and beyond. The current consumer movement began in the mid-1960s, but its momentum has diminished over the past fifteen years.

---

[3]Evelyn Iritani, "Wal-Mart Is Changing the Country's Retail Landscape," *Los Angeles Times,* September 12, 1998.

[4]Bob Ortega, *In Sam We Trust: The Untold Story of Sam Walton and How Wal-Mart Is Devouring America,* New York: Random House, 1998, p. 361.

The contemporary consumer movement was triggered by Rachel Carson's *Silent Spring,* which galvanized public opinion about environmental issues;[5] by Ralph Nader, who incited the public about automobile safety;[6] and by President Kennedy in a special message to Congress on March 15, 1962. In that message, he said that consumers had certain rights and these rights had been violated. They were the right to make intelligent choices among products and services; to have access to accurate information; to register complaints and be heard; to be offered fair prices and acceptable quality; to have safe and healthful products; and to receive adequate service.

President Kennedy's message, called by some the *magna carta* of consumers, reflected widespread consumer discontent at the time, a discontent that still exists despite the expansive protections in recent legislation. It seems paradoxical that the American consumer is the envy of the world for the quality and abundance of the products and services he or she consumes, and yet is dissatisfied with those products and services. Why the paradox? There are many explanations.

This is an age of discontent, of skepticism, and of challenge to authority. Today's consumers are better educated than those of the past, and they challenge practices that previous generations bore in silence. They question the authority of the uncontrolled marketplace. This is an age, too, of vocal expression of discontent; and consumers, fed up with actual or perceived bad treatment at the hands of manufacturers, advertisers, merchants, and repair services, are voicing their complaints.

Are complaints justified? Every consumer would say yes, because every consumer has been frustrated with a variety of consumption problems. Businesspeople, however, claim that dissatisfied consumers represent only a small fraction of the total. Nevertheless, people in business have become much more conscious of consumers and the importance of focusing attention on them. In *The Practice of Management,* Peter Drucker wrote forty-five years ago, "There is only one valid definition of business purpose: *to create a customer.* . . . It is the customer who determines what a business is. . . . The customer is the foundation of a business and keeps it in existence." [7] This idea was not generally translated into practice, and it remained for Peters and Waterman in a best-selling business book, *In Search of Excellence,* written in 1982, to highlight for business the importance of focusing attention on consumers.[8]

In Search of Excellence provoked widespread managerial thinking and action about the importance of consumers as major stakeholders. It reinforced for the business community how a strong focus on customer interests was instrumental in corporate profits. Wal-Mart was, of course, a classic illustration for any doubting managers. Then, in the 1980s and early 1990s, widespread questions about the ability of American companies to compete successfully in rapidly expanding

---

[5]Rachel Carson, *Silent Spring,* Boston: Houghton Mifflin, 1962.

[6]Ralph Nader, *Unsafe at Any Speed,* New York: Pocket Books, 1966.

[7]Peter F. Drucker, *The Practice of Management,* New York: Harper, 1954, p. 37.

[8]Thomas J. Peters and Robert H. Waterman Jr., *In Search of Excellence: Lessons from America's Best-Run Companies,* New York: Harper & Row, 1982.

global markets focused attention on successfully meeting customer needs as one important strategy to meet foreign competition. Today, most statements of corporate missions set forth as a major objective the satisfaction of consumers.

Materialism

A fundamental underpinning of consumerism is the value of materialism widely held in this society. Materialism refers to the high value consumers place on material goods. Ours unquestionably has been a materialistic society from its very beginning, although, early in our history, materialism was modified considerably by austere religious views about spending money. Throughout our history, this value has been significant in stimulating production and motivating individual initiative, technical innovation, and consumption of goods. While there are modifications of this value by renewed emphasis on nonmaterial things, the basic force of materialism is strong.[9]

Momentum of the Consumer Movement

In the past forty years, one consumer statute after another passed Congress. Table 16-1 shows the expansion of federal spending in this period on regulatory activity concerning consumers. Spending increased from $318 million in 1960 to over $14 billion in 1999. In the meantime, state and local governments also expanded significantly their regulatory activity concerning consumers.

Consumer Advocates

One phenomenon of today's consumerism, in contrast with that of the past, is the rise and influence of consumer advocates. These self-appointed promoters of the consumer are numerous.

Probably the most publicized and highly influential is Ralph Nader. His role has been partly like that of the muckrakers of the past. But it goes much further, to active representation of the consumer in the courts, government agencies, legislatures, and corporations. Nader has been fiercely attacked by businesspeople, many of whom consider him a dangerous radical. Some businesspeople view Nader as being obsessed with what he considers business abuses of the public and as pursuing a vendetta against business. Most people, however, including many businesspeople, believe he has sought to achieve his objectives through, not against, our legal and political systems. They see his motivation as reform of the system to benefit consumers. Many observers believe he has distorted or exaggerated facts in numerous cases, but others believe his work has resulted in needed legislation.

---

[9]For a critic of materialism, see "Delectable Materialism: Second Thoughts on Consumer Culture," Chapter 14 in David A. Crocker and Toby Linden, eds., *Ethics of Consumption,* Boston: Rowman & Littlefield Publishers, 1998.

TABLE 16-1 **Summary of Spending on Federal Regulatory Activity**
(Fiscal Years, Millions of Current Dollars in Obligations)

	1960	1970	1980	1990	1995	1996	1997	(Estimate) 1998	1999
Social Regulation									
Consumer safety and health	$250	$710	$2,349	$3,795	$5,193	$5,475	$5,726	$6,233	$6,367
Job safety and other working conditions	35	128	753	1,002	1,201	1,172	1,238	1,279	1,373
Environment	21	214	1,651	4,164	5,175	4,546	5,054	6,210	6,112
Energy	12	64	550	462	582	539	521	509	515
Total social regulations	$318	$1,116	$5,303	$9,423	$12,151	$11,732	$12,539	$14,231	$14,367

Source: Melinda Warren and William F. Lauber, *Regulatory Changes and Trends: An Analysis of the 1999 Federal Budget,* St. Louis: Washington University, Center for the Study of American Business, November 1998, p. 2.

Nader graduated cum laude from Princeton and then got a law degree at Harvard Law School in 1958. His first major move into consumerism was in 1965 with the publication of his book *Unsafe at Any Speed.*[10] This book dealt with what he called dangerous designs in American cars, especially General Motors' Corvair. General Motors hired private investigators to seek evidence to discredit him and faced a lawsuit for invasion of privacy that the company settled in 1970 for $425,000. This money provided the financial support for Nader's Center for the Study of Responsive Law, which he started in 1968.

Nader founded Public Citizen in 1971. He says it is the public's eyes and ears in Washington. "We fight for safer drugs and medical devices, cleaner and safer energy sources, a cleaner environment, fair trade, and more open and democratic government." "We stand up for you," he adds, "against thousands of special interest lobbyists in Washington."[11]

Over the years, his network has pushed for much legislation to protect consumers. For example, he was instrumental in the creation of the National Highway Traffic Safety Administration and the Consumer Product Safety Commission, passage of the Freedom of Information Act, a 1996 Supreme Court decision upholding the right of people injured by defective medical devices to sue for compensation, and defending tobacco industry whistleblowers. In addition, Public Citizen has been active in many other areas such as campaign finance reform, automobile safety, food safety, drug safety, and initiating litigation on behalf of consumers.[12]

Nader founded a Museum of American Tort Law, located in Winsted, Connecticut, where he was born. The museum will show such things as a

---

[10]Nader, *Unsafe at Any Speed.*
[11]"More About Public Citizen," http://www.citizen.org/newweb/more_about.htm, July 29, 1998.
[12]Ibid.

vintage Corvair, defective toys and other dangerous products removed from the market, and reenactments of famous tort trials. "It is a tribute," he says, "to a major chapter in American history, the great struggle for health and justice in the environment, workplace and marketplace."[13]

Nader's influence has been waning in recent years. This may be due to the fact that he is a victim of his own success. As he says, "Our success has made corporations smarter and tougher."[14] Clearly, Congress in the past twenty-five years has established formidable protections for consumers in major areas and that does not leave as much to be done. The success of the Republicans in gaining control of both houses of Congress and their commitment to reforming the federal regulatory process has also slowed the consumer movement.

There are many other important consumer advocacy groups. To mention a few, the Consumer Federation of America, founded in 1967, brings together about 200 organizations (mostly state and local) with consumer interests. Consumers Union, founded in 1936, is basically an organization that disseminates information to consumers, especially through its magazine *Consumer Reports*. A few others whose names indicate their activities are Accuracy in Media, Action on Smoking and Health, Advocates for Highway & Auto Safety, American Heart Association, Citizens for Reliable & Safe Highways, Citizens for a Tobacco-Free Society, Friends of the Earth, National Citizens' Coalition for Nursing Home Reform, and Public Voice for Food and Health Policy.

Fundamentally, consumer advocates are reformists. On balance, they probably have served the best interests of consumers, business, and the community. However, many of them are polemicists, and their "factual" assertions, arguments, and policy recommendations must be examined critically in that light.

Business-Oriented Interest Groups and Organizations

To round out the picture of the interest groups that address consumer issues, we should mention many groups inside and outside of business organizations that have responded to consumer advocates, sometimes positively and sometimes negatively, and also have initiated programs in the interests of consumers. For example, business organizations such as the U.S. Chamber of Commerce, the National Association of Manufacturers, and the Business Roundtable vigorously advance the business point of view, especially in legislative debates. These and other business advocacy groups were discussed in Chapter 11.

The Consumer's Protective Shield

Today there is a massive statutory shield to protect consumers from abuses, real and imagined, from the operation of the free competitive market. In this book we have dealt mostly with federal regulations, but there are other signifi-

---

[13]Jonathan Rabinovitz, "Nader's Museum of Liability: Corvairs, Pintos and Implants," *New York Times*, July 28, 1998.

[14]Quoted in Rich Thomas, "Safe at This Speed?" *Newsweek*, August 22, 1994.

cant protections. A primary one is the legal system, which we will discuss later in the chapter. Every state and local government has extensive laws to protect consumers, ranging from uniform electrical connections to fraudulent billing. An important protection exists in the dissemination of information in the mass media and the growth of investigative reporting.

Well over fifty federal agencies and bureaus are directly active in consumer affairs. The six most important ones are the Federal Trade Commission (FTC), the Consumer Product Safety Commission (CPSC), the National Highway Traffic Safety Administration (NHTSA), the Food and Drug Administration (FDA), the Food Safety and Quality Service (FSQS) of the Department of Agriculture, and the Environmental Protection Agency (EPA). We shall discuss briefly activities of the first five in this chapter. The last two chapters dealt at length with the EPA. This list of agencies might well include the Securities and Exchange Commission (SEC), which protects investors; the Department of Energy, which is concerned with nuclear waste hazards; and the Federal Deposit Insurance Corporation (FDIC), which protects depositors of financial institutions.

To get a sense of the scope and complexity of these agencies, which is important, we have chosen three for a brief analysis, as follows.

The Consumer Product Safety Commission (CPSC)

This agency, created by Congress in 1972, is directed by six major statutes. These laws mandate it to:

1. Protect the public against unreasonable risks of injury and death associated with consumer products.
2. Assist consumers to evaluate the comparative safety of products.
3. Develop uniform safety standards for consumer products and minimize conflicting state and local regulations.
4. Promote research and investigations into the causes and prevention of product-related deaths, illnesses, and injuries.

This is a formidable charge. The CPSC regulates every consumer product except guns, boats, planes, cars, trucks, foods, drugs, cosmetics, tobacco, and pesticides, which are in the province of other government agencies. Even with these exclusions, the agency's mandate is enormous, since it must oversee 15,000 classes of products, work with thousands of manufacturers, and address the complaints of millions of consumers.

Unfortunately, from the time of its creation in 1972, the CPSC has faced serious barriers in achieving its mandated goals. While it was the Nixon administration that gave it birth, the political environment was difficult. It became embroiled in political battles in both the Ford and Carter administrations. President Reagan wanted to abolish it but could not. Instead, he drastically cut its budget. Currently, the agency is threatened with substantial budgetary cuts by the Republican-controlled Congress. So lack of resources will likely continue to hamper its operations.

By far, most of the activity of the agency concerns the development with industry of voluntary safety standards. For example, it has worked with manufacturers to set specific standards for bicycles, bunk beds, toys, lawn mowers, cigarette lighters, swimming pool covers, spas, and thousands of other products. It has also set limits on the amount of chemicals in products, such as methylene chloride in paint strippers, paint thinners, spray paints, and adhesive removers.

The CPSC has banned products that do not meet specified standards. Examples include hazardous toys, charcoal lighter fluid, bicycles, and lawn darts. It has initiated recalls of products including playground equipment, toys using lead paint, and children's furniture. Toys and children's products are a prime concern of the agency. Other product categories in which recalls were made include home electrical appliances, gas furnaces, fireworks, and smoke detectors. In addition, imported products are inspected and some have been detained. They include mostly toys, fireworks, bicycles, and children's sleepwear.

An agency with such a broad mandate, limited resources, and political embroilment has attracted many critics. Critics claim that the agency relies too much on voluntary agreements and industry self-policing. They argue that the recall program should be severely cut back or stopped because the agency expends too many resources on the program, costs to manufacturers are substantial, and the program saves few lives. They say that it would be better if the agency spent its money on informing consumers about product safety rather than on regulating the products themselves. Of course, these are debatable propositions.

The National Highway Traffic Safety Administration (NHTSA)

This agency was created by Congress, in 1966, and has authority to

1. Mandate minimum safety standards for automobiles, trucks, and their accessories.
2. Establish fuel economy standards.
3. Administer state and community highway safety grant programs.
4. Conduct research, development, and demonstration of new vehicle safety techniques.

The agency has initiated many automobile safety features. A short list of programs to protect occupants would include air bags, safety belts, energy-absorbing or collapsible steering columns, penetration-resistant windshields, recessed door handles, breakaway rearview mirrors, padded dashboards, crushable front ends, passenger compartment designs to resist crushing, and tire standards. The agency can order recall of defective products.

Automobile companies have complained about the costs of many of the agency's mandates, but there is no doubt that the regulations have saved thousands of lives. Some critics claim that some of the programs cost too much and that less expensive alternatives exist for saving lives, such as better lighting on highways, limiting highway speeds, installing breakaway traffic lights and signs, padding abutments, and so on.

I want to let you in on one of the best kept secrets in Washington, a town usually thought of as a sieve: federal regulation of passenger automobiles is by far the most extensive case of government influence on a consumer product. There is no close second. Moreover, that regulation is extremely burdensome and the outlook is for more rather than less.

Specific regulations cover almost every aspect of the vehicle, including design, production, and operation. Government is directly involved in setting standards of such basic items as engines, bumpers, headrests, seat belts, door latches, brakes, fuel systems, and windshields, as well as the type of fuel that can be used.

Source: Weidenbaum, "The Automobile Industry," in a speech before the National Automobile Dealers Foundation, Orlando, Florida, October 20, 1998, conveniently found in *Vital Speeches of the Day*, November 15, 1998.

The Food and Drug Administration (FDA)

This agency was created by Congress in 1906 and operates under no less than twenty-six major legislative enactments. These include its original legislation, the Food and Drug Act of 1906, and amendments. For example, the original legislation gives it power to regulate in interstate commerce misbranded and adulterated foods, drinks, and drugs; the Public Health Service Act of 1944 gives it authority to ensure safety, purity, and potency of vaccines, blood, serum, and other biological products; the Nutrition Labeling and Education Act of 1990 mandates the agency to develop uniform nutrition labeling on packaged food items; and the Generic Drug Enforcement Act of 1992 permits it to oversee the generic drug industry.[15]

The FDA is an active and power watchdog of the public health and it is continuously embroiled in heated controversies. For example, the agency has been constantly pressed to speed up its new drug authorizations. It has responded and has substantially reduced the time needed to approve. Congress expressed its interest in speeding the FDA's approval process and President Clinton signed legislation in November 1997 to accelerate the review system for experimental medical devices and to give desperately ill patients the ability to get experimental drugs outside of clinical trials. The FDA has the difficult task of balancing vital needs with safety approval precautions. Former Commissioner David Kessler has lamented that people want new drugs in a hurry, but if anything goes wrong, they blame the FDA for moving too fast.

---

[15]*Congressional Quarterly's Federal Regulatory Directory*, Washington, D.C.: Congressional Quarterly Inc., 1994.

Another important current issue concerns tobacco. In August 1996, President Clinton announced he would allow the FDA to regulate nicotine as an addictive drug and restrict advertising as a means to reduce teenage smoking. The industry argues that only Congress can give the FDA authority over tobacco. The issue of nicotine regulation is unresolved, but action is proceeding on advertising as discussed in the case at the end of the chapter.

Food Safety Issues

Americans probably have the world's safest food supply. Food is relatively cheap, plentiful, and wholesome. But is it safe enough? Studies estimate that each year thousands of lives are lost and millions of illnesses are created by foodborne diseases. The cost of this is estimated to be in the tens of billions of dollars.[16]

There are many important issues in this area, but space permits discussion of only a few. We review briefly in the following the overlapping jurisdictions of federal agencies responsible for food safety, the food safety inspection system, the so-called Delaney paradox, food labeling, and the question of "how safe is safe."

Overlapping Federal Agency Jurisdictions

In testimony before Congress, the General Accounting Office (GAO) concluded: "The existing federal system to ensure a safe food supply is fragmented, characterized by a maze of often inconsistent legal and regulatory requirements implemented by 12 different federal agencies."[17] The GAO has found inconsistencies and illogical differences in inspection approaches to food safety, budgets, staffs, and authorizing laws.

Two agencies have primary responsibility for food safety—the Food Safety and Inspection Service (FSIS) of the Department of Agriculture and the FDA in the Health and Human Services Department. The FSIS has jurisdiction over meat, poultry, and some egg products. The FDA regulates all other foods. These agencies work closely with the Customs Service, the Centers for Disease Control and Prevention, and other agencies that do research on airborne diseases. The Environmental Protection Agency (EPA) is responsible for pesticides, fungicides, and rodenticides that may affect food safety.

In light of periodic outbreaks of diseases caused by food contamination, and a substantial increase in imported fruits and vegetables, more attention has been focused on the food inspection system. The FSIS and the FDA employ

---

[16]U.S. General Accounting Office, "Food Safety: Federal Efforts to Ensure the Safety of Imported Foods Are Inconsistent and Unreliable," Washington, D.C.: General Accounting Office, April 1998.

[17]Robert A. Robinson, "Food Safety: Fundamental Changes Needed to Improve the Nation's Food Safety System," Testimony before the Committee on Agriculture, Nutrition, and Forestry, U.S. Senate, October 8, 1997, p. 1.

two different systems for imported foods. The FSIS has statutory authority to require exporters of meat and poultry to the United States to have food safety systems in their countries equivalent to the system in the United States. The FSIS also inspects incoming shipments for safety. The FDA, on the other hand, relies on inspections of foods for safety by selecting and testing samples at ports of entry. The FDA system has been widely criticized as much less protective of the food supply. The GAO recommends that legislative authority be given to the FDA to use the "equivalence standard." In addition, the FDA needs much better information to help inspectors at ports of entry to target potential problems.[18]

The substantial increase in imported foods increases problems of detecting contaminants in foods. For example, imports of broccoli have grown by 833 percent from 1980 to 1995, tomatoes have increased by 150 percent, fresh vegetables by 53.9 percent, fresh fruits by 37.6 percent, and fish and shellfish by 22.1 percent.[19] The volume alone overwhelms detection resources. Then, too, the source of a contagious virus may be elusive. For example, in 1997, several thousand students were thought to have been exposed to Hepatitis A virus in a frozen strawberry dessert served at five schools. The berries were harvested in the spring of 1996 in Mexico, frozen by a food processor in San Diego, and packed into cups by a company in Clovis, California. Hepatitis A can be transmitted through tainted water or ice or the hands of food workers. The source of the contaminated berries could have been anywhere in this food chain. It may be noted also that the Department of Agriculture requires that only U.S.-grown commodities be used in school lunch programs. These berries somehow avoided that restriction.[20]

In 1997, in an effort to improve the inspection system for food safety in the United States, the federal government introduced the Hazard Analysis and Critical Control Point (HACCP) system. This system, first initiated for meats and poultry, was expanded to include fruits, vegetable juices, and seafood. The system requires food processors to identify points during food processing where contamination can occur. Various methods are then defined by the companies and government inspectors to test for food contamination. With this system, government inspectors will focus less on hands-on inspections and more on oversight of quality assurance methods.

The National Academy of Sciences concluded in a study that the food safety system today provides an "acceptable" level of protection for consumers, but it could be improved. It recommends replacement of fragmented authorities with one national food law. It also suggests the appointment of a "food safety czar."[21]

---

[18]U.S. General Accounting Office, "Food Safety."

[19]Ibid., p. 13.

[20]Editorial, "Holes Cannot Be Tolerated in U.S. Food Safety System," *Los Angeles Times,* April 3, 1997.

[21]Ricardo Alonzo-Zaldivar, "Panel Presses Congress on Need for 'Food-Safety Czar,'" *Los Angeles Times,* September 21, 1998.

The Delaney Clause and Food Additives

The Delaney clause is one of the most stringent and controversial consumer protection laws. This clause, a 1958 amendment to the Food, Drug, and Cosmetic Act (FDCA) of 1938, allows no flexibility in its prohibition against the addition to food of any substance known to produce cancer in any species, in any dosage, and under any circumstances. Applying this clause has raised difficult administrative problems, but strong efforts to alter it have been stopped in Congress and the courts. A fundamental problem in modifying this clause is political. Defenders have only to accuse politicians supporting change of favoring more cancer. This is a terrifying charge for any politician.

The FDA has primary responsibility for food safety with respect to around 2,700 "direct" food additives and thousands more of "indirect" additives that may get into foods through ingredients in packaging materials. The issue, therefore, is not a negligible one. For example, the Delaney clause is an open invitation for ingenious toxicologists to find cause for outlawing even the most innocuous substances. Experimenters have created tumors with hundreds of common food substances. New instruments are capable of detecting traces of substances at the level of one part in a trillion. The result is that almost everything anyone eats can contain traces of carcinogens.

The FDA has sought to avoid banning substances that are in minuscule quantities in foods and cause no harm. These efforts, however, have been rebuffed by court decisions that point to the zero tolerance wording in the legislation. The courts have said that if there is to be any change in the law, it is up to Congress, not the judiciary.[22]

To complicate matters, this clause conflicts with another law, the Federal Insecticide, Rodenticide, and Fungicide Act (FIFRA), passed in 1972. This act, among other things, gives the EPA authority to regulate pesticides. FIFRA did not embody the concept of zero tolerance since that would ban a large number of important pesticides. Concentrations of pesticides in most raw fruits and vegetables are well below allowed tolerances, and concentrations of pesticides in processed foods are also below allowances in the raw products. But Delaney permits zero tolerance, hence the "Delaney paradox." Pesticide levels acceptable to the EPA in raw fruits and vegetables cannot be legally accepted when appearing in processed foods made from the same crops.[23]

Widespread dissatisfaction with this situation led to passage of the Food Quality Protection Act of 1996 (FQPS) to correct the problem. Since rescinding the Delaney clause was politically unthinkable, Congress finessed the issue in this way. The new law specifies that before both raw and processed foods can be offered for sale, the pesticide safety level must be at the point where there is "a reasonable certainty that no harm will result from aggregate exposure."

---

[22]*Kathleen E. Les et al., v. William K. Reilly,* U.S. Court of Appeals for the Ninth Circuit, No. 91-70234, 56 Fed. Reg. 7750, July 8, 1992; cert. denied, U.S. Supreme Court, February 22, 1993.

[23]Daniel M. Byrd, "Goodbye Pesticides?" *Regulation,* Fall 1997, p. 59.

This, of course, requires that the EPA establish safety levels, which will vary among hundreds of products, a complex and expensive task. Undoubtedly, this law, together with the Delaney clause, which still is in force, will continue to be controversial.

Food Labeling: How Safe Is Safe?

Both in the preparation of legislation and in the bureaucracy, the troubling question of "how safe is safe?" arises. Most scientists believe that the cancer threat from pesticides, for example, is minuscule compared with many other daily risks, such as those from smoking. Such comparison of risk raises tantalizing questions about safety. Furthermore, there are enough uncertainties about what is known about pesticides and other food hazards, as well as what happens in the processing and distribution of foods, to raise questions about food safety. This subject is far too big and complex to be fully treated here, but a few comments are appropriate.

The case of Alar, a chemical used to regulate the growth of some red apples, illustrates a worrisome type of food safety problem. In February 1989, a public interest group published a report that said schoolchildren faced serious risks from eating chemically treated apples and apple products. The story was aired on talk shows and in the newspapers. Immediately, school boards removed apples from school lunches, grocery stores stopped selling apples, sales of apples and apple juice plummeted, and the FDA and EPA were accused of failure to stop the use of Alar.

The scientific community almost unanimously said the risks of cancer from eating apples treated with Alar were virtually nil. An ad hoc group of fourteen prominent scientists called the risks from approved agricultural chemicals negligible or nonexistent and said flatly that the "public's perception of pesticide residues and their effects on the safety of the food supply differs considerably from the facts."[24] The fact is that Alar does produce a possible carcinogen (daminozide), but in minute quantities. Anyway, only 5 to 10 percent of apple orchards were treated with Alar at the time.

A troubling aspect of the Alar incident is that a complicated scientific issue was decided by individuals throughout the country rather than by officials charged with the responsibility for determining what should and should not be tolerated in foods. The case was decided not upon any hard evidence but by a frightened public acting on incorrect media reports. Professor Bruce Ames, chairman of the biochemistry department at the University of California, Berkeley, tells us that many foods contain natural toxins at much higher levels than residues of dangerous pesticides. Fruits and vegetables produce such substances, he says, to repel insects, fungi, and other predators. Ames points out that up to 10 percent of a plant's weight is made up of natural pesticides. The

---

[24]Malcolm Gladwell, "A Consuming Matter of Apples," *Washington Post National Weekly Edition,* May 17, 1989.

ordinary potato contains 150 chemicals before it is sprayed with pesticides. Most scientists affirm that by the time a food gets to the market, very little pesticide residue remains.[25]

Nevertheless, there are troubling aspects to potential hazards of contaminants in the food supply. For example, there are thousands of chemicals, animal drugs, and microbiological organisms in food, some of which may be dangerous to human beings. But which ones, and how dangerous? Identifying and testing them is a gigantic task that has only partly been accomplished. Critics point to the fact that restrictions in foreign countries on the use of pesticides and additives are not as strong as in this country, and we import as much as 25 percent of our fruits and vegetables. Little of this produce is tested when it arrives on our shores. Critics also claim that the EPA has no way to measure the combined effects on humans of ingesting many different pesticides. A significant concern of the FDA is the growing microbiological contamination of food.

This area swirls with controversy that will continue. This is partly because not nearly enough is known about linkages between cancer and human health with specific food contaminants, doses that humans can safely tolerate, the risks to humans of adding chemicals to the food of animals, which natural and human-introduced chemicals are hazardous to consumers, and how to identify sources of serious contamination in a long food production and processing chain.

Products Liability Law

Consumers have legal recourse to compensation for injury of person, property, or reputation by individuals or corporations. This includes, of course, automobile accidents, medical malpractice, professional malpractice, or defective products. An area of special concern to both consumers and business is products liability, so we briefly discuss this area here.

For most of our history, consumers had little recourse in being compensated for defective products. Today, manufacturers or other sellers of products can be held liable for defective products under four fundamental theories of law, namely, negligence, breach of warranty, strict liability, and joint-and-several liability.

Negligence

Under this theory, manufacturers have an obligation to do what a reasonable person could be expected to do. Not only the manufacturer but all those in the stream of events leading to the final sale to a customer must exercise reasonable

---

[25]Gisela Bolte and Dick Thompson, "Do You Dare to Eat a Peach?" *Time*, March 27, 1989; and John F. Ross, "Risks, Where Do Real Dangers Lie?" *Smithsonian*, November 1995.

care. They can be held liable today even for injury resulting from unintended but reasonably foreseeable misuse.

The law has not always been this generous to consumers. Until a few years ago, manufacturers were well protected from consumer liability suits. An injured consumer tried to collect damages through either contract law or caveat emptor (let the buyer beware). Under contract law, the courts would accept the defendant's argument that in the absence of a direct contract between the manufacturer and the consumer, called *privity*, the plaintiff had no case against the producer but had to go to the retailer. If retailers lost a suit, they would sue the wholesaler, and the wholesaler, in turn, the manufacturer. This chain seldom resulted in redress to consumers. This doctrine was based on an English decision in 1842.[26] Under the caveat emptor principle, the vendor was liable only when there was an agreement that provided for that liability. These views were developed at a time when consumers generally dealt face to face with manufacturers of the products they bought. As the distribution chain evolved in industrial society, that experience, of course, became rarer and rarer.

This legal protective wall for manufacturers was broken by the milestone case of *McPherson* v. *Buick Motor Company,* in 1916.[27] McPherson was injured when a wooden spoke in a wheel of his Buick collapsed. General Motors claimed that the car was bought from a dealer and the company had no liability. The court disagreed and said the company was negligent in not properly inspecting the wheel. Furthermore, the court said, General Motors was responsible irrespective of who was in the chain of events prior to the purchase.

This legal philosophy has been vastly stretched in subsequent decisions. For example, General Motors was held responsible by the court for designing products that minimized risks in collisions. If it did not do so, it was liable for damages.[28] The New Jersey Supreme Court said, in effect, that the manufacturer had the responsibility for warning of dangers that were not only undiscovered but scientifically undiscoverable at the time the products were first introduced for use in the workplace.[29] This is a puzzling rule for a company to follow. However, it may provide major protection for injured consumers, as it did for workers injured by inhaling asbestos.

Warranties

A manufacturer or seller can be held liable for a breach of warranty, either explicit or implied. An express warranty is an explicit claim made by the manufacturer to the seller. It can be stated on a card or on labels, packages, or advertising.

---

[26]*Winterbottom* v. *Wright,* 15 Eng.Rep. 402 (Eng. 1842), 177.

[27]217 N.Y. 382, 111 N.E. 1050 (1916).

[28]*Larson* v. *General Motors Corporation,* 391 F.2d 495 (8th Cir. 1968).

[29]*Beshada et al.* v. *Johns-Manville Products Corporation,* 90 N. J. 191, 447 A.Zd 539(1982).

The Magnuson-Moss Warranty Improvement Act of 1974 sets forth federal standards for written consumer product warranties.

When a product is sold, there is an automatic implied warranty that it is fit for the ordinary use to which it is intended. The landmark case about implied warranties is *Henningsen* v. *Bloomfield Motors, Inc.*[30] In this case, Henningsen bought a Plymouth automobile. A few days after purchase, the steering mechanism failed and his wife, who was driving, crashed and was injured. The dealer and the company claimed that when the purchase contract was approved by Henningsen, he had signed a disclaimer appearing on the back of the contract. (Included in eight inches of fine print was a sentence saying there was agreement that there were no warranties express or implied by either the dealer or the manufacturer on the vehicle or its parts.) The court said that the automobile company was legally responsible for making cars good enough to serve the purpose for which they were intended.

Strict Liability

This legal weapon makes it possible for injured consumers to hold all those in the chain of distribution responsible for defective products. This theory puts the focus on the product, not the reasonableness of the producer or seller. Anyone who sells any product in a defective condition that is "unreasonably" dangerous to a consumer is liable for the harm caused. If there are no defects in the design of the product, but the product is "unreasonably" dangerous, a producer will still be held liable for injury if customers are not properly warned about its use.

The landmark case in the development of strict liability was *Greenman* v. *Yuba Power Products, Inc.* The court said that "a manufacturer is strictly liable when an article he places on the market, knowing that it will be used without inspection, proves to have a defect that causes injury to a human being."[31]

Joint-and-Several Liability

This is a further extension of products liability law, also discussed briefly in Chapter 14 in connection with Superfund litigation. Here is another illustration of its application. The driver of a bumper car was struck by the bumper car driven by her fiancé. The jury found the fiancé 85 percent responsible for the injury, the plaintiff 14 percent responsible, and Disney World 1 percent responsible. Later, but before the trial, the plaintiff married her fiancé. Under Florida law, the husband was immune from suit by the wife. As a result, Disney World had to pay for all the damages not attributable to the plaintiff.[32]

---

[30]N.J. Supreme Court, 161 A.2d 69 (1960).
[31]Supreme Court of California, 27 Cal. Reptr. 697, 377 P.2d 897 (1962).
[32]*Walt Disney World Co.* v. *Wood*, 515 So. 2d 198 (Fla. 1987).

Expansion of Products Liability Suits

Many forces joined in recent years to generate a rapid growth of products liability suits. Among them have been the aggressiveness of some trial lawyers in pressuring consumers to bring suit, the development of more complicated products, and the feeling that if anyone is injured by a product, they deserve to be paid for damages incurred. In addition, juries have become more willing to punish manufacturers when they perceive outrageous wrongdoing.[33] The result has been tens of thousands of liability suits, a large number of which have been associated with asbestos and silicon gel breast implants. Many products liability cases are settled out of court, but no one knows how many.

Punitive Damage Awards

Punitive awards capture public attention because some of them are spectacular. In the last chapter, we noted the nature of these awards and gave examples. Here are a few more. In September 1994, an Alaskan jury hit Exxon with the largest jury punitive damage award in history—$5 billion for the damages caused by the eleven-million-gallon spill of the *Exxon Valdez* in Prince William Sound in 1989. In September 1997, a jury in Louisiana awarded punitive damages of $3.5 billion in a Louisiana railway fire in 1987. Then there was the highly publicized case of $2.7 million awarded to a woman who was scalded by a cup of carryout coffee at McDonald's. The award was later reduced to $640,000 by a judge. Most huge punitive awards are subsequently reduced substantially by judges.

Huge punitive awards are very few relative to the total of products liability suits. But the total number of products liability suits (estimated at well over 100,000 annually) attests to the fact that consumers in large numbers seek and get some relief for damages incurred. And products liability remains a large and threatening potential for all people in business from medical doctors to giant corporations. High liability insurance costs confirm that.

Business Wants Products Liability Reform

The business community, stung by increased liability suits, rising liability insurance costs, differing state liability laws, and high-profile business bankruptcies because of products liability awards (e.g., Dow Corning, A. H. Robins, and Johns Manville), has pressed Congress for years to reform and make uniform the nation's products liability standards. Opponents of congressional action

---

[33]Damages are given to plaintiffs for injury, and punitive awards to punish defendants. Compensation may be awarded for economic (out-of-pocket) loss, medical expenses, lost income, and noneconomic loss such as pain and suffering. Punitive damages penalize outrageous wrongdoing that is malicious, willful, wanton, or evil. All these injuries are called torts, and the legal system to protect individuals is the tort system.

have been powerful consumer groups, plaintiffs' lawyers, and some conservative thinkers.

The business community seeks a number of reforms. First, business wants Congress to pass legislation that will establish uniform liability standards across the states. Second, business wants to eliminate a manufacturers' liability when products made today may cause injuries in the future that cannot be reasonably foreseen. Third, business wants reform of strict liability to shift the burden of proof to consumers rather than the current system where manufacturers must prove they were not negligent. Fourth, business wants a cap on total punitive awards. Fifth, business wants to eliminate joint-and-several liability. Finally, business wants judges to determine punitive damages, not juries. This is because judges award lower punitive damages than juries. The Supreme Court has moved a little in the direction of restraining damage awards, as noted in Chapter 7.

After many years of debate, Congress in 1996 sent a products liability bill to President Clinton, which he vetoed. He rejected the measure saying it was tilted against victims of defective products. In 1998, a bill to place limits on products liability lawsuits was before the Senate. Business groups opposed the bill because it did not address some of their central concerns. Several powerful senators opposed the bill because it limited damage awards for manufacturers and sellers of guns.

State Activities

A number of states have recently introduced reforms. Many have enacted laws that cap punitive damages. For example, Connecticut limits punitive damages in products liability cases to twice the compensation damages awarded. Louisiana virtually eliminates punitive damages in civil suits. A powerful protection for consumers is the way states attorneys general are banding together to file class-action suits. When confronted by the attorneys general, many companies settle without admitting wrongdoing.[34]

Impact of Products Liability on Business

The impact of the current products liability laws varies among companies. Most are concerned about the possibility of large liability awards. Some have dropped products, such as football helmets and off-road vehicles, for fear of liability suits. Many try to settle suits by out-of-court settlements, a practice that has grown in recent years. Arbitration, in which both parties to a dispute accept an arbitrator to decide competing claims, is also a much-used alternative. Probably the most significant alternative has been improvement in the quality of products in order to compete better in domestic and global markets, avoid liability suits, and limit the chances that regulators will order a product's recall.

---

[34]David Morrow, "Transporting Lawsuits across State Lines," *New York Times,* November 9, 1997.

False and Deceptive Advertising

Advertising is ubiquitous. Consumers cannot escape it on TV, in the media, on billboards, on packaging, and on the Internet. Tens of billions of dollars are spent each year to advertise consumer products. The states have been especially active in recent years in protecting consumers against abuses in advertising. At the federal level, the dominant agency concerned with advertising is the Federal Trade Commission (FTC). It, too, has been active in this area. The FDA, the USDA, and the Department of Labor also deal with certain types of false and deceptive advertising. For example, the Department of Labor reviews claims of companies regarding the manufacture of their products in the United States.

Fundamentally, the purposes of advertising are to make the consumer aware of a product or service, inform the customer of its characteristics, and then persuade the customer to buy it. A wide range of policy issues flows from these simple purposes. For example, what should consumers be told about product contents, use, maintenance requirements, and warranties? What is the impact of advertising on social values? How should products be advertised? How far should government go in regulating advertising?

These are significant issues. We discuss here only false and deceptive advertising to illustrate but one dimension of the issues. Advertising is false when its claims are explicitly, literally untrue. A few years ago, a dishwasher manufacturer advertised that the washer would completely clean dishes, pots, and pans "without prior rinsing or scraping." That was clearly untrue, said the FTC, and the company had to stop making that claim. On the other hand, puffery is not objectionable to the FTC. If a restaurant claims that "we serve the best hamburgers in town," that is acceptable because consumers know it is an exaggeration and are not deceived. However, if an advertisement says, "Our hamburgers are the lowest priced in town," the FTC wants factual evidence that the statement is true. In dealing with this subject, one is reminded of the words attributed to Mark Twain: "When in doubt, tell the truth, it will amaze most people, delight your friends, and confuse your enemies." Some American advertisers apparently have not heard or been convinced of Twain's recommendation.

Federal Trade Commission Guidelines

Over the years, the FTC has developed guidelines concerning various aspects of advertising, such as use of endorsements and testimonials, use of the word "free," allowances and other merchandising payments and services, bait-and-switch advertising (that which is offered to get the consumer to buy something else), and false and deceptive advertising.

In a policy statement on deceptive advertising, the FTC said: "The Commission will find deception if there is a representation, omission or practice that is likely to mislead the consumer acting reasonably in the circumstances, to the consumer's detriment."[35] Several recent high-profile cases illustrate the application of this definition.

In May 1997, Jenny Craig Inc. settled FTC charges of deceptive advertising by changing its advertising of weight-loss claims. The FTC said Jenny Craig could not substantiate claims made about weight loss, weight loss maintenance, price, and safety. For example, the company claimed that nine out of ten customers would recommend the Jenny Craig program to a friend, and represented it had surveys backing up the claim, when it did not. Jenny Craig agreed to stop that claim, to substantiate weight-loss claims in its advertising, to reveal all costs associated with its program, and to include a disclaimer that weight loss is temporary for most dieters.[36]

In another case, the FTC and state officials charged a number of companies with deceptive advertising of automobile lease arrangements. For instance, the FTC charged that advertising of Mazda automobiles violated fair trade and truth-in-advertising laws by deceptively stating the true costs of leasing. The commercials said down payments were only a few dollars, but flashed only briefly on the TV screen was the disclosure that consumers would be required to pay at least $900 in fees at the lease signing. Another case involved Mitsubishi ads, including TV commercials, quoting credit terms of $750 down and $199 a month. But in a mass of unreadable fine print was a final balloon payment of $7,320.[37] That was deceptive, said the FTC.

States Move Aggressively

States have been more active in recent years than the federal government in reviewing false and deceptive advertising. The states attorneys general have been aggressive not only in challenging individual companies but in joining with other states in bringing multistate lawsuits against large national advertisers.

Here are a few illustrations of actions taken by states. Texas challenged Sara Lee for suggesting that its "light" cheesecake is low calorie. Several states challenged Kellogg Co. for its advertising of the nutritional benefits of its cereals. Quaker Oats settled a challenge by the state of Texas over its claims that eating oatmeal reduces cholesterol. Seven states sued Mobil for claiming that its Hefty garbage bag is biodegradable.

There are many other important issues in advertising; for example, using images of sexuality, medical issues, the overcommercialization of life in the United States encouraged by advertising, and special problem areas such as alcohol and tobacco advertising. The latter are considered in the case that follows this chapter.

---

[35]"FTC Policy Statement on Deception," Federal Trade Commission, http://www.ftc.gov/bcp/policystmt/ad-decept.htm, December 25, 1998.

[36]FTC, "FTC Reaches Settlement with Jenny Craig to End Diet Program Advertising Litigation," http://www.ftc.gov/opa/1997/9705/jcraig-2htm.

[37]Bruce Ingersoll, "Three Ad Agencies Settle FTC Charges of Deceptive Car-Leasing Commercials," *The Wall Street Journal,* January 21, 1998.

Ethical Standards for Advertisers

The American Association of Advertising Agencies (AAAA) has a laudable ethics code for all its members. The code appears to be one of the most ignored in the corporate world, but some of its major provisions are worth noting as follows:

> Specifically, we will not knowingly create advertising that contains:
> a. False or misleading statements or exaggerations, visual or verbal
> b. Testimonials that do not reflect the real opinion of the individual(s) involved
> c. Price claims that are misleading
> d. Claims insufficiently supported or that distort the true meaning or practicable application of statements made by professional or scientific authority
> e. Statements, suggestions, or pictures offensive to public decency or minority segments of the population.

Food Labeling

Prior to FDA food labeling requirements mandated in 1994, food processors seized on the public's interest in health to sell products by proclaiming their health benefits. Some products claimed they would lower cholesterol, ward off heart disease, reduce weight, and so on. Going down an aisle in a grocery was like going into a drug store, said former FDA Commissioner David Kessler. Pressure on Congress to do something led to passage of the Nutrition Labeling and Education Act of 1990. This law gave the FDA and the USDA authority to ensure truthful and uniform nutritional labeling on foods regulated by the two agencies. In conformance with this act, the FDA in November 1992 issued detailed rules covering 15,000 product classes, which went into effect in 1994. The result is the labeling on foods that today is familiar to all consumers.

Since that time, the FDA has mandated labeling for other products. The agency issued labeling rules for bottled water that went into effect in May 1996. Bottlers are required to state the precise source of the bottled water as well as the amount of some minerals in it. In 1997, the FDA proposed labeling requirements for nonprescription drugs. The proposals are to make labels easier for consumers to read and understand. The proposal is for a standard format that sets forth (1) active ingredients and purpose of the drug, including its different uses; (2) specific warnings, including when to consult a doctor before using the drug, and potential side effects; and (3) directions for use. All of this should be in plain and simple language, said the FDA. The design should be easy to read with a minimum type size and style that is readable.[38]

---

[38]Marlene Cimons, "New Labeling Proposed for Patent Drugs," *Los Angeles Times*, February 27, 1997.

In September 1998, new labeling rules became effective for fresh-squeezed fruit and vegetable juices. If the juice is not pasteurized, it must contain this warning: "Warning. This product has not been pasteurized and therefore may contain harmful bacteria that can cause serious illness in children, the elderly, and persons with weakened immune systems." [39] Health advocates want the FDA to mandate labels concerning caffeine content of various foods, but the FDA has not yet acted.

Patients' Bill of Rights

No other issue concerns consumers more than provisions for their health care. Today there are millions of Americans without health insurance, and many of those with health insurance do not have all the protections they need. On March 26, 1997, President Clinton established the Advisory Commission on Consumer Protection and Quality in the Health Care Industry. This Commission was charged with the responsibility to advise the president on measures needed to ensure quality health care for consumers and workers. As part of their work, the president asked for a "consumer bill of rights." It was sent to him in November 1997. Following are the eight areas of consumer rights and responsibilities drafted by the Commission:

1. Consumers have the right to receive accurate and readable information about their health plans, professionals, and facilities.
2. Consumers have the right to a choice of health care providers that will assure high-quality health care.
3. Consumers have the right to access emergency health care services when and where the need arises.
4. Consumers have the right and responsibility to fully participate in all decisions related to their health care. If they are not able to participate, they have the right to be represented by family members and conservators.
5. Consumers have the right to considerate, respectful care from all members of the health care system at all times and under all circumstances.
6. Consumers have the right of access to their medical records and assurance that they will be held in confidence.
7. All consumers have the right to a fair and efficient process for resolving differences with their health plans, health care providers, and institutions that serve them.
8. In a health care system that protects consumers' rights, it is reasonable to expect consumers to assume responsibility for staying healthy. [40]

---

[39] Eleenna De Lisser, "FDA Is Putting the Squeeze on Makers of Fresh Juice," *The Wall Street Journal*, September 22, 1998.

[40] "Consumer Bill of Rights and Responsibilities: Executive Summary," http://www.hcqualitycommission.gov, December 28, 1998.

Shortly after receiving this report, the president directed all federal health plans, which he said served 85 million Americans, to come into substantial compliance with the recommendations. Not all programs of federal agencies ensure patients these rights. For instance, Medicare, administered by the Department of Health and Human Services, does not ensure access to specialists and adequate levels of participation in treatment decisions.[41]

When the president ordered all federal agencies to implement the consumer bill of rights, he asked Congress for legislation to set national standards for protection of consumers. The House passed legislation in July 1998 that defined patients' rights and regulated HMOs, but the Senate rejected a similar bill and the legislative initiative collapsed. One stumbling block was a coalition of powerful interest groups—HMOs, insurance companies, and employers—that strongly opposed the cost of new federal mandates.

Dissatisfaction with HMOs is growing and consumers not only want new rights but also the ability to sue HMOs, a right not mentioned in the Commission report. Here again, powerful pressure groups are opposed to legislation that would facilitate rights to sue HMOs.

Concluding Observations

There is no question that today business is increasingly concerned about the interests and demands of consumers, government regulations (federal, state, and local) concerning them, and pressures of consumer advocacy groups. This medley of forces will become more complex in the future as the population grows, product choices of consumers expand, technology changes the nature and content of products, and competition intensifies both at home and globally. We can expect, therefore, even more attention to consumers in business, government, and society.

---

[41]"President Clinton Issues Directive Aimed at Ensuring that Federal Health Plans Come Into Compliance With the Patients' Bill of Rights," http://www.pub.whitehouse.gov/uri-res/ I24?urn:pdi://oma.eop.gov.us/1998/2/26/1.text.1.

ADVERTISING ALCOHOL AND TOBACCO

It has been said that a drink is the best thing to take for a headache—provided that it is taken the night before. Of course, the person accepting this advice might want to have a cigarette—defined in an adage as "a fire at one end, a fool at the other, and a bit of tobacco in between." In fact, alcoholic beverages and tobacco products have more in common than being sources of humor.

- Both contain powerful, addicting drugs—alcohol and nicotine, respectively—that are a source of pleasure but may have pernicious effects on bodily organs.
- Both imperil users. In the United States, there are more than 100,000 alcohol-related deaths and more than 430,000 tobacco-related deaths yearly.
- Both sustain massive economic networks of producer corporations in oligopolistic industries, advertising agencies, broadcasters, publishers, retail stores, farmers, labor unions, and trade associations. Just as alcohol and nicotine spread through the body, so the interests that purvey them weave through the economy. Of the two industries, tobacco is by far the largest with U.S. sales of $156 billion in 1998 compared with $29 billion for alcoholic beverages.[1]
- Both are "right-of-passage" products; that is, their use is associated with adulthood. This creates a marketing climate with unique legal and ethical restraints against targeting underage users.
- Both are heavily promoted by slick ads that associate their use with images of the good life and satisfaction of needs.
- Both are the target of campaigns to ban or curb advertising.

---

[1]*Value Line Investment Survey*, Edition 10, February 12, 1999, pp. 1535 and 1582.

Part I: Advertising Alcoholic Beverages

Back in the 1950s and 1960s, alcoholic beverage advertising was unsophisticated. Most beer ads, for instance, the Hamm's beer animations of bears at play, were low-key and simple. Ads for distilled spirits and wine were similarly unsophisticated. But after 1970, all this changed with the injection of powerful techniques from the world of cigarette marketing. In that year, Philip Morris, the largest U.S. tobacco company, acquired Miller Brewing Company. In those days, Miller was a small brewer, with only 4.2 percent of the domestic beer market. But Philip Morris quickly revolutionized beer marketing by introducing market segmentation, target marketing, and image-oriented lifestyle advertising. By 1980, Miller had become the nation's second largest brewer. More important, other beer, wine, and distilled spirits marketers adopted its cutting-edge advertising methods, and advertising in the industry was transformed. When the ads began to attract greater attention, some of it was from people opposed to drinking.

The number of American adults who drink has remained almost constant at about 60 percent since the first survey was taken in 1939. Of Americans who drink, 45 percent prefer beer, 32 percent wine, and 18 percent hard liquor.[2] Despite more sophisticated advertising, domestic consumption of alcoholic beverages is stagnant. Per capita consumption has been in decline for more than twenty years, and, even with overall population growth, beer production has not risen and production of distilled spirits and wine has declined by more than half.[3] The downward trend is caused by aging of the population and concerns about health effects of heavy drinking. This mature and stagnant market generates fierce competition for market share in all three segments—beer, wine, and distilled spirits—much of it manifested in clever ad campaigns. Companies spend more than $2 billion each year advertising alcoholic beverages.[4]

The Attack on Alcohol Advertisements

A strong anti-alcohol movement exists in the United States. The nation's brief experiment with prohibition ended in 1933, but a 1994 poll found that 21 percent of Americans still want to turn back the clock and ban alcohol again.[5] These people are the foundation of the movement; its leaders are activists in church, health, and citizens' groups. Its greatest success to date has been getting all states to raise the legal drinking age to 21. Now, it wants to ban or limit alcoholic beverage advertising. There are three basic reasons.

---

[2]Leslie McAneny, "Drinking a Cause of Family Problems for Three Out of Ten Americans," *Gallup Poll,* June 6, 1997.

[3]Bureau of Labor Statistics, *Statistical Abstract of the United States,* 118th ed., Washington, D.C.: Government Printing Office, 1998, Table nos. 249 and 1245.

[4]"Comprehensive Alcohol Abuse Prevention Act of 1997," H. R. 1982, 105th Cong., 1st Sess., H. R. 1982 (1997), Sec. 102(6).

[5]Leslie McAneny, "Alcohol in America: Number of Drinkers Holding Steady, but Drinking Less," *The Gallup Poll Monthly,* June 1994, p. 14.

First, advertising increases consumption. Many ads are designed to attract new drinkers and promote additional drinking. The Michelob beer campaign based on the slogan "Put a little weekend in your week" advocated drinking on weekdays, not just on weekends. Commercials such as Philip Morris's classic Miller Lite "Tastes Great—Less Filling" spots attempt to reposition beer as a competitor to soft drinks, telling consumers that light beers are low-calorie drinks that can be consumed more often than regular beer. A recent campaign by the Wine Marketing Council suggests that wine goes with television viewing. Studies show that, overall, advertising does not affect aggregate consumption of alcoholic beverages.[6] However, this does not deter critics who believe that when alcohol ads saturate the media, they create a climate of undeserved social approval for drinking. One critic of the ads argues this way:

> To pretend, as alcohol marketers do, that the advertisements do not have any effect on consumption is disingenuous at best . . . [C]onsider that [companies] spend hundreds of millions of dollars advertising their products. One would think they have some faith in that investment. Try finding an advertising agency modest enough to confess that marketers have been wasting all (or even some of) that money . . . [T]o suggest that it does not help bring in new consumers and encourage current users to consume more begs credulity. Trusting one's eyes and ears makes more sense.[7]

Second, the ads encourage children and teenagers to start drinking. By age eighteen, a typical American teenager has seen 100,000 beer commercials on television.[8] The cumulative mass of alcohol ads is an irresistible lesson for children that drinking is fun and leads to social acceptance. Researchers report that fifth- and sixth-grade children who can describe alcohol ads have more positive attitudes toward drinking than less knowledgeable children.[9] And many ads are attractive to children. For example, in 1998, Budweiser spots featuring the lizards Frankie and Louie were the favorites of children aged six to seventeen.[10]

Third, sophisticated lifestyle advertising plays on emotional needs for popularity, success, achievement, and romance and associates alcohol with fulfillment of these needs. Sexual images are a staple of alcohol marketing. In non-Western societies, marketers sometimes use imagery associated with Western values to sell. In Malaysia, an ad campaign for Carlsberg beer features a blond, Danish model in a white bathing suit. Strangely enough, in Zimbabwe, a

---

[6]For an overview of this research see Hae-Kyong Bang, "Analyzing the Impact of the Liquor Industry's Lifting of the Ban on Broadcast Advertising," *Journal of Public Policy & Marketing,* Spring 1998.

[7]George A. Hacker, "Liquor Advertisements on Television: Just Say No," *Journal of Public Policy & Marketing,* Spring 1998, p. 139.

[8]William Beaver, "What to Do About Alcohol Advertising," *Business Horizons,* July/August 1997, p. 88.

[9]Joel W. Grube, "Television Beer Advertising and Drinking Knowledge, Beliefs, and Intentions among Schoolchildren," *American Journal of Public Health,* February 1994.

[10]Kathy DeSalvo, "FTC Investigates Alcohol Company's Ad Practices," *SHOOT,* September 25, 1998, p. 39.

This advertisement associates Bud Dry with fun, companionship, and female sexuality.

brandy named "Robert E. Lee" is sold with images of Confederate flags.[11] This advertising works if people wanting to be popular, successful, or trendy buy the beverage trying to fulfill their desire.

Critics claim that alcohol advertising is targeted not only at young drinkers, but at other inappropriate groups, including heavy drinkers and minorities, whose members are at greater risk of alcohol abuse. An example of objectionable targeting is the heavy advertising of malt liquors in inner-city black neighborhoods and in black media. Malt liquor has a higher alcohol content than regular beer and ads for it appeal to drinkers looking for a high. In 1991, G. Heilman Brewing Company introduced PowerMaster brand malt liquor on inner-city billboards with pictures of young black men and the slogan "Bold Not Harsh."[12] Critics felt the slogan was a not-so-subtle hint that it had a big alcohol kick. Criticism of PowerMaster was so strong that Heilman eventually withdrew the brand. In 1998, United States Beverage Company introduced a malt liquor called Phat Boy. "Phat" is a slang word used by teens for something hip, cool, or exciting. Phat Boy was marketed with graffiti-style ads as "the new malt liquor with an attitude." It came in large 40-ounce bottles, each of which had nearly as much alcohol as a six-pack of regular beer. After an outcry by activists, the company dropped the brand, although the reason it cited was poor sales.[13]

---

[11]David H. Jernigan, "Thirsting for Markets: Corporate Alcohol Goes Global," *Multinational Monitor*, July/August 1997, pp. 34–35.

[12] George G. Brenkert, "Marketing to Inner-City Blacks: PowerMaster and Moral Responsibility," *Business Ethics Quarterly*, January 1998.

[13]Melanie Wells, "Phat Boy Brew on Way Out," *USA Today*, September 14, 1998, p. 12B.

Alcohol Marketers Defend Their Advertising

The industry defends its ads. First, it says, ads are not the cause of alcohol abuse. As noted, studies fail to show that advertising increases consumption. So commercials and billboards cannot be blamed for what one critic calls "the nether side of drinking—car wrecks, spousal abuse, rapes, crime, and addiction related to excessive alcohol consumption."[14] Alcoholism is a complex disease caused by personality, family, genetic, and physiological factors rather than by viewing ads. So the main result of restraints would be to deprive moderate drinkers of product information, not to help alcoholics. As one advertising executive notes, trying to stop problem drinking with an ad ban "makes as little sense as trying to control the Ku Klux Klan by outlawing bed linens."[15] Ad restrictions would also muzzle a competitive weapon. Without advertising, starting a new national brand would be almost impossible and established brands would have an insurmountable advantage. Innovative products such as the ice beers introduced in the past decade would be hard to introduce.

Second, anti-alcohol groups assume that the public is too stupid to make responsible decisions. The idea of curbing ads is condescending. Consumers are intelligent and skeptical, and are not fooled by the association of alcohol with attractive images. Would the critics expect brewers and vintners to associate their products with root canals, traffic congestion, or income taxes? An ad ban would wrongly imply to millions of responsible drinkers that they were doing something wrong by having a beer or a glass of wine.

Third, the beer, wine, and spirits industries have voluntary codes of advertising behavior. The policies in these codes are extensive and specific. For example, the Beer Institute's *Advertising & Marketing Code* prohibits depictions of excessive consumption, intoxication, and drinking while driving. Models in beer ads must be over 25 and "reasonably appear" to be over 21 years old. No ads should be placed in media where the audience is primarily under 21 years old, and beer ads should never show "any symbol, language, music, gesture, or cartoon character that is intended to appeal primarily to persons below the legal purchase age." No depictions of Santa Claus or sexual promiscuity are permitted.[16] However, compliance with these codes is voluntary. The Beer Institute simply refers complaints about ads and leaves action up to the company.

Fourth, alcoholic beverage companies deflect critics by broadcasting public service announcements that preach moderation and by setting up education and community-action projects such as designated-driver programs. There are many such programs. The Distilled Spirits Council of the United States, for example, sponsors college campus programs in which students teach other students about moderation and also has a program to train bartenders how to serve drinks responsibly.

---

[14]Hacker, "Liquor Advertisements on Television," p. 139.

[15]Eric Clark, *The Want Makers,* New York: Viking Press, 1988, p. 285.

[16]The Web site for the *Code* is http://www.beerinst.org/education/code.html.

Finally, the industry does not deny the practice of targeting younger drinkers, minorities, and other groups with advertising themes. The Anheuser-Busch frogs and lizards have strong appeal to legal buyers age 21 to 29, who are the heaviest beer drinkers. The puzzle faced by the company is that this critical group of beer consumers shares many interests and behaviors with teenagers below the legal drinking age. With respect to ads aimed at minorities, the industry believes this practice is legitimate. Market segmentation and the targeted advertising that makes it work is standard in many industries. When toy companies make black or latina dolls, social critics applaud, but when brewers make products that appeal to minority communities, critics argue that these consumers are too gullible and naive to withstand manipulation, implying that members of these groups are not as astute as, say, white male consumers. The real problem is that the product is alcohol, not that the ads have ethnic or racial appeal.

Proposals to Limit Alcohol Advertising

Today there is little government regulation of alcohol ads, and, in recent years, federal courts have weakened that which does exist. Two federal agencies have some power over the claims that companies make. Under a 1935 law, the Bureau of Alcohol, Tobacco and Firearms regulates container labels to prevent false claims, obscene images, and the use of words such as "strong" and "extra strength." Originally, this law prohibited statements of alcohol content on labels so that companies could not start strength wars. But in 1995, the Supreme Court held that forbidding this information violated bottler's speech rights,[17] so alcohol content can now be stated on labels. A second agency, the Federal Trade Commission, has the power to stop "deceptive" and "unfair" advertising claims, and now and then it flexes its muscles regarding alcohol ads. For instance, in 1998, a television ad for Beck's beer showed people on a sailing ship holding beer bottles. One person, holding a bottle, balanced on a bowsprit over the ocean. The FTC held that the ad was "unfair" because operating a vessel under the influence of alcohol is dangerous and the ad was "likely to cause substantial injury to consumers."[18] Industry critics have petitioned a third agency, the Federal Communications Commission, to allow counter-advertising with anti-drinking themes, but so far the agency has refused.

Recently, two cities, Baltimore and Chicago, banned alcohol ads on billboards. The Chicago ban was struck down in court. Until 1996, Rhode Island banned price advertising for alcoholic beverages, claiming it was justified in doing so to promote temperance. However, the Supreme Court struck the ban down, saying that price advertising is protected by the First Amendment's

---

[17]*Rubin* v. *Coors Brewing Company,* 115 S.C. 1585 (1995).

[18]Federal Trade Commission, *Complaint: In the Matter of Beck's North America, Inc.,* http://www.ftc.gov/os/1998/9808/9823092.cmp.htm.

free-speech guarantee.[19] Altogether, the body of government regulation covering alcohol advertising imposes very few restraints.

Critics want stronger measures. Over the years, they have focused attention on some specific restrictions. In 1997, Rep. Joseph P. Kennedy II (D.-Mass.) introduced a bill for a Comprehensive Alcohol Abuse Prevention Act that pulled together a range of these ideas, including the following.[20]

- Alcohol ads would be prohibited in video games or films and on billboards within 1,000 feet of schools and playgrounds.
- In publications with 15 percent or more readers under age 21, ads would be restricted to text and black and white only; no images would be allowed.
- No television ads could be broadcast between the hours of 7:00 A.M. and 10:00 P.M.
- Hats, T-shirts, coffee mugs, and other promotion items with the brand name of an alcoholic beverage would be prohibited.
- On college campuses, companies would be prohibited from using brochures, giving away free drinks, and sponsoring concerts, dances, or sports events. Ads in college newspapers could contain only product names and prices.
- The tax deductibility of ads for beer, wine, and spirits under the Internal Revenue Code would end.
- Health warnings would be required on beer, wine, and spirit labels. (In the past, ad opponents have wanted health warnings in alcohol advertisements as well.)
- In a separate bill, Rep. Kennedy would require the Federal Communications Commission to write a voluntary advertising code for limiting children's exposure to alcohol ads.[21]

Kennedy's bills were opposed by powerful industry lobbies and failed to come to a vote. Yet the ideas in them have not lost favor among those who want ad restrictions, and they will continue to resurface.

Part II: Advertising Tobacco Products

About 47 million Americans, or 23 percent of the adult population, smoke cigarettes, and another 10 million use other tobacco products. This is less than in many other countries. The World Health Organization estimates that about

---

[19]*44 Liquormart v. Rhode Island,* 116 S.Ct. 1495 (1996).

[20]H. R. 1982.

[21]"Voluntary Alcohol Advertising Standards for Children Act," H. R. 1292, 105th Cong., 1st Sess. (1997).

33 percent of the global population over age fifteen smokes, including 47 percent of men and 12 percent of women.[22] In recent years, the number of adult smokers in the United States has held steady, but the number of underage smokers has slowly increased, reversing a twenty-year downward trend. Overall, however, smokers are smoking less and cigarette consumption in the domestic market continues to decline.

Tobacco use has been compared with an epidemic. Cigarette smoke contains forty-three carcinogens, which is why it is associated not only with lung cancer but with cancers in many sites such as the bladder, kidney, and pancreas.[23] Each year, more than 430,000 Americans die of smoking-related diseases, a number equivalent to the lives that would be lost if two Boeing 747s filled with passengers crashed every day, 365 days a year. Worldwide there are an estimated four million annual deaths, and the number is predicted to rise to ten million by 2020. By that time, smoking will be responsible for one of every eight deaths around the globe.

Notwithstanding, the tobacco industry spends enormous sums to advertise its products. In the United States, it spent almost $5 billion in 1995, according to the Federal Trade Commission.[24]

The Tobacco Industry's Grim Marketing Environment

In early America, smoking was mostly confined to southern states, but during the Civil War, Union troops occupying the South picked up the habit and brought it home with them, creating national demand for smoking tobacco. In the century after the Civil War, smoking grew to be widely accepted, and by the 1950s, the majority of men, and about one-third of women, smoked.

From the beginning, suspicion of adverse health effects hung over cigarettes, and by the 1940s, much advertising focused on trying to allay smokers' fears. For instance, one Chesterfield slogan was, "Not a cough in a carload." Manufacturers also introduced filters and advertised that these made cigarettes safer by removing harmful substances from smoke. However, in 1954, the Federal Trade Commission banned health claims of all kinds in cigarette ads. Unfortunately, this removed an important incentive for cigarette makers to compete with safer cigarettes. After this action, companies could no longer claim their brands were healthier than competing brands. In particular, smaller companies trying to get a share of the market could no longer use safety features and health claims as a competitive weapon. So advertising changed. It began to focus on allaying smoker's fears through pleasant imagery.[25] Ironically, this imagery has been attacked ever since as misleading for depicting smoking as decent and pleasurable.

---

[22]World Health Organization, "Tobacco Epidemic: Health Dimensions," *Fact Sheet,* May 1998.

[23]It has even been found that environmental tobacco smoke causes lung cancer in pet dogs. See John S. Reif et al., "Passive Smoking and Canine Lung Cancer Risk," *American Journal of Epidemiology,* February 1, 1992, pp. 234–39. Dogs with shorter noses are at greater risk.

[24]Alissa J. Rubin, "Tobacco Ads' Impact Debatable, Except to Some Lawmakers," *Los Angeles Times,* March 19, 1998, p. A5.

[25]John E. Calfee, "The Ghost of Cigarette Advertising Past," *Regulation,* Summer 1997, p. 42.

In 1964, the Surgeon General of the United States released a report warning of a strong association between smoking and lung cancer.[26] It stated that death rates for male smokers were 170 percent those for male nonsmokers and that mortality increased with the number of cigarettes smoked and the number of years a person smoked. This report was a turning point for the industry, putting it on the defensive and soon ending the growth of demand for its product.

Since then, the environment for marketing tobacco has further deteriorated. In 1965, Congress required health warnings on cigarette packages, and in 1971, it prohibited cigarette ads on radio and television. Medical research on the ill effects of smoking accumulated, and in 1985, the Surgeon General called for a "smoke-free society" by the year 2000—a futile hope, but nonetheless a drag on marketing.

An additional burden to the industry is a steady stream of lawsuits by sick smokers. Since the 1950s, there have been more than 900 such suits, and they have always carried the potential to drain industry assets. Companies have fought them off with two main lines of defense. First, they argue that even if medical research establishes a statistical association between smoking and cancer, it cannot prove that smoking caused cancer in individual cases. And second, warning labels on cigarette packs and stories in the media have educated smokers about risks. Therefore, smokers voluntarily accept these risks and are responsible for their own health problems.

Until recently, these arguments had never failed the industry in court, but there are ominous portents. Four of six cases that went to juries between 1996 and 1999 resulted in verdicts against companies, including an $80 million punitive damages verdict against Philip Morris awarded to the family of a Marlboro smoker who died of lung cancer. These courtroom reverses are largely attributable to the use as evidence of newly disclosed internal memos showing that the cigarette companies knew smoking was dangerous and addictive, but continued to create ads that implicitly denied its hazards. It remains to be seen if these verdicts are exceptions or the beginning of a trend.

The Case against Tobacco Advertising

The attack on cigarette advertising is similar to that on alcohol advertising. For one thing, say critics, smoking is harmful, and advertising increases tobacco consumption. It depicts smoking as an attractive, worthwhile pastime and leads people to take alarming risks by starting, smoking more, and switching to low-tar brands instead of quitting. The pervasiveness of advertising makes smoking seem mainstream and unexceptional.

Second, tobacco ads are designed to recruit smokers in certain segments of society. Demographic groups show variation in their smoking rates, and the

---

[26]Department of Health, Education, and Welfare, *Smoking and Health: Report of the Advisory Committee to the Surgeon General of the Public Health Service,* Washington, D.C.: Government Printing Office, 1964.

tobacco companies tailor brands and advertising appeals to groups with relatively more smokers such as American Indians, blacks, blue-collar workers, youth, and the less educated. In other cases, tobacco companies have obviously targeted groups such as Hispanics with relatively low smoking rates, either to recruit new smokers or simply because the groups have unique identities that can be targeted. Critics object to targeting because of the implication that the industry is creating victims. "When [tobacco companies] decide they want to sell to a certain segment of the population," says one, "what they are deciding is that they want that segment to die at a higher rate."[27] There are many examples of targeting.

Blacks smoke at a rate of 27 percent, about 1 percent higher than whites, and much advertising is aimed at them. In 1990, R. J. Reynolds tried to introduce a new mentholated brand, Uptown, with ads featuring black couples in urban settings. The brand failed when R. J. Reynolds was attacked by black leaders for promoting death and disease in the black community. Comedian Jay Leno joked that the name Uptown was chosen because the name Genocide had already been trademarked.

Although only 19 percent of Hispanics smoke (compared with 26 percent of whites), cigarette companies use Spanish-language advertising to reach them in ethnic publications and neighborhoods. Three special brands have been successfully introduced for Hispanic smokers—Rio, Dorado, and L&M Superior.

In the early 1960s, less than one in every four women smoked, but the rate began to rise when the first modern brand aimed at women, Virginia Slims, was introduced in 1967 by Philip Morris. Other "female" brands followed. To attract women, marketers used new production technologies to make slim and ultra-slim cigarettes (Capri and Superslims), flavored smokes (Chelsea and Spring Lemon Lights), and decorated cigarettes in packs with pastel colors, flowers, and other feminine touches (Newport Stripes 100s and Eve). Marketing themes targeting women focused on the symbolism of thin models and thin cigarettes to reinforce the belief that a benefit of smoking is appetite suppression. Ads also emphasized the theme that smoking was a way for women to express independence and self-fulfillment. Brown and Williamson's Misty Lights, for example, are advertised using the slogan "slim 'n sassy."

Although the tobacco companies deny it, critics believe that cigarette ads also target young people. About 90 percent of smokers start before age twenty-one and 82 percent before age eighteen. Brand loyalty for cigarettes is higher than for any other major consumer product. About half of all smokers never change brands.[28] Therefore, attracting beginning or young smokers pays big dividends. There is no question that tobacco ads register on youth.

---

[27]Philip Wilbur, quoted in Michael F. Jacobson and Laurie Ann Mazur, *Marketing Madness,* Boulder: Center for the Study of Commercialism, 1995, p. 172.

[28]Department of Health and Human Services, *Reducing the Health Consequences of Smoking: 25 Years of Progress,* Rockville, Md.: DHHS, 1989, pp. i, 161.

Research found that six-year-olds were as familiar with Joe Camel as they were with Mickey Mouse.[29] The theory is that children are especially vulnerable to ad psychology and fall into the grip of nicotine addiction before they grasp the consequences.

Third, tobacco ads, like beer and wine ads, employ clever "lifestyle" themes. These associate a dangerous product with success, adventure, romance, status, fun, and masculinity or femininity. The strong, ruggedly independent Marlboro cowboy or the slightly rebellious, sassy, and attractive Virginia Slims woman is geared to satisfying strong emotional needs in targeted personality types. Smokers then buy a particular brand to meet an emotional need. Cigarettes as physical objects are essentially the same, and all function adequately as nicotine containers. However, brand advertising endows them with psychological utility. Thus, awkward, immature adolescents buy Camels, Kools, or other brands hoping to get not simply the cigarettes, but also the social acceptance and sophistication promised by the images in ad campaigns. Young smokers start not to get nicotine, but "to belong, to rebel, to express their individuality, to take risks, to appear more grown up, to be cool, and so on."[30]

Cigarette Makers Defend Ads

Tobacco companies point out that there is no proof that advertising increases consumption or that its elimination would reduce smoking. In the United States, the long-term trend has been decline and stagnation in per capita cigarette consumption even as advertising expenditures increase. Analysis of ad bans in thirty foreign countries since the 1970s shows that bans are generally accompanied by consumption declines, though not always. In the United States, for example, smoking increased in the years after the 1971 ban on televised cigarette ads went into effect. Moreover, even when consumption has declined, researchers are unable to show that advertising bans caused the decline. Ad bans usually reflect high levels of antitobacco sentiment in countries that adopt them, and declining use may be related to that sentiment rather than the ban itself.[31]

Advertising, says the industry, is used not to increase consumption and encourage new smokers, but as a weapon of brand competition. In the United States, the cigarette market is mature. Everyone is familiar with cigarettes, so advertising to inform potential buyers of their nature and availability is no longer cost-effective. Since the market is also shrinking, there is a ferocious battle among sellers, in which one competitor can grab a larger share only at the expense of a rival. This is why the tobacco companies spend $5 billion a year on

---

[29]Suein L. Hwang, "Doctor Whose Study Tied Joe Camel to Kids Takes an Odd Journey," *The Wall Street Journal,* February 21, 1997, p. A1.

[30]Gerard Hastings et al., "Tobacco Marketing: Shackling the Pied Piper," *British Medical Journal,* August 23, 1997, p. 439.

[31]DHHS, *Reducing the Health Consequences of Smoking,* p. 179.

marketing, to promote brand switching and steal revenue from rivals. Restrictions on advertising would lock in the dominance of the largest companies—Philip Morris with 48 percent of cigarette sales and R. J. Reynolds with 25 percent. Without the weapon of advertising, it would be difficult to launch new brands or reposition and reinvigorate older ones. Established brands would reign supreme.

In response to charges that targeting is reprehensible, the tobacco companies say new brands provide useful alternatives for the forty-seven million American smokers. They do not, for instance, directly target children with ads relating to unique life experiences such as first dates or Little League games. They argue that the influence of advertising is less than that of peer pressure, tobacco use by parents and siblings, and personality variables such as rebelliousness and extroversion, which research shows to be associated with smoking.

In fact, the cigarette companies have programs to discourage youth smoking. In 1998, Philip Morris began spending $100 million a year to run television ads aimed at ten- to fourteen-year-olds, encouraging them to resist peer pressure to smoke.[32] R. J. Reynolds runs a program called "Right Decisions, Right Now" that provides posters and curriculum materials to schools and claims to reach 3.3 million students each year. It also runs public-service commercials featuring teenage celebrities. Both companies participate in an industry program called "We Card" that has trained more than 70,000 retail store clerks how not to sell tobacco to persons under age eighteen. These programs are dismissed by critics as trivial and done mostly to improve corporate image. However, the $100 million per year spent on antismoking ads by Philip Morris approaches the roughly $135 million it spends annually to advertise its top brand, Marlboro.

Tobacco firms also reject the argument that their advertising plays unfairly on emotional needs. Surveys going back to the 1970s show that more than 90 percent of both teenagers and adults believe cigarette smoking harms health.[33] Thus, they freely choose risk exposure. Cigarettes are not marketed differently from other products, and the ads are manipulative only in the sense that all advertising incorporates positive associations from life into product presentation. Millions see tobacco ads daily but do not become smokers. There is also pronounced skepticism toward ad content in American society. This makes it difficult for marketers of any product to manipulate consumers. Theories of subliminal manipulation and irresistible seduction are unprovable because they are wrong.

Finally, the industry, advertising agencies, and media corporations seek to define smoking and tobacco advertising as civil liberties. In a free society, the ideas of a legal industry, including those expressed in ads, are entitled to be heard. The government should not try to reach policy goals through censorship.

---

[32]Constance L. Hays, "Philip Morris Assembles a $100 Million Program to Try to Reduce Smoking's Appeal to Teen-agers," *New York Times*, December 3, 1998, p. C2.

[33]About such studies, see, for example, DHHS, *Reducing the Health Consequences of Smoking*, p. 119.

There is no monopoly on truth about smoking; it will emerge from lively exchange in the marketplace of ideas, not from government edicts.

The Endgame for Tobacco Advertising

In 1995, the FDA declared that it had jurisdiction to regulate tobacco products because they were "nicotine delivery devices" and nicotine was a drug. It drafted sweeping regulations trying to prevent youths from initiating the smoking habit.[34] The rules set up by the agency banned vending machines, self-service displays in stores, and mail-order sales. They limited ads in youth-oriented publications to black-and-white only and required warning statements such as "ABOUT 1 OUT OF 3 KIDS WHO BECOME SMOKERS WILL DIE FROM THEIR SMOKING." Billboards near schools were prohibited. Cigarette brand names could no longer be used on merchandise such as hats or T-shirts. And the tobacco companies were required to run public service anti-smoking ads that had to be submitted to the FDA for prior approval. However, the tobacco industry was outraged that the FDA would restrict its right to advertise a legal product and, in any case, believed that the agency lacked authority to regulate tobacco since Congress had never specifically granted it. It sued to stop enforcement of these regulations, and, in 1998, a federal court invalidated them for exceeding the FDA's statutory authority.[35]

Meanwhile, tobacco firms faced a problem in the legal arena. State governments were suing them to recover billions of Medicaid dollars paid out to treat smokers' illnesses. In addition, hundreds of lawsuits for lung cancer victims were winding through the courts. The potential cost of all these cases frightened the cigarette makers, and, in 1997, they reached a negotiated settlement with state attorneys general and victims' lawyers to resolve their legal liability and limit the payout.

This settlement ended the state Medicaid lawsuits for $368.5 billion to be paid by the industry to state governments over twenty-five years. It also imposed many advertising restrictions. It prohibited the use of human figures and cartoons, sponsorship of sports events, and the use of brand logos on promotional items. In return, the industry would get immunity from punitive damages based on its past conduct and, although sick smokers could still sue, jury awards against all companies could not exceed an annual cap of $5 billion. These were very unusual, indeed unprecedented, arrangements. No industry had ever been granted such special protections from the law. So in order for the settlement to work, Congress needed to legislate changes in products liability law.

In 1998, a bill was introduced in the Senate to enable the settlement, but the politicians in Congress could not resist adding new elements to the deal.[36] One provision sought to raise $516 million over twenty-five years from a federal tax

---

[34]U.S. Food and Drug Administration, "Regulations Restricting the Sale and Distribution of Cigarettes and Smokeless Tobacco to Protect Children and Adolescents," 61 FR 44396, August 28, 1996.

[35]*Brown & Williamson* v. *Food & Drug Administration*, 153 F.3d 155 (1998).

[36]The National Tobacco Policy and Youth Smoking Reduction Act, 105th Cong., 2nd Sess. (S. 1415), 1998.

increase of $1.10 per pack of cigarettes. Another part of the bill gave the FDA authority to regulate tobacco. The tobacco industry bolted. It feared that bureaucrats in the FDA were getting the power to regulate it out of business. And the proposed taxes would raise the price of a cigarette pack to $5. Steven F. Goldstone, CEO of RJR Nabisco, attacked the bill in these words.

> . . . Washington has rushed to collect more tobacco revenues while playing the politics of punishment—not only destroying the negotiated settlement but threatening to injure farming communities, retail store owners, and everyone else who participates in this $50 billion industry, as well as every adult who chooses to use tobacco products . . . What would this do . . . to the family of a smoker who makes $25,000 a year? . . . [I]t would increase his tax bill by almost $1,000 a year—more than he will then pay in federal income taxes.[37]

Fed up, the industry ran a massive lobbying campaign to kill the Senate bill, including $40 million in advertising that painted it as a disguised tax hike and more Big Government. The bill died.

After renewed negotiations, the industry reached a second settlement with the states late in 1998, this time agreeing to pay $246 billion over twenty-five years and submitting to specific advertising restrictions. The agreement banned all outdoor advertising, transit advertising, in-store ads larger than fourteen square feet, cartoons, logos on promotional items, brand-name event sponsorships (with one annual exception), and sale of packs with fewer than twenty cigarettes. In addition, the industry was required to run $25 million of anti-smoking ads every year for ten years. It also agreed not to run ad campaigns targeting children and not to lobby against state laws that limit ads in schools.

Although at first glance the deal seemed to shackle the industry, opponents disliked it. Ralph Nader called it "a sweetheart deal" filled with "laughably weak" and "inconsequential marketing restrictions."[38] It still allows image ads with human figures in magazines and newspapers. Philip Morris can still sponsor a Virginia Slims tennis tournament. And many other promotional activities are left untouched. The billion dollar payments seem huge, but they are tax deductible and spread out over twenty-five years, making them affordable. Moreover, most observers thought they failed to cover even half the Medicaid costs of smoking illness. And, since the companies immediately raised prices on cigarette packs to cover payout costs, the deal is essentially a tax increase on smokers.

Are Restrictions on Alcohol and Tobacco Ads Constitutional?

Images and statements in advertising are speech. Therefore, proposals for muzzling liquor and tobacco companies raise constitutional issues. The First Amendment protects speech from government-imposed curbs, but courts

---

[37]Speech to the Washington Press Club, Washington, D.C., April 8, 1998, pp. 2, 9.
[38]Ralph Nader, "Marlboro Man Still in the Saddle," *Los Angeles Times*, November 24, 1998, p. B14.

have distinguished *noncommercial* speech from *commercial* speech. The former is defined as speech in the broad marketplace of ideas, encompassing political, scientific, and artistic expression, and is broadly protected. The latter refers to speech intended to stimulate business transactions, including advertising, and has received less protection.

In both areas, the general principle used by courts to test restrictions is that the right to speech must be balanced against society's need to maintain the general welfare. The right of free speech is assumed to be a fundamental barrier against tyranny and is not restricted lightly. Courts will not permit censorship of speech unless it poses an imminent threat to public welfare, as it would, for example, if a speaker incited violence or a writer tried to publish military secrets.

With respect to commercial speech, however, various restrictions are allowed. For example, ads for securities offerings can appear only in the austere format of a legal notice and, as noted, tobacco ads are barred on radio and TV. Would courts approve additional restrictions on alcoholic beverage and tobacco advertising?

The most important legal guidelines for weighing restraints on commercial speech are those set forth by the Supreme Court in 1980 in the *Central Hudson* case.[39] Here the Court struck down a New York regulation banning advertising by public utilities, a regulation intended to help conserve energy. Justice Lewis Powell, writing for the majority, set forth a four-part test to decide when commercial speech could be restricted.

First, the ad in question should promote a lawful product and must be accurate. If an ad is misleading or suggests illegal activity, it does not merit protection. Second, the government interest in restricting the particular commercial speech must be substantial, not trivial or unimportant. Third, the regulation or advertising restriction must directly further the interest of the government. In other words, it should demonstrably help the government reach its public policy goal. Fourth, the suppression of commercial speech must not be more extensive than is necessary to achieve the government's purpose.

All measures to ban or restrict alcohol and tobacco ads could be immediately challenged and would have to pass the four-part *Central Hudson* test.

Conclusion

Should government use restrictions on speech to protect citizens from the dangers of alcohol and tobacco? Because of the settlement between the states and cigarette makers, the tobacco industry has voluntarily agreed to restrict its advertising, but not to end it. Critics want similar restrictions imposed on the alcoholic beverage industry as well. Historically, the free-speech principle has

---

[39]*Central Hudson Gas & Electric Corp.* v. *Public Service Commission,* 447 U.S. 557.

been revered in American society. Every power given to government to censor the expression of unpopular ideas is an encroachment on the notion that truth emerges best through the unrestricted expression of competing claims. Do the American people need government protection against the blandishments of alcohol and tobacco marketers?

Questions

1. Are some beer, wine, liquor, or tobacco ads misleading? What examples can you give? What specifically is misleading?
2. Do alcoholic beverage and tobacco companies that fight for their right to advertise also generally fulfill their corresponding ethical duty to be informative and honest?
3. Would the restrictions on alcoholic beverage marketing in Representative Kennedy's proposed Comprehensive Alcohol Abuse Prevention Act meet the criteria for speech restraints in the *Central Hudson* guidelines?
4. Although the tobacco industry has voluntarily agreed to advertising restrictions, some believe in the need for further limits or a complete ban. Do you agree? What additional constraints or how extensive a ban would meet the criteria in the *Central Hudson* guidelines?

Human Resources

17

The Changing Face of Organizational Life

Ford Motor Company
www.ford.com

enry Ford (1863–1947) was a brilliant inventor. After incorporating the Ford Motor Company in 1903, he designed one car after another, naming each chassis after a letter of the alphabet. In 1908, he began selling the Model T, a utilitarian, crank-started auto that came only in black. An early Model T cost $850, but Ford introduced the first moving auto assembly line and, by 1924, mass output lowered the price to $290. He sold 15.5 million of them before production ended in 1927 and the Model A was introduced.

Hidden behind the success story of the Model T, and less known, is the darker side of Ford Motor Company.

Henry Ford was an obstinate man, obsessed with power, iron-willed, dictatorial, and cynical about human nature. He spied on his employees in their homes to see if they smoked or drank. Believing that workers were motivated by fear, he created a tense atmosphere marked by frequent dismissals that were capricious and arbitrary. Managers arrived at work to find their desks chopped to pieces. One morning, an entire department of eighty-four office workers came in to find their desks gone. Many managers had no job title; this made it less likely that they would establish a power base. Sometimes two managers were given the same duties and the one failing to thrive in the competition was fired. Shy by nature, Ford hired sadistic lieutenants to carry out these petty assassinations while at a safe remove he set the tone. In his autobiography, he wrote that a "great business is really too big to be human."[1]

As the firm grew, Henry Ford's authoritarian style became embedded in its informal culture. Independent managers left and he was surrounded by sycophants who would have jumped into the Detroit River if Ford had asked. They, in turn, were ruthless and autocratic with their subordinates.[2]

This internal atmosphere left power in Ford's hands, but it hindered adaptation to external forces. Despite warnings in the form of fast-dropping market share in the mid-1920s, Ford Motor Company failed utterly to anticipate a sea change in the auto market. It clung to the spartan Model T even as consumers turned to the styling changes, closed body design, and model hierarchy offered by General Motors. Finally, in 1927, Ford had to suspend production, stilling its great River Rouge assembly plant for seven months while the Model A was hurriedly designed. It never recovered the market share it once held.

Although the company regained its footing and made successful new models over the years, authoritarianism remained firmly entrenched. In 1945, Henry Ford himself felt its sting

when he was ousted in a coup engineered by family members. He was replaced by his grandson, Henry Ford II, who also proved to be an autocrat.

In the early 1980s, Ford suffered three years of disastrous losses, mainly due to heightened international competition. Japanese auto companies had captured 20 percent of the domestic market. The company studied Japanese management and decided to emulate its focus on teamwork and continuous quality improvement. It set out to make an innovative world-class sedan using teams similar to those used by Japanese car makers.

In Japanese management philosophy, competing personalities and individualism are thought to hamper productivity. So Ford tried to change its corporate culture. Over the years, it had tended to select autocrats for management positions. A study of 2,000 Ford managers classified 76 percent as "noncreative types who are comfortable with strong authority" (as compared to about 38 percent of the population).[3] To facilitate change, thousands of managers went to workshops on participative management.

Ford was rewarded for its efforts when the innovative Taurus sedan appeared in 1985. It was a quick success and became the best-selling car in America between 1993 and 1995. In 1994, Ford made an extraordinary $5.3 billion in profits, a sum exceeded by only one other company in the world (Royal Dutch/Shell with

[1]Henry Ford, *My Life and Work*, Garden City, N.Y.: Doubleday, 1923, p. 263.

[2]Anne Jardim, *The First Henry Ford: A Study in Personality and Business Leadership*, Cambridge, Mass.: MIT Press, 1970, pp. 114–15.

[3]Melinda G. Builes and Paul Ingrassia, "Ford's Leaders Push Radical Shift in Culture as Competition Grows," *The Wall Street Journal*, December 3, 1985.

$6.2 billion). Yet in that year, a new Ford chairman, Alexander Trotman, started a radical change program, called Ford 2000, to prepare the company for an even more competitive global car market.

Ford 2000 restructured Ford, changing it from an organization divided by regions and countries to one focused on products. Old bureaucratic hierarchies were abolished. Layers of middle management disappeared. Tasks were defined in meetings instead of by superiors. Promotions, reassignments, and performance reviews were done by committees. Product design, engineering, and manufacturing, once separate parts of the organization, merged. Now teams with members from these three areas develop vehicles. This cut costs and speeded timetables for new models.

The changes were traumatic for workers. More than 25,000 managers left hierarchical slots and moved into team structures. Jobs were eliminated and early retirements encouraged. But Ford 2000 was not a reincarnation of its founder's philosophy that the company was "too big to be human." Instead, it was impelled by external forces.

Competition is relentless in the global automobile industry. Ford is the second-largest car producer in the United States, with a 20 percent market share. Japanese firms have seized 31 percent of the American market. In Europe, where Ford has an 11 percent share, six other companies have shares of between 10 and 17 percent and Japanese manufacturers have an 11 percent share, making rivalry intense. Ford has 18 percent of the market in Australia and 16 percent in Taiwan, but it has only small shares elsewhere in Asia and in rising markets such as Brazil.[4]

Inroads against competitors are excruciatingly difficult due to a worldwide production overcapacity in the industry. Because of the potential for oversupply, car companies cannot easily raise output to increase revenue. For the same reason, and because brand loyalty in consumers is declining, they cannot raise prices. The only way to raise profits in this industry climate is to cut costs and increase net income on each car sold. Leaner organizations save money. So does new technology, and Ford is using new manufacturing techniques to raise productivity. It uses computers that not only design cars, but then automatically cut the tools and dies used in their production, and subsequently configure the assembly lines from which they emerge. Like other car companies, it uses lean manufacturing techniques, where suppliers do part of the work by delivering parts and modular assemblies just as they are needed on the line. When Ford 2000 began in 1994, its cars averaged $875 in profits; by 1997, this rose to $1,020.[5]

Although many jobs were eliminated by Ford 2000, the company's total workforce increased from 325,000 in 1992 to 364,000 in 1998 due to acquisitions and expansions. In this respect, Ford is like many other companies that simultaneously cut and add workers in a dynamic growth

---

[4]Ford Motor Company, *Form 10-K,* 1998, p. 5.
[5]John Lippert, "New CEO Aims to Keep Ford Profitable," *The Plain Dealer,* November 8, 1998, p. 1H.

process. Despite overall job growth, there are feelings of insecurity at Ford. In early 1999, the company eliminated 2 percent of its worldwide workforce and announced its intention to cut further. Ford uses incentives that encourage white-collar employees to leave or retire early. To thin the ranks of older workers and bring in younger, lower-paid replacements, the company plans to reduce its management ranks 10 percent by identifying low and average performers and encouraging them to resign or retire. These managers are told that they will not be promoted and that, if they stay, their jobs cannot be guaranteed. However, if they leave voluntarily, they receive a generous deal.

This short history of Ford Motor Company illustrates how a set of forces—leadership of a founder, changes in management philosophy, international competition, and technological change—can shape the workplace. In this chapter, we discuss a number of such external forces and illustrate how they affect the welfare of the 3.7 billion mortals who toil in the global economy.

The Nature and Meaning of Work

Those who work are performing a timeless, basic task. We define *work* as sustained effort done to produce something of value for other people. At an elemental level, work is essential. Humans must manipulate their environment to live. The underlying moral basis of work is that each person is a burden on society and should contribute a fair share of the expenditure of human energy necessary for survival.

Work has an important psychological dimension. The clinician Karl Menninger saw work as one of two constructive outlets for aggressive impulses, the other being play.[6] Psychoanalyst Harry Levinson speaks of work as a central means for accomplishing the "twin unconscious drives of love and hate." "The carpenter who hammers nails," says Levinson, "is not only discharging his aggressions but also building a shelter."[7] Besides giving expression to inner drives, work can bring a sense of mastery, placate a stern conscience, or divert attention from harmful anxieties.

The psychological value of work is underscored by the apparent strains on those who lose their jobs. Studies show that fired and laid-off workers are at greater risk of accident, illness, suicide, and marital problems than those who stay employed. A landmark study of the years 1922 to 1971 showed an inverse relationship between economic conditions and admission to mental hospitals.[8] Another study found that suicides rose and fell with the unemployment rate

---

[6]Karl Menninger, *The Vital Balance*, New York: Viking, 1963, p. 141.

[7]Harry Levinson, *Executive*, Cambridge, Mass.: Harvard University Press, 1981, p. 29.

[8]Harvey M. Brenner, *Mental Illness and the Economy*, Cambridge, Mass.: Harvard University Press, 1976.

between 1940 and 1984.[9] Despite the salutary benefits of work, however, the workplace is often highly stressful and competitive. Even emotionally healthy people have difficulty adapting to its pressures, frustrations, and conflicts.

The meaning of work has been different in other societies, past and present. In ancient Greece and Rome, work—in the sense of hard physical labor—was associated with degradation and slavery. Aristotle, for example, believed that hard labor deprived a person of the leisure necessary to develop character. Early Christians moved away from this disdain for work. They believed that manual labor was approved of by God and served worthwhile ends, including "to obtain food, to remove idleness, to curb concupiscence, and to provide for almsgiving."[10] Doctrinal changes after the Protestant Reformation in the sixteenth century led to changes in the Christian work ethic. A belief arose that God called every person in the community to labor. Hard work, discipline, thrift, and sober diligence glorified God and were necessary for salvation. If strenuous labor led to material rewards, even great wealth, it was a sign of God's approval. This set of ideas became known as the *Protestant ethic*. It began as a religious teaching in medieval Europe and was carried across the Atlantic to the American colonies.

Today, the work ethic in the United States has lost most of its religious overtones, but in the colonial period, farmers and artisans, who had to work tirelessly to survive, were motivated by the message of religious duty in the Protestant ethic. In this era, workers also took great pride in their skills and crafts. Mundane tools such as saws, shovels, and knives were ornately engraved and fondly passed from father to son.

After 1850, the industrial revolution attracted farmers and immigrants to cities, where they hoped to toil their way to riches. Instead, they often found alienating work with low wages, long hours, tedium, danger, and pitiless supervision. In the early twentieth century, business applied "scientific management" to factories. This was an approach to work developed by Frederick Taylor, an engineer who increased productivity by using time and motion studies to make tasks specialized, routine, efficient, and quick. Gone were the days of decorated shovels. Taylor ushered in an era of utility.

In reaction to this treatment of workers as machines, a school of applied psychology encouraged employers to increase productivity by recognizing the social needs of workers. Both approaches survive today and are deeply ingrained in managerial practice. During World War II, the driving motive behind work became patriotism. Then, from the end of the war through the 1960s, work was seen by Americans mainly as a source of status and income.

But by the 1970s, work was increasingly a means of self-fulfillment. In a 1983 survey, salary and regular promotions ranked seventh and eighth on a list

---

[9]Bijou Yang, "The Economy and Suicide: A Time-Series Study of the U.S.A.," *American Journal of Economics and Sociology*, January 1992.

[10]Gerald F. Cavanagh, *American Business Values: With International Perspectives*, 4th ed., Upper Saddle River, N.J.: Prentice Hall, 1998, p. 112, citing Thomas Aquinas, *Summa Theologica*, II-II, qu. 87, art. 3.

of ten indicators of career success, behind self-fulfillment measures such as "achievement of personal life goals" and having the "opportunity and means for achieving a fulfilling, happy home and social life."[11] In a similar survey in 1991, high income and promotions ranked eleventh and fourteenth on a list of job attributes; "interesting work" ranked second, behind having health insurance.[12] As these surveys show, most workers want to fulfill a variety of inner needs beyond religious duty or material success.

External Forces Changing the Workplace

Those who work today, especially those who work in large corporations, are swept up in turbulence caused by five environmental forces (1) demographic change, (2) technological change, (3) structural change, (4) competition, and (5) government intervention. These powerful forces interact and together create more rapid change than the country has seen since the 1930s. A discussion of each follows.

Demographic Change

Population dynamics slowly but continuously alter the labor force. Out of a 1999 population of 272 million Americans, about half, or 139 million, composed the civilian labor force as either working or unemployed (the rest were retired, disabled, students, homemakers, children under age 16, or not counted because they got unreported wages). This is the third largest labor force in the world, though it pales in comparison to China's 718 million workers and India's 408 million.[13]

Historically, the American labor force has grown rapidly and continuously. It continues to grow, but more slowly now. Between 1986 and 1996, the number of workers grew by 2.1 percent each year. But over the years until 2006, it is projected to grow by only 1.1 percent a year, due to slower growth in the general population.[14] Amid this slower overall workforce expansion, however, the number of workers in some demographic categories is growing faster than in others, producing incremental but significant changes. Table 17-1 shows data for the 1996 labor force and projects current trends to the year 2006.

---

[11] George F. Breen, *Middle Management Morale in the '80s,* New York: American Management Association, 1983, p. 16.

[12] Larry Hugick and Jennifer Leonard, "Job Dissatisfaction Grows; 'Moonlighting' on the Rise," *Gallup Poll Monthly,* September 1991, p. 9.

[13] Figures are from the U.S. Bureau of Labor Statistics and World Bank, *World Development Indicators 1998,* Washington, D.C., CD-ROM, 1998, Table 2–3. Figures for China and India are for 1996.

[14] Howard N. Fullerton Jr., "Labor Force 2006: Slowing Down and Changing Composition," *Monthly Labor Review,* November 1997, p. 24.

TABLE 17-1   **The Changing Civilian Labor Force: 1996–2006**
(in thousands)

	1996	Percent of Labor Force in 1996	2006	Percent of Labor Force in 2006	Percent Change in Numbers
Total	133,943	100	148,847	100	11.1
Men	72,087	53.8	78,226	52.6	8.5
Women	61,857	46.2	70,620	47.4	14.2
White	113,108	84.4	123,581	83.0	9.3
White male	61,783	46.1	66,008	44.3	0.7
Black	15,134	11.3	17,225	11.6	13.8
Hispanic[1]	12,774	9.5	17,401	11.7	36.2
Asian[2]	5,703	4.3	8,041	5.4	41.0
Median age	38.2		40.6		

[1] "Hispanic" persons may be of any race.
[2] "Asian" includes Asians, Pacific Islanders, Native Americans, and Alaskan natives.
Source: Bureau of Labor Statistics.

Table 17-1 shows that on a proportionate basis, both Hispanics and Asians are increasing their numbers faster than whites and blacks. By 2006, Hispanics will replace blacks as the second largest ethnic group in the labor force. Asians are the fastest-growing group, but they will remain the smallest ethnic category at only about 5 percent. Since the 1970s, women have increased participation more rapidly than men and, although this trend is slowing and nearing an end, it will continue until 2006. The long-term participation rate for men will decline because the male labor force is on average older and men are withdrawing from the labor force in greater numbers than women.

These changes mean that the workforce continues to become more diverse in gender and ethnicity. In percentage terms, the change will not be great. White males, for example, will decline by only 1.8 percent, and because of rising participation by white females, whites will decline by only 1.4 percent overall. Hispanics will increase by 2.2 percent and Asians by 1.1 percent. Blacks will increase in number but will remain about 11 percent of the workforce. These are modest overall shifts. However, businesses in very cosmopolitan areas will experience more rapid diversity increases than these national rates suggest.

The workforce is also aging. High fertility rates following World War II created a "baby-boom" generation born between 1946 and 1961. As this generation entered the labor market in the 1970s, the median age of the workforce began to decline, reaching a low of 34.6 years in 1980. The baby boomers are now a bulge of workers in their late thirties to mid-fifties that makes up 45 percent of all workers. There are so many baby boomers that, as they age, the median age of the entire workforce rises. It stood at 38.2 years in 1996 and will rise to 40.6 years in 2005. Because the nation's fertility rate has been declining, generational cohorts of workers following the baby boomers are smaller. This means that there are fewer entry- and lower-level workers, while the statistical crowd of baby boomers, now seasoned in middle-management positions, confronts a bottleneck at the top, competing for fewer and fewer vacancies where the organizational pyramid constricts.

The graying of the workforce in developed nations is worldwide, and aging trends are more rapid in Europe and Japan. European Union nations have an average birth rate slightly below the replacement rate of 2.1 births per woman. In Germany, for instance, the rate is only 1.3.[15] Because fewer younger workers will arrive in the next ten to twenty years, these countries face a challenge in filling entry- and lower-level jobs. While some developed nations face population declines and all have aging workforces, some third-world nations have explosively growing, relatively youthful populations.

The United States, which will average net immigration of 820,000 persons yearly to 2006, may have a long-run competitive advantage in labor costs.[16] Japan and European countries have much more restrictive immigration laws. The Japanese want to preserve racial purity and have difficulty integrating non-Japanese into their workplaces. Many European nations are strongly ethnocentric and prohibit most immigration. But immigration brings an influx of younger workers who are less costly and more adaptable.

Technological Change

Recently, Yellow Cab installed a new navigation system to manage its fleet of 450 taxis in Dallas. Signals from a global positioning device in each cab are relayed by satellite to dispatchers, who can see their exact street routes on a monitor. When a customer calls, the system finds the closest cab and calculates the fare to a destination. This technology increases Yellow Cab's efficiency in many ways. Not only does it save gas, but a payola system in which dispatchers gave more lucrative runs to drivers who kicked back some of the fare has disappeared. Now, the closest cab gets the call, no matter who is driving it.[17]

Technological change has many impacts on work. It affects the number and type of jobs available. Invention of the airplane, for example, created new job titles such as pilot and flight attendant. Web masters, or employees who design and update Web sites, emerged with the rise of the Internet. New machines are used by management to raise productivity and reduce costs.

---

[15]Peter G. Peterson, "Gray Dawn: The Global Aging Crisis," *Foreign Affairs*, January–February 1999, p. 45.

[16]Charles Bowman, "BLS Projections to 2006—A Summary," *Monthly Labor Review*, November 1997, p. 3.

[17]Art Pine, "Technology May Not Drive Nation's Productivity, but It Can Hail a Taxi," *Los Angeles Times*, December 27, 1997, p. A20.

Robots in auto manufacturing made American companies more competitive in cost and quality with Japanese car makers. Automated teller machines at banks simultaneously increased daily transactions and reduced the number of employees necessary to do them. Computer makers such as Dell Computer Corp. take orders over the Internet, reducing the need for telephone sales representatives.

Automation has a turbulent impact on employment because it creates jobs for the architects of the machine age while displacing traditional manufacturing and service jobs. Overall, the number of jobs available in the United States has continuously increased, and this is projected to continue. But automation causes significant job loss in less-skilled manufacturing and service occupations. In the coal-mining industry, for example, mechanization has eliminated 300,000 pick-and-shovel jobs since the 1950s. The movement to robotics in the 1980s put almost 40,000 robots on U.S. assembly lines and eliminated roughly two-thirds of all assembly-line jobs by 1990. In service industries, the blows have been softer, but still telling. Between 1987 and 1997, 20 percent of telephone operators were eliminated due to automation of their services, even as the average number of daily conversations increased by more than 600 percent.[18]

High-tech industries, which are the source of the innovations that erase jobs, are not immune to the implications of the labor-saving, work-reorienting devices they create. In fact, job growth in the technology sector is slower than in the rest of the economy as a whole. Between 1988 and 1996, the twenty-eight industries defined by the Bureau of Labor Statistics as "high technology" created 400,000 new jobs, an increase of only 5 percent, and less than 3 percent of all jobs created in the nation. Low-tech industries were more prolific, creating jobs almost three times as fast (an increase of 14 percent). Among the twenty-eight high-tech industries, only five that deal in services added jobs, doing so at a much more rapid rate than the general economy. However, the other twenty-three industries do some manufacturing and, like low-tech manufacturing industries, were rapidly automating and innovating and, as a result, shed more than 600,000 production workers in the period under study.[19] In sum, most technology industries are sluggish job creators, not the dynamos many people believe them to be.

Structural Change

The American economy is being reconfigured by three structural trends common to industrialized nations. The long-term action of these trends dramatically reshapes the job landscape.

---

[18]Stephen Franklin, "Telephone Operators Are Among Those Being Displaced by Technology," *San Jose Mercury News,* September 6, 1998; Bureau of the Census, *Statistical Abstract of the United States 1:1998,* 118th ed., Washington, D.C.: Government Printing Office, 1998, Table 918.

[19]William Luker Jr. and Donald Lyons, "Employment Shifts in High Technology Industries, 1988–96," *Monthly Labor Review,* June 1997, pp. 14–15.

First, the agricultural sector has declined from predominance to near in-significance as an occupation. In colonial America, farming occupied 95 percent of Americans, but today it employs only 2.8 percent as fewer and fewer large farms deliver the nation's food supply using intensive and highly automated crop and animal agriculture.[20] In the 1920s, for example, the largest poultry farm in the country had a flock of 500 chickens; today, up to 100,000 birds are raised in a single, long, narrow poultry building, and multibuilding operations raise several million birds at once. The Bureau of Labor Statistics predicts that agricultural workers will dwindle further, to 2.4 percent of the labor force by the year 2006.

Second, employment in the goods-producing sector has declined for many decades.[21] In 1950, industry jobs dominated the workforce, occupy-ing 78 percent of workers, but by 1996, they lost their prominence and oc-cupied only 19 percent. By 2006, they are predicted to slump further to 16 percent. There are many reasons for the fall of manufacturing work, but perhaps the two most significant are automation and relocation of assem-bly to lower-wage countries. In steel production, for example, competition from Japan, Korea, and Brazil caused a steady drop in U.S. jobs from a peak of 620,400 in 1953 to only 112,000 in 1997.[22] Since 1970, however, the amount of steel made per hour by each U.S. worker has more than doubled because of automated production techniques. Structural change away from manufacturing is also pronounced in other industrialized nations.[23] Ger-many, for example, lost 15 percent of its manufacturing jobs between 1991 and 1996.[24]

Third, there is explosive growth in the service sector, which includes jobs in retailing, transportation, health care, and other occupations that add value to manufactured goods. Service jobs increased from 10 percent of the work-force in 1950 to 71 percent in 1996 and are predicted to grow to 74 percent in 2006. An example of this explosive growth is in business computer services that employed 271,000 people in 1979 and grew by 263 percent to employ 984,000 in 1994.

---

[20]Sector employment figures in this section are from James C. Franklin, "Industry Output and Employment Projections to 2006," *Monthly Labor Review,* November 1997, Table 1, and from various editions of the *Statistical Abstract of the United States.* Sector employment percentages for 1996 do not total 100 percent; the missing increment of 7.2 percent includes private household wage and salary earners and nonagricultural self-employed.

[21]The goods-producing sector includes primarily manufacturing, but also mining and construction.

[22]Bureau of the Census, *Statistical Abstract of the United States: 1998,* Table 1256.

[23]Todd M. Godbout, "Employment Change and Sectoral Distribution in 10 Countries, 1970–1990," *Monthly Labor Review,* October 1993.

[24]Nathaniel C. Nash, "In Germany, Downsizing Means 10.3% Jobless," *New York Times,* March 7, 1996, p. C3.

Occupational Structures of Other Nations

The occupational structures of industrialized nations are remarkably similar. The eight nations below have all seen long-term job losses in agriculture and industry and steep growth in service sector employment. The percentages are for 1996.

	Agriculture	Industry	Services
Australia	5%	22%	73%
Canada	4	22	74
France	5	25	70
Italy	7	32	61
Japan	5	33	62
Sweden	3	19	72
United Kingdom	2	27	71

Source: Bureau of Labor Statistics.

Because of these structural trends, the fastest-growing occupations are those requiring more education. Less-skilled occupations predominate in the declining manufacturing sector, although even there traditional blue-collar jobs such as tool-and-die maker now require math and computer skills. Women, Hispanics, and blacks are underrepresented in the fastest-growing occupations in part because their educational attainments are, overall, less than those of white males. This raises problems for employers who are pressured to show equity in job categories.

Structural change has been a major factor in the decline of labor unions. Before the wave of protective legislation passed in the 1930s, unions represented only 5 percent of industrial workers, but this tripled to 15 percent by 1940 and reached a zenith of 25 percent in the 1950s.[25] Unions were instrumental in raising wages and increasing benefits for blue-collar workers, and these improvements rippled through the entire manufacturing sector because nonunionized companies needed to approximate the welfare levels of union workers if they wished to prevent unionization.

In the 1970s, however, union membership in the private sector began a long slide as structural change eroded its base of factory workers. Employment shifted to service industries and to industries employing knowledge workers who were hard for industrial unions to organize and to low-wage countries where unions were illegal or weak. By 1997, unions represented only 10 percent of private sector employees in the United States, and as the ranks of factory workers continue to thin, so do union rosters.[26] The upward push on wages and benefits that unions

---

[25]Bureau of the Census, *Statistical Abstract of the United States: 1956,* Washington, D.C.: Government Printing Office, 1956, Table 271.

[26]Bureau of Labor Statistics, News Release, "Union Members Summary," January 30, 1998, p. 2. When public sector and agricultural workers are included, unions represented 14 percent of workers.

provide for both members and nonmembers has weakened commensurately. Today, the United States has lower union representation of the private labor force than any other developed economy. In Europe, on the other hand, although union membership declined during the 1990s in every European Union nation, roughly a third to a half of all workers remain unionized, with the exception of France, where union membership is only slightly higher than in the United States. This is a major reason that labor costs are generally higher in Europe than in the United States.[27]

Competitive Pressures

Competition has always been strong in the U.S. economy, but recent trends have intensified it. Customers demand higher quality, better service, and faster new-product development. Deregulation of large industries such as airlines, telecommunications, trucking, and electric utilities has stirred formerly complacent rivals. Foreign trade grew from just 9 percent of the U.S. economy in 1960 to 26 percent in 1996.[28] U.S. firms increasingly have been challenged by foreign competitors in both domestic and foreign markets. These foreign competitors have many advantages, including lower labor costs, a strong dollar, and, sometimes, higher worker productivity.

American workers, and workers in other developed nations including Japan and those of the European Union, are increasingly exposed to a global labor market that contains pools of low-cost workers. In less-affluent, less-industrialized countries, wages are lower for many reasons, including oversupply of labor relative to demand, low living standards, local currency devaluations, labor policies of authoritarian regimes where workers have no political power, and wage competition among countries seeking to attract jobs.

In 1997, the average hourly compensation for a manufacturing worker in the United States was $18.24 an hour. This was not the highest in the world; that distinction went to German workers making $28.28 an hour, and workers in Japan and many European nations also outearned Americans. But elsewhere, an hour of labor cost far less, for example, $0.48 in Sri Lanka, $1.75 in Mexico, $5.29 in Portugal, and $5.89 in Taiwan.[29] Given this wage discrepancy, companies in some industries can no longer afford to do low-skilled manufacturing or service work in the United States and contract to have it done in a foreign country.

To match competitors who take advantage of cheap foreign labor, American firms must either contract to have work done overseas themselves, and many have, or they must increase the productivity of domestic labor by reducing employees to a minimum and applying technology to enlarge their output. Either way, there are generally fewer jobs for American workers in the occupation affected.

---

[27]Greg J. Bamber and Russell D. Lansbury, eds., *International & Comparative Employment Relations*, rev. ed., London: Sage Publications, 1998. See Appendix, pp. 357–59.

[28]Thomas Boustead, "The U.S. Economy to 2006," *Monthly Labor Review*, November 1997, p. 7.

[29]Department of Labor, News Release, "International Comparisons of Hourly Compensation Costs for Production Workers in Manufacturing, 1997," September 16, 1998, p. 8.

Government Intervention

Historically, a strong laissez-faire current in American economic philosophy made governments at all levels reluctant to interfere with the *employment contract,* or the agreement by which an employee exchanges his or her labor in return for specific pay and working conditions. Today, government intervention is extensive and growing, but this is a twentieth-century trend.

Before 1860, the number of persons employed as wage earners in factories, mines, railroads, and other workplaces was relatively small. But with industrialization, their numbers skyrocketed. Between 1860 and 1890, the number of wage earners rose from 1.33 million to 4.25 million, an increase of 320 percent.[30] This rapid growth in numbers, which would continue into the 1930s, created a new class interest, and it was an aggrieved one. In the hard-hearted wisdom of the day, employers treated workers as simply production costs to be minimized; there was relentless downward pressure on wages and reluctance to improve working conditions.

Liberty of Contract.   Prior to the 1930s, there was little government intervention on behalf of workers, and what there was consisted mostly of feeble state safety regulations and laws to limit working hours. In the late nineteenth and early twentieth centuries, strong majorities on the Supreme Court adhered to the *liberty of contract doctrine.* This doctrine held that employers and workers should be free from government intervention to negotiate all aspects of the employment contract, including wages, hours, duties, and conditions.[31] For many years, the Court struck down state and federal laws that interfered with this theoretical freedom. Such laws were regarded as "meddlesome interferences with the rights of the individual."[32]

The great flaw in the liberty of contract doctrine was that it assumed equal bargaining power for all parties, whereas employers unquestionably predominated. For employers, liberty of contract was the liberty to exploit. Employees could be fired at will and had to accept virtually any working conditions. Unchallenged dominion of employers opened the door to the negligent treatment of workers that invited and fueled the labor union movement, a social movement to empower workers. Employers resisted demands for kinder treatment of workers and bitterly fought the rise of unions.

---

[30]Arthur M. Schlesinger, *Political and Social Growth of the United States: 1852–1933,* New York: Macmillan, 1935, p. 203.

[31]The liberty of contract majority first emerged in *Allgeyer* v. *Louisiana,* 106 U.S. 578 (1897), where Justice Rufus W. Peckham grounded it in the due process clause of the Fourteenth Amendment, which states that no state can deprive a person of life, liberty, or property without due process of law.

[32]Justice Rufus W. Peckham, writing for a 5–4 majority in *Lockner* v. *New York,* 198 U.S. 61 (1905). The decision struck down a 1897 New York State law limiting bakery employees to sixty-hour weeks.

Turn-of-the-century cartoonist Art Young drew this cynical view of the topsided employment contract in the days before labor unions and laws protecting worker rights.

Waves of Regulation. It was not until the 1930s that government regulation of the workplace began to redress the huge power imbalance favoring employers. One major step was the Norris-LaGuardia Anti-Injunction Act of 1932, which struck down a type of employer–employee agreement called, in the colorful language of unionists, a "yellow dog contract." These were agreements that workers would not join unions. Employers virtually extorted signatures on them when workers were hired, and hapless applicants had little choice but to sign if they wanted the job—and jobs were scarce in the 1930s. If union organizing began, companies went to court, where judges enforced the agreements. The Norris-LaGuardia Act outlawed yellow dog contracts, overruling a 1908 Supreme Court decision that upheld them under the liberty of contract doctrine.[33]

The new law encouraged unions. It was soon followed by the National Labor Relations Act of 1935, which guaranteed union organizing and bargaining

---

[33]*Adair* v. *United States,* 291 U.S. 293 (1908).

rights, and by other laws that fleshed out a body of rules for labor relations. After the 1930s, employers still dominated the employment contract, but company power over wages and working conditions was increasingly checked by unions.

Figure 17-1 shows how this first wave of federal workplace regulation, which established union rights, was followed by two subsequent waves. A second wave, between 1963 and 1974, moved federal law into new areas, protecting civil rights, worker health and safety, and pension rights. A third wave, between 1986 and 1996, again broadened the scope of federal law to address additional, and somewhat narrower, employment issues. During this period, Congress enacted the following laws.

- A provision in the Comprehensive Omnibus Budget Reconciliation Act of 1986 allows separated workers to continue in group health plans for up to eighteen months at their own expense.
- The Immigration Reform and Control Act of 1986 protects work rights of legal aliens and prohibits hiring illegal aliens.
- The Worker Adjustment and Retraining Act of 1988 requires companies with more than 100 workers to give sixty days' notice prior to plant closings or large layoffs.
- The Employee Polygraph Protection Act of 1988 prohibits the use of lie detectors to screen job applicants and narrows grounds for using the tests to detect employee theft or sabotage.
- The Drug-Free Workplace Act of 1988 requires companies with federal contracts to take measures against drug abuse.
- The Americans with Disabilities Act of 1990 prohibits discrimination against the disabled and requires employers to make reasonable accommodations for people with substantial physical or mental impairments.
- The Family and Medical Leave Act of 1993 gives workers the right to take up to twelve weeks of unpaid leave for family reasons such as childbirth or illness.
- The Health Insurance Portability and Accountability Act guarantees that preexisting medical problems will continue to be covered by health insurance when workers switch jobs.

Altogether, approximately 200 federal laws have been enacted since the 1930s, including amendments to original statutes, so only the major ones are shown in Figure 17-1. These laws have been based on the dominant perspective of 1930s reformers that the relationship between labor and management is antagonistic. Based on this model, a broad and complex regulatory structure has been created over nearly seventy years to counterbalance the perceived weakness of workers in the employment contract with corporations.

Federal regulations are only part of the growing web of regulation that fetters employers. State courts and legislatures have created additional rules that

FIGURE 17-1

This figure shows the historical march of major statutes (and one executive order) regulating labor–management and employer–employee relations. Note the existence of three rough clusters or waves of intervention. Space prohibits a description of each law.

A Chronology of Major Workplace Regulations

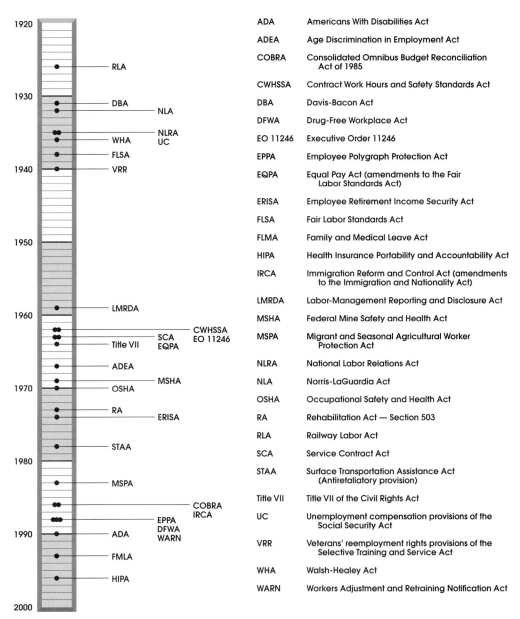

ADA	Americans With Disabilities Act
ADEA	Age Discrimination in Employment Act
COBRA	Consolidated Omnibus Budget Reconciliation Act of 1985
CWHSSA	Contract Work Hours and Safety Standards Act
DBA	Davis-Bacon Act
DFWA	Drug-Free Workplace Act
EO 11246	Executive Order 11246
EPPA	Employee Polygraph Protection Act
EQPA	Equal Pay Act (amendments to the Fair Labor Standards Act)
ERISA	Employee Retirement Income Security Act
FLSA	Fair Labor Standards Act
FLMA	Family and Medical Leave Act
HIPA	Health Insurance Portability and Accountability Act
IRCA	Immigration Reform and Control Act (amendments to the Immigration and Nationality Act)
LMRDA	Labor-Management Reporting and Disclosure Act
MSHA	Federal Mine Safety and Health Act
MSPA	Migrant and Seasonal Agricultural Worker Protection Act
NLRA	National Labor Relations Act
NLA	Norris-LaGuardia Act
OSHA	Occupational Safety and Health Act
RA	Rehabilitation Act — Section 503
RLA	Railway Labor Act
SCA	Service Contract Act
STAA	Surface Transportation Assistance Act (Antiretaliatory provision)
Title VII	Title VII of the Civil Rights Act
UC	Unemployment compensation provisions of the Social Security Act
VRR	Veterans' reemployment rights provisions of the Selective Training and Service Act
WHA	Walsh-Healey Act
WARN	Workers Adjustment and Retraining Notification Act

Source: Adapted from General Accounting Office. "Testimony: Rethinking the Federal Role in Worker Protection and Workforce Development," 1995, p. 5.

employers must follow. Legislatures in many states have enacted laws that go beyond federal requirements. For example, Vermont gives workers twenty-four hours of leave to attend school functions and go to medical appointments. Arizona, North Carolina, and Texas ban discrimination based on genetic test results, and Louisiana bans discrimination due to the sickle cell trait. In Maine, workers must be paid one week's wages when companies close.

Federal laws typically apply only to firms with more than a specified number of employees—often as many as 50 or 100. Many states enact laws that extend the same employee protections to smaller firms. The federal Family and Medical Leave Act, for example, entitles employees of firms with fifty or more workers to take as long as twelve weeks of unpaid leave for family matters such as adoption, illness, or birth. But Oregon lowers the size of the company to twenty-five workers and Vermont to fifteen. The federal law requiring sixty-day advance notification of plant closings applies only to companies with 100 or more workers, but in Hawaii, employers with fifty or more workers must give forty-five day notice. These state actions enhance worker protections and make them more expensive.

State courts have added additional worker protections. While federal courts often decide issues of constitutionality and statutory interpretation, they have not expanded workplace rights beyond the statutes. State courts, on the other hand, have used doctrines of common law to establish new employee rights in the absence of legislation. A leading example of the power of state courts is how, in recent years, they have revised the doctrine of employment-at-will, shriveling perhaps the most fundamental right of an employer—the right to hire and fire.

Erosion of the Employment-at-Will Doctrine.   In the United States, there is a body of common law, or law derived from judicial decisions, that governs employer–employee relationships. In general, this law holds that employers and employees may enter voluntary employment contracts and that either party may freely end these agreements anytime.

While employed, an employee must act "solely and entirely" for the employer's benefit in all work-related matters or be liable for termination and damages. Furthermore, the law stipulates that when a conflict arises between an employee and an employer, the employee must conform to the employer's rules. The common law in this area is derived from paternalistic English common law that, in turn, was influenced by Roman law that framed employment in terms of a master–servant relationship. Under this body of law, employers have had extensive rights to restrict employee freedom and arbitrarily fire workers.

Until recently, an extreme interpretation of the employment contract prevailed. It resounds in the oft-quoted statement by a Tennessee judge more than 100 years ago: "All may dismiss their employees at will be they many or few, for good cause, for no cause, or even for cause morally wrong without being thereby guilty of legal wrong."[34] *Employment-at-will,* therefore, was traditionally

---

[34]*Payne* v. *Western & Atlantic R.R. Co.,* 81 Tenn. 507 (1884).

defined as an employment contract that could be ended by either party without notice and for any reason.

With the rise of government intervention since the 1930s, absolute discharge rights have eroded. Federal and state laws take away the right to fire employees for reasons related to union activity, race, sex, national origin, religion, and physical disability. In addition, courts in many states have introduced three common-law exceptions to termination at will.

First, employees cannot be fired for complying with public policy. In *Petermann* v. *International Brotherhood of Teamsters*, a California worker was asked by a supervisor to lie to a legislative committee investigating unions.[35] The worker answered questions honestly anyway and was fired. The court struck down the firing, stating that there was an overriding public interest in ensuring truthful testimony at legislative hearings. In another case, *Sabine Pilot Service, Inc.* v. *Hauck*, a deck hand was ordered to pump bilge off the Texas coast each day. The worker read a placard stating that this was illegal and, after phoning the Coast Guard for confirmation, refused to do it. He was fired. A Texas court held, however, that an employer could not fire a worker for refusing to disobey the law.[36]

Second, courts have limited the employer's ability to fire if an implied covenant of good faith is breached. In *Cleary* v. *American Airlines*, an employee of eighteen years was fired.[37] Company policy contained a specific statement that the firm reserved the right to fire an employee for any reason, but the court was convinced that the purpose of the firing was to avoid payment of a sales commission to Cleary. It awarded him punitive damages.

A third check on freedom to fire is recognized where an implied contract exists. Daniel Foley was employed by a subsidiary of Chase Manhattan Bank. His superiors made oral statements that his job was secure and for seven years gave him regular promotions and raises. One day, Foley learned that his new supervisor was being investigated by the FBI for embezzling money from Bank of America. He told a vice president. Shortly afterwards, the new supervisor fired Foley. However, a California court ruled that Foley had been promised permanent employment while his performance was satisfactory. It held, in *Foley* v. *Interactive Data Corp.*, that the company violated an implied contract.[38] Because of this decision, companies began removing implied promises of job tenure, such as references to "permanent employees," from employee manuals.

The states vary in the extent to which these exceptions to employment-at-will are adopted. Only five states have failed to take up any of the new exceptions and eight states have adopted all of them. The great majority have adopted one or two, and the overall trend is toward greater restriction on the

---

[35] 344 Cal. App. 2d 25 (1959).
[36] 687 S.W.2d 733 (Tex. 1985).
[37] 168 Cal. Reptr. 722 (1980).
[38] 205 Cal. App. 3d 344 (1985).

employer's ability to terminate. One state, Montana, now has a law that permits employers to discharge workers only for "good cause."

Worker Protection in Other Industrialized Nations.   The level of benefits and protections for U.S. workers is high, but not exceptional in comparison to other industrialized nations. Elsewhere, workers benefit from similar and even greater welfare guarantees. Cultural differences are evident in how worker rights are provided, but in every nation where strong welfare measures are in place, labor costs are high.

Japanese workers are now among the world's most expensive. In 1997, the average hourly compensation for a manufacturing worker in Japan was $19.37, compared to $18.24 for an American counterpart.[39] The fringe benefits of permanent employees in the large companies that employ about 40 percent of the Japanese workforce typically include company housing, family allowances, meals, child education expenses, and paid vacations. Many Japanese men in these large firms enjoy virtual lifetime employment. When they die, Japanese workers are often buried in corporate cemeteries. These benefits are provided voluntarily by paternalistic Japanese companies.

Japanese history and culture in part explain why companies are so generous. Japan's long feudal period shaped cultural patterns based on values derived from the spread of ancient Chinese culture to the islands, including belief in rigid status hierarchies, strong duties of loyalty owed to rulers, emphasis on group rather than individual welfare, and the belief that a paternalistic government should provide for citizen welfare. Later, these values molded the relationship between modern workers and the industrial corporation. Just as the feudal Japanese vassal owed fealty to a lord, workers were asked to give loyalty to their company and place work group interests above individual interests. In return, the company had a duty of parent-like beneficence and generously helped workers.

In the United States, pugnacious unions had to demand federal laws protecting their right to organize, then they fought companies for higher wages and benefits. But in Japan, the centuries-old Confucian tradition of harmony in relationships prevented similar fissures from developing. Unions never grew strong and unified. Most today are company unions, and they rarely strike or make strident demands. In Japanese politics, corporations work closely with government ministries to promote economic growth; they do not struggle with dozens of regulatory agencies enforcing workplace rules as do U.S. companies. Similar approaches to worker welfare are found elsewhere in Asia in the more affluent and developed nations of Singapore, Taiwan, and South Korea.[40]

---

[39]Department of Labor, News Release, "International Comparisons of Hourly Compensation Costs for Production Workers in Manufacturing, 1997," Table 2. All country wage figures in this section are taken from this table.

[40]Sanford M. Jacoby, "Social Dimensions of Global Economic Integration," in Sanford M. Jacoby, ed., *The Workers of Nations: Industrial Relations in a Global Economy*, New York: Oxford University Press, 1995, pp. 21–22.

Industrialized nations in northern Europe also give high wages and comprehensive benefits to workers. This is reflected in average hourly compensation for manufacturing workers of $22.02 in Denmark, $21.92 in Austria, $23.79 in Norway, $22.82 in Belgium, $24.19 in Switzerland, and, highest of all, $28.28 in Germany. These countries have powerful unions organized to negotiate wages and benefits over entire industries. Many European countries have strong socialist parties, giving unions longstanding political strength. In France, for example, unions pressure the government to enforce a 39-hour workweek law prohibiting even managers, programmers, or engineers from working past 7:00 PM without paid compensation. A special labor police unit raids companies to catch violators. Top executives who condone lawbreaking are fined up to $1 million and may be imprisoned. To protect themselves, many employers require managers and professionals to punch time clocks.[41] The intent of the law is to reduce high unemployment by forcing companies to hire more workers, instead of stretching the existing labor force to fit needs. Now, the French government is trying to reduce the workweek to 35 hours.

Throughout Europe, the result of such labor market rigidities has been persistent, high unemployment. Faced with these practices, European multinationals outsource jobs to countries with more flexible labor markets. In 1998, the unemployment rate in the European Union averaged 10.2 percent, higher than in many third-world countries.[42]

The benefits and protections achieved by German workers are unmatched, which is why Germany has the highest labor costs in the world. A complex network of laws, union agreements, and customs makes the labor market inflexible. Workers are entitled to generous government pensions, health insurance, sick leave, unemployment, and paid vacations. When Chrysler Corp. merged with Daimler-Benz in 1998, Chrysler workers were amazed to learn that the German autoworkers had a union contract giving them a 35-hour workweek, a medical plan with no deductible that allowed them to choose their own physicians, and fully paid sick leave for up to four weeks.[43] In Germany, laws prescribe the hours when factory machines can run, prohibit most labor during an official Sunday "pause" (exceptions are gas station attendants and bakery clerks), and require that workers be given 30 days' paid annual vacation and six months' notice before termination. The average German works only 40.1 hours per week, compared to 42 hours in the United States (the Chrysler workers average 50.5 hours). Recently, German unions have experimented with more flexible arrangements and the German government has proposed scaling back social benefits, including pensions and sick pay. But major rollbacks of entitlements for workers in Germany and other affluent European nations are not likely.

---

[41]Gail Edmondson, " 'I'm Shocked! There Are People Working in Here!' " *Business Week*, March 16, 1998, p. 50.

[42]International Labor Organization, Press Release, "ILO World Employment Report 1998–99," September 1998, p. 4.

[43]Harry Kelber, "One Carmaker, Two Unions," *Progressive Populist*, July 1998, p. 9.

Turbulence in the Workplace

The combined impact of the five major forces changing the workplace creates uncertainty and anxiety. For some workers, opportunities are greater, for others, there are fewer rewards. The vicissitudes of work life are illustrated by corporate downsizing and growing income inequality. Because of changes going on today, a new employment contract between workers and companies may be emerging.

Corporate Downsizing

In recent years, corporations have reduced the size of their workforces, often by announcing huge job cuts. This phenomenon is given many names in the press and management literature, including downsizing, restructuring, and reengineering. Downsizing occurs for many reasons. When IBM announced layoffs of 60,000 workers in 1993, it was reacting to technology shifts in computing that reduced revenues from its traditional mainframe business. When AT&T made 34,000 layoffs in 1996, it was responding to the imperative of a deregulation law opening its long-distance business to regional phone company competitors. When Citicorp and Travelers merged in 1998, they announced layoffs of 10,400 workers, some made redundant by the merger and others made unnecessary by automated tellers and rising Internet sales of investments and insurance.

Some companies have been shrinking for years. Since 1978, General Motor's American workforce has steadily declined from 520,000 to 220,000. To reduce costs, GM has moved about 20 percent of its manufacturing from the United States to Mexico. In 1998, assembly workers in GM *maquiladoras* earned $11,000 to $12,000 a year in wages and benefits, more than twenty times the Mexican minimum wage and a coveted income in that country.[44] Moreover, Mexican workers are not unionized. The average United Auto Workers member at GM's Flint Metal Center makes almost $100,000 a year in wages and benefits, and union rules allow machines to run fewer hours and at slower speeds than in Mexico. GM has fallen behind its competitors in the global race to reduce the cost of making an automobile. The company will continue to close American plants and send work to Mexico, and it plans to wave the layoff wand at another 50,000 workers in the next few years.[45]

Critics say that making workers bear the burden of adjustment to powerful global forces is unfair. Historically, mass layoffs were used only as a last resort and were an embarrassing sign of management failure. Today layoffs are no longer a source of shame; in fact, top executives sometimes make record salaries in downsizing years and stockholders are enriched by short-term price jumps in their shares after big job cuts.

---

[44]Warren Brown and Frank Swoboda, "At GM, a Stalled Revolution," *Washington Post National Weekly Edition,* July 20–27, 1998, p. 20.

[45]"Can These Adversaries Avoid Another Collision?" *The Wall Street Journal,* July 29, 1998, p. A2.

Lavish executive compensation can look obscene in contrast to the real pain of economic adjustment passed on to workers. Their suffering is illustrated in a story about a secretary named Linda, told by a manager conducting a mass layoff in which workers were called without notice to a conference room and read a prepared statement that terminated them.

> We avoided looking at each other as I spoke. When I finished, she didn't move for several long seconds; then she stood up and paced the length of the room and started wringing her hands. "What am I supposed to do?" she pleaded, not waiting for the answer that we couldn't give. "I am a single mother, my parents are gone, and I just closed on a house two weeks ago. I *need* my job," she said as the tears started to flow. My reaction was to offer some comfort, at least offer some words of encouragement, but we had been strictly warned by the company attorney not to do anything of the sort. It was for the good of the company that we restrain ourselves, lest we make some passing promise that would end up in court later. We all just sat there until she gathered her papers and walked out.[46]

This portrait of suffering at the hands of a heartless corporation is like many that find their way into the news. It is factual, but to generalize from it about the fortunes of American workers is misleading. The trauma for a person of losing a job can be terrible. However, more workers are finding jobs than losing them, because the economy is creating more jobs than are being lost by downsizing. Although approximately forty-seven million jobs in the United States were permanently lost between 1979 and 1997, more than seventy-eight million jobs were created—a net gain of thirty-one million jobs.[47] And since the recession of 1981–1982, the unemployment rate has declined from a high of 11 percent to a low 4.3 percent in early 1999.

In recent years, displaced workers have fared well in finding new jobs. Between 1995 and 1997, for example, 3.6 million American workers who had been on their jobs for more than three years lost those jobs because plants closed, work was outsourced to low-wage countries, positions were abolished in corporate restructurings, or market losses cut demand for products. By early 1998, three-fourths of them were working again, and, among these, more than half were paid the same amount as or higher than in their last jobs. Only about a quarter suffered pay cuts of 20 percent or more.[48]

Downsizing is a complex response to global forces. Multinationals in all countries feel pressure to make cost-cutting workforce reductions to meet the competition. American firms operate in a more flexible labor environment than their European and Japanese competitors, and they are better able to reduce employment, so in the last two decades, American firms have shed the most employees. European firms, on the other hand, have to contend with powerful unions and laws that protect job security and make outsourcing to

---

[46]Alan Downs, *Corporate Executions,* New York: Amacom, 1995, p. 76.

[47]Figure derived from historical labor force data and a Bureau of Labor Statistics News Release, "Displaced Worker Summary" August 19, 1998.

[48]Bureau of Labor Statistics, "Displaced Workers Summary," p. 1.

foreign countries more difficult. They have been slower and less extensive in their workforce adjustments.

Japanese firms, gripped by cast-iron traditions of paternalism toward workers, have the most difficult time of all. In 1998, Mitsubishi Motors Corp., which has weakened as a competitor in the global automobile industry, had a ¥102 billion ($480 million) net loss and was carrying ¥2 trillion of debt. These figures dictated a need for deep cost and spending cuts. The company decided to reduce the number of models in its product line, lower production, and cut staffing. It announced layoffs of 2,200 workers, 1,000 in the United States and 1,200 in Southeast Asia. Yet, none in Japan were let go. Why not?

The Employment Security Law of 1947 makes it illegal to fire regular employees, so large Japanese companies cannot simply lay off workers as American firms do. Instead, they hire more temporary workers and may transfer personnel to other units or to supplier firms in the *keiretsu.* When all else fails, they simply shame entrenched but superfluous workers into leaving with demotions, inconsequential assignments, or embarrassing slights. This form of workplace ostracism is called *murahachibu,* a term used in medieval Japan to describe how villages shunned social outcasts.

> It is almost imperceptible at first—a barbed comment, perhaps or an oversight. Then one afternoon, the middle manager who has worked for his company since college fails to get his usual cup of green tea from the office lady down the corridor. A week later he fails to be invited to the regular morning meeting. Next his telephone disappears. His computer goes, too. Colleagues are suddenly too busy for lunch. Memoranda detailing company social events do not reach his desk. Finally, the desk itself vanishes.[49]

Downsizing is a complex phenomenon of workforce restructuring, in which some firms are cutting workers, others are adding them, and many are doing both. It is more difficult to restructure workforces in some nations than in others, but global companies in every nation see their staffs shriveled by winds of economic change. Corporations cannot control structural and technological forces that define markets, and they cannot compete if locked into outmoded, excessively labor-intensive practices to avoid hurting workers. One strength of the American economy compared to, for example, the German and Japanese economies, is the relative ease with which labor is shifted from declining sectors to rising ones. It would be hardest on workers in the end if American firms, bloated with highly paid and aging workers, grew uncompetitive with foreign rivals.

Wages

External forces have also had an impact on trends in wages and compensation for workers. Income growth has slowed for all but the highest paid workers, and income inequality is rising.

---

[49]"Gang Sackings," *The Economist,* November 14, 1998, p. 74.

Following World War II, wage earners in the American economy experienced rapid income growth and rising standards of living. Between 1948 and 1973, the average worker's compensation (including wages plus benefits) rose 3 percent yearly. This was enough to double the standard of living every twenty-five years. Rising compensation did not make American workers uncompetitive. The real measure of competitiveness is worker output compared with worker cost. Worker output is called productivity, which is measured as output per hour of work. Even when a nation's workers get comparatively high wages, they can be low cost if their productivity is high enough. Between 1948 and 1973, the productivity of American workers rose an average 2.5 percent yearly, one of the highest rates in the world.

Then, beginning in the late 1970s, compensation and productivity trends began to diverge. Productivity growth remained strong. In manufacturing, for example, it increased an average of 2.6 percent each year between 1979 and 1995, a rate higher than in the past and higher than in most other industrial nations.[50] However, wages were flat or climbed slightly for most of the period, beginning to rise only after 1996.[51] Overall, worker compensation rose, though more slowly than productivity, only because employers increased medical benefits.

The overall stagnation of wages obscures a growing inequality. Over the long-term, from 1979 to 1996, the pay of high-income professionals, technology workers, and executives has been rising, while the pay of low- and middle-income workers has been level or has fallen. On a scale of zero to 100, with zero representing a situation in which all persons get the same wage and 100 representing a situation in which one person gets all income, the United States has risen from 34.2 in 1979 to 38.6 in 1996.[52] The precise cause of growing wage inequality is elusive, but experts agree that competition in global labor markets, the shift away from manufacturing, computerization of work, and the declining influence of unions as wage-setting institutions are all important. Demographic change is less of a factor. Although immigration increases the supply of unskilled workers, the Council of Economic Advisors has estimated that this influx is responsible for less than 1 percent of declining wages among less-educated workers.[53]

---

[50]Christopher Sparks and Mary Greiner, "U.S. and Foreign Productivity and Unit Labor Costs," *Monthly Labor Review*, February 1997, p. 28.

[51]*Economic Report of the President: 1997*, Washington, D.C.: Government Printing Office, 1997, pp. 147–49; Christopher Farrell, "A Rising Tide," *Business Week*, August 31, 1998, p. 74.

[52]Jared Bernstein and Lawrence Mishel, "Has Wage Inequality Stopped Growing?" *Monthly Labor Review*, December 1997, p. 3. The statistic representing wage inequality is the Gini index.

[53]*Annual Report of the Council of Economic Advisors: 1995*, Washington, D.C.: Government Printing Office, February 1995, p. 181.

How Income Is Distributed in Other Nations

The Gini index is a measure of income equality. If the Gini index is zero, all persons in a country will have equal incomes. If the number is 100, one person in the population receives all income, the rest get nothing. So the higher the number, the more unequally income is distributed.

Gini index figures supplied by the World Bank show that income inequality varies greatly between nations. Inequality in the United States is markedly greater than in Europe, but far lower than in many Latin American countries. Elsewhere around the world, inequality varies widely.

Region and Nation	Gini Index	Region and Nation	Gini Index
North America		**Asia**	
Canada	31.5	Australia	33.7
United States	40.1	China	41.5
		Malaysia	48.8
Europe		Philippines	42.9
Denmark	24.7	Thailand	46.2
Finland	25.6	Vietnam	35.7
Norway	25.2		
Sweden	25.0	**Middle East**	
France	32.7	Egypt	32.0
Germany	28.1	Israel	35.5
Italy	31.2	Jordan	43.4
United Kingdom	32.6		
		Eastern Europe	
Latin America		Bulgaria	30.8
Brazil	60.1	Czech Republic	26.6
Chile	56.5	Hungary	27.9
Columbia	57.2	Russian Federation	31.0
Guatemala	59.6		
Honduras	53.7	**Africa**	
Mexico	50.3	South Africa	58.4
Nicaragua	50.3		
Paraguay	59.1		

Source: *World Development Indicators 1998*, CD-ROM, Washington, D.C.: World Bank, 1998, Table 2–8.

A Revised Employment Contract

In the current turbulent setting of work, the outlines of the traditional job are fading. Yesterday, work was done in eight-hour days on rising trajectories of pay and power within hierarchical, pyramid-shaped, corporate organizations. The largest of these organizations, firms such as IBM, AT&T, and General Motors, were insulated in a domestic market and protected by their market power from fierce competition. They could offer unwritten promises of lifetime employment and did so, although economic crisis could abrogate these commitments, as it did during the 1930s depression years.

But, in general, the unwritten employment contract was an exchange of the worker's time, skill, and loyalty for a career of growing compensation, status, and security within the company. Now, though, this contract equation no longer works. Competitive and global forces have altered every aspect of it. Downsizing has flattened organization structures, extending work hours for remaining employees and removing many higher positions in the pyramid to which they could have aspired. For all but the top 20 percent of workers, the long-term trend in real compensation has not matched overall economic growth. And there is less job security. The story of one giant company's metamorphosis illustrates how this works in practice.

> When Jack Welch became CEO of General Electric in 1981 the corporate culture reinforced loyalty. Employees went to work at GE right out of college, stayed for 40 years, retired in communities of GE people, and attended GE alumni clubs until rigor mortis set in.
>
> Welch, however, saw that the company was a ponderous bureaucracy. Long before other business leaders, he also saw that international competition would become fierce and firms such as GE would be uncompetitive unless they raised productivity and cut costs.
>
> Welch began to remake GE. There were mass layoffs. As jobs vanished he got the nickname "Neutron Jack," comparing him to the neutron bomb that left buildings standing but killed everyone in them. He believed that obese managers were less productive and so plant managers hid overweight employees when Welch visited their facilities.
>
> Above all, Welch thought that the concept of loyalty in GE's culture retarded change, so he rooted it out. At meetings he told employees it was out of fashion. He instructed staff never to use the word "loyalty" in any company document, press release, or publication. He wanted each GE worker to prove their value every day and said people who knew they could be fired worked harder. Old timers at GE said Welch was callous and subhuman.
>
> GE has turned in an extraordinary profit performance and other big company CEOs have been forced by global trends to follow Welch's example of breaking the loyalty bond. Today Welch continues to lead GE. Thousands of GE managers who thought they would also be there are gone.[54]

Despite recent turbulence in employer–employee relations, the outlines of a new employment contract are emerging. In the new contract, employees will trade their time, energy, and skills for compensation and the opportunity to work in a company that provides learning, training, and perhaps feelings of self-worth in team settings. Unlike the old contract, the employee will not give a high level of loyalty and the organization will not promise long-term employment. In a competitive global economy, companies will need a lean and highly flexible workforce. To promote adaptive and rapid decisions, they will move further away from hierarchy and toward more

---

[54]For more of this story, see Thomas F. O'Boyle, *At Any Cost: Jack Welch, General Electric, and the Pursuit of Profit* (New York: Knopf, 1998), chapter 3.

participatory management, team-oriented work, and flexible hours. To attract ambitious people, they will need to provide training and education for workers who expect to move sequentially from one employer to another over their working lifetimes. The security of these employees will lie in their marketability, not in promises of long-term security by their immediate employer.

Concluding Observations

In this chapter, we discuss the action of five powerful forces external to the workplace but changing it—demography, technology, competition, structural shift, and government. These forces are not likely soon to diminish in importance. Demographic change is uncontrollable, but since it is slow and predictable, it can be accommodated. Technological change, because it is often rapid and unpredictable, is perhaps the most radical and disruptive force. Computers now furrow the commercial landscape in many directions, just as railroads, electricity, and automobiles did in their time. The importance of competition is elevated now in developed nations, where great corporations rush to automate and send their work to low-wage countries. As manufacturing jobs flow to low-wage workers, the world's richest economies are increasingly dominated by service occupations. Finally, the role of government is changing. In both the United States and Europe, the primary role of government has been to slowly and steadily increase protections and benefits for workers. Now this long-term trend has slowed in the United States. In Europe it has reversed. In Japan, where cultural traditions have protected workers from exploitation, values are slowly changing to permit more labor market flexibility.

How will workers fare in the caldron of change in which these external forces put them? Experience suggests that fortunes will be mixed. Yet it is likely that if the global economy prospers, the benefits for workers will outweigh the inevitable dislocations.

DRUG TESTING IN THE WORKPLACE: EMPLOYERS' RIGHTS VERSUS EMPLOYEES' RIGHTS

There is a long record in the United States of drug use in the workplace. However, it was not until the 1980s that drug testing by employers began. The initiative came from the federal government.

The U.S. Navy began the first random drug testing as a result of its discovery of widespread drug use following an accident on the *USS Nimitz* in 1982. Other branches of the federal government quickly followed. In 1986, President Reagan issued Executive Order No. 12564 requiring all federal agencies to develop a "drug free workplace" by establishing a program to test for the use of illegal drugs by employees in sensitive positions.

A Conrail engineer who had been smoking marijuana rolled his string of locomotives past a warning light and onto the same track as a high-speed train carrying 600 people. The collision, in 1987, killed 16 people and injured 176. In 1989, the *Exxon Valdez*, a large oil tanker, struck a rock formation and spilled millions of gallons of crude oil in the pristine waters of Prince William Sound in Alaska. There was enormous loss of animal life and destruction to the economic and social fabric of the area. Alcohol was partly responsible for this disaster. Such accidents resulted in the passage of the Omnibus Transportation Employee Testing Act of 1991, requiring the Department of Transportation to test employees in safety-sensitive transportation jobs for drug and alcohol use.

The Department of Energy, the Department of Defense, and the Nuclear Regulatory Commission all have private-sector drug-testing requirements in their security-sensitive workplaces. Other laws and regulations prompt drug testing. The Occupational Safety and Health Act, for instance, requires employers to provide safe working environments.

The result of such incidents and laws was a rapid expansion of drug testing in public and private workplaces. In 1983, only six firms in the *Fortune* 500

627

were testing their workers for drugs. By 1987, 20 percent of major firms were testing, and by 1996, over 80 percent.[1]

Issues

Controversy has accompanied the evolution of drug testing. Issues have arisen over why drug tests are needed, who should be tested, what tests should be given, and how tests should be conducted. At the heart of this case is a conflict between employer and employee rights. As noted later, these issues are complicated by a bramblebush of federal and state laws.

Costs of Drug Addiction

The true cost of drug use at work is unknown and estimates vary widely. A few examples reveal major dimensions of this cost. The Department of Labor estimates that substance abuse in the workplace costs $100 billion annually. The Department reports that "Drug-using employees at General Motors average 40 days of sick leave annually, compared to 4.5 days for non-users. . . . The State of Wisconsin estimates that expenses and losses related to substance abuse average 25 percent of the salary of each worker affected."[2]

Alcohol is the most serious drug abuse problem in the workplace. It is estimated that in the early 1990s, up to 40 percent of industrial fatalities and 47 percent of industrial injuries were linked to alcohol consumption.[3] More recent estimates are not available. The prevalence of alcohol and drugs varies widely among occupations. For example, 17 percent of construction workers reported using illegal drugs at least once during the month before they were polled. Among food preparation employees, it was 16 percent, and for laborers, it was 13 percent. The least frequent drug users were police and detectives, 1 percent, and teachers, 2 percent.[4]

The behavior of drug-addicted employees can be costly both to employers and employees. Included in the costs are lost productivity, higher insurance premiums, excessive absentee and sick leave rates, the loss of trained workers who are fired or die, the administrative costs of antidrug programs, extra

---

[1]Data are from American Management Association surveys reported by Kirstin Downey Grimsley in "Great Résumé, Interview, References—Now Here's the Cup," The Washington Post National Weekly Edition, May 18, 1998.

[2]U.S. Department of Labor, "Working Partners for an Alcohol- and Drug-Free Workplace," http://dol.gov/dol/asp/public/programs/drugs/backgrnd.htm, November 6, 1998.

[3]Beverly A. Potter and J. Sebastian Orfali, Drug Testing at Work, Berkeley, Calif.: Ronin Publishing, Inc., 1998, p. 24.

[4]Data are from a study of 33,505 workers from 1991–1993 by the U.S. Department of Health and Human Services, reported by Stuart Silverstein, "Substance Abuse in Decline, but Still Heavy in Some Fields," Los Angeles Times, April 22, 1996.

plant security, property damage, a decline in employee morale, tarnishing of the company image, lawsuits, and theft of company property.

Behavior of Drug-Addicted Employees

Drug-addicted employees tend to exhibit one or both of two pernicious effects. The first is distortion of time, which is seen in the inability of the employee to follow normal time patterns for job activities. The second is lack of motivation, which is seen as disinterest in normal performance standards. Both effects stem from imbalances of brain chemistry caused by the chronic presence of marijuana, cocaine, or other drugs in the bloodstream.[5] Supervisors are trained to suspect drug abuse when employees show patterns of behavior such as

- Frequent tardiness and absences from work, especially on Mondays and Fridays and near holidays.
- Poor concentration, forgetfulness, missed deadlines, and frequent mistakes.
- Mood changes, including a wide range of states that interfere with personal relationships such as depression, withdrawal, hostility, and overexcitability.
- Risk taking and frequent accidents.

A Comprehensive Procedure for Drug Abuse in the Workplace

The National Institute on Drug Abuse recommends that drug testing be part of a larger comprehensive program directed at correcting workplace drug abuse. The main elements of such a program include (1) a clear policy statement, (2) training of supervisors and others involved in a drug abuse program about their responsibilities, (3) employee education and training, (4) drug testing methods and procedures, and (5) counseling of employees who test positive.[6]

Drug Testing Programs

Companies must choose which kind of testing to use. There are a variety of drug testing methods such as the following.

---

[5]William F. Banta and Forest Tennant, *Complete Handbook for Combating Substance Abuse in the Workplace,* Lexington, Mass.: Lexington Books, 1989, p. 45.

[6]For the details of these elements of a comprehensive system, see National Institute on Drug Abuse, *Comprehensive Procedures for Drug Testing in the Workplace,* Washington, D.C.: U.S. Department of Health and Human Services, Alcohol, Drug Abuse, and Mental Health Administration, 1991.

Employee searches may include searches of lockers, workstations, desks, and purses. They seldom include bodily searches, which anger workers and create litigation. Drug-sniffing dogs are extremely effective in locating contraband. But searches are often ineffective. For example, drugs can be secreted in common areas so that employee ownership is concealed.

Surveillance can detect drug use, but has many pitfalls. It is difficult to keep undercover agents a secret. Spying can shatter employee morale. Surveillance agents can make mistakes, such as striking an employee, that can result in expensive lawsuits.

Written drug tests are available from a dozen or more vendors of employment tests. They ask job applicants and employees whether they have used drugs, what kind, and how often. The validity of these tests is unproven, but they are the least expensive type of drug test.

Polygraphs, or lie detectors, were used frequently at one time, but no more. The accuracy of the results is open to question. Furthermore, the Employee Polygraph Protection Act of 1988 so severely limits their use that most employers no longer use them for drug testing.

Fitness-for-duty exams, sometimes called performance tests, detect impaired acuity. In one test, for example, workers sit in front of a computer screen and turn a knob to keep a moving point centered between two lines. Such tests measure impairment but they do not show the cause, which may be drugs, alcohol, fatigue from staying up with a sick baby all night, or emotional upset. Advocates of performance tests believe they are less physically intrusive than other forms of testing. Critics argue that poor performance invites an employer to ask intrusive questions about private off-work behavior.

Blood tests are useful primarily for alcohol abuse testing. They are expensive and exceptionally intrusive and, because of legal challenges, are rarely used by employers. Their main advantage is that they can determine the approximate time a drug was used.

Saliva tests exist to test for marijuana use, but are unreliable. They are useful only up to three hours after marijuana is smoked, and rinsing the mouth can remove detectable residues.

Hair analysis tests can detect use of cocaine, marijuana, or other illegal drugs for as long as three months prior to removing a 1 ½-inch growth of hair for testing. However, it takes about seven days for substances indicative of drug use to appear in the hair. Few companies use it.

Urinalysis is the most commonly employed testing method. Before discussing urinalysis in some detail, the options about whom to test and the drugs to be tested should be noted.

Employees Who Might Be Tested

Employers have many testing options. Here are some of the major ones.

- *Those in Safety-Sensitive Positions.* This might refer to national security but also those who could jeopardize the safety of themselves or other employees or the public at large. Included also would be people handling substantial amounts of money or carrying firearms.

- *Those Who Provide Cause.* When employees are frequently absent on Mondays or take periodic unexpected absences, have frequent accidents, display erratic behavior, or show inconsistent job performance, they may be singled out for drug testing.
- *Those Who Have Gone through Rehabilitation.* When employees have gone through a drug rehabilitation program, they may be subject to periodic drug testing.
- *Those Who Apply for Employment.* Job applicants, especially for sensitive positions, may be tested.
- *Random Testing of All Employees.* Random testing has grown significantly in recent years to the point where one-third of all major companies reportedly employ it.[7]

Drugs of Abuse Tested by Employers

In 1988, the National Institute for Drug Abuse (NIDA) issued guidelines on drug-abuse programs for public sector employees. Five drugs were identified for testing: tetrahydrocannabinol, the psychoactive ingredient in marijuana; cocaine; opiates; amphetamines; and phencyclidine. Many employers add to this list other drugs, such as barbiturates, benzodiazepines, methadone, methaqualone, and propoxyphene. Employers also test alcohol, a legal drug, and the most commonly abused drug.[8] All these drugs can be tested in urine samples. Alcohol can be tested by breath or saliva and confirmed by blood tests.

Urinalysis

There are several basic types of urine tests. The first is the *immunoassay test.* This is an inexpensive test costing about $15 that can be done quickly with modest laboratory equipment and technician training. However, this test is not always 100 percent accurate. For example, it may register positive if a person has recently used any of ten common over-the-counter drugs.

If the test is positive, a second and much more accurate test may be used to confirm. It involves a different chemical process called *chromatography*. It is more time-consuming and more expensive (about $25 per test) and requires a highly trained technician to interpret results. It is not, therefore, used for mass

---

[7]*Annual Corporate Membership Survey,* Washington, D.C.: Institute for a Drug-Free Workplace, May 1992, cited in Mark A. de Bernardo, *Workplace Drug Testing: An Employer's Development & Implementation Guide,* Washington, D.C.: Institute for a Drug-Free Workplace, 1994, p. 5.

[8]Ibid. pp. 37–38.

screening but is held in reserve to double-check a positive result on an immunoassay test.

A third test may be done with a *mass spectrometer*. It is the most accurate test, and the most expensive (about $100 per test). Gas chromatography/mass spectrometry tests are so sensitive that they have detected cocaine and a by-product, cinnamolycocaine, in the urine of people who have drunk one or two cups of coca leaf teas imported from Peru. Five doctors writing in the *Journal of the American Medical Association* cautioned that individuals in urine-testing programs should be warned not to drink these teas.[9]

One shortcoming of urine tests is that they can be thwarted by employees who tamper with a sample. A small amount of table salt, bleach, laundry soap, ammonia, or vinegar causes screening tests to miss drug residues in the urine. For this reason, employees giving urine samples must be closely supervised.

A significant problem with urine testing is that it cannot indicate whether an employee is "high" or impaired. Cocaine and heroin can be detected up to three days after last use and marijuana up to two months after last use. This means that a person who used cocaine at a party on Saturday night could be nailed by a drug test on Tuesday morning when feeling hale and working productively. But if a colleague had taken LSD that morning and was hallucinating and dangerous, the LSD could not be detected with a simple immunoassay test. An immunoassay test cannot detect hallucinogens such as LSD.

Implementing the Drug Test Program

Once a company has chosen from among the options, the Institute for a Drug-Free Workplace recommends the following steps:

1. Identify any federal or state laws with which you must comply.
2. Write a clear, consistent, and fair policy that includes the conditions under which drug testing is to be conducted and the consequences of a "positive" drug test result.
3. If applicable, consult with union representatives and bargain in good faith on the terms and conditions of the drug testing program.
4. Identify and contact a certified laboratory to set up a drug testing contract. If possible, go for a visit.
5. Contract with a collection site to receive testing samples.
6. Develop and implement a system to protect the confidentiality of employee drug test records.
7. Designate the person who will receive the test results from the laboratory, and make sure that person is aware of confidentiality issues.

---

[9]Ronald Siegel, Mahmoud A. Elsohly, Timothy Plowman, Philip Rury, and Reese T. Jones, "Cocaine in Herbal Tea," *Journal of the American Medical Association*, January 3, 1986, p. 40.

8. Have your policy reviewed by legal counsel.

9. Notify employees 30 to 180 days before the testing program goes into effect.

10. Establish procedures for review of all "positive" drug test results by a medical review officer.

11. Communicate to employees that management also is fully subject to the policy, the specifics of the testing program, what is expected of them as employees, the company's reasons for promoting a drug-free workforce, and the adverse employment consequences of a policy violation.[10]

Why Corporations Favor Drug Testing

First, federal and state laws require drug tests for certain workers and companies. For example, the Drug-Free Workplace Act of 1988 requires private employers with federal contracts over $25,000 to have comprehensive policies designed to prevent drug abuse. The Department of Transportation, the Department of Energy, the Department of Defense, and the Nuclear Regulatory Commission all have private-sector drug-testing requirements in their security-sensitive workplaces. Most states and many cities have laws concerning drug testing.

Second, drug tests have produced positive results. For example, SmithKline Beecham, a major testing laboratory, reported that the percentage of employees who tested positive for illegal drug use declined from 18 in 1987 to 5 in 1997. (Sixty percent of the positive results showed marijuana use. Cocaine was next with 16 percent, followed by 9 percent for opiates, 5 percent for amphetamines, 3 percent for barbiturates, and others, 6 percent.)[11]

The Department of Labor reported major improvements in job-related performance as a result of substance abuse treatment. For example, one manufacturer reported a 30 to 35 percent decrease in industrial accidents. An electric supply company said absenteeism was reduced 39 percent and productivity rose by 36 percent. The Southern Pacific Transportation Company reported that injuries dropped 71 percent.[12]

Reductions in workplace drug use also will reduce health costs and potential liability suits for employee errors. It is difficult to put a dollar sign on such cost reductions, but savings can be substantial not only to the company but to worker well-being.

Third, corporate drug testers argue that urinalysis is a practical method of testing for drug use. Although urine tests are intrusive, they are less so than

---

[10]de Bernardo, *Workplace Drug Testing*, pp. 51–52.
[11]Grimsely, "Great Résumé, Interview, References."
[12]Department of Labor, "Working Partners."

some alternatives such as drug-sniffing dogs, polygraphs, searches through handbags and desks, undercover investigations, entry and exit searches, and closed-circuit TV monitors in restrooms. When done correctly, urine tests are reliable. Good programs follow the Rule of Two, in which two positive tests are required before action is taken. The first test, an inexpensive screening test, is followed by a second, more sophisticated confirming test on the same vial of urine. Cutoff levels for positive results can be set reasonably high to avoid unnecessarily stigmatizing innocent employees. Errors can also be minimized by using proper procedures for specimen collection and laboratory analysis. We have already noted the effective procedures needed to ensure testing accuracy.

Fourth, there is a social responsibility argument for drug testing. As employers screen applicants and employees, it will become harder for drug abusers to make a living. Employees have no right to use marijuana, cocaine, hallucinogens, PCP, heroin, and designer drugs. Their use is illegal and creates crime, illness, broken families, and broken lives. Thus, business is helping society by combating drug use. From an individual standpoint, if companies can catch a drug-using employee early, it might save his or her career. Many companies refer employees who test positive to assistance programs for treatment rather than terminate them.

Why Some Employees Oppose Drug Testing

As compelling as these arguments are, drug testing in general and urine testing in particular raise difficult questions. Critics point out that the right of an employer to protect assets and property must be balanced against the rights of individual employees to a reasonable amount of privacy. Opponents make telling points.

First, urine testing is intrusive and an invasion of privacy. To avoid false positive results based on the presence of other drugs in the urine, employees are asked to list all prescription and over-the-counter drugs taken in the last thirty days. This reveals their private, off-duty lives and medical histories. Also, chemical analysis of urine (or blood) can reveal more than drug use. Employers could test it and discover medical conditions such as pregnancy, clinical depression, diabetes, and epilepsy. For all these reasons, civil libertarians believe urine testing smacks of Big Brother.

Second, urine testing is inherently demeaning whether a sample is taken with visual or passive supervision. An author of a law journal article put it this way: "[I]n our culture the excretory functions are shielded by more or less absolute privacy, so much so that situations in which this privacy is violated are experienced as extremely distressing, as detracting from one's dignity and self-esteem."[13]

Third, the tests are unjust because they violate ethical standards of fair treatment. Testing is a dragnet; many innocent people are tested for each drug

---

[13]Charles Fried, "Privacy," *Yale Law Journal*, January 1968, p. 487.

user detected. A presumption of guilt is placed on everyone, and workers must prove their innocence. If there is an overriding safety justification to prohibit drug abuse—for example, among bus drivers or railroad engineers—then it may be prudent. But indiscriminate testing of applicants and employees who are not in critical safety-related positions is an evil greater than the drug abuse it seeks to remedy.

Fourth, urine tests are imperfect. Inaccuracies arise from lab errors, mixed-up specimens, and false positives that are due to legal drugs in the body. Errors are too frequent and cast suspicion on employees or cost them their jobs. If scrupulous collection and laboratory procedures are followed, testing is very accurate. But not all companies and labs are that scrupulous. For example, follow-up confirmatory tests after a positive on a simple screening test are expensive, and not every firm is willing to undertake the extra expense for job applicants.

Finally, drug tests can be misleading and cannot meet reasonable evidentiary standards. The ACLU says "they cannot detect impairment and, thus, in no way enhance an employer's ability to evaluate or predict job performance."[14] The ACLU adds, "Even a confirmed 'positive' provides no evidence of present intoxication or impairment; it merely indicates that a person may have taken a drug at some time in the past.[15] Emphasis should be placed on employee assistance programs not drug testing, says the ACLU.

Employee Approval of Some Drug Testing

The above arguments against drug testing refer principally to general as well as random testing of a workforce. Both the ACLU and the AFL-CIO resist invasive and unjustified drug testing. However, surveys show that most employees endorse drug testing for selected occupations, such as airline pilots, truck drivers, construction workers, and those in safety-sensitive jobs.[16]

Drug Testing and the Law

Legal precedent on drug testing is relatively new and still developing, but the clear trend is to uphold it where it is part of a previously announced and carefully formulated policy. Here is a short briefing on legal issues.

Since the Bill of Rights of the U.S. Constitution restrains only government actions, public employees are protected by these provisions but employees in private

---

[14]American Civil Liberties Union, *Drug Testing in the Workplace,* Briefing Paper No. 5, undated.
[15]Ibid.
[16]Marci M. DeLancey, *Does Drug Testing Work?* 2nd ed., Washington, D.C.: Institute for a Drug-Free Workplace, 1994, pp. 49–50.

businesses are not. This is a major legal difference; public employers must meet stricter guidelines for testing. The Fourth Amendment guarantees protection to public employees against "unreasonable searches and seizures," and courts have generally held that urine tests and other forms of testing, such as blood tests for HIV antibodies, are a form of search and seizure. The Fifth Amendment guarantees "due process of law" and protects against self-incrimination. Public employers must guard against firings that violate these rights.[17] Since 1988, federal agencies have adhered to testing guidelines issued by the Department of Health and Human Services. These guidelines attempt to elevate due process for government employees to an impeccable level and stipulate testing procedures in detail.[18]

There have been many court challenges to federal urine-testing programs, and those that have reached the Supreme Court have been upheld. But the decisions also show that some of the justices have grave misgivings about drug testing and do not believe it is permitted by the Fourth Amendment.

In *Skinner* v. *Railway Labor Executives' Association*, the Court was asked to decide whether railroad workers could be forced to submit to mandatory urine and blood tests for drugs.[19] In a 7–2 decision, the Court held that the clear public interest in railroad safety outweighed the privacy rights of employees. But in a strong dissent, Justice Thurgood Marshall compared the decision with the Court's 1940s decisions upholding the assignment of Japanese to relocation camps during World War II, and noted that "when we allow fundamental freedoms to be sacrificed in the name of real or perceived exigency, we invariably come to regret it."[20]

A second case decided by the Supreme Court, *National Treasury Employees Union* v. *Von Raab*, involved a urine-testing program of the U.S. Customs Service.[21] It required applicants for positions in which they would interdict drugs, carry guns, or work with "classified" material of interest to criminals to submit to urine tests. In a 5–4 decision, the majority argued that the national drug crisis, together with the special gravity of drug enforcement work, justified weighing the public interest in drug-free customs agents more heavily than the interference with the agents' civil liberties. Thus, testing was "reasonable" under the Fourth Amendment. Justice Antonin Scalia, writing in dissent, warned that the Court was too cavalier in sacrificing basic constitutional privacy rights. He quoted these famous lines written by Justice Louis Brandeis in 1928: "The greatest dangers to liberty lurk in insidious encroachment by men of zeal, well-meaning but without understanding."[22]

In 1995, the Court decided a third case and remained divided about the issue. In a 6–3 decision in *Vernonia School District* v. *Acton*, it upheld the

---

[17]These rights are extended to state, county, and local employees through the Fourteenth Amendment.

[18]National Institute on Drug Abuse, *Comprehensive Procedures for Drug Testing in the Workplace.*

[19]57 LW 4324 (1989).

[20]At 57 LW 4333 (1989); the relocation camp cases are *Hirabayashi* v. *United States*, 320 U.S. 81 (1943); and *Korematsu* v. *United States*, 323 U.S. 214 (1944).

[21]489 U.S. 656 (1989).

[22]In *Olmstead* v. *United States*, 227 U.S. 479 (1928).

requirement that all student athletes in an Oregon high school submit to urine testing. The majority in *Vernonia* was willing to balance the privacy right of individuals against the legitimate needs of government agencies, in this case, the "substantial need of teachers and administrators for freedom to maintain order in the schools."[23] Writing in dissent, however, Justice Sandra Day O'Connor argued that random drug testing such as that on the high school athletes intruded on privacy where individual grounds for suspicion of wrongdoing did not exist. The Founding Fathers, she stated, clearly intended the Fourth Amendment to prohibit general searches of the population such as this and, therefore, such random drug tests were unconstitutional.

These three cases reveal an undercurrent of discomfort and opposition even though the Court approved testing in all three situations that came before it.

Trends in court decisions since then have tended to side with Justice O'Connor. The school board in Anderson Indiana ruled that all students who were caught fighting or had violated important school rules should be tested for drugs and alcohol. The case was appealed to the U.S. District Court of Appeals in Chicago. The court struck down this policy saying it was the type of unreasonable search prohibited by the Fourth Amendment. The case was appealed to the U.S. Supreme Court and without comment the court turned down the appeal in March 1999.[24]

Although the Fourth Amendment only applies to government as an employer, the discretion of private sector employers is limited by other legal guidelines. First, many state and local governments have adopted laws that regulate drug testing. These laws vary considerably. For instance, San Francisco prohibits drug testing under most circumstances but permits tests for pre-employment, for suspicion of use, and after accidents. Florida permits testing of job applicants and employees but if they are tested, the employer must follow specific procedures set forth in the Florida Drug-Free Workplace Act. Many states prescribe mandatory precise testing procedures. Second, private employers are open to common-law actions by employees based on doctrines such as negligence, defamation, assault and battery, emotional distress, invasion of privacy, or wrongful discharge. Employees have sued over drug testing using all these legal theories. Some have won in court, but there is no overall trend to prohibit drug testing programs. Union contracts also may circumscribe drug testing.

Questions

1. Should urine testing (or other types of testing) be permitted among public and private employees to prevent drug abuse? Why or why not?
2. If you believe that urine testing in some form might be acceptable, write down the outlines of a sound testing program. Who should be tested?

---

[23]*Vernonia School District* v. *Acton,* 115 S.Ct. 2391 (1995).
[24]*Anderson Community Schools* v. *Willis,* No. 98–1183 (1999).

Employees? Job applicants? Should there be random testing? Should people in all job categories be tested?

3. As a manager with responsibility for conducting a testing program, what would be your response to the following situations?

    a. An employee who tests positively for marijuana on a Monday morning but has a spotless ten-year work record.
    b. An airline pilot who refuses a random test.
    c. A job applicant who tests positively for cocaine use.
    d. An employee who tests positively for cocaine use.
    e. An employee who comes to your office the night before an announced urinalysis testing and admits that he regularly uses a hallucinogenic drug off the job.
    f. A productive worker who gives no outward sign of drug use but who is named as a drug abuser at work in an anonymous tip.
    g. An employee involved in a serious work accident who refuses to take an immunoassay test based on her belief in the right to privacy.
    h. The recommendation of the union that management be given the same test as workers.

18

Civil Rights at Work

Johnson Controls, Inc.

www.jci.com

Johnson Controls, Inc., of Milwaukee was founded in 1885 by Professor Warren Johnson to manufacture his new invention—the electric room thermostat. The company has grown into a large multinational with locations on every continent. In 1998, it had 88,000 employees and, with $11.3 billion in revenues, it ranked 136 on the *Fortune* 500, just ahead of Microsoft.

Over the years, the company diversified by moving into auto components. It makes seats, instrument panels, consoles, and other parts and delivers them just-in-time to the assembly lines of the big auto firms. In addition, it is the largest manufacturer of lead-acid batteries in the United States. It was battery making that got the company into a landmark legal fight.

Medical research in the 1980s found that small amounts of lead that were harmless to adults could damage a fetus and cause stillbirth, low birth weight, and retardation. In response, Johnson Controls banned fertile women from certain battery-making jobs where workers breathed particles of lead. Ending a woman's lead exposure when pregnancy was discovered was not prudent because inhaled lead stays in the body a long time—it takes five to seven years for just half of it to be excreted.

Unless women proved that they were infertile, Johnson Controls moved them to other jobs. But sometimes the new jobs paid less and women voluntarily sterilized themselves to avoid losing income. For example, Gloyce Qualls, age 34, was removed from a job welding auto battery posts and given a safer job putting vents in motorcycle batteries. She elected to have a tubal ligation to regain her old job. Elsie Nason, age 50, also chose sterilization after being transferred to a lower-paid job.

What happened at Johnson Controls was typical in firms with so-called fetal protection policies. Many companies, including General Motors, Ford, Dow Chemical, DuPont, and Monsanto, had them. It was believed that if impaired children were born, they could sue corporations for exposing them to lead in the womb. So the policies protected stockholders along with fetal health.

However, some women thought that rules barring them from battery-line jobs were sexist. Eight women at Johnson Controls, joined by their union, filed a legal challenge. They argued that Johnson Controls' policy violated Title VII of the Civil Rights Act of 1964, which bans employment discrimination based on sex. The company responded that it was a "business necessity" to keep fertile women away from lead to prevent future lawsuits. In addition, the company argued, Title VII allowed exceptions to its general rule against sex discrimination. These exceptions, called *bona fida occupational qualifications* (BFOQs), exist when workers of one or the other sex cannot do a job the right way precisely because of their sex. An advertising agency, for example, can screen out men applying for a job modeling woman's bathing suits. Johnson Controls felt that infertility should qualify as a BFOQ in battery making.

Two lower courts agreed with the company.[1] But in 1991, a unanimous Supreme Court held that the fetal protection policy caused illegal sex discrimination.[2] Women could not be excluded from any battery-making job. The opinion, written by Justice Harry Blackmun, author of *Roe* v. *Wade,* said that the exclusion of women from work based on their ability to get pregnant violated Title VII. The policy was not neutral as the law required because it did not bar men. Moreover, wrote Blackmun, Title VII had been amended some years before to make job actions based on pregnancy illegal. No BFOQ exception existed either, because pregnancy did not hinder the woman's ability to make batteries as efficiently as men. The Court concluded that Johnson Controls should inform women of risks and then let them decide.

Justice Blackmun also stated that for Johnson Controls, obeying federal civil rights law was a defense against future lawsuits by children impaired in the womb. But *The Wall Street Journal* challenged Blackmun, asking: "Is there a jury in the land that would tell an injured child who sues a corporation that, sorry, your mother decided to risk it and you must pay the price?"[3]

Before the decision, Johnson Controls had acted to lower lead exposure

---

[1]See 680 F.Supp. 309 (DC-EDW 1988) and 886 F.2d 871 (7th Cir. 1989).

[2]*Automobile Workers* v. *Johnson Controls, Inc.,* 111 S.Ct. 1196. There were three concurring opinions.

[3]"Justices Adopt Fetal Position," *The Wall Street Journal,* March 22, 1991.

in its factories but no available technology eliminated it. It also returned to a voluntary fetal protection policy. Feminist groups were elated; women could chart their own destinies. Gloyce Qualls, however, had married and regretted that she could not have children.

This story illustrates the strong protections available in federal civil rights law for women—and for other protected groups—who claim discrimination. In this chapter, we discuss employment discrimination and explain the laws and methods used to fight it over the years.

A Short History of Workplace Civil Rights

The American nation was founded upon noble ideals of justice, liberty, and human rights. Yet, for most of our history, business practice openly diverged from these ideals and widespread discrimination based on race, color, sex, national origin, religion, and other grounds occurred. In fact, significant protection from unemployment discrimination has existed for only the last 35 years of our 220-year history. The gap between ideals and practice has narrowed, but not closed.

The Colonial Era

Employment discrimination can be dated from 1619 when European slave traders first brought African natives to the nation's shores. When the colonies declared their independence from England in 1776, there were already 500,000 slaves, mostly in the southern colonies. In the northern colonies, there was considerable anguish about slavery because it clashed with the ideals of those who had founded them to escape from religious persecution and government tyranny in Europe. These ideals were expressed in the Declaration of Independence in the following words.

> We hold these truths to be self-evident, that all men are created equal, that they are endowed by their Creator with certain unalienable Rights, that among these are Life, Liberty, and the pursuit of Happiness.

These "unalienable" rights are *natural rights,* that is, rights to which a person is entitled simply because he or she is human and that cannot be taken away by government. Natural rights exist on a higher plane than *civil rights,* which are rights bestowed by governments on their citizens. Natural rights are a standard against which the actions of governments and employers must be measured and can be found wanting.

This statement in the Declaration distills a body of doctrine known as the American Creed, which historian Arthur M. Schlesinger Jr. defines as incorporating "the ideals of the essential dignity and equality of all human beings, of inalienable rights to freedom, justice, and opportunity."[4] In the language of the time, the phrase "all men" was a reference to free, white males. Thomas Jefferson included in the original draft a strong statement condemning slavery as a "cruel war against human nature itself, violating its most sacred rights of life & liberty."[5] But this offended slave owners and had to be deleted to preserve unity in the coming revolution against England. Despite the limited inclusiveness of the Declaration's language, its statement of natural rights, notes Schlesinger, challenged whites to live up to its ideals and, if anything, "meant even more to blacks than to whites, since it was the great means of pleading their unfulfilled rights."[6]

The Constitution also reflected this bifurcated view of civil rights. When it was ratified in 1789, it sanctioned the practice of slavery in five clauses. Article 1, section 2, for example, counted slaves as three-fifths of a person for purposes of apportioning seats in the House of Representatives.[7] Yet the Bill of Rights contained ringing phrases protecting a wide range of fundamental rights.

Civil War and Reconstruction

Beginning at about the time the Constitution was ratified, an anti-slavery movement originated in a small sect within the Church of England. This movement grew rapidly and, in a century's time, its moral arguments largely swept slavery from the world stage.[8] In the United States, the issue of slavery rose to a crisis in the Civil War fought between 1860 and 1865. In 1865, President Abraham Lincoln issued the Emancipation Proclamation that freed an estimated four million slaves. Following the war, Congress passed three constitutional amendments designed to ensure that the rights of former slaves would be protected in the race-conscious southern culture.

- The *Thirteenth Amendment* in 1865 abolished slavery.
- The *Fourteenth Amendment* in 1868 was intended to prevent southern states from passing discriminatory laws. It reads, in part: "No State shall make or enforce any law which shall abridge the privileges or immunities of citizens of the United States; nor shall any State deprive any person of life, liberty, or property, without due process of law; nor deny to any person within its jurisdiction the equal protection of the laws."
- The *Fifteenth Amendment* in 1870 prohibited race discrimination in voting.

---

[4]Arthur M. Schlesinger Jr., *The Disuniting of America*, New York: Norton, 1992, p. 27.

[5]Edward S. Corwin and J. W. Peltason, *Understanding the Constitution*, 4th ed., New York: Holt, Rinehart and Winston, 1967, p. 4.

[6]Schlesinger, *The Disuniting of America*, p. 39.

[7]See also article 1, section 9, limiting taxation of slaves; article 1, section 9, prohibiting Congress from ending the slave trade before 1808; article 4, section 2, requiring return of fugitive slaves to owners; and article 5, prohibiting amendment of article 1, section 9, before 1808.

[8]Thomas Sowell, *Race and Culture: A World View*, New York: Basic Books, 1994, pp. 210–14.

These amendments were supplemented by a series of civil rights acts passed by Congress, most notably one in 1866 to protect blacks against employment discrimination and another in 1875 to protect them from discrimination in transportation and accommodations. Altogether, these amendments and statutes created a formidable legal machinery to implement the rights to which blacks were entitled under the American Creed. If this machinery had been allowed to function, a century of painful employment discrimination against blacks and other groups might have been prevented. But it was not to be.

There was tremendous resistance to the new laws in the South, but at first much enforcement was possible because of the continuing presence of the Union Army, an occupying force that kept a temporary lid on southern resistance to black rights, which was formidable and violent. Because the troops protected voting rights, for example, 16 blacks were elected to Congress and about 600 to state legislatures. But the presidential election of 1876 ended the era of southern rehabilitation. In the race, the Republican candidate Rutherford B. Hayes lost the popular vote to his Democratic opponent Samuel J. Tilden, but the vote was close in the electoral college and returns from three southern states were contested. Hayes agreed to an "understanding" that if the electoral votes from these southern states were cast for him, he would withdraw the remaining federal troops. History records that Hayes won the election and the soldiers left. An important check on racism went with them.

White racism reasserted itself in the South in many ways. *Racism,* defined broadly, is the belief that each race has distinctive cultural characteristics and that one's own race is superior to other races. It persists when myths and stereotypes about inferiorities are expressed in institutions of education, government, religion, and business. Racism leads to social discrimination, or the apportioning of resources based on group membership rather than individual merit. It insulates the power of a privileged group—for example, white Americans—from challenge.

Southern states adopted segregationist statutes called Jim Crow laws. These laws institutionalized the idea that whites were superior to blacks by creating segregated schools, restrooms, and water fountains; in literacy tests that disenfranchised blacks; in restrictive covenants, or deeds, that prevented whites from selling property to blacks in certain neighborhoods; and in discriminatory hiring that kept blacks in menial occupations.

Other Groups Face Employment Discrimination

In the meantime, other groups aside from blacks faced extensive and institutionalized employment discrimination as well. Native Americans were widely treated as an inferior race. In the nineteenth century, the federal government spent uncounted millions of dollars to destroy their societies and segregate them on reservations. A large population of roughly 90,000 Hispanics suddenly became residents of United States territory when Mexico ceded Texas in 1845 and huge tracts of southwestern land in 1848. Soon these Mexican-Americans were victims of a range of discriminatory actions. They were legally stripped of extensive land holdings and exploited in a labor market where discrimination confined them to lesser occupations. They suffered great violence; more Hispanics were killed in the Southwest between 1850 and 1930 than blacks were lynched in the South.[9]

Beginning in 1851, Chinese laborers began to enter the country. They settled in western states and many owned placer mines. In 1863, several thousand began working on the construction of the Central Pacific Railroad as "coolies" (a word of that era used as a synonym for Chinese labor). Some started businesses such as laundries and restaurants. By the 1870s, there were 100,000 Chinese in western states; in California there were 75,000, about 10 percent of the population. Although prejudice existed against them, their presence was tolerated until economic depression set in and the white majority felt them competing for jobs and customers. Then economic and racial discrimination began in earnest. Special taxes passed by state legislatures were used to confiscate their mines and ruin their commercial businesses. Some towns ordered all Chinese to leave. San Francisco passed an ordinance requiring city licenses for all laundries, then denied licenses to Chinese laundries.[10] The California state constitution, adopted in 1874, prohibited Chinese from voting and made it illegal for corporations to hire them. Finally, Congress banned the immigration of Chinese laborers in 1882.

The earliest Japanese immigrants found similar inhospitality. By 1880, there were only 124 Japanese in the United States, but their numbers increased rapidly as employers sought replacements for the cheap Chinese labor supply that had been cut off. By 1900, about 100,000 Japanese immigrants had arrived, most in California. Japanese laborers were typically paid 7 to 10 cents an hour less than whites. Like the Chinese, they ultimately threatened white labor and soon faced violent prejudice in cities. They turned to agricultural work in California's fertile inland valleys, but powerful white farmers resented their presence. California passed laws prohibiting Japanese land ownership and, in 1924, Congress banned further Japanese immigration. Although employers wanted to utilize Japanese labor, social attitudes frequently made this impossible. For example, in 1925, Pacific Spruce Corporation brought thirty-five Japanese to the small lumber town of Toledo, Oregon, to work in its sawmill. A mob of 500 men, women, and children swarmed the mill and the company had to load the Japanese on trucks that took them to Portland.[11]

As this brief sketch of nineteenth- and early twentieth-century employment discrimination shows, neither the American Creed nor the fine legal mechanism put in place after the Civil War worked to stop racism. Why not? The former was eclipsed by broad public prejudice. The latter had to be enforced against the

---

[9]John P. Fernandez, *Managing a Diverse Work Force*, Lexington, Mass.: Lexington Books, 1991, p. 165.

[10]In *Yick Wo* v. *Hopkins*, 118 U.S. 356 (1886), the Supreme Court struck down the ordinance as a violation of the equal protection clause of the Fourteenth Amendment. Had the Court followed up on this precedent, it could have struck down Jim Crow laws in the South.

[11]Herman Feldman, *Racial Factors in American Industry*, (New York: Harper, 1931), pp. 89–90.

grain of southern racism and was, in any case, soon dismantled by the Supreme Court in two landmark cases—the *Civil Rights Cases* and *Plessy* v. *Ferguson.*

The Civil Rights Cases

The Civil Rights Act of 1875 was passed to prevent racial discrimination in "inns, public conveyances on land or water, theaters and other places of public amusement."[12] The law set a fine of up to $1,000 or imprisonment up to one year for violation. Still, there was widespread discrimination against freed slaves by business and soon a series of cases reached the Supreme Court. Two cases involved inns in Kansas and Missouri that had refused rooms to blacks. And in one case, the Memphis and Charleston Railroad Company in Tennessee had refused to allow a woman "of African descent" to ride in the ladies' car of a train. These cases were consolidated into one opinion by the Supreme Court in 1883 and called the *Civil Rights Cases.*[13]

The Civil Rights Act of 1875 was based on the Fourteenth Amendment and, in the Court's opinion, Justice Joseph P. Bradley focused on its wording. Because the amendment reads that "no state" shall discriminate, Bradley held that it did not prohibit what he referred to as a "private wrong." If race discrimination was not supported by state laws, it was a private matter between companies and their customers or employees and the Fourteenth Amendment did not prohibit it. For this reason, Congress lacked the authority to regulate race bias among private parties; therefore, the Civil Rights Act of 1875 was unconstitutional.

The *Civil Rights Cases* so narrowed the meaning of the Fourteenth Amendment that it became irrelevant to a broad range of economic and social bias. Congress and the courts could no longer use it to strike down much of the most brazen race discrimination. It was not necessarily a wrong decision; in fact, many constitutional scholars believe that the Court made a reasonable decision for that day given the clear reference to state action in the Fourteenth Amendment. But in dissent, Justice John Marshall Harlan argued that "the substance and spirit of the recent Amendments of the Constitution have been sacrificed by a subtle and ingenious verbal criticism."[14]

Plessy v. Ferguson

Southern states had passed so-called Jim Crow laws that sanctioned race segregation. If the Fourteenth Amendment could not prohibit private individuals from depriving each other of basic rights, did it not still clearly prohibit states from enacting laws that abused the former slaves? The answer was no.

One such law was the Separate Car Act passed by Louisiana in 1890. This statute required all Louisiana railroads to "provide equal but separate

---

[12]An Act to Protect all Citizens in their Civil and Legal Rights, 18 Stat. at L., 335, sec. 1.
[13]109 U.S. 835 (1883).
[14]109 U.S. 844.

accommodations for the white, and colored races, by providing two or more passenger coaches for each passenger train, or by dividing the passenger coaches by a partition so as to secure separate accommodations."[15] This law, like other Jim Crow laws, was based on the *police power* of the state, a presumed power inherent in the sovereignty of every government, to protect citizens from nuisances and dangers that might harm public safety, health, and morals.

On June 7, 1892, Homer Plessy, who was seven-eighths Caucasian and one-eighth African, bought a first-class ticket on the East Louisiana railroad to travel from New Orleans to Covington. Boarding the train, he took a vacant seat in the white coach. He was asked by the conductor to move to the "non-white" coach. Plessy refused and was taken to a New Orleans jail.

Plessy brought suit, claiming he was entitled to "equal protection of the laws" as stated in the Fourteenth Amendment. In 1896, in *Plessy* v. *Ferguson,* the Supreme Court disagreed, holding that as long as separate accommodations for blacks were equal to those of whites, blacks were not deprived of any rights. Justice Henry B. Brown, writing for the majority, argued that laws requiring race separation "do not necessarily imply the inferiority of either race to the other" and were a valid exercise of police power by state legislatures because they enhanced "comfort, and the preservation of the public peace and good order."[16] This ruling completed the destruction of the Fourteenth Amendment as a mechanism that could guarantee civil rights by imposing upon it the perverse interpretation that legitimized "separate but equal." This doctrine, which became the foundation for legal apartheid in the South, stood for fifty-eight years until reversed in 1954 by the Court in its famous school desegregation case, *Brown* v. *Board of Education.*[17]

Plessy is in retrospect notorious and some say one of the worst decisions ever made by the Court because of its consequences. The justices missed an opportunity to read the Fourteenth Amendment in a way that would protect blacks from the schemes of white racists. They must have thought that a decision striking down Jim Crow would be unpopular and widely disobeyed and may have sought to prevent the Court from being weakened by disregard for its opinions. As in the *Civil Rights Cases,* Justice Harlan was a lone dissenter who kept the light of the American Creed flickering by lecturing the majority.

> Our Constitution is color-blind and neither knows nor tolerates classes among citizens. In respect of civil rights, all citizens are equal before the law. The humblest is the peer of the most powerful. The law regards man as man, and takes no account of his . . . color when his civil rights as guaranteed by the supreme law of the land are involved.[18]

---

[15]Act 111 of 1890, quoted in Richard Epstein, *Forbidden Grounds: The Case against Employment Discrimination Laws,* Cambridge, Mass.: Harvard University Press, 1992, pp. 99–100.

[16]*Plessy* v. *Ferguson,* 163 U.S. 540 (1896), at 544 and 550. John H. Ferguson was the judge who denied Plessy's constitutional claim in a New Orleans Criminal Court.

[17]347 U.S. 483.

[18]163 U.S. 537.

The Plessy *decision made possible this photograph taken in North Carolina in 1950. These water fountains symbolize a much larger universe of discrimination, including employment discrimination.*

Long Years of Discrimination

The nation's civil rights laws were now hopelessly crippled. Southern legislatures were emboldened by *Plessy*. Now needing no special moral justification, Jim Crow laws spread. Black workers faced the most blatant discrimination. They were not allowed to hold jobs such as streetcar conductor or cashier where they would have any authority over whites. Labor unions refused to admit blacks, and a few that did limited them to low-pay occupations. The Brotherhood of Locomotive Engineers, for example, barred blacks from being locomotive engineers. In South Carolina, a law prohibited blacks and whites from working in the same room or using the same plant entrances in the cotton textile industry. Such custom spread to the North. A study of economic opportunity for blacks in Buffalo, New York, told the following tale.

> A [black] man tells of being made a moulder in a foundry, later to be replaced by a white worker and reduced to the grade of moulder's helper, and finally dismissed when he made a complaint. Another man was given a chance to try out for a skilled-labor job in a stone-cutting concern and, having made good, was given the position temporarily, losing it, however, a few days later when the superintendent "came down through the shop" and, seeing him so employed, told the foreman to put another man on the work.[19]

---

[19]Quoted in Feldman, *Racial Factors in American Industry*, p. 36.

The Civil Rights Act of 1964

This kind of open discrimination continued in the South. A study of 175 firms in New Orleans in 1943 found that almost all of them hired blacks, but then 93 percent segregated their workforces and 79 percent segregated job categories.[20] In the North, many companies refused to hire blacks at all. A study of fourteen plants in Chicago in 1952, for example, found that ten of them, or 71 percent, excluded blacks.[21]

In the late 1950s and early 1960s, a new civil rights movement arose. Under the leadership of blacks such as Martin Luther King, this movement was nonviolent and again focused on making America live up to the ideals in the American Creed. "The American people are infected with racism—that is the peril," said King. "Paradoxically, they are also infected with democratic ideals—that is the hope."[22] The pressures of this movement led to many social reforms, among them passage of the Civil Rights Act of 1964, which is today the cornerstone of the structure of laws and regulations enforcing equal opportunity. Its Title VII prohibits discrimination in any aspect of employment. It reads, in part:

> It shall be an unlawful employment practice for an employer:
>
> 1. To fail or refuse to hire or to discharge any individual, or otherwise to discriminate against any individual with respect to his compensation, terms, conditions, or privileges of employment, because of such individual's race, color, religion, sex, or national origin.
>
> 2. To limit or classify his employees or applicants for employment in any way which would deprive any individual of employment opportunities or otherwise adversely affect his status as an employee, because of such individual's race, color, religion, sex, or national origin. [Section 703(a)]

Title VII also created the Equal Employment Opportunity Commission (EEOC), an independent regulatory commission, to enforce its provisions. All companies with fifteen or more employees fall under the jurisdiction of Title VII and must report annually to the EEOC the number of minorities and women in various job categories.[23] If bias exists, employees can file charges with the EEOC. The agency then attempts to resolve charges through conciliation or voluntary settlement, but if that fails, it can sue in a federal court. In

---

[20]Logan Wilson and Harlan Gilmore, "White Employers and Negro Workers," *American Sociological Review*, December 1943, pp. 698–700.

[21]Lewis M. Killian, "The Effects of Southern White Workers on Race Relations in Northern Plants," *American Sociological Review*, June 1952, p. 329.

[22]Quoted in Lani Guinier, "[E]racing Democracy: The Voting Rights Cases," *Harvard Law Review*, November 1994, p. 109.

[23]A 1972 law extended coverage of Title VII to federal, state, and local government employees, so today Title VII covers most workers. Workers at firms with fewer than fifteen employees can sue under state and local civil rights laws or, for race discrimination, may seek remedy under the Civil Rights Act of 1866.

1998, there were 58,124 charges filed under Title VII leading to the recovery of $83 million in monetary benefits to workers suffering discrimination.[24]

The overall purpose of Title VII, which is clear from the congressional debates that preceded its passage, was to remove discriminatory barriers to hiring and advancement and create a level playing field for all workers. As originally enacted, it did not require that minority workers be hired simply because they belonged to protected groups. It did not require employers to redress racially imbalanced workforces or change established seniority systems. No whites would be fired, lose their seniority, or be adversely affected. Simply put, from the day the law went into effect, all bias was to end. Job decisions could be made only on merit.

Disparate Treatment and Disparate Impact

Title VII made overt, blatant employment discrimination illegal. It enforced a legal theory of *disparate treatment.* Disparate treatment exists if an employer gives less favorable treatment to employees because of their race, color, religion, sex, or national origin. For example, a retail store that refused to promote black warehouse workers to sales positions, preferring white salespeople to serve predominantly white customers, would be guilty of this kind of discrimination. Disparate treatment violates the plain meaning of Title VII.

Although the intention of Title VII was to create a level playing field by prohibiting all discrimination, given the entrenched prejudices of employers in the 1960s, expecting that bigotry would instantly vanish was futile. The statute would need to evolve, and it did.

When Title VII went into effect, employers could no longer engage in outwardly visible displays of discrimination. "Whites only" signs came down from windows and discrimination went underground where it was disguised but just as invidious. Instead of openly revealing prejudicial motives, employers hid them. Minority job applicants were simply rejected without comment or were found less qualified in some way. Or employers introduced job requirements that appeared merit-based but were in fact pretexts for discrimination. Female applicants had to meet height, weight, and strength requirements that favored men. Southern blacks were given tests that favored better-educated whites.

This kind of discrimination was hard to eradicate under the existing provisions of Title VII because employers would not admit a discriminatory motive and claimed that their job criteria were neutral and merit-based. The flaw in Title VII was that it contained no weapon to fight *disparate impact.* Disparate impact exists where an employment policy is apparently neutral in its impact on all employees but, in fact, is not job-related and prevents individuals in protected categories from being hired or from advancing. To combat disparate

---

[24]U.S. Equal Employment Opportunity Commission, "Title VII of the Civil Rights Act of 1964 Charges: FY 1992–FY 1998," http://www.eeoc.gov/stats/vii.html.

impact, the courts initially used a case-by-case judicial test for discrimination. First, the applicant or employee made a charge alleging bias. Then the employer had to set forth a reason why it was a "business necessity" to engage in the practice. Then the burden of proof shifted back to the employee to prove that the employer's reason was phony, which was frequently hard.[25] This back-and-forth dance in which each individual case was separately considered was awkward and time-consuming for the courts and placed the difficult burden of proving the employer's secret motive on individual plaintiffs who lacked the legal resources of corporations. Some other way to fight hidden employer racism was needed. The Supreme Court would create it.

The Griggs Case

The Duke Power Company had a steam-generating plant in Draper, North Carolina, where workers had been segregated by race for many years. The plant was organized into five divisions and blacks had been allowed to work only in the lowest-paying labor department. The company had openly discriminated against blacks, but when Title VII took effect, it rescinded its openly race-based policies and opened all jobs to blacks.

But it also instituted a new policy that required a high school diploma to move up from the labor department to the coal handling, operations, maintenance, or laboratory and test departments. Now, black workers could apply for formerly white-only jobs that paid more only if they had finished high school. Alternately, they could take an intelligence test and a mechanical aptitude test and if they scored at the same level as the average high school graduate, they could meet the high school diploma requirement. But since blacks in the area were less educated, this requirement frustrated their ambitions. Instead of rejecting blacks for being black, Duke Power now rejected them for lacking education. Black workers filed suit, alleging that the education and testing requirements had the effect of screening them out and were, in any case, unrelated to the ability, for example, to shovel coal in the coal handling department.

In *Griggs* v. *Duke Power,* decided in 1971, the Supreme Court held that diploma requirements and tests that screened out blacks or other protected classes were illegal unless employers could show that they were related to job performance or justified by "business necessity." They were unlawful even if no discrimination was intended. The *Griggs* decision, and the legal theory of disparate impact it created, was necessary for Title VII to work. If employers had been permitted to use sinuous evasions and substitute proxies for direct racial bias, Title VII would have been ineffective.

In 1978, the EEOC defined illegal disparate impact for employers with a guideline known as the *80 percent rule.*

---

[25] This sequence was set up in *McDonnell Douglas* v. *Green,* 411 U.S. 792 (1973).

A selection rate for any race, sex, or ethnic group which is less than four-fifths (4/5) or (eighty percent) of the rate for the group with the highest rate will generally be regarded . . . as evidence of adverse impact. . . .[26]

This rule is met if a company has hired minorities at the rate of at least 80 percent of the rate at which it hires from the demographic group (usually white males) that provides most of its employees. If, for example, it hires 20 percent of all white applicants, it must then hire at least 16 percent (80 percent of 20 percent) of black applicants. If it hires less than 16 percent of blacks, this statistical evidence defines unlawful disparate impact. The company is now on the defensive. It must show that the employment practices it uses, such as tests or applicant screening criteria, are a *business necessity.* Using the business necessity defense, it must prove that the test or practice is "essential," and the need for it is "compelling."[27]

With the addition of the theory of disparate impact by the judiciary, Title VII had evolved beyond its original meaning and could be used to strike down a broader range of discrimination. Title VII finally gave blacks and others a potent legal mechanism to get the civil rights on the job that Congress had tried to give them during the Reconstruction era. In a sense, broken promises were repaired. There is little in Title VII that would have been needed if, a century before, the Supreme Court had given good-faith construction to Reconstruction-era laws.

Affirmative Action

Affirmative action is a phrase describing a range of policies to seek out, encourage, and sometimes give preferential treatment to employees in the groups protected by Title VII. The broad use of affirmative action was rejected when Title VII was drafted and its congressional backers assured the business community that blacks and others would not have to be given preference over whites. Title VII was designed as a stop sign to end discrimination, not as a green light to engineer racially balanced workforces. Yet no sooner had President Lyndon Johnson signed it than civil rights groups argued that its philosophy of equal opportunity was too weak; blacks and others were so disadvantaged by past rejection that they lacked the seniority and credentials of whites. They could not compete equally in a merit system, and preferential treatment was needed to get justice.

Executive Order 11246

The origin of most affirmative action in corporations is Executive Order 11246, issued by President Johnson in 1965.[28] As originally written, the order simply

---

[26]29 CFR 1607.4 D (1989).

[27]Epstein, *Forbidden Grounds*, p. 212, citing *Williams* v. *Colorado Springs School District*, 641 F.2d 835, 842.

[28]Now codified as 41CFR60 (1998).

required federal contractors to refrain from discrimination. It imposed penalties for noncompliance and established an agency in the Department of Labor, the Office of Federal Contract Compliance Programs (OFCCP), to enforce its provisions.

However, in 1971, the Labor Department issued Order No. 4, which requires federal contractors to analyze major job categories—especially officials and managers, professionals, technicians, sales workers, office and clerical workers, and skilled crafts workers—to find out if they are using women and minorities in the same proportion as they are present in the area labor force. If protected groups are underrepresented, companies must set up goals and timetables for hiring, retention, and promotion. About 200,000 corporations, employing more than 20 percent of the labor force and including nearly all of America's largest firms, have contracts to supply goods and services to government. So in effect, Executive Order 11246, as revised by Order No. 4, imposes widespread affirmative action.

The OFCCP, with one exception, does not establish rigid hiring goals for companies. The exception is in the construction industry, where, since 1980, it has mandated a goal of 6.9 percent females. In other industries, however, it requires contractors to set hiring goals and make a "good faith" effort to achieve them. Adequate progress is usually defined as a final hiring total that meets the 80 percent rule.

The OFCCP conducts zealous compliance reviews. Teams descend on a contractor, looking around, interviewing employees and managers, and auditing all kinds of records from interview notes to payroll slips. Each year the agency does more than 3,000 such audits. At the San Diego Marriott Hotel & Marina, OFCCP team members walked around restaurants, banquet halls, and the front desk and failed to see a single black woman working in a visible position. A look at job applications soon revealed that most black women had been rejected for positions where they would interact with hotel guests. Some were better qualified than whites who were hired. Once this information surfaced, the hotel gave job offers, back pay, and benefits—a package worth $670,000—to 34 black women.[29] In extreme cases, the OFCCP can disqualify corporations from receiving federal contracts.

The Supreme Court Changes Title VII

From the beginning, affirmative action was controversial. Philosophically, it challenges the American Creed in several ways. It affronts the ideal of equality of opportunity by substituting equality of result. It affronts the ideal of achievement based on merit. And it affronts the ideal of individual rights before the law by substituting group preferences. When affirmative action first started, it posed more than a philosophical problem. Corporations were

---

[29]Office of Federal Contract Compliance Programs, "OFCCP Egregious Discrimination Cases," http://www.dol.gov/dol/esa/public/media/reports/ofccp/egregis.htm.

alarmed by its potential for generating lawsuits. If they failed to remedy race and sex imbalances in their workforces, they faced penalties for violating federal laws. If they used affirmative action to increase numbers of minorities and women, they feared reverse discrimination suits by white males.

Affirmative action was bound to provoke fierce legal challenges, and the Supreme Court used these attacks to read revolutionary changes into Title VII. The first high-profile challenge came from Allan Bakke, a white male denied admission to the medical school at the University of California at Davis. In the entering class, 16 places out of 100 had been reserved for minority students. Bakke argued that he was better qualified than some minorities admitted and had suffered illegal race discrimination under Title VII because he was white. In *Regents of the University of California* v. *Bakke,* the Supreme Court ruled in his favor.[30] In a muddled, divided, and verbose opinion, the justices forbade strict quotas. Yet they also held that race and ethnicity could be one factor considered in admissions. This kept affirmative action alive, but failed to resolve the dilemma of employers, who still feared reverse discrimination lawsuits.

Then a second case arose from a Kaiser Aluminum and Chemical Corporation plant in Louisiana. The Kaiser plant was near New Orleans where 39 percent of the workforce was black. Few blacks worked at the plant before passage of Title VII, and even with it, by 1974, only 18 percent of the plant's workers were black. Moreover, less than 2 percent of skilled crafts workers were black because Kaiser required previous craft experience and seniority. Blacks had little of either since crafts unions excluded them. Kaiser had federal contracts and, to comply with Executive Order 11246, it adopted an affirmative action plan in 1974 to raise percentages of black workers. One goal was to bring blacks into skilled craft positions, so the plan reserved 50 percent of crafts-training openings for them. This was clearly a race-based quota.

In 1974, a white laboratory analyst, Brian Weber, who had worked for Kaiser for ten years, applied for a crafts-training program that would place him in a more skilled job and raise his yearly pay from $17,000 to $25,000. To pick the trainees, Kaiser set up dual seniority ladders—one for blacks and another for whites. Names were picked alternately in descending order from the top of each ladder, starting with the black ladder, until positions were filled, with the result that seven blacks and six whites were chosen. Weber was too low on the white ladder and was not selected, whereas two blacks with less seniority than Weber were chosen (see Figure 18-1). This was a classic case of reverse discrimination.

Weber brought suit, claiming that the selection procedure violated the clear language in Title VII that prohibited making employment decisions based on race. He claimed that his Fourteenth Amendment rights to equal treatment under the law had been abridged. Justice William J. Brennan delivered the opinion of the Court in 1979 in *United Steelworkers of America* v. *Weber,* ruling that Kaiser's affirmative action plan embodied the "spirit of the law," which was to overcome the effects of past discrimination against blacks.[31]

---

[30]438 U.S. 265 (1978).
[31]443 U.S. 193.

Figure 18-1

Selection of crafts trainees at Kaiser. Kaiser and the union selected thirteen crafts trainees. All candidates met minimum qualifications, but black applicants numbered 6 and 7 had less seniority than whites numbered 7, 8, and 9.

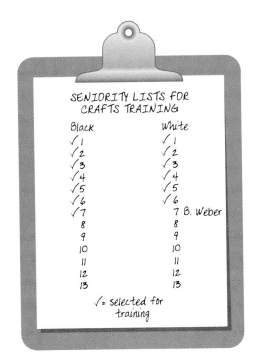

The Court also established important criteria for judging the legality of affirmative action programs that it would frequently use in later years. First, a plan must be designed to break down historic patterns of race or sex discrimination. Second, the plan must not create an absolute bar to the advance of white employees. In the *Weber* case, for example, some whites were still admitted to training. Third, the plan must not require the discharge of white workers. And finally, the plan should be flexible and temporary, so that it ends when goals are met.

The *Weber* decision added an entirely new meaning to Title VII. Henceforth, Title VII no longer stood guard over a neutral playing field. Now, it permitted the very thing that its drafters assured the nation it would not do—it permitted race-conscious preferential treatment for members of protected groups. A strong dissent in *Weber* by future Chief Justice William Rehnquist attacked the majority for adding this meaning to Title VII in contravention of its language, which clearly forbade *all* race discrimination, including that against whites. He referred to Brennan's opinion as "a tour de force reminiscent not of jurists such as Hale, Holmes, or Hughes, but of escape artists such as Houdini."[32]

The *Weber* case squarely raised the issue of reverse discrimination and confirmed that affirmative action plans were legal even if they adversely affected whites. After *Weber*, companies no longer worried about lawsuits by angry white workers. Affirmative action spread.

---

[32]47 LW 4859.

One year after *Weber*, the Supreme Court upheld race-conscious "set-aside" programs in *Fullilove* v. *Klutznick* in 1980.[33] To spur the economy, Congress in 1977 established a $4 billion fund for public works construction. Ten percent of the fund was reserved, or "set aside," for minority contractors, who had to be given contracts sometimes even when they were not low bidders. When the set-asides were challenged by white contractors, the Court ruled that they were an appropriate remedy for past discrimination against minority contractors.

The *Bakke, Weber,* and *Fullilove* cases showed that a majority on the Supreme Court supported affirmative action. But in each case, there were strong dissents. And even among the justices who supported affirmative action, there was disagreement about its legitimate scope. Thus began many years of contentious jurisprudence in which the Court defined the limits of affirmative action and then began to back away from it.

In the 1980s, a liberal majority on the Court tried to define the permissible boundaries of affirmative action. It held, for example, that seniority systems could not be overridden during layoffs to retain recently hired blacks.[34] In several other cases, it confirmed its decision in *Weber* by upholding affirmative action plans with hiring quotas for blacks.[35] It also upheld affirmative action to increase percentages of women in skilled crafts work.[36] Throughout, a minority of conservative justices vigorously dissented from the decisions of the liberal majority.

By 1988, however, President Ronald Reagan, an opponent of affirmative action, had appointed three new associate justices and a conservative bloc of five justices emerged to dominate the liberals on affirmative action cases. In three cases decided in 1989, this group whittled down the scope of race-conscious preferences.[37] The five first struck down a program awarding 30 percent of city construction work in Richmond, Virginia, to minority contractors, holding that the city had not adequately documented the existence of the discrimination this program was said to remedy.[38] Next they changed the rules and shifted the burden of proof in disparate impact cases. Previously, neutral-seeming practices that led to disproportionate exclusion of minorities were assumed to be illegal unless the company could prove that they were a "business necessity"—an extremely difficult task. Now, said the Court, in a decision favoring an Alaskan salmon cannery where whites dominated the better-paying jobs, the

---

[33]448 U.S. 448.

[34]*Firefighters Local Union No. 178* v. *Stotts*, 467 U.S. 561 (1984); and *Wygant* v. *Jackson Board of Education*, 476 U.S. 267 (1986).

[35] *Local 28* v. *EEOC*, 478 U.S. 421 (1986); *Local No. 93* v. *City of Cleveland*, 478 U.S. 450 (1986); and *United States* v. *Paradise*, 480 U.S. 149 (1987).

[36]*Johnson* v. *Transportation Agency, Santa Clara County, California*, 480 U.S. 616 (1987).

[37]This bloc included Chief Justice William Rehnquist and Justices Anthony Kennedy, Sandra Day O'Connor, Antonin Scalia, and Byron White. These five joined to dominate the liberals William Brennan, Thurgood Marshall, Harry Blackmun, and John Paul Stevens. Kennedy, O'Connor, and Scalia were Reagan appointees.

[38]*City of Richmond* v. *J. A. Croson Co.*, 488 U.S. 469 (1989).

burden was on nonwhites to prove that neutral-seeming rules caused discrimination.[39] Finally, in a case involving the Birmingham Fire Department, which had adopted an affirmative action plan because only 42 of 5,453 firefighters and none of 140 officers were black in a city that was more than 50 percent black, the Court held that white firefighters passed over for promotions were entitled to bring reverse discrimination lawsuits.[40]

Advocates of affirmative action were infuriated, and soon Congress sent a clear message of its intent to the Supreme Court by passing the Civil Rights Act of 1991. This statute reversed the Court's decisions that had narrowed the grounds for affirmative action. Among other things, it shifted the burden of proof in statistical disparity cases back to employers and it restricted the ability of whites to challenge preferential hiring and promotion plans.

Since 1991, there has been a clear majority on the Court for ending affirmative action. Two more justices likely to stand with conservatives on civil rights cases, David Souter (1990) and Clarence Thomas (1990), were appointed by President George Bush; then, two liberal-leaning justices, Ruth Bader Ginsburg (1993) and Steven Bryer (1994), were appointed by President William J. Clinton. Although a five-to-four majority to end affirmative action has existed for many years, the Court has not yet done so, although, in 1995, the five conservatives set up a "strict scrutiny" standard that was more difficult for existing affirmative action programs to pass. The case, *Adarand* v. *Pena,* is a case study following this chapter.[41]

In 1997, the Court was about to take up the case of a white teacher laid off by a school district anxious to promote racial diversity. The school district retained an equally qualified black teacher. This situation seemed unlikely to pass the strict scrutiny test under which affirmative action is justified only as a remedy for past discrimination, not as a tool to promote other goals such as diversity. However, before the case was argued, five civil rights groups raised $308,000 to settle it and it was withdrawn.[42] Later in 1997, the Court refused to hear an appeal by opponents of Proposition 209, a California ballot measure amending the state constitution to prohibit preferential treatment by state agencies based on race, sex, color, ethnicity, or national origin.[43] Its refusal allowed the measure to stand. The future is uncertain, but if the five-member majority in favor of restricting or eliminating affirmative action remains intact, new tests of affirmative action are likely to limit its use further.

The Affirmative Action Debate

The legal debate about affirmative action parallels an ethical debate in society. This debate revolves around three basic ethical considerations.

---

[39]*Wards Cove Packing Company* v. *Atonio,* 490 U.S. 642 (1989).
[40]*Martin* v. *Wilks,* 490 U.S. 755 (1989).
[41]132 L.Ed. 2d 158 (1995).
[42]*Piscataway Township Board of Education* v. *Taxman,* No. 96–679, 118 S.Ct. 595.
[43]*Coalition for Economic Equity* v. *Wilson,* 122 F.3d 692 (9th Cir.), *cert. denied,* 118 S.Ct. 397 (1997).

First, there are *utilitarian* considerations. Utilitarian ethics require calculations about the overall benefit to society, as opposed to the costs, of affirmative action. Advocates argue that preferential treatment policies benefit everyone by making fuller use of talent and shoring up political stability (because poor, unemployed, and abused people riot). Critics say that affirmative action has been ineffective or that its meager benefits are outweighed by the fairness problems it raises.

Pinning down the overall effect of affirmative action is difficult. For example, three studies of the impact on blacks when federal contractors changed their hiring practices to comply with Executive Order 11246 showed only small employment increases of 0.8 percent to 1.2 percent.[44] But studies of its effect in some industries show remarkable gains. Statistics cannot resolve the utilitarian argument about whether affirmative action, on the whole, is a net benefit or cost to society.

Second, ethical theories of *justice* raise questions about the ultimate fairness of affirmative action. Norms of distributive justice require that fair criteria be used to assign benefits and burdens. It is widely believed that economic rewards should be distributed based on merit, not on race, ethnicity, or sex. On the other hand, norms of compensatory justice require that payment be made to compensate for past wrongs. Past and current discrimination has handicapped women and minorities and placed them at a disadvantage. It has been estimated from the study of wage gaps, for example, that discrimination in employment has cost blacks $500 billion since 1929 and unjustly enriched whites by the same amount.[45] Thus, discrimination in favor of blacks may be justified to compensate for past deprivation. In 1963, President Lyndon Johnson used a colorful analogy to make this point.

> Imagine a hundred-yard dash in which one of the two runners has his legs shackled together. He has progressed ten yards, while the unshackled runner has gone fifty yards. How do they rectify the situation? Do they merely remove the shackles and allow the race to proceed? Then they could say that "equal opportunity" now prevailed. But one of the runners would still be forty yards ahead of the other. Would it not be the better part of justice to allow the previously shackled runner to make up the forty-yard gap or to start the race all over again?[46]

However, with affirmative action, the penalty for past injustices falls on the current generation of white males—the least racist of any generation. Retributive justice requires that punishment be proportional to the crime committed.

---

[44]Robert Rank and Eleena de Lisser, "Research on Affirmative Action Finds Modest Gains for Blacks over 30 Years," *The Wall Street Journal*, February 21, 1995, p. A2.

[45]Richard F. America, "Has Affirmative Action Repaid Society's Debt to African Americans?" *Business and Society Review*, Summer 1995, p. 58.

[46]Quoted in Robert A. Fullinwider, *The Reverse Discrimination Controversy: A Moral and Legal Analysis*, Totowa, N.J.: Rowman and Littlefield, 1980, p. 95.

By what proof can it be shown that this generation should inherit the guilt of past generations?

And third, affirmative action may be debated in light of ethical theories of *rights.* Advocates of affirmative action argue that it is appropriate to mint a new civil right for women and minorities, the right to preferential treatment and to exercise it until equality prevails. Discrimination in favor of protected groups is benevolent of intention, unlike the evil discrimination of whites in the past. Opponents of the right to preferential treatment argue that it destroys a more fundamental right—the right of all individuals to equal treatment before the law. Affirmative action can result in rewards being taken from persons who did not discriminate and given to persons who suffered no discrimination.

There is no easy solution to the contradictory appeals of these ethical arguments. Affirmative action is a complex policy with important benefits, but also highly visible drawbacks.

Other Important Antidiscrimination Laws

The problem of employment discrimination is so deep and persistent that, in addition to Title VII and Executive Order 11246, other laws have been necessary to protect women, ethnic or racial minorities, and other disadvantaged groups. They include the following.

The Civil Rights Act of 1866 was passed after the Civil War to protect the employment rights of freed slaves. It provides that "All persons . . . shall have the same right . . . to make and enforce contracts . . . as is enjoyed by white citizens."[47] Soon after its passage, the Supreme Court narrowly interpreted it to protect only state employees. For nearly a century, it remained on the books as an emasculated law, but it was revived by the Supreme Court in 1968.[48] Since then, it has been widely used by civil rights attorneys. It protects millions of workers in firms with fewer than fifteen employees against all forms of racial discrimination in employment. Employees of such small firms are not covered by Title VII.

The Equal Pay Act of 1963 prohibits pay differentials between male and female employees with equal or substantially equal duties in similar working conditions. It does not override pay differences that are due to legitimate seniority or merit systems. It also covers nonwage benefits.

The Age Discrimination in Employment Act of 1967 protects people over age 40. After that age, it is illegal to discriminate against a person in hiring and job decisions because of their age. As the workforce ages, age bias complaints are the fastest-growing kind of discrimination charge. The average charge is brought by a white male in his fifties, dismissed in corporate downsizing, believing that his age was the reason.

The Vietnam-Era Veterans' Readjustment Assistance Act of 1974 requires federal contractors to develop affirmative action programs for hiring, training, and promoting the nation's 6.9 million Vietnam veterans.

---

[47] 42 U.S.C. Sec. 1981, rev. stat. 1977.
[48] *Jones* v. *Alfred H. Mayer Co.,* 392 U.S. 409 (1968). This case overturned the *Civil Rights Cases.*

The Pregnancy Discrimination Act of 1978 prohibits employment discrimination based on pregnancy, childbirth, or related medical conditions. If a woman can still work, she cannot be made to resign or go on leave for any pregnancy-related condition, including having an abortion. If she is temporarily unable to perform her regular duties, the employer must try modifying her work assignments or grant leave with or without pay.

The Immigration Reform and Control Act of 1986 makes employers responsible for checking the residency status of workers. Companies with four or more employees must document the immigration status of new hires and job applicants. Hiring an undocumented alien carries a fine of $250 to $10,000 per offense, and repeat offenders can be imprisoned for up to six months. There is a flaw in this statute: employers are not required to verify the authenticity of documents that establish legal status. So a huge black market exists for phony driver's licenses, green cards, and birth certificates.

The Americans with Disabilities Act of 1990 protects workers with mental and physical impairments, including those with AIDS, from job discrimination and extends to them the protections granted to women, ethnic, racial, and religious minorities in Title VII. In interviews, employers can ask only about the ability to do specific work. Companies must make "reasonable accommodations" for disabled workers, including, for instance, provision of devices that allow deaf workers to communicate visually and readers for blind workers. Companies must also try to accommodate persons with mental illnesses such as major depression, manic depression, schizophrenia, and obsessive-compulsive disorder. For example, employers have been required to install soundproofing and set up room dividers for schizophrenic workers who have heightened sensitivity to noise and visual distractions.[49] However, companies are not required to make accommodations imposing an "undue burden" on the business.

The Civil Rights Act of 1991 amended five existing civil rights laws, including Title VII, to extend their coverage in employment situations. This encouraged civil rights lawsuits. Employment discrimination cases are difficult to prove, the evidence is often subtle or hidden in voluminous employment records, and they can take years to complete. Before this law, awards were limited to reinstatement and back pay, so the attorneys trying them were, in effect, low-paid crusaders. Then the 1991 act allowed plaintiffs in class actions to recover up to $300,000 in pain and suffering in addition to back pay and permitted their lawyers to bill losing corporations double their fees. It also allowed cases to be tried before juries, which are more sympathetic to plaintiffs than judges. The result was that more lawyers were attracted to bias litigation and the number of civil rights cases doubled between 1992 and 1996.[50]

Altogether, this is a thorough body of legislation that, with Title VII and Executive Order 11246, protects *everyone* in the workforce from discrimination.

(continued)

---

[49]Robert Fear, "Employers Told to Accommodate the Mentally Ill," *New York Times*, April 30, 1997, p. A15.

[50]David Segal, "Striking Gold in Those Bias Lawsuits," *Washington Post National Weekly Edition*, February 3, 1997, p. 29.

> ### Other Important Antidiscrimination Laws   *(concluded)*
>
> Sexual orientation is one area in which federal law does not yet provide specific protection against discrimination. Civil rights laws protecting homosexuals and lesbians from bias at work have been enacted by at least eight states and more than 90 cities. In 1996, the Supreme Court struck down a Colorado initiative that prohibited Colorado cities from passing ordinances to protect gay rights.[51] The Court held that the initiative violated the equal protection clause in the Fourteenth Amendment. This made it clear that the Court put discrimination due to sexual orientation on the same plane as discrimination based on other motives such as racism. However, no federal law specifically prohibits job bias against gays and lesbians.

Women in the Workplace

More women are entering the workforce. There are many reasons. Since the 1960s, contraception has allowed women to plan and limit childbearing. Changes in values have freed women from restrictive attitudes that discouraged working for pay outside the home in traditionally male occupations. Women receive more education. In the United States, for example, they now get the majority of bachelors' and master's degrees. This enables them to find higher-paying, more interesting work.

The number of working women began to rise early in the century. In 1910, women were only 21 percent of the labor force, and this number crept up very gradually until World War II, when it jumped to 35 percent as women replaced men in defense factories. After the war, the percentage of working women, what statisticians call the "participation rate," resumed its slow growth—never more than 1 percent a year and now less than that.

Today, 59 percent of all women work and they comprise 46 percent of the labor force. These figures are records and some believe they reflect a recent and striking social change, but the trend they represent is almost a century old. What is new is the tendency for married women with children to hold jobs. Single women and married women without children have always worked in large numbers but left their jobs for childbearing. However, in the 1960s, the number of women continuing to work while raising children began to grow. In 1960, only 25 percent of mothers worked; today more than 70 percent do.[52] If there is any dramatic element of social change in the gradual trend of women to participate more in the labor force, it is found in this subtrend. The presence of so

---

[51]*Romer* v. *Evans,* 517 U.S. 620 (1996).

[52]U.S. Department of Labor, *Equal Pay: A Thirty-Five Year Perspective,* Washington, D.C.: Department of Labor, June 10, 1998, pp. 16, 53.

many mothers at work creates pressure to modify workplaces and forces millions of women to balance motherhood with job demands.

The trend for more women to work is worldwide. Except for sub-Saharan Africa, in developed and developing nations alike, women are a growing percentage of workers. The experience of European Union countries, for example, closely parallels that of the United States; the percentages of women in their labor forces and the rise in participation rates is comparable. Some non-western nations have far fewer working women. Where strong religious and cultural values discourage independent work by women outside the home, the percentages of women in the labor force are lower, for example, in Islamic nations. Only 14 percent of workers in Saudi Arabia and the United Arab Emirates are women, 15 percent in Oman, 22 percent in Jordan, and 29 percent in Kuwait (compared with 46 percent in the United States). But Islamic women are entering the workforce more rapidly than in the United States and Europe. Since 1980, women have increased by 4 percent in the U.S. labor force, but by 6 percent in Saudi Arabia, 9 percent in the United Arab Emirates, 8 percent in Oman, 7 percent in Jordan, and 16 percent in Kuwait.[53] In some socialist countries such as Vietnam, and in the nations formerly comprising the Soviet Union, women have for decades comprised half the labor force and their participation rates have not risen.

The only part of the world where women are declining in the workforce is sub-Saharan Africa. There, strong cultural and religious traditions subordinate females. Women have little access to education. They are directed into heavy manual labor and into traditionally female work where they experience discrimination and sexual harassment. The largest concentration of the world's very poor countries is in sub-Saharan Africa; these nations have not participated in the growth of world trade and most are in long-term economic decay. To remedy this, many governments have cut back spending and directed resources toward industries that attract international trade. Men move into better-paying jobs in modernizing sectors while women are vulnerable to unemployment as old areas of the economy flounder. Thus, as economies decline and change, the percentage of women in African labor forces has fallen.

Gender Attitudes at Work

Throughout recorded history, men and women have been socialized into distinct sex roles. Men were traditionally aggressive, logical, dominant, and the breadwinner. Women were objects of sexual desire and homemakers; they were expected to be emotional and submissive. For centuries, these stereotypes dominated perceptions of the sexes and they were carried from family and social life into the workplace, where they defined male–female relationships.

---

[53]*World Development Indicators 1998*, CD-ROM, Washington, D.C.: World Bank, 1998, Table 2.3.

However, in the 1960s, a worldwide women's movement gained force and challenged male domination in Eastern and Western cultures. Its advocates argued that women could do men's jobs and attacked cultural impediments to equality. Because of this movement, two competing values clashed in the workplace. The new feminist perspective asserted that working women were entitled to the same jobs, rights, and ambitions as men. Yet men who believed in traditional sex-role stereotypes thought that women were too emotional to manage well; lacked ambition, logic, and toughness; and could not sustain career drive because of family obligations.

There is no evidence that stereotypes of male and female behavior have a biological basis. Sex-difference studies done over many years show genetic and hormonal differences between men and women, but do not convincingly show behavioral differences. Some studies document, for example, greater aggressiveness in men and greater willingness of women to express a range of emotions. Yet other studies contradict such findings and find that, from a statistical standpoint, behavioral overlap is usually more significant than behavioral similarities.[54] The lesson of sex-difference studies is that differences are small. There is much overlap between men and women in aggressiveness, emotions, and other personality traits. Individual capacities are varied and unpredictable.

These observations are confirmed by studies of men and women in management. Some studies bear out stereotypes, but others fail to support them. One survey of higher-level managers found that men tend to use a command-and-control leadership style, whereas women use an "interactive" style with more emphasis on participation, information sharing, and enhancing the self-worth of subordinates.[55] This result confirms a stereotyped view of sex differences. Another study, however, found that female managers were more committed to their careers than males; they were, for example, more willing to rank work over family and more willing to move for promotion.[56] This contradicts the stereotyped view that women are less steady workers because of family obligations. Still other studies show that women are not different in the way they work. An analysis of the decision styles of 300 managers, for example, found that female managers, like male managers, were predominantly "left-brain" and tended to use the same decision methods as men.[57] Another survey of men and women found that over a wide range of values and attitudes toward work, there were few sex differences and those that did exist were "of rather small magnitude."[58] In sum, there is no persuasive body of evidence that men and women behave differently as managers.

---

[54]Cathy Young, "Sex & Sensibility," *Reason,* March 1999.

[55]Judy B. Rosener, "Ways Women Lead," *Harvard Business Review,* November–December 1990.

[56]Warren H. Schmidt and Barry Z. Posner, "The Values of American Managers Then and Now," *Management Review,* February 1992.

[57]Alan J. Rowe and James D. Boulgarides, *Managerial Decision Making,* New York: Macmillan, 1992, p. 49. "Left-brain" thinking refers to logical thinking, as opposed to "right-brain" thinking which is defined as nonlogical, or emotional, thinking.

[58]Joel Lefkowitz, "Sex-Related Differences in Job Attitudes and Dispositional Variables: Now You See Them, . . . ," *Academy of Management Journal,* April 1994, p. 343.

The Persistence of Traditional Stereotypes

Despite lack of evidence for behavior differences at work, stereotypes persist. Some surveys document a decline in negative stereotyping. One revealing survey of male business executives was done in 1965 and then repeated twenty years later in 1985. The results, published in the *Harvard Business Review*, showed sexist attitudes receding. The number of men expressing an "unfavorable basic attitude" toward female executives fell from 41 percent in 1965 to 5 percent in 1985. The number agreeing that "women rarely expect or want authority" fell from 54 percent to 9 percent. And the number who believed that "the business community will never wholly accept women executives" fell from 61 percent to 20 percent.[59] Other surveys have shown similar changes in male thinking.[60]

However, a gap still exists between how men and women perceive the career chances of women. A survey of female executives and male CEOs at 1,000 large American corporations found a remarkable divergence of opinion about why women advanced so slowly into top jobs. For example, 52 percent of the women felt that male stereotyping stopped their advance, while only 25 percent of CEOs saw this as a problem; 49 percent of women felt that their exclusion from informal male networks was a problem, but only 15 percent of the CEOs agreed.[61]

Discriminatory Treatment of Women

In this section, we discuss four areas of work life in which women are treated differently than men.

Occupational Segregation

Women are more likely to work in some jobs than others. Within corporations and in the economy as a whole, traditionally female jobs generally are lower in status and pay than typically male jobs. Women also have less occupational diversity than do men.

In the 1960s, when married women first began to work in large numbers, two-thirds of women worked in clerical, sales, or low-level service occupations such as domestic worker. Another 15 percent worked in the professions, mainly as teachers and nurses. Since then, women have entered nontraditional

---

[59]Charlotte Decker Sutton and Kris K. Moore, "Executive Women—20 Years Later," *Harvard Business Review*, September–October 1985.

[60]See, for example, Alma S. Baron, "What Men Are Saying about Women in Business: A Decade Later," *Business Horizons*, July/August 1989, p. 52.

[61]Belle Rose Ragins, Bickley Townsend, and Mary Mattis, "Gender Gap in the Executive Suite: CEOs and Female Executives Report on Breaking the Glass Ceiling," *Academy of Management Executive*, February 1998, p. 34.

TABLE 18-1   The Top Ten Occupations of Women: 1997

Occupation	Women as a Percentage of Total Number of Workers in Occupation
1. School teacher (except post-secondary)	75.7
2. Secretary	97.9
3. Cashier	78.4
4. Manager or administrator	44.3
5. Registered nurse	93.5
6. Sales supervisor or shop proprietor	38.4
7. Bookkeepers, accounting, and auditing clerks	92.3
8. Nursing aide, orderly, or attendant	89.4
9. Waitress	77.8
10. Salesperson	65.7

Source: Bureau of Labor Statistics.

occupations. They flow most freely into growing occupations where demand for labor reduces barriers to entry such as sex discrimination. For example, they have moved in large numbers into manager and administrator positions in service industries. Because manufacturing has declined since the 1960s, women have had far less success in occupations such as operator, machinist, and mechanic.

Table 18-1 shows that most women still work in jobs regarded as traditionally female. Except for managers and administrators and sales supervisors, the percentage figures in the right-hand column confirm the predominance of women in each occupation. Although women are moving into nontraditional occupations, they do so in small numbers. For example, women are now 26 percent of physicians, but the total number of female physicians is just 6 percent of the number of women working as secretaries.[62]

Labor statisticians have developed a *difference index* to measure occupational differences between men and women over time and throughout the labor force. Between 1985 and 1995, the difference index fell from 58 to 54.[63] This means that because women are so highly concentrated in a few traditionally female occupations, for men and women to have an equal share of every occupation, 54 percent of women would have to switch to another occupation. The index has fallen more slowly in the 1990s, showing that the movement of women into nontraditional jobs has slowed; overall, it is dropping so slowly that it will be decades before any approximation of parity in occupations across the board is achieved. An indefinable part of this slowness in achieving parity can be explained as discrimination.

---

[62]In 1997, there were 2,990,538 women working as secretaries and 189,688 women physicians.

[63]Barbara H. Wootton, "Gender Differences in Occupational Employment," *Monthly Labor Review,* April 1997, p. 17. See this article for a description of the difference index.

Subtle Discrimination

Women face discriminatory male attitudes. Many workplace cultures are based on masculine values. In them, the expectation is that women will behave according to traditional male–female stereotypes. Traditional men are conditioned to see women mainly as lovers, wives, or daughters; they subconsciously expect female coworkers to act similarly and be supportive and submissive.

In blue-collar settings, sexism may be blatant; some men will openly express biases. In managerial settings, sex discrimination is usually subtle, even unintentional. Men assume that women are secretaries. In groups, men address other men first. They discount or ignore women's ideas. They make women uncomfortable with locker room humor. They fail to include women in after-hours socializing. This kind of more subtle sexism can be invisible to men, but women instantly detect it. When Bank of America, a corporation in which 25 percent of top executives were women, merged in 1998 with NationsBank, a company in which none of the top officers were women, the chairman of NationsBank, who was to be CEO of the new combination, sent employees a video tape bragging about having "the best men in banking." The top ten female executives at Bank of America resigned when they were offered positions with reduced authority. "They harbor a feeling about women that they should have bumblebees on their shoulders and be playing tennis at the club," said one departing woman.[64]

Masculine work values underlie many kinds of differential treatment. For example, Deborah Tannen studied the linguistic styles of men and women at work.[65] According to Tannen, men and women learn different ways of speaking in childhood. Boys are taught by peers and cultural cues to use words in ways that build status and emphasize power over other boys. Girls, on the other hand, use language to build rapport and empathy with their playmates. Unlike boys, girls will ostracize a playmate who brags and asserts superiority in a group. Later in life, these conversational styles carry over into the workplace, where they can place women at a disadvantage. In meetings, women may be reluctant to interrupt or criticize the ideas of another, whereas men push themselves into the conversation and engage in ritual challenges over the validity of ideas. Men hear women make self-effacing or apologetic remarks and conclude that they lack self-confidence. Tannen thinks that the female linguistic style makes it harder for women to make a firm impression in male-dominated groups and negotiations, so they are more often interrupted in meetings and overlooked in decision-making groups. One corporate CEO talking about his experience with women in upper management seems to confirm Tannen's thesis.

> If a woman wants to be as assertive as men, she can get just as much air time. In many cases she can do better than a man. But sometimes mentally their knees

---

[64]"Female Executives Have Left Bank of America," *Los Angeles Times,* December 3, 1998, p. C2.

[65]Deborah Tannen, "The Power of Talk: Who Gets Heard and Why," *Harvard Business Review,* September–October 1995.

buckle in an area where they are toe to toe. . . . If they want to be forceful, they are just as good. I'd say there is a gender bias that there's less tough, aggressive women than men.[66]

Compensation

Women are paid less than men. Before the Equal Pay Act was signed in 1963, newspapers openly ran help-wanted ads with separate male and female pay scales for identical jobs, and in that year, across all occupations, the average woman earned only fifty-nine cents for every dollar earned by a man. The Equal Pay Act has been effective in narrowing the wage difference between the sexes. By 1998, women earned seventy-six cents for every dollar earned by a man. Why though, after thirty-five years of enforcing the law, does any discrepancy remain?

Overall, women have entered the labor force more recently than men, so they are younger and have less seniority. In addition, they have less education and take more degrees in lower-paying fields such as education and nursing. Therefore, it is argued that eventually, as women stay in the job pipeline and receive more degrees in fields such as engineering and business administration, their pay will equal men's pay.[67] Indeed, the earnings gap narrows when women and men of similar age, occupational experience, and educational background are compared. But it does not disappear. In one study of all men and women holding degrees in 130 major fields, women were paid equally with or made more than men in only 11 fields employing just 2 percent of the women. In all the remaining fields, women averaged only 73 percent of men's pay.[68] Nothing in the statistical analysis of men's and women's characteristics, besides sex, accounts for this shortfall in women's pay. Unmeasured or hidden factors, among them discrimination, are responsible.

The pay gap between men and women is worldwide. A study by the International Labor Organization showed that women were paid less than men for comparable work in every nation. Depending on the country, they earned between 50 percent and 96 percent of men's wages in 1995.[69]

Top-Level Promotions

Women have great difficulty reaching top management. In 1998, women were 10.6 percent of officers in a survey of *Fortune* 500 companies.[70] The number of

---

[66]Anonymous interviewee cited in Ragins, Townsend, and Mattis, "Gender Gap in the Executive Suite," p. 38.

[67]Diana Furchtgott-Roth and Christina Stolba, "'Comparable Worth' Makes a Comeback," *The Wall Street Journal,* February 4, 1999, p. A22.

[68]Daniel E. Hecker, "Earnings of College Graduates: Women Compared with Men," *Monthly Labor Review,* March 1998, p. 63.

[69]ILO, Press Release, "Women Work More, but Are Still Paid Less," August 25, 1995, p. 1.

[70]A survey by Catalyst, cited in Keith H. Hammonds, "You've Come a Short Way, Baby," *Business Week,* November 23, 1998, p. 82.

women officers has been increasing; for example, it was up from 8.7 percent in 1995, but some large corporations such as Exxon and General Electric had no women officers and, even in companies that did, women executives earned only 68 percent of the salaries of their male counterparts and were less likely to be in line positions with profit-and-loss responsibility.[71] This situation leads some to say that women have hit a "glass ceiling," or an invisible barrier of sex discrimination thwarting career advancement to the highest levels.

One recent survey of male CEOs and female top managers found that the women believed the most important barrier they faced was "male stereotyping and preconceptions," while the CEOs believed the most significant barrier was lack of experience and felt that women had not been "in the pipeline" long enough. The CEOs believed promotion processes were neutral and that as women gained more seniority, they would prevail. Yet women saw the process as tilted against them. The authors concluded that "the majority of CEOs surveyed apparently are unaware of the corporate environment faced by their women employees."[72]

Like the pay gap, the glass ceiling is worldwide. The International Labor Organization estimated in 1995 that at the existing rate of progress, it would be 475 years before parity between men and women was achieved in executive positions.[73]

Sexual Harassment

Many working women experience sexual harassment. Various forms of harassment exist, and same-sex harassment is prohibited by the same laws that bar male–female harassment.[74] However, the major problem for employers is harassment of women by men. In a landmark book, *Sexual Shakedown*, Lin Farley defined this form of harassment as "unsolicited nonreciprocal male behavior that asserts a woman's sex role over her function as a worker."[75]

Sexual harassment of women encompasses a wide range of behavior. It can be very subtle, as when older men treat younger women like daughters, a tendency that can make a female manager's job uncomfortable. More direct forms of harassment are staring, touching, joking, and gratuitous discussion of sex. The most serious forms include demands for sexual favors or physical assaults. These behaviors reinforce male power in work settings. By treating a woman as a sex object, a man places her in the stereotyped role of submissive female, thereby subordinating and marginalizing her. The message is, "You're

---

[71]Joann S. Lublin, "Even Top Women Earn Less, New Study Finds," *The Wall Street Journal,* October 10, 1998, p. B18.

[72]Ragins, Townsend, and Mattis, "Gender Gap in the Executive Suite," p. 37.

[73]ILO, "Women Work More," p. 2.

[74]See *Oncale* v. *Sundowner Offshore Services,* 523 U.S. 75 (1998).

[75]New York: McGraw-Hill, 1978, pp. 14–15.

FIGURE 18-2

*The EEOC
guidelines on
sexual harassment.*

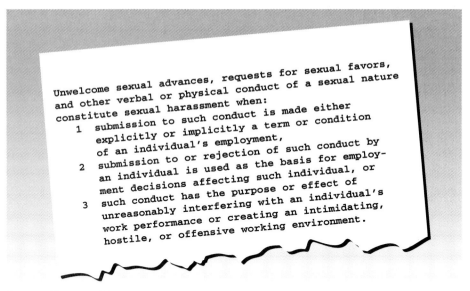

Unwelcome sexual advances, requests for sexual favors, and other verbal or physical conduct of a sexual nature constitute sexual harassment when:

1 submission to such conduct is made either explicitly or implicitly a term or condition of an individual's employment,

2 submission to or rejection of such conduct by an individual is used as the basis for employment decisions affecting such individual, or

3 such conduct has the purpose or effect of unreasonably interfering with an individual's work performance or creating an intimidating, hostile, or offensive working environment.

Source: 29 CFR 1604.11(a).

only a woman, that's the way I see you. And at that level you're vulnerable to me and any man."[76]

For many years, women had little recourse when they were sexually harassed. Corporate cultures condoned harassment, policies against it were nonexistent, and, short of battery or rape, there was no precedent for legal action. Now that has changed. In 1980, the EEOC issued guidelines (see Figure 18-2) making sexual harassment a form of sex discrimination under Title VII. This gave women a powerful legal weapon to aim at offending men and the employers who condoned them.

The EEOC guidelines define two situations where harassment is illegal. One is the *quid pro quo,* when submission to sexual activity is required to get or keep a job. The other is a *hostile environment,* where sexually offensive conduct is so pervasive that it becomes unreasonably difficult to work. The range of conduct that can create a hostile environment has expanded to become very broad, but is not subject to precise definition. At first, courts often held that coarse language, innuendo, and pin-ups were part of some work environments and that Title VII could not magically dignify the manners of male workers throughout America.[77] Then, in a landmark case, a female welder named Lois Robinson, one of only seven women among 1,010 skilled craftsworkers in a Florida shipyard, complained that suggestive and lewd pinups, drawings, and cartoons created a hostile working environment. A Florida

---

[76]Cynthia Cockburn, *In the Way of Women: Men's Resistance to Sex Equality in Organizations,* Ithaca, N.Y.: ILR Press, 1991, p. 142.

[77]See, for example, *Rabidue* v. *Osceola Refinery Co.,* 805 E.2d 611 (CA-6 1986).

court agreed with her, holding that even if men enjoyed this decor, it never-theless created an abusive climate for Robinson.[78]

In 1993, the Supreme Court set up a test for hostile environments. Teresa Harris, a manager in a Nashville company that rented forklifts, filed an EEOC complaint due to the behavior of the company president, Charles Hardy. Over several years, Hardy engaged in a pattern of vulgar and demeaning behavior that targeted Harris as a woman. He made derogatory remarks such as "You're a woman, what do you know?" and "We need a man as the rental manager." He made her serve coffee in meetings. He asked Harris and other female employees to fish coins out of his front pants pockets and sometimes threw objects on the floor, asking the women to pick them up while he commented on their breasts and clothing. He proposed negotiating Harris's raise at a Holiday Inn and suggested that she try giving sexual favors to get forklift rentals. When Harris complained and threatened to quit, Hardy apologized and she stayed, but his boorishness resumed.

Other women at the company testified that Hardy's behavior was all part of a ribald, joking atmosphere that everyone understood and enjoyed. Did Forklift Systems contain a hostile working environment? A lower court did not think so, ruling that although it was a close call and Hardy was a vulgar man, there was no proof that his conduct created a situation so intimidating that it interfered with Harris's ability to do her job.[79] However, when the case reached the Supreme Court, the justices created new criteria for defining a hostile environment.

In *Harris* v. *Forklift Systems*, they held that the guideline was whether sexual harassment created "an environment that a reasonable person would find hostile or abusive." There was no "mathematically precise test" for what constituted a hostile environment, but harassing conduct should be examined with respect to its "frequency" and "severity," whether it is "physically threatening or humiliating," and whether it "unreasonably interferes" with work.[80] The Supreme Court sent the *Harris* case back to a lower court for rehearing based on these criteria, and, a year later, that court ordered the company to set up a sexual harassment policy and to pay Harris's attorney fees. Forklift Systems appealed, but the litigants ultimately made a nonpublic, out-of-court settlement to end the case.

In the year following the *Harris* decision, the number of harassment charges filed with the EEOC jumped by 21 percent. In 1998, the agency resolved more than 17,000 complaints. Women filed most of the charges, but 13 percent came from men.[81] In 1998, the Supreme Court further elaborated the law of sexual harassment. It made corporations liable to damages for sexual harassment when

---

[78]*Robinson* v. *Jacksonville Shipyards,* 760 F.Supp. 1486 (M.D. Fla. 1991), at 1524.

[79]*Harris* v. *Forklift Systems, Inc.,* No. 3–89–0557 (M.D. Tenn. 1990).

[80]510 U.S. 23 (1993).

[81]Equal Employment Opportunity Commission, "Sexual Harassment Charges," www.eeoc.gov/stats/harass.html.

employees create a hostile environment. They can escape liability only if management proves that it tried hard to prevent and remedy harassment and, in addition, that the aggrieved employee neglected to make a complaint.[82] Now, most companies have a formal policy to prohibit sexual harassment and open complaint channels. Many companies take out sexual harassment insurance policies offered by Lloyd's of London and several American firms. A policy with coverage of $25 million has a deductible of $25,000 and costs $15,000 annually.[83]

Corporate Efforts to Promote Diversity

Employment decisions are now closely regulated to protect workers from discrimination. While companies, particularly smaller ones, try simply to comply with all the laws and regulations, many large firms have broadened their efforts beyond legal compliance to promotion of diversity. In 1998, three out of four *Fortune* 500 corporations had one or more programs to manage diversity.[84] *Diversity management* refers to a range of programs that increase worker diversity and change corporate cultures to make them hospitable to employees regardless of race, ethnicity, gender, age, religion, sexual orientation, or disability.

Managing diversity can pay off in many ways. First, it can lower costs of recruiting, turnover, absenteeism, and lawsuits. Minorities and women have higher turnover than white men and often have higher absenteeism due to the presence of barriers the corporation fails to see and remove. Less frustration raises both tenure and productivity and can prevent discrimination charges. The average such complaint that goes to trial by jury is lost and the company pays $600,000.[85] Second, diversity can improve understanding of markets and customers. At Merck, an anticoagulant drug sold poorly in Hispanic markets until a Hispanic manager in the company noticed that the package insert was written only in English. After translation into Spanish, sales rose. The idea was simple, but nobody else thought of it.[86] Third, diversity efforts can reduce friction between workers with diverse backgrounds. There is evidence that diverse teams also make better decisions because they consider more perspectives.[87] Finally, some managers think that strategizing in a global economy requires diversity. "It is clear to me," says John H. Bryan, head of Sara Lee

[82]*Burlington Industries, Inc.* v. *Ellerth*, 524 U.S. 742 (1998). See also *Faragher* v. *City of Boca Raton*, 524 U.S. 775 (1998).

[83]"More Firms Insuring for Harassment," *Los Angeles Times*, January 24, 1998, p. D1.

[84]"Competitive Practices for a Diverse Workforce," *Fortune*, July 6, 1998, p. S12.

[85]Gail Robinson and Kathleen Dechant, "Building a Business Case for Diversity," *Academy of Management Executive*, November 1997, p. 24.

[86]Margaret A. Hart, *Managing Diversity for Sustained Competitiveness* (New York: The Conference Board, 1997), p. 5

[87]Faye Rice, "How to Make Diversity Pay," *Fortune*, August 8, 1994, p. 79.

Corporation, "that a group of older, white male executives of the same nationality, men with backgrounds which are quite similar, represent a dangerously narrow profile of exposure for a management in a world changing as rapidly and dramatically as ours is today."[88]

Specific examples of corporate actions illustrate the range of diversity initiatives in companies.

- *Top management commitment* is critical. When Jim Adamson arrived as CEO of Flagstar, the parent corporation of Denny's restaurants, the company had a reputation for terrible bigotry. It had settled a federal lawsuit for discriminating against black customers and its Annapolis, Maryland restaurant made the news by failing to seat six black Secret Service agents for breakfast. Under a "blackout" policy used by some district managers in the chain, restaurants closed if too many black customers entered. At his first employee meeting, Adamson announced a broad diversity program. "And I will fire you," he warned, "if you discriminate."[89]

- *Recruitment and hiring practices* are important. Sara Lee sets affirmative action goals that go beyond even ambitious EEO/AA requirements. At Sara Lee, 40 percent of MBA recruits each year must be women and 40 percent must be black. Denny's uses a computerized interviewing technique to screen out racist applicants. Job seekers call an 800 number and answer a variety of questions, including, for example, "Do you like dealing with people of different races?" People take longer to tell a lie, so the software registers deviation from average response times for each question. If there is hesitation, the company probes the issue in subsequent face-to-face interviews.

- *Training programs* sensitize employees to prejudices and cultural differences. Merck developed a training system in which every employee participates in a one-day training session led by other employees. These sessions encourage workers to verbalize their feelings about such topics as prejudice, diversity, and affirmative action.

- *Mentors* can be assigned to women and minorities to overcome isolation in firms where the hierarchy is predominantly white and male. Xerox Corporation, for example, assigns mentors to female and minority employees.

- *Social identity groups,* also called support groups or networks, exist at many companies. At DuPont, for example, there are more than 100 networks in plants and offices around the world for blacks, women, Hispanics, Asians, gays and lesbians, and the disabled.[90]

---

[88]John H. Bryan, "Diversity: A Strategic Business Imperative," *Vital Speeches of the Day,* November 1, 1998, p. 45.

[89]Faye Rice, "Denny's Changes Its Spots," *Fortune,* May 13, 1996, p. 133.

[90]"Do They Get It," *Across the Board,* March 1998, p. 32.

- *Data collection* is sometimes needed to understand the facts of discrimination. Four times a year, Allstate Insurance Co. surveys its 50,000 employees to learn how they feel they are being treated. Related to data collection is measurement. Because of the pervasive philosophy in business that what gets measured gets done, many companies quantify diversity goals. The Quaker Oats Company created a statistic called the "best-practices index" that registers points for every program and action taken in each of its plants. The head of its diversity management program argues that "Most CEOs may not know a lot about diversity, but they understand numbers. They can tell the difference between a facility with 1,000 points on the best-practices index, and a facility with 500 points."[91]
- *Policy changes* establish new rules. Following a public relations disaster when tapes of executives making racially biased remarks were leaked to the press and a $115 million settlement of a race discrimination lawsuit, Texaco embarked on a program to change its corporate culture. An Equality and Tolerance Task Force was set up to create and monitor change. Many policies changed as a result. One example is a new rule that no human resource committee meeting can take place unless attended by a minority or a woman. If such a committee member is sick or delayed, the meeting is postponed.[92]
- *Reward systems* encourage managers to achieve diversity goals. At General Foods, managers are evaluated in four equally weighted areas, one of which is diversity. Division managers at Exxon are required as part of their performance reviews to present career development plans for ten females and ten minority males.

Resistance to diversity projects comes from white males who feel blamed for problems and see their opportunities fading and from some women and minorities trying to deemphasize their differences and assimilate into the dominant organizational culture. Yet, growing diversity in workforces and markets ensures that these programs will spread because there is a business rationale for them. Nondiscrimination has moved from a social responsibility, to a legal duty, to a business imperative. In the end, it may be the latter consideration that closes any remaining gap between the promises of natural rights in the Declaration of Independence and the abridgement of them in practice.

---

[91]Hart, *Managing Diversity for Sustained Competitiveness*, p. 8, citing Vice President of Diversity Management I. Charles Mathews.

[92]Richard F. Brenner, "Crisis and Opportunity at Texaco," in Hart, *Managing Diversity for Sustained Competitiveness*, p. 20.

Concluding Observations

Workplace discrimination has existed throughout American history. The first national effort to end it began during the Civil War, with the Emancipation Proclamation freeing slaves, and included constitutional amendments and civil rights laws passed after the war. This effort floundered because societal values did not permit enforcement of the laws.

In the 1960s, a second effort to eradicate discrimination began with passage of the Civil Rights Act of 1964. Since then, more laws and thousands of agency and court decisions have greatly reduced, but not eliminated, job bias against minorities and women. Today, the accumulated corpus of antidiscrimination law is massive, complex, and controversial where it embodies preferential treatment. But overall, and unlike the reconstruction-era effort, it works. Along with government, corporations are taking a wide spectrum of actions—both voluntary and legally mandated—to make progress.

Yet more still needs to be done. There is widespread evidence of continuing discrimination. Research on wage gaps, studies of job applications, and the continued existence of many discrimination suits attest to it.[93]

---

[93]William A. Darity Jr. and Patrick L. Mason, "Evidence on Discrimination in Employment: Codes of Color, Codes of Gender," *Journal of Economic Perspectives,* Spring 1998.

ADARAND v. *PENA*

This is the story of an affirmative action case that made its way to the Supreme Court. When the Court announced that it would hear *Adarand v. Pena*, there was considerable speculation about the outcome. The plaintiff, a white male, argued that preferential treatment for minority and female contractors was unconstitutional. Would the justices agree?

In the end, the nine-member Court issued a lengthy (21,800 words), split decision showing itself to be as fractured as the public in its thinking. It divided 5 to 4, with six separate opinions—a majority opinion, two concurring opinions, and three dissents. The result? Affirmative action lived on but became harder to justify.

The Guardrail Subcontract

In 1987, Congress appropriated a huge sum, more than $16 billion, to the Department of Transportation (DOT) for highway construction across the nation.[1] Ten percent, or $1.6 billion, was earmarked for small businesses run by "socially and economically disadvantaged individuals."[2] Socially disadvantaged persons were defined as "those who have been subjected to racial or ethnic prejudice or cultural bias" and economically disadvantaged persons were defined as those "whose ability to compete in the free enterprise system has been impaired due to diminished capital and credit opportunities as compared to others in the same business area who are not socially disadvantaged."[3] It was to be presumed that black, Hispanic, Asian Pacific, subcontinent Asian, and Native American persons and women were both socially and economically handicapped. Any small business with 51 percent or greater ownership by persons in these categories could be certified as a *disadvantaged business enterprise,* or DBE. Then, Congress put monetary incentives to hire DBEs into the highway construction law. The story here illustrates how these incentives worked.

In 1989, Mountain Gravel & Construction Company received a $1 million prime contract to build highways in the San Juan National Forest of southwest Colorado. It requested bids from subcontractors to install 4.7 miles of

---

[1]The Surface Transportation and Uniform Relocation Assistance Act of 1987, P.L. 100–17.
[2]Section 106(c)(1).
[3]Section 106(c)(2)(B).

Randy Pech
of Adarand
Constructors.

guardrails. Two small companies that specialize in guardrail installation responded. Adarand Constructors, Inc., a white-owned company, submitted the low bid and Gonzales Construction Company, a firm certified as a DBE, submitted a bid that was $1,700 higher. Ordinarily, Mountain Gravel would have chosen the low bidder, but the prime contract provided that it would be paid a bonus, up to 10 percent of the guardrail subcontract, if it picked a DBE. On this subcontract, the bonus payment was approximately $10,000, so even by accepting a bid $1,700 above the low bid, Mountain Gravel came out $8,300 ahead. Gonzales Construction, the high bidder, got the nod.

The part of the prime contract that caused Mountain Gravel to reject Adarand Constructors' low bid was called a *subcontractor compensation clause*. It provided that a sum equal to 10 percent of the subcontract would be paid to Mountain Gravel, up to a maximum of 1.5 percent of the dollar amount of the prime contract, if one DBE subcontractor was used. If two DBE subcontractors had been used, the extra payment could have been as much as 2 percent of the prime contract.

Losing the guardrail job angered Randy Pech, the white male co-owner and general manager of Adarand Constructors. "It was very discouraging to run a legitimate, honest business," said Pech, "to go to a lot of trouble of bidding on a project—to know you did a great job and come in the low bid—and then find out they can't use you because they have to meet their 'goals.'"[4] Pech's lawyer, William Pendley, spoke more bluntly about the subcontractor compensation clause. "It works like a bribe," he said.[5] This was not the first

---

[4]Quoted in Marlene Cimons, "Businessman Who Brought Lawsuit Praises Ruling by Justices," *Los Angeles Times*, June 13, 1995, p. A15.

[5]David G. Savage, "'Colorblind' Constitution Faces a New Test," *Los Angeles Times*, January 16, 1995, p. A17.

time Adarand Constructors had faced this situation. It was one of only five Colorado contractors specializing in guardrails. The other four, Cruz Construction, Ideal Fencing, C&K, and Gonzales Construction, were minority-owned and, by virtue of that, designated as DBEs. These four competitors were all stable businesses at least ten years old and, on nonfederal highway projects, they sometimes beat Adarand Constructors with lower bids. Yet when federal highway dollars were being spent, Adarand Constructors frequently lost—even with the lowest bid. Later, it would be documented that because of the subcontractor compensation clause, prime contractors had rejected the company's low bids five times to favor its DBE competitors. Mountain Gravel's bid estimator verified that Adarand Constructors' low bid on the 4.7 mile guardrail job would have been accepted if the extra payment had not existed. Fed up, Randy Pech sued the federal government.

In his suit, Pech claimed that the subcontractor compensation clause violated his constitutional right to equal treatment under the law. This right is found in the Fifth Amendment of the Constitution, which reads: "No person shall . . . be deprived of life, liberty, or property, without due process of law." Although this wording does not literally state that citizens are entitled to equal treatment, the Supreme Court has held that its meaning protects citizens from arbitrary or unequal treatment by the federal government in the same way that the Fourteenth Amendment prohibits states from denying "equal protection of the laws" to their citizens. Pech did not seek monetary damages, but requested an injunction, or a court-ordered halt, to any future use of contract clauses providing extra payments on subcontracts given to DBEs.

Things got off to a bad start for Pech when the U.S. District Court for the District of Colorado ruled against him.[6] The court held that it was within the power of Congress, when it enacted the highway bill, to use race- and gender-based preferences to compensate for the harmful effects of past discrimination. Pech appealed to the Tenth Circuit Court of Appeals, but, two years later, it affirmed the district court's decision.[7] Pech then took the next step and appealed to the Supreme Court, which agreed to decide the case. Because the lawsuit named Transportation Secretary Federico Pena as a defendant, it was entitled *Adarand* v. *Pena*.

The Constitution and Race

The Court was being asked to decide whether classifying citizens by race in order to treat them differently was constitutionally respectable for the federal government. This was not a new question; neither was it one that has ever been resolved with clarity. Affirmative action has deeply divided the Court, but it is not the first race-based classification scheme to raise constitutional problems.

---

[6]*Adarand Constructors, Inc.* v. *Samuel K. Skinner,* 790 F.Supp. 240 (D.Colo. 1992). Then-Secretary of Transportation Skinner was named as the defendant.

[7]*Adarand Constructors, Inc.* v. *Federico Pena,* 16 F.3d 1537 (10th Cir. 1994). By this time, Pena was Secretary of Transportation.

Between 1884 and 1893, the Court decided a series of challenges to exclusionary laws passed by Congress stopping the immigration of Chinese laborers and restricting the civil rights of resident Chinese. At first, the justices struck down laws that treated Chinese differently from American citizens.[8] Eventually, however, the Court went along with a wave of public hysteria over the Chinese and in key decisions upheld laws that denied them equal treatment.[9]

A few years later, in 1896, the Court had an opportunity to strike down the Jim Crow laws of the old South in *Plessy* v. *Ferguson*, but failed to do so. Instead, it upheld the Louisiana statue requiring segregation of whites and nonwhites in separate railroad cars and fixed in place the infamous "separate but equal" doctrine. In a lone dissent that rang across decades, Justice John Marshall Harlan called the Constitution "color blind" and said that race was not a valid criteria for making law.

> In respect of civil rights, common to all citizens, the Constitution of the United States does not, I think, permit any public authority to know the race of those entitled to be protected in the enjoyment of such rights. . . . [T]he common government of all shall not permit the seeds of race hate to be planted under the sanction of law.[10]

During World War II, the Court was once again called upon to decide the question of a race-based government action. In early 1942, President Franklin Roosevelt issued an executive order, which Congress ratified, requiring the relocation of 70,000 persons of Japanese descent, both American citizens and resident aliens, from homes on the West Coast to inland evacuation camps. This policy was challenged as depriving the Japanese-Americans of their Fifth Amendment guarantee of equal protection of the laws. However, the Court was once again willing to uphold a racial classification scheme used by government. In the majority opinion, Justice Black conceded that "all legal restrictions which curtail the civil rights of a single racial group are immediately suspect" and must be subjected "to the most rigid scrutiny."[11] Nevertheless, the evacuation order passed this "rigid scrutiny," because the president and Congress were taking emergency actions in time of war to prevent sabotage and avert grave danger. In dissent, Justice Frank Murphy argued that the evacuation "goes over 'the very brink of constitutional power' and falls into the ugly abyss of racism."[12]

In 1954, the Court finally reversed its decision in *Plessy*. In the landmark school desegregation case, *Brown* v. *Board of Education*, it agreed that under the "separate but equal" doctrine, the states had provided grossly unequal

---

[8]*Chew Heong* v. *United States*, 112 U.S. 536 (1884); and *United States* v. *Jung Ah Lung*, 124 U.S. 621 (1888).

[9]*Lee Joe* v. *United States*, 149 U.S. 698 (1893).

[10]163 U.S. 554, 560.

[11]*Korematsu* v. *United States*, 323 U.S. 214.

[12]323 U.S. 242.

schools for blacks.[13] During oral arguments in the case, Thurgood Marshall, destined to be the first black Supreme Court justice, invoked the principle of a color-blind Constitution. A unanimous Court struck down "separate but equal" as a violation of the equal protection clause in the Fourteenth Amendment.

The *Brown* decision, however did not mean that the Court saw a completely color-blind Constitution. In the 1970s, suits by whites who had suffered reverse discrimination as a result of affirmative action began to reach its docket. In the first such cases, a divided Court upheld affirmative action, but was obviously troubled by it and tried to define its limits. There was also an ideological split among the justices, with a liberal bloc condoning race-based affirmative action and a conservative bloc inclined to severely limit or prohibit it.

The Fullilove Case

In 1980, the Court heard for the first time a challenge to a set-aside program for minority businesses. In the Public Works Employment Act of 1977, Congress authorized $4 billion in federal grants for public works projects such as dams, bridges, and highways. At least 10 percent of this sum was set aside for businesses owned by "minority group members," who were defined as "Negroes, Spanish-speaking, Orientals, Indians, Eskimos, and Aleuts."[14] The law was challenged by several associations of white contractors, who claimed to have lost business and argued that the set-aside violated their constitutional rights to equal protection. But in *Fullilove* v. *Klutznick*, the Court held that Congress could use racial classification schemes to strike at racist, exclusionary practices used by prime contractors on federally funded projects.[15]

Over the years, courts have developed standards for testing the constitutional validity of laws that classify citizens. All such laws must withstand one of three levels of scrutiny by a skeptical judiciary. The lowest level is "ordinary scrutiny," which requires that government prove its classification scheme is "reasonably" related to a "legitimate interest." For example, classifying citizens by income for purposes of tax collection would pass this minimum test. The second level is "intermediate scrutiny," a heightened standard requiring that the law be "substantially related" to an "important government objective." In the past, intermediate scrutiny was typically used for laws related to gender, for example, the law drafting men for military service, but not women.

The final, and most exacting, level of scrutiny, called "strict scrutiny," is reserved for racial classifications regarded as pernicious and undesirable.

---

[13]347 U.S. 483.
[14]Section 103(f)(2).
[15]448 U.S. 448.

When strict scrutiny is used, it is presumed that the law in question is unconstitutional unless the government can prove that it serves a "compelling" government interest and is "narrowly tailored," that is, not more extensive than it needs to be to serve its purpose. There are no fixed definitions of the words "reasonably," "substantially related," and "compelling," but they represent an escalating standard of proof.

The majority opinion in *Fullilove* showed that neither Chief Justice Warren Burger nor the five other justices who joined and concurred with him were particularly alarmed about race-based set-asides for minority contractors. The chief justice subjected the minority business program in the Public Works Employment Act to only an intermediate level of scrutiny. This was unusual for a race-based classification, but reflected much thinking at the time that discrimination against whites to make up for past racism was not as harmful as old-style, direct discrimination against minorities.

The Croson and Metro Cases

After *Fullilove,* nine years passed before the Court looked at set-asides again. During the interim, President Ronald Reagan appointed three new conservative justices and the liberal bloc lost its ability to form a five-member majority on affirmative action cases. Hence, in 1989, the Court struck down an affirmative action contracting plan used by the city of Richmond, Virginia. This plan required that 30 percent of city construction work be awarded to minority contractors. In *Richmond* v. *Croson,* the Court held that because the city's plan was a suspect racial classification, it should be subject to strict scrutiny.[16] And when the two tests required by strict scrutiny were applied, the plan could not pass constitutional muster. First, although the population of Richmond was 50 percent black and less than 1 percent of city contracts were awarded to black firms, the city had not proved a "compelling" interest because it had never conducted studies to show that this statistical discrepancy was caused by race discrimination. Without proof of past discrimination, no "compelling" justification for race-based remedial action existed. And second, the plan was not "narrowly tailored"; in addition to giving preference to black contractors, it entitled Hispanic, Asian, Native American, Eskimo, and Aleut contractors located anywhere in the United States to take advantage of preferential bidding rules. This scheme of inclusion was too broad. The Court ruled that for white contractors, the Richmond plan violated the Fourteenth Amendment guarantee of equal protection under the law.[17]

---

[16]*City of Richmond* v. *J. A. Croson Co.,* 488 U.S. 469 (1989).

[17]The Fourteenth Amendment protects American citizens from unjust actions by state governments. It reads: "No State shall . . . deny to any person within its jurisdiction the equal protection of the laws." The city of Richmond, being chartered by the state of Virginia, was therefore a governmental actor falling under the reach of the Fourteenth Amendment.

In the wake of the *Croson* decision, more than 200 set-aside plans around the country were dropped or changed for fear that they would be challenged and struck down. In Richmond, the percentage of contract dollars awarded to minority businesses plummeted from 30 percent to "the low single digits."[18]

A year later, in 1990, the Court confronted a case in which white-owned broadcasters challenged a congressional statute requiring that the Federal Communications Commission give certain preferences to minority radio and television companies when it issued broadcast licenses. Congress declared that its purpose was to promote diversity in programming. In *Metro Broadcasting* v. *FCC*, a five-member majority of the Court composed of four remaining liberals and the usually conservative Justice Byron White held that "benign race-conscious measures" undertaken by Congress to compensate victims of discrimination need be subject only to the standard of "intermediate scrutiny."[19] Creating diversity in broadcasting was an "important governmental objective," and preferences for nonwhite and female broadcasters were "substantially related" to achieving this objective. In dissent, Justice Anthony M. Kennedy sought to refocus the Court on the mistake made in the *Plessy* case. "I regret," he wrote, "that after a century of judicial opinions we interpret the Constitution to do no more than move us from 'separate but equal' to 'unequal but benign.'"[20]

Two Lines of Precedent

This was where matters stood until 1994, when *Adarand* came before the Court. The Supreme Court likes to follow precedent and generally adheres to the rule of *stare decisis* (STARE-ray da-SEE-sis), a Latin term meaning to stand as decided. The judicial system is based on the principle that once a matter of law is settled, courts should follow the established path. Judges believe that this should be the case even though a court would decide the question differently if it were new. *Stare decisis* preserves one of the law's primary virtues, its predictability.

However, two different precedents had been established for minority preferences in contracting. In *Croson*, the Court had applied strict scrutiny to a city plan and declared it unconstitutional. But *Adarand* was not about a city plan; it involved a plan enacted by Congress. Traditionally, the Supreme Court recognizes that Congress represents the will of the American people and thus its actions deserve great deference. Supreme Court justices, who are appointed rather than elected, are reluctant to substitute their views in place of congressional intent. The line of precedent closest to the issue in *Adarand*

---

[18]Paul M. Barrett and Michael K. Frisby, "Affirmative-Action Advocates Seeking Lessons from States to Help Preserve Federal Programs," *The Wall Street Journal,* December 7, 1994, p. A18.

[19]497 U.S. 547.

[20]497 U.S. 637–38.

was that emerging from *Fullilove* and *Metro*. In both cases, the Court had applied only intermediate scrutiny to congressional affirmative action plans and in both cases the plans were upheld. This result was consistent with the Court's studied deference toward Congress.

The Decision in *Adarand*

Attorneys for each side in *Adarand* v. *Pena* presented thirty minutes of oral argument before the nine justices on January 17, 1995.[21] On June 12, 1995, the Supreme Court released a 5–4 decision in favor of Adarand Constructors.[22] The majority opinion, written by Justice Sandra Day O'Connor, departed from the line of precedent running from *Fullilove* and *Metro* and instead returned to *Croson* and ruled that the Department of Transportation plan giving preferences in bidding to minority subcontractors would have to withstand the test of strict scrutiny. The majority held that the plan was a race classification and presumed to be unconstitutional unless it was "narrowly tailored" to meet a "compelling government interest." Justice O'Connor wrote as follows.

> . . . [W]e hold today that all racial classifications, imposed by whatever federal, state, or local governmental actor, must be analyzed by a reviewing court under strict scrutiny. In other words, such classifications are constitutional only if they are narrowly tailored measures that further compelling governmental interests. To the extend that *Metro Broadcasting* is inconsistent with that holding it is overruled.[23]

Justice O'Connor justified departing from the *Fullilove* and *Metro* precedents by citing Justice Felix Frankfurter, who fifty-five years earlier had written that "*stare decisis* is . . . not a mechanical formula of adherence to the latest decision, however recent and questionable, when such adherence involves collision with a prior doctrine more embracing in its scope, intrinsically sounder, and verified by experience."[24] The Court's longstanding, deep suspicion of any race classification, wrote O'Connor, should override the recent efforts of some liberal justices to apply more lax scrutiny to forms of discrimination they called "benign." She expressed deep skepticism about the ability of Congress to distinguish between race classifications generated by "benign" or remedial motives and race classifications resulting from illegitimate motives or racially charged politics.

[21]This oral argument can be heard in CSPAN's recorded archives at http://www.cspan.org/guide/courts/historic/oa072598.htm.
[22]132 L. Ed. 2d 158.
[23]132 L. Ed. 2d 182.
[24]132 L. Ed. 2d 184, citing *Helvering* v. *Hallock*, 390 U.S. 106, at 119.

However, the majority was unwilling to say that no scheme of race-conscious preferences could withstand strict scrutiny. Using affirmative action might still be possible for the government. O'Connor wrote:

> Finally, we wish to dispel the notion that strict scrutiny is "strict in theory, but fatal in fact. . . ." The unhappy persistence of both the practice and the lingering effects of racial discrimination against minority groups in this country is an unfortunate reality, and government is not disqualified from acting in response to it.[25]

This completed the majority opinion. The Court did not uphold or strike down the Transportation Department's subcontractor bidding clauses. Instead, it remanded, or returned, the case to the Tenth Circuit Court of Appeals to be redecided using the strict scrutiny test instead of the lesser test of intermediate scrutiny.[26] The result of this tougher review would determine whether the equal protection rights of Randy Pech at Adarand Constructors had been violated. Thus, as in many cases that come before the high court, the justices avoided the underlying issue and decided only matters of law.

Justice Scalia Concurs

Justice Antonin Scalia, a conservative and longtime foe of affirmative action, wrote a concurring opinion in which he agreed with the application of strict scrutiny but took the extreme position that "government can never have a 'compelling interest' in discriminating on the basis of race in order to 'make up' for past racial discrimination in the opposite direction."[27] He elaborated:

> Individuals who have been wronged by unlawful racial discrimination should be made whole; but under our Constitution there can be no such thing as either a creditor or a debtor race. The concept of racial entitlement—even for the most admirable and benign of purposes—is to reinforce and reserve for future mischief the way of thinking that produced race slavery, race privilege and race hatred. In the eyes of government, we are just one race here. It is American.[28]

Justice Scalia concluded that it was very unlikely and probably impossible that the Department of Transportation program could pass the strict scrutiny test.

Justice Thomas Concurs

Justice Clarence Thomas, the Court's only black member, agreed with the majority opinion, but wrote separately to underscore the principle that the

---

[25]132 L. Ed. 2d 188.
[26]16 F.3d 1537, vacated and remanded.
[27]132 L. Ed. 2d 190.
[28]132 L. Ed. 2d 190.

Constitution requires all races to be treated equally. In his eyes, there was no moral difference between a law designed to subjugate a race and a law passed to give it benefits.

> That these programs may have been motivated, in part, by good intentions cannot provide refuge from the principle that under our Constitution, the government may not make distinctions on the basis of race. As far as the Constitution is concerned, it is irrelevant whether a government's racial classifications are drawn by those who wish to oppress a race or by those who have a sincere desire to help those thought to be disadvantaged.[29]

Many observers of Justice Thomas's appointment believed that he was not the most qualified jurist available for the Supreme Court at the time and that his race played a part in President Bush's decision to nominate him. Whether that is correct or not, Thomas used his concurrence in *Adarand* to argue that affirmative action degraded the very individuals it tried to help.

> So-called "benign" discrimination teaches that because of chronic and apparently immutable handicaps, minorities cannot compete with them without their patronizing indulgence. Inevitably such programs engender attitudes of superiority or, alternatively, provoke resentment among those who believe that they have been wronged by the government's use of race. These programs stamp minorities with a badge of inferiority and may cause them to develop dependencies or to adopt an attitude that they are "entitled" to preferences.[30]

The Dissenters

Three separate dissenting opinions were written, joined in by four justices. In the first, Justice Stevens, joined by Justice Ginsburg, objected to the departure of the majority from established precedent and argued that the Court had a duty to uphold the intermediate scrutiny standard. Stevens also disagreed with the majority that all discrimination was the same in principle.

> There is no moral or constitutional equivalence between a policy that is designed to perpetuate a caste system and one that seeks to eradicate racial subordination. Invidious discrimination is an engine of oppression, subjugating a disfavored group to enhance or maintain the power of the majority. Remedial race-based preferences reflect the opposite impulse: a desire to foster equality in society. No sensible conception of the Government's constitutional obligation to "govern impartially" . . . should ignore this distinction. . . . The consistency that the Court espouses would disregard the difference between a "No Trespassing" sign and a welcome mat.[31]

A second dissent was written by Justice Souter, in which Justices Ginsburg and Breyer joined. Souter objected to the Court's departure from the

---

[29]132 L. Ed. 2d 190.
[30]132 L. Ed. 2d 191.
[31]132 L. Ed. 2d 192, 193.

Fullilove and *Metro* precedents. He argued that more deference was owed to Congress and affirmed his approval for laws that try to redress persistent racism.

The third dissenting opinion came from Justice Ginsburg, joined by Justice Breyer. She wrote to underscore the lingering effects of "a system of racial cast" in American life. According to Ginsburg:

> White and African-American consumers still encounter different deals. People of color looking for housing still face discriminatory treatment by landlords, real estate agents, and mortgage lenders. Minority entrepreneurs sometimes fail to gain contracts though they are the low bidders, and they are sometimes refused work even after winning contracts. Bias both conscious and unconscious, reflecting traditional and unexamined habits of thought, keeps up barriers that must come down if equal opportunity and nondiscrimination are ever genuinely to become this country's law and practice.
>
> Given this history and its practical consequences, Congress surely can conclude that a carefully designed affirmative action program may help to realize, finally, the "equal protection of the laws" the Fourteenth Amendment has promised since 1868.[32]

A Final Decision

The Supreme Court elected to decide principles of law and declined to settle the underlying question of whether the subcontractor compensation clause was unconstitutional. Therefore, the case went back to the Tenth Circuit from where it had come. The Tenth Circuit also declined to render a decision and promptly sent the case down to the U.S. District Court in Colorado where it had originated back in 1992.

On June 2, 1997, almost two years after the Supreme Court's decision, and eight years after the loss of the guardrail contract, the district court issued an opinion. Judge John L. Kane Jr. applied the strict scrutiny test to the subcontractor compensation clause and the result invalidated the clause. The clause passed the part of the test that required the government to show a compelling interest. Judge Kane held that there was sufficient evidence of bias in contracting before Congress when it passed the law and Congress had the power to remedy national problems of this scope. But the clause failed the test of narrow tailoring. Judge Kane held that basing findings of social and economic disadvantage solely on race was unfair. Under the existing criteria for selecting DBEs, a multimillionaire who immigrated from Hong Kong and became a U.S. citizen one day before applying would automatically qualify, but a poor white man who had lived in the United States his entire life could not. So the set-aside program was overinclusive and unconstitutional. Since Colorado

---

[32]132 L. Ed. 2d 212.

was administering the program for the federal government, Judge Kane issued an injunction ordering the state to stop using the objectionable regulation. Adarand Constructors had won.

Resistance

Colorado refused to comply. Governor Roy Romer argued, somewhat disingenuously, that a federal court order did not apply to a state government. Adarand Constructors immediately sued the state to force it to obey. Colorado's attorney general believed that Governor Romer's defiance was wrong and refused to defend the case, so Romer hired other attorneys willing to do so with a straight face. When the case came before Judge Kane, Colorado argued that it had made changes in the way the subcontractor compensation clause was administered so that it was now narrowly tailored; for example, white male contractors could apply for DBE status.

Judge Kane was furious. Instead of retrying the entire issue, he declared that Adarand Constructors had suffered years of discrimination and financial hardship at the hands of a government enforcing an unfair, unconstitutional law. He decreed that Adarand Constructors was eligible for DBE status and instructed the company to apply to the state as a financially disadvantaged white contractor. In April 1998, Pech filed papers to make this official.

Meanwhile, the *Adarand* decision had set off a national debate. The federal government has approximately 160 preference programs for businesses certified as disadvantaged. In the year that *Adarand* was decided, $10 billion in contracts was earmarked for minority and female vendors through various methods. Opponents of affirmative action felt that, because of the decision, preferential treatment programs for minority contractors could no longer be justified and should end.

There was no doubt that *Adarand* cast a shadow over these arrangements, but their supporters had no intention of conceding their unconstitutionality. Instead, President Clinton promised to "mend, not end" affirmative action. What he had in mind was to revise the complex maze of regulations that enforced affirmative action so that the programs would withstand legal challenge.

There were some direct assaults on affirmative action. Preferences in federal highway contracts met a fierce attack in Congress when Senator Mitch McConnell (R-Kentucky) tried to end race-conscious contracting in highway construction. The Intermodal Surface Transportation Efficiency Act (ISTEA) of 1997 was a giant appropriations bill that reserved 10 percent of highway funds, or about $17.3 billion, for DBEs. When the district court ruled in favor of Adarand Constructors, McConnell decided that this $17.3 billion set-aside was unconstitutional. In March 1998, he introduced an amendment "to prohibit discrimination and preferential treatment based on race, color, national origin, or sex, with respect to [federal highway] funds."[33] McConnell spoke in its favor.

> . . . I rise today to introduce my amendment to bring the federal highway program into compliance with the Constitution and with the recent landmark case of Adarand versus Pena . . .
>
> ISTEA mandates that "not less than 10 percent" of federal highway and transit funds be allocated to "disadvantaged business enterprises" ("DBEs"). Firms owned by officially designated minority groups are presumed to be "disadvantaged." The government has placed the stamp of "disadvantage" on groups with origins ranging from Tonga to Micronesia to the Maldive Islands.
>
> And . . . what is the reward for these government-preferred firms? The reward is a $17.3 billion quota. In other words, if the government decides that you are the preferred race and gender, then you are able to compete for $17.3 billion of taxpayer-funded highway contracts. But if you are the wrong race and gender, then—too bad—you can't compete for that $17 billion pot.
>
> Frankly, I am astonished that any member of this Senate would ever think such a provision is fair, prudent, or constitutional . . .
>
> It is time to end the divisive discriminatory practice of awarding highway and transit construction contracts based on race, gender and ethnicity of a company's ownership. Respect for our Constitution, our courts, our States, and our individual citizens demands no less.[34]

Not everyone agreed. Senator Carol Moseley-Braun (D-Illinois) rose to defend the program.

> I rise in strong opposition to the pending amendment that would dismantle the Department of Transportation's affirmative action programs . . .
>
> The program . . . is no more and no less than a structural response to a structural distortion of our society that is caused by 200 years of slavery and segregation and, frankly, the status of women and an age-old tradition that set women apart as second-class citizens as well.
>
> The DBE program addresses these underlying realities. It helps to weave thousands of small businesses into the fabric of our economy and our society. It creates for us a stronger Nation.
>
> Now who are the disadvantaged business enterprises? In 1996, DBEs . . . received slightly less than 15 percent of the Federal-aid highway construction money. Of that small slice, again, here we are—14.8 percent . . . These are women, minorities, Hispanics, Asians, Native Americans—these are all the majority minority of the population that is described as 'minorities' in the debate. They got all of 14 percent of Federal highway spending. . . . And 85 percent went to the traditional white male business owners. Now that is just the reality . . . Racism and sexism are indeed unhappy, but still very real, phenomena in our society. The DBE program is one of our responses to those lingering effects, and it works.[35]

---

[33]Amendment No. 1708, 144 Cong. Rec. S1395.
[34]Ibid. at S1396 and S1397.
[35]Ibid. at S1419, S1420.

A polarized debate over the McConnell amendment went on for eight hours in the Senate. McConnell cited a study predicting that ignoring low bidders on highway contracts and giving preference to higher-bidding DBEs would cost taxpayers $1.1 billion extra over the next six years.[36] Senator Max Baucus (D-Montana) pointed out that nine months after another state, Michigan, had dropped affirmative action bidding in its state highway program, the percentage of highway dollars going to minority firms dropped to zero, whereas on federal highway projects in Michigan, minority- and women-owned firms continued to receive 13 percent.[37] There were similar results in other states and cities. Ultimately, the amendment lost when 58 senators voted against it, but the Clinton administration realized that the rules needed to be changed to protect the DBE program against foes in both the judiciary and Congress.

In 1999, the Department of Transportation issued revised rules for using DBEs in federal highway construction contracts.[38] These new regulations ran 64,500 words in the *Federal Register,* the equivalent of about 125 pages of the book you are now reading. They state that the 10 percent of highway funding, or $17.3 billion, reserved for DBEs is not a "quota" or a "set-aside," but an "aspirational goal at the national level" and the DBE participation level in each state receiving highway funds may be higher or lower. To meet DBE goals, the states are required to first use "race-neutral" measures, that is, to do things to help all small contracting businesses, including both DBEs and white-male-owned companies. These measures do not require race-gender classification and include, for example, training and advice in bidding and contract work, bonding assistance, and breaking large contracts into pieces that small businesses can more easily handle. However, if such methods do not fully achieve DBE goals and "egregious" discrimination exists, then "race-conscious" methods that give preferences to DBEs, including set-asides on which only DBEs can bid and mandatory contract goals for DBE participation, can be used.

The states are also required to do studies that pinpoint discriminatory practices, so that there will be a compelling rationale for race-conscious actions if they are needed. The rules also tighten qualifications for persons designated as "economically disadvantaged." From now on, this status will be denied to persons with a net worth of $750,000 or more. This is calculated as personal net worth minus the value of their primary residence and their ownership interest in the contracting business. The rules now allow white males to apply for socially or economically disadvantaged status. However, unlike minorities and women who are still automatically included (unless worth more than $750,000), the burden is on white males to prove that they have suffered financial hardship from discrimination. The use of the subcontractor compensation clause at issue in the *Adarand* case is nowhere mentioned in the new rules. Overall, these changes amount to a scaling back of affirmative action in highway programs.

---

[36]Ibid. at S1396.

[37]Ibid. at S1404.

[38]Department of Transportation, "Participation by Disadvantaged Business Enterprises in Department of Transportation Program," 64 FR 5096–5148.

Who Is Disadvantaged?

Any person who is a citizen and falls into one of the following categories is presumed to be socially and economically disadvantaged (beginning in 1999, persons with a net worth of $750,000 or more were disqualified). If the person has 51 percent ownership or greater in a company applying for a federal highway construction contract, that company qualifies as a "disadvantaged business enterprise" and can receive preferential treatment on federal highway contracts.

Black. Includes persons having origins in any black racial groups in Africa.

Hispanic. Includes persons of Mexican, Puerto Rican, Cuban, Dominican, Central or South American, or other Spanish or Portuguese culture or origin, regardless of race.

Native American. Includes American Indians, Eskimos, Aleuts, or Native Hawaiians.

Asian-Pacific Americans. Includes persons whose origins are from Japan, China, Taiwan, Korea, Burma (Myanmar), Vietnam, Laos, Cambodia (Kampuchea), Thailand, Malaysia, Indonesia, the Philippines, Brunei, Samoa, Guam, the U.S. Trust Territories of the Pacific Islands (Republic of Palau), the Commonwealth of the Northern Marianas Islands, Macao, Fiji, Tonga, Kirbati, Juvalu, Nauru, Federated States of Micronesia, or Hong Kong.

Women. All women are included.

Source: 13 CFR 121, Sec. 124.103(b), 64 FR 5128.

Postscript

At this writing, the application of Randy Pech for DBE status in Colorado is pending. The State of Colorado has appealed the district court's injunction back to the Tenth Circuit.

Questions

1. What constitutional issue is raised in the *Adarand* case?
2. What requirements must an affirmative action program now meet to be constitutional?
3. Was the decision of the Court majority correct? Why or why not?
4. In a concurring opinion, Justice Scalia said that race classifications by government were never legitimate. In dissenting opinions, Justices Stevens,

Souter, and Ginsburg argued that race-conscious remedies were justified. What were their arguments? With whom do you agree? Why?

5. Following the *Adarand* decision, the district court held that the affirmative action program in federal highway contracts was unconstitutional. Do you agree with this decision? Why or why not?

6. Will the Department of Transportation's new rules for helping DBEs get highway construction contracts pass the strict scrutiny requirement?

PART 9

Corporate
Governance

Reforming Corporate Governance

D ebate over high salaries usually focuses on CEOs, but corporate directors also receive generous compensation. There are fifteen directors on GE's board. Five insiders, including chairman and CEO John F. Welch, are company executives and receive no additional pay for board service. However, ten outside directors get the following compensation package.

- An annual retainer of $75,000.
- A $1,400 fee for each board meeting. There were eight meetings in 1998; attendance was 97 percent.
- A $2,000 fee for board committee meetings. Four major committees

of the board met between three and ten times in 1998.
- A travel allowance for attending meetings.
- A life insurance policy of $150,000.
- Two liability insurance policies to cover legal expenses and damages from lawsuits. In recent years, GE's shareholders have sued its directors a number of times. A 1998 suit, for example, sought damages for alleged negligence in design and building of nuclear power plants.
- Stock options for 6,000 shares of GE common shares each year. Every year, on the last trading

day in January, GE stock is priced. Directors do not buy GE stock at this time, but get the right to buy it at this price later—as much as ten years later. For example, on January 30, 1998, GE shares traded for $77.50 each. A current director could wait until 2008 to exercise the option to buy 6,000 shares at this price. If the price of the stock rises to $300 per share, the director would make a pretax profit of $222.50 per share, or $1,335,000 on 6,000 shares. Every year, each outsider is given the option to buy, later, 6,000 more shares at the January trading price of the year in which the option was granted. Directors do not have to exercise these options. They do not own the stock until they decide to buy it. If the share price falls after they get the options, they will simply choose not to exercise them. Ordinary investors who buy GE stock must accept the risk that its price will fall. GE directors with options do not have that risk; they enjoy the investment equivalent of shooting fish in a barrel.

On retirement, more is lavished on GE directors. If they have served five or more years and retire from the board, they receive two additional benefits.

- An annual, lifetime pension of $75,000, which continues for a surviving spouse if the director dies. Alternatively, the director can opt for a life insurance benefit of $450,000.
- GE donations totaling $1,000,000 among up to five charities of the director's choosing.

Of the ten outsiders on GE's board, there are one black, one Hispanic, and two women. Most are current or former CEOs of large corporations, but among them there are a college professor, a retired university president, and a former U.S. Senator—Sam Nunn of Georgia. Their average age is 61. Most are millionaires in GE stock; the average holding is approximately $32,000,000.[1] GE's monthly board meetings usually last one day—sometimes two—so outside directors have time to serve on an average of 3.3 other corporate boards each. They are with some of America's most prominent firms, including Anheuser-Busch, Bristol-Myers Squibb, Citicorp, Coca Cola, Exxon, Goodyear Tire & Rubber, Kellogg, Lockheed Martin, J. P. Morgan, Philip Morris, and Texaco.

GE is generous in director compensation, but it can afford to be. Between 1980 and 1999, it created $300 billion in shareholder wealth, more than Microsoft, Intel, Wal-Mart, or any other U.S. firm. Its revenues in 1998 were $100.5 billion; net earnings were $9.3 billion.[2] To put director compensation in perspective, total retainers and fees of outside board members were only eight one-hundredths of one percent of net earnings.

What is the compensation of GE's board chairman and CEO John Welch? In 1998, he received $10,104,944 in

---

[1]Figures on compensation and share ownership are taken or derived from General Electric Company, *Notice of 1999 Annual Meeting and Proxy Statement,* Fairfield, Conn.: General Electric Company, 1999. The stock value is calculated at a share price of $110 which prevailed early in 1999.

[2]General Electric Company, *1998 Annual Report,* Fairfield, Conn.: General Electric Company, 1999, p. 26.

compensation and options for 500,000 GE shares that he can exercise on retirement. His salary was a little more than one percent of net earnings. He currently owns 6.7 million shares of GE, worth $736 million. Every day that the stock rises $1 per share, he goes to sleep $6.7 million richer.

We begin this chapter with a definition of governance and contrast it with management. Then the corporate charter as the legal basis for governance authority is described. This is followed with a review of current structures of boards in the United States and selected foreign countries, and the board duties ascribed to directors. We then note the more important specific criticisms of boards and recommendations for reforming them. Special attention is then given to compensation of CEOs. Employee governance activities are next discussed. Finally, we examine the question: to whom are directors accountable?

Corporate Governance Defined

Corporate governance is the overall control of activities in a corporation. It is concerned with the formulation of long-term objectives and plans and the proper management structure (organization, systems, and people) to achieve them. At the same time, it entails making sure that the structure functions to maintain the corporation's integrity, reputation, and responsibility to its various constituencies.

In this definition, governance is the concern of the board of directors. However, top management is also clearly involved. But management has other dimensions that are quite distinct from the operations of the typical board of directors. Management is a hands-on operational activity. It is concerned with supervising day-to-day action and the prudent use of scarce resources to achieve desirable aims. The typical board of directors does not become involved in such activities. While governance is shared by boards and top management, our focus in this chapter is essentially but not exclusively on boards of directors.

The Corporate Charter

The corporate charter is the legal authority for corporate managers and directors to function in conformance with the above definition. All American corporations except a few quasi-public enterprises chartered by the federal government (for example, the Tennessee Valley Authority) are chartered by the state in which they incorporate. At the Constitutional Convention of 1787, the Founders debated a federal chartering power but decided that existing state controls were adequate to regulate corporate activity.

All states have general incorporation laws and compete with one another to attract the tax revenues of large corporations. Delaware is the longtime victor in this competition and charters almost half the largest industrial corporations in this country. The attraction of Delaware, despite the fact that costs of incorporation there are higher than in most states, is the business-friendly corporate laws in the state. It has been said that Delaware will not be underregulated, meaning that its laws are less restricting of corporate activities. Also, its Chancery Court, which handles only business cases, is very accommodating to corporate interests.

Corporate charters specify the rights and responsibilities of stockholders, directors, and officers. Fundamentally, corporate charters lodge control over the property of the enterprise in stockholders who own shares in the assets of the company and vote those shares in naming a board of directors to run the firm. The directors have a fiduciary responsibility to protect the interests of the shareholders. They are responsible for appointing officers to run the day-to-day affairs of the company. The legal line of power runs from the state, to shareholders, to directors, to managers.

The charters also include detailed provisions about such matters as annual meetings, methods of choosing directors, and authority of directors to issue stock. For instance, charters are specific about calling meetings of shareholders, declaring dividends, electing and removing officers, proposing amendments of the articles of incorporation, and so on. Such charter provisions are meant to protect the interests of shareholders. A vast body of law that seeks to do the same thing has also been created over time.

The Structure of Boards of Directors

In 1997, the average corporate board of manufacturing companies had ten members, and financial firms had twelve.[3] Giovanni Agnelli, the founder of Italy's huge Turin-based Fiat conglomerate, once observed: "Only an odd number of directors can run a company, and three are too many."[4] This is an extreme position, but most small firms and many large ones do have small boards of directors. Banks and other financial institutions tend to have large boards, but the general trend is for smaller boards.

Board membership may include both inside (management) directors and outside (nonmanagement) directors. In recent years, the number of outside directors on boards has grown. In 1997, the average manufacturing company had eight outside directors, and financial companies had ten. The number of

---

[3]These and the following numbers about boards are derived from The Conference Board, *Corporate Directors' Compensation in 1997*, Report No. 1203-97-RR, New York: The Conference Board, 1998. This report surveyed 650 companies in three industry sectors.

[4]Quoted in Paul Betts, "Heads Begin to Roll at Fiat," *Paris Financial Times*, June 18, 1990.

women on boards rose from about 10 percent in 1973 to 67 percent in 1997 in financial companies, 64 percent in service companies, and 56 percent in manufacturing concerns. Both minority and foreign national directors increased significantly during the same period.

In the past, board members were usually suggested by the CEO to the board for approval. Today, nominating committees on most boards have this responsibility, but the CEOs still play a prominent part in the process. Once selected, the names of the nominees are presented to the shareholders in the annual call for the stockholder meeting, and management solicits the proxies of the stockholders. A *proxy* is a permission given by each stockholder to the management to vote the stock as management sees fit. Most stockholders give their proxies to management, which in turn votes the stock at the annual meeting.

In this model, which differs from the classical legal line of appointment, managers and directors of larger corporations (who typically own small percentages of total stock outstanding) choose directors. In very small companies, the stockholders generally choose directors, who in turn choose managers. The majority of stockholders in these small companies often are the managers as well as board members.

Boards are divided into committees. Today, virtually all companies have audit committees to review for the board the financial affairs of the company. Most boards have compensation committees that make recommendations to the board concerning pay and bonuses for top executives. Two-thirds or more have executive committees authorized by the board to decide on its behalf matters needing attention between board meetings. Other possible committees include public affairs, corporate ethics, employee pensions and benefits, human resources, environment, science and technology, corporate contributions, legal affairs, and social responsibility. Few, if any, boards have all these committees, even in the largest corporations.

Board Structures in Selected Foreign Countries

Board structures in European countries are considerably different from those in the United States. In Germany, for example, "two-tier" boards are prominent. The upper tier exercises broad supervision of the company. This board is composed of representatives from banks, major shareholders, trade unions, suppliers, purchasers, and employees. The lower board manages the detailed operations of the company and is appointed by the upper board.

In Germany and France, the largest holders of stock are usually the state, other companies, families, and banks. The state has more equity holdings in France than in Germany. Most boards are "insider systems," in contrast to those of the United States and the United Kingdom, because of the high concentration of stock ownership represented on the board.[5] In some European countries,

---

[5]Guillermo de la Dehesa, "Corporate Finance, Corporate Ownership, Corporate Control, and Corporate Governance," in *Proceedings of the December 8th, 1995, Meeting of the International Academy of Management at the Harvard Business School.*

such as Germany, participation of workers on the board is mandated by law. In Scandinavia, having independent boards even in small companies is traditional and the CEOs do not sit on the board. There are proposals before the European Union to standardize corporate governance systems in all countries in the Union, including two-tier boards, and to mandate worker participation.[6]

The board structure and powers in Japan differ radically from European experience. The board of directors in Japanese companies is not top management nor does it have much power. Virtually all the members are employees of the company who are ready to retire. They are promoted to the board by the president. Even boards of large companies have but one or two outside directors among a total number of directors ranging from twenty to fifty. (There is a trend today in Japan to reduce the size of boards.) The president is by far the most powerful decision maker in the company. He has a management committee composed of about ten "inside" senior directors to help in top management decision making.[7]

The Duties of Directors

Charters require that corporate affairs be "managed" by a board or "under the direction of a board." The board of directors clearly is the ultimate corporate authority except for matters that must have the approval of shareholders, such as the election of the board itself or an increase in capitalization.

The Business Roundtable, in an important policy statement in 1990, set forth the responsibilities of corporate boards of directors.[8] Overall, said the policy statement, "the principal responsibility is to exercise governance so as to ensure the long-term successful performance of their corporation." Specific responsibilities are as follows:

1. Select, regularly evaluate and, if necessary, replace the chief executive officer. Determine management compensation. Review succession planning.
2. Review and, where appropriate, approve the financial objectives, major strategies, and plans of the corporation.
3. Provide advice and counsel to top management.
4. Select and recommend to shareholders for election an appropriate slate of candidates for the board of directors; evaluate board processes and performance.
5. Review the adequacy of systems to comply with all applicable laws/regulations.

In a similar statement in 1978, the Business Roundtable advocated these specific studies for boards: "It is the board's duty to consider the overall impact of

---

[6]Morten Huse, "Researching the Dynamics of Board–Stakeholder Relations," *Long Range Planning*, April 1998.

[7]Toyohiro Kono and Stewart R. Clegg, *Transformations of Corporate Culture*, New York: Walter de Gruyter, 1998.

[8]The Business Roundtable, *Corporate Governance and American Competitiveness*, New York: Business Roundtable, March 1990.

the activities of the corporation on (1) the society of which it is a part, and (2) the interests and views of groups other than those immediately identified with the corporation. This obligation arises out of the responsibility to act primarily in the interests of the share owners—particularly their long-range interests."[9]

Cutting across these functions, it seems to us, are requirements to make sure that there is an appropriate flow of information to the board and that internal policies and procedures of the company are fully capable of responding to board decisions. Peter Drucker has added the following other dimensions to these functions if a board is to be effective: asking critical questions; acting as a conscience, a keeper of human and moral values; serving as a window on the outside world; and helping the corporation to be understood by its constituencies and by the outside community.[10]

How individual boards and members perform these duties will vary much. Jay Lorsch, a professor at Harvard Business School, observes, "Traditionally, corporate leaders have considered a powerful, active board to be a nuisance at best and a force that could improperly interfere in the management of the company at worst. They have preferred directors who are content to offer counsel when asked and to support management in times of crisis."[11] That is becoming less true as pressures have led to more active boards. Still, many companies' boards today perform in the traditional way.

Two scholars interviewed eighty CEOs and corporate directors representing some forty companies in twenty-three industries during the period 1992 to 1995 to learn what directors thought of their jobs. Among other things, they asked how they saw the importance of different duties. The results are shown in Table 19-1. It is not surprising that maximizing shareholder wealth is considered more important than any other function. It is not surprising that formulating corporate strategy is not high but ratifying corporate strategy is. If management is doing its job, it should be formulating strategy for board review, not the other way around. It is noteworthy that safeguarding stakeholder interests ranks high among the executives interviewed.

In light of what was said above about the structure of foreign boards of directors, it is not difficult to understand how they would array the importance of the functions in Table 19-1. In France, Germany, and especially in Japan, for example, concern about employees would rank high.

Core Criticisms of Boards of Directors

Historians may look back on the 1990s as a decade when corporate boards were under siege. Not only have criticisms of boards been widespread, but stockholder activists have succeeded in ousting some boards.

---

[9]The Business Roundtable, *The Role and Composition of the Board of Directors of the Large Publicly Owned Corporation,* New York: Business Roundtable, 1978, pp. 11–12.

[10]Peter F. Drucker, "The Bored Board," *Wharton Magazine,* Fall 1976.

[11]Jay W. Lorsch, "Empowering the Board," *Harvard Business Review,* January–February 1995, p. 107.

TABLE 19-1 **Board Responsibilities as Seen by Directors**
On a Scale of 1 to 5 with 1 Not Important and 5 Very Important

Maximizing shareholder wealth	4.50
CEO succession planning	4.40
Evaluating management performance	4.36
Determining top management compensation	4.29
Safeguarding stakeholder interests	4.19
Ratifying corporate strategy	4.12
Selecting new directors	3.95
Advising top management	3.84
Determining top management responsibilities/authority	3.76
Looking after a firm's reputation	3.30
Auditing top management decisions	3.17
Formulating corporate strategy	3.09
Mediating between top management and stakeholders	2.48
Buffering top management from outside pressures	2.05

Source: Don O'Neal and Howard Thomas, "Developing the Strategic Board," *Long Range Planning,* June 1996, p. 316.

Individual stockholders, and institutional investors, complain that in too many companies, board performance in enhancing equity investment is inadequate. Some critics assert that other stakeholders, such as employees, communities, and society as a whole, are not given the attention in decision making they deserve. Indeed, it is said, decisions are often made that are diametrically opposed to the best interests of these groups. It is asserted that boards do not evaluate properly the performance of managers and permit all sorts of unethical practices to go on in their companies. Board members do not spend enough time on company business and are, in effect, rubber stamps of the company's chief executive officer. To make matters worse, directors are egregiously overpaid.

Individual shareholders still stridently voice criticisms, but the real pressure for board reform comes from government agencies such as the SEC and organized groups like the large pension funds. Even friends of directors such as the National Association of Corporate Directors and the Business Roundtable have urged board reforms.

Institutional Investor Participation in Governance

An old, but still expressed, concern of corporate reformers is to give individual stockholders more influence in governance. Except in smaller corporations, that is difficult. Power has shifted to management, as explained years ago by Adolph Berle and Gardner Means in their seminal book *The Modern Corporation and Private Property.*[12] In recent years, there has been an extraordinary increase in pension fund stock holdings. The total assets of pension

---

[12]New York: Macmillan, 1932.

funds, public and private, rose from $70 billion in 1980 to $6.2 trillion in 1998. The total investments in corporate equities rose from $267.5 billion in 1980 to $3.512 trillion in 1998.[13] Today, a large percentage of the stock of many American corporations is owned by pension funds. This ownership gives them power to influence corporate governance, and they have used it.

Before the mid-1980s, pension fund managers were passive investors and usually went along with the decisions of corporate managers. Their activism in corporate governance began in April 1985 when Jesse Unruh, treasurer of the State of California and manager of the state's two large pension funds, decided to wield the ownership power of the funds to influence governance. His motivation stemmed from losses incurred when managers at Disney and Texaco paid "greenmail" to get rid of corporate raiders.[14] Unruh proclaimed, "We can't just sit there and watch the action pass by, and yet that's exactly what we're all doing." He added, "Up to this point, we have all been used and generally abused by everybody—corporate raiders, arbitragers (takeover speculators) and management—because we are all so ignorant and ineffective in these situations."[15] Unruh's ire led to formation of the Council of Institutional Investors (CII) by thirty-one pension fund managers who controlled at that time approximately $200 billion of assets. The CII endorsed a "Shareholder's Bill of Rights" that demanded a voice in all "fundamental decisions which could affect corporate performance and growth."[16]

Because of the large holdings of institutional investors, they are increasingly rightfully concerned about the governance of the companies in which they have a large share of stock. Their interest, however, is not unchallenged. One CEO undoubtedly spoke for other CEOs and directors when he said: " . . . we have a group of people with increasing control of the *Fortune* '500' who have no proven skills in management, no experience at selecting directors, no believable judgment in how much should be spent for research or marketing—in fact, no experience except that which they have accumulated controlling other people's money."[17]

Should pension fund managers seek to influence corporations? If not, why not? If so, in what way? There are many pension fund managers whose interest is essentially short-term improvement in the values of the stocks they hold. If they are not satisfied with the management of the companies whose stock

---

[13]Board of Governors of the Federal Reserve System, *Flow of Funds Accounts of the United States: Flows and Outstandings, Third Quarter 1998,* Washington, D.C.: Board of Governors of the Federal Reserve System, December 11, 1998.

[14]"Greenmail" is a name given to a transaction in which a company agrees to buy back a corporate raider's stock at a premium price over the market. Some critics use harsher words, such as "legalized corporate blackmail."

[15]In Debra Whitefield, "Unruh Calls for Pension Funds to Flex Muscles," *Los Angeles Times,* February 3, 1985.

[16]"Council of Institutional Investors", New York: Council of Institutional Investors, undated.

[17]Charles Wohlstetter, "Pension Fund Socialism: Can Bureaucrats Run the Blue Chips?" *Harvard Business Review,* January–February 1993, p. 78.

they hold, the shares can be sold. This is possible when the shares owned in any one corporation are small. But, when a pension fund such as the California Public Employee's Retirement System (CalPERS) owns a large percentage of stock in any one company, it is essentially "locked in" as an owner-investor of that company. Fundamentally, said former manager of CalPERS Dale Hanson, the security owner should take the long view of investment, not the short view. In this light, it makes sense to seek to influence companies whose performance is deficient but whose long-term promise is bright. CalPERS and other major pension fund managers agree.

The largest pension funds do not attempt day-to-day management of companies but seek to encourage them to improve their procedures and, on occasion, basic strategies. For example, CalPERS had some influence, along with other pension funds, over top management changes at General Motors, IBM, and Eastman Kodak. How much is not publicly known. Other large pension funds also have initiated change in top management. For example, Teachers Insurance and Annuity Association–College Retirement Education Fund succeeded in ousting the entire board of Furr's/Bishop's Inc., a cafeteria company.

CalPERS

CalPERS is the nation's largest public pension fund, with assets of more than $135 billion, and since Unruh's day it has been a leader in pension fund governance activism. CalPERS's initiatives have developed through several stages and are still evolving. The earliest focus was the elimination of greenmail and other techniques used by companies to combat hostile takeovers. Then, beginning in 1993, the fund identified each year a list of ten companies in its portfolio whose stocks underperformed general stock market indexes. CalPERS urged the boards of targeted companies, sometimes privately and sometimes publicly, to improve governance and enhance long-term stock performance. Surveys show that targeted companies outperform the Standard & Poor's 500 Index.[18]

Stock performance is a major ultimate goal of the fund, as Kayla J. Gillan, general counsel of CalPERS, explained:

> In CalPERS' view, companies operated with long-term shareholder returns as the primary goal will, ultimately, also reward other stakeholders. Companies driven by short-term goals do not reward anyone in the long-term. We believe that companies that elevate these other stakeholders to the same level as shareholders are really simply diffusing accountability. When a company is accountable to any one of the diverse group of interests, the company is really not accountable to anyone.[19]

---

[18]CalPERS, "Why Corporate Governance Today?" http://www.calpers.ca.gov/invest/corpgov/whycg.htm, January 2, 1999, pp. 3–4.

[19]Kayla J. Gillan, "CalPERS—Corporate Governance," speech delivered to the Institutional Investor Conferences, Corporate Governance Presentation, Rome, Italy, March 11, 1997, reproduced in *Vital Speeches of the Day*, May 15, 1997.

New Governance Guidelines

In 1997, CalPERS embarked on a new program called "Corporate Governance Core Principles and Guidelines." This is a set of standards for a model corporate board. The fund said, in initiating these standards, "CalPERS does not expect nor seek that each company will adopt or embrace every aspect of either the Principles or Guidelines . . . (the purpose is) to advance the corporate governance dialogue by presenting the views of one shareowner, but not to attempt to permanently enshrine those views."[20] Here are brief descriptions of some principles and guidelines:

- Majority of board should be independent directors.
- Independent directors meet periodically without the CEO.
- When the CEO is also the chair of the board, the board should elect an independent "lead" director.
- Some board committees, such as director nomination, board evaluation, and CEO evaluation, should be entirely composed of independent directors.
- No director can serve as a consultant to the company.
- Director compensation is cash and stock of the company.
- The board regularly evaluates itself.
- The board regularly reviews the CEO's performance.
- The board establishes guidelines limiting the number of other board seats each director may hold.
- The board should consider setting tenure rules.
- When selecting a new CEO, the board should consider separating the CEO and board chair positions.
- Generally, the retiring CEO should not continue on the board.

When the standards were first prepared, some of the proposals were much more stringent. For example, directors should not be retained when reaching seventy years of age. It was also proposed that the 300 largest U.S. companies be graded on the degree to which they met the standards. Since then, however, CalPERS trustees have softened the proposals in response to criticisms about their rigidity. Recommendations are now "guidelines" rather than mandatory standards.

Foreign Activism

CalPERS has extended its governance principles to foreign countries, including the United Kingdom, France, and Japan. The principles for these countries

---

[20]CalPERS, "Corporate Governance Core Principles & Guidelines," April 13, 1998, Sacramento, Calif., p. 3.

reflect structures, customs, and practices that differ from those for the United States. To illustrate, for Japan, the fund sets forth these principles:

- Shareholders, especially institutions, have a duty to exercise their responsibilities as corporate owners.
- Japanese boards should consider the interests of all shareholders.
- Boards should include directors who are independent.
- Boards should have a majority of nonexecutive directors.
- Size of boards should be reduced.
- Independent auditors should be appointed.
- Positions of chairperson and CEO should be held separately.[21]

Foreign Pension Fund Activism

Stockholder activism has risen in Europe in the past few years, and some of the largest European corporations have felt the fire of shareholder demands. For example, pension funds in the Netherlands for the first time are investigating governance activities of companies on the Amsterdam market. Managers of Hermes, a large British pension fund, now talk with company managers about improving shareholder performance.[22] Toshiba Corp, Takai Bank, Asahi Bank, and Sony Corp. in Japan recently significantly reduced the number of directors on their boards in response to shareholder demands.[23]

Comments on Some of the Proposed Board Reforms

Many other thoughtful proposals for reform have been made in recent years from such organizations as the National Association of Corporate Directors. Most of them are similar to those of CalPERS. Each of the proposals deserves evaluation, but space limits discussion to only a few.

Selecting Directors

The selection process varies among boards. In some, the CEO makes recommendations to a nominating committee, the committee accepts the suggestions, and the board approves. In others, the nominating committee makes selections, which are then discussed with the CEO and the board.

---

[21]For details, see "Corporate Governance Market Principles, Japan," http://www.calpers.ca.gov/invest/corpgov/egjapan.htm.

[22]Julia Flynn, Thane Peterson, Karen Lowry Miller, William Echikson, and Gail Edmondson, "Bosses under Fire," *Business Week*, November 30, 1998.

[23]Miki Tanikawa, "Shareholder Rights? In Japan?" *Business Week*, November 9, 1998.

If the board had an outside director as chairperson, it would be his or her responsibility to ensure that the nominating committee was finding appropriate people for membership. The advice and counsel of the CEO would still be sought, of course. But this process would end the misperception, if there was one, that board members were appointed by the CEO and therefore were in some sense beholden to that person.

There are some suggestions that the board be composed almost completely of independent outside directors. In our experience serving on boards, this would be a mistake. It is important that the board be well-informed about the details of the operation of the business. Insiders should be present to provide company information to the board.

Evaluating the CEO's Performance

Most boards, as shown in Table 19-1, say this is one of their major functions. There is a question, however, about how well-defined are the board's objectives for evaluation, how comprehensive, and how thorough are evaluations in practice. Too frequently, evaluation is casual, if performed at all, and any negative feedback is minimal.

There are, however, many companies whose boards have detailed evaluation criteria. Criteria for an effective evaluation of CEOs would include the following:

- The board should develop a clear job description for the CEO position.
- The board and the CEO should meet and agree upon the CEO's performance objectives.
- The performance evaluation should be conducted annually.
- Specific board meetings should be established for the CEO evaluation.
- The long-term performance of the company should be compared with similar organizations.
- The CEO's performance should be evaluated against the goals set for the company.
- The CEO should appraise his or her performance and present it to the board.
- The CEO should have an opportunity to discuss the evaluation with the entire board.[24]

Board Self-Evaluation

This is an extremely important function that too few boards perform satisfactorily if at all. The Conference Board Study referred to above found that of 112 companies reporting, only 17 percent had a formal evaluation process in place. Board

---

[24]Report of the NACD Blue Ribbon Commission on *Performance Evaluation of Chief Executive Officers, Boards, and Directors,* Washington, D.C.: National Association of Corporate Directors, 1994.

self-evaluation should certainly not be self-serving. It should be reasonably objective and, when well done, serves many purposes other than satisfying the demands of institutional investors. For one thing, it presents a picture of how well the board is performing its duties. It should help members to anticipate issues that the board may face in the future. It could improve the relationships among individual directors and between the board and top management of the company.

There are, of course, many ways to perform a self-evaluation. For example, a questionnaire may be completed by outside directors, the full board may discuss specific questions, and an outside consultant may be asked to conduct a survey. The preferred methodology should invite responses to specific questions. Companies that make such evaluations usually have such a list. Here are areas of assessment that should be included:[25]

- Board procedures.
- Quality of board discussions.
- Board relationship to senior management.
- Evaluations of the CEO.
- Board role in company strategy.
- Director selection and retirement.
- Preparation to deal with an unforeseen crisis.
- Board leadership.
- Director compensation.
- Definition of independence of outside directors.
- Adequacy of information given to board.

Understanding and Approving Major Company Strategies

It is difficult to understand how a board can feel comfortable in its performance unless it is certain that it understands, reviews, and approves the major strategies designed for the company. In a number of companies, this process is conducted at a two- or three-day offsite meeting of the board to discuss only strategy.

The question arises, of course, at what point does such a legitimate process encroach upon the detailed management of the company? This is a difficult line to draw, but one that must be understood and drawn in such a way that the CEO feels comfortable.

Separate the CEO and Board Chairman

In 72 percent of large American corporations, the CEO is also the chairperson of the board. Some observers believe the two jobs should be separated, but there is much opposition to the idea, especially among CEOs.

---

[25]Most organized evaluations are based on some listing of areas for board evaluation. For example, see ibid.

Many directors believe that when CEOs also chair the board, they have too much power. The power to control the agenda and the information that directors get is overwhelming, they say.

After a three-year study in which hundreds of directors participated, Professor Jay W. Lorsch of the Harvard Business School concluded that separating the two jobs would go a long way to help directors perform better. It would help prevent crises because, with an outside director as chairperson, the board would likely get more and better information about company affairs. Also, in the event of a crisis involving the CEO, the board would be more organized to deal with it. But beyond that, splitting the jobs would underscore the notion that managers serve at the discretion of directors, not the other way around. At board meetings, directors would feel freer to raise questions and be critical of management.[26] Many top executives support this view.

Critics of this proposal point out that although the two top people usually get along well, there are many unpublicized cases of failure. If the CEO and chairperson positions are split, and if rivalry or dislike develops between the two, then the split works to the detriment of the business and the board functions less well. CEOs say that to split the roles would complicate their jobs. They are concerned that their immediate predecessors might be appointed chairperson. That situation would indeed be fraught with danger and should not be permitted by a board where the split has taken place.

Ram Charan, a consultant to corporate CEOs and boards of directors, is critical of the separation of the two jobs. He says: "Separating the role of CEO and chairman can create confusion and blur accountability. Outsiders might begin to wonder who is really in charge or whether the CEO is on the way out. Any misperceptions outside can erode the CEO's decision-making power internally as well."[27]

Compensation Issues

Compensation of Directors

It has been said with some justification that directors get paid too much for what they do, but not enough for what they should do. What are the facts?

The Conference Board survey showed that the median 1997 basic annual compensation of outside directors was $33,000 across all industry groups. For larger companies with assets over $10 billion, the average was $72,630, and for some, such as the GE board members discussed at the beginning of the chapter, compensation was much higher. In very small companies, directors may not get any compensation. In large firms, the high in the Conference Board survey was $145,050.

---

[26]Jay W. Lorsch, *Pawns or Potentates* (Boston, Mass.: Harvard Business School Press, 1989).

[27]Ram Charan, *Boards at Work: How Corporate Boards Create Competitive Advantage*, San Francisco, Calif.: Jossey-Bass Publishers, 1998, p. 51.

Giving stock options in the form of compensation is growing. Among companies in the Conference Board survey 84 percent use this form of payment for outside directors. As at General Electric, many other benefits are given to board members. Most firms pay for director liability insurance; some provide life and other insurance, medical benefits, donations to directors' charities, and pensions.

Among the firms surveyed, only 19 percent provided pensions, a decline from 30 percent in 1996 caused by intense criticism. Critics claim that pensions make directors less independent, are far too generous, and lead directors to hang on too long to their membership. Corporations argue that pensions, as well as other compensation, are needed to attract and retain outstanding directors. However, a prestigious commission established by the National Association of Corporate Directors (NACD) agreed with critics and was influential in reducing the number of pensions granted and their generosity.

The basic recommendation of critics seems to be that compensation should be adequate and that it should be tied in some way to the long-range, not the short-range, performance of the company. What is adequate will vary among companies and will always remain controversial. How to link pay to performance is challenging. This probably can be done better through stock options that cannot be redeemed for a specified time in the future.

Compensation of CEOs

Virtually all corporations have compensation committees that set the pay and benefits of top executives. What is perceived as excessively generous pay and benefits for CEOs has today inspired widespread popular outrage. This is not a new phenomenon. In 1939, President Franklin D. Roosevelt railed against the "entrenched greed" of corporation executives, and the criticism has periodically arisen since.

How Much Are CEOs Paid?   First of all, it must be recognized that it is difficult to accurately calculate the exact amount of all pay and benefits paid to a chief executive. The salary paid to a CEO as well as annual bonus is clear enough and publicly reported. Problems arise in calculating the value of stock options, which are a large part of most CEO compensation, and other benefits such as deferred pay and perquisites. A stock option, as noted previously, is a right to buy the company's stock at a fixed price and conditions determined by the board of directors. Usually the price is set at or close to the current price and there is a limit on the time granted to the receiver to buy the stock, usually ten years. Thus, if the stock of XYZ corporation today is $10 and rises to $50 dollars within the time limit, say, ten years, the CEO can buy that stock at $10 and reap the gain between this price and the future market price. If the stock does not rise above $10, the option is worthless.

In 1997, according to Standard & Poor's Compustat, the average salary and bonus of CEOs of the 365 largest companies in the United States was $2.2 million, a slight drop from $2.3 million in 1996. The decline was due to the fact that

TABLE 19-2   The Top-Paid Chief Executives in 1997

	1997 Salary and Bonus (Thousands of Dollars)	Long-Term Compensation	Total Pay
1. Sanford Weill, Travelers Group	$7,453	$223,272	$230,725
2. Roberto Goizueta, Coca-Cola	4,052	107,781	111,832
3. Richard Scrushy, HealthSouth	13,399	93,391	106,790
4. Ray Irani, Occidental Petroleum	3,849	97,657	101,505
5. Eugene Isenberg, Nabors Industries	1,675	82,872	84,547
6. Joseph Costello, Cadence Design Systems	584	66,258	66,842
7. Andrew Grove, Intel	3,255	48,958	52,214
8. Charles McCall, HBO & Co.	1,725	49,684	51,409
9. Philip Purcell, Morgan Stanley Dean Witter	11,274	39,533	50,807
10. Robert Shapiro, Monsanto	1,834	47,491	49,326

Source: Jennifer Reingold, Richard A. Melcher, and Gary McWilliams, "Executive Pay," *Business Week,* April 20, 1998, p. 64.

many executives deferred bonuses or took stock options instead of additional cash compensation.[28] Stock options are the source of big money for executives of American companies because of a soaring stock market. The ten highest-paid CEOs in 1997 are shown in Table 19-2. The numbers in the table are huge, but that is not the entire story. Many executives hold unexercised stock options with current and prospective values in the millions. For example, Henry Silverman, CEO of Cendant, has nonexercised stock options of $833 million. The value is based on the stock price at the end of the company's fiscal year. Michael Eisner, CEO of Walt Disney, has unexercised options valued at $591 million; Echard Pfeifer of Compact Computer, $242 million; Richard Scrushy of HealthSouth, $216 million; and Lawrence Ellison, CEO of Oracle, $201 million.[29]

Pearl Meyer & Partners, an executive consulting firm, examined the equity holdings of CEOs of the 200 largest publicly traded companies. They eliminated the highest and lowest 10 and found the remainder held an average of $57.8 million. Included were shares owned outright or in options. The largest was William H. Gates of Microsoft with $35 billion. The second was Sumner

---

[28]Jennifer Reingold, Richard A. Melcher, and Gary McWilliams, "Executive Pay," *Business Week,* April 20, 1998.

[29]Ibid.

M. Redstone of Viacom with $4.1 billion. The third was Philip H. Knight of Nike with $3.68 billion. The fourth was Michael S. Dell of Dell Computer with $2.34 billion.[30]

Criticisms of CEO Compensation.   Critics complain that CEO compensation often has little or no correlation with company performance, as measured by stockholder returns or profits. Most studies of linkage find some correlation between company size and CEO compensation, but very little relationship between compensation and company performance.[31] There are many examples of both cases. For instance, in 1997, there was a positive correlation between high CEO pay and high company stock performance at SunAmerica, Compaq, and Pfizer. There were also instances of high performance and low pay. Examples were Microsoft, Marshall & Lisley, and State Street Boston. On the other hand, there were cases of high compensation and low performance; for example, Occidental Petroleum, Kodak, and Mattel.[32]

The year 1997 brought downsizing in many companies. Critics complain there is something unseemly about high and growing executive compensation at the same time companies discharge thousands of workers. Executive pay is rarely cut when employee reductions are made. This raises a significant question: Should the CEO's compensation be reduced when large layoffs are announced, or should the CEO be rewarded for making a difficult decision to cut employee costs in the hope that the result will be higher company profitability?[33]

Critics charge that in too many compensation committees, the members are CEOs of other corporations, cronies of the CEO, and/or consultants who have profited from business with the company. In such cases, it is alleged, the bias is clearly in favor of boosting CEO compensation.

In Defense of CEOs.   Executives defend high compensation on several grounds. First, stock options have been a large part of compensation in recent years. As a result, the bull market in stock prices in the 1980s and 1990s provided opportunities for executives to exercise options given years before at low prices. If these past option grants are exercised and compensation is calculated for the year in which they are exercised, say the CEOs, of course the amount looks large.

Second, CEOs and their defenders say many large compensation packages were justified by gains of stockholders during their tenure. In some cases, this is correct. Michael Eisner, CEO of Walt Disney, for example, became head of

---

[30]Reported by David Cay Johnston, "The Chiefs Stock Up," *New York Times,* February 15, 1998.

[31]See, for example, Graef Crystal, "Almost Any Way You Figure It, Executive Pay Remains Irrational," *Los Angeles Times,* December 3, 1995; and Michael C. Jensen and Kevin J. Murphy, "CEO Incentives—It's Not How Much You Pay, but How," *Harvard Business Review,* May–June 1992.

[32]Adam Bryant, "Flying High on the Option Express," *New York Times,* April 5, 1998.

[33]Molly Baker, "I Feel Your Pain?" *The Wall Street Journal,* April 12, 1995.

that company in 1984 when net income was barely at the break-even point and its stock price was low. By 1992, revenues of the company were $7.5 billion and profits were $816 million. Eisner cashed options in 1992 with a value of $175 million. He had received the options at $3.59 and sold them at $40. By 1997, the company's net income reached $22.5 billion, the price of the stock soared, and shareholders profited. So did the value of Eisner's stock options. During the 1990s, U.S. corporations successfully expanded globally, and that significantly increased total revenues and profitability. Many CEOs were responsible for devising and implementing strategies that produced these results. They are now being compensated accordingly.

Third, boards of directors point out that if they do not pay their CEOs what executives in comparable companies get, they stand to lose them, and that would be costly. Anyway, they say, the compensation is not out of line with other professionals, such as top lawyers and Wall Street investment bankers.

What Should Directors Do about Compensation?   There are several reforms that can be introduced to improve the system for setting executive compensation. First, the compensation committee membership must be made independent from the influence of the CEO and other biased interests. The committee should be composed solely of outside directors and in large companies have an outside compensation consultant.

The criteria for determining compensation should be designed to provide greater incentives for the CEO to meet company objectives, which, among other things, should be formulated with the long term in view. This can be done in a number of ways. For example, if stock options are given, the time after which they may be exercised can be extended. Cash compensation may be related to achieving specific goals, such as corporate profits.

Other Reforms and Proposals for Reform.   In response to widespread criticism, and to restrain unnecessary and unwanted congressional legislation, the SEC issued new regulations concerning executive pay in June 1992 that require companies to show in charts and graphs precisely all details of senior executive compensation. The board of directors compensation committee is required to explain the performance factors used in determining pay. As we have said, there is no generally accepted formula for calculating the value of unexercised options. However, the SEC now requires that companies calculate and report to stockholders a range of values.

Criticism of compensation also initiated action by Congress. A tax law introduced January 1, 1994, bars publicly held corporations from deducting as a cost of doing business a top officer's compensation in excess of $1 million a year. Nevertheless, many corporations pay executives more despite the fact that it is not tax deductible as an expense. The Financial Accounting Standards Board (FASB), an organization that sets guidelines for accounting practices, has been considering what to do about stock options. The recommendation to them is to account for stock options as an expense, the same as other compensation. The big problem, of course, is how the cost of the options should be calculated.

Employee Governance Activities

Employees traditionally have not had much impact on corporate governance, although historically there have been many efforts to empower them through stock ownership. For example, Albert Gallatin, who served as secretary of the Treasury under presidents Jefferson and Madison, created an employee ownership plan in his Pennsylvania Glass Works as early at 1795.[34] In recent years, employee stock ownership has increased significantly but has led to minimal representation on corporate boards of directors.

Employee stock ownership has expanded through employee stock ownership plans (ESOPs), 401(k) pension plans, and stock option plans. An ESOP is an employee ownership plan made possible by tax breaks created in the Employee Retirement Income Security Act of 1974 and subsequent legislation. Through the framework established by the law, a company sets up a trust. The trust then borrows money to purchase newly created stock and the company repays the loan by making tax-deductible contributions to the trust. The stock is placed in an account to be distributed to employees as the loan is repaid. There are other methods to set up an ESOP.[35]

The most notable recent ESOP was created in 1994 when employees of United Airlines acquired 55 percent of the company's stock and received three of the twelve seats on the airline's board of directors. During the wave of merger takeovers in the 1970s and 1980s, a number of companies gave large blocks of stock to employees as defenses against takeovers. Altogether, it is estimated by the National Center for Employee Ownership (NCEO) there are today about 11,000 ESOPs with 7.7 million employees.[36]

Employee stock ownership has expanded through 401(k) plans. These are saving plans spelled out in the Internal Revenue Code, section 401(k), that allow employees to save and reinvest pretax income. Employees can invest in company stock in these plans.[37] The NCEO estimates there are about 2,000 companies with such plans covering about two million employees.

Stock options are given to six million employees in about 3,000 companies according to the NCEO. Employees are also indirect stockholders through public and private pension funds.

With such vast holdings, it is remarkable that so few employees sit on corporate boards of directors. Both unions and employees have shown little enthusiasm for representation on boards. Some union leaders believe representation would permit them to have some say in the strategic direction of the

---

[34]For a history, see Jeff Gates, *The Ownership Solution: Toward a Shared Capitalism for the 21st Century,* Reading, Mass.: Addison-Wesley, 1998.

[35]For a complete description of ESOPs, see *The ESOP Reader: An Introduction to Employee Stock Ownership Plans,* Oakland, Calif.: The National Center for Employee Ownership, 1998.

[36]These and the following data on stock ownership are from National Center for Employee Ownership, "A Statistical Profile of Employee Ownership," http://www.nceo.org/library/eo_stat.html.

[37]For details, see ibid. pp. 57–63.

company and provide them with better information about financial operations. But they have not actively sought seats except in a few instances. Managers have little interest in employee representation on their boards.

The extent to which employees will seek direct representation on boards of directors in the future is unknown. There is, of course, indirect influence through pension fund activism, but will massive employee stock ownership lead to demands for board seats? If it does, corporate governance will change, and that, in turn, will raise new issues of social responsibility.

To Whom Are Directors Accountable?

Jay Lorsch in his study found that " . . . the majority of directors felt trapped in a dilemma between their traditional legal responsibility to shareholders, whom they consider too interested in short-term payout, and belief about what is best, in the long run, for the health of the company."[38]

The laws are clear that directors are accountable to stockholders. It is their duty to protect stockholder interests and provide an adequate return on their investment. But to which shareholders do directors owe this responsibility? Short-term stock traders? Corporate raiders interested in a "fast buck"? Large institutional investors who focus on short-term appreciation in their portfolios? Investors in friendly leveraged buyouts? Employees in stock option plans? Individual long-term stock investors?

In response to unfriendly takeovers in the 1980s, twenty-five states, not including Delaware, enacted laws that broaden the legal authority of boards to consider in their deliberations stakeholders other than shareholders. These other stakeholders may be communities, governments, suppliers, lenders, employees, and others. What these states are saying, and others will likely follow, is that corporations exist to provide more than a return to owners. This legal position, in contrast to the stark doctrine of stockholder supremacy, focuses the accountability of directors on the overriding role of the corporation in society. Directors obviously face difficult problems in balancing claims of different stakeholders and in defining their responsibility to them.

These considerations inject considerable ambiguity into the question: To whom are directors accountable? Lorsch suggests that directors should develop decision criteria for dealing with the dilemmas they face.

Concluding Observations

The roles of boards of directors of our corporations have changed dramatically in the past few years, a trend destined to continue in the future. Years ago,

---

[38]Lorsch, *Pawns or Potentates*, p. 49.

membership on a typical corporate board of a large corporation was viewed as an honorary position with few responsibilities and a chance to get away from the office to socialize with peers. Today, more and more boards are asserting their authority over corporate governance.

In this chapter, we have discussed reforms that have been suggested for more effective board governance. The successful implementation of these reforms will improve corporate governance. This, in turn, will improve our economic strength at home and abroad and raise the standard of living of the American people.

U.S. v. MICHAEL R. MILKEN

Introduction

Michael R. Milken has been called a "financial genius" with the stature of J.P. Morgan, a generous philanthropist, and a devoted family man. His entrepreneurship in building the junk bond market was instrumental in the development of many successful companies. He therefore holds a place of importance in the history of corporate governance. On the other hand, government prosecutors, in one of the most sensational financial trials of the century, filed an indictment in 1990 and said he was a felon who violated many security laws. His defenders say he might have been guilty only of minor technical violations of the securities law. Which characterization is most fitting? We discuss this question in this case.

Background

Michael Milken was born in Encino, California, July 4, 1945, to Ferne and Bernhard Milken. Bernhard Milken was an accountant and, from an early age, Michael watched his father prepare tax returns. After graduating from Birmingham High School in neighboring Van Nuys in 1964, Michael entered the University of California Berkeley, where he majored in business administration. He graduated from Berkeley in 1968 and enrolled for an M.B.A. at the Wharton School of the University of Pennsylvania, which, at that time, was renowned for its curriculum in finance and accounting.

Milken was a superior student, brilliant, hardworking, and intensely ambitious. While at Berkeley, he did not engage in the so-called free speech movement sweeping the campus at the time, but chose to work hard on his studies (he graduated Phi Beta Kappa) and then found a job with Touche Ross, an accounting firm. One of his fraternity brothers at Berkeley (he was a Sigma Alpha Mu) said, "he was monomaniacal about money. To be a millionaire by age thirty was his goal. I thought I shared the same goal, but Mike was different. He wanted to be *rich*."[1]

---

[1]Robert Sobel, *Dangerous Dreamers: The Financial Innovators from Charles Merrill to Michael Milken*, New York: Wiley, 1993, pp. 62–63.

In 1969, while at Wharton, Milken had a summer job at the Philadelphia offices of Drexel Harriman Ripley and later joined the firm's New York office. This company traced its origins to 1871 when it was Drexel, Morgan and Company. The two firms later split and eventually became Drexel, Burnham and Lambert, one of the most powerful investment bankers on Wall Street. Throughout his career in the investment business, Milken remained with Drexel.

The Financial Markets in the 1970s and 1980s

When Milken joined Drexel in New York, the bond market was in the doldrums. Interest rates on high-grade corporate bonds rated AAA had risen from an average of 4.49 percent in 1965 to 7.04 percent in 1970, remained at that relatively high level through the mid-1970s and began to rise again, reaching 14.17 percent in 1981. The doubling of rates resulted in a drop of bond prices of about 50 percent. Prices of low-rated bonds fell even more. In 1974, stock prices fell significantly, with the result that investors looked to places other than bonds and stocks to put their money.

Since they did not find other investment opportunities that suited their interests, they placed their money in low-paying money market funds. At the same time, pension and insurance company funds were swelling in size. The result was a rising amount of available cash for investment. There were three major sources of potential but not satisfied demand for these funds. (1) Small and medium-size firms found difficulty in raising money. Neither the bond nor stock markets were hospitable for new offerings, and banks were loath to lend them money. (2) Deregulation of the S&Ls, especially the Garn–St Germain Depository Institutions Act of 1982, which permitted the S&Ls to invest up to 40 percent of their assets in nonresidential real estate, opened a significant potential demand for securities. (3) The relaxed regulatory atmosphere of the Reagan administration accommodated the thirst of promoters for money to acquire other companies for profit through leveraged buyouts. (The word "leverage" refers to the use of bonds or debt to pay for the common stock of a company to be taken over. The acronym LBO encompasses a variety of financial transactions concerned with acquisitions and mergers.)[2]

The growing supply of and unsatisfied demands for money established a foundation for the sale of bonds, especially low-grade or junk bonds. High-grade bonds could be sold, but junk bonds were not well-regarded as investments.

---

[2]For a fuller definition of LBO, see Carolyn Kay Brancato and Kevin F. Winch, *Leveraged Buyouts and the Pot of Gold: Trends, Public Policy, and Case Studies,* report prepared by the Economics Division of the Congressional Research Service for the Subcommittee on Oversight and Investigations of the Committee on Energy and Commerce, U.S. House of Representatives, Washington, D.C.: U.S. Government Printing Office, December 1987.

Michael R. Milken

(Junk bonds are simply securities bearing high-interest rates to reflect a higher risk. They carry low ratings or are unrated by investment-rating services.) Conservative investment bankers avoided underwriting such securities, and that opened the door for new financial entrepreneurs. All they had to do was persuade holders of cash to invest in the low-grade bonds, not an easy task in light of the investment atmosphere of the times.

Thus Milken began his career at the relative bottom of the stock and bond markets and at a time when available money supply was growing but demand could not be met, especially among small, medium-size, and newly formed firms.[3] Milken was a superb salesperson and believed he had logic on his side for persuading people to invest in junk bonds.

The Case for Investment in Junk Bonds

Milken's interest in junk bonds extended back to his Berkeley days. There he studied research findings of W. Braddock Hickman, published in 1958, that concluded that lower-rated bonds, under certain circumstances, would yield more to an investor than higher-rated securities. If investors bought lower-rated bonds at their lows and held them to maturity, the net yield would be greater than on higher-rated securities. One reason for this is that at the bottom of the market cycle for bonds, the price of lower-grade bonds falls much more than for higher-grade bonds. Since the default rate in the past for lower-grade bonds was not high, an investor who held them through to maturity, or

---

[3]Ibid. for a detailed discussion of the financial conditions of the 1970s and 1980s.

sold at the top of the market, received net returns higher than if he or she had purchased higher-grade bonds.[4] Thomas R. Atkinson of the National Bureau of Economic Research confirmed the Hickman research and added an additional finding, that most defaults of bonds occurred one year before they reached their highs.[5]

Milken's interest at Drexel focused on the junk bond market, but he had to persuade buyers to invest in them. As Robert Sobel, a professor at Hofstra University, wrote:

> Milken had to convince the potential buyer that the rating was not reflective of their true value, and that the yield justified a purchase. Such bonds couldn't even be efficiently priced, since most had thin markets. Milken had to sweat out every sale in those days, while the gentlemen salesmen of highly rated bonds made their placements with ease. A Milken spiel must have sounded to them like the line of a tout at a bucket shop.[6]

Milken's Activities at Drexel

Milken's focus on junk bond sales paid off and he was a major contributor to Drexel's profits. However, in 1973, Drexel needed a cash infusion, which it got by merging with Burnham & Co. to become Drexel Burnham Lambert. Milken's success was appreciated by Burnham, who became president of Drexel, and when he was asked by Milken for permission to establish a bond unit to concentrate on junk bonds, it was granted. A compensation arrangement was made that eventually yielded extraordinary income to Milken. He could keep $1 for every $3 he made for Drexel and distribute it as he saw fit to pay personnel in his unit. In addition, his unit would receive fees for any new business it attracted. By 1976, Milken made $5 million a year under this arrangement.[7]

In 1978 Milken moved his department to Beverly Hills, California. There, his operation became the center of the junk bond market.

Growth of the Junk Bond Market

In 1970, total junk bonds outstanding were $7 billion, mostly low-grade securities exchanged for formerly high-rated bonds downgraded as a result of financial difficulties of the issuing company. By 1978, the total junk bond market

---

[4]W. Braddock Hickman, *Corporate Bond Quality and Investor Experience,* Princeton, N.J.: Princeton University Press, 1958.

[5]Thomas R. Atkinson, with the assistance of Elizabeth T. Simpson, *Trends in Corporate Bond Quality,* New York: National Bureau of Economic Research, 1967.

[6]Sobel, *Dangerous Dreamers,* p. 72.

[7]Ibid., p. 75.

had grown in $9.4 billion, a larger proportion of which was for new issues. Thereafter, the total rapidly increased until it reached $15 billion in 1980, $59 billion in 1985, and $210 billion in 1990.[8]

Milken gradually dominated the junk bond market. Robert Sobel wrote:

> . . . he [Milken] virtually owned the junk market, and anyone wanting to play there had to go through him. He not only bought and sold the bonds, but he also knew where they were. This meant that he could contact a customer and talk him into a buy, and then call the owner of the bond and invite him to sell. Milken could set prices within a very wide band, since buyer and seller would have no precise idea of how much the bond was worth. Only Milken could know when to deal with those bonds, and only he had pricing power. His customers lacked this information and control.[9]

During the 1970s and early 1980s, there was a boom in mergers and acquisitions. Generally, this arrangement was consummated when a company or person bought enough of the stock of a company to gain control of it. When the acquisition was without the approval of the management and stockholders of the targeted corporation, the action was called "hostile." Each case was different in detail, but junk bonds were frequently used to help an individual or a company finance the purchase of enough stock to control a company.

The hostile takeover movement was highly distasteful to traditional investment bankers, corporate leaders, employees of the company acquired, and the public. This was partly due to the fact that hostile takeovers often were designed only to enrich the "raider." To prevent a hostile takeover, a management might incur substantial debt to pay off the raider by buying his stock at a price much higher than he paid for it. Or, if the hostile takeover succeeded, a corporation might be loaded with excessive debt to pay for the raider's stock; employees might be discharged and careers ruined to cut costs; and sometimes the company sold in pieces with the hope that sales would yield profits for the raider. The issuance of junk bonds became associated in the public mind with such repugnant activities.

In reality, the vast majority of junk underwritings were for corporate restructuring and expansion. Sobel calculated that of 1,100 junk issues between 1980 and 1986, only 3 percent were used in unwelcome takeovers.[10] Milken helped finance well-known corporate raiders such as Victor Posner, Carl Icahn, and T. Boone Pickens. His name became linked with hostile takeovers. Milken also helped finance newly developing firms that became successful giants, such as Turner Broadcasting, MCI Communications, and McCaw Cellular.

---

[8]Edward A. Altman, "Defaults and Returns on High Yield Bonds: An Update through the First Half of 1991," in the Merrill Lynch magazine, *Extra Credit*, July/August 1991, p. 19; printed in Sobel, *Dangerous Dreamers*, p. 127.

[9]Sobel, *Dangerous Dreamers*, p. 93.

[10]Ibid., p. 128.

The Ethical Climate in the 1970s and 1980s

The late 1970s and 1980s, with but minor bumps, were boom years in financial markets. Vast opportunities existed to make enormous sums of money and large numbers of people became rich virtually overnight. The era was stamped with human greed. Ivan Boesky, a well-known and large-securities trader who was later sent to prison for insider trading and other crimes, said to a graduating class at the University of California Berkeley in 1986, "Greed is all right, by the way. I want you to know that. I think greed is healthy. You can be greedy and feel good about yourself."[11]

There were many investment bankers who held steadfastly to high ethical standards, but there were others who did not. Many were guilty of insider trading (using confidential information to acquire stock before the information became available to the public), conflicts of interest, misinforming clients, and fraud. Many were prosecuted and sent to jail.[12]

The U.S. Government Indictment of Milken

In the late 1980s, a series of prosecutions for illegalities darkened the financial markets. Among those prosecuted was Ivan Boesky, who, in November 1986, pleaded guilty to a series of financial crimes and was given a prison sentence. He freely cooperated with government prosecutors and pointed fingers at Drexel and Michael Milken, with whom he had frequent dealings. Drexel was investigated in late 1988 and agreed to accept government charges of wrong-doing and paid a large fine. Part of the agreement was to give Michael Milken a leave of absence. In January 1990, Drexel filed for bankruptcy and, in that year, Milken was charged with criminal acts.

In the meantime, the junk bond market collapsed. Savings and loan institutions and others dumped junk bonds on the market and prices plummeted. There was no one around like Milken to maintain liquidity in that market.

In March 1990, Benito Romano, U.S. District Attorney in New York, who followed Rudolph Giuliani after he left to run for mayor of New York, brought a 98-count, 110-page, indictment against Michael Milken, his brother Lowell, and Bruce Newberg, a close associate in the Beverly Hills office. The indictment contained charges of unlawful securities trading including price manipulation, fraud in the sale of securities, mail fraud, wire fraud, tax fraud, devious schemes to defraud, and other related crimes "in a pattern of racketeering activity."[13]

---

[11]Quoted in James Steward, *Den of Thieves*, New York: Simon and Schuster, 1992, p. 261.
[12]Ibid.
[13]*United States of America* v. *Michael R. Milken, Lowell J. Milken, and Bruce L. Newberg, Indictment,* U.S. District Court, Southern District of New York, S 89 Cr. 41 (KBW), undated. The charges described in this case are from this document unless otherwise specified.

The Boesky Arrangement

The first indictment concerned a charge of secret arrangements between Milken and Ivan Boesky, a major security trader, that the government claimed resulted in a series of illegal securities trades. The illegal activities included trading profits from "insider trading,[14] buying and selling bonds to support hostile takeovers without disclosing the purposes of these actions, bogus and fraudulent stock and bond trading, mail fraud, and violating the federal tax and securities laws to defraud investors." Space permits but a very few and brief illustrations of the government's charges of illegality.

Fischbach Corporation

An illustration of the unlawful actions of the Boesky and Milken arrangement, said the government, was the takeover of the Fischbach Corporation. This was a construction business, including electrical and mechanical contracting. Victor Posner, a well-known corporate raider, wanted to acquire Fischbach through the Pacific Engineering Corporation (PEC), which he controlled. In early 1980, PEC filed a Schedule 13D form with the Securities and Exchange Commission disclosing that it had acquired over 10 percent of Fischbach's common stock.[15] Fischbach's management resisted the attempted thrust of PEC and threatened to sue. PEC and Fischbach resolved their differences in a standstill agreement that barred PEC from acquiring more than 24.9 percent of the stock unless a third party not connected with PEC or Posner declared an acquisition of 10 percent or more of Fischbach's stock. If that happened, then the standstill agreement was no longer effective. PEC then proceeded to acquire 24.8 percent of the stock.

In December 1983, Executive Life Insurance Co., a purchaser of large quantities of junk bonds from Milken, filed a 13D with the SEC revealing it had acquired 14.4 percent of Fischbach's stock. This purchase of stock, of course, was enough to end the standstill agreement. However, Fischbach said that insurance companies had to file a 13G, not a 13D, which was correct, and since Executive Life did not do so, the standstill agreement still was in force. This was enough to throw the issue into the courts.

The government claimed that Milken then caused Boesky to buy over 10 percent of Fischbach's stock, which he disclosed on a 13D to the SEC. The government charged that Milken agreed to cover any losses of Boesky in the transaction. This action, of course, nullified the standstill agreement. The government claimed that Boesky did not reveal on his 13D that the shares were

---

[14]Insider trading, a violation of the securities laws, takes place when people who have access to confidential information use that knowledge to trade in securities for their own benefit prior to the release of the information to the public.

[15]The Williams Act of 1968 requires, among other things, that anyone acquiring 5 percent or more of a company's common stock must disclose that fact, state the purpose of the acquisition, and whether any additional shares are to be bought.

bought on behalf of Drexel Enterprises. This was illegal "stock parking." (Stock parking refers to a person or company buying securities from or on behalf of another person or company without revealing the owner's identity.) Thus, said the government, filing falsely and fraudulently deceived Fischbach and the public. Drexel also bought shares of Fischbach for its own account and later sold them to PEC. In February 1985, Drexel underwrote and sold $56 million of junk bonds to finance the further acquisition of Fischbach by Posner and his group. Posner was able to take control of Fischbach in September 1985.

Fischbach shares dropped in the market and Boesky's losses were substantial. He pressed Milken for reimbursement of losses, because Boesky said Milken had said he would cover any losses. Milken later arranged a series of trades in the junk bond market that resulted in profit for Boesky.

Altogether, charged the government, this experience revealed a secret conspiracy among Milken, Drexel, and Boesky's organizations to commit unlawful acts. Among the illegal actions were concealing the purposes of the transactions, unlawfully breaking the standstill agreement, and fraud in the sale of securities.

Golden Nugget

During the first half of 1984, Golden Nugget, a Las Vegas casino, and one of Milken's clients, decided to acquire MCA and quietly began accumulating MCA shares. Golden Nugget bought several million shares at a cost of approximately $99 million but only up to 4.9 percent of MCA's outstanding stock. Then the casino decided it did not wish to go through with the acquisition. It wanted to sell its shares but did not want to dump them on the market for fear of depressing the stock price, which had risen substantially on rumors of the takeover. The casino called on Milken for help; he in turn called on Boesky to buy large amounts of Golden Nugget's stock with the promise, Boesky said, to take care of any losses. "These purchases and sales," said the government, "were done to conceal from the investing public that Golden Nugget was selling its MCA common stock, and thereby to artificially support the price of that stock during the period of those sales."[16] Milken was accused of committing mail fraud as shown in mailings that confirmed the trades of Golden Nugget and Boesky.

Diamond Shamrock Corporation

In this case, Diamond Shamrock Corporation and Occidental Petroleum Corporation in January 1985 had agreed in principle to merge the two companies. Drexel was hired to advise Occidental on the merger. At about the same time, the government charged that Milken caused Boesky to buy approximately 3.6 million shares of Diamond common stock and sell "short" about 10,000 shares

---

[16]*Milken Indictment,* p. 21.

of Occidental common stock.[17] The profits and losses to Boesky were to be split with Drexel. Shortly thereafter, Milken caused Boesky to buy 180,700 shares of Diamond and sell short 327,100 shares of Occidental, and to split profits and losses. Neither Diamond nor Occidental knew about these trades. Boesky lost money on the trades and shortly thereafter, said the government, Milken conducted a series of "sham and bogus trades at artificial prices" with Boesky to repay money owed to Boesky on the Occidental and other company losses. Furthermore, Milken had Drexel " . . . reimburse the Boesky organization secretly for certain of these losses, enabling the Boesky organization falsely and fraudulently to claim the entirety of these losses on its federal income tax returns."[18]

The government alleged that Milken knowingly committed securities fraud by using inside information to profit. He violated his duty to Occidental, engaged in fraudulent security trading, and committed tax and mail fraud, said the government.

Storer Communications, Inc.

Storer, a cable and VHF television station in Miami, Florida, agreed to a leveraged buyout by Kohlberg, Kravis, Roberts & Co. (KKR), an investment firm in New York, in December 1985. KKR sought the help of Milken in the $1.5 billion LBO with bonds and preferred stock. Drexel earned a fee of $49.6 million. (This was the largest LBO up to that time but was surpassed a few years later when KKR bought R. J. R. Nabisco for $25.1 billion.) Milken caused Boesky to buy 124,300 shares of Storer common stock and secretly agreed to share profits and losses with him. The government charged Milken not only with insider trading but also with failing to disclose the stock acquisition to Storer and KKR. Boesky ultimately made $1.1 million on the trade.

Very briefly, here are a few similar charges. Wickes Companies, Inc., was in the home-products business with headquarters in Santa Monica, California. Milken caused Boesky to buy 1.9 million shares of Wickes to lift the stock price to a point that triggered a commitment to redeem preferred stock. This was alleged to be illegal stock manipulation. Princeton/Newport Partners, located in Princeton, New Jersey, and Newport Beach, California, was engaged in investing the assets of the partners in securities and commodities. Milken was accused of causing them to commence a series of trades to manipulate the price of securities underwritten by Drexel. Transactions were also arranged to generate "bogus tax losses which Princeton/Newport fraudulently used to reduce the federal income tax liability of its partners."[19]

---

[17]Selling short means that stock is sold that is not owned in anticipation of a decline in the stock price. Usually the sold stock is borrowed from a broker for delivery to the purchaser. If the stock later does decline in price, the short seller "covers" the trade by buying the stock and giving it to the broker. If the stock price rises, the short seller, of course, loses.

[18]*Milken Indictment*, p. 28.

[19]Ibid., p. 63.

David Solomon, the head of a mutual fund, was an important client of Milken's. In December 1985, he needed to offset capital gains with losses for his personal account. The government charged that Milken helped him by selling him bonds that Drexel had in its inventory and later buying them back at a lower price. Milken also agreed to include Solomon in deals at a later date to make up for his losses in the bond transaction. Milken was charged with fraud. The government charged that Milken and his associates (Lowell J. Milken and Bruce L. Newberg) participated in criminal activities that showed a pattern of racketeering activity in violation of RICO and as a result made all their earnings subject to forfeiture.[20] The government calculated that for the years 1984 through 1987, total fees and trading profits amounted to $1.845 billion.[21]

In Defense of Michael Milken

A comprehensive defense of Milken was made by Daniel Fischel, a professor of law and business at the University of Chicago Law School, and formerly on the defense team of Milken, in his book *Payback*.[22] Fischel wrote that the government did not produce evidence that Milken had " . . . engaged in any conduct that had ever before been considered criminal. After the most thorough investigation of any individual's business practices in history, the government came up with nothing. In fact, the government never established that Milken's 'crimes' were anything other than routine business practices common to the industry."[23] He concluded: "The unholy alliance of the displaced establishment and the 'decade of greed' rich-haters, aided by ambitious but unscrupulous government lawyers like Rudy Giuliani, combined to destroy him. The whole episode is a national disgrace."[24]

Here is a sampling of the defense as set forth by Fischel and others. As noted above, the government claimed that Boesky bought Fischbach stock on the initiation of Milken who promised Boesky he would cover any losses. Boesky did not reveal on the 13D he filed with the SEC that Milken had an interest in his purchase. This was stock parking. But, said Fischel, this was common practice. Historically, such practice has either been ignored or treated only as a minor technical infraction of the security laws. No one ever suggested this was a serious crime. Furthermore, even if Milken had promised to

---

[20]RICO refers to the Racketeer Influenced and Corrupt Organizations Act passed by Congress in 1970. It was directed at Mafia activities and it is not at all clear that Congress intended it be applied to so-called white-collar crimes. The law is harsh. If one is convicted of crimes under this law, he or she can be penalized of all property and profits made in the alleged illegal activities.

[21]*Milken Indictment*, p. 88.

[22]Daniel Fischel, *Payback: The Conspiracy to Destroy Michael Milken and His Financial Revolution*, New York: Harper-Business, 1995.

[23]Ibid., p. 158.

[24]Ibid., p. 189.

cover losses, that was no infraction of law. Stockbrokers often help clients cover losses suffered from their recommendations. This is done, among other things, to keep clients happy.

The arrangement of Boesky and Milken was quite innocent, said Fischel. The attempted takeover of Fischbach was well-known and Boesky simply asked Milken for his advice about the wisdom of an investment. There was speculation that Boesky bought the stock hoping that Fischbach management would buy his shares well over his cost. This had been done with Executive Life when the company bought back its shares at a premium with the hope that the standstill agreement would, therefore, not be nullified. There was no conspiracy here.

Both Boesky and Milken claimed there was no agreement that Milken would cover Boesky's losses. It is true that Boesky became concerned when the price of Fischbach fell on the market and called Milken about it. Milken's reply was, "Don't worry about it." That certainly was no commitment to cover Boesky's losses. (Boesky ultimately lost approximately $2 million, which was later covered by profitable investments recommended by Milken.) This was a routine accommodation for a client.

There were no explicit agreements for stock parking or reimbursement for loss. "Such ambiguous disputes," said Fischel, "should not be the basis of criminal felony prosecutions."[25] The Golden Nugget case is another illustration of Milken wanting to help a client. There was no proof that Boesky, who bought the casino's shares of MCA, was acting as an agent of Milken.

In the Occidental Petroleum case, Milken was accused of insider trading by having Boesky trade in Occidental common stock to make a profit. Boesky suffered losses because the merger with Diamond Shamrock never occurred. If there was insider trading, asks Fischel, why did Milken not inform Boesky that the merger was off so that he could get out?

The charge of tax fraud in the Solomon case, said the defense, made no sense. The loss of Solomon was a real loss and no fraud was committed when he so declared on his income tax. There was no evidence that Milken had agreed to help Solomon make up that loss.

To conclude, Fischel argued that the government was unable to present any evidence that crimes had been committed by Milken. Furthermore, the offenses with which he was charged "had rarely, if ever, been subject to criminal prosecution at the time of Michael's acts."[26] No witnesses linked Milken to securities manipulation, he said.

Milken Pleads Guilty

On April 24, 1990, Milken pled guilty to six felonies. Four involved Boesky and two involved Solomon. One concerned the failure to disclose Drexel's in-

---

[25]Ibid., p. 79.
[26]Ibid., p. 169.

terest in Boesky's organization holding securities of Fischbach Corp. A second concerned defrauding investors in the Golden Nugget case. A third related to a criminal conspiracy with Boesky to park securities to conceal the true owners. A fourth involved security fraud in the Golden Nugget case. A fifth involved assisting Solomon to file false tax returns. A final one dealt with mail fraud related to dealings with Solomon.

Fatico *Hearings*

On September 27, 1990, the court announced that it would conduct *Fatico* hearings. These are hearings, said Judge Kimba Wood, that permit the plaintiff and defendant to present a limited amount of additional information to enable the court, before determining the sentence, "to have as full a picture as possible of Michael Milken's character in sentencing him on the six counts to which he pled guilty."[27]

The government made six charges, of which the court accepted only two as being convincing and relevant to the purpose of the *Fatico* hearings. They involved the obstruction of justice and concealing transactions to clients as required by law.[28]

Storer

As part of the financing of the LBO of Storer by KKR, Drexel agreed to sell PIK preferred stock. (PIK means that dividends would be paid in preferred stock, not cash.) Warrants were issued as "sweeteners" to induce investors to buy the stock. The warrants permitted holders to purchase Storer common stock at a profit if the merger was successful. Approximately 67 million shares were issued, each worth 7.4 cents a share at the time.

The government claimed that Milken did not use the warrants to sell the preferred stock. Rather, he allocated substantial amounts of the warrants to Drexel-affiliated partnerships in which he and his family had sizable interests. Some he offered to employees of Drexel clients to curry their favor. By late 1988, the partnerships had earned approximately $270 million in profits.

The contention of the government was that Milken's interests were concealed from KKR and Storer and they should have been revealed. This point is supported, said the government, by the fact that Drexel's salespeople did not know the warrants were available.

The defense argued that the distribution was within the discretionary power of Drexel as it saw fit in marketing the Storer securities. Furthermore,

---

[27]*U.S.* v. *Milken*, U.S. District Court, S.D. New York, December 13, 1990, p. 110. *Fatico* was established by *United States* v. *Fatico* in 1979.

[28]The discussion of these charges is from *United States* v. *Michael R. Milken, Lowell J. Milken, and Bruce L. Newberg*, U.S. Dis. Ct., S.D. New York, 759 F.Supp. 109 (S.D.N.Y. 1990).

the CEO of Drexel knew about the warrants and gave his approval to Milken to distribute them as he did because it did not violate Drexel policy. Furthermore, KKR representatives knew that Drexel had no obligation to offer the warrants to any particular investor. Finally, the sale of the preferred stock was crucial to getting the Storer board to approve the merger.

The loss of Solomon was indeed real and no fraud was committed when he so declared on his income tax. There was no evidence that Milken had agreed to help Solomon make up that loss.

The Blue Ledger Book

This document contained entries between Milken and David Solomon, a mutual fund manager and substantial purchaser of Drexel's junk bonds. The books held evidence, said the government, of bogus security trades to generate phony losses for Solomon's personal account. The losses were used in the 1985 tax returns of Solomon and, of course, were illegal.

Terren Peizer, a close associate of Milken, testified that Milken came to him, a few days after subpoenas were served on Milken, and asked him whether he still had the ledger book. Peizer said yes, and Milken then said to give it to Lorraine Spurge, one of Milken's closest confidants. Thereafter, the book disappeared. On another occasion, Peizer testified he was looking for documents in response to the government's subpoena. Milken said to him, in unambiguous words, "if you don't have them, you can't provide them."[29] James Dahl, another close associate of Milken, testified that Milken went with him to the men's room, turned the water on, and said to Dahl, "there haven't been any subpoenas issued and whatever you need to do, do it."[30] Then he turned off the water and looked to Dahl for response. Dahl said okay and went out. There had been no subpoena for Dahl to produce the documents at that time, but Milken had received subpoenas prior to this interchange.

The defense argued that there was no witness who testified that Dahl had been given specific directions by Milken to withhold documentary evidence. Furthermore, both Peizer's and Dahl's creditability was in doubt because their testimony on other facts proved to be wrong. A number of perfectly legal interpretations of these discussions is possible, argued the defense. For example, Dahl might have misinterpreted Milken's meaning because of the noise of the running water, or Milken merely was telling a trusted employee that a subpoena had been issued.

The government presented other charges, but Judge Wood said they were not relevant to the purpose of the *Fatico* hearing. The defense also presented evidence about the longtime and substantial charitable generosity of Milken.

---

[29]Ibid., p. 114.
[30]Ibid., p. 113.

Milken Pays $47 Million in Security Case

In January 1998, the Securities and Exchange Commission (SEC) filed charges against Michael Milken for violation of his lifetime ban from the securities business. The ban was a penalty levied in connection with his felony conviction discussed in this case. The SEC said Milken and his company MC had acted as a broker in securities transactions concerning deals involving three corporations—MCI Communications Corporation, News Corporation, and New World Communications. Furthermore, said the SEC, Milken did not register as a broker. Fees in the transactions totaled $45 million, not an unusual sum in light of Wall Street's acceptance of fees based on a percentage of the total amount of money involved, which was substantial in this instance. Without admitting or denying the allegations of the SEC, Milken returned $47 million, $45 million of fees and $2 million of interest on fees.

Source: Peter Truell, "Milken Settles S.E.C. Complaint for $47 Million," *New York Times*, February 27, 1998.

Comments of Judge Wood on the *Fatico* Hearing

Judge Wood said she found the testimony of Peizer and Dahl to be creditable and Milken was guilty of obstructing justice. Also, she found that Milken had deliberately concealed from KKR information about his disposition of Storer warrants and thus violated the law. She noted in detail in her résumé of the *Fatico* hearings the reasons for these conclusions and why she excluded the other charges made by the government at that hearing.[31]

Judge Kimba Wood's Sentencing Opinion [32]

Judge Wood handed down her sentencing opinion on November 21, 1990. She noted,

> It is unusual for a judge to be presented with both such a wide range of possible sentences and such a stark contrast between the defendant's version and the government's version of the defendant's conduct.
>
> Defendant has claimed that his wrongdoing consisted of a few instances of over-zealous service to his clients, mere technical disclosure violations and . . . accommodating a client (the Solomon tax help) who needed tax losses.
>
> The government in contrast claimed defendant was one of the most villainous criminals Wall Street had ever produced and he abused his position as head of the

---

[31]Read how Michael Milken defends himself in "My Story—Michael Milken," as told to James W. Michaels and Phillis Berman, *Forbes,* March 16, 1992. Duplicated in http://www.forbes.com/archive/milken.htm.

[32]The following quotations are from Judge Kimba M. Wood, *Opinion, United States* v. *Michael Milken*, U.S. Dist. Ct, S.D. N.Y., November 21, 1990.

most powerful department in one of the most powerful firms on Wall Street to regularly distort the securities market and enrich himself and Drexel, and, finally, that he obstructed justice.

The judge said, in connection with the defense, although the crimes benefited Milken's clients, that was no excuse for violating the law. "There is no escaping the fact that your crimes also benefited you." The argument was not accepted that the violations were merely technical and that the defendant's conduct was not really criminal or only barely criminal.

"These arguments," said Judge Wood, "fail to take into account the fact that you may have committed only subtle crimes not because you were not disposed to any criminal behavior but because you were willing to commit only crimes that were unlikely to be detected. . . . Your crimes show a pattern of skirting the law, stepping just over the wrong side of the law in an apparent effort to get some of the benefits from violating the law without running a substantial risk of being caught. . . . You did not order employees to destroy or remove documents, but you communicated the advisability of their doing so in subtle terms that preserved some deniability on your part."

In determining Milken's sentence, she said, "I have taken into account that long before your current legal problems you took a significant amount of your own personal time to serve the community by working with disadvantaged children rather, for example, than using all your personal time to acquire possessions. You also successfully encouraged your colleagues at work to do the same." Furthermore, she added " . . . competitors found you to be forthright, honorable and honest in your dealings with them over the years." But on the other side, she said, " . . . you were head of your department and . . . you used

---

Michael Milken's Social Programs

Despite the heavy fine paid to the government, Michael Milken was left with sizable assets. He has used some of his money to fund a series of social, educational, and medical programs. Here are a few.

First, he cofounded the Milken Family Foundation with his brother to support his programs.

Shortly after he left prison, he was diagnosed with prostate cancer (now in remission). This led him to found and become chairman of CaP CURE, an organization dedicated to finding a cure for prostate cancer and stimulating public awareness of the disease. CaP CURE is the world's largest private source of research funding for this disease. He committed himself to giving $5 million each year for five years and to raising additional funding. By early 1998, CaP CURE had made $50 million in grants for prostate cancer research.

He established the Milken Institute, a think tank dedicated to research into social trends.

Many of his efforts focus on the educational world, where he initiated a number of programs. One is the annual Milken Family Foundation National

Educational Conference, where awards of $25,000 are given to 150 outstanding individuals from the field of education.

The Foundation paid one-third of the cost of $30 million to infuse new life into an old school now called the Milken Community High School located in Sepulveda Pass, Los Angeles. It is the nation's largest non-Orthodox Jewish high school.

The above are nonprofit endeavors. A large profit-oriented enterprise is Knowledge Universe (KU). This organization was started in January 1996 with capital of $500 million provided by Milken, his brother Lowell, and Lawrence Ellison, CEO of Oracle Corp. This company, growing largely through acquisitions, currently has assets over $4 billion.

The goal of KU "is to provide a very broad range of services and products serving the lifelong learning needs of individuals, corporations and education systems."[33] Milken said he hoped KU would be a "model for the best education has to offer." He said he wanted the company "to show what possibly can be done, and to serve as a model that other people can look at . . . to energize the public school system."[34] In pursuit of this vision, KU now includes many other companies.

> Productivity Point International, Inc., designs and delivers computer training skills. In 1998, it trained over one million students.
>
> MindQ Publishing, Inc., develops and markets learning systems that turn desktop computers into a classroom for professionals.
>
> TEC Worldwide, Inc., helps CEOs meet constant environmental changes.
>
> Children's Discovery Centers, Inc., operates 250 preschool and childcare centers.
>
> LeapFrog Toys makes educational products for children.
>
> Bookman Testing Services, Inc., is a leading provider of proficiency tests.
>
> CRT Group, now called Spring, is the largest vocational training firm in the United Kingdom.
>
> Sigma Consulting, Nextera Enterprises, and The Planning Technologies Group are three firms that provide business consulting services.[35]

others in your department to effect unlawful schemes. By your example, you communicated that cutting legal and ethical corners is, at times, acceptable."

Judge Wood made it clear that her sentence was not only to punish for criminal acts but also "to be effective in deterring others from committing them." She then sentenced Milken to ten years in prison, three years probation, and community service. Milken served less than two years of his prison sentence. He paid a total of $1.1 billion in penalties.

---

[33]Knowledge Universe, "About KU," http://www.knowledgeu.com/about.html, January 16, 1999.

[34]Debora Vrana, "Education's Pied Piper with a Past," *Los Angeles Times*, September 7, 1998, p. A14.

[35]Ibid. and Knowledge Universe, "KU Companies," http://www.knowledgeu.com/companies.html, January 26, 1999.

Concluding Comment

It is somewhat troubling to read the documents in this case and see two distinct pictures of a man. Can they be balanced?

Questions

1. Describe the state of the financial markets when Milken first began his career with Drexel.
2. What was the basis of Milken's conviction that junk bonds were good investments?
3. What was going on in the financial markets that helped Milken persuade managers to use junk bonds in their financing and enabled him to market these securities?
4. What were the basic charges of the U.S. District Attorney of New York against Milken?
5. What was the basic response of the defense to these charges?
6. Do you agree or disagree with Judge Woods's sentencing opinion?
7. Do you believe this was a case of (a) violation only of minor technicalities, (b) occasional unethical behavior, or (c) demonstrable criminal acts?

CREDITS

Art and Photo Credits

Chapter 2   Page 41, *Photo,* Bettmann Archive.

Chapter 3   Page 53, *Photo,* Sheeler, Charles. "American Landscape." 1930. Oil on Canvas, 24 × 31'' (61 × 78.8 cm). The Museum of Modern Art, New York. Gift of Abby Aldrich Rockefeller. Photograph © 1996 The Museum of Modern Art, New York. Page 77, *Photo,* Library of Congress.

Chapter 4   Page 87, *Photo,* From *The Best of Art Young* by Art Young. Copyright © 1936 and renewed 1964 by Vanguard Press, Inc. Reprinted by permission of Vanguard Press, Inc., a division of Random House, Inc. Page 94, *Photo,* Sue Coe. "Modern Man Followed by Ghosts of His Meat." © 1988 Sue Coe. Courtesy Galerie St. Etienne, New York. Page 106, *Photo,* Joel Gordon.

Chapter 5   Page 120, *Photo,* Reprinted with permission from Merck & Co., Inc. Page 157, *Photo,* Courtesy of Union Carbide.

Chapter 6   Page 182, *Figure,* The Conference Board, *Building the Corporate Community Economic Development Team,* Research Report 1205-98-RR, New York: The Conference Board, 1998, p. 14.

Chapter 7   Page 203, *Photo,* Courtesy of Pinecastle Boat & Construction Company. Page 235, *Photo,* Courtesy of M. Marshall, M.D./Custom Medical Stock Photo.

Chapter 9   Page 310, *Figure,* Melinda Warren and William F. Lauber, *Regulatory Changes and Trends: An Analysis of the 1999 Federal Budget,* Center for the Study of American Business, Washington University, Regulatory Budget Report 21, November 1998, p. 5.

Chapter 14   Page 511, *Photo,* Stephen Tuttle/U.S. Fish & Wildlife Service.

Chapter 15   Page 546, *Photo,* David E. Lilienfeld, "The Silence: The Asbestos Industry and Early Occupational Cancer Research—A Case Study." *American Journal of Public Health,* vol. 81, no. 6, June 1991.

Chapter 16   Page 585, *Photo,* Joel Gordon.

Chapter 18   Page 645, *Photo,* Elliot Erwitt/Magnum. Page 673, *Photo,* Gaylon Wampler/Sygma.

Chapter 19   Page 714, *Photo,* AP/Wide World Photos.

Text Credits

Chapter 1   Page 7, *Box,* Source: www.pg.com/docCommunity/activity/index.html

Chapter 5   Page 158, *Exhibit,* Courtesy of Union Carbide.

Chapter 6   Page 178, *Box,* Anne Faircloth and Caroline Bollinger, "Fortune's 40 Most Generous Americans," *Fortune,* February 2, 1998.

Chapter 8   Page 265, *Table,* Source: http://www.ti.com/corp/docs/ethics/brochure/qtest.htm

Chapter 9   Page 315, *Exhibit,* Melvin A. Brenner, James O. Leet, and Elihu Schott, Airline *Deregulation,* Westport, CN: Eno Foundation for Transportation, Inc., 1985, p. 83.

Chapter 12   Page 415, *Table, Fortune,* August 3, 1998.

Chapter 14   Page 487, *Box,* Poster reprinted in Ralph K. Andrist, ed., *Confident Years: 1865–1916,* New York: American Heritage/Bonanza Books, 1989, p. 293.

Chapter 19   Page 697, *Table,* Don O'Neal and Howard Thomas, "Developing the Strategic Board," Long Range Planning, June 1996, p. 316. Page 706, *Table,* Jennifer Reingold, Richard A. Melcher, and Gary McWilliamson, "Executive Pay," *Business Week,* April 20, 1998, p. 64. Page 725, *Box,* Peter Truell, "Milken Settles S.E.C. Complaint for $47 Million," *New York Times,* February 27, 1998.

Index